# The IDM Marketing Guide:

## Best practice in direct, data and digital marketing

# Volume 2

# The IDM Marketing Guide: Best practice in direct, data and digital marketing

Published by

## The Institute of Direct Marketing

1 Park Road, Teddington, Middlesex TW11 0AR

Tel:        +44 (0)20 8977 5705
Fax:        +44 (0)20 8943 2535
Website:    www.theidm.com

The IDM has made every effort to ensure that all the information contained in The IDM Marketing Guide is as accurate and up to date as possible. However, readers will appreciate that the data is only as recent as its availability, compilation and printing schedules will allow, and is subject to change during the natural course of events. If critical, please check.

ISBN-13:   978-0-9518692-8-4
ISBN-10:   0-9518692-8-0

Typeset by C&H Prototype Ltd, Teddington, Middlesex

Printed and bound in Great Britain by Imperial Printers UK Limited

# Foreword

■-■-■-■-■-■-■-■-■-■-■-■-■-■-■-■-■-■-■-■-■-■-■-■

**THIS IS A BIG BOOK**. Three volumes. Fifteen hundred plus pages. More than fifty authors.

Size isn't everything, I know. But we needed the size to contain the content. This 2006 edition is a clear twenty per cent bigger than its immediate predecessor in 2002. And the first edition in 1992 now looks a very slim volume indeed.

That's how much we have all learned in the last decade and a half. The old truisms and lessons of direct marketing remain to be applied – and will always be applied successfully – but they are now joined by all the new applications of digital marketing. The mailing pack has not been superseded by the new technologies; far from it – indeed its efficacy is often enhanced by those technologies. At the IDM we now talk of direct, data and digital marketing and this Guide reflects all three disciplines – with a proper expansion of coverage of the last of them where so much has been learned in the last few years.

This is a businesslike Guide. It proceeds always from the general to the particular, through twelve sequenced sections and fifty eight chapters. It offers step-by-step guides, checklists and case histories ... and it offers them in plain useable English rather than the tiresome management-speak that bedevils so many marketing textbooks.

So the emphasis is on practicality not theory. It gives you ideas, techniques, lessons and experiences that can affect your own marketing programme immediately. It can certainly help you avoid the pitfalls and misconceptions that surround this new discipline of ours; for it is written by experts whose expertise has been proven in today's marketplace.

Indeed, on behalf of the Institute I would like to thank and acknowledge all the authors who have kindly donated their time and shared their many years of collected, hard-won experience in contributing to this Guide.

Ten thousand copies of this Guide's predecessors are still around on the shelves of agencies and marketing departments throughout Europe. Keep this new edition close to hand for it will quite certainly serve you well in the years to come.

Robin Fairlie
Editor-in-Chief

# Explanation of icons used throughout this Guide

 Case study

 Definition

 Example

 Further reading

 Money saver

 Note / Checklist

 Quotation

 Remember

 Talking point

 Tip

 Warning

# Contents

---

## Volume 2

---

### Section 5    Planning your integrated communications

---

**Chapter 5.1    Direct mail**

Brian Thomas

---

**Chapter 5.2    Press ahead and get some good results**

Beverly Barker

---

**Chapter 5.3    Door-drop marketing, now with new improved targeting**

Nick Wells

## Chapter 5.8    Best practice search engine marketing

Mike Rogers

## Chapter 5.9    Email: marketing's most abused communications tool

Will Rowan

## Chapter 5.10   Mobile marketing: A mainstream medium for every brand

Jonathan Bass

## Chapter 5.11 Integration – bringing the media plan together – or making it all work – really well!

Beverly Barker

## Section 6 Customer acquisition

## Chapter 6.1 ROI-driven customer acquisition

Joanna Reynolds

## Chapter 6.2 Success factors for customer acquisition on and offline

Joanna Reynolds

## Chapter 6.3    Recording and analysing the results

Joanna Reynolds

# Section 7    Customer retention

## Chapter 7.1    Customer loyalty – more a philosophy than a technique

Neil Woodcock

## Chapter 7.2    Customer experience: getting under the skin

David Williams

## Chapter 7.3    Retention and loyalty: how do your customers measure up?

Mark Say

## Section 8   Campaign planning and management

### Chapter 8.1   Campaign planning and management: – converting strategy into action plans

Kate Boothby

### Chapter 8.2   Testing, testing, testing

Robin Fairlie and David Hughes

### Chapter 8.3   Campaign data: maximising the return of your campaign through excellent use of data

Scott Logie

**Chapter 8.4    Essentials of the printing process**

Philip Moreland, John Hughes

# Guide Overview

---

## Volume 1

---

Section 1   Introduction to DDD marketing

---

Section 2   Gaining the customer insight

---

Section 3   Strategic planning and proposition development

---

Section 4   Customer management, tools and techniques

---

## Volume 2

---

Section 5   Planning your integrated communications

---

Section 6   Customer acquisition

---

Section 7   Customer retention

---

Section 8   Campaign planning and management

---

## Volume 3

---

Section 9   Working with suppliers and partners

---

Section 10  Designing your communications

---

Section 11  Managing the customer experience

---

Section 12  Compliance and best practice

---

**Index**

**Glossary of terms**

**Trade and professional organisations, other useful addresses and further information**

**Further reading**

# Section 5: Planning your integrated communications

------------------------------------------------

**I**t **is** a major theme of this Guide that marketing in the 21st Century can no longer be (as it has in the past been for many companies) a matter of using a single medium of communication to advertise one's wares. Not only does such an approach ignore the opportunities afforded by a burgeoning list of new media; it also misses the vital point that in today's world customers expect – demand – to be able to communicate with their suppliers through whatever medium they happen to find most convenient, at whatever moment the need to communicate strikes them. And when they do so, they expect to receive a consistent message regardless of the medium used; hence the insistence, in the title of this Section, on the need for *integration* of marketing communications across media.

However, we can't ignore either, that optimum use of each of the rapidly growing number of media (and no doubt there are more still to come) requires a specific skill-set, such that it is improbable that any single individual marketer can claim full across-the-board competence. (And not too many 'full-service' agencies can either.) We have therefore dealt here, chapter by chapter, with the fundamental principles underlying the use of each medium in turn – starting with the traditional direct marketing media, and progressing to the more recent electronic arrivals.

And finally we wind up the Section, in chapter 11, with a piece on integration, pulling together the specifics of individual media and dealing with the principles behind such terms as Integrated Media Communications (IMC) and Media Neutral Planning (MNP).

# Direct mail

## This chapter includes:

------------------------------------------------

- ❏ **Introduction**

- ❏ **The importance of direct mail**

- ❏ **Direct mail functions**

- ❏ **How direct mail works**

- ❏ **Customer acquisition – external lists**

- ❏ **The two kinds of mailing list**

- ❏ **Lists and responsiveness**

- ❏ **List brokers**

- ❏ **Briefing your list broker**

- ❏ **Testing lists**

- ❏ **Deduplication**

- ❏ **Royal Mail services**

- ❏ **10 ways to succeed with cold mailing**

- ❏ **Mailing your own customers**

------------------------------------------------

## About this chapter

**D**irect mail is the oldest direct marketing medium. In terms of expenditure, it is second only to telemarketing. This chapter deals principally with the unique characteristics of the direct mail medium; the strategies, tactics, tools and philosophies that it shares to a greater or lesser degree with other media are more fully described elsewhere in this Guide, in chapters devoted to strategy and techniques etc.

## Brian Thomas, F IDM

brianthomas2@btconnect.com

Brian has been in marketing and management for almost 40 years. He held senior positions with GUS, ICI, Fine Art Developments and Early Learning before switching to the agency side in the 1980s.

He was Managing Director of THBW, helping this agency grow into the largest independent direct marketing agency in Britain.

THBW was merged into Ogilvy & Mather Direct (now Ogilvy One) with Brian continuing as Managing Director. During the next three years he helped build O & MD into the largest direct marketing agency in Europe.

After a sabbatical Brian became Chairman and Managing Director of Saatchi and Saatchi Direct in 1988, continuing in this role until 1991 when he left to become an independent direct marketing consultant.

Brian is one of the course directors for the UK residential courses for the IDM Diploma in Direct and Interactive Marketing. He also runs a number of public courses and seminars for the IDM. Between 1981 and 1998 he ran all the Direct Marketing courses and seminars presented by the Chartered Institute of Marketing.

In 1999 Brian was twice honoured by the Institute of Direct Marketing, receiving their award of 'Educator of the Year' in June and being elected an Honorary Fellow of the Institute in November.

# Chapter 5.1

# Direct mail

## Introduction

As an addressable medium direct mail offers marketers a number of advantages over broadscale communications such as press and television advertising:

- The message can be varied for each individual, though in practice addressees would be grouped into segments having similar characteristics, needs or budgets

- The timing can easily be varied to enable messages to be delivered at a time that is relevant for each prospect

These differences make addressable media more powerful than traditional mass media and consequently there has been a considerable shift in budget allocations over the past few years. Whereas many consumer advertisers used to spend upwards of 80 per cent of their budgets on TV, today there are many fields where direct communications (of all types) take more than 50 per cent of marketing budgets.

As of today (and it may be different tomorrow) these are the addressable media:

- Direct mail
- Online advertising
- Email
- Fax
- Mobile phones (SMS, MMS)
- Landline telephones

These media, although all different, have one thing in common – they can be used at every stage of the acquisition, retention and recovery cycle. That is because they can be targeted to individuals; information permitting, they can be used to send the right message to the right customer at the right time.

**The media of dialogue**

What else is special about addressable media? Well, they are *two-way* media. They are media that can also be used by customers to communicate with us.

In this chapter however, we will stick to *outbound* communications and specifically direct mail.

# The importance of direct mail

Direct marketing continues to grow dramatically. The Direct Marketing Association (DMA) UK Census 2003/2004 estimates that in the financial year 2002/2003, expenditure on direct marketing was £12.1 billion – an increase of 45 per cent in four years. Direct mail accounts for more than 20 per cent of total media spend in direct marketing, as the following table 5.1.1 shows:

Table 5.1.1 **Direct marketing media expenditure**

| Medium | Amount spent in 2002/2003 £million | | % of total (of £12,065 million) | Rank |
|---|---|---|---|---|
| DR ads in national and regional press and magazines | £1,113 | £1,113 | 9.2% | 5 |
| Inserts – press and magazines | £1,170 | | 9.7% | 4 |
| Direct mail | £2,531 | | 21.0% | 2 |
| Door-to-door | £797 | | 6.6% | 7 |
| Telemarketing | £3,461 | | 28.7% | 1 |
| DRTV | £1,575 | | 13.1% | 3 |
| DR radio | £175 | | 1.5% | 9 |
| Outdoor and transport | £288 | | 2.4% | 8 |
| Cinema | £5 | | 0.1% | 10 |
| 'New' media | £950 | | 7.9% | 6 |
| Total | £12,065 million | | | |

Direct mail is the most versatile of the addressable media. Apart from the comparatively small number of people who have opted out of receiving direct mail through the Mailing Preference Service (in February 2006 this was 2.7 million people – six per cent of UK Adults), its adult coverage is almost universal and the medium is equally appropriate to B2C and B2B marketing. It is less intrusive (and more popular) than any of the other addressable media and it costs nothing to receive.

**Table 5.1.2      UK direct mail volumes 1990 – 2005 (million items)**

|      | Consumer | Business | Total |
|------|----------|----------|-------|
| 1990 | 1544 | 728 | 2272 |
| 1991 | 1435 | 687 | 2122 |
| 1992 | 1658 | 588 | 2246 |
| 1993 | 1772 | 664 | 2436 |
| 1994 | 2015 | 715 | 2730 |
| 1995 | 2198 | 707 | 2905 |
| 1996 | 2436 | 737 | 3173 |
| 1997 | 2700 | 887 | 3588 |
| 1998 | 3123 | 891 | 4014 |
| 1999 | 3283 | 1062 | 4345 |
| 2000 | 3516 | 1148 | 4664 |
| 2001 | 3706 | 1233 | 4939 |
| 2002 | 3940 | 1293 | 5233 |
| 2003 | 4240 | 1198 | 5438 |
| 2004 | 4221 | 1197 | 5418 |
| 2005 | 4002 | 1132 | 5134 |

*Source: Royal Mail*

The above table shows that B2C and B2B direct mail volumes grew steadily from 1990 to 2003 and then in 2004 for the first time, a slight (0.37 per cent) decline was recorded. The decline accelerated during 2005 by a further 5.2 per cent against the previous year.

Trade press pundits have been quick to seize on this trend as an indication that direct mail is on the way out, but their assessment is flawed for two reasons:

1.  Better targeting means that direct mail volumes will from now on continue to decline although direct mail will remain one of the most important media in the DM mix.

2.  Given the massive increase in the use of email for business communications the fact that mailings are showing only a marginal decline indicates that direct mail is still recognised by marketers as a hugely powerful medium.

**Trend in reverse?**

Further evidence of the resilience of direct mail is seen in the data released by the Direct Mail Information Service in mid-March 2006. In the final quarter of 2005 (October to December 2005) direct mail volumes increased by 0.7 per cent year on year, while expenditure in the same period showed a 2.4 per cent increase. .

The above table, together with much similarly informative material, can be accessed on the Direct Mail Information Service website at www.dmis.co.uk

# Direct mail functions

Because it is mainly used to stimulate a direct response, direct mail is sometimes thought of as a method or branch of marketing. In fact direct mail is an *advertising medium* that can be used:

- In place of broadscale media such as television and print advertising

- In combination with such media

- In combination with other direct media such as telephone, email, SMS and so on

- As a standalone medium

The functions that can be performed specifically by direct mail include:

- **Enquiry generation.** Though its high cost-per-contact compared with broadscale media means that it should only be used in this role when the audience is carefully targeted using sophisticated profiling techniques. Some marketers still use mailings as a blanket medium but this is not only wasteful, it is also bad for the image of direct mail as such communications are truly 'junk mail'.

- **Direct sales.** Even where a product or service is unknown to prospects beforehand, direct mail can nevertheless sell unaided. This is because, unlike several other media, it is capable of delivering very detailed and complex messages.

- **Enquiry conversion.**

- **Appointment generation.**

- **Information**. Requests for information can be fulfilled by phone, but when samples or expensively printed brochures are involved only direct mail can deliver these.

- **Research**. As the cost of field canvassing rises, postal and phone surveys are becoming increasingly attractive.

- **Drive to web**. Often a mailing is intended to get the interested prospect to log on to a website for more information, and in acquisition programmes, provide vital information about themselves too.

# How direct mail works

In the planning stage it can be helpful to think of a direct mailing as a call by a salesperson. The process is:

- Arrange the appointment (attract **A**ttention)

- Explain the benefits (create **I**nterest)

- Demonstrate the product (engender **D**esire)

- Answer questions and reassure the prospect (build **C**onviction)

- Close the sale (generate **A**ction)

As we can see the five stages of the sales call correspond with the classic sales process of **AIDCA – Attention – Interest – Desire – Conviction – Action**

If we consider the various elements of a mailing pack we can see how each relates to this sales process:

## The outer envelope

This effectively makes the appointment – and just as a telemarketer would do when phoning for an appointment, the envelope often works better by exposing the key benefit that is promised to the prospect.

If your customers are used to receiving highly relevant and interesting mailings from you, your company logo may be sufficient to get your mailing opened. As in all direct marketing applications it is sensible to test in your own situation. However, more often than not, the envelope with the overprint achieves a higher response.

Before we leave envelopes let's talk about *postal indicia* – the franking, PPI or postage stamping of your mailings.

In some cases using real postage stamps rather than preprinted indicia generates a higher response, especially with business-to-business mailings. When using real stamps it is obviously sensible to use a plain envelope – here the stamp implies that this is a real personal letter. This level of subterfuge is acceptable but beware of other sneaky tricks.

For example, printing 'Private and Confidential' or 'Strictly Personal' on your envelope will sometimes gain you a small increase in response, but companies that have carried out post- mailing research find that many recipients are irritated or feel cheated by this pretence. It is clearly not a smart idea to increase your response from say 3 to 3.3 per cent while irritating 50 per cent of the rest of your prospect file.

## Now, what about the contents of your envelope?

First of all let's list them. You may well use any or even all of the following:

- Letter

- Product brochure or leaflet

- Testimonial leaflet

- Guarantee or 'Customer Charter'

- 'Lift letter'

- Incentive or special offer leaflet

- Response form

- Reply envelope

Let's take these in turn:

## 1. Letter

This is the one essential piece and the only piece that can do the job on its own. What the letter can do is personalise the entire communication based on the information we have about this prospect. This could be something as simple as knowing their job function or as complex as a complete buying history.

For example:

'Dear Mr Smith,

*Here is your copy of our new catalogue. You'll find our new range of security lighting on pages 420 to 435'.*

You may then add some more pointers, perhaps based on the buying or enquiry history of this customer or, through profiling other customers of the same type.

The job of the letter is to say exactly what the salesperson would say – so it is obvious that sending the same letter to the whole list would be less effective than a number of different letters sent to differing segments of the file.

The beauty of the letter is that, not only is it the piece that most benefits from being personalised, it is also the easiest and cheapest piece to treat in this way.

## 2. Brochure

As the letter is your sales message, the brochure is the *demonstration*. It thus benefits from pictures and captions, showing the product in use. The introduction of human faces is usually highly beneficial here. It is not generally necessary to vary the brochure for each customer segment, although there are some obvious exceptions to this. You would not usually expect to send the same brochure for a complex IT product to an IT director and an office manager. However the segmentation will probably be less complex than with the letter.

What comes next? Well, returning to our sales call analogy, we have explained the benefits this product or service will deliver to the prospect, we have demonstrated how it works using pictures and captions and we have hopefully made them want to either buy or at least know more. So we might now be ready to take the order. But in real life, the prospect is likely to have some questions and personal considerations:

- Why should I buy this from you when I have never heard of you?

- What happens if it does not work as you promise?

- Can I trust you to deliver on your promise of after-sales service?

These and similar questions would of course be answered by the salesperson only if asked, but in a mailing you are not present so you have to assume they will be asked. This is where the fourth letter in our mnemonic (c for conviction) comes into play. As we are not standing face to face with the prospect it is wise to assume that some additional doubts will need to be addressed, and this is where the additional enclosures prove their worth.

### 3. Testimonial

*"Why should I buy this from you when I don't know your company or its reputation?"*

This question and others like it can often be answered by the use of one or more testimonials. Consider the following from an advertisement by *Borland* the software house, for C++, a compilation tool for software authors:

The copy says that Borland C++ is the best product available – however, any producer is going to say that about their product, so readers are often sceptical of advertisers' claims.

What makes this ad work so well is the statements from clients of Borland:

> "C++ is fundamental to the object-orientated revolution ... and Borland is clearly the leader ... customers of our operating system told us that fundamental to their future plans was C++, and Borland C++ specifically."
>
> *Assistant General Manager for Personal Systems Programming, IBM*

The ad used three further testimonials from WordPerfect Corporation, Hewlett-Packard, and Micrografix.

Your advertising claims are much more credible when they are affirmed by a respected third- party. They give prospective buyers a great sense of security, especially when buying from an unknown supplier.

### 4. Guarantee

A powerful guarantee may also answer such questions from sceptical prospects. So another leaflet stating your guarantee or 'Customer Charter' may also be worth including.

### 5. 'Lift letter'

The lift letter is simply another opportunity to restate the benefits, overcome concerns and answer questions. It can be a very valuable addition at marginal cost. It is called a lift letter because it lifts response levels.

There are several possibilities, but typically a lift letter would be an A5 single sheet letter folded to A6 with a statement on the outside saying something like: *'Only to be opened if you are thinking of saying no to this offer'*. Inside, the letter starts on the lines of: *'Frankly I'm amazed. This is a completely risk-free opportunity for you to try this new product at our cost'*. And so on.

There may be some other factors preventing your prospect from responding such as:

*"I think I can probably get this elsewhere at the same price."*

This brings us to:

## 6. The incentive

If your product is clearly more expensive the price argument may be irrefutable but if you can offer some added-value element, it may be possible to overcome the price difference.

## 7. Response form

The prospect is now interested in ordering, or sending for more information, so we need to make this as easy as possible. We must not try to force prospects to fit into our system, but give every opportunity for them to respond in the way they prefer. This may mean offering up to five ways of responding – if you cannot deal with these you should change your system!

Ideally, prospects should be able to choose their method of response from:

1.  **Mail** – completing and posting the order form – in which case there are two things we should do:

    a)  try to ensure their name and address details are preprinted on the form – this not only removes a job from the prospect and thus makes it easier to respond, it also means that all responses can be actioned without delay as they are all complete, accurate and easy to read

    b)  provide a postage-paid reply envelope.

2.  **Phone** – offering a toll-free phone number – some mailers have found that the free number does not increase response but this generally means that their offer is very compelling. If you are offering unsecured loans to people who are desperate for money, the cost of a phone call will not deter them from responding. However, in most cases, paying for the call increases the number of responses.

3.  **Fax** – although not used so much since the growth of email, the fax-back form is still a useful way of encouraging response – especially in business-to-business mailings. Again you should pay for the call.

4.  **Email** – virtually all businesses and many consumers use email regularly today and this is definitely a response route you should offer.

5.  **Website** – it depends on your target audience but today a large percentage of UK homes, and virtually all businesses have internet access. Let those who prefer it take up your offer on the web. It is easier and quicker to keep a website up to date than to keep reprinting brochures.

**Expectations**

You should aim to turn round orders and information requests in 24 hours. Customers ordering by post may be prepared to wait a little longer, but those ordering by the other four methods will have much less patience.

This is especially so when an order or information request is placed by website or email and the system sends an automatic acknowledgement. This usually arrives within an hour or so of the request being received, and of course it sets up a very high expectation of rapid delivery.

If you are not able to turn round information requests or orders rapidly it is essential to manage expectations by quoting a delivery time. It makes sense to quote a slightly longer time than you anticipate – this not only ensures that you avoid disappointing customers, it also sets up a pleasant surprise when your product or information arrives earlier than expected.

# Customer acquisition – external lists

In terms of the cost-per-contact direct mail is an expensive medium and for this reason it is most cost-efficient when used to contact existing customers – for retention, development and customer care programmes, and for getting back in touch with lapsed customers or unconverted prospects.

The targets for acquisition mailings include lapsed or dormant customers and previously unconverted prospects, not simply new 'suspects'.

By definition, suspects are not on the customer or prospect database and so an external mailing list must be rented or compiled. In direct marketing jargon an external list is a cold list. Direct mail can be highly effective using cold lists provided these have been carefully sourced and matched against your existing customer profile. There are some 6,000 business and consumer external lists readily available for direct mail in the UK. To gain an impression of the range of lists available, look at the classified pages of *Precision Marketing* every week and visit list brokers' and managers' websites.

Cold mailing must compete with broadscale media such as press, inserts, door-to-door, TV etc. – so it must compete for its share of the acquisition budget on performance.

A four-piece direct mail package (rule of thumb) costs-per-contact:

- 28 times more than a consumer magazine full-colour page

- 10 times more than a consumer loose insert

- 8.5 times more than a business magazine full-colour page

- 5 times more than a business loose insert

Costs include production

The fact that cold list mailings are used regularly for customer acquisition, despite these cost differences, is testimony to their power.

So why is direct mail such a powerful medium? How can it justify outlay costs that can be almost 30 times as high as other media?

There are many reasons for direct mail's success; among them:

✔ **Accurate targeting**. Targeting is often based on past behaviour or declared interests, in addition to profiling.

✔ **Personal and relevant**. Good creative execution exploits the one-to-one communication possibilities and first-class targeting helps to ensure the message is more likely to be relevant.

✔ **Unique creative flexibility**. Direct mail offers the opportunity to appeal to all the senses: Sight? Touch? Feel? Sound? Taste? Direct mail can offer colour, movement, visual demonstration, sampling, high participation, involvement devices and so on.

✔ **Ease of reply**. Direct mail offers unique opportunities to dramatise postal response (e.g. personalised acceptance forms, uniquely numbered draw entries, formal invitations, prepaid or stamped reply envelopes) as well as the whole range of phone, fax, website or email response opportunities.

✔ It is **Involving**. The attention given by recipients to direct mail and its lack of format limitations allows it space and time to follow the AIDCA formula mentioned above and to handle potential sales objections by answering recipients' likely questions. Technical and complex subjects can be clearly explained.

✔ **Discreet.** No need to tell the world of a new product launch; direct mail is private. It enables the advertiser to let a privileged few in on the secret.

✔ **Highly testable**. Direct mail is a highly testable medium, producing reliable predictors. Testing is covered thoroughly in chapter 8.2.

✔ **Quality of recipient**. Many companies that use long-term lifetime value analysis report that direct mail respondents tend to be better long-term customers. This is felt to be because mailing, being such a copy-intensive medium, tends to recruit a more considered customer than one generated through a medium with high emotional appeal such as direct response television.

Although widely used in acquisition, direct mail is not always the most cost-efficient way to recruit new customers. However, when the target can be tightly defined, and when mailing lists of prospects can be obtained at the right cost, direct mail can be a very powerful acquisition tool.

For example, when Range Rover launched their new model in the mid 1990s, they targeted existing and former Range Rover owners, but also owners of other luxury cars such as Mercedes, Jaguar and so on.

A series of mailings was sent consisting of three teaser postcards followed up by an invitation to a unique launch event, where the new vehicle could be seen in use, being driven by celebrity teams in various remote locations around the world.

This classic campaign, costing more than £30 per contact, was hugely successful, generating almost 100 per cent response and resulting in the sales of three months' output of cars from the launch events alone. The success was, of course, partially due to the extremely attractive series of mailings; but an equally important factor was the precise targeting of prospects.

An insurance company seeking new customers for motor insurance would not find cold direct mail the most cost-efficient recruitment medium – unless it had enough data to be able to segment the list and mail only those whose insurance was due for renewal.

This is why many insurance companies begin the acquisition process with some sort of broadscale advertising – DRTV, press ads run in the motoring pages, loose inserts in appropriate magazines, posters alongside roads and so on, following this with direct mail to responders.

# The two kinds of mailing list

### 1. Compiled lists

The following are examples of compiled lists:

- Shareholder lists

- Directory lists

- The Times Top 1,000 companies

### 2. Responsive lists

The following are examples of lists which are the natural by-product of doing business, e.g. customers, enquirers and members. Examples include:

- Gardening catalogue buyers

- Subscribers to specific magazines

- Lifestyle survey respondents

People generally have to do something specific to find their name on a responsive list. In contrast, you might have to do something specific to *avoid* your name appearing on a compiled list. For example, registering with the Mailing Preference

Service (MPS), having your phone listed as ex-directory, or more probably today, registering your number with the Telephone Preference Service (TPS) – see more on this topic later in this chapter under 'List Brokers'.

Responsive lists are usually better for achieving high response rates and compiled lists are usually better for achieving high market coverage. Generally speaking, compiled lists are much more important in B2B marketing than they are in B2C marketing. That is because achieving high coverage of a market or market sector can be critical when generating sales leads. Also in B2B marketing, buying decisions are often made by more than one person so whereas only one will request information and thus appear on a responsive list, we may wish to communicate simultaneously with several members of the decision-making unit (DMU), and these can often be defined by job function.

# Lists and responsiveness

Responsive lists can be subdivided into two types. It is impossible to generalise to the extent of declaring one type of list to be better than another. It all depends on the application. Even then, it will usually be advisable to test alternative types of list before committing to one or the other. (More about testing lists later.)

## 1. Buyers and enquirers

More often than not, the most responsive lists of all will be lists of enquirers, buyers or former buyers of products that are closely related to your product. Buyers who responded by mail or phone will generally respond better than in-store buyers. It is not usually possible to rent direct competitors' lists, of course. However, if you are selling subscriptions to a gardening magazine, you will be interested in buyers of seeds, plants and gardening tools.

Don't ignore enquirers. They are often better responders than buyers. However, with enquirers the conversion ratio will often be less good.

List exchanges

Some frequent mailers swap lists on a one-time-use basis. This practice was pioneered by US magazine mailers because it was found (not surprisingly) that the best potential magazine subscribers were people who already subscribed to another magazine. The practice has since been adopted by charity fundraisers. Naturally, only supporters who have consented to their names being used are mailed. There are two advantages of list exchange:

1.   The cost is lower than commercial rental

2.   It is often possible to select individuals based on precise buying behaviour

Affinity group mailings

The most transparent form of list rental or exchange is the third-party or affinity group agreement. Instead of just renting a list, the owner agrees to endorse the list user's offer by enclosing a covering letter. To all intents and purposes, the mailing comes from the list owner, not the user. Endorsed mailings are very powerful but take time and patience to negotiate. Usually, the list owner will receive a commission on sales as well as a rental fee. Sometimes the product will be rebranded specially for the affinity group, e.g. the Manchester United credit card from MBNA.

## 2. Profile-matching responder lists

In consumer marketing, these are lifestyle questionnaire responders. Lifestyle databases will often provide highly responsive selections in considerable quantities.

There are two successful ways to use lifestyle databases. The first is to authorise the database owners to profile your customer list against their database. They can then produce a selection that best matches your customer profile. This works because the lifestyle databases are so large (containing 10 million or more names) that many of your customers are certain to have responded to their questionnaire. However, to produce a robust profile you will need to provide at least 3 to 5,000 names of your own customers.

Alternatively, you can make selections based on specific questionnaire responses. For example, if you are running a promotion to win new readers for the *Sunday Telegraph,* you will be interested in targeting survey respondents claiming to read the *Sunday Times* or *Observer,* while avoiding reaching those who already read your paper.

In B2B marketing, controlled circulation magazine readerships provide an excellent source of profile-matched names. To continue receiving the magazine, readers have to answer a questionnaire giving detail of their company, their job title, purchasing responsibilities and so on.

40 million names!

By analysing lifestyle database responses by postcode, it is possible to discover how lifestyle types are clustered within different postcode sectors or geodemographic neighbourhood types. The likely profiles of non-responders can then be inferred. The result is a hybrid database of responder names and non-responder names (the majority). The latter names are derived from the electoral roll. It is important not to confuse such a database with one of genuine questionnaire respondents. The latter will be much more responsive although it cannot provide blanket coverage. Geo-demographic targeting systems can also be used to produce lists that match the client's customer profile. Always use responsive lists if you can – they pull far more replies. (NB: For a full coverage of lifestyle and geodemographic systems, see chapters 2.5 and 2.6.)

When coverage counts, use compiled lists. But in B2C marketing, direct mail coverage is rarely an issue. The fact is that cold direct mail is far too expensive to use with less than highly refined targeting. Quality, not quantity, is the key ingredient of success.

With two important exceptions, cold consumer mailings are best confined to responsive lists. The two exceptions are localised mailings and 'wealth list' mailings. A retail store (depending on its type) can best define its target market by catchment area. In this situation, selections by postcode from the electoral roll would be the obvious choice. However, now that consumers can opt out of having their electoral roll data used for marketing purposes, the ER is not so powerful or comprehensive.

Wealth lists can be derived by collecting FTSE 100 or 200 shareholder names and 'merge-purging' them to produce a deduplicated list of private shareholders. During the merge-purge process, the aggregate shareholdings of the recurring names are totted up. Thus the shareholders can be assembled into a wealth list, segmented by the value of their shareholdings. This type of list is valuable to companies and trade associations selling services of interest to shareholders or even just to wealthy people.

## B2B compiled lists

If you are responsible for generating leads for a field salesforce, you will probably not wish to rely on business magazine subscribers and other responsive lists. Leads will be needed in each sales territory and in predictable numbers. Ideally, you want a market universe list giving 100 per cent coverage of the relevant market or market sector.

The prime data source for limited companies is Companies House. This provides details of a very high percentage of the 600,000 or so registered limited companies that are actively trading. The details are quite extensive but, unfortunately, do not include good contact data, being confined to directors (with unspecified responsibilities) and the address of the registered office.

For smaller companies, non-companies and branch trading addresses, other sources are used. The task of compiling and verifying the data is undertaken by specialist business database providers. These companies make extensive use of phone research to check details and add contact names. You will find details of several business database providers in the 'Business Lists' section of *Precision Marketing*.

Key factors used for profiling businesses are number of employees, SIC and location. Number of employees is the most reliable size indicator within a given market sector. SIC stands for Standard Industrial Classification. This divides businesses into a total of 503 classes and 142 subclasses. It was revised in 1992 to bring it into line with an EU-wide system.

Often it is possible to infer information by the presence of another, apparently non-related piece of data. For example, a company wished to target companies whose premises were built no later than 1992. This piece of information is rarely available but they were able to find a high 'hit rate' of appropriate companies when they discovered that they could identify through a third-party, the date on which the company's telephone number was first registered at that address. If this date was 1992 or earlier clearly the premises had to have been built by then. Good data providers can often suggest similar solutions to seemingly intractable problems.

## *Who supplies mailing lists?*

Mailing lists can be purchased or rented from a variety of sources. Chief among these – and certainly the most professional – are the following:

- List owners

- List managers

- List brokers

- List compilers

We now look at these list sources, followed by checklists for choosing your supplier and making your list selections.

### List owners – usually the data compilers

The owner of a list is normally the organisation which compiled or generated, and continues to maintain, the list or database from which your selection will be taken.

List owners may make their list available for multiple usage or rent it for a once-only mailing.

### List managers – the owner's exclusive agents

List owners often appoint exclusive agents to administer the rental or sale of their lists. Some managers have many list owners on their books.

Lists are often advertised in trade media such as *Precision Marketing* and *Direct Response* and are also listed in 'lists of lists' available from list brokers.

### List brokers – the user's representatives

When you approach a list broker you can expect advice on mailing list selections, applications and efficiency etc. That is because brokers tend to act on behalf of users rather than owners, although they also supply lists. List brokers and list managers are often the same people.

### List compilers – for your special needs

List compilers, as their name suggests, literally build lists from scratch – using data gleaned from directories, phone enquiries, questionnaires, personal visits and so on. Normally, list compilers undertake specific list building tasks and are commissioned by users. Again compilers can be independent or specialist divisions of list brokerages. Because they often require expensive telephone research, compiled lists can often cost more than existing lists. But this can often be a good investment as the following example shows:

List compilation – an example

A supplier of wireless internet access (wi-fi) networks for airports wanted to mail operations directors and IT managers of major airports around the world. No up-to-date list was available so a specialist compiler built the list using telephone research. The resulting list was naturally expensive but proved highly effective when mailed.

Beware of buying on price alone!

Many studies have been done to identify the most important factors in the success of a direct mail campaign, and have shown that the most important is targeting. Your product may be the best of its kind; your offer may be hugely powerful; your creative treatment may be stunningly attractive; yet all that is totally irrelevant if your mailing goes to the wrong person.

Clearly therefore, list buying is no place to shop for bargains! Of course, once you have identified a list that reaches your chosen target, you can negotiate on price, but do not look for cheap lists – this is definitely one area where 'you get what you pay for'.

## List brokers

It is also important to ensure you deal with a reputable company. The best way to do this is to obtain a list of the members of LADS. (List and Database Suppliers Group) from the DMA (UK). You'll find full information at www.dma.org.uk. Searching under 'Directory' will provide a list of DMA members under any given category, and contact details are available on each.

Recognised brokers have a commission-sharing agreement that enables each of them to access any lists managed by any of the others. You may want to brief more than one broker as they are unlikely to come up with identical solutions to your problem.

On the whole, once you have found a broker who is bright and efficient, it may pay dividends to remain loyal while you are getting a good service and good ideas.

Some brokers are stronger on consumer experience and others are stronger on business mailings. It is a good idea to ask if they can give you a handful of client names you can contact to check them out. Some have international dealings, but a few have a great deal more international list experience than others.

Always ask for a warranty that the list is being offered to you legally. A list warranty must exist for each rented list and will be held either by the list owner, the list manager or, increasingly, the DMA's list warranty register.

Recognised brokers obey a standard code of practice and seek to give list data in a standardised way. They subscribe to the Mailing Preference Service which allows consumers to have their names removed from lists offered for rental.

The Mailing Preference Service (MPS) is a facility which allows consumers to register their desire not to receive direct mail (or a positive desire to receive certain categories of direct mail). The Code of Practice of the Direct Marketing Association (DMA) places an obligation on list owners to warrant that their list has been cleaned against the MPS within the last 90 days; it is a function of the list broker to obtain such a warranty and provide it to the list user. The Telephone and Fax Preference Services have a similar function, but these now have a legal status: it is illegal to make an unsolicited approach by phone or fax to any number that has registered with TPS or FPS more than 28 days previously. (For more on 'Preference Services' see chapters 12.1 and 12.2.)

Lists may also be screened against a deceased register such as 'Mortascreen', but if not, you can have the mailing file screened against it, although there is no legal or voluntary code requirement to do so.

If you are offering credit, your mailing file may be screened against a database of debtors or potential debtors. For example, you can have CCJs deleted. CCJs are County Court Judgements for unpaid debts (less than seven years old). This work is undertaken by credit reference bureaux. Experian offers both credit reference and mailing list services.

There are numerous B2B suppression files available for both UK and international business lists. Inputting 'business suppression file' into Google instantly produces a listing of many options including that offered by the REaD Group. This file incorporates the REaD Group's consumer and SoHo data, Dun & Bradstreet's complete UK Business File, plus gone aways from Experian, Wegener and other sources.

At their best, recognised brokers are capable of giving a standard of service and a quality of advice that compares favourably with a good media independent. Some will have a fair knowledge of package insert opportunities as well as solus mailing opportunities. Package inserts (referred to as third-party inserts in chapter 5.2) are leaflets inserted in other companies' statements, bills or product despatches.

You may be asked to pay a small charge for speculative list proposals and you will certainly need to know your buying and selling terms.

Before attempting to buy or rent a mailing list be sure you understand the various selections which may be offered to you. The price you pay, needless to say, depends greatly on the combination you order. (More on selections within lists later.)

The main trade terms you need to know even before consulting a list owner or broker are these:

- **Single rental**

    One authorised use only – only respondents to your campaign become yours for further use. (Brokers insert 'seeds' into a list so they will know if this agreement has been broken. A seed is a name and address of someone known to the broker/owner and if you have contracted for a single mailing and the seed receives more than one, this will be reported. Conversely, should you be renting out your own list, make sure that you seed it for this reason.)

There is another good reason for seeding a list. If you or one of your colleagues is added to the list you will know when the mailing arrives and can alert the call centre or post room to expect responses.

- **Multiple rental**

  Use for a two- or three-shot mailing campaign at a negotiated rental cost. This can be considerably cheaper than negotiating each list extraction separately.

- **Outright purchase**

  You buy the names, addresses and any associated data, but you may not resell or rent out to anyone else. This is a quick but not always ideal way of building a database. Many of the names will never buy from you and it may be better to mail the list once with a compelling offer that attracts most of those interested to contact you – once they have responded, and subject to the provisions of the data protection legislation (see chapter 12.1) you can add them to your own database for future contact.

- **Phone only**

  If you require phone numbers, or more particularly if you wish only to make telephonic use of a list, state this clearly.

- **Gross billing**

  You pay for the entire list, with no further adjustment for names not used. See 'net names' below.

- **Net names**

  You pay only for usable names, i.e. names remaining after deduplication (see further below) with your customer database and any other lists you are using. Usually 15 per cent is the maximum reduction offered, but this is negotiable.

- **'Nixies' (Royal Mail returns)**

  Mailings returned undeliverable or gone away etc. are termed 'nixies'. A rebate is usually offered in exchange for your returning the nixies to your list broker, as this enables the owner to clean the list. The rebate may cover all nixies or only nixies over an 'acceptable' level. Bear in mind that most people don't return mailings addressed to previous occupants. Three per cent nixies may equal 12 per cent 'actual' gone aways. It is essential to print a return address on the envelope as without this, Royal Mail are not obliged to return those not delivered. You should also ensure each list used is coded on any reply device (as it should be anyway for response analysis) so that you can benefit from this rebate. The rebate will normally cover the postage cost, and in some cases the list rental cost, of the undelivered items.

## *Briefing your list broker*

By now you will have a good idea of the information you need to supply to your list broker – and what information you require in return.

Figure 5.1.1 provides a useful reminder to make your list briefing a more profitable experience.

Remember, your broker's interpretation of your requirements will be a reflection of your brief, so the more comprehensive the brief, the more accurate and detailed will be the proposal.

Figure 5.1.1    **Briefing your list broker**

| Client | Some list buyers seek to keep hidden the names of their clients. However the client's name and reputation may be important to your negotiations. Furthermore, the list owner may need to know this in order to avoid conflicts from competitive companies – neither company for example, would wish to mail the same list on the same day. If any information you divulge is confidential make this clear at the start. |
|---|---|
| **Product/ service** | Obviously your list adviser can give you better advice if they have details of your product or service and to whom it is likely to appeal. |
| **Objectives** | You should provide as much detail as you can about required response - in terms of both volume (per cent response rate) and quality of respondent. |
| **Creative** | Tell your broker how the communication will look and what it will offer. Include details of intended personalisation, incentives and response routes (e.g. post, phone, email and drive to web.) |
| **Data processing** | Share your intentions regarding data capture and retention, and how the captured names will subsequently be handled. |
| **Target prospect** | Include anything you know about the profile of your ideal customer in terms of demographics, lifestyle etc. for consumer. For business mailings your profile should include company type and size, SIC code (if relevant), position of prospect (e.g. finance director or office manager). |
| **Allowable cost** | How much you can afford to pay for each lead or order. Your list broker can advise on the feasibility of your plan if you wish. |
| **Tests** | If you are testing lists your broker can advise on minimum quantities for each list.  The minimum is usually 5,000 names. |
| **Previous history** | If you have any previous direct mail or advertising experience that you can share with your broker this can be helpful in arriving at the best lists for you.  If you give previous response data make sure you get your broker to sign a confidentiality agreement. |
| **Timing** | The earliest and latest dates when the names will be mailed – essential so the list owner can avoid the names being mailed simultaneously by competitive companies. |

## *The response to your brief: the list proposal*

The response to your brief will vary according to what output you have requested and what is normal for the supplier. It may range from a catalogue of mailing lists with a two-line description of each, to a combination of selections from various mailing lists with full details and costings. It would be sensible to indicate in your brief, the degree of detail you require in the proposal.

Essential information about a mailing list should be requested if not volunteered and should include the headings in the checklist (figure 5.1.2):

## Figure 5.1.2 **What the list proposal should tell you**

| | |
|---|---|
| **Source and correct name of list** | Lists often go under several titles, sometimes offered by different brokers. Make sure you know the true source of all lists offered. |
| **Description** | Type of customers (eg affluence, age) if known; any profile obtained from research, questionnaires; list owner's assessment. |
| **Total numbers available** | Even if only a test quantity is required you need to know the sizeof the total list in order to calculate the roll-out potential of your best performing tests. |
| **Demographics** | eg Mr, Mrs, Ms or Miss, marital status, socio-economic grouping may be available. |
| **How collected** | You need to know not only the source but also the method of collection, eg free sample requests, orders, competition entrants. |
| **Recency** | You should be told when names were obtained (affects their likely accuracy), and possibly any uses to which the list has been put, especially if recent. |
| **How supplied** | In which output format are names offered, eg disk, tape, other. Is mailing to be carried out by list owner on your behalf? |
| **Timing** | When lists become available, earliest and latest dates. |
| **Conditions and restrictions** | Any restrictions, eg by type of product which may be offered – usually must be non-competitive with list owner. |
| **Terms** | When payment due, to whom payable etc. |

### Selections within lists

Your list broker's response to your brief should not only include list selections but selections *within* the recommended lists.

These can be as simple as *gender* or *recency*. Recency refers to the date of the *last* response from the person on the list. The more recent names are newer or more active buyers. Furthermore, their contact details are more likely to be up to date. It is common practice to specify 'less than 12 months old'.

Figure 5.1.3 shows a downloaded data card from the prospectswetenhams.com website. You will see that the selection factors offered include geographic, gender, age, recency, newspaper readership, order value, method of payment and multi-buyers.

## Figure 5.1.3    **Example of a typical list data card**

Now available through Prospect Swetenhams on a list rental basis, the Expert Verdict file comprises individuals who have purchased the latest technological developments from the innovative Expert Verdict, mail order catalogue.

The merchandise offers stylish and performance focused household products and gifts, which appeal to affluent individuals who delight in gadgets and electrical items.

This file offers an even mix of males and females, predominantly aged 35-64 who are significantly more affluent than the national average with household incomes in excess of £40,000 per annum.

With their significant disposable incomes but busy work and social schedules, mail order has become an invaluable means for purchasing products and services. These buyers value the convenience afforded to them by shopping via mail order without forgoing on quality and service. It is not surprising then that a significant percentage of the file is comprised of repeat purchasers and the average order value is high.

For leisure and relaxation these consumers enjoy sport, fine wines, foreign travel, DIY and home computing. Other interests include Motoring, Home computing, Technology and Stocks and Shares.

Having been recruited via classic direct marketing methods, this high quality data source will work well for non-competing mail order, fundraising, publishing and travel & leisure mailers

### Volumes

| | |
|---|---|
| 0-12 month buyers | 35,523 |
| 13-24 month buyers | 16,454 |

prospect swetenhams

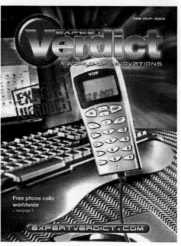

### Users

Expert Verdict offers advertisers an excellent opportunity to tap into an affluent and highly mail responsive consumer group.

### Computing Services
The very nature of this file, the high level of computer ownership and the general affluence of the target audience makes this list and ideal recruitment ground for a variety of computing services and offers, especially if they have an educational slant.

### Mail Order
A superb data source for non-competing mail order companies. These individuals enjoy purchasing products via mail order and will respond well to a range of high quality products.

### Fundraising
The high level of affluence across this file makes it an ideal choice for fundraisers. Profiling indicates that these buyers are very much family orientated and have a strong awareness of social concerns. Test the list for both donor and trading campaigns.

### Publishing
These well-educated buyers will be very receptive to subscription, book club offers that include special interest topics such as wine, gardening, DIY, foreign travel, personal computing and hobbies.

### Travel & Leisure
The affluence of the file suggests that overseas travel & leisure promotions are likely to be of interest to these mail responsive individuals. As profiling suggests that 94% of the file have children, customers are likely to be particularly interested in holidays for the whole family.

### Profile

| | |
|---|---|
| Females | 48% |
| Males | 52% |
| Home Owners | 84% |
| Credit Card Owners | 93% |
| Children | 95% |
| Car Ownership | 72% |

*Source: www.prospectswetenhams.com*

## Selections

Title/Prefix

Recency

Gender

Age

Multi-buyers

Credit Card Usage

Product Type

Order Value

Geographic Location

**Updates**
This file is updated on a monthly basis
This file is MPS screened on a monthly basis

**Minimum Order**                     5,000
Delivery 7 working days maximum

Cancellation charge £100 flat fee + delivery +
£10/000 plus selection charges

**Net Names**
Applicable on order of 20,000+ 85% + £10/000
run on charge. Net names must be confirmed
within 4 months of date of invoice. After this
time net name credits will become null and
void.

**Payment**
30 days from date of invoice

## Rates

| | |
|---|---|
| List Warranty | 000754 |
| DMA List Broker Commission | 20% |
| **Base Rental** | |
| 0-12 month buyers | £120/000 |
| 13-24 month buyers | £100/000 |
| Charity Discount | £10/000 |
| **Selections** | |

£5/000 with the following exceptions:

| | |
|---|---|
| Hotline Names (0-6 month) | £10/000 |
| Age | £10/000 |
| Multi-Buyers | £10/000 |
| Credit Card Payment | £10/000 |
| Product Type | £20/000 |
| Order Value | £10/000 |
| Newspaper Readership | £20/000 |
| Mutually Exclusive | £10/000 |
| Soft Option | £15/000 |
| **Product Endorsement** | £25/000 |
| (Subject to approval) | |

**Remail Rate**
£20/000 discount on base price

| **Production** | |
|---|---|
| Disk | £30 |
| CD-ROM | £30 |
| E-mail | £30 |
| Carriage | £35 |
| Keycoding | £3/000 |
| Running Charges | £10/000 |

# Testing lists

There are two ways you can test lists. The first way is to pretest a small sample to check its accuracy or the level of duplication with your customer database. Pretesting is more often used in business mailings or when a list is to be purchased outright.

Consumer lists are usually tested by mailing samples from them. Your list broker will probably submit a test schedule with four or five lists, suggesting you should test 5,000 names from each list. Why 5,000? A good question. The usual answer is that the minimum rental price is based on a quantity of 5,000.

Cheaper online

Some online suppliers (such as marketingfile.com) waive the minimum order quantity requirement. This can be very useful if you only want to rent a small number of names.

## Test samples

The next question you must ask yourself is what size sample you need. The answer will depend on how much response you expect and how important it is that the test produces an answer that is almost certainly right. The bigger the expected response rate, the smaller the sample you will need – this is because test results are never absolute but have to be read in conjunction with an allowance we call error tolerance. This is a plus or minus amount that has to be applied when reading a test. The larger the response the smaller will be the error tolerance.

Of course this is a very simplified explanation and to really understand the factors involved in reading a test result you must study chapter 8.2 on testing. This will explain in detail how to calculate sample sizes and how to judge the reliability of a test.

What if you don't know what response rate to expect?

There is always a way. Say you already do direct response advertising in the press. You know what the average response costs. You would not be testing mailing unless you thought it might do just as well, or nearly as well. Take this cost and work out what response you would need per thousand mailings to equal it. Now you have your expected response rate.

No previous response experience? Well, how much can you afford to pay for a sale or for a lead? How many responses will you need per thousand mailings to produce sales or leads at your allowable cost? The answer will give you your expected response rate for the purpose of determining the sample size.

## What kind of sample?

You will probably ask for an *nth name sample*, that is (for all practical purposes) a random sample of the whole list. But, with a big list, you may only want to test the most recent names, or females, or people in the North West. Make sure you specify exactly what you want and that you know what rollout potential the specified segment of the list offers you. If you do test a subset of the list remember that your results can only be extrapolated into a rollout to the same subset of names. In other words if you have tested a sample of recent buyers you can only project this result into an estimate of what the rest of the recent buyers will produce, not across the entire list.

Figure 5.1.4    **Sample list test plan**

| List | Test quantity selection | Description/ potential | Rollout |
|------|------------------------|------------------------|---------|
| Lawnmower owners | 6,000 | <2 years old | 49,000 |
| Greenhouse owners | 6,000 | random | 23,000 |
| Greenhouse enquirers | 6,000 | <12 months old | 78,000 |
| Garden furniture buyers | 6,000 | over £200 purchase value | 21,000 |
| **Total** | 24,000 | | 171,000 |

## Post-analysis

After your tests, you may still want to refine your selection from the best lists, particularly if they offer you more names than you can afford to mail. You may use post-analysis in which the responders are profiled against a sample of the mailing base to see how they differ.

For example, you may find that responders are more likely to live in houses than flats; that they are more likely to live in certain postal districts; that they are more likely to belong to certain geodemographic neighbourhood types and so on. This could enable you to get a higher response from your rollout than you got from any of your tests simply by specifying the exclusion of names with poor performance characteristics.

To do this you will need to obtain counts by title (Mr, Mrs etc.), address type, area, geo-demographic  profile and so on *within the complete file used to address the mailing*, so that you can profile responders against the mailing base and see how they differ. Doing this may also enable you to rescue lists that performed a little below par. This sort of analysis can also be done by CHAID – see chapter 2.4.

Using post-analysis will allow you to make correct selections within lists (see 'selections within lists' above) instead of guessing.

---

**Murphy's Law of list testing**

Without post-analysis – and often it is not worth doing unless the lists are big – you will generally find that the rollout response is slightly lower than the test response.

Many explanations for disappointment at rollout have been offered, some more convincing than others. One partial explanation is internal duplication, i.e. if every tenth name on an alphabetical or postcode sequence file is a duplicate, this will depress response in a rollout but not in an *nth* name test. This theory has waned in popularity as more lists have become duplicate free.
(See two articles by David Dupin in the *Journal of Database Marketing Vol 7 No 3,* and in *Interactive Marketing Vol 2 No 2* on testing from single and multiple lists respectively – Ed.)

The most important thing about Murphy's Law of lists is to allow about 10 per cent for it and underestimate your rollout result by this amount for financial calculations. But not for fulfilment print runs – otherwise Murphy will ensure your rollout goes 10 per cent over forecast instead.

---

# Deduplication

We have referred to the mailing file or mailing base before. This is not the sum total of the lists you ordered. It is this total *less those names that have been deleted* because they are (a) already on your database, or (b) also on one of more of the other lists, or (c) have been deleted as part of a suppression process, using MPS or other suppression files dealt with earlier. You will need to use a bureau to undertake the deduplication task (or merge-purge). They will need appropriate address management and merge-purge software to do this. They will also correct or delete any undeliverable addresses that they find, using the Postal Address File (PAF).

Lists that include a high proportion of duplicates ('dupes') also tend to work well. That is because they are:

(a)     More likely to match your customer profile.

(b)     More likely to be responsive.

It is important to ensure that these good lists are not included at the end of the merge-purge process. If they are, even more names will be deleted from them. The result? You will be demanding a better *net names* deal from your most valuable list owners and may sour relations with them. A way of avoiding this is to include these lists early in the chain and delete more of the dupes from the other lists. On the other hand, with a very large merge-purge you may wish to make small cost savings by instructing the bureau to delete from the most expensive lists first.

## *Royal Mail services*

Most media rates are roughly *pro rata*. That is, if you buy a full page it will probably cost you twice as much as a half page. If you buy two minutes of airtime, it will cost you four times as much as a 30-second spot. Or at least those are the rates that media owners will quote you. However, although the rate card costs will work like this, your media buyers should be able to negotiate better discounts on the larger spaces or time slots.

Direct mail is different. What you pay for postage depends, firstly, on the weight of your mailing pack. Most cold mailings are designed to fit within the lowest weight band (60g). Unless your mail is pre-sorted, you will pay the prevailing 60g second-class rate. (However, for forthcoming changes in the charging methodology of Royal Mail, under the heading of 'pricing in proportion' (previously known as size-based pricing) see chapter 11.3.)

## *10 ways to succeed with cold mailing*

1. Test. Only direct marketing allows you to be wrong three times out of four and still be a winner. Test four lists with 5,000 mailings to each. Three fail. One works. Rollout 120,000 mailings to the successful list. 125,000 of your 140,000 mailings work.

2. Think media strategy first (can direct mail work?), lists second (can we reach the people we want?), creative work last. The most successful direct mail copy is written for a highly specific audience.

3. Brief your list broker as carefully as your creative team. Given that targeting the right prospect is the most important factor, the chances are, your broker can make a major contribution to your success. Allow time for things to go wrong – preferably at least four weeks from list order to mailing date, and if you are producing copy that takes account of specific factors within this list, you need to allow much longer.

4. Specify how you want the lists – disk, CD-ROM, email. Do you want a code number to appear through the envelope window?

5. 'Nixies' are mailings that have been incorrectly addressed (usually to a person who used to live at that address or occupy that desk) and have been put back into the post with the message 'Return to Sender'. Remember the 'nixies' arrive before most of the positive response. Three percent of 20,000 mailings looks a lot. Do a rough count before making that hysterical call to your list broker. At least you remembered to print a return address on the envelope. (Did you? If not Royal Mail is not obliged to return them). Also when counting nixies, remember that not everyone who receives an incorrectly addressed mailing is sufficiently conscientious to 'return to sender'. The total of nixies returned can be considerably less than the actual number of incorrect addresses.

6.  Avoid the automatic choice of a 5,000 test quantity. Use chapter 8.2 to get it right. Remember to specify an 'nth' name sample of the list segment you want to test and roll out. Don't forget Murphy's Law. Discount your test result by 10 per cent before making your rollout business projection.

7.  Will the cost of pre-sorting the mailing be recoverable in Royal Mail discount? Check first before specifying your requirements.

8.  If you are dealing with a large number of lists or have a large database, your final mailing quantity may be considerably less than the number of names ordered. Have you requested a net names deal? Consider requesting counts of titles, job titles, postal districts, address or company types etc. on the complete mailing file so that you can undertake post-analysis.

9.  Remember list selection is an art, not just a science. A list of vitamin supplement buyers was the best source of classical record club members. Why? *Possibly* because both groups included many people lacking in self-confidence.

10. Never consider external mailing lists in isolation. They are simply an alternative to email lists, print, broadcast, online and other advertising media. Keep comparing the results.

# Mailing your own customers

There are two types of customer mailings:

1.  Seasonal (bulk) mailings

2.  Series (time-sensitive) mailings

When you send Christmas cards to all your friends, that is a seasonal (bulk) mailing. When you send a birthday card to each of your closest friends at the right time, each one is a series (time-sensitive) mailing. This type of mailing is also called an event-driven mailing.

## Seasonal (bulk) mailings

These are used for marketing communications that need to be addressed to a number of customers at the same time. For example:

•   Issue of new catalogue

•   Announcement of January sale

•   Launch of new product

Seasonal mailings are cheaper and simpler to organise than series mailings. They can also be driven by smaller amounts of customer data. However, it is wrong to think of them as mass mailings. A seasonal mailing may go to only one customer segment or may be despatched at different times to different segments. For example, some mail-order companies have found that by timing their catalogue mailings to coincide with previous customer buying patterns they get more orders. Alternatively, the message may be varied by segment. There may even be slight changes on an individual basis: for example, there may be a reference to the customer's unused credit limit or a reference to the customer's last transaction.

Seasonal mailings may be considered as an alternative to series mailings for certain tasks. For example, lapsed customers could be mailed in bulk to recover their custom with a new 'welcome back' offer. Alternatively, they could be mailed one by one at set intervals since their last transaction. Both methods can be used in combination:

## Series, then seasonal

If, despite many renewal invitations (series mailings), you allow your *Time* or *Newsweek* subscription to expire you can expect two or three further invitations in the weeks immediately ahead. If you still fail to respond, you will next be mailed on a seasonal basis some months in the future.

## Series (time-sensitive) mailings

Series mailings may compete with email and the phone or may be used in combination with these media. The most common application is *prospect conversion*. A series of communications will be used to complete the conversion process. Typically, a fulfilment mailing (giving the prospect the requested information) will be followed at predetermined intervals by reminder mailings and a reminder phone call or email.

For customer mailing programmes, series communications offer two main advantages:

1. Ideally, they target the right people at the right time

2. Their relevance conveys recognition of the individual customer

Applications for series mailings include:

- Anniversary mailings

- Event mailings

- Score-driven mailings

We can take the case of a bank to show examples of these applications:

- An anniversary mailing could be used to remind the customer that it is *her* car's third birthday. Why not consider taking out another loan to replace the car?

- An event mailing could follow a customer's change of address notification. Congratulating the customer on *his* new home, the mailing could offer finance to meet the cost of new furniture or other expenses.

- Recipients of score-driven mailings are selected because there has been a change in their circumstances. The bank may use a dynamic scorecard that reviews a customer's credit status or other characteristic on a month-by-month basis. A change in the score may lead to an invitation to apply for a credit card or a personal loan on special terms.

Series mailings also have their disadvantages:

1.  They require more historical data and may require advanced statistical modelling.

2.  They are more expensive – because they are sent out in smaller batches they do not offer the same economies of scale.

3.  They raise the penalty for getting personal data wrong. Any errors will be twice as irritating to customers because greater knowledge of the customer's circumstances has been assumed.

# Press ahead and get some good results

## This chapter includes:

- - - - - - - - - - - - - - - - - - - - - - - - - - - - - - - - - - - - - - - -

❏ **Brief overview of the UK press marketplace and lots of web addresses**

❏ **Summary of how the press is traditionally used**

❏ **Review of the obvious strengths and weaknesses of the press**

❏ **Media planner's master checklist**

❏ **Tips for reading media research data**

❏ **Inserts – planning checklist**

- - - - - - - - - - - - - - - - - - - - - - - - - - - - - - - - - - - - - - - -

## About this chapter

**T**his chapter reviews the range of national, regional and local newspapers, including free sheets, and also magazines. It considers the various ways in which direct marketers use press advertising, and the tools available to the advertiser who wishes to optimise spend. Finally it looks at the use of loose inserts, and the relative response available from this source versus standardpress advertising.

### *Beverly Barker*

Beverly is an entirely over qualified communications planner having started in the business as a broadcast buyer with Ogilvy & Mather in 1984 and, after moving through a succession of agencies that were assortedly acquired and merged to make the large conglomerates of today, spent from 1992-2002 as Head of Direct and Interactive at Carat Direct.

Beverly now combines academia with practical commercial operations, working as a senior lecturer in Marketing at London Southbank University and a regular tutor for the IDM, alongside being a Managing Partner in Everythingville, where she provides a strategic customer insight consultancy to both UK and International clients in customer management, customer insight, proposition development and integrated communications planning.

## Chapter 5.2

# *Press ahead and get some good results*

85 per cent or more of all display press advertising now carries a response mechanism of some type: coupon, tipped-on reply card, telephone/fax number or URL. Within 'classified' sections this increases to virtually 100 per cent.

## The UK print marketplace

According to TGI (2005), over 80 per cent of the population look at some form of printed media during the course of the average month. Within the newspaper arena, around 50 per cent of the population read a paper, with slightly more taking up the weekend editions.

Figure 5.2.1 **TGI : % coverage of UK population (adults aged 15+) by press publication type**

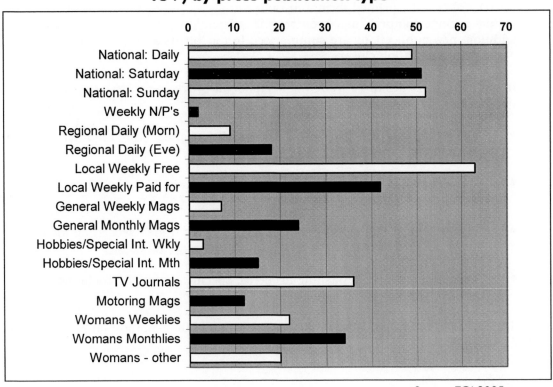

Source: TGI 2005

There are nearly 10,000 titles to consider. Titles come and go and they are broadly classified into four groups:

- Major national newspapers

  ✔ 13 major national dailies, including the Scottish national editions – each with a number of different supplements and editorial sections, providing nearly 50 different publishing environments

  ✔ 13 major Sunday papers, again with a plethora of supplements, totalling over 40 publications

  ✔ Five to six niche titles all classified as nationals, such as the *Sunday Sport, Racing Post* and *Sport First*

- Regional/local newspapers

  ✔ Plus a further 1,200-plus regional/local newspapers, some paid for, some free, and with numerous additional supplements and extra sections

- Consumer press

  ✔ An estimated 3,200 titles are published each year and the business is still growing

- Business press

  ✔ There are 5,142 B2B magazines published in the UK by some 700 companies

Besides standing in your local WH Smith and reviewing the contents of their shelves, the best way to keep abreast of the available titles is to subscribe to BRAD, either in its printed format or online at www.brad.co.uk. Publication listings include comprehensive contact and sales and readership information. In addition, new publications are summarised in the 'births and deaths' editorial, along with publication closers.

In addition, there are three trade bodies that can provide extensive details about the market:

- The Newspaper Publishers Association (NPA) representing the interests of the national press. (http://www.npa.co.uk)

- The Newspaper Society, the 'voice of Britain's regional press'. (http://www.newspapersoc.org.uk)

- The Periodical Publishers Association (PPA), the trade association for UK magazine and B2B media publishers. (http://www.ppa.co.uk)

- The Association of Publishing Agencies, specifically for the consumer market. (http://www.apa.co.uk)

The following brief market summary details some of the common jargon grouping classifications:

## *The national press*

National newspapers can be classified two ways:

- By **the frequency of publication – 'dailies'** (publishing six days a week) and 'Sundays' (printed weekly). However, the Saturday editions are assuming greater importance, and becoming the primary weekend purchase for many people. In addition, when the *Daily Star* launched its Sunday edition in 2005, it made a positive effort to reduce the degree of demarcation between weekdays and weekends, publishing the fact that the Star was now available seven days a week. Figures 5.2.2 and 5.2.3 detail current circulations for daily and Sunday newspapers.

- By **the nature of the overall editorial style and the type of readers** that the publications attract – 'popular' (or tabloid), 'mid-market' and 'quality'. The largest selling newspaper is the *News of the World*, published by News International. This, along with its sister title, *The Sun*, is categorised within the popular sector which represents over 50 per cent of all newspapers sold each week (see figure 5.2.4 below).

Official sales are published by the Audit Bureau of Circulation (ABC). These figures are calculated through careful auditing of sales distribution and are released to give:

- Monthly averages for daily and weekly publications

- Biannual averages for monthly titles

- Annual averages for less frequent publications

ABC breaks the total circulation down geographically detailing UK only, Republic of Ireland and overseas sales. They also identify full-rate sales, lesser-rate (i.e. discounted) sales, prepaid non-postal subscription sales and multiple copy (bulk) sales.

The ABC is divided into two divisions: newspapers and consumer magazines and business-to-business, with a subsidiary ABC ELECTRONIC auditing websites and electronic media. From the ABC website you can view the latest circulation figures for a wide range of publications (see: http://www.abc.org.uk).

Figure 5.2.2 **National daily newspapers average sales**

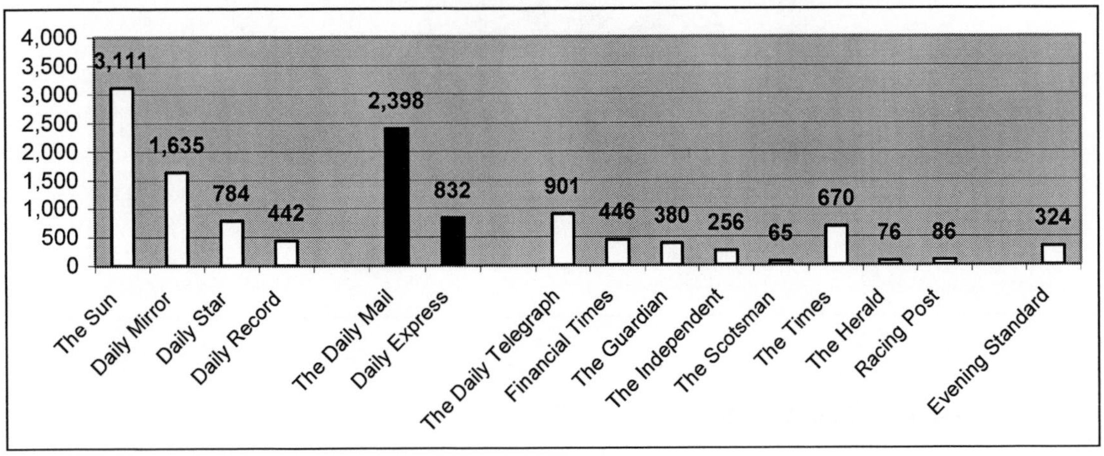

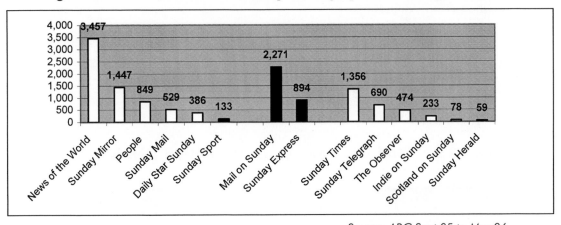

Source: ABC Sept 05 to Mar 06

Figure 5.2.3 **National Sunday newspapers average sales**

Source: ABC Sept 05 to Mar 06

## Share of circulations

There is a wider choice of quality titles, with five dailies and six Sundays; however, the combined circulations of the quality titles are much smaller, and represent less than 23 per cent of the total number of copies sold. Figure 5.2.4 shows the share of circulation by market segment:

Figure 5.2.4 **Share of circulation**

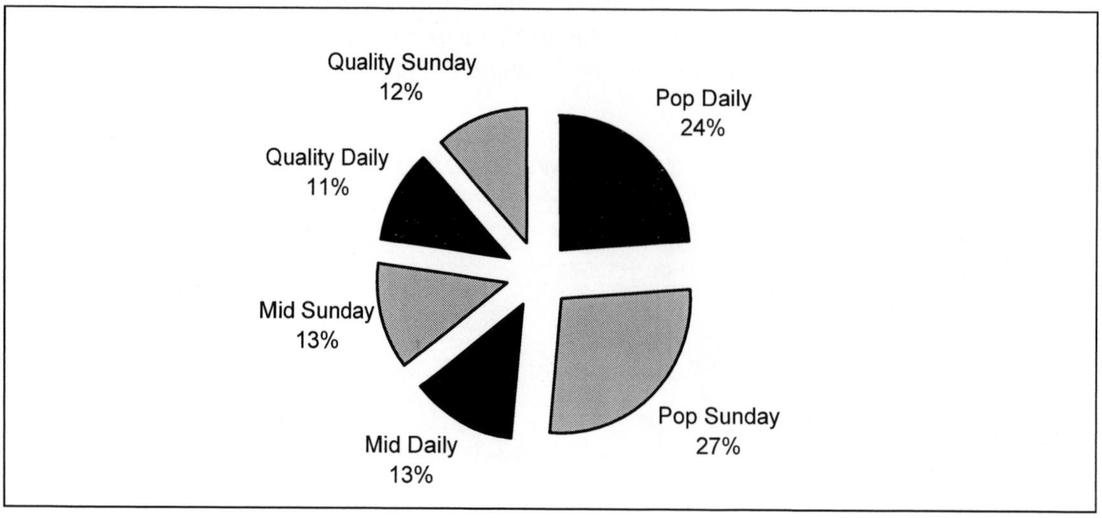
Quality Sunday
12%
Pop Daily
24%
Quality Daily
11%
Mid Sunday
13%
Mid Daily
13%
Pop Sunday
27%

*Source: ABC Sept 05-Mar 06*

## Trends in circulation

Newspaper sales were at their peak in the 1960s, and have been in steady decline since. There are many factors that account for this, some sociological – with the changes in leisure-time pursuits, and some reflecting the proliferation of media over the period, including:

- The explosion in broadcast news, be it breakfast news or dedicated news channels
- The explosion in local radio stations, and of course...
- The internet

Figure 5.2.5 **National newspaper circulation trends**

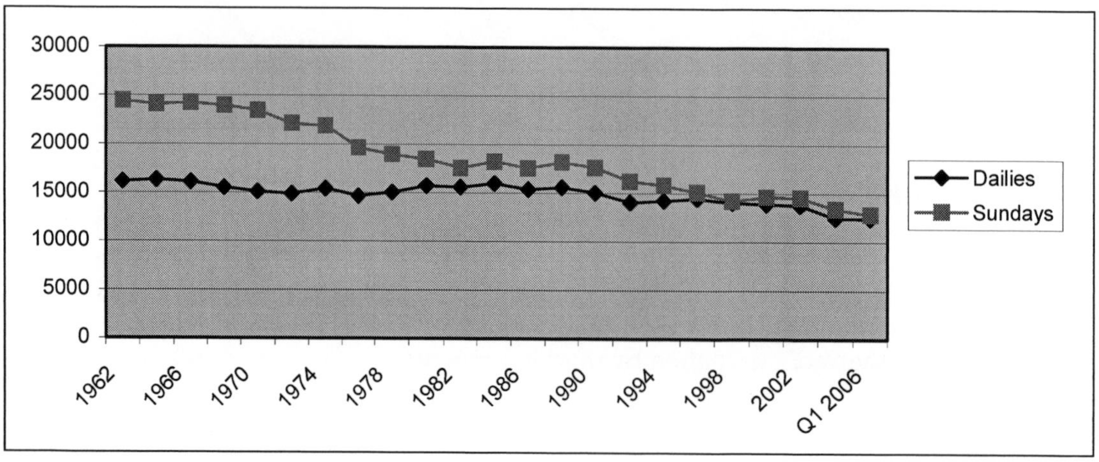
30000
25000
20000
15000
10000
5000
0
1962
1966
1970
1974
1978
1982
1986
1990
1994
1998
2002
Q1 2006
Dailies
Sundays

*Source: ABC*

Publishers continuously strive to increase their sales, either by attracting readers to change their choice of paper, or by activating new readers. Some of the tactics employed include:

- Reduced cover price offers to encourage trial
- Reduced price subscription offers to encourage loyalty

- Makeovers of publication style to improve modernity and appeal

- Tactical use of sales promotions and competitions

- Inclusion of varying additional sections to increase value perception and reflect consumer leisure demands; this is currently reflected in the continued rise in popularity of the Saturday reading package

For the advertiser the most important statistics to know are:

**The number of copies sold**

Year-on-year the individual circulations change, which is why all direct marketers should ensure that they are always working with the most accurate data for their results analysis and forecasting. Historic evaluation should be based upon the actual circulations delivered at the time of the advertising, and future plans should reflect what you think the circulation will be, i.e. where you believe the trends are going.

**The profile of the readers and the number of readers in a particular profile set (how many of your target group read the publications)**

On average every newspaper bought is read by two to three people, e.g. the *News of the World* records nearly 10.4 million readers and reaches more than 20 per cent of all adults each week. Research from the National Readership Survey (NRS) identifies the readers, their socio-demographic profiles and their product purchasing habits. It is reviewed in detail later in this chapter.

## *Regional press*

There are over 1,200 regional newspapers and supplements, ranging from paid-for dailies to free weeklies. The planner tends to use the term 'regional' for those titles covering the country's major conurbations and large towns, some of which assume near-national importance, such as the *Birmingham Mail*, *Yorkshire Evening Post*, *Bristol Evening Post* and *London Evening Standard*. The term 'local' is the collective noun for the majority of the free weeklies.

The majority of regional papers are published daily, varying between morning and evening appearance, and there are around 150 different titles, with approximately 470 weekly paid-for papers and a further 629 weekly free titles. The Newspaper Society includes an up-to-date analysis of the market structure that can be accessed via facts and figures/regional press: structure/daily/weekly and Sunday newspaper information tables (http://www.newspapersoc.org.uk/ Default.aspx?page=7). You can also find a wealth of related data, case studies and regional insights on this site.

Figure 5.2.6 **Generalised structure of the non-national press market**

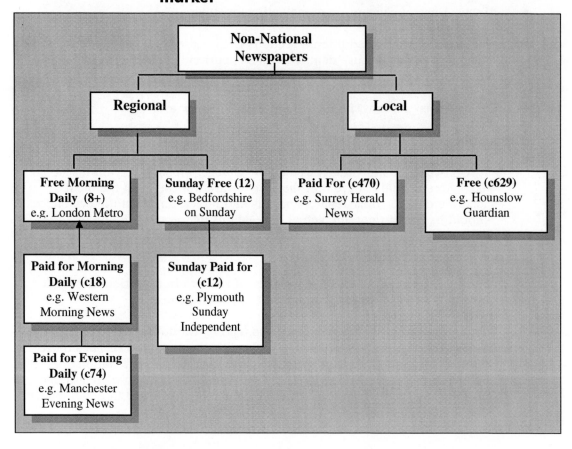

Regional newspapers have not traditionally appeared on space schedules of national direct marketers. For many, the relative cost-per-thousand for the circulation is much higher than for the nationals, as the examples in table 5.2.1 demonstrate:

Table 5.2.1 **Comparison of national and regional press cost-per-thousand**

| Publication | Circulation (thousands) | Rate card ^ Page mono | CPT* £s |
|---|---|---|---|
| Daily Mirror | **1,671** | **£12,000** | £7.18 |
| Manchester Evening News | **143** | **£2,000** | £13.99 |
| *CPT = Cost per 1,000 circulation | | ^ Rate card = the published cost from BRAD | |

Being more expensive, regional newspapers would need to be more responsive, to deliver the same anticipated cost-per-lead, or would need to be twice as efficient in delivering conversion to sales to equal the cost-per-sale.

However, for any brand with regionalised distribution patterns, or particular variations in customer penetration by region, these titles are invaluable. They will incur less wastage and are therefore very useful for providing effective regional upweights and as such they then *do* deliver the improvements in response and conversion that are required to deliver a superior return on investment.

Regional publishers are very keen to make sure that marketers and advertisers are aware of the wealth of regional publications. For example, The Scottish Newspaper Publishers Association (SNPA) represents the publishers of 100 weekly and biweekly newspapers and 30-plus free distribution newspapers and can be found easily on  http://www.snpa.org.uk/

## Local newspapers – town, village and parish

Local newspapers serve medium and small towns, with some publishers targeting separate editions to individual villages and parishes. They are normally weeklies and often distributed free, being known in the trade as free sheets. They are very effective in delivering prospects that match localised distribution and sales requirements. Local car dealers, cable networks, slimming clubs and shop and supermarket promotions all benefit from being able to target locally, thereby reducing unnecessary coverage (wastage) and enabling more tailored creative executions to be designed. Local free newspapers are generally distributed by hand to the door of every householder in the vicinity, which in itself has led to the development of a parallel advertising opportunity, that of newshare door-to-door distribution – loose inserts and leaflets posted through the letterbox alongside the local newspaper (see chapter 5.3).

## The magazine market

The magazine marketplace is huge. There are more than 3,200 consumer magazines and over 5,000 business-to-business titles.

Within the consumer sector, genres range from broad lifestyle (e.g. *Woman's Own* – mixing fashion, home décor, cookery and family issues) to highly specific interest groups (e.g. *Cat World*, *Golf Monthly*, *Yachting Monthly* and *Mother and Baby*).

There is also a wide assortment of retailer and manufacturer magazines picking off targets based upon their lifestyle behaviour and whether they  shop at Boots, Sainsbury's, Waitrose or M&S, or drive a Volvo.

Table 5.2.2 below is an extract from BRAD and details all of the major consumer classifications. However, to get a real feeling for the true breadth of this area, stand back and take a fresh look at the shelves of your local WHSmith.

Table 5.2.2     **BRAD consumer publication classifications**

| | | |
|---|---|---|
| Buying and selling | Health and fitness | Music |
| Computing | Home entertainment and electronic equipment | News and current affairs |
| County town and local interest | Home interests | Outdoor pursuits |
| Education and careers | Leisure interests | Personal finance |
| Entertainment and leisure guides | Men's magazines | Sport |
| Ethnic and expatriates | Motorcycling | Travel and tourism |
| Food and drink | Motoring | Women's magazines |
| General interest | | Youth |

## Women's magazines: a market within a market

Within the broad category of consumer magazines, women's publications form a huge segment, which in itself can be subdivided by the editorial platform. BRAD lists seven main subcategories: *business women, hair, parenthood, wedding and brides, women's lifestyle and fashion, women's weeklies and women's associations*

Each section offers a wealth of opportunity for targeting prospects and customers very closely.

For example, within the women's weeklies section there are 23 titles currently. Each sets out to satisfy a slightly different reader interest, from the competition companion and entertainment gossip styles of *Chat* and *Heat*, to the classics, such as *Woman* and *Woman's Own* focusing on real life, makeovers, family relationships, health and consumer issues. The circulations in this genre range from *Woman's Way* at 27,000 to *Take a Break* at 1,156,000, as detailed in figure 5.2. 7:

Figure 5.2.7     **Women's weeklies circulations July to December 2005 (ABC)**

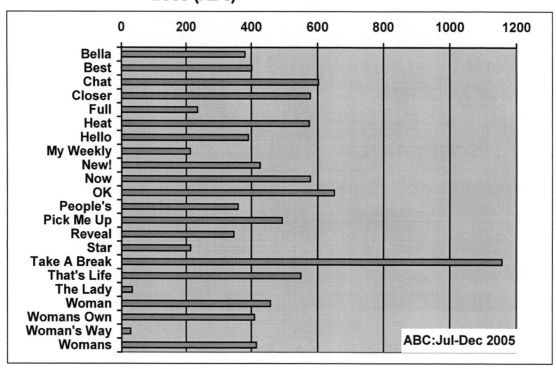

Broadly speaking, these titles offer a national platform, with the opportunity to target by age and social demographics. However, because of the close 'fit' between editorial content and reader interests and lifestyle, women's magazines form very strong relationships with their readers. From a practical point of view, this can enhance the pulling power for relevant offers, making them more cost-effective than their rates might suggest.

## Consumer interest magazines: food to football

Outside of the women's sector there are literally thousands of titles covering every conceivable sport, hobby and pastime, and usually more than one title competing in each sector.

Special interest magazines form a natural channel for niche marketing, often delivering responses economically albeit usually in small volumes.

These can be researched either via the BRAD, PPA or APA websites, which will provide comprehensive details including, in many cases, a hyperlink back to the publisher's site, or by going directly to a publication's site.

If an interest is widely subscribed to, e.g. gardening, its participants can often be reached more economically through national media; e.g. the Daily Mail reaches more gardeners than all the specialist garden magazines combined.

However, the quality of customer generated from the specialist publication can often be far greater, opening up the opportunity for increased lifetime value (LTV) through repeat purchases and cross-selling to relevant line extensions.

Consumer magazines can be highly cost-effective vehicles for loose inserts. Subjects either directly related (e.g. rose catalogues in gardening magazines) or indirectly related (e.g. warm clothing offers to readers of outdoor pursuits) can do equally well.

Figure 5.2.8 **Main users of customer/contract publishing**

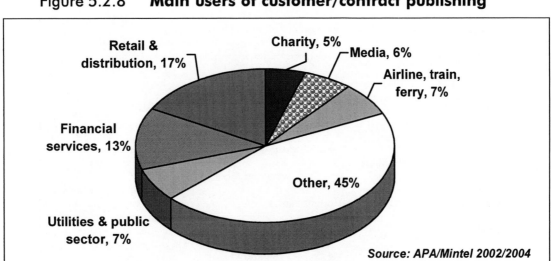

Source: APA/Mintel 2002/2004

The vast majority of contract publications are aimed at the consumer, accounting for 68 per cent of the magazines covered by the APA/Mintel survey. One-fifth was looking to reach business and the remainder were targeting both consumer and business segments.

Relationship management is crucial in the customer publishing market, the most commonly cited objectives being to engender loyalty, to provide information to existing customers and sell them more.

Many of these titles are distributed free of charge although a few have commercialised sufficiently to justify a cover price. In addition, over half of those in the market now take advertising from third parties, giving advertisers the opportunity to reach prospects in a variety of ways.

## Business and trade magazines – over 5,000 titles

Business magazines cover every trade, industry and profession – and every job function from production to finance. Table 5.2.3 summarises the wealth of choice. Most are monthly or quarterly, although a few trades have weeklies and some dailies (such as in the licensed trade). There is a further breakdown between *paid-for* and *free* subscriptions. The latter, known as *controlled circulations*, are despatched only to bona fide registered members of an industry or profession, who must complete a signed subscription form annually.

Because of the high level of subscriber information available in the business-to-business sector, there is a further opportunity open to direct marketers; that of direct mailing or emailing the magazine readers, or even linking with a publisher's website. Most publishers will make their subscription lists available, and very often there is a high degree of additional selectivity that can be overlaid, e.g. selecting subscribers by job title, region, number of employees and size of factory. Using the opportunities in combination can produce very good results.

## Table 5.2.3    BRAD business magazine classifications

| | | |
|---|---|---|
| Aeronautical | Energy | Medicine and health packaging |
| Agriculture, forestry and fishing | Entertainment industry and technology | Printing |
| Architecture | Environment and conservation | Property |
| Arts | Exporting and importing | Rail transport |
| Antiques and dealers | Fashion, clothing and textiles | Security and crime prevention |
| Building | Finance and financial services | Recruitment |
| Business management | Food and drink processing | Retailing and wholesaling |
| Business services | Furnishings and woodworking | |
| Catering and hospitality | Government, church and public services | Road transport |
| Chemical industry | Legal | Sciences |
| Computing | Leisure industry | Ships and marine |
| Corporate and organisation journals | Licensing, wine and tobacco | Social sciences |
| Education and training | Manufacturing | Telecommunications |
| Electrical industry | Materials | Transportation industry |
| Electronics | Media, marketing and advertising | Travel industry |
| | | Veterinary |

# Press advertising and the direct marketer

Direct marketers use press advertising in five distinct ways corresponding to the strengths of the medium. These are:

1.  To make direct sales (one-stage)

2.  To produce volume enquiries (two-stage)

3.  To reach niche audiences

4.  To support other response media

5.  To build awareness

These objectives can also be combined, e.g. to make direct sales and build awareness, or to produce volume enquiries and support other media. However, over time, awareness accrues from press advertising whatever its primary objective.

## Objective no 1: direct sales

The use of press advertising to generate direct sales is a well-established method of business. The boom began in the 1970s with the growth of telephone and credit card advertising and has continued into the 21st Century, due to the evergrowing appreciation for the effectiveness and convenience it affords.

A large proportion of mail order or off-the-page advertisements appear in the supplements of national newspapers. The higher quality colour reproduction works well to enhance the appeal of many products; for instance a collectible plate, a floral dress or a stack of CDs. In addition, the environment is more conducive to leisurely repeat reading, which can help to increase the effectiveness of the advertising.

All direct sale offers, especially cash-with-order, are carefully monitored by the ASA and publisher watchdogs, such as SHOPS, the Safe Home Ordering Protection Scheme (the replacement for  the old MOPS, the Mail Order Protection Scheme). SHOPS is a not-for-profit organisation owned by the Newspaper Publishers Association (NPA) and the Direct Marketing Association (DMA) and is there to protect the consumer when buying directly from advertisements and catalogues inserted in the national newspapers.

All the major publishing groups run such reader protection schemes to offer readers additional insurance. Advertising copy that has not been approved by the appropriate group will not be published, even if the space has been booked. Off-the-page offers may be cash-with-order (i.e. payment by cheque or postal order), free trial or payment by credit card and direct debit.

Many organisations have built their businesses through response advertising in the national press as it is a highly effective acquisition medium. It is not unknown for a single advertisement (one insertion) to 'pull' several hundred enquiries for the advertiser to handle, be it mail, telephone or personal follow-up. Increasingly, a very wide spectrum of organisations designs their advertising to generate responses, whether for reasons of research, customer care or sales.

## *Objective no 2: volume enquiries (two-stage)*

So what makes press advertising so good at generating cost-effective replies? One theory is that because the press is a news medium, readers regard it not only as an important source of news and information about products and services, but also for the 'news' contained in advertising. For many product categories the number of individuals likely to reply to an individual advertisement combines favourably with the relative cost of press advertising to deliver cost-efficient leads. The financial industry has certainly found it a highly useful acquisition tool, effectively generating regular volumes of leads to their call centres. It does not, of course, work for everyone.

The business press also promotes volume enquiries but adds an extra dimension; their 'directory' effect. Readers turn to magazines to locate suppliers of specific goods, much as they would use a directory; consequently some businesses find that they cannot afford not to advertise there!

## *Objective no 3: reaching niche audiences*

Press advertising can find prospects that cannot easily be identified by any other means, in two ways:

✔    Self-selection (hand-raising)

✔    Specialist targeting

Where a target audience is highly specialised, but cannot be categorised via a mailing list or niche magazine, the national press can encourage interested prospects to identify themselves by returning a coupon or making a telephone call. This process is known as *hand raising* or targeting by self-selection.

**Application: home is where the computer is**

Take the case of someone starting up a business from home or a small rented office. Although the SOHO (small office, home office) market is quite well established, until an individual has subscribed to their first computer magazine or requested a catalogue from a mail-order stationery supplier, they are not very easy to identify. They may however be your perfect prospect, ready to buy a business computer, software package, desk or insurance policy. The news or business pages of the national press are probably the best place to try and reach them.

As the business progresses, they may subscribe to a selection of related magazines (e.g. managerial, financial, technical or legal advice) and their own trade or industry publications, be it architecture, dentistry, accountancy, freelance writing, rabbit breeding or whatever.

At this point our SOHO prospect can be reached via a number of routes. Our campaign could incorporate elements of both mass and specialist press options, plus direct mail information from subscription data. Through evaluation we will be able to identify the relative cost efficiencies, both in the short and long term, of the different vehicles for different messages – but right up there at the beginning of the relationship – the press will be the most effective way of enabling these suspects to reveal themselves.

### Objective no 4: support other media

Press advertising, with its high visibility and wide coverage, can provide effective support for other response media such as direct mail or direct response TV.

It is often used to carry detail that cannot be conveyed in image-oriented TV or radio commercials, e.g. for cars, financial services and travel. It may also be used to promote the 'call to action' by providing the necessary coupon or application form.

In some cases the role is reversed and the press is employed to generate the broad appeal for a product or service – with other media such as direct mail, inserts, door-to-door or telephone marketing being used to generate the sales lead. This is frequently seen in the business arena where display advertisements in trade magazines are used to draw attention to a product or service and contact is made with decision makers via direct mail or personal follow-up.

### Objective no 5: to build awareness

Essentially all advertising has to generate some degree of awareness to be able to create any subsequent related behaviour. In direct marketing terms we have noted that press awareness can be turned to immediate response. Similarly, many brand advertisers will now incorporate contact details within their image ads, enabling people to enquire for further information directly, instead of visiting a store or dealership for instance. Smart advertisers will add the enquirers' names to their prospect database and develop a recontact strategy if it seems profitable.

We are straying into non-direct advertising here. Awareness is a very real objective in its own right and requires skilled planning. However, many advertisers see a measurable uplift in response when their overall levels of awareness are higher. Running integrated campaigns can be highly beneficial, but it is important to have clearly identified objectives for each element to enable them to be planned and measured accurately.

## Features and advantages of press advertising

There are some generalised strengths and weaknesses associated with print media and a number of specific issues relating to the various sectors of the marketplace or to the format in which the advertiser accesses the audience, i.e. whether through space or inserts. Firstly we have categorised the general features:

✔ Year-round availability

✔ National/local cover: *Sunday Times* versus *Wandsworth Guardian*

✔ Mass or niche audiences: *News of the World* versus *Cat World*

✔ Entry cost

✔ Reader relationships and environments: motoring, gardening or fashion etc.

✔ Lead times

✔ Creative versatility

✔ Response times and publication shelf life

✔ Rates and data availability

✔ Reader research

✔ Test opportunities

✔ Competitive activity

✔ Two-dimensional image

But to see how they impact upon an individual direct marketing campaign we must understand that effectiveness varies and it will do so by:

✔ Size of audience

✔ Allowable costs

✔ Complexity of message

✔ Environment and intrinsic qualities of publication or position

✔ How much any wastage costs

## Year-round availability

Press media is always available. Published schedules allow you to plan campaigns to commence and, in theory, finish on specific dates. However, some publications and advertising sites are very heavily demanded, therefore it may not be possible to get an insertion on the exact date that you intended due to a lack of availability. This is mainly a problem with specific magazine and newspaper sites such as the outside back cover (OBC), inside front cover (double-page) spread (IFCDPS) or the front page solus sites on the main new section of the newspapers, and with specific highly demanded insert slots such as in the run-up to Christmas.

## National/local cover

The diversity of print publications means that whatever the scale of the task required, there is probably a vehicle to match it. An advertiser, such as a motor manufacturer, who needs to launch a new car and build rapid awareness, will find the high volume coverage of the national press very effective; as will the direct marketer who wants to take advantage of a sales window and maximise lead generation over a short period of time. Conversely, the motor dealership can concentrate its activity on those local prospects that will find the showroom's location convenient.

## Mass or niche audiences

Due to the breadth of the marketplace, there is a diversity of reader profiles to choose from, but as any direct marketing statistician will confirm, no targeting method is perfect. With the national press it is often quite rudimentary, the overriding profile being driven by the *majority* of readers, not the *totality*, therefore high-earning professionals read popular tabloids and an aspiring student will digest *The Times*. But the *loose* targeting of the national press is also its strength. We use its coverage to encourage prospects to identify themselves, a process we call hand raising, as mentioned previously.

## Reader relationships and environments

Editors develop strong relationships with their readers and an advertiser can gain an implied endorsement through careful selection of the advertising environment. For example, an investment company will probably attract *higher-value investors* by placing their ads within financial editorial (be it the money section of <u>The Daily Telegraph</u>, or *Money Week magazine*) because the readers are actively seeking an investment solution. However, the same company could probably attract a *greater number of investors* from an advertisement placed in general editorial, by stimulating hand raising from a broader group, but the average investment level is likely to be lower. As to which solution will be the best for your campaign will depend upon your business objectives.

Likewise, special features and supplements are often attractive opportunities because they deliver interested prospects – but it is important to ensure that your company is not going to be the subject of bad PR or at the bottom of any league tables that may be published in the report! The reader relationship will work to your disadvantage in that case.

## Entry cost

The cost of reaching audiences through space advertising, especially in national newspapers, is probably the lowest of any media.

The relatively low cost-per-thousand (CPT) of reaching the audience through the publications circulation, combined with relatively simple origination and low production costs, compare favourably to direct mail packages that may cost as much as 50 pence each to produce and deliver. Table 5.2.4 shows some typical newspaper costs-per-thousand circulation (based on mono 25cm x 4 column space):

### Table 5.2.4 **Typical newspaper costs-per-thousand**

| Publication | Circulation (ABC) | Position* | Rate card mono 25 x 4 | CPT £'s | Response % to deliver £10 CPR |
|---|---|---|---|---|---|
| Daily Mail | 2,394,052 (Feb 2001) | Guaranteed position | £17,300 | 7.23 | 0.07% |
| | | ROP | £12,500 | 5.22 | 0.05% |
| Daily Express | 950,523 (Feb 2001) | Guaranteed position | £10,670 | 11.23 | 0.11% |
| | | ROP | £8,500 | 8.94 | 0.09% |
| Evening Press (York) | 42,546 Jun to Dec 2000 | Guaranteed position | £1,000 | 23.50 | 0.23% |
| | | ROP | £770 | 18.09 | 0.18% |
| Croydon Guardian | 112,904 - VFD | ROP | £1,050 | 9.29 | 0.09% |
| * ROP = Run of paper | | | | | |

The low-cost argument is less persuasive for specialist media with smaller circulations, but often this is compensated for by the high responsive and improved LTV that is often seen from special interest markets.

### Lead times – relatively simple set-up procedures

Compared to most media, press advertising takes less time to set up, especially mono executions. New press technology means copy deadlines are remarkably short, especially for the national press, which can often be accessed the day before publication, i.e. 'short term', if there is availability. Colour reproduction is more complex, of course, although technology is constantly being introduced to simplify the process. However, special positions and highly demanded sections need careful planning, as the supply on any one day is not infinite.

Don't let shorter lead times mislead you into leaving space reservation too late. Booking time for some monthlies can be up to four months in advance of the cover date and several months longer for specific sites, e.g. inside front cover (IFC), half-page under contents, first right-hand page and facing specific editorial.

### Creative versatility

There is a lot of choice – small space sizes can be utilised to optimise frequency, fractional space can dominate editorial environments, double-page spreads (DPS) deliver dramatic pictorial effect – and a gatefold attached to the front cover could extend the design area further still.

In every planning process there comes a point when the title selection has been refined and you know what creative messages you are going to want to put over. At this point it is well worth spending time reviewing your chosen publications to see exactly what positions can be attained. For example, is there a site available next to 'contents' – is it landscape or portrait?

### Response times and publication shelf life

There is a clear correlation between the shelf life of a publication and the pattern of response it generates. Response tails (what percentage of the overall response arrives when) are something that every direct marketer should track and once you know the various patterns, you can predict the end result based upon the first few days' activity – a very useful facility.

As a rule of thumb, a large proportion of daily newspapers are 'binned' the following day and therefore about 60 per cent of total telephone responses will be delivered in the first day or two. The remaining 40 per cent will tail off within five days or so. Sunday publications by contrast generate comparatively little of their overall response on the first day (even if a Freephone number (0800) is included) – it seems that everyone wants to call from the office on a Monday morning, which will generally be the high spot for the response tail, with the remainder trickling in over the rest of the week.

Figure 5.2.9    **Theoretical response tail for media of varying on-street durations**

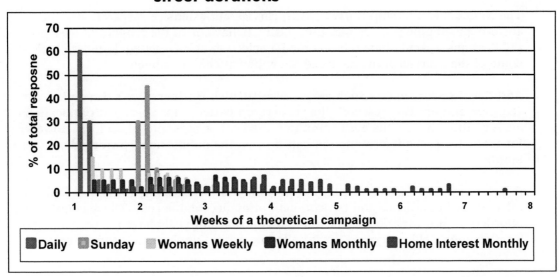

Monthly magazines generate response more slowly, firstly because it can take up to four weeks for the full circulation to be achieved. Then, some readers will dip in and out of that copy until the next issue supersedes it; others will be kept for reference, some discarded after a final scan and some passed to secondary readers.

The response tail may therefore be many weeks or months. In a few cases, response can trickle in a year or more later – therefore it is important that advertising carries the necessary closing dates, small print or other legalities if your offer is likely to remain in circulation that long.

When working with call centres, it is important to plan call volumes as accurately as possible. Understanding when your advertising will actually be 'on-street' and when the expected responses are going to be delivered is vital to ensuring good call management. In addition, the evaluation reports should respect the timescales over which you can take a true reading on the effectiveness of your advertising, and when it is just an insightful snapshot. There is a management measure that can be usefully built around this principle known as 'the 50 per cent day', this being the day when you anticipate 50 per cent of the response to have been generated – by taking a reading at this point you are able to determine whether your activity is under or over performing, and you can consider contingency action.

## *Rates and data availability*

Through vehicles such as BRAD it is possible to reference the core statistics related to almost every title published, helping the planner to put together a well budgeted and detailed schedule. Schedules should include:

✔   Rate card details – cost for a single-column centimetre (SCC), page mono, page colour or special position premium, dependent upon what is appropriate for the schedule

✔   Mechanical data – column widths, page sizes, screen/film requirements and insert delivery requirements etc.

✔   Publication data – copy and print calendars, cover dates, on-street dates and copy deadlines etc.

## Reader research

The National Readership Survey (NRS) carries out extensive research into the socio-demographic profiles and purchasing behaviour of the readers of over 300 publications, essential for refining media selection and targeting. Later we look at some of the sources of the data and show how it can be applied.

Additional sector reports such as the BBS (British Businessman's Survey), CapiBus and AgriBus research the readership patterns for specialist publications such as those in the business computer, medical or agricultural sectors. However for many titles, the information is based upon the publication's own reader studies.

A lack of syndicated data should not prevent you from testing a title that looks to offer the right audience and environment at an acceptable cost. The accountability afforded to direct marketers means that you will ultimately have a true reading of a publication's efficiency and potentially unearth an uncluttered seam of gold.

## Test opportunities

Press advertising offers plenty of inexpensive test opportunities. For direct marketers developing customer acquisition programmes, testing print advertising is as important as direct mail testing. The various standard techniques for testing across all media, including press advertising, are covered in chapter 8.2.

Remember, the professional direct marketer is the one who realises it is necessary to test, not the one who makes a lucky guess at the result.

Press testing – some rules of thumb:

✔ When testing a publication, use your control advertisement where possible.

✔ If your control advertisement is particularly expensive, experiment with smaller or cheaper spaces.

✔ Different media and copy often produce widely varying ongoing customer performance (the so-called 'back end'). It is therefore wise to calculate back-end results carefully before setting on control advertisements and media.

✔ Never rely on single press test results. The more critical the decision, the more tests should be carried out (say, four to six at least). Fewer tests than this may yield inexplicably contradictory results.

✔ Where two advertisements regularly produce similar, satisfactory results regard this as a good outcome. It could mean you have a second winner!

In summary, testing in press helps you to compare the response-inducing power of advertising in newspapers and magazines. The important points are to be aware of the deficiencies and to retest frequently.

# So what are the drawbacks of the press?

## It is a passive medium

Some marketers must use direct mail, telephone or personal follow-up to transform a press enquirer into a long-term customer, gaining the necessary signature or private details required to finalise a deal.

## It is very public

Everything printed is highly visible and recorded by monitoring companies such as ACNeilsen/MMS. When you run a pilot programme in the press, everyone knows.

## It's two-dimensional

The 'visual only, no audio' argument is often levied at the press, and in some cases creative options can seem limited compared to other print media such as direct mail.

## Competitive clutter ...

This is definitely a factor to consider within many publications, as are mail-order ghettos. The financial section of most national papers will definitely be bursting with competitive offers; however, the readers will expect to be able to refer to these pages to find solutions to their needs, e.g. telephone numbers for motor insurance companies to call for quotes and investment companies detailing their interest rates. The competitive clutter has now created environments from which many companies dare not be excluded, such as the financial section of the *Daily Mail* on a Wednesday, which acts as a veritable directory for the reader.

# Media planning using space advertising – the media planner's checklist

We can now appreciate the benefits of press advertising and how it can be used. However, before contemplating a schedule we need to understand the *who, what, how* and *when* to ensure that the final decisions deliver the campaign objectives – the *why*.

**Marketing objectives:**

- Number of responses (enquiries/sales)

- Enquiry-to-sales

- Required/anticipated expected conversion ratio

- Allowable cost-per-enquiry/sale

- Other objectives, e.g. awareness and support

- Tests

**Target audience:**

- Demographic profile, age and location etc.

- Interests/lifestyle

- Purchase behaviour/propensity

- Media/audience research – research data (NRS, TGI, BBS)

**Competitor analysis:**

- MMS/ACNeilsen

- Observation

**Results analysis:**

- Past performance

**Production/creative:**

- Lead times required for production

- Colour and other special features

**Budget:**

- Media

- Production

- Follow-up materials

- Fees

**Candidate media:**

- Coverage of target market

- Cost-per-thousand circulation

- Editorial environment

- Test facilities, rollout potential

**Specifics:**

- Creative execution – format, size and colour etc.

- Position etc.

So let's look at some of those issues in detail and see how, by understanding exactly what it is that we want to achieve, the media selection will start to come together.

## What are the marketing objectives?

The objectives of direct marketing media are normally numeric and response-based, e.g. the required number of enquiries and sales and allowable costs-per-enquiry/per-sale. Media planners may also be required to estimate the ratio of telephone to postal responses (to facilitate efficient call handling); enquiries to sales; likely returns; bad debts; spin-off retail sales; and, particularly with business media, the number of sales appointments that may result or the expected number of publishers' 'reader service' enquiries. *Objectives therefore must be SMART: Specific, Measurable, Achievable, Realistic and Time bound.*

Other objectives might include awareness and support for non-press media. When planning any campaign schedule, however single-minded, details of any other media activity should be noted, to ensure that any cross-media effects can be taken into account.

## Who is the target audience?

Target audiences can be described in many ways, such as socio-economic classifications (ABC1), geodemographics – age (all adults aged 45-plus), interests (cat lovers) and likely purchase behaviour (car owners with January insurance renewal). For business prospects, industry, job description, title, and areas of purchasing responsibility, are all criteria that may be applied. The more detailed the description, the more accurate the targeting can be. To help identify the most accurate 'pictures' of your likely customers, it is possible to profile your existing customer base and segment according to the Recency, Frequency and Value behavioural indicators related to the key objectives – see chapter 2.3)

The art of media planning is then to understand the profile of target prospects and match them to the media that they 'consume' with the greatest degree of interest and attention. Media research is a useful tool with which to commence this process and there are a number of surveys that can be used. For press planning the key consumer sources are:

1. TGI – Target Group Index

2. NRS – National Readership Survey

And for B2B audiences, the BBS is of great value.

### 1. TGI – Target Group Index

TGI is based upon a sample of 25,000 individuals and focuses on product purchases, embracing 500 product fields and over 4,000 brands. It records a comprehensive profile of the individuals, including their media consumption, enabling media planners to evaluate the match between a prospect's purchase and reading habits.

The TGI extract in table 5.2.5 below shows the profile of people who have credit cards.

- The first row, *Totals*, tells us that 13,212 individuals responded positively to the question, "Do you have a credit or charge card?" – the 'target group' in this instance. This sample is extrapolated to reflect its share of the population overall, indicating that over 24.6 million individuals (*Target '000's*) have a credit card, which is 52.8 per cent of the population, as indicated in the fifth column – *Penetration %*. Because this is the 'universe', i.e. the entire base, the *Index*, in column six is recorded as 100.

- By reading down the index column we can see at a glance the socio-demographic bias of the average credit card holder versus the profile of the population as a whole, in this case:

  ABC1 is aged 25 to 64, with a household income of £15,000-plus, working full-time, with a slight male bias.

## Table 5.2.5 **TGI Extract**

**Target: credit card/charge card**
**Population: 24,602 (000)**

| | Sample size | Target '000s' | Target profile % | Pop. penetration % | Index |
|---|---|---|---|---|---|
| Totals | 13,212 | 24,602 | 100 | 52.87 | 100 |
| 15-19 | 178 | 382 | 1.55 | 9.44 | 18 |
| 20-24 | 552 | 1,278 | 5.19 | 44.08 | 83 |
| **25-34** | 2,140 | 4,687 | 19.05 | 54.2 | 103 |
| **35-44** | 2,936 | 5,256 | 21.36 | 62.28 | 118 |
| **45-54** | 2,786 | 4,931 | 20.04 | 65.06 | 123 |
| **55-64** | 2,410 | 3,570 | 14.51 | 61.1 | 116 |
| 65-99 | 2,210 | 4,497 | 18.28 | 49.52 | 94 |
| **AB** | 2,945 | 7,783 | 31.64 | 74.41 | 141 |
| **C1** | 4,876 | 7,766 | 31.57 | 61.32 | 116 |
| C2 | 3,053 | 5,008 | 20.36 | 49.05 | 93 |
| DE | 2,338 | 4,046 | 16.45 | 30.65 | 58 |
| engaged | 102 | 217 | 0.88 | 38.07 | 72 |
| married | 9,954 | 18,034 | 73.3 | 61.51 | 116 |
| h/h income 1-9999 | 1,786 | 2,968 | 12.06 | 35.15 | 66 |
| h/h income 10-14999 | 1,886 | 3,168 | 12.88 | 52.88 | 100 |
| **h/h income 15-24999** | 3,363 | 6,148 | 24.99 | 64.33 | 122 |
| **h/h/ income 25-34999** | 2,434 | 4,645 | 18.88 | 73.43 | 139 |
| **h/h income 35-39999** | 763 | 1,612 | 6.55 | 74.46 | 141 |
| **h/h income 40-49999** | 715 | 1,569 | 6.38 | 79.81 | 151 |
| **h/h income 50-99999** | 881 | 2,067 | 8.4 | 81.89 | 155 |
| **men** | 6,417 | 12,946 | 52.62 | 57.11 | 108 |
| women | 6,795 | 11,657 | 47.38 | 48.84 | 92 |
| work - not | 5,403 | 9,203 | 37.41 | 42.13 | 80 |
| work 1-8 part-tm | 203 | 314 | 1.28 | 47.01 | 89 |
| **work 30+full-tm** | 5,693 | 12,462 | 50.65 | 65.64 | 124 |
| work1-29part-tm | 2,115 | 2,935 | 11.93 | 51.55 | 97 |

*Pop. = UK Population

Using the same data, in table 5.2.6 we can see how individual publications perform in terms of delivering coverage of our audience and reducing wastage:

✔ **Coverage** – the title delivering the greatest number of card holders is the *News of the World*, reaching over 4,468,000 of them (18.16 per cent coverage). The research also shows us that those individuals represent 42 per cent of the paper's total readership (*Profile %*), therefore the publication has, statistically, 58 per cent of readers who are not in the target group.

✔ **Wastage** – the number of publication readers that are not within the target group. The titles delivering the least wastage are easily identified through the *Profile Index*, an expression of the *Publication Profile* % compared to the *Population profile* %, in this case 52.8 per cent as defined above. *The Sunday Telegraph* affords the least wastage statistically with an index of 142, with nearly 75 per cent of its readers having a credit card (i.e. 74.84 , 52.87 = 142). However, on the issue of coverage, a single insertion in that paper will only reach 6.5 per cent of our target group (see *Coverage %*), although it can be seen that that is still a sizeable audience of 1,606,000 (see *Target '000s'*).

**How does this inform your selection?**

Which title should be selected for your campaign will depend upon your overall objectives. If you are seeking to create new card holders, then *The Sunday Telegraph* may not be the answer as nearly 75 per cent of the readers already have a card. However, the remaining 25 per cent demonstrate the same profile as those with a card and therefore represent good prospects, although there may be entrenched reasons as to why they have not got a card already. If you are seeking to encourage someone to change card providers, then it is a very good place to go. Conversely the *News of the World* may provide greater scope for acquiring 'new to category' customers, but within a switching strategy an insertion in this publication would deliver a high percentage of wastage:

## Table 5.2.6    **TGI Extract**

| Target: credit card/charge card<br>Population: 24,602 (000) | | | | | |
|---|---|---|---|---|---|
| | Sample size | Target '000s' | Coverage % | Profile % | Profile index |
| Totals | 13,212 | 24,602 | 100 | 52.87 | 100 |
| | | | | | |
| **Sunday Telegraph** | 785 | 1,606 | 6.53 | 74.84 | 142 |
| Scotland on Sunday | 111 | 178 | 0.72 | 74.48 | 141 |
| Daily Telegraph | 876 | 1,821 | 7.4 | 73.75 | 140 |
| Sunday Times | 1,107 | 2,356 | 9.58 | 72.96 | 138 |
| Independent on Sunday | 222 | 454 | 1 .85 | 72.41 | 137 |
| Financial Times | 319 | 517 | 2.1 | 71.41 | 135 |
| Times | 814 | 1,244 | 5.06 | 69.85 | 132 |
| Independent | 224 | 461 | 1.87 | 69.01 | 131 |
| Guardian | 414 | 754 | 3 .06 | 67.93 | 128 |
| Observer | 396 | 736 | 2 .99 | 67.34 | 127 |
| Evening Standard | 296 | 679 | 2 .76 | 65.79 | 124 |
| Mail on Sunday | 2,206 | 4,013 | 16.31 | 64.78 | 123 |
| Daily Express | 805 | 1,554 | 6.32 | 64.59 | 122 |
| Daily Mail | 2,276 | 3,677 | 14.95 | 63.16 | 119 |
| Sunday Express | 886 | 1,466 | 5.96 | 62.52 | 118 |
| Sunday Post | 627 | 895 | 3 .64 | 48.69 | 92 |
| Daily Mirror | 1,728 | 2,685 | 10.91 | 45.41 | 86 |
| Sunday Mirror | 1,427 | 2,738 | 11.13 | 45.19 | 85 |
| People | 1,040 | 1,593 | 6.48 | 44.09 | 83 |
| Sunday Mail | 452 | 862 | 3.5 | 43.45 | 82 |
| **News of the World** | 2,553 | 4,468 | 18.16 | 42.92 | 81 |
| Sun | 2,460 | 4,108 | 16.7 | 42.68 | 81 |
| Daily Record | 396 | 714 | 2.9 | 39.78 | 75 |
| Daily Star | 362 | 620 | 2.52 | 39.37 | 74 |

## 2.    NRS – The National Readership Survey

The NRS tells the media planner about the readers of almost 300 titles including the national newspapers, the major regionals and a large proportion of consumer magazines. It is based upon interviews with a demographically representative sample of 38,000-plus adults aged 15-plus.

Information contained within the NRS includes:

✔ Socio-demographic data of all readers and their household. Marital status and number of children etc. of readers

✔ Readership habits by population/demographic groups

✔ Numbers of regular readers per title and what else they read

✔ Purchasing habits of readers, for brands, products and services, (although not in the detail seen on the TGI,) and therefore reading habits of purchasers of particular brands or services

## Using NRS for targeting

Taking our credit card brief, the core proposition may mean that targeting by age band, rather than lifestyle, is a better way of describing our target audience. This could be because our strategy is to attract people at the early stages of their career ladder. This would alter the title performance as detailed in the NRS extract below in table 5.2.7:

### Table 5.2.7    NRS extract

Target: ABC1 20 to 44 inc. £15 to 30,000
Population: 3,598 (000)

|  | Sample size | Target '000s' | Coverage % | Profile % | Profile index |
|---|---|---|---|---|---|
| Totals | 1,850 | 3,598 | 100 | 7.73 | 100 |
|  |  |  |  |  |  |
| Guardian | 73 | 141 | 3.92 | 12.7 | 164 |
| Scotland on Sunday | 18 | 29 | 0.81 | 12.13 | 157 |
| Evening Standard | 37 | 114 | 3.17 | 11.05 | 143 |
| Sunday Mail | 77 | 177 | 4.92 | 8.92 | 115 |
| Observer | 49 | 96 | 2.67 | 8.78 | 114 |
| Daily Record | 71 | 151 | 4.2 | 8.41 | 109 |
| Daily Express | 76 | 198 | 5.5 | 8.23 | 106 |
| News of the World | 411 | 767 | 21.32 | 7.37 | 95 |
| Mail on Sunday | 240 | 446 | 12.4 | 7.2 | 93 |
| Independent | 28 | 46 | 1.28 | 6.89 | 89 |
| Daily Mail | 238 | 391 | 10.87 | 6.72 | 87 |
| Sunday Times | 102 | 215 | 5.98 | 6.66 | 86 |
| Daily Star | 52 | 104 | 2.89 | 6.6 | 85 |
| Times | 80 | 115 | 3.2 | 6.46 | 84 |
| Sun | 360 | 617 | 17.15 | 6.41 | 83 |
| Daily Telegraph | 66 | 148 | 4.11 | 5.99 | 78 |
| Sunday Express | 83 | 141 | 3.92 | 6.01 | 78 |
| Sunday Mirror | 173 | 366 | 10.17 | 6.04 | 78 |
| Daily Mirror | 205 | 346 | 9.62 | 5.85 | 76 |
| Independent on Sunday | 23 | 37 | 1.03 | 5.9 | 76 |
| Sunday Post | 59 | 104 | 2.89 | 5.66 | 73 |
| People | 116 | 192 | 5.34 | 5.31 | 69 |
| Financial Times | 22 | 35 | 0.97 | 4.83 | 63 |
| Sunday Telegraph | 41 | 95 | 2.64 | 4.43 | 57 |

## 3.   BBS – The British Business Survey

The British Business Survey is conducted by BMRC (British Media Research Committee) among 3,000 individuals representing a universe of 1.55 million, and covers 140 titles, including national press plus selected business-to-business magazines. The fieldwork is carried out on the basis of an April to March calendar and is released in the second quarter each alternate year (http://www.bbs-survey.com).

This survey gives a good insight into the business behaviour of the respondents; for example, their purchasing responsibilities as shown in figure 5.2.10:

**Figure 5.2.10**

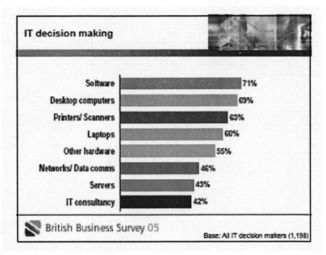

## The candidate media list

When you have surveyed the research you will discover that different titles have different claims to secure your objectives – depending on whether you want volume coverage of your chosen market, highest penetration/reduced wastage by title, or the lowest cost-per-target prospect.

Table 5.2.8 below shows how the ranking of candidate media will differ depending upon the evaluation criteria:

Table 5.2.8 **Ranking of candidate media**

| | Rank by target **Coverage** | | | Rank by reader **Profile** | | | Rank by target **Cost-per-thousand** (CPT*)* Based upon 'guestimate' cost | | |
|---|---|---|---|---|---|---|---|---|---|
| | Publication | **Cover** % | | Publication | **Profile** % | | Publication | **£ cost – full page colour*** | CPT |
| 1 | Cosmopolitan | 11.2 | 1 | Marie Claire | 43.2 | 1 | Hello | £2,000 | £3.3 |
| 2 | Marie Claire | 8.7 | 2 | Company | 42.3 | 2 | Company | £2,000 | £5.6 |
| 3 | Woman's Own | 7.8 | 3 | Cosmopolitan | 40.3 | 3 | She | £3,000 | £6.8 |
| 4 | Bella | 7.6 | 4 | New Woman | 38.3 | 4 | Sainsbury's Magazine | £5,000 | £8.0 |
| 5 | Sainsbury's Magazine | 7.3 | 5 | She | 32.1 | 5 | Prima | £5,000 | £8.3 |
| 6 | Prima | 7.1 | 6 | Hello! | 27.8 | 6 | OK! | £1,000 | £9.3 |
| 7 | Hello! | 7.1 | 7 | Harpers & Queen | 27.2 | 7 | New Woman | £3,000 | £9.6 |
| 8 | Woman | 6.8 | 8 | Essentials | 27.1 | 8 | Essentials | £4,000 | £11.4 |
| 9 | Best | 5.9 | 9 | Prima | 26.6 | 9 | Cosmopolitan | £11,000 | £11.5 |
| 10 | Vogue | 5.5 | 10 | Sainsbury's Magazine | 26.2 | 10 | Family Circle | £4,000 | £11.7 |
| 11 | She | 5.2 | 11 | Sky Magazine | 25.4 | 11 | Marie Claire | £9,000 | £12.1 |
| 12 | Sky Magazine | 4.5 | 12 | OK! | 24.6 | 12 | Woman's Own | £12,000 | £18.0 |
| 13 | Company | 4.2 | 13 | Vogue | 24.3 | 13 | Harpers & Queen | £3,000 | £19.9 |
| 14 | Essentials | 4.1 | 14 | Family Circle | 20.5 | 14 | Best | £10,000 | £20.0 |
| 15 | Family Circle | 4.0 | 15 | Woman | 19.1 | 15 | Vogue | £10,500 | £22.5 |
| 16 | New Woman | 3.7 | 16 | Best | 18.8 | 16 | Bella | £15,000 | £23.3 |
| 17 | Harpers & Queen | 1.8 | 17 | Woman's Own | 17.0 | 17 | Woman | £14,000 | £24.3 |
| 18 | OK! | 1.3 | 18 | Bella | 16.3 | 18 | Sky Mag | £10,000 | £26.0 |

*To amplify the example the page colour costs are 'made up', they are not rate card nor estimated negotiated rates.

In practice you will take note of all three indicators, although each will have a different value to you as follows:

- **Coverage**

  Is a useful guide if the objective of your campaign is to reach the greatest number of target prospects. This might be the case when launching a new product such as a car, when it is important to get your message to as many prospects as possible ahead of any competitive 'spoiler' campaigns.

- **Profile %**

  Indicates how many of a publication's total readership is actually in your target group. Selecting titles with the highest profile per centage in a ranked table helps to reduce wastage and should improve the response rate from a schedule.

- **Cost-per-thousand**

  Is a good guide to the potential cost-per-response. From the table above a ranking is generated by dividing the 'guestimated' cost for a colour page by the number of target individuals that the publication reaches, i.e. the *Target '000s'*. For this example the advertising buying rates have been exaggerated to create a ranking of cost-per-thousand from £3.30 to £26. As such, the rate of response from *Sky Magazine* would theoretically have to be eight times greater than that from *Hello* to achieve a better cost-per-response, given that the cost of reaching each 1,000 readers in *Sky Magazine* is 7.8 times that of *Hello*, or £26 versus £3.30.

**Circulation data**

Although publications may be selected on the basis of the readership information, results analysis and forecasting tend to be more accurate if based upon the most current circulation figures and trends rather than readership figures. As we have seen previously, a publication's circulation can change greatly over the period of a year but the profile of readers is unlikely to be altered notably.

## *Monitoring competitive activity*

Monitoring competitive activity can give a good insight into a market and how it uses the media. This is particularly useful to direct marketers since experienced exponents *never* repeat media patterns that are unsuccessful!

There are two chief ways to assess competitive activity:

- Collect all, or the main, publications, on a regular basis and review the advertising therein – this is not absolutely accurate but it can give you a good indication of what types of business are using which titles.

- Buy a competitive analysis report from a specialist supplier such as AC Neilsen/Media Monitoring Services (MMS) – such services are well established, reporting on all the major media options, including TV, cinema, radio, newspapers, magazines and outdoor advertising. Alongside this they also maintain a large national panel through which they monitor direct mail, door-to-door and third-party inserts, giving a very detailed picture of a competitor's marketing tactics. Within the business-to-business arena there are also a number of sectors that are regularly reviewed, among them the medical and agricultural publications.

Both can provide a detailed view of a competitor's advertising including details of insertions by media, date, position and estimated expenditure etc.

You can also subscribe to a cuttings service that will supply periodic reviews of creative executions from your competitors.

Further information on these services can be attained from: ACNeilsen/MMS, Madison House, High Street, Sunninghill, Ascot, Berkshire SL5 9NP.

## Examining relevant results

Where prior results are available it is important to study these objectively. Careful results analysis, preferably going back several years, can reveal a great deal about your customers and prospects and fresh interpretations can often be made:

✔ Look especially at media that were once effective and then suffered diminishing returns, or those that are showing demonstrable improvement over time.

✔ Investigate issues such as the following:

✔ Have they been overused? Was the frequency too high?

✔ Were they used properly? What was the offer, format or reply mechanism?

✔ Are they ready for a retest?

✔ Has the level of competitive activity changed?

✔ Has the publication changed its readership profile or circulation? Has another publication become more popular with your same target audience?

Table 5.2.9 shows part of a typical direct marketing results report. Reading from left to right it shows publication, insertion date, costs, circulation, number of replies, percentage response, number and percentage of orders, percentage conversion to orders, cost of fulfilment, total cost including fulfilment, initial revenue generated, allowable cost and profit/loss per insertion.

The revenue from future years (lifetime values) would be a major consideration in assessing these results; hence the allowable cost may exceed the revenue at this initial recruitment stage.

Table 5.2.9    **Example press response analysis**

| Publication | Insertion Date | Cost £s | Circ '000s' | Responses | Response % | Orders to date | Order % | Conv % | Cost-per-order | Fulfilment £s @ £20 | Cost inc. fulfilment | Revenue £s | Allowable @ £39.99 X 3 | +/- £ | Current Rank |
|---|---|---|---|---|---|---|---|---|---|---|---|---|---|---|---|
| Marie Claire | Nov | 9000 | 445 | 356 | 0.08% | 170 | 0.038% | 48% | 52.94 | 3400 | 12400 | 6798 | 20394.9 | 7994.9 | 1 |
| Company | Dec | 2000 | 181 | 145 | 0.08% | 44 | 0.024% | 30% | 45.45 | 880 | 2880 | 2111 | 5278.68 | 2398.6 | 4 |
| She | Dec | 3000 | 226 | 203 | 0.09% | 62 | 0.027% | 30% | 48.39 | 1240 | 4240 | 2479 | 7438.14 | 3198.1 | 3 |
| New Woman | Dec | 3000 | 261 | 235 | 0.09% | 71 | 0.027% | 30% | 42.25 | 1420 | 4420 | 3691 | 8517.87 | 4097.8 | 2 |
| Hello! | Jan | 2000 | 510 | 153 | 0.03% | 31 | 0.006% | 20% | 64.52 | 620 | 2620 | 1240 | 3719.07 | 1099.1 | 7 |
| Cosmopolitan | Jan | 11000 | 476 | 238 | 0.05% | 125 | 0.026% | 53% | 88.00 | 2500 | 13500 | 4999 | 1496.25 | 1496.3 | 6 |
| Essentials | Jan | 4000 | 296 | 148 | 0.05% | 60 | 0.020% | 41% | 66.67 | 1200 | 5200 | 2519 | 7198.2 | 1998.2 | 5 |
| Best | Feb | 10000 | 510 | 153 | 0.03% | 57 | 0.011% | 37% | 175.44 | 1140 | 11140 | 2735 | 6838.29 | -4301.7 | 8 |

## Budget and timing requirements

Next on our media planner's master checklist comes the small matter of the budgeting, which may be for a campaign, a season or a calendar or financial year.

In the main there are two ways in which a budget is determined:

- Fixed budget – allocation, calling for maximum possible number of responses, leads, sales or whatever the main criterion is

- Task-related budget – amount required to achieve predetermined number of responses with a known or forecast cost-per-response

Combinations of these are also frequently used, whereby a fixed budget is expanded to take advantage of early successes, the 'extra' being effectively task-related. Task-related budgets usually come with a caveat to 'minimise the cost per response'.

### How direct media planning differs from awareness

General marketers entering direct marketing will by now begin to see that media planning for direct marketing differs from that for general awareness in numerous respects, as the simplified summary in table 5.2.10 demonstrates:

### Table 5.2.10 Media planning for direct marketing and general awareness

| Direct | Awareness |
|---|---|
| Objectives numerical and data-based | Objectives target coverage and frequency levels or increases in claimed awareness/recall levels |
| Accountability judged through actual customer and prospect interaction, be they enquiries or sales etc. | Accountability predominantly judged through consumer research into claimed levels of spontaneous and prompted recall of brand |
| Planning based primarily on results data | Planning based primarily on research data |
| Initial schedules based upon readership profiles and cost, with ongoing activity reflecting actual response analysis | Schedules constructed and evaluated via readership data deriving coverage and frequency statistics for target audience |
| Frequency balanced to minimise reductions in response rates (attrition) and avoid diminishing returns | Frequency optimised to drive repeat exposure and stimulate memorability and recall in concise campaign periods |
| First insertions tend to record best results | Initial insertions viewed as stepping stones to achieving required repetition of message to achieve recall |
| Broadest range of cost-efficient titles considered for testing with accountability providing backstop | Tendency to limit core activity to researched publications to underpin coverage and frequency modelling |
| Efficacy normally results-based – cost- per-lead/sale etc. | Efficacy predominantly measured through research – reading, noting, recall etc. |

Figure 5.2.11 shows a graph demonstrating a typical diminishing return from direct response advertising. Whereas awareness of a company/offer grows with the number and frequency of insertions in a given medium, direct responses to individual advertisements fall dramatically with repetition (all other factors, e.g. seasonality, being equal).

Figure 5.2.11 **Diminishing returns from direct response advertising**

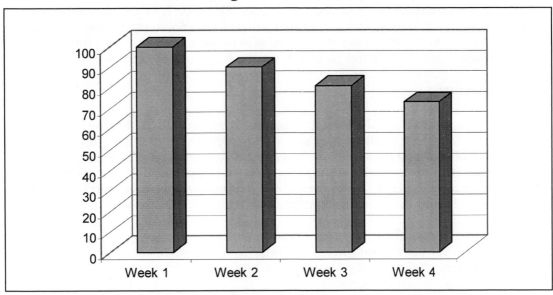

If the maximum response is achieved with the first insertion, subsequent ads will show a steady decline as the prospect pool reduces.

However, some products, especially at the launch stage, can positively benefit from increasing awareness as demonstrated in figure 5.2.12, and in these cases the pattern of attrition may not hold true.

When using the press to build awareness, the planner will calculate what frequency level is required to achieve recognition of the proposition and what percentage of the target group they can afford/need to reach, i.e. they will set the coverage and frequency targets. As the schedule unfolds, subsequent insertions reinforce the message, delivering multiple impacts to heavy/regular readers and building frequency.

Figure 5.2.12 **Coverage build over time**

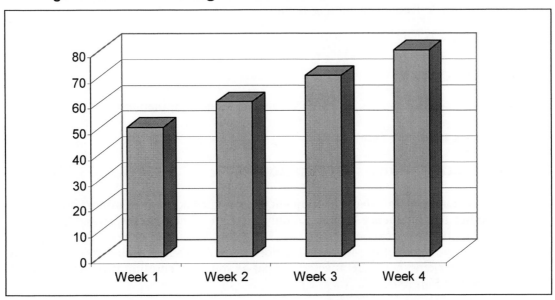

Coverage is built through the breadth of unduplicated readers reached over time with the diversity of title selection and as new readers dip into titles that may be used more than once.

## *Finalising the media plan*

So far we have talked only of selecting media titles – we have not decided space sizes, positions, timing, weight and frequency of insertions, or the use of colour. Of these the most critical are what space size to use where, and how the individual insertions should be timed, i.e. the frequency of exposure.

### Frequency

Direct marketers normally seek to maximise response and experience shows that response is highest when an offer is fresh to readers of a given medium. The phasing of subsequent insertions therefore becomes critical. If the initial advertisement theoretically achieves the maximum response, the media planner must calculate the time period over which subsequent insertions can be slotted. This will depend upon the marketplace and the product or service.

Purchasing patterns for financial products such as insurance may be annual events for individuals, but for the marketer someone new is coming into the market every week. Therefore advertising frequency can be at least weekly, and even daily for some products.

For gifts and self indulgences (e.g. exercise bikes, books, music, collectible plates and jewellery) the market will take longer to refresh. By taking a look at competitive data it can be seen that these sectors often leave between 6 and 12 months before repeating the same product offer to the same audience.

For a product with a major purchase window, such as the launch of a car or selling Christmas-related gifts, marketers will weigh up the balance between achieving the lowest cost-per-response from every insertion, versus gaining the maximum number of people over the campaign period.

For some campaigns the optimum frequency can only be determined through testing, and so a plan should be constructed to include insertions with structured phasing, to enable the planner to understand the relevant dynamics efficiently.

Direct marketers use a number of techniques to reduce the effects of response attrition due to frequency, among them:

✔    Copy variants

✔    Change day of the week

✔    Change positions, e.g. from TV page to holiday supplement

✔    Vary space size (see below)

### The effect of readership duplication

When considering the effects of frequency upon a schedule it is important to remember that frequency builds not only through successive insertions in an individual title *but also between titles*. For example, 60 per cent of *Sun* readers also read the *News of the World*. Therefore, an advertisement placed in both titles over one weekend could be affected almost as much as running two consecutive days in *The Sun* itself.

Duplication is often the explanation for poor response when all other indicators suggest that a good response could be expected.

## The effect of space size

An important way to reduce frequency and maintain response ratios is to begin with a large space or to take large spaces less often. Larger spaces normally result in more responses, although not in direct proportion to increased costs. The term 'large' is of course relative, with 'small' generally applying to spaces ranging from 5cm by 1 column (a 5x1) up to perhaps 20 x 3, or 25 x 4. Full pages and double-page spreads (DPS) are classified among the larger sizes.

Experience suggests that the relationship between increased space size and response is the square root of the increased space! i.e. doubling the space can yield approximately 1.4 times more response, *not twice as many*. Unfortunately, *the relationship between the cosst of different space size is generally linear – i.e. doubling the space does cost twice as much*, so the increased response will lead to more costly response.

The following graph in figure 5.2.13 outlines this principle, demonstrating the variation between linear projections and those following the Sainsbury's formula; that is the square route formula devised by Philip Sainsbury, statistician, to explain the correlation between space size and response rate.

Figure 5.2.13 **Probable response change with space size**

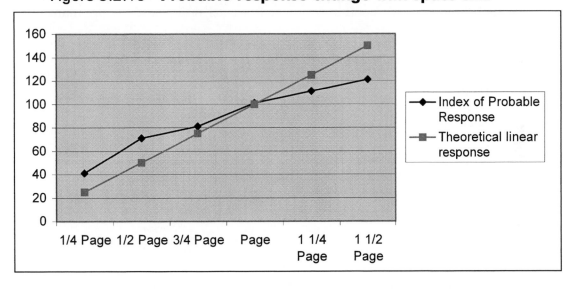

In practice, space size will be determined by a number of criteria:

✔ Direct sales (one-stage) ads normally require larger spaces than two-step lead generators because of the need for detailed sales copy, payment details and often the inclusion of a response coupon

✔ Complex offers, especially financial investment products, require larger spaces to explain and include mandatory information

✔ Large spaces may be used to optimise the seasonal potential, especially during short seasons

✔ Larger space sizes are more impactful and will generate a higher degree of awareness alongside the immediate response

✔ Small spaces may be deployed to enable daily advertising, such as for motor insurance

✔ Space size can be used to maximise or restrict the number of responses to levels which can be handled

✔ Larger space sizes are usually a prerequisite to copy testing

## The effect of colour

Colour is often thought to be essential to the presentation of certain products, to attract attention, demonstrate detail or convey style, but it should be remembered that the readers of newspapers are used to mono reproduction. Colour can boost response and therefore a planner must evaluate the potential for increased response versus the increased cost of advertising, and construct the schedule that most appropriately satisfies the objectives.

## Paying for position?

Position is very important. However, the planners should ensure that in selecting any specific site they are able to measure the results and compare them to other placements. All of the positions described below will carry a premium of at least 10 per cent over the price for a run of paper/magazine sites. Those that are in shortest supply – i.e. outside back covers, inside front covers or solus on TV, could demand premia in excess of 40 per cent. The planner must evaluate whether the anticipated uplift in response is greater or equal to the premium charge.

The following are usually considered to be superior positions:

✔ Front cover

✔ Back cover

✔ Front of publication

✔ Outer edges

✔ Right-hand pages

✔ Facing or next to editorial

✔ Next to letters, TV or horoscopes

There are a number of well-known ways to try and reduce the cost of media, as listed below. However, blindly taking advantage of what appears to be 'cheap' media is a common error. Your aim should be to select the best possible position in the right media, at the right time. Knowing that what you are buying *is what you want*, e.g. by testing individual newspaper insertions on each day of the week, it may transpire that there is no perceptible difference in response. Knowing this, the buyer can confidently negotiate discounts for 'run-of-week' space. The same degree of latitude may be confirmed in respect of positional placement.

Ways to reduce media costs:

- **Off season:** e.g. some advertisers automatically pull out during holiday periods. However, many sectors do not reflect the same seasonal pattern and good response rates can combine effectively with lower media costs on offer.

- **Run-of-paper/run-of-week:** better deals are available if the media owner retains some flexibility as to when and where your ad is inserted.

- **Forward bookings:** as well as discounts for volume, lower rates may be available for advanced reservations that help the publisher to forward plan.

- **Standby:** good rates are usually available if you leave an ad with a publisher for them to run when it suits them.

- **Short-term buying:** holding a proportion of the budget in reserve for short-term buying, and being able to make quick, sometimes instant decisions, can be a vital factor in securing low-cost space. However, as outlined above, it is important that you know how the space will work for you and whether the reduced price really represents value.

## Loose inserts

Inserts take many forms, including single sheets, leaflets, four- or six-page folds, catalogues (from eight to 64 pages), cut-out shapes, product mini-samples, postcards, newsletters, unaddressed direct mail packs, sample magazines, perforated questionnaires, credit card-sized information cards, or any number of alternative creative formats. They can be classified according to the method of enclosure:

- **Loose** – enclosed with the host (or carrier) publication, or delivered alongside it

- **Bound-in** – stapled or glued into the publication

- **Tip-on** – attached to a space advertisement usually by means of a gummed strip

Once inserts are being considered, it is important to think through all of the related *non-press* methods of distribution that are also available, including door-to-door and third-party enclosures (e.g. in non-competing statement envelopes or actual product despatch).

The media planner should contemplate all of the routes available for a campaign, from space through to inserts, to ensure that the best formats are used to maximise the potential response and to avoid unnecessary duplication and gain all potential economies of scale for printing and price negotiation stages.

### Why inserts work

Inserts work because they draw immediate attention to themselves, often before the reader has had a chance to study the news, views and space advertisements inside a publication. Familiar criticism is that inserts simply drop out onto the floor or get shaken into the waste bin. But even as an insert is being picked up to be discarded, it is being noted and this leads to a greater number of individuals becoming involved with the sales message. Reading and noting studies exemplify this as detailed in table 5.2.11, demonstrating that inserts are remembered by a far greater number of people.

### Table 5.2.11 Comparison of reading and noting scores

| Advertising format | Size\position | Average noting score |
|---|---|---|
| Space | DPS colour | 39 |
| | Page colour | 33 |
| | Page mono | 27 |
| Loose inserts | 48 pages | 87 |
| | 4 pages | 83 |
| | 4 pages | 79 |

Partly for this reason, inserts are generally more responsive than space, and common statistics show that if a creative execution were to run in both page format and as an insert, the insert would achieve four to five times greater level of response. The following response index in table 5.2.12 is calculated on the same principle as outlined in the Sainsbury formula, and can be used as a guide for forecasting.

### Table 5.2.12 Response index by size and format

| Size | Response index |
|---|---|
| 1\2 page | 122 |
| 1\2 page colour | 141 |
| Full page mono | 171 |
| Full page colour | 200 |
| Loose insert | 1000 |

## The role of inserts

Inserts are effective for many products, whether consumer or business-to-business, and can be contemplated for a number of reasons, among them:

✔ To generate higher volume of response from each publication

✔ To show a wider product selection (such as gadget catalogues or music/book offers)

✔ To include a questionnaire that can be signed, thereby speeding the sales conversion process

✔ To enable detailed/mandatory information to be included without overly detracting from the sales headline (such as with some complicated financial products)

✔ To enable greater creative flexibility

✔ To test multiple copy treatments in a single controlled environment

✔ To test a small proportion of a high circulation publication before planning an expensive rollout

✔   To deliver specific targeting requirements

✔   Cost-efficient responses

## High volumes of enquiries

A large-scale insert campaign, taking in national newspapers, consumer and business-to-business magazines, can deliver a cumulative circulation in excess of tens of millions each month. Coupled with the increased responsiveness, a huge volume of the enquiries and sales can be generated very quickly. A motor manufacturer launching a new car might consider this approach to ensure that he got the maximum number of prospects into a test-drive before the competition launched theirs.

## Increased product

With catalogues there is a definite correlation between the diversity of product offering and the number of sales achieved; the more that is offered the greater the likelihood that different individuals will find something interesting. The same is true of single product offers such as music, books or flowers. 'Buy one get one free' is a good offer if there are two things that you want, and again extended product range makes such introductory offers stronger.

Inclusion of questionnaires and reply forms to improve conversion
Some products end up with a very extended sale process. If an enquirer needs to be sent a form to be returned to the company prior to assessment and approval, it results in a four-stage process and can have a detrimental effect on the overall conversion. People get bored, forget, find another solution or are otherwise diverted from their initial interest. Including the forms within the insert cuts out 'stages' and there can be a notable improvement in conversion. Entire application forms, full product specifications and details of extensive product ranges can all be included if appropriate.

## Inclusion of detail

Some products, particularly those including financial terms, can look horribly boring when all the small print is laid out. The creative scope of inserts allows for the inclusion of as much copy as the advertiser feels will be useful, informative, interesting or convincing to prospects.

## Creative flexibility

Inserts offer immense creative flexibility, similar in many ways to that of direct mail. Existing brochures, catalogues and direct mail packs can all be used, along with paper-engineered flip-out boxes, or other interest-grabbing initiatives. At a more practical level, even simple single-sheet inserts can gain immense standout in mono environments. And, of course, inserts can carry such devices as scratch-off panels, lucky numbers and mini-samples etc.

## Measurable test campaigns with good rollout potential

Inserts provide the ideal test vehicle. For example, the *News of the World* can deliver a circulation of nearly four million. This offers two major opportunities for inserts.

We can test the viability of using the entire title with a sample; say 100,000 inserts, which at potentially 0.1 per cent response rate would deliver 100 leads/ sales. If these proved to meet our requirements we have a huge rollout opportunity.

We can book half a million inserts and run five different creative formats. As the environment would be constant for all executions, we can learn a lot about the comparative strengths of different propositions very quickly. Successful products and creative can then be rolled out to the full circulation.

### Broad or niche coverage/targeting

En masse, inserts can build coverage into any campaign and minimise frequency. However, niche and tightly targeted opportunities also exist:

### Geodemographic targeting

Many publications will accept inserts into specific TV regions or tightly-defined towns and areas within their distribution networks. Others, such as the *Radio Times*, have invested in geodemographic systems such as ACORN that allow for the detailed analysis of their wholesale areas and the geo-profiling of inserts.

### Lifestyle targeting

Special interest titles and third-party carriers can be used to target specific lifestyles such as gardeners, golfers, anglers and new mothers.

### Occupation targeting

With business-to-business titles there are many opportunities to target prospects by occupation and influence. Some business journals break down their circulation by industry type or job category for insert advertisers.

### Cost-efficient responses

In judging the efficiency of inserts, the total cost should include the price paid to a publisher/carrier and the price of producing and printing the insert.

Printers tend to work to volume-related price bands and publisher rates are generally negotiable around confirmed volumes on set dates, although some opportunities exist for short term if an advertiser is set up for rapid delivery of preprinted material. Rate card prices for loose inserts vary between £20 and nearly £100 per thousand, specialist magazines (including business-to-business journals with small circulations) generally being more expensive than large circulation newspapers. The planner must evaluate the cost comparisons between space and insert in the context of the anticipated response and the overall campaign objective. It can often transpire that the best schedule includes a mixture of formats.

## *Testing with inserts*

One method of testing, not so far mentioned, is the use of inserts for testing space advertisements.

Your campaign may be destined to use space formats, but testing creative executions by the split copy method discussed above may not be possible or may be too slow. In this instance, inserts can be used to replicate your space advertisements and test numerous elements quickly. Response rates from inserts are usually higher than from space advertisements, ensuring robust response volumes.

A practical example of how to do this would be a test of several different propositions for a newspaper campaign destined to use small space sizes – say 20 cm x 2 columns. You could turn each advertisement into the front of a postcard and print a Freepost reply address on the reverse.

The results will give an inflated response rate compared to that which you should expect for the space advertising rollout, (potentially by between five and 10 times the volume), but they will give a good indication of the difference between copy A, B, C and D, or G etc.

## Planning and carrying out your insert campaign

As with all marketing activity, the starting point is to define your objective, the role of the advertising and the target audience.

Industry research sources such as TGI and NRS, as described earlier, can be used to identify the readership patterns of your chosen target audience.

Assuming the campaign is to maximise pre-Christmas sales for a high street department store by offering the convenience of direct sales from a gift-orientated magazine-style catalogue, TGI can then be used to define the demographics of the target audience and look at their readership patterns. If the bias is towards homes and gardening press, we can look in BRAD to find all of the related titles that could be used for our campaign, e.g. *Gardeners World*, *The English Garden* and *Gardens Illustrated*.

On the same basis, we can consider statement and product mailings by home-orientated and gardening-orientated companies, e.g. for seeds, plants, trellises and even wellingtons! These could include *Parks* (garden plants and trees), *Van Meuwen* (seed catalogue) and *Cannock Gates* (trellising and rose arches). Third-party programme managers, the equivalent of the publication sales representative, can provide profile information about their customers to help us refine selections beyond the obvious lifestyle interest implied by the company's products.

Third-party programmes are normally accessed direct through the list/database owner, via a programme manager or by an experienced list broker.

Having come up with our candidate publication/third-party selections we have a great deal of detail to progress through before we can finalise our insert schedule.

## Managing the detail

### Availability?

✔ First you must establish whether your chosen publications have the availability to take your inserts within your required campaign period. The majority of publishers/carriers will take up to *three* non-competing inserts in an edition/mailing/product despatch etc. But many existing users will be pre-booking up to a year in advance.

### Size and specification?

✔ The next variable is mechanical specifications. Before confirming a schedule you must confirm what size, weight, paper type, format and delivery requirements are acceptable. There are an infinite number of permutations as to what is acceptable to publishers/carriers in terms of dimensions, paper stock and total weight, and changes in technology mean that what was true last year may not be consistent this year. Inevitably the planner will have to telephone around to finalise all the information required.

✔ You may be working with an existing piece of artwork or may be looking to brief the optimum specifications to the designers. Print economies can obviously only be achieved if an insert design is acceptable to all of your selected titles.

## Suitability for insertion?

✔ There are wide variations in inserting techniques and distribution methods employed by publishers and carriers. National newspapers have to consider the accumulated bulk of inserts when their publications are bundled up. Poly-wrapped subscriber magazines and third-party carriers will be concerned with any additional costs of postage resulting from substantial weight increases. New technology introduced by many publishers has made the process more automated, which would be a cost saving if it were not for their requirement to amortise the investment costs of the machinery. Some publishers and carriers still rely on hand-inserting – theoretically a more expensive process and one that can place limitations on volumes. Folds must be planned with the insertion method in mind, the least acceptable being the concertina or fan-type fold.

## Delivery details?

✔ Deadlines, delivery addresses and preferred methods of packaging and palliating have to be understood and planned for by the media planner.

The following checklist may help when planning delivery:

✔ Check the delivery deadline for the specific issue booked.

✔ Check the delivery address – it will be the publisher's printer and is unlikely to be the same as that of the publisher.

✔ Check the packaging instructions – how does the printer want to receive the inserts: pallets or cartons etc?

● Pallets must be in good condition to allow them to be stacked.

● Pallets should be well wrapped to avoid damage during transit and storage.

● Inserts that are unable to be palletised due to their shape or size should be packed appropriately in cartons.

● Inserts should be packed with the minimum number of turns, i.e. all copies stacked in the same direction if possible.

✔ Pallets or cartons should be clearly marked with:

● Name of advertiser

● Name of insert

● Number of inserts

● Name of publication

● Date of planned insertion

- Copy of the insert if practicable

- Name, address and contact name of advertiser's printer

✔ Inserts should not be delivered earlier than requested by the publication's printers – with some printers it is necessary to book an appointment for the delivery.

✔ Inserts should be accompanied by a delivery note/instruction sheet detailing:

- Address of the publication's printer/binder

- Description of the insert, including the name of the advertiser and the insert specification (e.g. 4-page leaflet or 16-page catalogue)

- Total quantity delivered and number of inserts per pallet or carton

- Name of publication and date of insertion. This is very important as many publications use the same printer

- Editions, regions, quantities and any other inserting instructions

## Analysing insert campaigns

As confirmation, printers/media owners should produce a *certificate of insertion* detailing the number of inserts that were actually inserted. It is recommended that no invoice be paid until a certificate of insertion has been received.

Where schedules have been planned to target defined regions it is obviously important to break down the total responses according to these regions. This is best accommodated at the planning stage by using regional response codes on coupons and for customers to quote on the telephone. It is also possible to sort regional response by postcode analysis of enquiries. Systems such as CACI can be used to do this.

# Door-drop marketing, now with new improved targeting

## This chapter includes:

------------------------------------------------

- [ ] **What do we mean by door-drop marketing?**

- [ ] **Door drop's unique advantages**

- [ ] **Public attitudes to door drops**

- [ ] **Door drops and sampling**

- [ ] **Door drops and redemption coupons**

- [ ] **Door-drop targeting**

- [ ] **The four methods of distribution**

- [ ] **Door drops and creativity**

- [ ] **How much will it cost?**

- [ ] **Choosing your door-drop supplier**

------------------------------------------------

## About this chapter

**D**oor-drop marketing is now a viable medium for new customer acquisition programmes after decades of being a short-term promotional tool. What has made the difference is the improved targeting that results from geodemographic and lifestyle area selections. Also, the realisation that customers can be persuaded to identify themselves when responding to offers, even though these may be redeemed in stores.

In communication terms, door-to-door has the extended reach of the national press, the impact and immediacy of inserts, and the creative flexibility enjoyed by direct mail - to say that anything can be home delivered, from a pin to an elephant, would be only a slight exaggeration.

In this chapter, we explain door drops in general terms and invite you to consider how the medium can best serve your needs.

### Nick Wells

Nick Wells is CEO of CD Marketing Services which includes Circular Distributors and Lifecycle Marketing. CD Marketing Services is owned by the Royal Dutch Post Office which includes TNT and has a revenue exceeding £7 billion. Nick is on the Board of their international division European Mail Networks. Nick is past chairman of The Institute of Sales Promotion (ISP) and a Fellow of the ISP; he has served on the Board of the Direct Marketing Association (DMA), and its executive committee.

Nick Wells
Managing Director
Circular Distributors Ltd
CD House, 1-3 Malvern Road
Maidenhead, Berkshire SL6 7QY
Tel: 01628 771232
Fax: 01628 770705

# Chapter 5.3

# Door drops, now with new improved targeting

## What do we mean by door drops?

**D**oor-drop distribution is the business of delivering unaddressed material to houses in defined geographical areas (usually based on postcode sectors and micro sectors). It differs from mailed communications in that mail is delivered to named persons at specific addresses.

Research by RSGB, commissioned by Royal Mail, suggests that unaddressed items account for approximately one-third of what goes through Britain's letterboxes. While it is impossible to calculate the exact number of items delivered, it is commonly estimated to be in excess of thirteen billion per year, of which the majority is delivered by the three leading suppliers; Circular Distributors (CD), Royal Mail Door-to-Door, and The Leaflet Company.

The chart below shows the growth of the medium from 2000 to 2004:

Figure 5.3.1

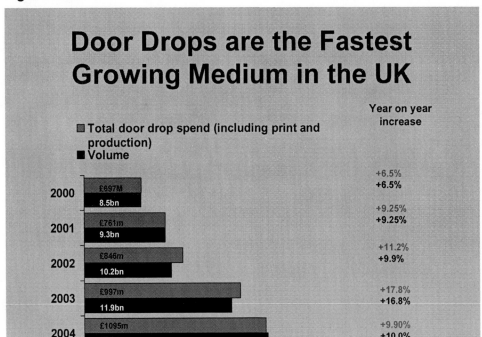

Source DMA door-to-door council July 2004.

## Door-drop marketing's unique advantages

The fundamental strength of door-drop marketing is that a leaflet, brochure or sample is delivered through the letterbox, thus offering direct communication to the customer right into the home. It also offers creative freedom, because there are virtually no restrictions as in press advertising - for example, in size, shape, colour or design. With door drops there is no duplication of coverage, because only one leaflet or sample per household is delivered, and it is possible to cover as few or as many households as appropriate to meet the marketing objective. Coverage of virtually every household in the UK is available and vitally, in an age of increased media fragmentation, each household can be reached once only or more often with absolutely controlled frequency.

Door drops are perhaps most powerful when combined with other media. They are commonly used as a follow-through to a press or TV campaign and are at their most effective when the advertising has been running for a couple of weeks. Then, when a follow-up leaflet reflecting the image created by the advertising arrives through the letterbox, there is instant recognition and the door-dropped item can play its proper role of triggering purchase.

## Public attitudes to door drops

Door-drop marketing has been subjected to a great deal of attitude research and some of its findings may surprise you. Research by BMRB Omnibus Survey in December 2003 suggests that most are very aware of the samples, coupons and offers they receive through the letterbox, as this graph shows:

Figure 5.3.2

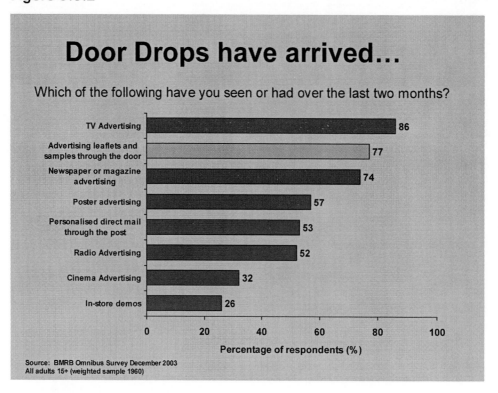

# Door Drops have arrived...

Which of the following have you seen or had over the last two months?

Source: BMRB Omnibus Survey December 2003
All adults 15+ (weighted sample 1960)

Key fact: door-drop leaflets and samples are second in saliency only to TV advertising.

Figure 5.3.3

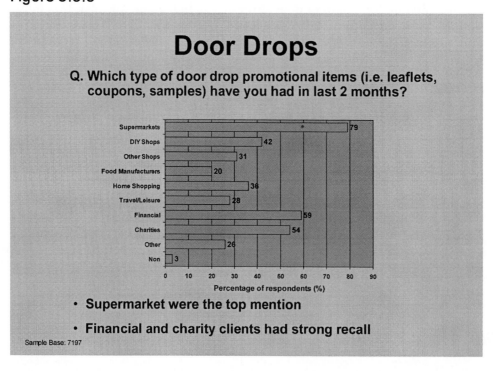

# Door Drops

Q. Which type of door drop promotional items (i.e. leaflets, coupons, samples) have you had in last 2 months?

- **Supermarket were the top mention**

- **Financial and charity clients had strong recall**

Sample Base: 7197

Key fact: particularly high recall to supermarket, financial and charity advertising through the letterbox.

Figure 5.3.4 **Immediate action - how best to describe what consumers do with items received through the letterbox**

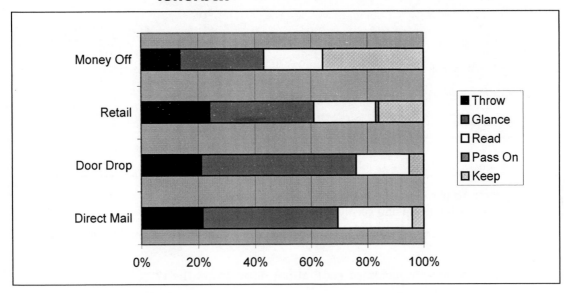

Key fact: 79 per cent of people keep, pass on, read or glance at door drops - the same as direct mail.

Figure 5.3.5 **Time leaflets kept**

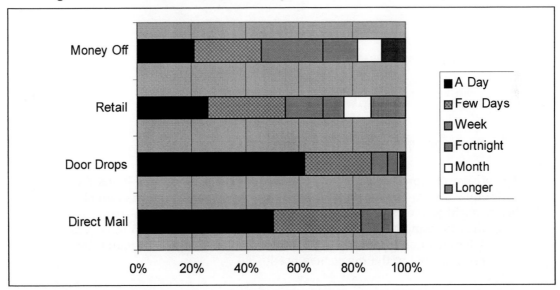

Key fact: 38 per cent are kept for at least a few days and 13 per cent are kept for a week or more.

Table 5.3.1    **Purchase or shopping action**

| Action ever taken as the result of media | | | | |
|---|---|---|---|---|
| | Door drops | Direct mail | TV | Press |
| Visited a shop | 27% | 22% | 26% | 29% |
| Sent for information | 20% | 22% | 11% | 25% |
| Bought a product | 15% | 17% | 20% | 22% |
| Any of these | 48% | 47% | 47% | 60% |

*Source: BMRB Omnibus/synergism*

Key fact: 48 per cent of consumers visited a shop, sent for information or bought a product having received a door drop.

**To summarise - "What is so good about door drops then?"**

- Useful

- Stronger

- Impactful

- Retained

- Effective

- Responsive

- Competitive

## *Who uses door drops?*

The advent of more accurate targeting in door-drop marketing helps the marriage with other media. For example, if a new shampoo/conditioner is launched with a heavyweight women's press campaign and a door-drop coupon drop to encourage trial, then by using NRS, TGI or demographic targeting (e.g. 25 to 45-year-old housewives with children), the distribution can be planned to match the readership profile of the magazines used.

Door drops are particularly appropriate for delivering information for public undertakings. It works for the privatised utilities, local authorities and the Central Office of Information. Leaflets communicating changes of services or timetables, or of policy, have all been distributed. Charities, motor insurers, household insurers and book clubs have used door-to-door very successfully, thanks to the effectiveness of targeting by postcode sector.

Door-drop marketing is now an established medium that plays a crucial role in UK marketing. Most of the major grocery manufacturers and retailers use it as part of their advertising and promotional strategies. It is also widely used by mail-order companies to recruit agents, and by financial service companies to sell products and policies. Many use it consistently as part of their strategic long-term brand-building programmes as well as for tactical applications, and it is particularly heavily used for new product launches.

Overall 84 of the top 100 spending advertisers in 2004 used door drops regularly, endorsing the claim that door-drop marketing is a mainstream medium.

## Door drops and direct marketing

Door drops were, until recently, associated in many people's minds only with massive distribution of sales promotion leaflets. These often incorporated money-off coupons but did not usually call for any other response. Today an increasing number of manufacturers ask customers to insert their names and addresses on coupons before redemption.

Asking consumers to include their names and addresses on redemption coupons not only discourages misredemption at the checkout - the consumer is less likely to misredeem if he has filled in correct address details - but can also begin to form the basis of a customer database. Label collection schemes, cash-back offers and many other forms of brand promotion necessarily require a name and address. The more progressive manufacturers capture such information at the handling house and keep it on file for future direct marketing activity. With the advent of large consumer databases, responses to door-to-door promotions can now be matched against existing databases.

Many retailers who use door drops ask for customers' names and addresses. For example, Beefeater has required those redeeming their vouchers to record their names and addresses.

Mail-order catalogue companies use door-to-door to recruit new customers, and financial institutions (life assurance companies, for instance) use door drops to generate immediate response. The medium is now as appropriate for this kind of marketing activity as the mail when either a reply coupon or phone response is required.

More recently, car manufacturers, appliance retailers, DIY chains and electrical retailers have used large-scale door-drop activity to generate footfall for their stores. Have a look at door-to-door's many advantages and applications and think how many of them have possibilities for the alert direct marketer:

- Low cost distribution of customer recruitment literature, including samples and discount offers.

- Unrestricted creativity - the escalation of cost with increased space, or weight, as experienced in press advertising or direct mail respectively, is much less significant with door drops. (But see section on costs at the end of this chapter.)

- Postcode sector targeting using geodemographic and lifestyle database information.

- High-speed coverage for most of the country with only a few simple phone calls or emails.

- Research/feedback facilities - a special benefit in the early stages of building a customer database.

- The missing link between image advertising and direct sales stimulation – with no need to buy or own a list before you can begin.

- Testing potential - as with inserts and direct mail, by using alternative or batched leaflets and by comparing local, regional and national results.

- Unduplicated coverage of target market (an advantage not shared by other unaddressed media, e.g. loose inserts, space ads or DRTV).

Clearly, door drops offer many interesting and unique opportunities for the direct marketer prepared to investigate what has now become an established direct response medium.

### Gillette - a close shave

Circular Distributors' two-day consumer 'opt-in' technique provided the perfect vehicle for delivering a free sample of a Sensor Excel razor safely into an appropriate household on behalf of Gillette. It was extremely important that the razors went to as few existing Gillette users as possible and was aimed specifically at the disposable market.

A bag, aimed to appeal to users of disposable razors, was delivered through the letterbox on the first day. The householder was asked to fill in some basic details and hang the bag back out on their doorknob on the second day if they wished to receive their 'free shaving pack'. The distributors then returned to every household, collecting the bags for future use and posting the free razor through the letterbox where requested.

The targeting involved working within chosen store catchments. A stunningly high 42 per cent of households responded to this offer, and the two-day sampling campaign added an estimated £30 million worth of incremental retail sales for trade customers over three years. A great example of how door drops can be used in a creative way to satisfy a complicated marketing objective.

## Door drops and sampling

Door-drop sampling has been a very popular medium for creating product trial for many years. As long
ago as 1954, four million bars of Sunlight soap were delivered to UK households. The activity worked so well that soon many major manufacturers were delivering product samples through the letterboxes of Britain's households and this continues to this day.

The expression 'trying is buying' is never more relevant than placing real products into the hands and homes of consumers and there is a wealth of evidence that shows once consumers try a brand that subsequent purchase of a full-size product follows on quickly.

Door-drop sampling can be divided into three methods:

- Letterbox sampling

- Personal call sampling

- Two-day consumer 'opt-in' sampling

## Letterbox sampling

This is simple and inexpensive. If an item can fit through a letterbox and the product is legal, non-toxic and doesn't contain nuts, door-drop marketing is a good option. It is ideal for the delivery of a multitude of products from shampoo to chocolate and toothpaste.

Presentation and packaging add value and attraction to samples. Many fmcg manufacturers have used 'replica' letterbox sampling, including Lever Fabergé, Procter & Gamble, Unilever Best Foods, Kellogg's, Gillette and Kraft Jacob Suchard. It is recommended that a coupon is included on the pack, so that once the consumer has tried the product, the coupon is there to encourage purchase. A name-gathering device can also be applied as part of a database-building scheme for ongoing consumer dialogue.

## Personal call sampling

Although more expensive this enables qualification of the consumer, i.e. only suitable consumers need be offered the sample. Information can also be collected via a sample doorstep call procedure carried out by interviewers. Personal call sampling reduces wastage and has been used by companies such as Unilever to build customer databases. The sample distributor often uses a hand-held computer to data capture the required details. (The same technique is also used in shopping precincts and other public places, when it is called field marketing.) The method is particularly favoured if the product costs are high. Nestlé used 'personal call' to deliver Felix to cat owners and Winalot to dog owners as part of a major Database-building operation in the UK that ran successfully for four years. Sampling can be expensive, especially when the advertiser is generous, so qualification of dog or cat ownership is important prior to placement. The upside is that return on investment from a newly converted 'loyalist' can be very profitable for the brand. In addition, doorstep interviews can also provide answers to simple questions for future targeted direct marketing activity.

## Two-stage consumer 'opt-in' sampling

With this activity, on day one a communication is delivered through the letterbox, asking the householder if they would like to receive a free sample. Consumers are requested to fill in certain details and leave the door-dropped communication (e.g. bag or door hanger) on their doorknob by the following morning (day two), when it is collected by the distributor. (See Gillette case history previously.) This technique enables the householder to actually request a free sample and identify themselves as the appropriate target market, eliminating wastage completely. It also offers the opportunity for all interested householders to get involved without having to be in during the day (unlike personal call). Information on the householder can also be gathered in return. This has proven to be a compelling and intriguing promotional technique that often yields very high response rate and householders seem to love it.

## The power of sampling 'try me and buy me'

The performance of door-drop marketing is especially remarkable where samples are letterboxed as the following research findings show:

Figure 5.3.6

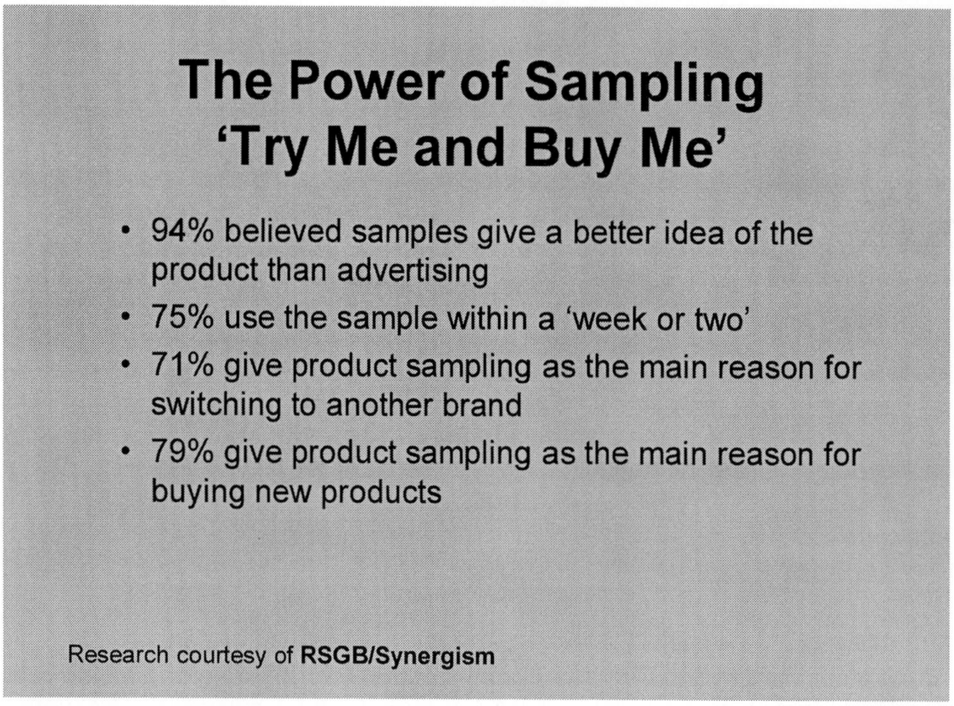

## The Power of Sampling
## 'Try Me and Buy Me'

- 94% believed samples give a better idea of the product than advertising
- 75% use the sample within a 'week or two'
- 71% give product sampling as the main reason for switching to another brand
- 79% give product sampling as the main reason for buying new products

Research courtesy of **RSGB/Synergism**

*Source: RSGB/Synergism*

## *Door drops and redemption coupons*

Coupons delivered via door drops are a particularly powerful sales promotion tool. According to NCH research, door-drop redemption levels average around 4.5 per cent, compared with only 1 per cent and 2 per cent respectively for coupons featured in magazines and newspapers. The response rate on door-drop coupons is bettered by in-pack and on-pack coupons and by direct mail, although this does not take into account the high cost of postage and personalisation when delivering by mail. Of all coupons delivered, just over 5 per cent are delivered by mail, 58 per cent by newspapers and magazines, and 37 per cent by door drops.

## *Door drop targeting*

When door-drop distribution first became popular with national marketers, its strength was as a low-cost non-discriminate means of reaching everyone, i.e. the mass market. Later, with the development of socio-economic classifications, a degree of targeting became possible. But in recent years targeting has become highly developed and now rivals direct mail in its geographic selectivity. The following geographic groupings are widely used in the distribution of door-drop advertising, each of which can be overlaid on the recognised socio-economic groups ABC1 and C2DE:

- TV regions

- Radio regions

- County boundaries

- Major urban areas/conurbations

- Marketing areas, e.g. Nielsen sales territories

- Catchment areas, e.g. around retail outlets

- By postcode sector (average of 2,500 households)

- By postcode micro sector (average of 700 households)

## Targeting with the aid of sophisticated databases

More recently, door-drop marketing now employs sophisticated computer techniques coupled to established consumer databases to target *areas with the highest penetration of likely prospects for a particular product, service or offer*.

To do this, first an advertiser needs to establish a geodemographic profile of their ideal prospect, using either research data or by profiling existing lists of known customers and prospects. To achieve this all that is required is the full postcode of the customer/prospect - names or addresses are not required.

The resulting data is then overlaid to create a detailed profile using one of the following databases:

- Mosaic

- Financial Mosaic

- ACORN

- Electoral roll

- Retail catchment areas

Finally, the best prospect postcode sectors are compared with the four possible door-drop methods of accessing households e.g:

- Solus door drop

- Shared door drop

- Door drop alongside local free newspaper

- Door drop by the postman (Royal Mail)

# The four methods of door dropping

## Solus Plus - undivided attention for an advertising message

Solus Plus gives total flexibility. The advertiser can choose their own timing, precise geographical area, postcode sectors and selection criteria. The message is delivered in a non-competitive environment with up to two other items. In some cases this is the only practical method to achieve coverage. For example, it is not possible with shared methods to make personal calls and place product samples in the hands of consumers, to qualify prospects on the doorstep, or to collect information about householders. Generally Solus Plus is more expensive than shared door drops. Nationally this service is offered by Circular Distributors and Royal Mail.

## Shared door drops - the low-cost option

Shared door drops offers the lowest cost method, because advertisers share with up to four non-competing brands or products. Flexibility nevertheless exists to choose by geographical area, postcode sector, TV region, socio-economic grouping and specialist profiling and ranking methods etc. Shared door drops allow the delivery of items weighing up to 100 grams, so this covers most items such as product samples, booklets, leaflets and direct response items.

## Local free newspaper door drops

Door-drop delivery with local free newspapers is a technique developed 20 years ago. It is a method that has grown rapidly, mirroring the development of the free newspaper business in the UK. 70% of UK households now receive at least one weekly free newspaper, and the medium's advertising revenue is now more than that of the paid-for weeklies. As many as 18 million households can be door dropped in this way.

The reliability of distribution by the reputable free newspaper publishers is backed by VFD (verified free newspaper distribution) which was founded by ABC (audit bureau of circulation) in 1981 to provide independent verification of circulation figures. Latest research indicates that VFD papers have an average certified distribution rate of 95 per cent. Unlike Solus Plus and shared door-drop methods free newspaper deliveries are usually completed within a three-day period. Most papers and accompanying door-drop items are delivered on a Wednesday, Thursday or Friday so if speed of campaign is vital, free newspaper door drops is the answer. Three companies dominate the national planning and distribution service of door-drop items with local free newspapers: Circular Distributors, The Leaflet Company and NLM (National Letterbox Marketing).

## Royal Mail door drops

Delivery of unaddressed material is undertaken by the Royal Mail; items are normally delivered by the postman at the same time that the normal post is letterboxed. Royal Mail's door-drop service is the only UK service that can reach every letterbox and this service is extensively used by direct response advertisers. This product is more fully described in a later chapter of this Guide.

# Door drops and creativity

Just as it is possible to cost-effectively deliver a wide variety of product samples e.g. breakfast cereals, health and beauty samples, snack and beverage products, so it is also practical to deliver a wide range of different promotional formats. The format limitations imposed by newspapers and magazines do not apply to door drops, nor do the weight, bulk and format limitations of direct mail apply. As long as a promotional item can be fitted through a normal letterbox then designers can create any type of novel, eye-catching shape. Indeed promotional items in the actual shape of the product have become particularly popular with many advertisers as this tactic ensures that when the product is seen on the retailer's shelf there is immediate recognition by the consumer - a vital function of image advertising.

**Figure 5.3.7**

Leaflets and samples can be shaped like the products they represent.

There is also evidence to show that large door drop formats, provided that they can be folded to go through the letterbox, are cost-effective in their response payback. Catalogues and magazines, often quarterly, are a format increasingly used by retailers who want to promote a wide range of merchandise in one vehicle - something that cannot be done in a press ad or a TV commercial.

Magazines prove highly effective when used by retailers to drive traffic through stores, encouraging loyalty among existing customers and promoting switching among others. There is no reason why manufacturers should not follow this example, as they have done in the US. The 'house' magazine is also a proven vehicle for direct marketers who wish to stay in close touch with customers - and this is further evidence of how different disciplines are drawing closer together from a creative point of view.

## What makes for effective door drops?

Over recent years CD has commissioned several pieces of research to establish the creative factors that determine consumer response. According to the research, when consumers receive a leaflet through the letterbox it is either thrown away, retained or, in the case of information leaflets, put to one side for perusal at a later time. During this sifting process, respondents weed out those items of little or no interest, typical examples being deliveries that are made at high frequency but promote items of low-frequency purchase, e.g. kitchens or double glazing, and also confusing or over-complicated material that does not immediately and clearly promote its value to consumers.

Money-off coupons, free samples, multifaceted offers and retailer booklets are considered generally more interesting by consumers. The conclusion is that the more immediate the reward and the less effort that is required to get it, the greater is the interest and the greater the response.

Three factors combine to make a good door drop:

- Impact

- Relevance

- Branding

As a result of the research, a number of creative guidelines were established for door-to-door. These are set out below in a useful checklist in table 5.3.2. Keep it handy - much of it applies to other forms of advertising such as inserts and even some direct mail activity:

### Table 5.3.2 The essential features of an effective door drop

- Brand recognition and message or reward must be almost instantaneous.

- Strong, simple visual clues (through the use of colour and shape) work best, and can also appear quite impactful and interesting to consumers. This creativity has to be either brand- or reward-related (or both).

- Teasers generally serve to confuse and annoy rather than arouse curiosity.

  Teasers that do work are related to a reward or attractive benefit. In other words, they have to demonstrate relevant creativity.

- Additional product information has to be communicated with simplicity and relevance.

- Consumers are not generally prepared to read detailed copy, but a product image can still be communicated through mood, tone and style of the leaflet.

- Information-style leaflets, e.g. booklets, should have a sense of size and quantity of information, and a quality soft-sell approach.

## How much will it cost?

The cost of door-drop distribution is dependent on six straightforward elements:

- Size and weight of the item

- Quantity of households to be door dropped

- Areas to be covered

- Door-drop method (e.g. Solus Plus, shared, with free newspaper or Royal Mail)

- Targeting system and data preparation

- Supplier

Very broadly, shared costs from specialist door-drop companies can be as low as £13.00 per thousand; Solus Plus £38.00 per thousand; and leaflets with free newspapers about £14.00 per thousand. These costs are for simple items weighing less than 10 grams. Heavier items are generally more expensive and agreed by negotiation and are subject to sight of intended material.

As with every other supplier sphere, buying door drops on price alone can lead to poor quality activity and poor results. Unless distributors, who are essentially a casual labour force, are properly remunerated and managed there will be trouble. It is therefore important to obtain client references and recommendations, for example from a business colleague or an advertising or media agency.

When buying door-drop services it also pays to ensure the chosen supplier is a member of the Direct Marketing Association; the DMA has a door-drop council that represents the unaddressed sector of the market in terms of protection and promotion. Members of the DMA must abide by the service level agreements that are set by the door-drop council; this provides guarantees of quality and recourse for advertisers in the case of a bad experience.

# Choosing your door-to-door supplier

As mentioned earlier, there are three large nationwide suppliers of door-drop services: Circular Distributors, The Leaflet Company and the Royal Mail. There are, in addition, a large number of smaller national players plus regional and local suppliers, all offering different levels and quality of service. Having arrived at your shortlist of door-drop distributors, probing questions should be asked about the operator's field structure. It is important to check the number of field-based managers within the coverage network and to ensure that they are wholly employed by the company and bound by proper contracts of employment. Specialists consider that full-time field managers are required for door-drop validation, in the form of back-checks interviews with householders to be carried out to ensure deliveries have been properly made, in the right areas at the right times.

Details should be requested about back-checking procedures, because this is a vital discipline and a reflection of the company's policy on field control and organisational standards. It is also important to ensure that back-checks are carried out independently of the subcontractor doing the distribution.

## Door drops and overseas markets

Pan-European distributions can be mounted through ELMA (the European Letterbox Marketing Association). Different countries in Europe offer differing levels of penetration, price and sophistication. It is worth noting that the UK is more advanced in terms of its targeting abilities than most other countries.

## Business-to-business?

Straightforward door-drop distribution is not usually effective for business purposes, and services in this area are limited. However, personal calls involving literature delivery with research feedback are available from organisations specialising in part-time field sales and demonstrator teams. Also the Royal Mail offer a service with their door-drop service that allows advertisers to include door dropping to business addresses when residential coverage is booked at the same time.

# Case study

And finally, an unusual, imaginative and profitable example of the use of door-drop marketing:

## Associated Co-op Creameries

This DMA Royal Mail Grand Prix winner proved the maxim that often the best work comes from the simplest concept. Associated Co-op Creameries (ACC) had a problem in that doorstep milk delivery was a shrinking market and was becoming a concept forgotten by many consumers. Potential customers needed to be reminded about the convenience of having Co-op milk delivered to their home.

The solution was found in ACC's backyard and led to one of the year's most evocative pieces of direct marketing. ACC and its agency partners Andrews Aldridge used a message in an empty bottle to communicate with a potential customer in the way they would communicate with a milkman. The apparently handwritten note, signed by a Co-op milkman, wished them 'good morning' and offered a free pint of milk if they took up the service.

The Co-op's milk bottle delighted the judges on many fronts. It had creative simplicity in using an instantly recognisable medium. Results were impressive too, with a 26 per cent increase on rounds that employed the door drop and a cost per response of less than 49 pence per new customer. The milk bottle has, not surprisingly, become a key weapon in ACC's acquisition armoury.

But perhaps the ACC campaign's biggest selling point for the judges was its effectiveness compared with other media. TV advertising of delivered milk, for instance, had clearly failed to stem the market's decline. As one judge summed up: "The milk bottle as a door drop achieved success where conventional advertising failed. It's a brilliant argument for why direct marketing is a better medium than any other."

# *Telemarketing*

## *This chapter includes:*

------------------------------------------------

- ❏ **Telemarketing today**

- ❏ **The applications of telemarketing**

- ❏ **Planning, implementing and evaluating campaigns**

- ❏ **Integration – optimising performance**

- ❏ **Best practice and regulatory requirements**

------------------------------------------------

## *About this chapter*

**T**his chapter explains how to get the most out of this most versatile and far-reaching marketing tool – the telephone.

The primary role of the phone within the marketing mix is to find, win, develop and retain customers:

| Find ⟶ Win ⟶ Develop ⟶ Retain |

Clever use of the telephone enables every step of this process to be planned, measured and controlled in order to reach and retain customers in the most profitable manner. Continuous learning ensures there is constant improvement and ultimately the know-how for success, time and time again.

The power of the phone lies not only in the hands of highly skilled advisors, but it is also ultimately the creative and analytical skills that the marketer brings to bear that really make the difference between an average and successful telemarketing programme.

## Natalie Calvert,
## Managing Director, Calcom Group

Natalie's wealth of call and contact centre experience has been developed over the past 20 years. An impressive range of international organisations have benefited from her business insights, passion and unrivalled expertise. Undertaking global and local assignments, she is totally committed to raising professionalism, standards and skills for sales, marketing and customer services. Over the past decade she has undertaken pioneering work in this area, including:

- Ambassador for the European Contact Centre Qualifications
- Chair of London First Call Centre Task Force
- Founder and Fellow of the Institute of Direct Marketing
- Chair of People Group for DMA Telecommerce Board

- Masters in Contact Centre Management Verifier
- Editorial Board for the *Journal of Database Marketing*
- CCA Standard Advisory Council Member

In 1992 Natalie founded Calcom Group, a highly respected and award-winning organisation that significantly improves the performance of its clients. Calcom's clients include companies such as Royal Bank of Scotland, Royal Mail, Department of Work and Pensions and LEGO. The team at Calcom is renowned for really making a difference to bottom-line business results and customer and employee satisfaction. In 2004 she developed and edited the *Gower Handbook of Call and Contact Centre Management*, with over 35 contributors from best-practice organisations. It has sold across the globe and during 2006 it will be re-released in Chinese.

# Chapter 5.4

# *Telemarketing*

Planned and controlled use of the phone to create a profitable relationship with customers and prospects.

Outbound has always been more than a sales tool – despite the common belief, some may say common misconception, that is all it is used for. However, an average of 27 per cent of sales still come through outbound telemarketing activity, with outsourcing (64 per cent), telecoms (28 per cent) and utilities (23 per cent) being the biggest users.

# Telemarketing today

## The changing consumer

Today's consumers are increasingly demanding and choice-driven. Having come to expect quality, reliability and functionality, they are now seeking distinctiveness and choice, control and responsiveness as key characteristics of the products and services that they are prepared to purchase (Source: *BT Best Practice 2005*).

A European financial services company found that customer defection rate had reached 12 per cent (three times the industry average) for their highest value customers because 'they were irritated at being sold to.'

*(Source: Henley Centre and BT Teleculture 2004)*

## The real challenge

The key to future success lies in *integration* with other marketing media, bold and creative use of the telephone, and going beyond compliance and best practice. But you cannot run before you can walk. First, back to basics.

## The marketing challenges

Outside influences are also driving the development of outbound.

| | | |
|---|---|---|
| ✔ | Technology | – Reducing costs |
| | | Improving data quality |
| ✔ | Operational size | – Larger call centres leading to economies of scale |
| ✔ | Telecoms costs | – Reducing costs of calling |
| ✔ | Outsources | – Growth leading to more availability of skills and resources |
| ✔ | Service | – More demanding customers leading to an increased need for organisations to differentiate their products through improved service advantage |

## The tough challenge

Over the past two decades the phone has played an instrumental role in most marketing campaigns; from inbound response handling through to outbound telephone account management. However, despite significant evidence that the phone as a marketing tool works, the real concern lies in the use of cold calling. The Telephone Preference Services (TPS) has increased to over 11 million consumers in the UK registered by Q1 2006 (Source: TPS). If the expected growth continues then forecasts estimate that by 2007–2009 the UK would have saturated its consumer market for outbound cold calling.

# The applications of telemarketing

## What is telemarketing?

Planned and controlled use of the phone to create a profitable relationship with customers and prospects.

## What does this really mean?

✔ Planned and controlled:      Always ensure clear measures, excellent tracking and reporting systems.

✔ Creativity:      Be innovative and ensure high levels of interest for your target audience.

✔ Profitable:      Understand the true costs involved and the return. The return on investment calculation will help support future activity and justify the use of the phone as a key marketing tool.

Set up test control groups to measure, compare and validate the results being achieved.

## What makes a call successful?

The *Teleculture 2000 Report* sets out that to be successful, outbound telemarketing is achieved through the *3R*s:

Relevant
Reputation
Relationship

So the three rules can be summarised as:

1. Make sure the call is highly *relevant* to the recipient

2. Build upon your organisation's *reputation* in each and every call

3. Whether targeting a prospect or customer, recognise the intrinsic values of creating a *relationship* from simple rapport-building through to enhancing customer loyalty

**Checklist**

**Relevance**
Targeted customers
Timely contacts
Relevant products and services

**Reputation**
Acting professionally
Legal and regulatory compliance
Supporting brand values

**Relationship**
Thanking and acknowledging
Loyalty-driven
Offering help
Respect

## Applications of outbound telephone marketing

The telephone has myriad roles, both inbound and outbound. All outbound calls, whatever their ostensible purpose, are marketing calls. Even if they are in response to a customer complaint, a request for information or to help solve a problem, marketing investment in these calls can help develop customer loyalty and lifetime value. Rather than be seen as a necessary but expensive cost, all outbound calling should be viewed as marketing investment and measured as such.

Use the phone in the outbound marketing mix for:

- Direct generation of sales and leads

- Setting appointments

- Customer acquisition

- Customer retention

- Customer upgrades

- Customer reactivation

- Customer care

- Welcome calling

- Warm-up to direct mail activity

- Follow-up to direct mail activity

- Direct response follow-up

- Charity fundraising and campaigning

- Complaint resolution

- Crisis management

- Traffic generation

- Investor relations

- Market evaluation and testing

- List building, cleansing and testing

- Database building and maintenance

- Lead generation, screening and qualification

- Selling

- Sales promotion

- Merchandising

- Telephone account management

- Credit approval

- Event attendance

- Customer service

**Table 5.4.1    What companies actually use the phone for**

| | |
|---|---|
| Customer service (non-sales) | 42 % |
| Sales to new prospects | 35% |
| Sales to existing customers | 34% |
| Customer satisfaction surveys | 33% |
| Customer service leading to cross-selling/upselling | 31% |
| Market research | 27% |
| Debt collection | 17% |
| Other | 15% |

Source:  The UK Contract Centre
Operational Review 3rd Edition

Each application has different requirements:

✔    Skill requirements (and sometimes people)

✔    Operational needs, i.e. time to contact, call duration and productivity rates

✔    Results, both in terms of cost and return

# Planning, implementing and evaluating campaigns

## Telemarketing is a six-stage process

Telemarketing is a cyclical six-stage process, starting with careful planning through to evaluating the last development.

Figure 5.4.1

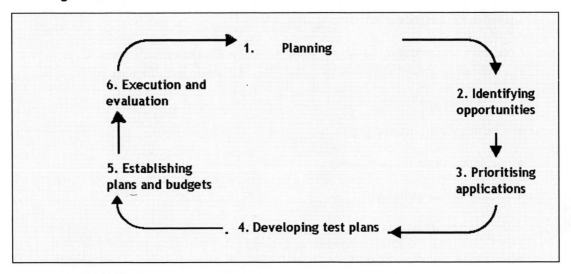

The six stages are:

1.    Planning

2.    Identifying opportunities

3.    Prioritising phone applications

4.    Testing

5.    Establishing plans and budgets

6.    Evaluation

## 1.    Planning

Begin with knowing what telemarketing is capable of (and what it cannot do) and how it can – and should – be strategically integrated into the marketing mix. Telemarketing must be given the same priority and weighting as other channels and integration is key – with mail, web and advertising – and cannot be overstated. Simply bolting on the phone as an added extra is not the answer; you will not achieve the results that are possible when the medium is intelligently integrated within the marketing strategy.

## 2.    Identifying opportunities

There are three ways to identify telemarketing opportunities:

•    Gut feel and experience

- Customer segmentation

- Customer Management Cycle Analysis (CMCA)

## Gut feel

The 'gut feel' is adopted by many, if not most users, but is *not* the preferred approach of the professional marketer. This solution also needs 'number' justification and proven methodology.

## Customer segmentation

Customer segmentation involves breaking down the customer base and prioritising each group in descending order, (1 = high 6 = low), in terms of:

- Volume available

- Geographic needs

- Seasonality requirements

- Marketing priority

- Propensity to work

- Other (market, business or operational, as appropriate to your organisation)

### Table 5.4.2

| | Volume | Geography | Seasonality | Market priority | Propensity for success | Other inhouse skill | Cost | Total |
|---|---|---|---|---|---|---|---|---|
| Key accounts | 1 | 3 | 4 | 3 | 6 | 2 | 1 | 20 |
| High-value medium accounts | 2 | 1 | 5 | 4 | 5 | 3 | 3 | 23 |
| Medium accounts | 3 | 2 | 6 | 6 | 2 | 2 | 2 | 23 |
| Small accounts | 6 | 6 | 3 | 5 | 1 | 3 | 6 | 30 |
| Third-party | 5 | 4 | 1 | 2 | 3 | 5 | 4 | 24 |
| Prospects | 4 | 5 | 2 | 1 | 4 | 6 | 5 | 27 |

In this example the following customer segments would be prioritised for activity:

1. Key accounts

2. High-value medium

3. Medium

4. Third party

5. Prospects

6.    Small accounts

## Customer Management Cycle Analysis

A different approach is Customer Management Cycle Analysis (CMCA), which, as the name suggests, plots the 'life cycle' of a customer and uses this to identify key points where telemarketing could be utilised. There is often scope for telemarketing throughout the life cycle, either on its own or integrated with other activity, but the two key applications are account management and customer service.

Most companies are harbouring many untapped opportunities for increasing the profitable use of the telephone and adding significant value to the business. It is worth investigating every opportunity along the sales and marketing chain to look for key areas in which to test an investment in telemarketing.

Examine the following:

- Extra pieces of information that could help to improve conversion at the next stage of the process. If so, what is the potential value of an increase?

- Can the connection being made help to increase customer loyalty? If so, what is the potential value of the additional retained customers?

- Generate opportunities to sell additional products and services. If so, what is the potential value of the incremental sales?

- What is the value of higher productivity? Are there savings in staff costs, or lower production costs? What is the value of these savings?

More and more companies are now realising that they have to develop a different sort of relationship with customers. At a time when much of a customer's relationship with a business is conducted remotely through the internet or automated inbound calls, telemarketing at an appropriate customer management life cycle juncture provides one of the few ways companies and their customers can build a real customer relationship. As research that has come out of the charity sector has recently shown, especially that conducted by the NSPCC, any point of contact helps build customer loyalty.

USE ALL PHONE CONTACTS TO BUILD CUSTOMER LOYALTY

Figure 5.4.2

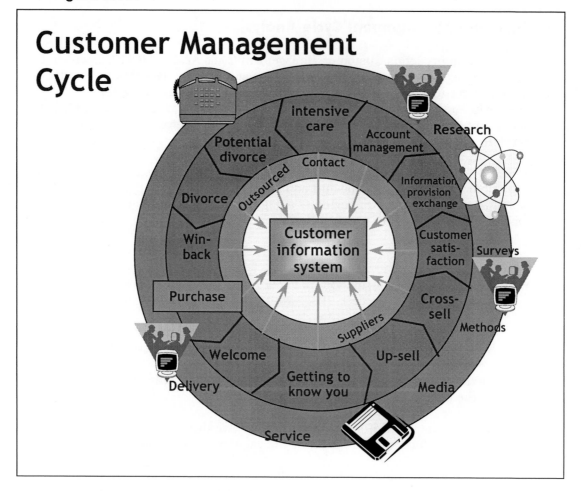

# Customer Management Cycle

## 3. Prioritising phone applications

Using CMCA, customer segmentation or, if you must, gut instinct, the next step is to prioritise call prospects. The highest priority should be given to those that will deliver:

• The highest profitable margin

• The highest volume

Calculate this using a break-even analysis described below. But it's not just about the break-even point: candidate uses for the phone should also be checked against the marketing plan to ensure they are consistent with the objectives that have been set, so that the choice of priorities is a combination of potential value and strategic fit.

Now set clear campaign objectives:

Checklist – campaign objectives

• Is the target audience existing customers or new prospects?

• Is the campaign designed to maximise number of responses, or generate a small number of quality leads?

- What are the specific objectives of the campaign? Is it about generating direct sales or qualifying the leads and passing them on to a salesforce? Is it about establishing a qualified mailing list for future activity? Is it about building the database? Is it an awareness-raising campaign?

- What media will be used?

- Timings.

- What other marketing activity at the same time could affect the response rates?

- What are the budgetary constraints?

- The advisors.

It is worthwhile taking time to devise a checklist template of campaign objectives, covering all the initial information needed. It will be handy, not just as a ready reference guide, but also as part of the briefing process for future campaigns.

## 4. Testing

So far, the planned use of telemarketing is all based on assumptions, however rational and evidence-based these may be. Now those assumptions must be tested, demonstrating that use of the phone, whether solus or integrated with other media, will cover its costs and provide an acceptable contribution to overheads and profits. Specifically with integrated campaigns, you'll have to show that the cost of adding the phone to the mix is covered by the *extra* revenue generated.

The importance of test campaigns prior to rollout against random sample and control (i.e. those not phoned) populations is vital here. Test, retest, and then test again.

### Table 5.4.3    Key testing areas

| Marketing | Process | Operations | Customer | People |
|---|---|---|---|---|
| Offer | Script | Timings | Contact strategy | Skills |
| List | Reporting | Conversions | Target audience | Staffing levels |
| Other media | Back office | Volumes | Decision making unit | Profile |

## 5.    Developing and managing operational plans and budgets

This requires a detailed operational plan with schedules and forecasts. Below is a useful checklist.

All telemarketing campaigns should be assessed against, and managed through, the following process:

1.    Define the overall campaign objectives

2.    Identify the potential for telemarketing application

3.    Create an outline budget and cost-benefit evaluation

4.    Eliminate or accept any risks involved

5.    Test the proposed approach

6.    Evaluate initial results and feedback

7.    Calculate actual cost-effectiveness of the activity

8.    Identify improvements and implement them

9.    Repeat steps 5 to 8 until the process is complete

10.   Document the final results and learning for future reference

All too often the basic planning process is sacrificed. A wise outbound manager will recognise that planning provides the key to effective performance and improvement, and time dedicated to planning and monitoring will ultimately determine the extent to which the activity fulfils its potential.

## Costs

All the applications of outbound calling have the potential to be highly profitable or just highly expensive, depending on the skill with which the telephone is integrated within the marketing activity.
But one of the great advantages of outbound telemarketing is that, regardless of the product or type of company, many of its costs can be accurately estimated. The main variations in costs come from:

- The length of the call

- The number of contacts per hour

- Skills required – cost of resource

- Data quality

Using a bureau, you can expect to pay a set up fee of £75 to £1,250 with an hourly charge of £15 to £30 per advisor. Other methods of charging include one-off project fees or costs-per-call. These tend to be harder to judge and can prove costly if not accurately estimated up front.

## Hardware

Most campaigns may well require appropriate technology: normally a campaign management system and a dialler system.
There are three main types of dialler system: preview, predictive and power.
*Preview diallers* (used, on average, on 23 per cent of campaigns) allow the advisor to preview contact information before the call is made.
*Predictive diallers* (39 per cent) automatically call a list of numbers and detect the tone at the receiving end (engaged, unobtainable, answerphone or live ring). They then predict at which point an advisor will become available to handle the next call. However, caution is needed when this system overdials and therefore there is a risk of a prospect or customer answering the phone to find no one at the other end – the 'silent call' currently the subject of so much controversy (see below).
*Power diallers* (10 per cent) work in a similar – but simpler – way to predictive diallers, with a certain degree of overdialling.

Diallers can have tremendous advantages. They can increase the average productive talk time per advisor per hour to well over 50 minutes, compared to the average of 10 to 15 minutes in a manual environment, increasing advisor productivity by 150 to 400 per cent for consumer calling and 30 to 60 per cent for business calls.

It is advisable to check the current Ofcom/DMA guidelines regarding diallers. Information may be found at the end of this chapter.

## Inhouse versus bureau

Doing the work inhouse might save money, perhaps as much as half of what a bureau will charge, but inhouse operations have their own issues. Telemarketing is a professional, highly trained job; it is not a responsibility you can pass to other members of staff and expect them to succeed at. To run a successful inhouse operation you will have to recruit a dedicated team and manager and invest time and resources. Here is a summary of the strengths of each:

## Table 5.4.4

| Inhouse | Bureau |
|---------|--------|
| Know-how of organisation | High levels of expertise |
| Existing product knowledge | Availability of staff |
| Access to data/systems | Good environment to learn (and make mistakes) |
| Usually high skill levels | Campaign peaks and troughs better managed |
| Integration with other departments and campaign earners | Highly flexible resource (switch on and off as needed) |
| Utilisation of existing infrastructure (i.e. consumer evening calling) | Good levels of testing |
| High profile | Usually strong reporting ethos |
| | Specialist hard and software available |
| | Neutral and objective |

Use bureaux to identify benchmarks, go through learning curves and establish success – then roll out inhouse.

## Scripting

There have been many debates on whether to script or not; here is a summary of why to script:

- Clear structure for call duration

- Establish what does and does not work

- Data capture

- Consistency

- Branding of organisation

- Share best practice

- Quality control

> The aim of a script is not to sound scripted!

The script must be good. Writing something that is intended to be spoken and heard by a customer is not like writing something that is intended to be read by another customer. It has a different quality and timbre. Because of this, speak the script into a tape recorder before attempting to put pen to paper.

> When composing your script:
>
> - Be colloquial and chatty – use words and phrases your audience uses in everyday speech: 'you'll', not 'you will'; 'might've', not 'might have'; and of course, 'bought' not 'purchased' but be wary of being too colloquial
>
> - Address prospects directly by using 'you' rather than talking about yourself ('I/we')
>
> - Don't worry about grammatically correct language – you want something that works
>
> - Allow for tone and inflexion – don't deliver in a monotone
>
> - Use role play extensively

The alternative to a script is the guide, which may be a printed document rather than an on-screen display. The guide will usually have been devised by experienced advisors but allows for some creative interpretation and improvisation. It is especially useful when the proposition is complex and invites questions from the prospect.

But ... no matter how good the script or guide, you *must* have a dedicated, motivated, skilful advisor delivering it. A great script in the wrong hands is as bad – no, worse – than a great adviser with a dud script.

When planning the content of the script:

- Always start with a clear objective

- Ensure the script answers these questions:

    1. Who's calling?

    2. Why are they calling?

    3. Where did they get my name/number?

    4. Why should I listen?

    5. What's in it for me?

- Follow the tried and test AIDCA formula:

    1. Attention

    2. Interest

    3. Desire

    4. Conviction

    5. Action

The target audience for the campaign will drive the style of your delivery. For instance, a financial services product targeted at people with high savings may require a very different style from that of a free mobile phone subscription.

> Run a workshop with an informed group to develop the script, a great way to gain buy-in.

## Managing the campaign

Whether you go for a bureau or an inhouse operation, managing the campaign is the same process. As a manager, you should:

Checklist

- Continually watch performance and judge it on an hourly basis. Know the hourly cost and look at conversion hourly. Keep tracks of costs.

- Always get regular reports on why prospects refuse the proposition. As your advisors are engaged in a conversation, the script should allow them to gather valuable information on why target prospects say no. You may find that the script can be changed or simple things added to it that could overcome these objections.

- Attend regular feedback sessions with the advisors. These are the people who can give you a real feel for what is happening out there.

- Listen in to live calls or review taped calls.

- Reward and praise success. If advisors are doing well, then tell them so and ensure they continue to be motivated.

- Provide advisors with as much information about products and proposition as possible. The more they know, the more confident they will be and the easier it will be to 'sell'.

- Attend training sessions.

Below is a sample project plan:

## Table 5.4.5

| ID | Task name | Duration | Start date | Finish date |
|----|-----------|----------|------------|-------------|
| 1 | Campaign implementation project | 55 days | Mon 11/02 08.00 | Fri 26/04 17.00 |
| 2 | Initiate | 13.7 days | Mon 11/02 08.00 | Thu 28/02 14.36 |
| 3 | Decision to use partners | 5 days | Mon 11/02 08.00 | Fri 15/02 17.00 |
| 4 | Identify steering group members | 3 days | Mon 11/02 08.00 | Wed 20/02 17.00 |
| 5 | Project kick-off with steering group and project manager | 1 day | Thu 21/02 08.00 | Thu 21/02 17.00 |
| 6 | Define project goal | 0.2 day | Thu 21/02 08.00 | Thu 21/02 09.36 |
| 7 | Define project objectives | 0.5 day | Thu 21/02 09.36 | Thu 21/02 14.36 |
| 8 | Define project team structure | 0.2 day | Thu 21/02 14.36 | Thu 21/02 16.12 |
| 9 | Define project workstream leaders | 0.1 day | Thu 21/02 16.12 | Thu 21/02 17.00 |
| 10 | Steering group signs off goals and objectives | 1 day | Wed 27/02 14.36 | Thu 28/02 14.36 |
| 11 | Define | 20.7 days | Thu 21/02 08.00 | Thu 21/03 14.36 |
| 12 | Confirm project managers | 1 day | Thu 21/02 08.00 | Thu 21/02 17.00 |
| 13 | Prepare scope management | 1 day | Thu 28/02 14.36 | Fri 01/03 14.36 |
| 14 | Steering group sign-off of scope document | 1 day | Thu 07/03 14.36 | Fri 08/03 14.36 |
| 15 | Define initial plan based on objectives and scope | 1 day | Fri 08/03 14.36 | Mon 11/03 14.36 |
| 16 | Project kick-off with workstream leaders | 1 day | Mon 11/03 14.36 | Tue 12/03 14.36 |
| 17 | Review project objectives from steering group meeting | 0.2 day | Mon 11/03 14.36 | Mon 11/03 16.12 |
| 18 | Define project tasks | 0.2 day | Mon 11/03 16.12 | Tue 12/03 08.48 |
| 19 | Assign tasks to workstream leaders | 0.2 day | Tue 12/03 08.48 | Tue 12/03 10.24 |
| 20 | Agree task deadlines | 0.2 day | Tue 12/03 10.24 | Tue 12/03 12.00 |
| 21 | Agree task interdependencies | 0.2 day | Tue 12/03 13.00 | Tue 12/03 14.36 |

| 22 | Prepare work breakdown structure | 2 days | Tue 12/03 14.36 | Thu 14/03 14.36 |
| 23 | Steering group sign-off of work breakdown structure | 1 day | Wed 20/03 14.36 | Thu 21/03 14.36 |
| 24 | Plan | 53.7 days | Mon 11/02 08.00 | Thu 25/04 14.36 |
| 25 | Identify project stream members (HR/finance/operations/IT) | 2 days | Tue 12/03 10.24 | Thu 14/03 10.24 |
| 26 | Project team agree task responsibilities, timings and resource requirement | 3 days | Tue 12/03 14.36 | Fri 15/03 14.36 |
| 27 | Prepare detailed project plan | 2 days | Fri 15/303 14.36 | Tue 19/03 14.36 |

*Source: Sitel Corporation*

## 6. Execution and evaluation

### Evaluating and measuring success

All data gathered from a telemarketing campaign is valuable and the:

- Numbers give you benchmarks against which to measure all activity

- Numbers provide planning information for future growth

- Numbers make it easier to secure budgets for future growth – they are hard to argue with

---

**Number crunching**

Data is important. People make their livings out of number-crunching sales and customer data. So the more recorded, the better your analysis will be, the better plans will be, and the more successful campaigns will be. It all comes down to numbers, both going into the planning in statistics and coming out at the other end as increased sales and ultimately in pounds and pence.

---

Most telemarketing activities are measured primarily on conversion rates, but again of course, this is only part of the equation for a profitable return on investment (ROI).

### Quality

Your success will be evaluated not just against quantitative accountable performance indicators, but on the quality of the contact handling and data collection. Quality can be measured via three methods:

- Dedicated quality management team

- Team manager monitoring

- External mystery shopping or post-contact research

The ideal world would give you a rounded perspective on all three views, but not every contact centre has this. Whichever solution you have available to you (the very minimum will be team manager monitoring), integral to success is a documented quality management assessment process that identifies the key quality thresholds to be achieved and indicates remedial action.

**The basic quality process involves:**

- Specifying the goal

- Creating a plan to achieve the goal

- Articulating the expectation and making assignments to the team and advisors

- Conducting follow-up at all levels

- Managing variance and taking action

**The sort of action you might take can include:**

- Side by side monitoring

- 'Buddying'

- Re-training

- Improved help screens or knowledge base

The quality process should also encompass advisor data capture and relevance of call outcome logging. During training, the quality process should be outlined to the advisors so that they are clear on the quality success measures and how they can impact on them.

With the campaign now set up and ready, it is possible to develop the *critical success factors* (CSFs). These can be divided into two lists of 'hard' and 'soft' measures.

## Critical success factors

**Hard measures:**

- Number of leads

- Number of effective calls

- Number of calls per hour, per advisor*

- Conversion ratios

- Mandatory information collection requirements

- Target number of sales/quality leads or other objectives

- Back office requirements and turnaround items such as mailing/quotation/ contract turnaround, email response targets, etc.

*As a pretty reliable rule of thumb, business-to-business outbound activity will average three to six contacts an hour; consumer activity should average eight to twelve.

Make sure you carry out activity at a time when prospects are likely to answer their phones. At its simplest, this means make business calls during the day and consumer calls in the evening/weekends. (Of course don't call during EastEnders or Coronation Street if your demographic profiles suggest your prospects are likely to be glued to their TV sets at this time.)

**Soft measures**

Soft measures will normally be those that cover qualitative issues that directly affect the respondent's experience and are often difficult to measure. These include:

- Attitude

- Quality of call

- Helpfulness

- Enthusiasm

There is much evidence to suggest that a company's reputation is built on these direct interactions with consumers and all the investment in the campaign can be won or lost by a poor experience when communicating through the outbound call. These quality issues are just as critical as the other more measurable elements, so assign them equal importance.

## The advisors

The human element in outbound telemarketing distinguishes it from every other direct marketing activity. Training advisors on how to give objective feedback when evaluating activities can help to ensure that opportunities for improvement are highlighted. After all, they are on the front line talking directly with potential customers.
It is often well worth going beyond the basic briefing process and involving advisors more actively in the feedback loop, providing them with updates and information on progress as well as the overall performance, and seeking their input on improvements.
Some companies will go as far as to provide incentives and rewards for advisors. This helps build a culture where the return on investment is focused at every level.
As well as standard briefing and training practices, some additional forms of advisor involvement can have an impact on results:

- Meeting real customers, prospects or clients

- Introducing incentives or competition to reward successful improvement suggestions

- Providing information on individual wins to customise the process

- Experiencing the product (where appropriate)

- Providing samples of relevant literature and letters

- Setting up campaign-specific recognition boards and certificates

- Inviting someone important to attend the briefing and debriefs

Above all, it is the power of customer connections that provides the best results, and anything that enhances the advisors' abilities to relate to the process from the customer's perspective will contribute to the outcomes. Help them appreciate the importance of their role. Be creative. Provide a relevant, meaningful and motivating experience for the advisors.

## *The integration effect*

The telephone is most effective when properly combined with other direct marketing techniques, especially direct mail and, increasingly, email. The figure below shows typical multiples that can be achieved by integrating phone and mail – especially with a direct mail warm-up call to verify the recipient's details (phone/mail/phone):

**Figure 5.4.3**

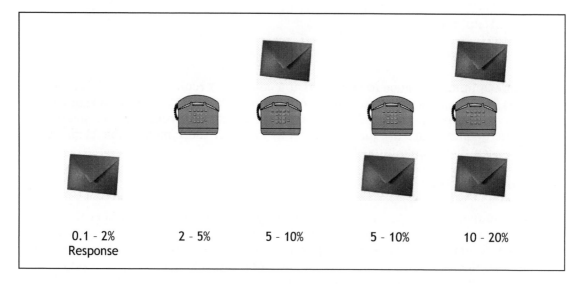

| 0.1 - 2%<br>Response | 2 - 5% | 5 - 10% | 5 - 10% | 10 - 20% |

Similar evidence comes from research conducted by Citibank in the USA. Integrating a freephone number with cold DM recruitment generated 7 per cent more sales than mail on its own. But adding outbound telemarketing generated 13 per cent more sales than just mail, almost doubling the effect of the mail and freephone combination.

The multiples that can be achieved will vary with every application – the mail/freephone/telemarketing option can generate up to 30 per cent more sales than mail alone.

Using the phone can be expensive so it is important to test carefully to determine the true potential for improvement in overall results.

Compared to other direct marketing techniques, the phone does well.

It delivers high performance in:

- Targeting

- Response

- Speed

- Control

- Testing

But, it has a *high cost* and delivers *low volume*.

But providing the case is made for the phone, then do not be afraid to go for it, and go for it in a big way. And remember, integration with other marketing techniques reduces the risk and spreads the cost.

In the first decade of the 21st Century, telemarketing is not just part of the integrated marketing mix, it is an essential part of the integrated marketing mix. Successful marketers (i.e. Orange, First Direct, American Express) understand this and give the same priority (and of course, time and resources) to the phone as they do mail, press and e-marketing.

## *Lead and appointment generation*

The phone/mail/phone (phone to verify details/mail them/make follow-up call) approach is particularly effective for lead and appointment generation, especially where the customer value is high. Spending 10 – or even 100 times more on this approach may seem excessive. But this investment can pay back.
To help visualise how this works, consider the following:
Consider the real value of a customer – say £3,000. Now imagine you have 10 per cent of this value to create a campaign to attract them – £300 per customer. Phone/mail/phone is a proven method for recruiting new customers, beginning with an initial phone call to verify the prospect's details.

The verification call

By investing in an initial phone call to verify the correct details, wastage is minimised and effective contacts are maximised. In some cases, the verification call can also prepare the ground so that the prospect is more receptive to the mail communication. Knowing that only qualified prospects are now on the mailing list, it is easier to justify an increased investment in written communications.

Now, you need to devise your phone/mail/phone campaign. But how do the costings work? The sums may look like this:

**Target £75,000**

- Average customer value = £3,000 (equivalent to 25 new customers).

- Marketing investment @10% = £300 each to invest.

- Based on a 25% conversion to sale, it would be necessary to create 100 appointments in total to create 25 new customers.

- Based on a conversion of lead/appointment of 20%, it would be necessary to contact 500 prospects to achieve 100 appointments and break even.

- So, the total cost to target 500 prospects and deliver 25 new customers would be £7,500. This provides a marketing investment of £15 per contact – more than enough to invest in a phone/mail/phone campaign of verification, a highly creative mailing and follow-up call.

### Case study

*Most telemarketing activities are measured primarily on conversion rates but this only forms part of the equation for a profitable return on investment.*

*This case study looks at a young business providing computer services to a small but distinct business sector. Its basic break-even calculation is typical of the way businesses think about telemarketing.*

*Cost by decision maker reached by telephone*

| | |
|---|---:|
| *(based on five contacts per hour)* | *£6* |
| *Number of contacts planned – 1,000 @ £6 each* | *£6,000* |
| *Estimated response rate of appointments made* | *4%* |
| *Cost per appointment* | *£150* |
| *Percentage of appointments converted to sale within six months* | *10%* |
| *Four sales at average value of £10,000 each* | *£40,000* |
| *Total profit @ £1,500 per sale* | *£6,000* |
| *Four sales deliver break-even @ £6,000 investment* | |
| *Cost:profit ratio* | *1:1* |

*Arriving at this calculation, the company was hesitant about investing as much as £6,000 as this was quite a large sum and therefore quite a big risk to a fledgling business. Their instinct, as is so often the case, was to reduce costs and minimise the risk, but this would have only reduced the contribution to the business and was unlikely to have delivered enough new business to justify the time and energy involved.*

*The company had actually been hoping to add £500,000 worth of new business in 18 months, and with this calculation found themselves hesitating to invest in just £50,000 worth of business. The numbers were realistic based on their experience of making telephone calls, and it was not easy for them to see how the telephone marketing activity could be justified. In addition, the market was so highly defined that only 3,500 companies fell within their selection criteria, so even on rollout, this approach could not deliver the business growth they were seeking.*

*After changing focus from short-term cost reduction to long-term value, the company happily signed off a test budget of £12,500 for the following phone/mail/phone campaign:*

| | |
|---|---|
| *Phone/mail/phone cost-per-contact* | *£25* |
| *Comprised:* | |
| *Data verification call* | *£1* |
| *Mailing* | *£19* |
| *Decision-maker contact call* | *£5 (six per hour)* |
| *Cost for 500 planned contacts @ £25 each* | *£12,500* |
| *Data verification calls* | *£500* |
| *Mailings* | *£9,500* |
| *Decision-maker contact calls* | *£2,500* |
| *Estimated response rate* | *15%* |
| *Number of appointments* | *75* |
| *Cost-per-appointment* | *£167* |

| | |
|---|---|
| Conversion to sale | 10% |
| Seven new customers with average value of £40,000 over 18 months | £280,000 |
| Value per customer @ £6,000 profit each over 18 months | £42,000 |
| Cost:profit ratio | 1:3.3 |

Now the company had a basis for investing in the test. The proposed approach also had the following safeguards built in:

- The campaign could be stopped at any time if the results did not support the investment.

- The fixed costs amounted to just £2,000 by negotiating for the mailing to be hand-created in batches of 50.

- 95% of waste was eliminated in the verification call.

- The decision-maker contact rate was confidently planned at a higher rate due to the verification having taken place, and due to the mailer that was designed to be 'unforgettable'.

- The data cleansing and warm-up mailing would make it possible to achieve at least the same number of appointments from half the size of the mailing list in question.

- Given the small size of their market sector, this approach also made it much more likely that they would achieve their overall objective of £500,000 on rollout to a universe of just 6,000 companies.

The company was rewarded for its courage by exceeding all the volume, response and conversion estimates after just 100 verifications, despatches and follow-up calls. The return on investment was 1:6, almost double the hoped-for improvement.

*Source: Calcom Group*

### Case study

It is sometimes easier to justify the high costs of investment in business-to-business activities due to the potentially high customer values. With high volumes and often more limited lifetime values associated with consumer marketing, it takes even more courage to adopt a bolder approach. Yet it can pay great dividends.

Take this real-life example of a company manufacturing and selling high-value home improvement products to individual consumers. The company had high acquisition costs and few opportunities to extend the customer lifetime value, and it was seeing ways to attract new customers more cost-effectively.

This was how the company typically approached conversion of prospect data

Per 10,000 prospects:

| | |
|---|---|
| Mail low-cost flyer to warm up @ £0.25 each | £2,500 |
| Cost of follow-up calls to convert to appointment @ £2 each | £20,000 |
| Conversion to qualified appointment @ 1% | 100 |

| | |
|---|---|
| Cost-per-appointment | £225 |
| Conversion to sale @ 40% | 40 sales |
| Average order value @ £2,500 revenue | £100,000 |
| Average profit per customer @ £1,000 | £40,000 |
| Return on investment (cost:profit ratio) | 1:1.8 |

The company wanted to improve the cost-effectiveness of its activity by lowering the costs of mailings and improving conversions. But this focus on cost didn't really provide much hope of significant improvement and instead the company decided to test a bolder approach by investing more in a full-colour glossy brochure for the initial mailing. While no savings could be made on the cost-per-contact on the follow-up calls, it was anticipated that there would be quite a significant uplift in conversion to appointments. The result would be to increase the ROI by more than 20%.

Projected results were then

Per 10,000 prospects:

| | |
|---|---|
| Mail low-cost flyer to warm up @ £0.75 each | £7,500 |
| Cost of follow-up calls to convert to appointment @ £2 each | £20,000 |
| Conversion to qualified appointment @ 1.5% | 150 |
| Cost-per-appointment | £183 |
| Conversion to sale @ 40% | 60 sales |
| Average order value @ £2,500 revenue | £150,000 |
| Average profit per customer @ £1,000 | £60,000 |
| Return on investment (cost:profit ratio) | 1:2.18 |

The test was successfully carried out, with some surprising results.
Per 10,000 prospects:

| | |
|---|---|
| Mail low-cost flyer to warm up @ £0.75 each | £7,500 |
| Cost of follow-up calls to convert to appointment @ £2 each | £20,000 |
| Conversion to qualified appointment @ 1.3% | 130 |
| Cost per appointment | £212 |
| Conversion to sale @ 45% | 58 sales |
| Average order value @ £2,650 revenue | £153,700 |
| Average profit per customer @ £1,000 | £66,700 |
| Return on investment (cost:profit ratio) | 1:2.93 |

The uplift to appointments was lower than expected at just 1.3%. This generated an additional 30 appointments per 10,000 mailed, but the appointment cost rose to £212. While this conversion was not as high as was hoped, it still delivered an improvement on the current cost per appointment.

But what was less expected was the upturn in conversion to sales, as well as an increase in the average order value. While the desired uplift in appointments had only been partially met, the new approach helped to ensure that more of the right kind of customers were appointed, and the *provision of more product information at the front end also increased the likelihood of a high spend.*

*The result was an uplift of more than 60% in the return on marketing investment from £1.80 per £1 spent to £2.93 per £1 spent.*

*Source: Calcom Group*

## Key to improved ROI

There are four important principles that are prerequisite to achieving the maximum return on the marketing investment:

### 1. Focus on improvements in value and profits, rather than just reducing costs

A purely cost-based method of evaluation is unlikely to show enough benefits to justify investment in a new approach. Calculate the real value of a customer and think about how you might invest to deliver significant improvements in conversions. Always measure through to final sales and profits, because improvements can be experienced at any of the lever points along the selling chain.

### 2. Recognise the importance of getting greater market share

Improved conversions deliver more than new opportunities for revenue and profit. They also provide the basis for increasing overall market share, by extracting more customers from an often limited universe of prospects. Generally, the smaller the pool, the greater the justification for increased investment in improved cost. This provides the organisation with the option to reduce the overall investment required to deliver the desired results or, if equipped to do so, the company can opt for maintaining the current level of investment in order to achieve higher growth.

### 3. Planning, testing and measurement are vital

Testing new approaches provides the only means for significant performance improvement. This means that marketers must understand the implications of a bolder, high-impact approach so that lever points can be measured and incentives for improvement attached to the most appropriate outcomes.

### 4. Go for the big picture

Small-scale changes deliver modest improvements, but significant improvement in ROI can only be achieved through a bolder approach overall. The telephone is the most powerful lever point in the process, and even minor increases in effectiveness can deliver a high uplift in ROI.

# *Best practice and legal requirements (selected)*

There are many best practice and legal requirements a telemarketing campaign must adhere to.

The Direct Marketing Association's Code of Practice on telemarketing contains the following requirements (and this is not exhaustive):

- Members must give the name of the advertiser at the beginning of the call and full contact details on request.

- Members must state at the beginning of the conversation all commercial purposes of the call.

- Members must take 'all reasonable steps' not to make outbound calls to minors.

- The Code of Practice proscribes the use of random number dialling, along with the process of random number scanning (or 'pinging') used to ascertain the status of numbers and build lists. Ofcom has powers to take enforcement action against both practices.

- Members must not make calls to unlisted or ex-directory numbers or call individuals at their place of work.

- Members must not contact people listed with the Telephone Preference Service and members must therefore operate an inhouse suppression file listing recipients who have indicated they do not wish to be contacted by phone. Members must have documented procedures to ensure that all such names have been blocked from telephone contact lists used by them or on their behalf. Members must ensure that no list containing individuals is used for telemarketing unless it has been cleared against this TPS file no more than 28 days before supply. However, members may use their own list (i.e. a list of those with whom they have an established relationship) without clearing this against the TPS file, as long as the individual has provided their telephone number (i.e. it is not sourced) and it has been clarified that the number may be used for marketing purposes). For more on TPS, see below.

- Members intending to initiate outbound marketing calls involving the use of an automated calling system (which makes calls without human intervention) must have obtained prior consent from the customer being called.

The DMA's Distance Selling Regulations require that an outbound call includes clear details of the goods or services being offered, including:

- A description of their main characteristics

- Price, including VAT, and additional non-optional costs such as postage

- Clear details on delivery arrangements

- A prominent statement explaining the existence of a right to cancel

- Details of any limitations on the offer, such as geographical or time limitations

- Information on payment mechanisms available

There are three sets of legislation that cover telemarketing, all of which are enforced by Ofcom:

1.    The Privacy and Electronic Communications Regulations 2003 (PECR) – an EC directive

2.    Data Protection Act 1998

3.    Communications Act 2003

(For further details on the effects of this legislation see Section 12.)

## PECR and Telephone Preference Service

The PECR cover all types of cold electronic sales calls, and are the legislative basis for the Telephone Preference Service.
The Telephone Preference Service allows members of the public to opt out of receiving cold calls. Advisors cannot call TPS-registered consumers – as the law and the DMA code make clear – first failing is a warning from Ofcom and, if that doesn't work, a £5,000 fine, although Ofcom has asked the government to increase this to £50,000.
In order to comply with the TPS (and therefore PECR) requirements, companies must screen their own lists against a suppression file of TPS-registered consumers. The only exception is where the company has an existing relationship with the customer. Provided they have not specifically asked you *not* to call them any more, you are allowed to call them, even though they may be TPS-registered.

## Data Protection Act

Someone may not be registered with the TPS, but they still have a legal right not to be contacted by any one named organisation – and that right derives from the Data Protection Act. So companies must operate another suppression file of those consumers who have asked not to be contacted.

## Communications Act

This covers the use of silent calls using predictive diallers, which the DMA describes as the biggest concern the contact centre industry has ever faced. The DMA Code of Practice deals with predictive diallers.
The new guidelines – published in March 2006 – require that:

•    Any abandoned calls carry a recorded message identifying the source of the call

•    Calling Line Identification must be presented on all outbound calls from automated calling systems, allowing the recipient to use the 1471 function

The total number of abandoned calls must be below three per cent of the total for any 24-hour period.

### In summary

Now let us add all this up. BT's *Best Practice in Outbound Contact* produced an excellent best-practice checklist, both externally and internally.

## Adopting best practice externally:

- Have consumer trust and confidence at the heart of every consumer communication

- Wear your 'consumer hat' – think how you would like to be contacted

- Know your customers' contact preferences (by channel and time where possible)

- Always act with courtesy – check it's OK to talk now and stop when requested

- Investigate multi-media contact – e.g. email and SMS

- Have meaningful conversations – deploy profiling and analytics where possible

- Keep contact histories – know what you have spoken to each customer about before

- Keep your promises – deliver what you say you will do

- Adopt mass-customised conversation that is different and appropriate to each contact

## Adopting best practice within your organisation:

- Work within the legislation and regulations – in letter and in spirit

- Adopt industry codes of best practice

- Ensure that your recruitment strategy helps you employ high-quality advisors

- Ensure your training (induction and ongoing) gives your advisors all the knowledge they need and empowers them to make decisions in the interest of brand reputation

- Respect data – pushing your advisors too hard will foster a 'numbers game' mentality

- Measure outcome not output (e.g. sales per contact, not calls per hour)

- Make sure there is joined-up communication between your call centre and the marketing department

- Keep your advisors briefed on changes and updates – you don't want the customer telling them about new initiatives

- Understand how your dialler works to minimise the risk of irritating your contacts. Follow best practice and Ofcom requirements on those calls you do abandon

- Keep your promises – if you promise 24-hour replies to email, then make sure you deliver

## *In conclusion: where does outbound telemarketing go from here?*

It has to be about the customer experience – integrating the phone with other media in the marketing mix and offering not just a sales call but a genuine *experience* to the customer that relates to the brand.

Outbound calling will evolve to combine its sales message with non-sales issues, such as customer service leading to cross-sell opportunities, market research, welcome calls or even complaint resolution.

Research shows that the more 'touchpoints' – opportunities a customer has to interact with a company, the more loyal that customer becomes. This can happen interactively via the web, but also in one-to-one contact with a human advisor on the phone. Every outbound call, if done well, will be enhancing customer loyalty and ultimately adding to the bottom line.

# Watching the response come in: DRTV and iTV

## This chapter includes:

------------------------------------------------

☐ **The UK TV marketplace**

☐ **The broadcast map**

☐ **Digital and interactivity**

☐ **DRTV and the direct marketer**

☐ **Planning and buying TV**

☐ **Using BARB data in buying airtime**

☐ **Interactive advertising opportunities**

☐ **Why are advertisers using interactivity?**

☐ **How are advertisers using interactivity?**

☐ **Skyview**

☐ **The overall planning process**

------------------------------------------------

## About this chapter

From this chapter you will learn about the following:

• The UK TV marketplace as it is today and how it may be in the future

• Technical details such as:
How TV is managed
How TV airtime is measured
How TV airtime is bought

• How response can be driven by TV
DRTV planning issues
DRTV buying tips
Received wisdom for DRTV creative executions

- The developing opportunities for interactive TV (iTV)
  What iTV is being used for
  The variety of interactive formats that can be used
  Case studies detailing many of the successful uses of iTV

## Beverly Barker

Beverly is an entirely over qualified communications planner having started in the business as a broadcast buyer with Ogilvy & Mather in 1984 and, after moving through a succession of agencies that were assortedly acquired and merged to make the large conglomerates of today, spent from 1992-2002 as Head of Direct and Interactive at Carat Direct.

Beverly now combines academia with practical commercial operations, working as a senior lecturer in Marketing at London Southbank University and a regular tutor for the IDM, alongside being a Managing Partner in Everythingville, where she provides a strategic customer insight consultancy to both UK and International clients in customer management, customer insight, proposition development and integrated communications planning.

## Chapter 5.5

# Watching the response come in: DRTV and iTV

## Direct response TV and interactive TV

**D**uring the 1990s there was a sea change in the use of TV as a direct marketing technique. Financial services, motor and travel providers, among others, found it a powerful means of initiating a direct relationship with individual consumers. Since then massive proliferation of channels has created a fragmented market resulting in a host of highly targeted and low-cost entry points; telephone technology has continued to evolve to drive ever more efficient call handling and computers have revolutionised the data processing and analysis of results. Since 1998 the market has also seen the introduction of digital broadcasting (DTV) and the potential for viewers to interact with advertising as it appears on screen, with the ability to request samples, brochures and sales calls at the touch of a 'red button'.

As a result this chapter will detail the latest in both DRTV techniques and interactive digital television (iDTV) opportunities.

# The UK TV marketplace

The first commercial TV stations started in 1955 with the launch of ITV, which started as a network of regional franchises, and in 1956 Gibbs SR toothpaste earned its place in history as the first product to be advertised. After that, nothing much changed until the 1980s, which saw the launch of Channel 4 (Ch 4) in November 1982 and the introduction of the first cable and satellite services.

Launching in 1989 with four channels, Sky's satellite services brought a new principle to television broadcast, that of providing channels themed to a specific genre. These included news, movies, sport and entertainment, rather than the all-encompassing remit required from the BBC, ITV or Ch 4.

Satellite stations have continued in this general manner, launching channels that seek to appeal to specific niche audiences, ranging from documentaries, music, religion, history, household design and baby care through to quizzes, competitions, mail order sales and even channels dedicated to individual football teams. All of these options were provided for reception through traditional 'analogue' technology up until October 1998 when Sky launched the first mainstream digital broadcast, Sky Digital.

## Table 5.5.1    Chronology of UK TV broadcast 1936 to 2005

| 1936 | – | First BBC Transmission |
|------|---|------------------------|
| 1955 | – | ITV launched, regulated by the Independent Television Authority |
| 1956 | – | 1st commercial = Gibbs SR Toothpaste |
| 1964 | – | BBC2 launched |
| 1969 | – | ITV goes colour |
| 1982 | – | Channel 4 and S4C launched. Commercial airtime sold by ITV |
| 1984 | – | First cable service is licensed |
| 1983 | – | TVAM started breakfast television service on ITV broadcasting seven days a week 0600 – 0930 |
| 1988 | – | ITV extended commercial broadcast to 24 hrs /day |
| 1989 | – | Sky television launches four channel services on the Astra Satellite |
| 1990 | – | Sky and BSB merge into BSkyB |
| 1990 | – | Discovery, the first cable exclusive channel launched |
| 1993 | – | New 10 yr ITV Franchises commence operation |
| 1993 | – | Channel 4 Sells Own Airtime |
| 1994 | – | ITV Sales Houses replace franchise holder sales teams |
| 1996 | – | BBC charter re-negotiated |
| 1997 | – | Channel 5 (now Five) launched |
| 1998 | – | Digital TV launched<br>= October – Sky Digital (Satellite DTH)<br>& November – ONDigital (Terrestrial) |
| 2001 | – | ITVDigital (formerly ONDigital) closed |
| 2002 | – | Freeview launched November 2002 to provide terrestrial digital service |

*Source: IPA/Carat*

Since then improvements in compression technologies mean that all digital platforms now have increased capacity, and operators are taking advantage of the associated reductions in costs to launch additional stations and services. As a result the late 1990s and early 2000s saw massive 'channel proliferation' as detailed in Figure 5.5.1 overleaf.

According to Ofcom, the UK Office of Communication, more than 370 channels were broadcasting in the UK at the end of 2005 (excluding the many time-shifted '+1' services), and they continue to receive applications with ideas for more new channels.

Ofcom is the independent regulator and competition authority for the UK communications industries with responsibilities across television and radio telecommunications and wireless communications services – www.ofcom.org.uk

Ofcom issued 156 new licences in 2004, with the entertainment, shopping, sport and adult genres accounting for over three-quarters of the total, and the majority being for services broadcasting on satellite and cable. That number is likely to continue to grow as new terrestrial, satellite and cable channels are launched, but will potentially contract again as the market finds its natural level between audience demand and commercial viability.

For the major UK broadcasters developing a portfolio of channels is an important tactic in their attempts to head off the threat of audience fragmentation posed by increasing multi-channel take-up (Ofcom1, 2005).

Figure 5.5.1 **Rapid growth in channel numbers throughout the late 1990s**

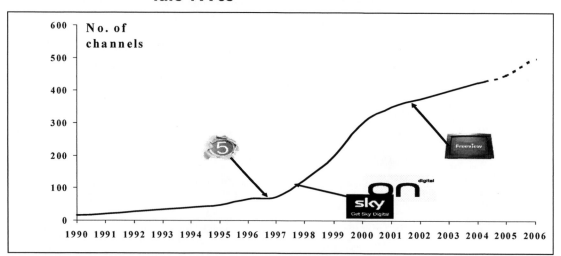

## Television audiences

Interestingly, despite the increase in programme provision and massive fragmentation of channel audiences, the average number of hours of television viewed by UK individuals has only increased marginally between 1980 and 2004.

Audience viewing data collected monthly by BARB and published in the IPA Trends in TV (table 5.5.2) indicate that the average UK household still watches around three and a half hours of TV a day. Although this equates to nearly 24 hours a week, it is less than the four and a half hours reported for American audiences across 2004/2005 (Nielsen Media Research, 2005).

**Table 5.5.2    Average hours of TV viewed per household 1980 to 2005**

| Year | Viewing Choice | Transmission Hours | Hours Viewed Daily |
|------|----------------|--------------------|--------------------|
| 1980 | ITV, 12am – 12pm BBC1 + BBC2 | 36 hrs | 3hr 22' |
| 1990 | ITV 24 hrs, C4, BBC1 + BBC2, Satellite | 228 hrs | 3hr 33' |
| 2000 | ITV, C4, C5, BBC1 + BBC2, Satellite, Digital and cable | 1000+ hrs | 3hr 37' |
| 2005 | as above | 1000+ hrs | 3hr 35' |

IPA, Trends in TV to Q3 05)
http://www.ipa.co.uk/media/tvtrends/2005/contents_summaryQtr3_2005.cfm

## Television regulation

Ofcom's duties fall into six specific areas:

1)    Ensuring the optimal use of the electro-magnetic spectrum

2)    Ensuring that a wide range of electronic communications services – including high-speed data services – is available throughout the UK

3)    Ensuring a wide range of TV and radio services of high quality and wide appeal

4)    Maintaining plurality in the provision of broadcasting

5)    Applying adequate protection for audiences against offensive or harmful material

6)    Applying adequate protection for audiences against unfairness or the infringement of privacy

For the broadcast TV area this includes:

- Issuing licences allowing commercial television companies to broadcast in and from the UK – whether received by conventional aerials, cable or satellite, or delivered by analogue or digital means. The licences vary according to the type of service, but they all set out conditions on matters such as standards of programmes and advertising.

- Regulating and monitoring broadcasters' performance against the requirements of the ITC's published licences, codes and guidelines on programme content, advertising, sponsorship and technical performance.

- Imposing penalties for failure to comply with licence requirements.

- Having a duty to ensure a wide range of television services are available throughout the UK, and that these are of a high quality and appeal to a range of tastes and interests.

- Having a duty to ensure fair and effective competition in the provision of these services.

- Investigating complaints and regularly publishing its findings.

The following codes of practice apply:

- **The Ofcom Broadcasting Code**

  This took effect in July 2005 and is based on a number of pre-existing codes from the merged commissions and authorities (see http://www.ofcom.org.uk/tv/ifi/codes/ for updates). It will remain in force until such time as Ofcom develops its own code.

- **Rules on the amount and distribution of advertising**

  Guidance on advertising, including information about teleshopping and self-promotional channels.

- **Code on sports and other listed events**

  Restrictions on broadcasting listed sports events.

- **Code on television access services**

  Requirements for the subtitling, signing and audio description of television services.

- **Code on electronic programme guides**

  Guidance on listing of public service and other channels and on disability access.

## ITC rules on amount and scheduling of advertising

The amount of advertising allowed is firmly regulated. Terrestrial broadcasters are allowed to average seven minutes of advertising per hour, with a maximum of seven and a half minutes per hour in peak time; and satellite broadcasters are allowed an average of nine minutes per hour, again with the leeway to transmit slightly more in peak. The content of the advertisements themselves are regulated and monitored by two different bodies, the CAP Broadcast Committee, without whose approval your advertising will not be broadcast, and the ASA who monitor commercials on behalf of the viewing public to ensure that advertising is legal, decent, honest and truthful as detailed below.

## Regulating the UK advertising industry – broadcast

The Committee of Advertising Practice (CAP) is the industry body responsible for the UK's advertising codes. The CAP's Broadcast Committee is contracted by the broadcast regulator, Ofcom, to write and enforce the codes of practice that govern TV and radio advertising. The committee comprises representatives of broadcasters licensed by Ofcom, advertisers, agencies, direct marketers and interactive marketers.

The code regulates the content of all TV and radio commercials on channels and stations licensed by Ofcom, including interactive television services, TV shopping channels and Teletext services. The remit does not cover programme sponsorship, advertising airtime allocation, the use of commercial breaks (except for advertisement content) or judgements about whether advertising is 'political' (and therefore prohibited). These are all regulated under the Broadcast Code and are the responsibility of Ofcom as detailed above.

Two sets of rules apply to broadcast advertisements – a set for TV and another for radio. In broad terms, they state that all types of broadcast advertising should not mislead, offend or cause harm. To control the implementation of the code of practice all TV commercials must be pre-approved by the Broadcast Advertising Clearance Centre (BACC) who are a specialist body responsible for the pre-transmission examination and clearance of TV advertisements.

## The BACC – Broadcast Advertising Clearance Centre

The BACC works on behalf of all major UK broadcasters to ensure TV advertising complies with regulatory codes, because it is a condition of the broadcaster's licence (as issued by Ofcom) that they will ensure that all the advertising which they transmit complies with 'codes' and that they have procedures in place to enable this to happen. BACC therefore has two principal functions:

- The examination of pre-production scripts

- The pre-transmission clearance of finished television advertisements (although a minority of local advertisements may be cleared by the broadcaster concerned)

Clearance of pre-production scripts is not compulsory, but the great majority of advertisers and agencies use the service, therefore it is unusual for a finished commercial to be rejected when viewed by BACC and only a small proportion require any amendment before being cleared.

The BACC is there to ensure that claims made in commercials are substantiated. They are concerned with proof of fact for your claims, whether it is the uniqueness of your 'unique' product or the purity of your 24-carat gold.

In addition they are concerned with a number of production issues, such as the speed of flashing lights, to ensure that they are not likely to induce an epileptic fit and for mail-order advertisers they will want to see confirmation of product stocks, credit agreements, call centre arrangements and sometimes bank guarantees. In 2004, BACC dealt with 28,320 pre-production scripts and 43,066 finished advertisements.

## The ASA – Advertising Standards Authority (Broadcast)

Ofcom have also appointed the ASA to be responsible for the investigation and adjudication of complaints against broadcast advertising.

The Advertising Standards Authority is the independent body set up by the advertising industry to police the rules laid down in the codes and to make sure all advertising, wherever it appears, meets the high standards required.

To monitor broadcast activity they have established the specific ASA(B).

The strength of the self-regulatory system lies both in the independence of the ASA and the support and commitment of the advertising industry, through the Committee of Advertising Practice (CAP), to the standards of the codes, protecting consumers and creating a level playing field for advertisers.

The website (www.asa.org.uk) will tell you more about the rules for advertising, let you complain online, and explain how the ASA is working to keep UK advertising standards high.

## The broadcast map

There are a host of opportunities available for advertisers, with a variety of different networks, channels and delivery systems.

There are four main delivery mechanisms for 370-plus channels: the traditional transmitter to aerial analogue signal, the newer transmitter to dish satellite systems, the transmitter to home cable systems and the newer ADSL to PC systems.

The following section looks at the content delivered on these different platforms and the audiences that interact with them.

Firstly, it must be remembered that despite all of the selections that are available, the only stations that are available universally are those that can be received via the traditional analogue system or the digital options. This includes only the traditional broadcast channels of BBC1 and 2, ITV, Channel 4 and Five.

Figure 5.5.2    **UK TV receiver homes profile, Q4 2005**

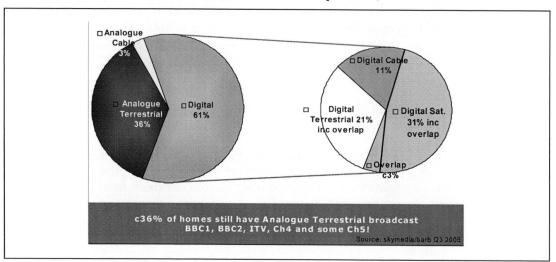

For around 36 per cent of UK homes these stations are the only options. In addition, these are likely to be the only stations that are picked up by the vast number of second, third or fourth TV sets that families often have; however, by the end of 2005 just under one in four homes had fully converted all its sets to receive digital broadcasts of one form or another (Ofcom, Q4 2005).

The profile figures for UK channel reception, as detailed in figure 5.5.2, changes quite quickly as the sales of digital terrestrial and satellite decoders continue to increase.

Figure 5.5.3 outlines the current estimates from Ofcom, based upon their estimation of market- driven growth and the gradual implementation of the digital switchover, with about 1.7 million in 2006 and a further 1million a year thereafter until 2012.

### Figure 5.5.3    Digital take-up – historic trend and future forecast

**Actual and forecast household penetration of digital TV (at year end)**

Source: Ofcom

The government digital rollout timetable clarifies that all regions will be converted between 2008 and 2012, as detailed in figure 5.5.4.

### Figure 5.5.4    UK regional switchover plans

Source: Department for Culture Media and Sport

Therefore, for the latest figures visit Ofcom digital television updates on http://www.ofcom.org.uk/research/tv/reports/dtv/ and download the quarterly digital report that will provide the latest consolidated figures for you.

## *The major station providers*

### The ITV Group

ITV1 remains the most watched commercial station in the UK, providing a broad spectrum of programmes across the day catering to all tastes, and taking the second largest share of viewing after BBC1.

ITV was launched in 1955 as a national network of franchises and, despite the merger of the majority of these companies over the last ten years, the programme provision is still broadcast under the traditional thirteen regional identities, providing advertisers with access to both national and regional airtime, as detailed in figure 5.5.5 below.

Figure 5.5.5   **ITV1 regional transmission map**

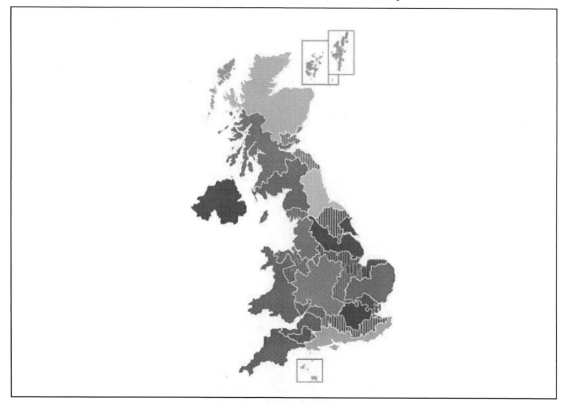

98 per cent of the population watch some ITV programmes each week and overall it takes about 30 per cent share of all viewing. Besides ITV1, the group also produces ITV2, a highly watched station that provides repeats of the popular ITV1 programmes, along with ITV3 and CITV, the new children's channel, all of which are available via the digital broadcast options.

### GMTV

GMTV can claim to be Europe's biggest breakfast broadcaster providing news, weather, celebrity gossip, and health and lifestyle information every weekday morning from 06:00 to 09:25.

At the weekends and during the school holidays the station is taken over by children's programming through Toon Attick, except for the very early hours of Sunday morning. GMTV promotes itself as 'not just a TV show – it's a national institution'.

As well as these main services, GMTV also runs GMTV2 which is only available on the digital platforms. They also run a highly interactive magazine website (www.gm.tv)

GMTV is owned jointly by ITV plc (75 per cent) and Disney (25 per cent) but as a franchise holder GMTV is managed independently, selling airtime through its own dedicated sales department in competition with the other commercial sales houses.

Figure 5.5.6     **Adult age and demographic profile of GMTV versus ITV and all TV viewing**

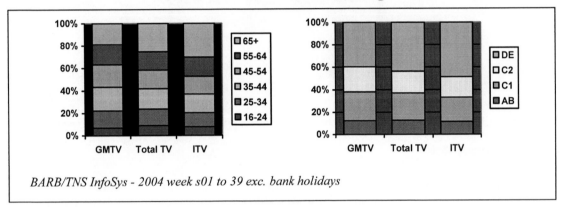

*BARB/TNS InfoSys - 2004 week s01 to 39 exc. bank holidays*

Research conducted by GMTV indicated that it has a unique relationship with its viewers, who feel that it is a 'part of their family' and their breakfast routine.

GMTV offers national coverage but can also be accessed via any one of the six macro regions (see figure 5.5.7). Some of the regions are more highly demanded than others and therefore the cost for accessing the regional audiences is not exactly pro rata to its share of the UK population, as detailed below.
For further details and updated figures regarding audience share, coverage, profile and attitudes visit gm.tv on http://www.gm.tv/sales/frames.htm?i=audience

Figure 5.5.7 **GMTV macro regions**

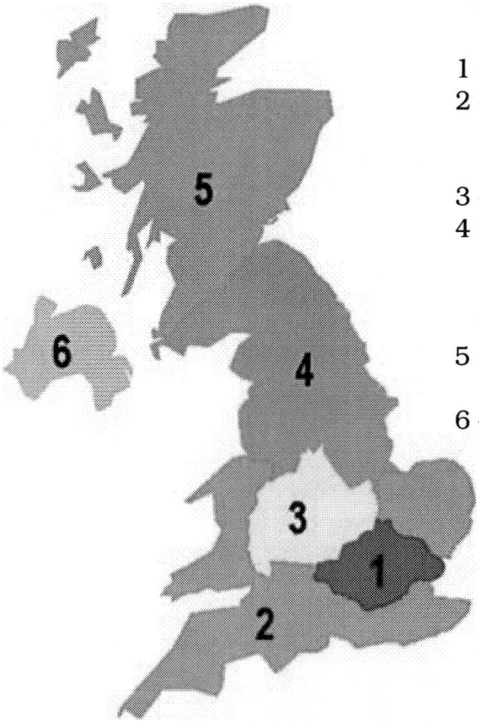

| Region | % of Pop. | % of Total Cost |
|---|---|---|
| 1 – London | 20.2% | 26.7% |
| 2 – Meridian, HTV, Anglia Westcountry, | 25.6% | 27.6% |
| 3 – Central | 16.0% | 16.3% |
| 4 – Yorkshire, Granada, Tyne Tees Border | 27.4% | 20.8% |
| 5 – Scottish, Grampian | 8.1% | 6.2% |
| 6 – Ulster | 2.7% | 2.3% |

## Channel 4

Channel 4 launched in 1982. The Channel Four Television Corporation was established under the Broadcasting Act 1990 and all its publisher/broadcaster functions were transferred over to the new Corporation in 1993. It transmits across the whole of the UK, except some parts of Wales which are covered by the Welsh language S4C. It is available on all digital platforms (terrestrial, satellite and cable) as well as through conventional analogue transmission. It is a publicly owned corporation whose board is appointed by Ofcom and is funded entirely by its own commercial activities and is required by the Communications Act of 2003 to:

• Demonstrate innovation, experimentation and creativity

• Appeal to the tastes and interests of a culturally diverse society

• Include programmes of an educational nature

• Exhibit a distinctive character

Channel 4 is a publisher/broadcaster. It does not produce its own programmes but commissions them from more than 300 independent production companies right across the UK, making it the major stimulus and outlet for Britain's highly successful independent production sector.

More than three-quarters of the UK's population watch Channel 4 services in the course of an average week and, as with GMTV, Channel 4 broadcasts nationally but offers six macro regions (see figure 5.5.8) to enable advertisers to test, upweight or downweight regions as dictated by their marketing requirements.

As well as the main Channel 4 service, the Channel Four Group operates a variety of pay channels, including the E4 entertainment channel, E4+1, and three film channels.

Through its Film Four division it produces and co-produces feature films for the UK and global markets. It also operates a wide variety of online and broadband services that cover entertainment, information, education, health, careers and many other areas.

**Figure 5.5.8    Channel 4 macro regions**

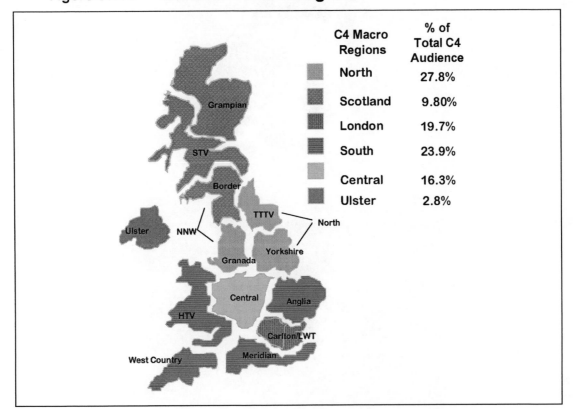

| C4 Macro Regions | % of Total C4 Audience |
|---|---|
| North | 27.8% |
| Scotland | 9.80% |
| London | 19.7% |
| South | 23.9% |
| Central | 16.3% |
| Ulster | 2.8% |

## Channel 5

Channel 5 launched on 31 March 1997 and is now part of the RTL group which operates 31 TV channels and 33 radio stations across 10 countries throughout Europe, making them the largest European broadcaster.

The group also provides over 260 programmes that are transmitted in over 40 countries, equivalent to 8,000 hours of programming each year.

Five has been very successful and is positioned as a 'mass, modern, youthful and energetic channel' with very strong morning programming, Milkshake, for children.

In addition, the peak evening shows have been popular with strong film and US series, such as CSI and House.

Advertising on Five is available in four key macro regions but the station cannot be viewed everywhere via the analogue transmission, reaching only about 70 per cent of the country, as detailed in figure 5.5.9.

However, this problem is overcome when viewers have digital cable, satellite or terrestrial decoders.

Figure 5.5.9 **'Five' broadcast map including macro regions**

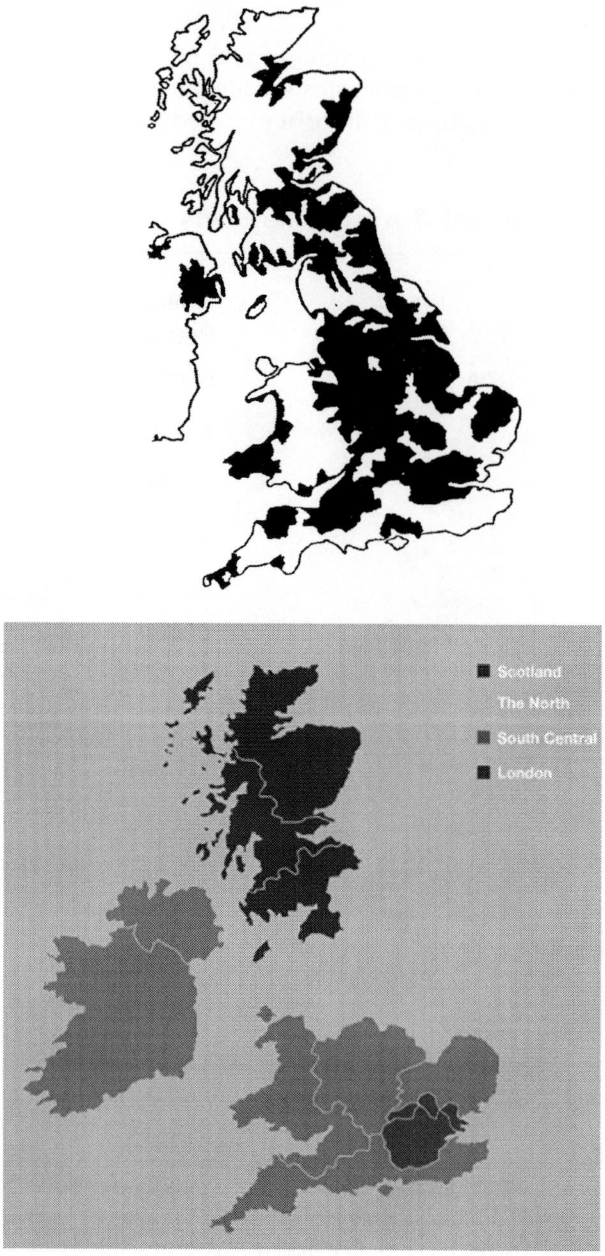

## Multi-channel homes

The ability to receive additional programme options via satellite or cable subscription gave rise to the term 'multi-channel homes', distinguishing them from homes that access only the traditional analogue terrestrial channels described earlier, and there has been a steady rise in the number of multi-channel homes over the last decade as detailed in figure 5.5.10.

Figure 5.5.10  **Digital and multi-channel penetration of UK households to Q4 2005**

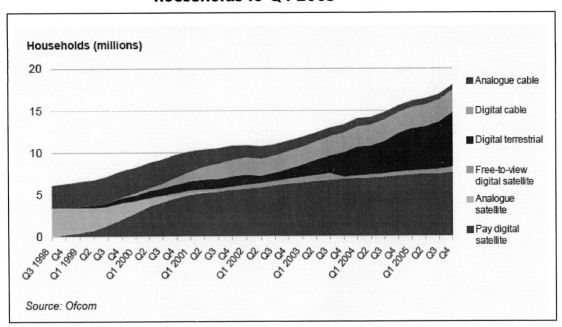

Source: Ofcom

As has been discussed, multi-channel homes are served by a variety of different platforms, using satellite, terrestrial, cable and ADSL technology and there are still a small number of cable homes that receive multi-channel options via an analogue system.

The plateau between 2001 and 2003 reflects the troubles experienced by the early digital terrestrial television (DTT) platform providers, firstly OnDigital and then ITVDigital. ITVDigital had been taken up by over one million homes at the time of its demise in 2001 and it was not until the launch of Freeview in November 2002 that the DTT option was available again. Freeview benefited from heavy publicity and ongoing support from both the BBC and ITV networks which renewed public confidence in the DTT solution.

Freeview research shows that their service is expanding the Digital TV (DTV) viewer base rather than attracting customers from rival DTV platforms. 52 per cent of Freeview customers are apparently from the ABC1 socio-economic category – 'a group considered less likely than the average consumer to subscribe to pay television', according to the BBC Corporation. Their research also indicated that increased programme choice and improved reception remain the primary drivers for a household to take up digital TV.

Table 5.5.3  **Multi-channel penetration as at Q4 2005 (Ofcom)**

|  | 2004 Q4 % of UK homes | 2005 Q4 % of UK homes |
| --- | --- | --- |
| Digital Cable | 10.1 | 10.8 |
| Digital Satellite | 30.8 | 32.8 |
| DTT | 18.5 | 25.7 |
| ADSL | 0.08 | 0.16 |
| Total Digital | 59.4 | 69.4 |
| Analogue Cable | 3.2 | 2.4 |
| Total Multi-channel | 62.6 | 71.8 |

Table 5.5.3 outlines the current estimates for the make-up of multi-channel homes as published by Ofcom. It is interesting to note that the uptake has not been even across the country and as detailed in figure 5.5.11 below, a number of regions have over 75 per cent of homes receiving digital TV. Visit www.ofcom.org.uk for quarterly updates.

Figure 5.5.11 **Penetration of digital TV in UK households, by ITV region**

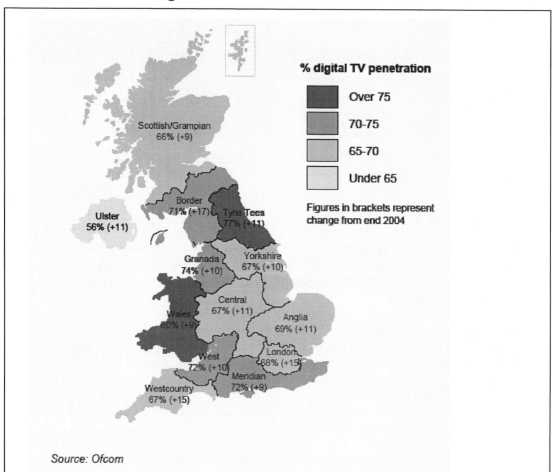

Source: Ofcom

# Digital and interactivity

The newest and potentially one of the most impactful changes to the television market in recent years has been the introduction of interactivity which is facilitated via digital TV network and which provides interactive television (iTV) advertising opportunities. This enables television to combine the power of a mass marketing medium with one that can also deliver one-to-one messages – giving advertisers the opportunity to take people from awareness, through consideration, on to purchase and potentially into loyalty; a very powerful formula indeed.

There are a number of benefits to digital broadcasting:

Broadcasters benefit from the reduced cost of production and the compression of bandwidths, enabling them to provide a greater range of channels more economically

Viewers report improvements in sound and picture quality and increased programme choice

The result is increased choice, fragmentation of audiences, greater targeting and the opportunity to engage the viewer with more information through the interactive elements that are now on offer

iTV services are only available via a digital television platform. Most digital households in the UK have upgraded their existing television with the addition of a set-top box, although a percentage have invested in bespoke digital TV sets with built in decoders. Currently, these platforms include Sky Digital (digital satellite television), ITV Digital (digital terrestrial television), NTL and Telewest (digital cable television) and services such as Video Networks' Homechoice (ADSL).

## Digital satellite television (DST)

Over 300 television channels are on offer via the DST service. Around 30 to 40 are 'free to air', i.e. they do not require a subscription payment to be viewed. These include the suite of BBC stations (BBC1, BBC2, BBC3, BBC4, BBC News 24, CBBC, and CBeebies). Other stations are available on a 'pay per view' arrangement, or monthly subscription payment. Such stations may include sports, movies or entertainment from Sky, or films from FilmFour, or the various ethnic or adult-orientated channels.

The majority of satellite broadcast is via the BSkyB digital services. 98 per cent of UK households are in a position to be able to receive digital satellite if they choose to; all they need is a Sky mini-dish and either a new digital television receiver or set-top box. The satellite link is one way (from the broadcaster to the dish), but the modem that is inside the set-top boxes connects to the viewer's telephone line, enabling full two-way interactive capability, also known as a return path, as detailed in figure 5.5.12. This offers viewers 'interactive' services through an operating system known as SkyActive.

BSkyB now have over eight million subscribers (Ofcom, Q4 2005), and their constant evolution means that to date they have benefited from the lowest 'churn rate' of all the digital platforms at just under 10 per cent.

Figure 5.5.12 **Digital system example for satellite broadcast**

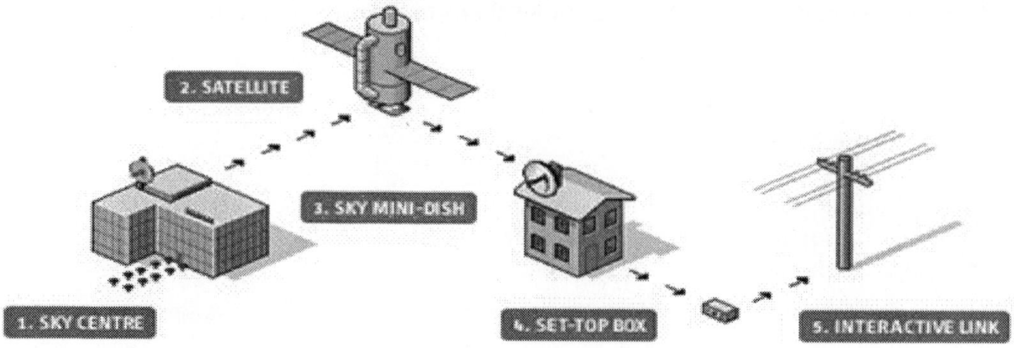

1 – Sky digital centre, Isleworth: content transmitted to satellites via uplink facility in Hampshire.

2 – Satellite: Geostationary satellites 22,300 miles up in space receive signals from Chilworth.

3 – Sky mini-dish: The mini-dish installed at the viewer's home receives signals from the satellites.

4 – Set-top box (Sky digibox): This unscrambles the satellite signal and plays it out through TV set.

5 – Return Path: Interactive services & data accessed through telephone line via a modem in a digibox.

*Source: skyinteractive.com*

In 1999 Sky launched an interactive shopping area in partnership with Open TV; however, by May 2001 they had acquired their former partner's shareholdings and set about forming the Sky Interactive service, designed to enable the closer integration of interactive services and the viewing experience. The interactive services include text and online information as well as shopping and gaming areas. The current incarnation of the interactive services is SkyActive, which incorporates a broad array of shopping, banking, messaging and gaming 'locations'.

The locations are similar to a basic intranet page but they are navigable on-screen via the remote control coloured buttons and alpha/numeric recognition, lacking the overall flexibility of the point and click mouse-driven web environment.

Sky's interactive area is known as a 'walled garden'. Walled garden is a term that appeared in the mid-to-late 1990s to define interactive content offerings 'walled off' from direct access to internet users. Walled-garden users may link to the internet from the walled gardens, but not vice versa. America Online is an example of a very successful walled garden.

Certain interactive TV middleware and software solutions enable cable and satellite providers to create their own walled gardens or 'portals'. Inside an iTV walled garden an interface allows the viewer to have access to news, sports information, email on TV, and other applications.

Sky Active offers an attractive environment to advertisers. Menu-driven zones enable advertisers to situate their offers within relevant editorial as detailed in figure 5.5.13.

Viewers can get more involved with their favourite shows, engage in live discussions, vote on issues and enter quizzes and competitions. They can also play games and place bets, download ringtones, shop for music, clothes or even cars, check their bank accounts, and email family and friends.

Figure 5.5.13 **Sky guide access screen and SkyActive listings page**

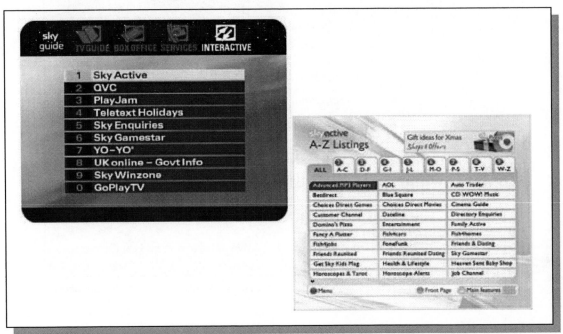

*Source: Sky.com/skyactive/homepage*

Sky Active offers an attractive environment to advertisers. Menu-driven zones enable advertisers to situate their offers within relevant editorial as detailed below.

## Free to air via satellite

Often referred to as 'Sky Churners' there are an estimated 450,000 ex-subscribers who use their set- top box to receive the free to air public channels. Sky also launched FreeSat in October 2004 which gives free access to over 200 non-subscription TV and radio channels for a one-off fee of around £160 for the installation of the set-top box and dish.

This move is predominantly motivated to get a foothold in the remaining market and ensure Freeview does not take the majority share of the remaining UK analogue homes, particularly in the areas that the Freeview signal cannot currently reach. A comparison of the basic package criteria is noted below in table 5.5.4.

As a retaliatory move, a competitive 'Free Sat' was mooted for launch in early 2006 through a BBC/ITV joint venture to cater for viewers unable to receive Freeview (BBC News).

Table 5.5.4    **Comparison of basic package criteria for Freeview and FreeSat**

|  | **Freeview** | **Sky** |
| --- | --- | --- |
| Price | £50 one-off payment for the reception box. This price is constantly heading lower. Freeview is available from high street retailers. | £160 one-off payment for installation of satellite dish and box. Sky's opening price is likely to fall, but the labour to install the dish will not. The service can only be ordered from Sky. |
| Channels | 30 channels, including the BBC digital channels, ITV1 and 2, Channel 4, 5, QVC and UKTV History. Additional channels can be added through a top-up service. 21 radio stations. | 116 channels, including BBC digital channels, ITV 1 and 2, Channel 4, 5, QVC, Fashion TV and other niche channels including the Wrestling Channel, The God Channel and the Horror Channel. Additional channels come from upgrading to a Sky subscription.81 radio stations. |
| Reception | 73% of all UK households get all channels; an additional 7% get limited channels. | 97% of the UK. |
| Equipment | Digital-capable aerial and set- top box. | Sky satellite dish and set-top box. |

Source: Cordilia.uk.com ( http://www.cordelia.uk.com/skyfreesat.html)

## Digital cable – NTL/Telewest

Digital cable (or DCable) is another way that viewers can receive digital TV. Digital services pass between the cable operator and the viewer's home via fibre-optic cables laid below the ground. Again, a set-top box is needed to receive and decode the digital signal. An 'always on' return path is enabled via the telephone line. Many urban and suburban households can receive cable services from a cable television provider, and there are over 11 million homes in the UK that are 'bypassed' by a potential connection (Ofcom, 2005).

Digital cable services were launched in 1999 and, according to Ofcom, by December 2005, the total number of UK cable households was 3,310,400, of which 1,942,800 subscribed to ntl and 1,367,600 to Telewest Broadband. Of these, 715,900 are digital cable subscribers.

On 3 March 2006 ntl and Telewest completed a merger creating the UK's largest residential broadband communications company and the country's leading provider of triple-play services, comprising telephone, television and broadband services, called ntl incorporated.

Figure 5.5.14  **UK cable coverage**

Some of the cheapest deals start at £16 per month for a free set-top box offering around 40 digital TV and radio channels and interactive services, through to a premium 'family pack' that provides 160 digital TV and radio channels for a monthly cost of around £30.

A smaller cable company, Wight Cable also offers cable TV services to around 8,000 subscribers in Scotland, Border, North West, and the Isle of Wight.

*(Source: ntl incorporated)*

Digital cable TV is present in 10.8 per cent of all TV homes, with analogue cable serving a further 2.4 per cent of TV homes. Digital and analogue cable combined account for 18.3 per cent of all multi-channel TV homes and 30.1 per cent of pay-TV homes. Although the share of homes looks low when taken on a national scale, the service can be seen to be very popular when viewed on a regional perspective.

The share of homes that ntl incorporated have among the homes that they bypass within their 'marketable areas', (termed 'in-franchise') averages 43 per cent share of all multi-channel TV provision in the old ntl areas and around 40 per cent across Telewest areas.

## Interactivity via cable

ntl incorporated provides a comprehensive walled garden within which branded interactive services are provided, and provide 'picture-in-picture' viewing to ensure that viewers remain in contact with the programme stream (figure 5.5.15).

Figure 5.5.15 **ntl incorporated offers games, entertainment and advertising**

*Source: ntl 2004/Telewest 2005*

The interactive area hosts many types of advertisers, such as:

* Shopping via WHSmith, Marks & Spencer, Asda and Dominos Pizza etc.

* Financial services from Abbey, HSBC, Lloyds and Norwich Union etc.

* Teletext holidays with Thomas Cook

* Betting with Blue Square, Ladbrokes and William Hill

Technically, cable is the best platform, as interactive content is served to the viewer's set-top box rather than being broadcast.

## Digital terrestrial television (DTT)

The digital terrestrial programme content includes all of the existing analogue terrestrial channels plus a number of additional stations such as those in the BBC and ITV digital packages (such as BBC News 24, BBC Knowledge, BBC Choice and ITV2), providing around 30 to 40 channels free to air. In addition, there are more than 20 subscription/pay per view channels available.

Digital Terrestrial Television (DTT) services can be received through a variety of systems. The most prevalent is Freeview, which is now installed in over 25 per cent of homes across the UK (Ofcom, 2005) and more than 10.5 million Freeview boxes and integrated TV sets had been sold by the end of 2005, with DTT accounting for seven out of every ten digital systems adopted throughout 2005 (Ofcom, 2006).

As discussed earlier, the first big commercial venture in the UK was OnDigital, later becoming ITVDigital before closing in 2001. In October 2002, the BBC, Crown Castle International and BSkyB joined forces to launch Freeview as the provider of the new UK Digital Terrestrial TV network, marketed under the name DTV Services Ltd. The marketing, particularly that by the BBC in support of its additional digital channels, (BBC3, BBC4, CBBC and Cbeebies), created a rapid growth in awareness of this option for the provision of digital services as detailed in figure 5.5.16:

Figure 5.5.16 **Percentage of UK adults aware of Freeview, 2004**

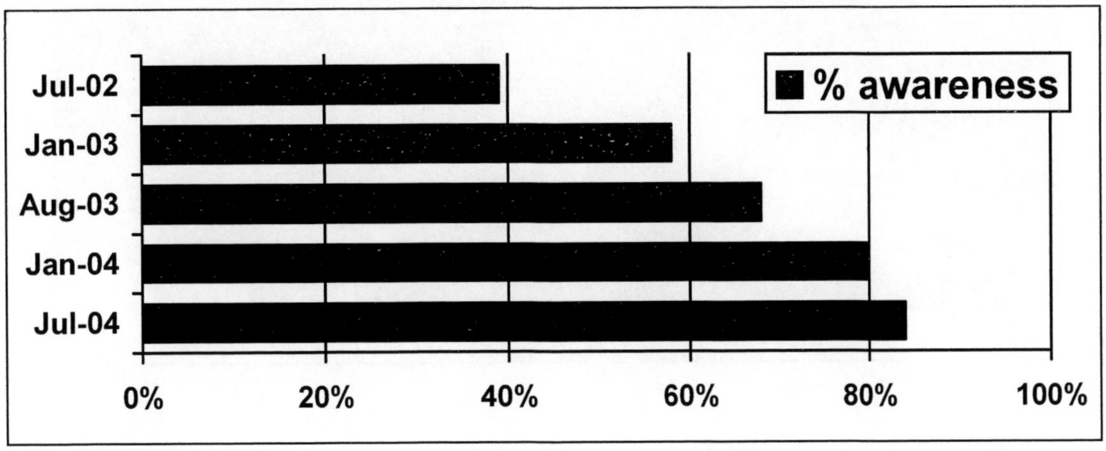

*Continental Research, 2004*

Totally free to view, the service is technically more stable than ITVDigital was, as the transmitter power has been increased. In addition, the channel 'multiplexes' are less compressed due to the fact that the new service provides a lower number of channels, delivering about 30 free digital TV channels, around 20 digital radio stations and a range of interactive services.

Reception works in a similar way to traditional TV, being broadcast from transmitters and received via a rooftop aerial, but because the signals are digital they need to go via a decoder to be converted and therefore a set-top box needs to be connected between the existing household TV and aerial.

The current set-top boxes costs between £30 and £140-plus. There are a number of manufacturers in this area and not all of the boxes have the same functionality. The basic boxes will support basic programmes, broadcaster interactive services and subtitles. Higher grade boxes will include electronic programme guides, built-in games and programme timers. The top-of-the-range boxes can include CD and DVD players, DVD recorders, hard-disk recorders and a modem that can support commercial interactivity as experienced via cable or satellite systems.

Alternatively, viewers can receive the signals via a new integrated iDTV (interactive Digital TV) system from brands like Philips, Panasonic, Sharp, Sony and Toshiba, which all have the technology of the set-top box built in. However, with the Freeview system there is no subscription or installation cost, nor any ongoing fees.

These terrestrial services bring increased channel choice and a number of interactive programme elements that can be accessed by viewers through the red button, such as the enhanced sports coverage provided for Wimbledon and detailed in figure 5.5.17.

Figure 5.5.17  **Additional programming available via Freeview**

## *Interactivity via Digital Terrestrial TV (DTT)*

Additional interactive services are available through Freeview, examples of which are shown in figure 5.5.18 and currently include:

- BBCi  : programme listings, news headlines, latest sports updates, weather reports, entertainment and cinema listings and video clips from any BBC TV channel

- Fun2Play games: an interactive channel with games such as Tetris, Darts, Binko, Ring Realms, and YooPlay games plus  the latest ringtones and java games, plus digital broadcast from JazzFM

- Teletext on channel 9: offers viewers up-to-the-minute national and international news, sport and racing, plus weather information and entertainment listings and a range of holiday and flight deals through Teletext Holidays.

Figure 5.5.18  **Examples of Freeview interactive screens**

BBCi News Multiscreen      Teletext Weather      YooPlay games on Ch.53

### The return path

DTT does not however offer a true return path in the same way that cable or a telephone connection to the back of a satellite set-top box do.

Without a proper return path terrestrial digital viewers are only able to respond to interactive ads by phoning in their responses. The original design for the

ITVDigital set-top box did include the facility to connect the domestic phone line to the box to create the return path, but unlike Sky digital subscribers, there were no clauses in the original ITVDigital contract stating that the phone line and the set-top box must be connected.

Accordingly, most ITV Digital subscribers did not have their phone lines and set-top boxes connected, rendering the return path ineffective. When relaunching the service, Freeview made no plans to offer the return path necessary for interactive advertising; consequently the majority of current Freeview receivers do not include the facility to connect the box at all.

## Top Up TV

Top Up TV, founded by two former executives of BSkyB, is a pay-TV service on the Freeview platform. For a £20 connection fee, and £7.99 a month, subscribers can watch 10 extra channels including E4, UK Gold and Discovery. Currently, Top Up TV has a take-up of an estimated 200,000.

## Internet Protocol Television (IPTV) – ADSL/broadband technology

The fourth platform, and potentially one of the most important, comes from the upgrading of the existing copper telephone lines into high-speed connections using Digital Subscriber Line (DSL) broadband technology. According to Tony Glover, Technology Editor of The Business, IPTV is 'the next big thing'. Microsoft has been partnering with telecoms and cable companies to offer IPTV in the US for many years and Ofcom predicts that IPTV will play a key part in the future of TV.

The majority of new broadband connections in the UK are supplied via asymmetric digital subscriber line (ADSL) technology, predominantly over BT's copper wire line network. Like 3G, ADSL broadband availability has been lowest in rural areas, so perhaps the most significant milestone for extending digital service accessibility came in August 2004 when BT announced the scrapping of 'exchange distance limits' whereby customers living more than six kilometres from a broadband-enabled exchange were unable to receive a service. The further exchange upgrades in 2005, combined with the removal of the six kilometre distance limits, will make basic ADSL broadband more widely available, potentially reaching up to 99.6 per cent of households.

IPTV promises to offer an unlimited number of channels, video-on-demand, gaming and other interactive services through the TV, and broadband internet connection through the PC. IPTV sends audio and video services directly to a TV set-top box which is connected to an ADSL or cable line. IPTV should not be mistaken for streamed video on a computer; the quality of IPTV on a TV set is far better; connection speeds and capacity, combined with video compression technology, enables standard and high-definition video to be delivered to the TV. IPTV can also mean more choice of programmes, more interactivity, more tailored and localised programming as well as targeted advertising, delivering live linear, live TV channels and unlimited on-demand content, thus competing directly with the existing cable and satellite companies. IPTV has many advantages including lower provider entry costs compared to the existing cable and satellite platforms, and the chance to offer a 'triple-play' service of voice, video and data, currently the cable company territory. Content production companies could cut out broadcasters completely by offering their content directly to the viewers, and Telco's could start producing their own content. It is all part of the larger changing TV technology landscape and, like personal digital video recorders (PVRs), gives people much more control over TV. Broadcasters see IPTV and PVRs as both a threat and an opportunity.

Figure 5.5.19 **Examples of Freeview interactive screens**

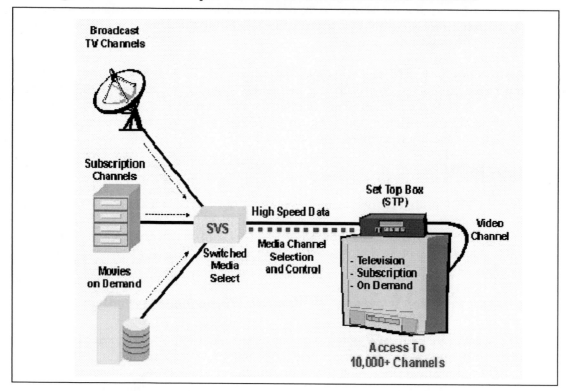

Ofcom estimated that nearly 40,000 homes in the UK were receiving IPTV digital services by December 2005 (Ofcom, 2005) through Homechoice.

## Homechoice TV

Homechoice TV uses this DSL system to connect with its customers and has the potential to extend its original West London footprint to around 2.4 million homes. Ofcom, 2005, reported that around 40,000 homes are connected to Homechoice TV to receive internet, movies and TV on-demand.

Delivered down a variety of broadband speed connections (1Mb, 2Mb or 4Mb), Homechoice has established a 'new' on-demand way to consumer TV. Their service offers a back catalogue of over 1,000 movies, complemented each week with the 'most popular' BBC and ITV1 shows which are available via 'replay' for seven days after they were first aired.

In addition, Homechoice supplies a selection of digital TV channels, high-speed broadband for the household PC and free phone calls, and expanded their potential distribution sufficiently in 2005 to justify undertaking a large-scale awareness drive for their services, supported by TV, press and poster advertising (mediaweek.co.uk).

## Yes TV

Yes Television bills itself as 'a leading provider of IP-based video-on-demand and personalised TV expertise' and provides solutions and consulting skills to operators who wish to deploy high quality video services for broadband. This includes residential video-on-demand (VOD) over ADSL, alongside hotels and hospitality services and residential broadband PC.

In addition, Yes Television has supplied video-on-demand (VOD) over BT's broadband mesh radio trial in Pontypridd, one of the first deployments of VOD over wireless in the world. Yes Television's residential VOD solution enables service providers to deliver a comprehensive next-generation pay- TV service over any IP-based network, including DSL, fibre to the home and wireless broadband networks (ibid).

## Personal video recorders (PVRs)

With all this talk of multi-channel TV and video-on-demand, it seems appropriate to take note of the fact that the use of home video systems and time shift viewing has an impact on how people use their television services. According to Continental Research (2004) the personal video recorder (PVR) market is currently dominated by Sky+, with an estimated 400,000 owners. There are other PVRs on the market that are compatible with both the Freeview and cable platforms, including the TiVo, and as demonstrated in figure 5.5.20, sales of both DVDs and PVPs are on the up.

The true difference between a VHS recorder or DVD recorder and a PVR such as the TiVo is that a PVR should have additional software which allows it to suggest viewing material based on the user's programme choices and personal profile.

However, most of the hard drive (HDD)-based recorders do not currently have this level of complex programme analysis and therefore the terminology seems to be used to include the 'dumb' recorder which carries out the basic programme recording/time slip functions as well.

Figure 5.5.20 **Sales of VCRs, PVRs and DVD recorders, 2001 to 2005 (Ofcom, 2005)**

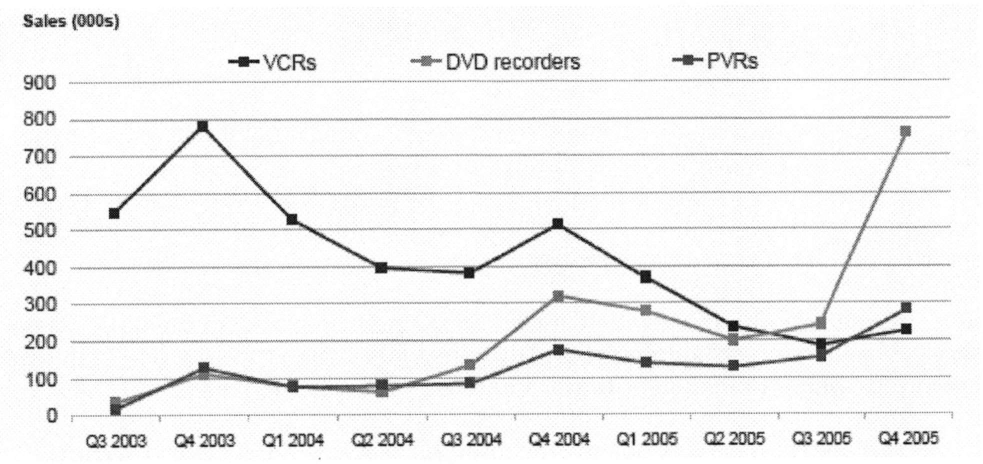

Sky+ is currently the main HDD-based unit in the UK and has the most PVR type features, enabling the bookmarking of favourite programmes or series and enabling audiences to 'binge' on their 'stack' of favourite programmes. It is also possible to archive off programmes from the PVR to traditional DVD or VHS. Unfortunately this is only available for Sky satellite users. Other digital terrestrial and cable users in the UK will have to wait for the release of products using an advanced EPG and software such as that being developed by the TV-Anytime forum.

Media owners, advertisers and ad agencies are keeping a keen eye on PVR's development and the impact it will have on the nature of TV viewing. Some argue the PVR will mean the end of TV advertising as we know it, and view the device as providing just another method of potential ad avoidance.

However, it should be remembered that viewers already use a number of avoidance techniques such as ...

- Channel surfing during ad breaks

- Watching text services during ad breaks

- Doing other things rather than watching TV, e.g. reading and talking

- Leaving the room

- Videoing and fast-forwarding through ads

Yet despite these techniques, TV still proves a powerful medium to communicate brand and sales messages. Some observers argue that PVR owners enjoy TV more, and as a consequence, are less likely to indulge in the avoidance techniques listed above.

In fact PVR users become very adept at 'ad sampling', using the multi-speed fast forward functions to almost never watch the ads before or during programmes. However, research has indicated that viewers halt the fast forward process to watch ads they enjoyed (PVRUK 2005).

As a result, they are just as susceptible to pick up advertising messages as those without a PVR. Sky and Disney have published data that reveals that ad and brand awareness in PVR homes is on a par with non-PVR homes, i.e. the PVR has not had a detrimental effect on ad effectiveness. Time and further research will tell us if this remains the case (Continental Research, 2004).

## Summary of digital services

With the variety of solutions being offered to UK consumers it is interesting to compare the actual levels of availability.

Telephone lines, broadband, mobiles and satellite services are the only digital services that have near total coverage.

Satellite remains the most widely available method of receiving digital television services, with coverage of almost all UK households, apart from a few built-up and hilly areas where line of sight to the satellite is unavailable.

Cable will always have a problem extending its reach while it relies on cable bypass. The unbundling of the BT network may be a great opportunity to change the situation.

DTT availability will remain close to 75 per cent population coverage until the phased switchover to DTT (and shutdown of analogue transmission) allows for a power boost to the digital signal. It is envisaged that the first phase of the digital switchover will take place in 2008, with the whole country converted by 2012 [Ofcom, 2005].

See http://www.dtg.org.uk/consumer/switchover_map.html for a region by region guide to planned switchover dates.

You can also download A Guide to Digital Television and Digital Switchover from http://www.digitaltelevision.gov.uk/.

And visit Digital UK (www.digitaluk.co.uk), an independent, not-for-profit organisation, established by the broadcasting industry to lead the switchover programme and communicate with the public.

Television in the UK is changing rapidly as broadcasters and viewers respond to the advances in digital technology. The predominant digital systems are Digital Satellite (synonymous with Sky), Digital cable (provided by Telewest and ntl) and Digital Terrestrial – DTT (mainly Freeview), and nearly 60 per cent of homes now receive their television broadcast through one of these digital systems.

**Table 5.5.5** **Summary of main digital services available in the UK, February 2006**

| Platform | Equipment | Availability | Brand | UK take-up (household) | Penetration | Price range |
|---|---|---|---|---|---|---|
| Satellite | Externally mounted receiver and set top box | Estimated 95-97% maximum | Pay: Sky Digital | 7.7m Q4 2005 | 30.7% | £15-£42.50 per month |
| | | | Free to view: Sky Solus | 0.6m Q4 2005 | 2.4% | Sky 'freesat' £150 one-off fee |
| Cable | Cable connection from network to house and a set top box | 51% | Pay: NTL, Telewest, Wightcable (Analogue & Digital) | 3.3m Q4 2005 | 13.2% | £16-£51 per month |
| Digital Terrestrial (DTT – Freeview) | Conventional TV aerial + a set top box or TV with built-in digital tuner | 73% | Pay: Top Up TV | Est 200,000 Q4 2005 | 0.8% | 7.99 per month |
| | | | Free to view: Freeview (DTT-only homes) | 6.3m Q3 2005 | 25.0% | DTT boxes from £30+ |
| TV over ADSL | Using existing telephone lines and set top box | 10% | Pay: HomeChoice, KIT (closed April 2006) | 38,000 Q4 2005 | 0.2% | £15-£44 per month |
| **Total digital TV penetration of UK households:** | | | **71.8% multi-channel 69.4% digital** | | | |

*Source: Ofcom, platform operators, service providers*

# DRTV and the direct marketer

Advertisers use DRTV in a number of different ways, the most identifiable of which are:

- To make direct sales (one-stage)

- Lead generator (two-stage)

- Product sampling

- Support of primary response activity

- Promoting direct brands (BRTV)

- Integrated branding

- Interactive TV

Today however, the traditional discriminators between DRTV and 'brand' commercials are blurring, but as with all advertising, if the campaign objectives are clearly laid out then they should deliver the required results. Do not mix your objectives.

In order to enjoy a successful DRTV experience, be very clear about your campaign objectives and make sure they feed through into creative and media briefing.

## Objective 1: Direct sales (one-stage)

This is the oldest and most traditional use for DRTV; to sell 'off the screen'. The main objective – to motivate viewers to call and purchase during or immediately after seeing the product or service advertised. Most advertisers in this category do not have any form of retail distribution other than direct sales.

The cost equation is all important. The cost of airtime, call handling, fulfilment and amortised cost of creative must be offset against revenue from sales. As airtime is a major cost, one-stage DRTV is mainly found in lower-cost 'off-peak' segments, (morning or afternoon 'daytime' or late night etc). There are also many lower cost satellite opportunities to access the peak-time segment, i.e. between seven and 10 pm, giving advertisers access to a wider audience.

One-stage activity must always maximise call generation and the TV buyers should be totally aware of call centre staffing arrangements throughout the day.

Creatively, the style and content is usually hard hitting. Ads are longer than average to ensure that they have time to develop their message and to persuade the viewer to act, following the 'Attention, Interest, Desire, and Action' (AIDA) model. They should hook viewers with interesting facts or appeals, establish a clear proposition, develop the selling benefits and deliver a clear call-to-action. Showing the telephone number at the beginning of the commercial is a good way to signal to the viewer that the message will seek a response. Research certainly shows that higher levels of response can be attained if the number is repeated throughout the commercial. (See BT/Ch 4 response/research).

Core attributes of direct sales ads are:

- Minimal branding, with the emphasis being on the product

- Predominantly low-cost/off-peak airtime

- Majority longer length commercials: 90 seconds to 120 seconds

- Typical advertising categories are music compilations, exercise equipment, collectibles and charities

## Objective 2: Lead generation (two-stage)

Lead-generation commercials are the starting point for a one-to-one dialogue with an advertiser's prospects. This will hopefully lead to sales, and for many companies cross-selling and upselling.

Media planning for two-stage is similar to that for one-stage direct sales. Cost-per-lead may be more generous, opening up more expensive day parts. However, call handling restrictions must still be closely adhered to. For example, evening peak airtime may look appropriate but not if the call centre is shut and there is no messaging service or IVR (interactive voice recording), no reference to directories or any hint that calling during the daytime is required.

Two-stage will be evaluated on a number of cost indicators, including the cost-per-lead, conversion rate from leads to sales, renewal or churn rates, initial sales value and overall 'lifetime value'. Analysis should identify where the cheapest and most expensive leads are coming from so that the planner can identify the best airtime for quality leads.

Creatively, the proposition tends to be straightforward and as a result commercials can be shorter. Most common are the 30" and 40" commercials, with 10"and 20" cut downs being used successfully alongside the full-length commercial as a cost-efficient reminder of the call-to-action. The tone is generally purposeful and businesslike.

Core attributes of two-stage advertisements are:

- Brand recognition and differentiation are important

- Core propositions spelt out succinctly  (e.g. low-cost insurance)

- Medium length commercials 30" to 60", often with shorter reminder ads

- Daytime still popular, based upon call centre requirements and cost efficiency

- Typical advertising categories are mail-order catalogues, financial services, motor insurance, life insurance, debt release/debt consolidation, solicitors for 'no win, no fee' compensation claiming

## *Objective 3: Product sampling*

Response TV is a useful mechanism to generate sample requests and build a database of interested prospects/customers, gaining insight that can inform the future marketing activity. This is often referred to as Sales Promotion TV (SPTV), as sampling offers and trial mechanisms are usually devised by the client's sales promotion agency.

- Media planning for sampling campaigns follows the main DRTV rules, using lower cost daytime airtime. Call capacity considerations remain important, although the majority of sampling campaigns run with automated call systems, which considerably increases the manageable call volumes, or through interactive response to the 'red button' (see objective 7 below).

- Sampling exercises are often phased within a brand launch or seasonal push, and therefore require the maximum number of samples to be distributed within a limited campaign period – often only a four-week window. This will determine that the planner uses a broader base of airtime options, but chooses the individual spots carefully to ensure maximum conversion to the target audience.

The creative needs to be persuasive and offer-based. For an established brand the style and tone should be absolutely in keeping with the brand personality. This is often achieved by running the existing brand commercial with a 10-second call-to-action tag line, ensuring of course, that it does not look disjointed. However, many samplers find that a dedicated commercial will perform better. It should be made clear that the commercial is offering a free sample. The telephone number, web address or impulse response instruction should be clearly displayed and voiced sufficiently to be remembered.

Evaluation should be on the basis of the number of samples requested and the cost-per-request, but evaluation should also monitor changes in the perception of the brand as a result of offering the free trial samples and look for any uplift in retail sales etc. A database relationship can also be developed through email or direct mail which can be used for many purposes including continuing to inform customers of important innovations.

Core attributes of product sampling ads are:

- Brand values contained within commercial

- Core 'sample' propositions made clear

- Medium length commercials: 30 seconds to 60 seconds, often utilising an existing brand commercial with a call-to-action tag line 10 second

- Airtime generally selected to deliver best conversion to target audience and run over limited campaign period

- Advertisers typically come from the FMCG area, including McVities, Kenco, Revlon and Lenor

## Objective 4: In a supporting role

Support TV campaigns are designed to raise awareness of specific direct response offers in other media such as direct mail, inserts or door drops, and maximise the response. The activity being supported is called the 'primary' activity, or alternatively the anchor medium (US).

It is planned for maximum coverage of the response medium's target audience. For example, if it is a product appealing to housewives, then airtime will be selected to deliver housewife audiences efficiently. The ratio of expenditure between primary and support activity is very important. The right media mix will be specific to an individual product and some pretesting may be required.

The creative objective for support TV is to raise awareness of a specific offer. This can be done with comparatively short time lengths of between 10" and 30". The style and tone of the commercials should be informative and draw attention to the offer. A good example of this type of ad is Reader's Digest's 'win it, don't bin it'.

Support TV is evaluated on its ability to uplift response from the primary media. Al Eicoff in his book Broadcast Direct Response Marketing cites uplifts in primary media of between 50 per cent and 800 per cent when support activity is correctly planned. However, beware of overspending on support media and having insufficient response media to capitalise on would-be responders. The web is now a primary medium to which to drive response and using TV to create awareness and drive respondents to the website is proving to be a highly successful strategy.

Successful users of support TV are invariably advertisers with well proven national response campaigns. The basic offer should be successful before support activity is contemplated: TV backing will not make a dead duck fly.

## Objective 5: Promoting direct brands

Direct brands are now well established, the most famous being First Direct and Direct Line. Their customer contact and distribution methods are entirely direct, but they invest heavily in developing a clearly differentiated brand personality. They are the most modern brand sector, capitalising on technology and modern lifestyle attributes to conduct traditional high street business without the overheads.

Direct brands require their media to build long-term brand awareness as well as short-term call volumes, but whichever the focus of a commercial, all of their advertising will emphasise that the consumer should access the company initially by telephone or the web.

Direct brands incorporate elements of the traditional awareness building airtime into their schedule, using peak time alongside daytime. Peak is highly demanded and much more expensive than off-peak, combined with which, it is generally seen to be less responsive, leading to more costly lead generation. However, the job of peak is to build coverage, creating awareness and understanding of the brand's core proposition. Therefore the media planner will often run a multi-level media plan, incorporating a specific brand-building strategy alongside harder hitting DR activity, be it DRTV in off-peak, direct mail, directories or press etc.

Creatively, direct brand commercials often exhibit classic brand advertising characteristics. They are short, often less than 30", with high production values. However, the distinguishing feature of a direct brand commercial is the message, i.e. that the advertiser should be contacted directly via the web or phone. Not surprisingly a telephone will normally feature prominently, e.g. the famous red telephone on wheels of Direct Line.

Direct brand commercials are not evaluated on their ability to generate leads alone – if they were, the expensive evening peak airtime would not be viable and would be pulled. They are evaluated on their ability to raise awareness of, and to position, the direct brand. Higher airtime cost is acceptable because advertisers here are investing in the equity of the brand more than in the generation of immediate response. The different elements of a multi-level campaign will be evaluated against appropriate criteria, e.g. awareness and positioning research for the branding element and overall cost-per-lead (or per-sale) for the response elements. Data analysis also enables the different streams of the matrix to be brought together to identify the correlation between building awareness and brand knowledge and the uplift in response generated from the response elements, such as directories or direct web traffic.

Core attributes of direct brands are:

- Brand values contained within commercial

- Core propositions made clear

- Shorter length commercials: 20 seconds to 40 seconds

- Traditional brand airtime including peak to raise and sustain brand awareness

- Typical advertising category is finance, including Direct Line, First Direct, Norwich Union and Eagle Star

## Objective 6: Brand ads – integrating response

Integrating a response device into a traditional brand commercial offers a way to involve the consumer and presents a greater level of approachability to your prospects. The objective should be to help differentiate the brand; the response may not be the primary objective, but simply part of the differentiating process – and could be constructed in the form of an offer, a sample, a competition or an outright gimmick, e.g. Tango.

Media planning will, in general, follow the rules of brand advertising, identifying the best airtime to reach the selected target audience. A youth brand will find youth and cult programmes to buy into, whether it is in peak or off-peak. Response may be via the web, a text message or telephone. If the phone is being used lessons of call management must not be overlooked; while the response may not be the primary requirement, it will give consumers a negative impression if call handling does not meet expectations.

Creatively, it is vital to remember that with this type of interactivity, the purpose is always, and only, to differentiate the brand, i.e. to develop a personality for the brand that makes it stand apart from its competitors. Depending on the brand's personality, creative work can range from the mundane to the truly bizarre. This advertising has to captivate, fascinate and build brand credibility – the response element only being effective if it reinforces this objective.

Evaluation of this type of TV activity is primarily via the traditional brand measures: product sales, changes in market share, and shifts in attitudes towards the brand itself. While high levels of consumer response indicate consumers' willingness to become involved in the advertising, these calls are not the purpose of the campaign.

Core attributes of response integration include:

- Audience-targeted airtime

- Brand-building commercials

- Examples include Tango, Pepperami and Martini

Note the youthful common denominator between the examples, young people being generally more prone to respond to interactive offers – as well as being more difficult to access through many other traditional media such as press.

### Objective 7: Interactive TV – iTV

There is now a whole host of interactive opportunities available on the digital networks. The first interactive ad was on Sky Digital, for Chicken Tonight, which ran an extended commercial with a prompt to access recipe cards via its website using a bit of button pushing on the viewer's remote control. Now there are numerous advertisers offering a range of options, from the direct purchase of a CD from Woolworths, through to online quotes for insurance, pre-booked test drives for new cars or requesting a free lipstick. Regulars in the interactive forum are Woolworths and Domino's Pizza who are partners on SkyActive, along with financial/home banking sites such as Abbey National and HSBC, among others.

These involve the viewer going purposefully to the interactive walled garden area of the digital service, where the advertising partners have built 'dedicated advertiser locations' (DALs). These can be reached via the navigation buttons on the handset, or by driving traffic from 'impulse response' (I-Ads) or banners in the walled garden. Interactive opportunities are described in greater detail later in this chapter.

# Planning and buying TV

When purchasing direct or impulse response advertising the buyer must first negotiate for a TV ad spot. It is therefore important to buy airtime that provides the right programme environment and audience profile and impact level – the actual number of people that are likely to view the slot. Knowing how many impacts a spot will deliver is also important in establishing the cost that will be paid for the airtime as the trading is generally done on the basis of cost-per-thousand (CPT). That base cost could range from £2 to £20 CPT depending upon the station, time of day and programme; and the CPT, when multiplied by the actual audience delivery, will equate to the gross cost of the airtime spot and will become one of the metrics for evaluating the ROI.

To identify the impact level, BARB provides in-depth minute by minute impact information and therefore can determine the estimated audience to any single ad spot; so let's take a look at BARB and how it measures television audiences and then look at how that data is used to plan and buy campaigns.

### The Broadcasters' Audience Research Board (BARB)

BARB is a quantitative study that provides estimates for the number and types of people watching channels and programmes at different times. The service only covers viewing within private households and provides a minute by minute analysis of the channels received within those homes which can be aggregated to be reported in a number of ways, such as nationally or regionally or whether viewed via analogue or digital platforms. BARB is an independent company whose shareholders are the BBC, ITV, Channel 4, Five, BSkyB and the IPA.

In summary BARB's remit is ...

- **To provide the agreed industry standard measurement of television audiences in the UK**
- **To enable broadcasters to evaluate programme and schedule performance**
- **To be a reference source for the TV industry**
- **To satisfy regulatory requirements**
- **To provide the commercial airtime currency**

So how do they collect the data? Viewing estimates are obtained from panels of television-owning households representing the viewing behaviour of the 24 million-plus households within the UK.

The panel homes are selected via a 'multi-stage, stratified and unclustered' sample design (BARB, 2005), meaning that the panel is fully representative of all television households across the whole of the UK, However, to understand the detailed picture of UK households it is necessary to conduct the establishment survey.

## The BARB establishment survey ...

- Is a continuous survey with 52,000-plus interviews per year

- Is a random probability survey, i.e. that any household within the UK has an equal likelihood of being selected for interview

- Ensures that any changes in the population can be identified and the BARB TV panel adjusted to ensure it continues to reflect the television-owning population

## The panel homes

- There are currently 5,100 panel homes with about11,000 viewers

- Panel homes have all their television sets, video cassette recorders etc. electronically monitored.

- All panel household residents and their guests register their presence when in a room with a television set on. Each individual does this by pressing the button allocated to them on the 'Peoplemeter' handset. (see figure 5.5.21)

## The viewing data

- A small black box meter, about the size of a hardback book, is connected to all television sets and automatically collects information about the channels that they are showing

- The black box meter system stores all daily viewing data for the household and downloads it automatically to the processing centre each night between 02:00 and 06:00

- The people meter data is overlaid with the live 'overnight' minute by minute television channel data to match the 'types of people' that viewed each channel at

**Figure 5.5.21 Peoplemeter Handset**

each stage throughout the day, providing useable viewing data by the following midday

- The published 'overnight impact data' represents the population as a whole and gives a first indication of the number of people who viewed television throughout the previous day

## The audience profile

- Video playback is also measured if it takes place within seven days of the original broadcast. This time shift viewing is added to the live data, along with the programme and advertising details, to produce the final, minute by minute 'consolidated audience impacts' eight days after the original transmission date.

- Three specialist research companies are contracted to provide BARB with the service:
RSMB: responsible for panel design and quality control
Ipsos-RSL: responsible for the establishment survey
ATR UK: responsible for metering the panel, data collection and processing.

## The BARB website (www.barb.co.uk) is a good source of information and provides:

- Weekly and monthly TV viewing summaries, top programmes by channel and ITV facts and statistics

- Background information of BARB services, news and industry developments

- Subscriber information to enable use of the detailed viewing data

- All BARB subscribers pay an annual registration fee, currently £3,850, plus a quarterly subscription fee or licence appropriate to their category of business as set out in their rate card

## *Using BARB data in buying airtime*

The number of individuals viewing an individual break are described as 'impacts' and the common industry jargon is then to describe those individuals in terms of 'ratings', as in a TVRating, or TVR, as described below:

Impacts are the actual number of people watching a programme or advertisement, generally over a specific rolling minute in the broadcast day.

Impacts can describe all viewers, i.e. all individuals, or other sub-demographic groups. BARB tracks 200-plus different audiences, covering most of the socio-demographic permutations such as ABC1 adults, women or men aged 55-plus, along with a number of lifestyle profiles such as dog shoppers, mobile phone owners and air package users. The most common 15 audiences are detailed in table 5.5.6:

Table 5.5.6 **Main TV audiences used in planning and buying**

| All individuals | All adults | All homes |
|---|---|---|
| Women | Men | ABC1 adults |
| Housewives | Children | Housewives and children |
| ABC1 women | ABC1 men | Adults 16 to 44 |
| Adults 45+ | Adults 16 to 24 | Men 16 to 24 |

*BARB, 2005*

The total population, or universe, is simply the population of a particular area or channel, by target group, that could have watched the programme or advertisement as opposed to those that actually did.

- Universe is usually expressed as a 'thousandth of'; therefore the universe for women in London would be 4,777, if there were actually 4,777,000 women in London

- The universe for men in Granada is 2,461, meaning there are 2,461,000 men in the Granada region

- The universe figures are supplied by BARB on the basis of the establishment survey information

A television rating (TVR) is the number of impacts delivered in one rolling minute expressed as a percentage of the total universe.

- Example: 10 adult ratings (10 TVRs) in London means 10 per cent of all the adults in London watching. If there are 8,921,000 adults in London (the universe), 10 per cent = 892,100 adults watching. Therefore 10 TVRs = 892,100 adult impacts (in London).

## Entry cost and TV buying

Airtime is sold mainly on the basis of an agreed cost-per-thousand for the campaign target audience:

$$\frac{\text{Total revenue (demand)}}{\text{Total audience (supply)}} = \text{Station price/CPT}$$

Cost-per-thousands are calculated monthly from the total revenue (amount paid by all advertisers for commercial minutage over the month) divided by the total audience (total number of impacts delivered over the month) – resulting in an expression of the average cost of delivering 1000 impacts.

## *Variations in price created by the supply and demand mechanism*

### Regional and channel cost variations

Due to the balance between supply and demand regional and channel costs vary:

- London is highly demanded therefore has more revenue and a higher station price.

- If the annual network CPT for 'all adult' ratings is called '100' with individual regional prices indexed against it, the North, Scotland and HTV are seen to be considerably cheaper than London and Meridian. Similarly, many of the smaller digital channels reflect the lower price point, again because of a lesser demand for their airtime, which can be due to the specific targeting that they offer and the quality of their programming.

- Indices for regional pricing will be calculated every month, but will generally show the same patterns.

Figure 5.5.22 **Regional cost variations (adult CPT)**

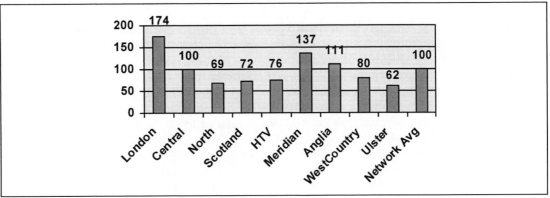

### Seasonal variations

- In the same way, if audience volumes increase, the price will decrease, and vice versa.

- Large audiences in January bring the average cost down. The demand for pre-Christmas airtime will put the price up again.

- Once again, when indexing monthly CPTs against the annual average, December and January are much cheaper than May, September and October.

- The absolute figures will vary year on year, especially if there is a major event such as the Olympics, a World Cup or an election, but the underlying pattern will hold true.

Figure 5.5.23 **Monthly cost variations (adult CPT)**

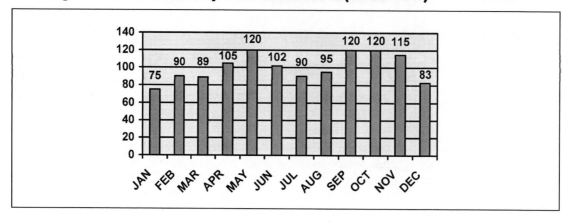

## Effects of day part

The TV marketplace divides the day into a number of time bands referred to as 'day parts'. These attract different audience levels and advertiser demand, the combination of which results in another price variation:

- Breakfast through daytime are lower cost day parts, attracting many DRTV advertisers for whom such prices make the cost-to-sales model work.

- Peak is more expensive because it contains higher quality programmes, delivers a broader audience profile, higher audience levels and is more in demand from a wide range of advertisers. Many advertisers use this to build campaign coverage quickly and are prepared to pay a premium for it. Conversely, off-peak is less expensive and reaches smaller audiences, as detailed in table 5.5.7, which provides an example of how day part costs will vary in relation to one another, where '100' is equivalent to the all-time average. It must be noted that individual channels will have their own pattern of cost variations and that the examples provided here are merely to explain the principle and may not be exactly the same as prices that you may currently be negotiating.

Table 5.5.7    **Day part cost variation**

| Day part | Description | Index of price versus average CPT |
|---|---|---|
| 07.00-09.30 | Breakfast | 60 |
| 09.30-12.00 | Coffee time | 60 |
| 12.00-16.00 | Daytime | 60 |
| 16.00-18.00 | Pre-peak | 100 |
| 18.00-20.00 | Early peak | 120 |
| 20.00-23.00 | Late peak | 125 |
| 23.00-00.30 | Post peak | 100 |
| 00.30-06.00 | Night-time | 50 to 30 |

You can see how the price movement by day part, by month, by region and by channel can affect your campaign results. To get the best price at the right time is the knowledge that underpins the TV buyer's skill.

# So – how much does a spot cost?

The cost of a spot is related to the number of views and the agreed CPT.

> Actual spot audience ('000) X station price/CPT = cost of spot airtime

As a result, it is virtually impossible to say "An average spot on X channel will cost you £Ys". A 30" spot in Coronation Street on ITV1 could cost between £80 to £120,000 depending upon the time of year, whereas the much lower audience ITV2 spot is more likely to be £800 to £1500. (See regional cost variations above.)

## TV buying options

Most DRTV advertisers will use 'all adults' as the target audience for their negotiations, response evaluation and forecasting as their campaigns are effectively eliciting hand raising from daytime audiences. By contrast, an interactive campaign for a youth brand such as Tango is more likely to buy directly against an audience of, say, 'men 16 to 24', and isolate the specific airtime that converts best to this group.

At the negotiation stage, the most common approach for these two scenarios would be to enter into a cost-per-thousand deal with the contractor to buy the target audience at an agreed price; however, there are at least four different routes that negotiators can take:

1. **Cost-per-thousand for agreed TVRs**

   **This is the most common currency by which TV is traded.**

   • For example, if a spot delivers 5,000,000 adult impacts at a CPT of £3 the cost is: (5,000,000 ÷ 1,000) x £3 = £15,000

2. **Spot pricing**

   **This is particularly prevalent with the smaller satellite and cable channels, where the impact levels are very low. DRTV advertisers can take advantage of such offers and test whether the set cost represents value once the results are evaluated. But it is always wise to check the basic maths.**

   • For example: if a 30" spot is offered for £200 it may look like a bargain. But if it only delivers 5,000 impacts then the CPT is very high: £200 ÷ (5,000 ÷ 1,000) = £40 CPT.

   • Even at £20 per spot, the CPT would be £4.

   • Using the CPT methods above, if campaign evaluation indicates that £3 CPT is the target, then the target cost of this spot would be £15.

3. **Per response (PI) deals**

   **These are available on a number of the smaller channels, and are based on the advertiser paying the TV contractor a fixed rate for each enquiry (inquiry in the US, hence 'PI'), lead or sale-generated.**

   - Example: if a week's activity generates 2,000 leads at an agreed price of £10 per lead, the advertiser will pay the TV contractor £20,000.

   - However, many TV contractors are wary of trading this way. To assist, the DRTV advertisers should allocate a dedicated telephone number to every station that they wish to agree a PI deal with, to ensure that responses and sales can be accurately reported.

4. **Guaranteed rating levels**

   **This is to ensure that coverage and frequency targets are delivered. This is particularly important for launch campaigns or if an advertiser is undertaking a regionalised advertising 'weight test'.**

   Over and above these basics the TV buyer can affect the price for an individual station through negotiation. The following are some of the elements that may be traded: advertising weight, regionality, share of budget by contractor, day part percentage, programming and position in break. In addition deals can be done on a number of different levels: by brand, by manufacturer, by agency, by calendar year or just ad hoc.

   - Table 5.5.8 shows clearly how the final buying price for TV airtime will impact on the resulting campaign efficiency:

**Table 5.5.8     Budget versus CPT**

| Budget | Airtime cost-per-thousand | Impacts obtained | Responses fixed at 0.03% | Cost-per-lead |
|--------|---------------------------|------------------|--------------------------|---------------|
| £10,000 | £5.00 | 2,000,000 | 600 | £16.66 |
| £10,000 | £4.00 | 2,500,000 | 750 | £13.33 |
| £10,000 | £3.00 | 3,333,333 | 1,000 | £10.00 |
| £10,000 | £2.00 | 5,000,000 | 1,500 | £ 6.66 |
| £10,000 | £1.00 | 10,000,000 | 3,000 | £ 3.33 |

# DRTV planning issues

Media planning for DRTV becomes highly detailed. The availability of minute by minute audience response information results in an ability to evaluate very small variations in criteria. However, the primary steps are:

- Evaluation of product and offer ! campaign objectives

- Strength of brand

- Nature of product (i.e. likely demand)

- Motivation to call (e.g. free video versus insurance quote)

- Review historical data on past performances if available

- Review competitive activity

- Define target audience

- Set response objectives – i.e. criteria for evaluation and check information flow

- Review media options and selection – day part, regionality, programming and channel etc – media planning

- Negotiate airtime costs – media buying

- Review telemarketing and fulfilment services

- Response forecasting, call handling volumes and impact management

- Evaluation

- In order to get everything done well one of the big steps with DRTV is to ...

- Plan well ahead

## Choice of product/service

As the earlier examples demonstrate, different types of product tend to be successful with different types of DRTV. Some products fall very clearly into place, e.g. music collections with one basic offer are suited to one-stage selling. Two-stage is more appropriate for insurance quotes, where there are many permutations of your product dependent upon the individual criteria of the respondent.

In addition, the allowable cost-per-lead or per-sale can determine whether DRTV will work successfully or not. Unfortunately only testing, experiment, experience – and watching others – will determine whether your product is suited to DRTV.

## Competitive activity

As with all media planning, competitive monitoring is a highly useful source of information. Full reports on schedules and audience delivery are available through the BARB data, and can be accessed through services such as MMS and BARB. In addition, show reels can be compiled of actual commercials that can help to understand the competitor's strategy. Commercials are archived by companies such as Xtreme Information, (http://www.xtremeinformation.com/) which can compile a tape of competitive commercials for review.

## Target audience

As we have seen, the audience research can tell us who is watching and at what time. The planner needs to understand the differences between taking the audience that a day part delivers because that is when the airtime is less expensive and the call centre is open, versus chasing a specific audience.

The latter may appear more costly when judging the initial media costs; however, the specific target audience may result in higher numbers, deriving a higher response rate, convert better to sales, remain with you for longer offering greater LTV, and therefore deliver a better overall cost of business for the advertiser.

## National versus regional access

TV audiences can be accessed both nationally through ITV, GMTV and Channel 4. Regionally, options include:

- 13 ITV regions

- The macro regions available on Channel 4, Channel 5 and GMTV

- The regionalised cable networks

Satellite provides a semi-national option, although with many specific lifestyle-targeting options.

- Selected regional activity or small satellite channels can be desirable for a number of reasons, such as for running test campaigns, for matching regional distribution or for upweighting or downweighting areas of sales strength or weakness.

## Mass or selective audiences

TV gives us access to many different types of audience. In addition to the regional opportunities there is a massive variation in the sheer scale of audiences that can be reached through one channel versus another. One ITV network spot in Coronation Street could reach 12 million adults, whereas the daytime repeat on ITV2 might deliver just 200,000 adults.

## Lead times

To guarantee the airtime that you want, at the best price, your booking should be made six to eight weeks before the month of transmission, i.e. by the advanced booking deadline (AB deadline). All sales houses publish their calendar of deadlines, an example of which is shown below. All campaigns booked after the relevant monthly deadlines below are subject to a premium. Check out the Channel 4 site (http://www.channel4sales.com/advertising-info/advance-bookings.aspx) to get the updated advance booking deadlines.

**Table 5.5.9**     **Channel 4 – AB deadlines**

|  | 2006 AB Day |
|---|---|
| January | Tue 15 November 2005 |
| February | Tue 13 December 2005 |
| March | Tue 10 January 2006 |
| April | Tue 7 February 2006 |
| May | Tue 7 March 2006 |
| June | Tue 4 April 2006 |
| July | Wed 3 May 2006 |
| August | Tue 6 June 2006 |
| September | Tue 4 July 2006 |
| October | Tue 1 August 2006 |
| November | Tue 5 September 2006 |
| December | Tue 3 October 2006 |

http://www.channel4sales.com/advertising-info/advance-bookings.aspx

Last-minute campaigns are generally subject to a price premium. However, in periods of lower demand, e.g. the summer, and across some smaller satellite channels, there are short-term opportunities. This is generally for the airtime that the contractor wants to get rid of rather than exactly the airtime that you want, but for some advertisers the two objectives come together successfully if the target audience is available during the airtime on offer.

An additional consideration is the production lead time required for TV. After concepts and storyboards are produced the commercial has to gain BACC approval – as described earlier. This will be done over a number of sessions where, firstly, the details of the script are approved, followed by approval of the actual commercial to ensure that it has not deviated from the approved script. Four weeks is generally the very minimum time allowable for this process. TV contractors will only transmit a commercial if it is received with a BACC consignment note and clock number.

## Media planning

The planner should select the best time of year and station mix to deliver the optimum test. Time bands should be designed to meet the communications objectives while combining cost efficiency with call centre availability. Test activity does not generally need to be any longer than two to four weeks.

However, one thing is true: low impacts and low demand will result in lower capital costs, and the proliferation of small channels presents the DRTV buyer with a multitude of low-cost entry points. As a consequence a month-long, daytime-only DRTV test schedule, using a 60-second commercial, across eight or so low-impact satellite stations, can be achieved for around £50,000.
To monitor such airtime it is vital that different telephone numbers are used for each station. Even if you wish to use a single vanity number at a later stage, individual tests should be monitored. At rollout the copy can be changed on the successful stations to use the single corporate number should it be strategically

important. Voiceovers and screen text are easily and cheaply edited and the BACC must see each execution and give it an individual consignment note. But the results will be worth it.

## Creative execution

The different types of response objectives call for different creativity treatments as discussed previously. However, to summarise there are a number of guidelines that good DRTV commercials follow:

- Be clear about your objectives

- Appeal directly to your target market – to the deliberate exclusion of everyone else

- Arrest viewers' attention immediately

- Have a powerful and motivating offer framed in an irresistible way

- Support selling statements with product facts and features; use TV to demonstrate them

- Employ a clear and simple response mechanism

- Capitalise on the brand's established personality

## Results of BT/Channel 4 research into effective DRTV – 1998

BT and Channel 4 collaborated on a series of research studies between 1993 and 1998 which provide a number of useful pointers as to what has worked for some DRTV advertisers. The following information outlines a number of results relating to use of day parts, time lengths, voiceovers, telephone numbers and the like, and may prove useful as a starting point for DRTV treatments.

| % by marketing category for top 6: 1998 versus 1997 | | |
| --- | --- | --- |
| | 1997 | 1998 |
| Finance | 28 | 21 |
| Office automation | 14 | 16 |
| Motors | 9 | 14 |
| Mail order | 1 | 12 |
| Charities | 0 | 5 |
| Retail | 5 | 5 |

- Financial advertisers continue to dominate DRTV activity, bringing new products to screen each year, such as debt consolidation, mortgages and personal loans.

| Response rate by marketing category 1998 | |
|---|---|
| Finance | 0.19% |
| Office automation | 0.09% |
| Motors | 0.02% |
| Mail order | 0.77% |
| Charities | 0.24% |
| Retail | 0.3% |

- The highest response rates are generally experienced by the mail-order advertisers. They are often employing the core one-stage techniques with longer, hard-hitting advertising.

- Charities, likewise, are highly successful, but have the opportunity to put over very compelling and emotional messages.

| Response index by day of week | | | | | | | |
|---|---|---|---|---|---|---|---|
| Day of week | Mon | Tues | Wed | Thurs | Fri | Sat | Sun |
| Response index | 87 | 139 | 104 | 99 | 116 | 58 | 90 |

- By day of week the research indicates Tuesdays and Fridays – but most importantly the DRTV advertiser must construct a test matrix to identify which days of the week are the most effective for their product or service.

- In addition it is important to identify the level of background noise that a call centre receives – i.e. the percentage of call capacity that is naturally taken up by ongoing calls that are not directly resulting from current advertising messages but result from the build-up of awareness of the proposition and call mechanism over time. Where possible background noise must be isolated from the ongoing activity to ensure that statistics are correctly interpreted.

| Response indices by duration/time length | | | | | |
|---|---|---|---|---|---|
| | 10" | 20" | 30" | 40-50" | 60"+ |
| % of all ads | 9 | 11 | 59 | 9 | 11 |
| Response index | 42 | 65 | 104 | 95 | 213 |

- The majority of DRTV ads are 30" in length; however, the evaluation indicates that the 60" commercials gained the highest response – however, this is fairly simply explained as the majority of the longer length ads are for mail-order products.

- In reality the commercial should be as long as it needs to be to put the message over effectively – and no longer.

- Commercials can be of almost any length from 2" to 3.5 minutes; however, they are generally produced in multiples of 10" and less than 2 minutes.

- Commercial length has cost implications (see below) – cut down reminders carrying the core proposition and response mechanisms are a highly effective way of increasing the efficiency of an ongoing campaign.

| Response indices by duration of phone no. on screen | | | | | | |
| --- | --- | --- | --- | --- | --- | --- |
| Seconds | <5 | 6-10 | 11-15 | 16-20 | 21-30 | 31+ |
| % of ads | 42 | 23 | 8 | 5 | 19 | 3 |
| Response index | 53 | 119 | 322 | 193 | 94 | 178 |

- In crafting the commercial, unsurprisingly the telephone number is also important along with the voicing of the number; however, looking at the statistics it would be difficult to tell this on occasions. If DRTV is to work, test out the number recollection – it is, after all, the point of the exercise.

With the above data, it is important to remember that these results are limited to those campaigns that happened to be transmitted during the research period, and are now a few years old. However, the patterns seen still hold and can be of guidance with the initial DRTV test, after which you will start to generate your own data with which to refine the activity.

Source: BT/Ch 4 research undertaken by Broadcast Monitoring Company, on ITV, C4, C5, Sky 1 and UK Gold in London between noon and midnight 6/7/98 – 26/7/98 inclusive, monitoring all television commercials with a phone number or web address over three weeks.

## The importance of avoiding lost calls

The issues of call handling and fulfilment are covered in detail in chapter 11.2; however, the media planner is responsible for ensuring that the call delivery reflects the call capacity and especially so with TV. Response to 'core' DRTV campaigns is one of the most immediate, with research showing that the majority of calls will have been received within 20 to 30 minutes.

Over time, a level of awareness may be created that will soak up some of the call capacity, generating 'background noise' – i.e. a percentage of calls that happen every day because the service or product is now better known. This happens particularly when an advertiser uses a 'memorable' number, such as Lombard Direct's 0800 2 15000.

Because of this, the media planner should develop a model that can assist in predicting what level of audience impacts can be bought without exceeding response-handling capacity. For example, if the call centre resource can handle 200 calls per 10 minutes and the response rate is estimated to be 0.025 per cent, then the maximum manageable level for each spot is 800,000 impacts. Any audience above this will produce lost calls and irritated prospects. The model can help identify time bands, regions and stations that can deliver within the required levels.

Once the contractors have supplied an initial schedule, it is important to estimate the response delivery and compare this to the call centre capacity. With multiple channels, all of the airtime needs to be combined and evaluated chronologically to ensure that there is not excessive bunching. Response rates are very difficult to estimate in the first instance, and will vary by all the usual variables; however, planners often start by benchmarking from industry averages.

Table 5.5.10    **Estimating 0.038 per cent response rate for advertiser 'X'**

| Station | Date | Time | Est TVR1 | Univ '000s | Impacts '000s | Est response rate | Est response '000s |
|---------|------|------|----------|------------|---------------|-------------------|--------------------|
| SKYNEWS | 04-Jun | 9.46 | 0.12 | 19,451 | 23,341 | 0.038% | 9 |
| SKYNEWS | 04-Jun | 10.13 | 0.14 | 19,451 | 27,231 | 0.038% | 10 |
| SKYSPORT | 04-Jun | 10.18 | 0.08 | 19,451 | 15,560 | 0.038% | 6 |
| SKYSPORT | 04-Jun | 10.27 | 0.11 | 19,451 | 21,396 | 0.038% | 8 |
| SKYONE | 04-Jun | 10.41 | 0.59 | 19,451 | 114,760 | 0.038% | 44 |
| TLC | 04-Jun | 10.45 | 0.03 | 19,451 | 5,835 | 0.038% | 2 |
| SKYONE | 04-Jun | 12.12 | 0.38 | 19,451 | 73,913 | 0.038% | 28 |
| SKYSPORT | 04-Jun | 13.07 | 0.53 | 19,451 | 1,03,090 | 0.038% | 39 |
| SKYONE | 04-Jun | 13.41 | 0.48 | 19,451 | 93,364 | 0.038% | 35 |
| SKYSPORT | 04-Jun | 14.42 | 0.22 | 19,451 | 42,792 | 0.038% | 16 |
| SKYNEWS | 04-Jun | 14.43 | 0.16 | 19,451 | 31,121 | 0.038% | 12 |

As soon as the first few days' responses have been generated the estimates should be updated to reflect the early findings. DRTV forecasting is an ongoing task reflecting the changing audience volumes and response activity to a specific campaign.

Whether using an inhouse team or a response-handling house/bureau, spot timings and estimated responses should be sent to them in advance to ensure the staff are fully briefed and ready to receive the calls. In addition, a call bureau should advise the media planning agency if it is handling other accounts that are likely to produce large volumes of calls and constrain its overall call handling capacity in any way, so that airtime can be adjusted accordingly.

Call reports must be analysed in conjunction with the airtime impact information. Through BT's Enhanced Information Statistics (EIS) reports, advertisers can independently monitor the performance of their response-handling house. BT can produce statistics that record the total numbers of calls made to a specific number and EIS statistics include:

- Call volume analysis

- Average call duration

- Time of day call analysis

- Effective call duration

- Geographic call analysis

- Enhanced graphic analysis

- Ineffective call analysis

- Repeat call analysis

See BT agile media for further information (http://www.agile-media.co.uk/prs-mc.htm).

Advertisers and their agencies must be prepared to invest time and energy in response planning. Although call handling appears to be the least glamorous part of a TV campaign it is in fact one of the most important. When the consumer interacts with your organisation, they are walking into your shop and experiencing your service. If they are contacting you for the first time then this is where those crucial first impressions are formed. If you fail the consumer here, the campaign fails. The work of everyone involved in other parts of the campaign may be totally wasted.

## Evaluation of the variables

DRTV offers a myriad of variables across which response performance can be analysed, to understand the comparative performance of different regions and stations, programmes, audience profiles, day of week, time of day, break position and position in break, and frequency of commercial rotation.

However, the first test must be to see if DRTV is effective for the product in question. A low-cost satellite test is probably the best route to start with, ensuring robust, manageable results are achieved from measurable impacts.

Once this is established then the above variables can be evaluated during a period of response refinement:

**Table 5.5.11    Examples of variables**

| Geographical regions/ station options | • ITV regions, Ch 4, CH5<br>• GMTC macros – e.g. North versus South<br>• Satellite music channel versus news channel |
| --- | --- |
| Media options | • Channel and station<br>• Programmes<br>• Genre (sport versus film)<br>• Audience profile<br>• Day of week<br>• Time of day<br>• Break position – end breaks versus centre breaks, etc.<br>• Positions in breaks – first ad, last ad or 'just in there somewhere' ad<br>• Effects of proximity pairing – commercials close to each other, in the same programme or clock hour versus more random spacing<br>• Short-term and long-term frequency effects over days, weeks and months |
| Creative options (Owing to production costs, it is often too expensive to create multiple creative executions) | • Commercial time lengths<br>• Phone number types<br>• Voiceovers<br>• Duration of phone number display |

DRTV is a highly involving and rewarding medium to plan and buy. It requires great attention to detail and team involvement to get it right, but the benefits of testing and understanding the impact of the TV variables can make the difference between a poor campaign and a great one.

# Interactive advertising opportunities

When contemplating interactive advertising it is important to consider the following:

- How can the marketing objective be met through interactive advertising

- What are current interactive applications that are available to marketers

- How advertisers have used interactive applications in the past

Figure 5.5.24 **Cumulative interactive campaigns**

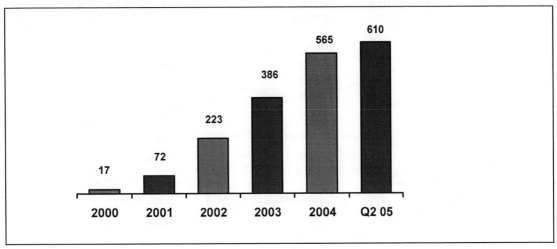

*Skymedia, 2005*

The first interactive advertisements appeared in 2000. By Q2 2005 there had been 610 individual campaigns recorded for 191 different clients across a mixture of channels including ITV, C4, Five, Sky and ids (see figure 5.5.24). The major users are the financial advertisers as detailed in figure 5.5.25, a trend that is also seen when analysing DRTV advertising.

Figure 5.5.25 **Top categories using interactive advertising**

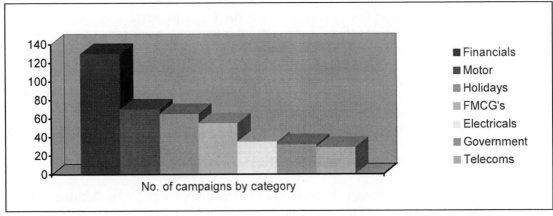

*Skymedia, 2005*

# Why are advertisers using interactivity?

The financial services category has contributed the largest number of campaigns over the first five years with over 130 campaigns to January 2005. A large proportion of the high street banks and the direct insurance companies utilise the services to provide online banking, customer service request facilities, telemarketing callback or product information requests. Motors and holiday advertisers have also contributed a high number of I-Ads.

A number of reasons have been cited by advertisers and media owners for using interactive television, of which a number are listed below:

Figure 5.5.26  **Some reasons given for using interactive TV**

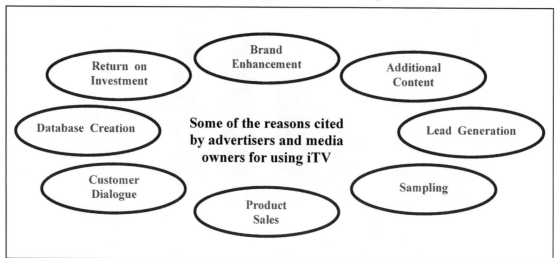

*Skymedia, 2005; ids, 2004*

Looking at specific objectives there is now a considerable databank of case studies that demonstrate how interactive has delivered for advertisers, for example ...

### 1. Increases DRTV response rates

- Canadian Tourist Board reported that the response rates and cost-per-response that they achieved through interactive TV were over three times better than those seen with traditional DRTV

- Extends the 30-second brand message

- KitKat reported that those individuals who responded to their on-screen invitation to play the KitKat game spent an average of 13 minutes interacting

### 2. Increases brand consideration

- Volvo's post-campaign analysis, conducted independently by Continental Research (2004) indicated an increase in spontaneous awareness among interactors versus non-interactors

### 3. Increases propensity to purchase

- The Volvo research also indicated that interactors were 10 times more likely to purchase than those who had only viewed the television advertisement

### 4. Increases actual purchases

- Suzuki tracked brochure requests versus actual sales to find out that they sold over £500,000 cars to interactors

It should be remembered that these anecdotes are not suggesting that the interaction causes the interactor to purchase, but more that those who chose to get involved in the interactive elements of the campaign were already interested in the products, and the opportunity to access more details at a key moment in their decision making process may have been key to converting them to actual purchase.

Encouragingly 73 per cent of those who have run an interactive advertising trail have made a subsequent repeat booking [ skymedia, 2005] indicating that they felt the result met or exceeded their expectations and campaigns have been rebooked to build upon previous successes.

# *How are advertisers using interactivity?*

The following topic will discuss in greater depth how others have used the services and how you might utilise these opportunities, including developing a long-term presence within the interactive area as a 'content partner' or combining interactivity with a short seasonal campaign through the inclusion of impulse response elements over the traditional linear commercial.

The opportunities offered by interactive advertisements (I-Ads) have been well exploited by traditional direct marketing brands as an enhancement of instant communication, and mirroring the DRTV marketplace, finance and travel advertisers are the biggest investors. However, brand–based advertisers, such as Procter & Gamble, British Gas, Coca Cola, and the motor manufacturers have found it a very engaging medium and been seen to spend heavily.

A good example of how motor advertisers are taking advantage of this is the Nissan Primera campaign, which included video streams, a demo of the DVD navigation system, audio explanation of the car's features and the opportunity to request a brochure or test-drive as detailed in figure 5.5.27 below:

### Figure 5.5.27 **Grabs from Nissan Primera interactive advertising**

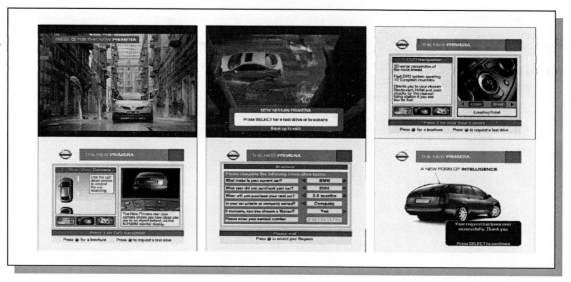

*Source: ids, 2003*

I-Ads can enhance branding power and are highly accountable, which partly explains why they have swiftly become an integral element of so many advertising plans. Increasingly, interactive advertising is of the jump-to variety on digital satellite. It is becoming more sophisticated, with multi-layer DAL applications being used to create enriching interactive experiences including games, film clips, flash animation and competitions. The core opportunities include:

- Impulse response and microsites allow advertisers to add a simple low-cost overlay to TV campaigns.

- Jump-to interactive advertising enables viewers to 'jump' from the broadcast to a microsite, dedicated advertiser location (DAL, satellite) or content partner site.

- Mini-DALs and DALs typically last for the campaign period only.

- A content partner site is the equivalent of a retail outlet. It occupies a permanent position within the interactive area of the digital TV service.

So let's take a look at some of the details involved in the different techniques summarised above.

### *Impulse response*

Impulse response (IR) and microsites are the simplest forms of IA. The viewer actually stays within the broadcast stream rather than moving into the interactive walled garden. They are accessible only from 'interactive airtime' and are bought individually from the sales point for each broadcaster, be it Ch 4, ITV, Five, Sky or Flextech channels etc.

Figure 5.5.28 details the stations that are currently interactively enabled to take IA in the form of impulse response, microsites and jump activity. Currently, ITV, Five, C4, Flextech, UKTV and Sky all use the same WML-based microsite and impulse response applications.

Figure 5.5.28 **Interactively enabled channels and date of activation**

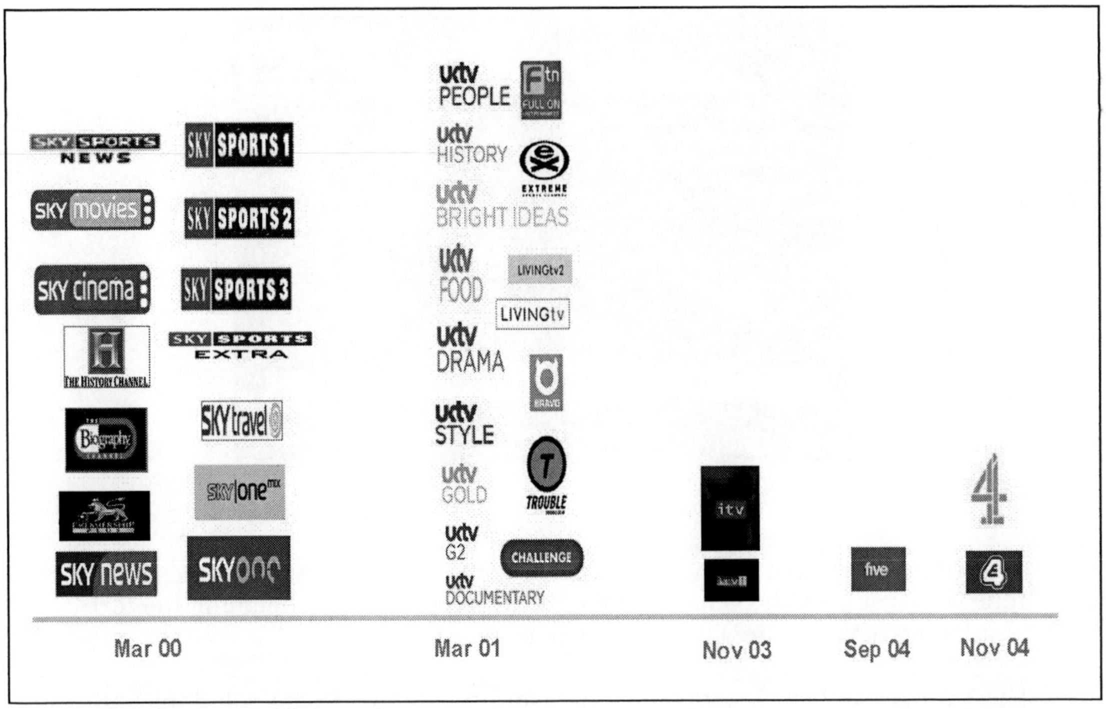

*Source: skymedia, 2005*

Once the impulse response (IR) has been activated the viewer can be engaged in a number of activities, from a straightforward request for a sample, through to a brochure or a callback request.

The advertiser can ask the viewer a maximum of nine questions, enabling the capture of names, addresses and other details such as telephone numbers, email addresses and responses to simple questions, or pick-lists that can be customised to the advertiser's needs and asked in any order.

Remember though that many viewers have their subscriber details logged with their cable or satellite company and therefore do not need to complete address details for the fulfilment of a sample, voucher or brochure requests

Simplistically put, IR ...

- Offers a graphical call-to-action or prompt, which is overlaid on the TV picture during the TV ad and allows the viewer to interact with a brand while the broadcast commercial continues in the background

- Facilitates data capture without leaving the broadcast stream

Impulse ads have had a dramatic impact on this market by offering a low cost and simple way of generating viewer response.

This product is suitable for response sampling or data collection campaigns and the instructions to the viewer appears as a small graphic overlay to an underlying television commercial, as demonstrated in figure 5.5.29 for the COI Gremlins campaign where a simple additional call-to- action button offers the viewer the chance to request a video giving more details of the adult learning programme.

Figure 5.5.29 **COI 'Gremlins' – a simple IR call to action added to national ad**

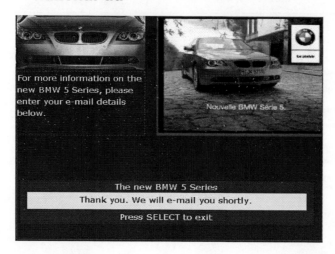

*Source: Press Red Ltd 2005*

IR ads have now been developed sufficiently to enable a 'black box' design approach that provides templates for the different options, detailing the text positioning options, sizes and colour palettes.

There are a number of companies that can provide the design solutions and who work with the broadcasters to ensure that advertisers have the right information to make the solution successful. These include companies such as Press Red Ltd (www.pressred.com) who have developed over 40 per cent of the I-Ads that have been broadcast to date via their BlackBox Designer®.

The black box approach is important for a technical area such as impulse response (IR) as it ensures that development matches the technical specifications that are required by the broadcasters, and minimises the risks of programming errors, or at its worst, a virus or bad programme pulling the broadcast system down.

With IR there is no need to develop and launch pages of content via a microsite or DAL (see below); however, many of the most engaging case studies that will be reviewed here have benefited from using a combination of the techniques.

## Microsites

Figure 5.5.30 **BMW microsite demonstrating ¼ screen broadcast**

*(Press Red Ltd)*

Microsites are an extension of the IR, delivered in the broadcast stream and incorporating the same functionality, giving the opportunity for simple requests or data collection.
However, they use the picture-in-picture features that reduce the commercial to a smaller proportion of the screen.

The commercial broadcast shrinks to 1/4 size leaving 3/4 of the screen available to the advertiser to increase their message with more product detail and data capture elements – see figure 5.5.30. Viewers can enter their details while still watching the broadcast commercial, providing the similar information as in the IR product.

## 'Jump-to' interactive advertisements

Jump-to ads also present the visual call-to-action overlaid on the TV ad, usually using the familiar 'press the red button' format. Viewers can press the red button during an ad to jump to a static page within a text service. The page can be in full colour and feature graphics and photo-quality stills. The programme audio usually continues to play in the background as with traditional text services. Upon completion of the details of an interactive advertisement, the data can be sent immediately to a call centre and a lead can be followed up within seconds. Domino's pizzas are still delivered within 30 minutes!

'Jump' landing sites can be made in a number of ways, including text pages as described above, mini-DALs and DALs. Jump-to advertisements that incorporate DALs or mini-DALs give advertisers the chance to create targeted leads by offering viewers many of the same facilities as the IR (request a brochure or a sample) but also extend the options from giving money to a charity or requesting a test-drive through to playing interactive games or watching short videos of the product.

## Mini dedicated advertiser locations (mini DALs)

Mini DALs are 'higher end' interactive ads, providing more flexibility for a brand, combining the detail of quality print with all the potential and power of a moving image and sound. A mini-DAL is a templated application, but uses richer graphics and can include bespoke audio and quarter-screen video.

There are three key formats for the mini-DALs:

1)   The 3/4 screen with 1/4 screen TV broadcast

2)   Full screen with dedicated audio

3)   Full screen with dedicated 1/4 screen video and audio as demonstrated in figure 5.5.31

Subject to commercial arrangements with each sales point, mini-DALs can be accessed by pressing the red button from interactive airtime on ITV, Ch 4, Five, Flextech, UKTV and Sky Channels. When on Sky, mini-DALs will be signposted on the SkyActive 'A to Z' listing of services and can also be accessed via a SkyActive or Sky Text advertising banner campaign.

Viewers who opt to do so become linked to the interactive area situated within the walled garden and therefore go outside of the broadcast stream. Here further information can be made available about products and services and there is the ability to capture the viewers' responses. The viewer can navigate around the interactive area using the red, yellow, blue and green buttons on the remote control and enter details using the alphanumeric keys. When inputting one's personal details, to save time and avoid non-completion, the default setting will be the details of the head of household.

This product offers more interactive capabilities, meaning more product information can be displayed. It is effectively a moving image brochure capable of facilitating an immediate response if required. The underlying structure of these sites means that they can be costed easily and put on air very quickly using wireless markup language (WML) content creation tools.

**Figure 5.5.31  Chrysler CrossFire Mini DAL demonstrating ¼ screen video window**

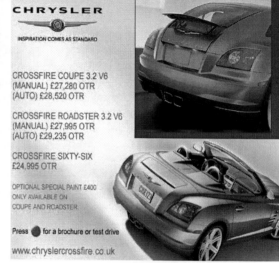

*(Press Red, 2005)*

## Dedicated advertiser locations (DALs)

This is a brand's ultimate interactive television experience. It is a visually rich service created to meet the bespoke needs of the advertiser. This product effectively gives the brand its own television channel. As with mini-DALs, DALs can be accessed by pressing the red button from an I-Ad. The viewer can jump to the bespoke video, audio or animation and extend the brand interaction beyond the traditional spot ad.

An excellent example of the use of a DAL is the Volvo S40 and the 'Mystery of Dalaro'. Volvo wanted to support the 'Mystery of Dalaro' campaign with interactive elements; therefore, a DAL was used to broadcast a spoof documentary, showcase the interior and performance elements of the car, and give viewers the opportunity to request a brochure or test-drive.

## Figure 5.5.32 **Volvo S40 – TV commercial with IA to DAL**

*(skyinteractive, 2005)*

The TV campaign was also accompanied by a viral email and supported the web campaign for which they made the eight-minute spoof documentary (skyintereactive.com/VolvoS40, 2005)

435,000 Sky Digital adults claimed to have pressed the red button to interact with this ad (IPSOS Tracker), costing five pence in telephone charges for every minute spent in the DAL. Spontaneous brand awareness was six times higher among interactors than among those who were just exposed to the linear television commercial, and spontaneous awareness of the advertisement itself was 12 times higher (Continental Research, 2004).

When questioned, interactors knew more about the S40, and had a higher intention to purchase. Research indicated that interactors perceived the Volvo S40 as ...

- Having attractive exterior styling

- A car they'd be proud to own

- Very safe

- High quality

As a result they demonstrated increased purchase intent – 'interactors were 10 times more likely to buy a Volvo S40 than those who saw the ad but did not interact' (Continental Research as cited by skymedia, 2005). The results for the Volvo S40 were very positive. Post-campaign analysis by Continental Research (2004) indicated that viewers consciously chose to interact with this ad, spending an average of six minutes in the application and that those who did so were 10 times more likely to buy a Volvo S40 than those who saw only the linear ad .

## Figure 5.5.33 **Volvo S40 – examples of DAL contents**

*Source: Skyinteractive, 2005*

## DALs for games

Because of the capacity for dedicated design within the DAL, a number of advertisers have developed games for viewers to interact with.

There is a good logic to this as the TV is overall an entertainment medium and research indicates games are a popular destination, whether in the form of free light-hearted ad-games, or more dedicated casino cards or other gambling sites.

A good example of this is KitKat who designed a campaign to relaunch KitKat and encourage the UK to 'take a break' at 15:00 on 21 March 2003.

The on-screen advertising included a response red button that migrated over to an interactive game, encouraging people to take a break. The game 'X-stream Salmon' was built within a DAL, offered three levels of skill, a leader board and a winning prize of a year's supply of KitKat.

Games have become a key part of the offering on Sky interactive with dedicated gaming areas including fixed-odds games, puzzle games and arcade-style games and there are three key 'pay as you play' platforms – Gamestar, YooPlay and GoPlay TV.

Gamestar currently generates 1.4 million plays a week. YooPlay and GoPlay TV generate about 210,000 plays a week, (BARB, 2005).Of 16 to 24 year old Sky subscribers, 35 per cent play games and 34 per cent of Sky subscriber households with children play games (skymedia/BARB, 2005).

### Figure 5.5.34 **KitKat X-stream Salmon**

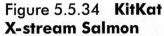

*(skymedia, 2004)*

Advertiser 'press red' games campaigns have been run in the past for KitKat, Crusha milkshakes and HSBC.

Companies such as Press Red Ltd can either develop bespoke games from a client brief or 're-skin' existing games with client branding, but remember DALs are definitely not quick and easy solutions and generally take at least eight weeks just to implement once all the designs have been finalised.

## Enhanced programming and sponsorship (EPS)

Enhanced TV (eTV) refers to interactivity relating to a channel, programme or event. Like interactive advertising, there is usually a call-to-action on the screen and pressing the red button on the remote control accesses interactive services.

For example:

- Ch 4 Big Brother 2005: 27.6 million votes with 5.4 million (20 per cent) through red button

- BBC Wimbledon 2004: 4.1 million-plus individuals accessed extra footage on digital satellite

- BBC Olympics 2004: 9 million individuals accessed extra content

- Euro 2004: 3 million-plus accessed the extra content

- The Eurovision Song Contest 2004: 990,000 individuals accessed extended content

New programmes are commissioned with eTV in mind and older programmes are having overlays built for them. Millionaire is a perfect example of how the simple TV question and answer format can be converted effectively to the TV interactive menu-driven format.

Enhanced TV content can be sponsored within the current ITC Sponsorship Guidelines and so brands now have the opportunity to integrate their message. Content can be developed to include bespoke functionality and branding within the interactive programme, enabling an unprecedented level of woven content.

## Content partner sites

A content partner site is the equivalent of a retail outlet. It occupies a permanent position in the interactive area of a digital TV service. Depending on how the site is constructed, viewers can browse products, find out more details or shop via the TV. Viewers can be prompted to visit the site by directional banners, located within editorial areas of the interactive content or by jump-to advertising, using the red button.

Within the content partner site advertisers can dedicate many pages of expanded information about their products, offering a chance to purchase or request a callback etc.

This is a tenure agreement for a permanent presence within a TV walled garden. Typically contracts last for between three and five years. To date content partners have been high street retailers and service providers including banks and insurance and utility companies.

HSBC interactive banking is a good example of this, along with many of the other advertisers appearing within SkyActive.

Functionally, the service offers 24-hour banking, including money transfer and bill payment. The site also offers product information and interactive services such as mortgage and loan calculators.

Aside from offering a range of banking services, HSBC was also concerned with creating an engaging televisual experience and not a website on TV.

The site therefore had to be functionally useful and accessible to a mass audience as well as entertaining. The service incorporates characters that the audience can identify with and mini commercials for different products as well as 'stings' to bridge different areas of the site and aid navigation. A new customer proposition has also been created: 'Take remote control of your money'. The success of the site was demonstrated almost immediately with HSBC registering 140,000 new accounts and 250,000 orders for product brochures in its first year, proving that the service is a good new business generator. HSBC's commitment to keeping the content fresh and entertaining ensures that the customer enjoys the experience, which in turn secures loyalty (Skymedia, 2004).

Other content partners have opted to use the service because it can take their services to the masses, in particular those who do not, or do not wish to have access to the internet.

The Lotto is a good example of this – with the TV commercial engaging the viewer, those who are interested there and then can be taken to the site via the jump facility, reducing the inertia that can set in over time. The site can also provide the opportunity for regular purchase.

## Figure 5.5.35 **Lotto using IA from TV advertising to take viewers to fully active content site**

## *Launch your own channel*

Advertisers can also develop a broadcast channel. There have been a number of channels developed already, one of the most successful of which appears to be Thomas Cook TV.

Creating original programming is an expensive business that needs to be fuelled by advertising revenues that have not been forthcoming for the most part because the new bespoke channels have small audiences and an inbuilt element of 'competitive' environment for many other advertisers.

Several interesting partnerships have occurred between broadcaster and advertiser. Granada and Boots teamed up to create 'Wellbeing' and Carlton Food

Network and Sainsbury's created 'Taste'; however these have not been successful. The genre that has developed well is the football channels such as MUTV from Manchester United.

## Summary

- Interactive advertising can be used to meet a wide range of objectives for brand, response or promotional aims.

- There are a number of different technical formats that can be used starting with the in-broadcast on-screen 'press red' prompts used for impulse response, microsite and jump activity. The more involving mini-DALS and DALS can deliver a wide range of experiences to those that interact, including videos and games.

- For long-term involvement many companies have become content partners on the SkyActive platform or established broadcast channels of their own.

- Visit the media owner websites regularly for new case studies and research findings.

# Creative considerations for digital executions

There is great scope within interactive advertising and therefore it is important to understand what has been done to date and see how their lessons may help future activity.

## Getting people to engage

The red button icon is very important as it is the first contact with the viewer. Research findings from both ids and Sky, in consultation with industry experts, agree on a number of guiding creative principles to ensure that the viewer will respond positively throughout their 'interactive journey' [ids 2005]. Ids research, (which incorporated expert in-depth interviews, creative analysis and campaign analysis of IA ads and the BMRB's audience interactors monitor (AIM) study in October 2004), centres on how viewers interact with IA and they have identified that IA can transform viewer behaviour from 'implicit to explicit advertising responses'. With interactive advertising, the viewer is invited to participate with the advertising content, to make conscious choices and beyond this, to make decisions to act on these choices, thus enabling the transition from viewer to consumer as reviewed in figure 5.5.36:

Figure 5.5.36  **How a viewer experiences IA**

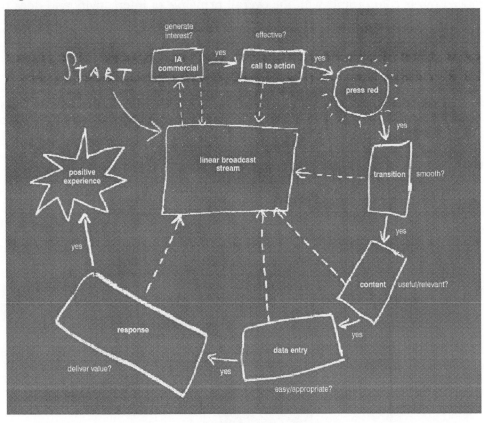

*[ids 2005]*

Much of the discussion about I-Ads is technology-led and heavily orientated towards response rates, but I-Ads have a considerable ability to engage the audience in many ways and when seen from the viewer perspective we can focus on the few but important steps that make up their journey and identify the creative techniques that will enhance the potential success.

Ids have translated this viewer perspective into a helpful model, as detailed in figure 5.5.37, that clarifies the interactive journey and helps to identify the strengths and weaknesses for the viewers.

Figure 5.5.37  **The interactive journey**

*Source: ids 2005*

## *The call-to-action – (CTA)*

The call-to-action is the overlay that appears during the commercial that indicates that the commercial is supported by interactive elements.

The most common and widely accepted form of overlay is the 'press red' red button, and both viewer comments and campaign results indicate that the viewer is still reliant upon the clear presentation of the red button to understand what is available and what to do. The customised 'press red' icon is also referred to as the 'trigger icon' or the 'trigger graphic'.

A number of designs have been tested on the assumption that the audience has moved on, is comfortable with the overall principle of interactivity and does not need the red icon, but research results have not supported this premise to date. Therefore …

## Keep it simple: use the red button

- Design: The red icon should be good and clear, with simple instructions and giving a very clear idea of what the viewer should do and what they should expect to happen once they interact.

- Location: The actual position on the screen is not seen to be of great importance, except that it should take into consideration and be complementary to the underlying commercial designs, and not obstruct anything of significance.

The following demonstrates two contrasting approaches to the inclusion of the red button icon as an overlay to the underlying commercial:

### Figure 5.5.38 **Example A**

Press ● Free home buying CD

2 Year fixed rate £80k repayment mortgage at 4.89% until 31/05/06. APR variable. Total £137,476.22.

**Example A:**
The offer for a free home-buying CD is made very clear and the detail is easily seen and absorbed. The creative would be rated 'good' because it is clear, concise and has a creative fit with the underlying ad design. The icon incorporates the simplest of incentives but reminds viewers that what is on offer is free.

### Figure 5.5.39 **Example B**

…utions is an introducer of …ge Company mortgages only and is a subsidiary of Kensington Group plc

HOMEOWNERS CALL FREE ON **0800 027 1907** LINES OPEN 24 HOURS

**Example B:**
Unfortunately an example of slightly poorer execution of the red button icon where there is less synergy with the underlying commercial.
The text has been positioned in an awkward way, with too many words covering various areas of the screen that are not complementary to the design of the TV commercial.

When the red button is designed in isolation this type of simple mistake can happen, with the icon blocks covering over something that was important, or even legally required.

## Voiceovers and on-screen call-to-action

As with early DRTV effectiveness research, case studies have noted that interactive response is enhanced when the offer and instructions are incorporated within the voiceover and the on-screen creative execution.

### Figure 5.5.40 **Incorporating instructions into commercial**

Examples include the Lotto (see figure 5.5.40) and programmes such as *Eurovision* on the BBC where statistics confirm a huge peak in interactions when Terry Wogan told viewers to vote.

The reason for the correlation between increased response and voiceover etc. is no doubt similar to that identified through the early Ch 4/BT DRTV study as described earlier, that driving new changes in behaviour often requires greater explanation in the early days.

Ids (2005) have produced data to support and 'evidence' these basic rules, demonstrating clearly that:

- CTA visibility: interactive ads with CTAs that were overly blended into the broadcast commercial achieved significantly lower response rates than average.

- Press red in the audio of the commercial: saying 'press the red button' in the audio of the broadcast commercial can increase response rates significantly.

- CTA clarifies fulfilment/offer: having a clear message in the CTA regarding the fulfilment/offer of the commercial increases the response rate considerably.

Figure 5.5.41  **Research data regarding Call to Action Techniques**

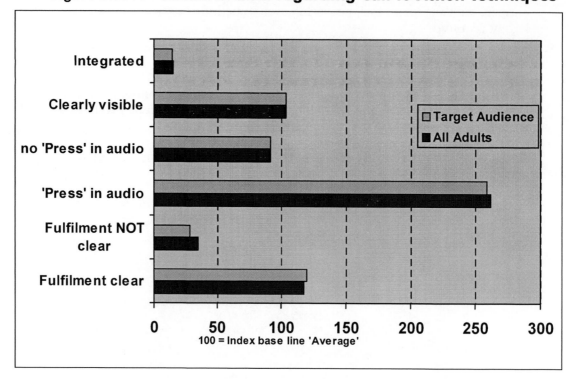

*Source: ids, 2005*

A guide for designing customised icons, '*Customised Icon Guidelines*' by Alex Black can be obtained from BSkyB Ltd, and includes information about the typography and colour palettes that can be used to format icons to ensure that they are TV/PAL compatible, and where and when advertiser graphics may or may not be included to ensure that the viewer has the correct and readable information.

These guidelines are important as it is easy to forget that the icons will be viewed on a TV screen, and therefore will be further away than a computer user would be from their PC screen, and that the images that may appear poor on a computer monitor may reproduce properly on a TV screen due to the differences in screen resolution. (Black, 2005, p.5)

### Transition

The transition is the moment that the viewer interacts – moving from the linear TV commercial through to the interactive content. Viewers will be met either with an impulse response page or a loading page for a DAL or mini-DAL. With impulse response ads the viewer should be given the opportunity to acknowledge that they have 'gone interactive' with a statement such as 'you have just pressed the red button to get ...'

Other interactive formats, such as DALs and mini-DALs, have a loading page, which appears on the screen while the interactive application is loaded. Issues at this stage include:

- **Loading time**: time taken for the interactive content to appear and become fully active

- **Creative continuity**: consistency of the loading pages and landing pages with the creativity

- **Clear text and instructions**: clear concise instruction reflecting that this is a televisual experience – not the detail enabled by the web

- **Not misleading**: deliver the promise of the broadcast commercial

## Loading time

If a loading page is being used it should also be of some value and keep the viewers interested and informed while they wait.

The main entry point is the first page of the DAL or mini-DAL and often includes a menu from which viewers can choose what they want to see or do next.

## Creative continuity

Creative continuity from TV ad to interactive area is key to a really good campaign – both in terms of thematic consistency and the quality of production, and must deliver what was promised.

The viewer expects it to be one interaction, and finds it disconcerting to have been engaged by one creative image only to be met with something different. Figure 5.5.42 shows the clear continuity maintained by the Jaguar X-Type interaction.

Another great example is the BMW Series ad featuring the giant tortoise, which is perfectly replicated in the interactive DAL which you can see by visiting the IDigital sales website, along with a number of other great examples (See: http://www.idigitalsales.co.uk/interactiveadvertising/iaExplained.cfm)

**Figure 5.5.42  Creative Continuity is expected and enhances viewer experience – Jaguar 118 OHA**

## Clear menu and text directions

Research has indicated that viewers do not like too much text and tend to scan the page to look for clear graphical directions, especially those in the older age groups.

Figure 5.5.43  **Peugeot 407 with clear menu**

It is important that the interaction represents a new form of televisual experience (ids, 2005), reflecting the need to navigate with the coloured buttons rather than the mouse and the more relaxed mindset at the time of entering the interactive area, compared perhaps to the more intent frame of mind that someone might experience when searching a website specifically for information. Interactive content that is simply re-versioned from the website is unlikely to be effective.

Therefore, a clear structure and simple navigation is most effective.

## Don't mislead

Icons should pass the 'Ronseal' test – it should do 'exactly what it says on the tin'. If it is purely a simple brochure request from impulse response say it is, if it's more information on-screen there and then, tell the viewer that.

Skymedia focus groups research indicated that in the Laguna ad (see figure 5.5.44) although the icon looks creatively great, the group reported that they thought it misled them as to what was gong to appear when they pressed red – in this case they were taken through to a static screen with data entry for a brochure whereas the icon had said 'press red for serious playtime'.

Figure 5.5.44 **Misleading Captions**

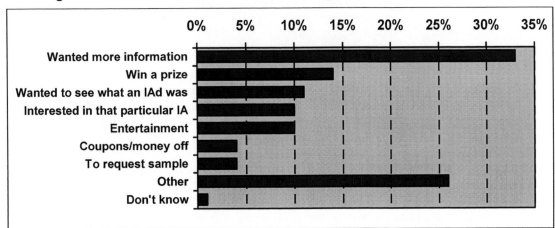

## *Good content can extend the 30′ ad*

The 'content' of an interactive commercial is all the different areas in a DAL or mini-DAL where viewers can find more information, view a video, order a brochure or enter a competition. Ids (2005) research indicates that having invited interaction, the content must be compelling to the target audience and meet or exceed expectations, therefore:

- **Information**: if the interactive ad does not yield information, there is great scope for viewer annoyance

- **Entertainment**: videos, games or competitions can increase response but they should not dilute the core marketing message

Interestingly, interactive experts often quote the fact that entertainment is a primary driver, extending the entertainment environment of TV; however, ids research indicates a discrepancy here, with what viewers actually think, which is that 'information is a must-have, and entertainment the nice-to-have' (ids, 2005).

Figure 5.5.45 **Reasons for interacting with an ad**

| | 0% | 5% | 10% | 15% | 20% | 25% | 30% | 35% |
|---|---|---|---|---|---|---|---|---|
| Wanted more information | | | | | | | | |
| Win a prize | | | | | | | | |
| Wanted to see what an IAd was | | | | | | | | |
| Interested in that particular IA | | | | | | | | |
| Entertainment | | | | | | | | |
| Coupons/money off | | | | | | | | |
| To request sample | | | | | | | | |
| Other | | | | | | | | |
| Don't know | | | | | | | | |

## *Data entry*

Data entry scenes are the areas where viewers can enter information about themselves to receive brochures, samples, callbacks or any other information that the advertiser has asked for. There is a concept that there has to be a trade-off between quantity and quality, that the more you ask the more viewers will drop out of the site, but it is possible to achieve both if the questions are asked well and are relevant; the trade-off probably comes between the level of incentive offered and the data required.

- **Data entry**: make it quick and easy – younger viewers are used to 'text' and can use the phonetic keys on a TV remote control with confidence; older viewers prefer drop-down menus and yes/no options (ids, 2005, p.10)

- **Data relevance**: viewers become unsettled when asked to enter personal data that does not appear to be necessary. For example, if the advertiser is giving away a brochure then the address is important – the home telephone number is not; also Sky viewers know that their subscription data holds this information.

Figure 5.5.46 shows that interactive ads which ask for viewers' telephone numbers or a combination of other personal questions have lower response rates, but also indicates that asking more questions does not have a negative effect on response rates. It can be concluded that it is the type of question that makes the difference.

Figure 5.5.46 **Correlation between requesting data, the number of data requests and response (ids, 2005)**

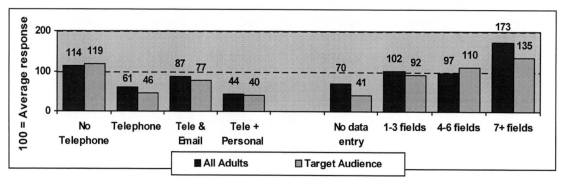

## Privacy

It is also vitally important to remember the data protection issues when constructing the data entry fields. Do you want to be able to contact the respondent again after fulfilment?  How secure are your systems for the transfer and storage of the data that you are requesting?

There is a general standard of data request and data encryption that is known as the Pretty Good Privacy [Blake, 2003], and details of these systems are available from www.pgpi.org (non- commercial release freeware) or www.pgp.com (McAfee commercial version) for automatic encryption and digital signatures for batch processing and FTP transfers. It is important to have encryption systems in place for enterprises, businesses, and departments requiring multiple encryption and digital-signature solutions managed from a single console to help comply with regulations and protect customer data.

## Response

Finally, whil data entry indicates a response, there is a high degree of dropout during the course of the interactive interaction. Therefore in this final section, the focus is on ensuring that the whole process is complete and looking at what lessons have been learned to ensure that positive result.

- **Speed**: interactions that are quick, intuitive and deliver value prevent viewer boredom and drop out

- **Good incentives**: free samples, vouchers and competitions heighten viewer interest and generate a positive effect if they are of value with no strings attached

- **Believability**: too good to be true equals hard sell, therefore offers must be believable, worthwhile and proportionate to the product

Figure 5.5.47 details the research results from ids, but in summary it demonstrates clearly the power of the 'free' incentive: simple but valuable reward of a sample or voucher

Figure 5.5.47 **Free as the CTA and types of fulfilment (ids, 2005)**

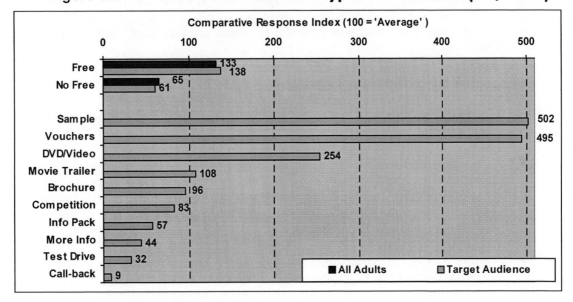

In summary – design should ...

- Be clear and concise, using red button iconography

- Be factual and simple with appropriate incentive

- Voiceover or demonstrate in the commercial what is required

- Do not be misleading or overstated; deliver what you promised

- Maintain creative continuity

- Don't ask irrelevant questions, and explain how data will be used

- Provide clear, intuitive navigation

- Make the experience valuable and enjoyable

- Remember this is TV

## Response results of interactive advertising

There are a number of case studies available on the Sky Media site; in addition, ids (Interactive Digital Sales) can supply response data based upon over 120 interactive campaigns. A number of the general findings are detailed below; however, for more information and access to all of ids' interactive research to date visit interactive digital sales (ids) at http://www.idigitalsales.co.uk or skymedia.com:

- Campaigns generate an average of 3,000-plus responses, peaking at 30,000 for travel brochure requests or free samples

- Response rates vary greatly by audience, offering and application. By category FMCG and retail generate the highest

- In 2002, the average interactive response rate was three times that of traditional DRTV, based upon 'all responses generated' and 'all adult impacts' delivered at the time of broadcast

- DRTV average response rate = 0.03 per cent – IA average response rate = 0.1 per cent

- Among specific TV audiences, response rates are noticeably higher than average, e.g. both a department store and a fruit juice brand targeted women aged 16 to 34 and achieved response rates 20 times higher than the average

## Response by advertising category

Response rates vary by category and differ further according to creative, response mechanism and campaign schedules:

- Categories such as FMCG, retail and travel, (offering free samples, competitions and brochure requests) tend to generate high response levels because of their direct calls-to-action and use of impulse overlays, based upon DDS weighted SkyDigital impacts/Sky Active responses/ids; indexed on average volume of responses.

- Motor and charity campaigns seem to have a lower than average response rate, but have been well received by advertisers for offering an alternative environment in which to communicate with their customers.

- Motor campaigns, for example, allow the viewer to see a demonstration of the car, request a test-drive, order a brochure and ask questions about car ownership. In a recent family car campaign viewers spent an average of four minutes within the DAL, representing a significant extension of the brand experience, yielding highly valuable conversion to sales.

## Response by type of offer

Ids research has shown that campaigns offering a free sample or coupon achieve more responses than information-based campaigns – hence the success of many FMCG advertisers. For example, a branded make-up sampling campaign in September 2002 generated nearly 2,000 requests in the first day alone, and 13,000 overall.

For charities the opportunity for respondents to sign up by 'paperless direct debit' has proven successful for Cancer Research UK, who rolled out their activity for a heavier weight campaign after an initial test.

Figure 5.5.48  **Summary of IA response rates by offer and application**

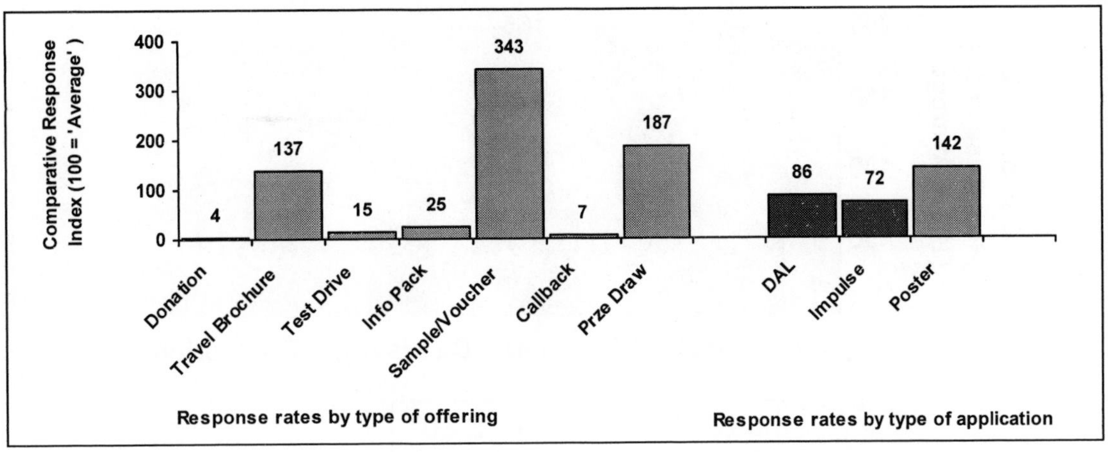

Response rates by type of offering          Response rates by type of application

Source: ids 2005

## Response by interactive application mechanism

In 2002, 54 per cent of the IA campaigns surveyed used a dedicated advertiser location (DAL).

- Multi-layered DALs, which deliver information and a big brand experience, were preferred by many brands to incorporate engaging elements such as interactive games, video and competitions.

- A flash campaign incorporating a promotion with Disney's *Lilo & Stitch* movie featured a film trailer, a toys promotion and a short survey. Respondents were within the branded application for an average of three minutes.

- The 'poster' application was favoured for direct calls-to-action, combining the speed of impulse response with a page of additional information and data capture options. Overall, poster campaigns were 42% more responsive than the average.

## Response by commercial length

Results of the IA research reflect those of traditional DRTV, concluding that the longer the commercial, the better the response efficiency. Of course this has to be balanced against the fact that longer commercials cost more. SkyActive estimates that the average time it takes viewers to press the red button is 17 seconds; therefore, the longer the spot, the greater the chance of a viewer picking up their remote control and pressing the red button. This is particularly pertinent for charity advertising, when the decision to interact may take longer (ids, 2003).

Figure 5.5.49   **Response rates for IA by commercial length**

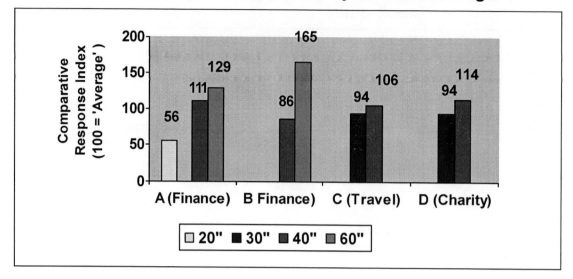

## Response by size of rating

Again reflecting traditional DRTV patterns, higher response rates are achieved from lower rating airtime. In fact spots in lower rating breaks were 59 per cent more responsive than the average. (Based upon DDS-weighted SkyDigital impacts/ Sky Active responses/ids; indexed on average response rate). One spot on UK Style during *Changing Rooms* at 21:45 achieved a 7.3 per cent response rate, yielding 150 brochure requests (SkyActive, 2004).

Intriguingly, according to Sky, in 2002 over 6,000 responses were generated in zero-rating breaks, i.e. where viewing levels were below the sensitivity of the BARB measurement, underlining one of the difficulties of panel-based methods to quantify TV viewing.

Figure 5.5.50   **Response rates for IA by size of rating**

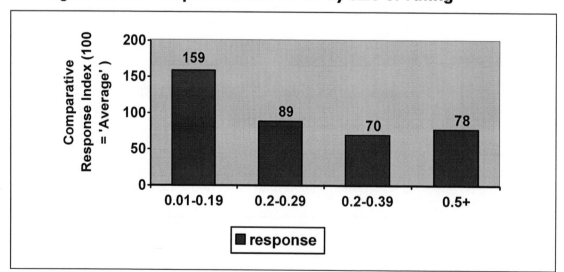

## Response by day part

Day part response patterns differ from those of traditional DRTV. Ids analysis of 2002 campaigns found that advertisements aired between 17:30 and 22:00 were the most responsive. Again however, substantial differences are apparent by category, (See figure 5.5.51). For example, the finance category appears to be more efficient during the evenings, with the Woolwich's springtime mortgage campaign being 49 per cent more responsive between 20:00 and 22:00, whereas the more female-targeted Tesco's credit card campaign excelled from breakfast time to 18:00.

**Figure 5.5.51  Response efficiency by time of day by category**

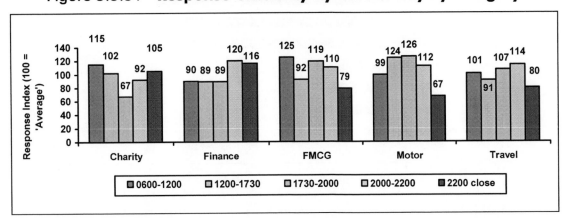

Finally we can add one further source of research to our planning knowledge – the types of people who interact with the I-Ads. BARB conducted some independent research in 2004, showing that those who have interacted with an interactive ad have a profile that is biased toward the younger and more upmarket viewers, and attitudinal research outlined a number of reasons why viewers engaged with interactive advertising, citing the main reason being 'curiosity'. This replicated the findings of the earlier BARB panel recontact study in July 2002, which indicated that 66 per cent of Sky Digital homes had seen an interactive advertisement, and that 49 per cent of those who had seen an interactive ad had pressed the red button to interact with it (SkyMedia, 2002).

**Figure 5.5.52  Interactors highest among the young (BARB 2004). Base: all respondents who have seen an interactive ad (1309)**

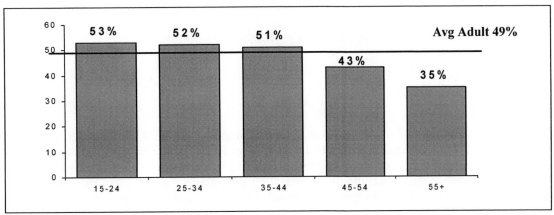

The profile of those interactors also demonstrated the young profile (figure 69 with over 50 per cent of all those aged 15 to 44 pressing the red button to access further info about the advertised product, compared to only 35 per cent of the 55-plus age group; and they were again more affluent, with the average family income of interactors being £40,563, 19 per cent more than the £34,149 for all Sky Digital subscribers.

### Figure 5.5.53  Reasons for engaging with interactive advertising

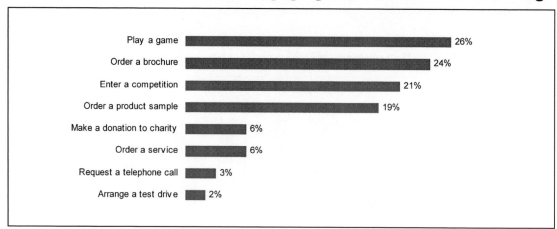

*BARB 2004, base: all respondents who have interacted with an ad (635)*

The BARB recontact study also undertook some attitudinal research, which indicated that:

- 89 per cent of those who did interact agreed that it was a convenient way to get additional information about products or services

- 88 per cent agreed that interactive advertising is an innovative way to advertise a product

- 78 per cent did not agree that interactive advertising is boring

- 67 per cent agreed they are more likely to interact with a TV ad when watching TV on their own

- 62 per cent rated their experience as good

- 56 per cent agreed that interactive advertising is a convenient way to make a purchase

- Only 11 per cent had a poor experience

## Skyview?

Sky has linked up with TNS to establish an ongoing panel of TV viewers. This is a panel of 20,000 satellite direct to homes, (7 to 9,000 of them being existing TNS panel homes) accounting for around 60,000 individuals in total and representative demographically, regionally and balanced across the subscriber profile. The viewing data from this panel will be merged with the subscriber data and a thorough review of purchasing data into a single source research. This will form the largest measurement panel of this type in the UK, possibly in the world.

Every set-top box will be downloaded with Skyview software which will enable the capture and analysis of data in far greater detail:

- Small channels and applications

- Promotional airtime effectiveness

- Second set-top box and Sky+ data

- Subscriber and viewing analysis

- Churn and upgrade/downgrade patterns

- TNS buyer data

Skyview is important for the further development of IA because:

- Lack of measurement has been a hurdle

- Online data has always been available, highlighting the stark lack of data and reducing comparability of campaign metrics

- There is only a very blunt measurement of response variations

- There is a need to understand who didn't interact as much as who did

# The overall planning process

So now we have a better understanding of what is available to us via interactive advertising and some of the lessons that have been learned to date it is possible to outline the essential planning steps that will be required.

## Planning considerations for digital airtime evaluation and selection buying considerations, set-up and airtime costs

Planning interactive advertising follows the same basic principles, as would any other media execution – although it is just currently made considerably more complicated by the ever-evolving technical capabilities.

**Identify the campaign and communication objectives**

- Response – branding – sampling – data collection

**Identify the target audience**

- Are they a good match with interactive users?

**Identify key accountabilities and campaign basics**

- Timing – start times and length of campaign etc.

- Budget

- Media mix – other ongoing activities – what will they/can they offer?

- Data requirements

**Calculate response**

- Target response volumes versus anticipated response volumes

- Do you have access to any past response data, either inhouse or via an agency or sales house that can assist?

- Use BARB data to estimate impacts and historic response information to estimate rates of response

- Plan your contingency – what will you do if it under/over delivers?

**Work with creative team to determine images, motivations and call-to-action mechanism**

- Determine interactive requirements

- What stations and platform/s should be used – satellite, terrestrial or cable?

- What Type of IA is appropriate? Impulse response – microsite – DAL – content partner or sponsorship via enhanced TV options?

- Deliver a clear call-to-action and maintain creative continuity if using IR, microsites or 'jump' and don't over promise

**Identify fulfilment requirements**

- Requirements from call centre and mailing house

- Organise production of fulfilment materials, samples required, questionnaire design and mailing pack etc.

**Interactive advertising campaigns must comply with the Ofcom regulations**

- The principal regulations are set out in the Code of Advertising Standards and Practice, which relates to content issues and the Guidance to Broadcasters on the Regulation of Interactive Television Services

**Manage the campaign closely**

- As per DRTV, ensure that airtime is being delivered correctly

- Ensure all data is being collated and dealt with correctly

- Collect and analyse data at least weekly – daily if possible

- Track performance against forecast

**Post-campaign evaluation**

- Produce post-campaign report

- If receiving name and address data on respondents organise for it to be profiled to gain clearer understanding of respondents, e.g. via Acxiom

- What follow-up activity is appropriate? Further research or communication in line with CRM?

**Useful links**

Adstream – www.adstream.com
Advertising Standards Authority (ASA) – www.asa.org.uk
Advertising Association – www.adassoc.org.uk
BSkyB – www.sky.com
CAP – www.cap.org.uk
Channel Four – www.channel4.com
Cosmetic Toiletry & Perfumery Association (CTPA) – www.ctpa.org.uk
European Advertising Standards Alliance (EASA) – www.easa-alliance.org
Financial Services Authority (FSA) – www.fsa.gov.uk
Five – www.five.tv
GMTV – www.gm.tv
Incorporated Society of British Advertisers – www.isba.org.uk
Independent Committee for the Supervision of Standards of Telephone Information Services (ICSTIS) – www.icstis.org.uk
Institute of Practitioners in Advertising (IPA) – www.ipa.co.uk
Interactive Digital Sales (IDS) – www.flextech.co.uk
ITV – www.itv.com
Media Guardian – www.mediaguardian.co.uk
Medicines Control Agency (MCA) – www.mhra.gov.uk
Ofcom – www.ofcom.org.uk
Proprietary Association of Great Britain (PAGB) – www.pagb.co.uk
Radio Advertising Clearance Centre – www.racc.co.uk
Turner Broadcasting – www.turner.com
Viacom (MTV) – www.viacom.com Profile of Interactors

## Station listing

GENERAL
ENTERTAINMENT

| | |
|---|---|
| 101 | BBC 1 |
| 102 | BBC 2 |
| 103 | ITV 1 |
| 104 | Channel 4 |
| 105 | five |
| 106 | Sky One |
| 107 | Sky Mix |
| 109 | UKTV Gold |
| 110 | UKTV Gold +1 hour |
| 111 | UKTV G2 |
| 112 | Living TV |
| 113 | Living TV +1 hour |
| 114 | Living TV 2 |
| 115 | BBC Three |
| 116 | BBC Four |
| 118 | ITV 2 |
| 119 | ITV 3 |
| 121 | Challenge |
| 122 | Challenge +1 hour |
| 124 | Bravo |
| 125 | Bravo +1 hour |
| 127 | Paramount Comedy |
| 128 | Paramount 2 |
| 130 | Sci-Fi |
| 133 | Discovery Real Time |
| 134 | Real Time +1 hour |
| 136 | Men & Motors |
| 139 | Sky Travel |
| 140 | Sky Travel +1 hour |
| 141 | Sky Travel Extra |
| 142 | UKTV Style |
| 143 | UKTV Style +1 hour |
| 144 | UKTV Style Gardens |
| 145 | UKTV Food |
| 146 | UKTV Food +1 hour |
| 147 | UKTV Drama |
| 148 | Travel Channel |
| 149 | Travel Channel +1 hour |
| 151 | S4C (C4 Wales) |
| 154 | Discovery Home&Health |
| 155 | Disc Home&Health +1 |
| 157 | Artsworld (encrypted) |
| 160 | Life TV |
| 161 | Life TV +2 hours |
| 163 | E4 |
| 164 | E4 +1 hour |
| 166 | TTV |
| 172 | Game Network |
| 178 | You TV |
| 181 | AVAGO |
| 184 | BEN |
| 187 | Reality TV |
| 188 | Reality TV +1 |
| 190 | Hallmark |
| 193 | E! |
| 196 | UKTV Bright Ideas |
| 199 | Ftn |
| 202 | Performance |
| 208 | Friendly TV |
| 214 | L!ve TV |

| | |
|---|---|
| 217 | nation 217 |
| 220 | Fashion TV |
| 223 | OBE |
| 226 | PokerZone |
| 229 | Biography |
| 232 | Hollywood TV |
| 235 | Get Lucky TV |
| 238 | Majestic TV |
| 241 | Soundtrack Channel |
| 244 | London TV |
| 247 | Classics TV |
| 250 | Real Estate TV |
| 253 | Wine TV |
| 256 | UKTV G2 +1 |
| 259 | Unlimited TV |
| 262 | Open Access 2 |
| 265 | Poker Channel |
| 270 | FX |
| 272 | Sky Vegas Live |
| 274 | Vegas 24/7 |
| 275 | Jackpot TV |
| 276 | Big Game TV! |
| 277 | Sound TV |

MOVIES

| | |
|---|---|
| 301 | Sky Movies 1 |
| 302 | Sky Movies 2 |
| 303 | Sky Movies 3 |
| 304 | Sky Movies 4 |
| 305 | Sky Movies 5 |
| 306 | Sky Movies 6 |
| 307 | Sky Movies 7 |
| 308 | Sky Movies 8 |
| 309 | Sky Movies 9 |
| 310 | Sky Cinema 1 |
| 311 | Sky Cinema 2 |
| 323 | FilmFour (encrypted) |
| 324 | FilmFour +1 (encr.) |
| 325 | Film4 Weekly (encr.) |
| 327 | TCM |
| 330 | Horror Channel |
| 333 | True Movies |
| 336 | Matinee Movies |
| 339 | Bad Movies |

SPORT

| | |
|---|---|
| 401 | Sky Sports 1 |
| 402 | Sky Sports 2 |
| 403 | Sky Sports 3 |
| 404 | Sky Sports Extra |
| 406 | MUTV (encrypted) |
| 408 | Sky Sports News |
| 410 | Eurosport UK |
| 411 | Eurosport 2 UK |
| 413 | Motors TV |
| 415 | At the Races |
| 417 | NASN (encrypted) |
| 419 | Extreme Sports |
| 421 | Chelsea TV (encrypted) |
| 423 | Golf Channel |
| 425 | Channel 425 |
| 427 | Wrestling Channel |

| | |
|---|---|
| 429 | Setanta Sports |
| 430 | Celtic TV (encrypted) |
| 431 | Rangers TV (encrypted) |
| 432 | Racing UK |
| 433 | Setanta Sports |
| 434 | Setanta Soccer |
| 437 | Prem Plus (encr.) |
| 438 | Setanta PPV 1 (encr.) |
| 439 | Setanta PPV 2 (encr.) |

MUSIC

| | |
|---|---|
| 440 | MTV |
| 441 | VH1 |
| 442 | MTV Hits |
| 443 | MTV Base |
| 444 | MTV Dance |
| 445 | MTV2 |
| 446 | VH2 |
| 447 | VH1 Classic |
| 448 | TMF |
| 449 | The Box |
| 450 | KISS |
| 451 | Smash Hits! |
| 452 | Magic |
| 453 | Q |
| 454 | Kerrang! |
| 455 | Chart Show TV |
| 456 | The Vault |
| 457 | B4 |
| 458 | The Hits |
| 464 | Classic FM TV |
| 467 | channel U |
| 468 | Fizz |
| 469 | The Amp |
| 471 | Scuzz |
| 473 | Flaunt |
| 475 | Musicians Channel |

NEWS

| | |
|---|---|
| 501 | Sky News |
| 504 | Bloomberg |
| 507 | BBC News 24 |
| 508 | BBC Parliament |
| 510 | CNBC |
| 513 | CNN |
| 519 | S4C 2 |
| 525 | ITV News |
| 528 | EuroNews |
| 531 | FOX News |
| 534 | CCTV-9 |
| 540 | SAW |

EDUCATIONAL

| | |
|---|---|
| 551 | Discovery Channel |
| 552 | Discovery +1hour |
| 553 | Discovery Travel & Living |
| 554 | Discovery Civilisation |
| 555 | Discovery Science |
| 556 | Discovery Wings |
| 558 | National Geographic |
| 559 | National Geographic+1hr |
| 560 | Adventure One |

| | | | | | | |
|---|---|---|---|---|---|---|
| 561 | History Channel | 661 | Ideal Vitality | 828 | Vectone Urdu |
| 562 | History +1 hour | 662 | Sky Travel Shop | 829 | MATV National |
| | UKTV Documentary | 663 | Gems.tv | 830 | Record TV (Brazil) |
| 565 | UKTV Doc +1 hour | 664 | Create & Craft | 831 | Vectone Punjab |
| 566 | UKTV People | 665 | Teletext Holidays | 832 | Vectone Tamil |
| | Animal Planet | 666 | Broadband UK | 833 | Vectone Bangla |
| 571 | Animal Planet +1 hour | 667 | Golf Pro-Shop | 834 | DW-TV (Germany) |
| 582 | UKTV History | 668 | IDMT | 835 | TVEi (Spain) |
| 583 | UKTV History +1 hour | 669 | Max TV | 836 | Islam Channel |
| 585 | Community Channel | 670 | One TV | 837 | Channel 'S' |
| 591 | UKTV People +1 | | | 838 | GEO UK |
| 592 | Teachers' TV | | | 839 | Zee Gujarati |
| | | **CHRISTIAN** | | 840 | Vectone Music |
| | | 671 | GOD Channel | 846 | Pub Channel (encrypted) |
| **CHILDREN'S** | | 672 | GOD 2 | | |
| 601 | Cartoon Network | 673 | Wonderful | | |
| 602 | Cartoon Network +1 hr | 674 | TBN Europe | **REGIONS** | |
| 603 | Boomerang | 675 | Daystar | 941 | BBC 1 Scotland |
| 604 | Nickelodeon | 676 | Revelation | 942 | BBC 1 Wales |
| 605 | Nick Replay | 677 | UCB TV | 943 | BBC 1 N.Ireland |
| 606 | Nicktoons | 678 | Inspiration Network | 944 | BBC 1 London |
| 607 | Trouble | 679 | Loveworld TV | 945 | BBC 1 North East |
| 608 | Trouble Reload | 680 | EWTN | 946 | BBC 1 Yorkshire |
| 609 | Jetix | | | 947 | BBC 1 E Yorks & Lincs |
| 610 | Jetix +1 hour | **SPECIALIST** | | 948 | BBC 1 North West |
| 611 | Disney Channel | 682 | Dating Channel | 949 | BBC 1 West Midlands |
| 612 | Disney +1 hour | 683 | GayDate TV | 950 | BBC 1 East Midlands |
| 613 | Toon Disney | 684 | Escape | 951 | BBC 1 East (East) |
| 614 | Playhouse Disney | 685 | Look4Love TV | 952 | BBC 1 East (West) |
| 615 | Discovery Kids | 688 | Gay Network | 953 | BBC 1 South East |
| 616 | CBBC Channel | 690 | Chat Box | 954 | BBC 1 South (So'ton) |
| 617 | CBeebies | 694 | Your TV | 955 | BBC 1 South (Oxford) |
| 618 | Nick Jr | 695 | Authentic TV | 956 | BBC 1 West |
| 619 | POP | 696 | Exchange & Mart TV | 957 | BBC 1 South West |
| 620 | Tiny Pop | | | 958 | BBC 1 Channel Islands |
| 621 | Toonami | | | 959 | BBC 2 England |
| | | **BOX OFFICE** | | 960 | BBC 2 Scotland |
| | | 700 | | 961 | BBC 2W (Wales) |
| **SHOPPING** | | to | Sky Box Office | 962 | BBC 2 N.Ireland |
| 630 | QVC | 761 | | 963 | ITV1 London |
| 631 | iBuy TV | | | 964 | Channel 4 |
| 632 | iBuy TV 2 | 763 | | | |
| 633 | TV Shop | to | 18 Plus Movies | | |
| 634 | Ideal World | 769 | | **ADULT (all encrypted)** | |
| 635 | price-drop.tv | | | 966 | Playboy TV |
| 636 | Express Shopping | 770 | Sky Box Office | 967 | Adult Channel |
| 637 | Thomson TV | | | 968 | Spice Extreme |
| 638 | Simply Shopping | **FOREIGN LANGUAGE** | | 969 | Television X |
| 639 | Best Direct | (* indicates encrypted) | | 970 | Television X 2 |
| 640 | Superstore TV | 800 | B4U Movies * | 971 | Television X 3 |
| 641 | Simply Ideas | 801 | B4U Music * | 972 | Climax3 – 1 |
| 642 | Shop Vector | 802 | Sony TV Asia * | 973 | Climax3 – 2 |
| 643 | TV Warehouse | 803 | Star News | 974 | Climax3 – 3 |
| 644 | bid tv | 804 | Star Plus | 975 | Sport XXX Babes |
| 645 | Thomas Cook | 805 | PCNE Chinese | 976 | Red Hot Rears |
| 646 | Gems.tv Gold | 807 | mta – muslim tv | 977 | Red Hot 40+ Wives |
| 647 | Tel Sell | 808 | Zee TV * | 978 | Red Hot Amateur |
| 648 | Best Direct+ | 809 | Zee Music | 979 | Red Hot All Girl |
| 650 | Shop on TV | 810 | Zee Cinema * | 980 | Red Hot Wives |
| 651 | Thane Direct | 811 | Bangla TV * | 981 | Red Hot Climax |
| 652 | TV Warehouse Select | 812 | ARY Digital * | 982 | Red Hot Only 18 |
| 653 | Vector 24/7 | 815 | PTV Prime * | 983 | Red Hot Movies |
| 654 | Stop + Shop | 817 | South For You * | 984 | Xplicit XXX |
| 655 | Yes | 818 | AlphaEtcPun * | 985 | Playboy TV |
| 657 | Screenshop | 819 | Al Jazeera | 986 | Adult Channel |
| 658 | Myphone.tv | 824 | Abu Dhabi TV | 987 | Spice Extreme |
| 659 | eeZee TV | 825 | TV5 (France) | 988 | Private Blue |
| | | 827 | ATN Global | | |

989 Private Girls
990 XXX TV
991 Amateur Babes
992 Gay TV
993 18 Plus XXX
994 XXX Housewives
995 Live XXX TV

SKY INFO
965 Sky Customer Ch
996 Channel Line-up
998 Sky Welcome
999 Sky Customer Ch

AUDIO
498 Music Choice
499 Music Choice (encrypted)
851 BBC Radio 1
852 BBC Radio 2
853 BBC Radio 3
854 BBC Radio 4 FM
855 BBC Radio 5 Live
856 Classic FM
857 Virgin Radio
858 Talk Sport
859 Classic Gold
860 The Storm
861 Planet Rock
862 Core
863 Capital Gold
864 XFM
865 BBC World Service
866 BBC Radio Scotland
867 BBC Radio Wales
868 BBC Radio Ulster
869 BBC Asian Network
870 BBC 6 Music
871 The Mix
872 WRN Europe
873 Premier Radio
874 Heart 106.2
875 UCB Europe
876 CrossRhythm
877 Oneword
878 Smooth FM
879 Solar Radio
880 Panjab Radio
881 BBC 7
882 PrimeTime
883 Sunrise Radio
884 UCB Bible
885 UCB Talk
886 UCB Inspirational
887 1Xtra BBC
888 TWR
889 BBC Radio nan Gaidheal
890 Pure Dance
891 Raaj Radio
892 RTE Europe
893 BBC Radio 4 LW
894 BBC R5 Live Sport Extra
895 Club Asia
896 Real Radio

897 EWTN
898 Big Blue (London only)
899 The Saint (South only)
900 Sukh Sagar
901 Asian Gold
902 BBC World Service Extra
903 The Villan (Midlands)
904 BBC Radio Cymru
905 Pulse Unsigned
906 Calvary Radio
907 GlobeCast
908 Gaydar Radio
909 Family Radio
910 RTE Radio 1
911 Arrow-Rock
912 Capital Disney
913 Apple FM
914 RTE 2FM
915 RTE Lyric fm
916 RTE R na Gaeltachta
917 Jazz FM
918 Akash Radio
919 Desi Radio
920 The Hits
921 Galaxy FM
922 Smash Hits!
923 Kismat Radio
924 Century Radio
925 Capital FM
926 Amrit Bani
927 LBC 97.3
928 Kiss
929 Heat
930 Magic
931 Q
932 MOJO
933 Kerrang
934 Radio
935 Spectrum 1
936 Liberty Radio
937 Yarr Radio
938 On Air

# Harness the power of radio!

## This chapter includes:

------------------------------------------------

- ❏ **The commercial radio marketplace**

- ❏ **The development of commercial radio**

- ❏ **Who listens to commercial radio?**

- ❏ **Who advertises on radio?**

- ❏ **What will digital mean for commercial radio?**

- ❏ **Radio as a communication medium**

- ❏ **Media planners' views of radio**

- ❏ **Using radio as an outreach medium**

- ❏ **Effectiveness of radio**

- ❏ **Get creative with radio!**

- ❏ **Useful places to go for more information**

------------------------------------------------

## About this chapter

**This** chapter will enable you to:

Understand the different kinds of radio stations, and the way they attract different audiences (plus the arrival of digital radio)

Understand how listeners use radio in their lives, and therefore the best roles it can play in media strategies

See the evidence for radio's effectiveness in different kinds of campaign, with advice on how to test the medium's effect

Get tips and advice on creativity – how to create the radio advertising that really engages and gets a response

### Andrew Ingram

**Founding Account
Planning Director
Radio Advertising Bureau**

Andrew@rab.co.uk
07966 262 551

Andrew joined the Daily Mail in 1981, selling space in the classified department, moving from there to display advertising. He then worked in quantitative research with AGB, and in qualitative research with Winstanley Douglas & Partners, of which he became a director in 1987. In 1988 he joined Davis Wilkins Advertising as an account planner, winning an IPA Effectiveness Award in 1992 for his paper on the launch of Direct Line Insurance.

With this background in media and research, he then became part of a unique project when the Radio Advertising Bureau (RAB) was set up in

1992. Andrew's eventual role as Account Planning Director meant he was responsible for the content of RAB events and publications.
Major publications include *Wireless Wisdom* (1994), *Understanding Radio* (1999), *An Advertiser's Guide to Better Radio Advertising* (2005) and *Engaging Radio Advertising for Dummies* (2006).

Andrew has been a judge in the D&AD Creative Awards, the IPA Business-to-Business Advertising Awards and the Sony Radio Academy Awards. In 2002 he was included in *Campaign* magazine's *Top Ten Brainiest Boffins in Media Research*. In 2003 he was a judge on the Media Week Awards Grand Prix.

These days Andrew works independently, and is often invited to give talks and seminars, increasingly in non-UK markets.

## Chapter 5.6

# Harness the power of radio!

## The commercial radio marketplace

Commercial radio is a relatively new medium, and has grown dramatically in the last twenty years, with new local, regional and national stations.

This has meant important changes in the make-up of the radio audience, and of the advertisers who now use the medium.

This chapter reviews the main factors affecting the growth of the medium, including a look at the way digital radio is beginning to affect the way consumers listen now and in the future.

## The development of commercial radio

Commercial radio is the youngest member of the UK's 'traditional' commercial media, having only started broadcasting in October 1973. The first ILR (Independent Local Radio) station on-air was LBC, followed a week later by Capital Radio, both in London.

Changes of government meant a stop-start development for some years, but a major step-change came in 1989, with the government's desire to make better use of the radio spectrum. This led to ILR stations being required to run different services on their FM and AM transmitters, which gave rise to the 'Gold' format stations playing oldies and classic hits.

In 1990 the first 'incremental' radio stations went on-air. They had to offer output not already available on ILR, such as specialist music or unique programmes for a specific section of the community.

The Broadcasting Act of 1990 led to the establishment of the Radio Authority, whose 'lighter touch' removed many of the technical, programming and local ownership requirements from ILR, and mergers and takeovers began to gather pace, leading to the development of today's major radio groups.

The Radio Authority introduced many new local radio licences during the 1990s, filling any remaining gaps in coverage, as well as creating new 'regional' licences. However, the biggest change came with the introduction of three 'national' licences, leading to the launch of Classic FM in September 1992, Virgin Radio in April 1993 and Talk Radio UK (later talkSPORT) in February 1995.

**Figure 5.6.1**

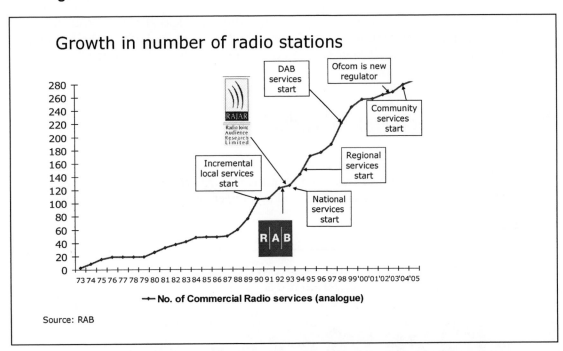

By the late 1990s the number of AM or FM frequencies remaining for further large-scale expansion of the radio market was limited and a new technology – Digital Audio Broadcasting (DAB) – was introduced.

Instead of having a different frequency for each radio station, DAB combined several services together into 'multiplexes'. Each multiplex was subdivided into further separate channels, allowing up to ten radio stations to be transmitted within the same amount of radio spectrum previously required by one single analogue FM station. Digital One, the national commercial DAB multiplex was launched in 1999 carrying the existing national analogue station brands in addition to some new digital-only station brands.

The Communications Act of 2003 saw Ofcom take on responsibility for regulating radio. In July 2004 Ofcom passed new legislation setting out rules for 'community' radio – highly localised services (typically with a radius of 5km) catering for a particular area or community of interest.

**Bold strategy for 'Make Autism Count'**

In 2005 the National Autism Society spent its entire budget on one day on radio, running many different ads on nearly 300 different stations. The event was also picked up by the radio news services. The aim of the campaign was to recruit new donors for the charity, but the campaign used an oblique strategy – they challenged listeners about the realities of autism, and asked them to go to the charity's website and answer a questionnaire about it. Results: 55,000 responses to the campaign, of which 35,000 were online where visitors were invited to become donors.

In the coming years, community radio is likely to significantly increase the number of independent radio stations across the UK, alongside the continued issuing of new FM licences. However, these will be run primarily for social gain in the community, not for profit, and only a limited number are likely to take advertising.

As of autumn 2005 there are nearly 300 analogue commercial radio stations (a combination of national, regional, local, incremental and community) broadcasting in the UK.

The UK is also world leader in DAB digital radio, with 130 stations currently broadcasting a combination of new formats and existing analogue radio brands, bringing much greater listener choice across most parts of the country.

## Who listens to commercial radio?

The growth of station choice across the country means that commercial radio is now a truly mass medium, reaching about two-thirds of the population every week, and this audience has always had a younger profile than BBC listeners.

Figure 5.6.2

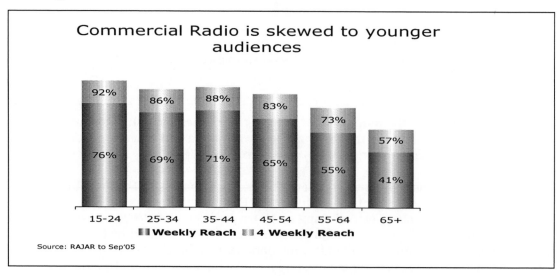

When RAJAR first posted listening figures in 1992 commercial radio was particularly strong in reaching the 15 to 44 year old age group, especially compared to the BBC. This listener group became known as 'the commercial radio generation' – people who had grown up, or were growing up, with commercial radio as their preferred choice of listening, in contrast to their predecessors who had grown up with only BBC stations available.

In 2005, this age group is still dominant in the commercial radio listening profile, but a number of factors have helped to increase the commercial listening among other demographics.

The first of these factors is the cohort effect – people who have grown up as commercial radio listeners, remaining as such even as they enter demographic breaks traditionally associated with listening to BBC stations.

## Figure 5.6.3

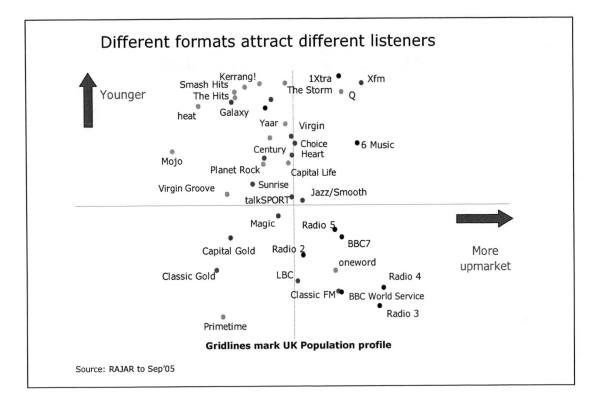

The other important factor has been the development of a greater variety of station formats catering for a broader set of tastes. The scatter chart shows how different stations attract very different audiences, allowing advertisers to target much more accurately.

# Who advertises on radio?

Because of its slow start in the seventies, radio was dubbed 'the two per cent medium' by advertising industry pundits, and growth was sluggish for many of the early years.

But 1992 was the pivotal year: the launch of a new audience research system (RAJAR), the launch of the first national station (Classic FM) and the launch of a unified business-to-business marketing strategy (Radio Advertising Bureau) created a tipping point for the industry.

As a result, many national advertisers began to reappraise the medium and growth from this sector helped advertising revenue to rise sharply through the nineties, and radio now carries about seven per cent of display ad revenue.

At the time of writing, commercial radio's top twenty advertisers – see table 5.6.1 – are mainly large corporate organisations with the emphasis on retailers, though the largest advertiser of all is COI Communications (government).

Since 1992, commercial radio advertising revenue has grown faster than the media market as a whole, making radio the fastest growing medium of the last decade.

**Figure 5.6.4**

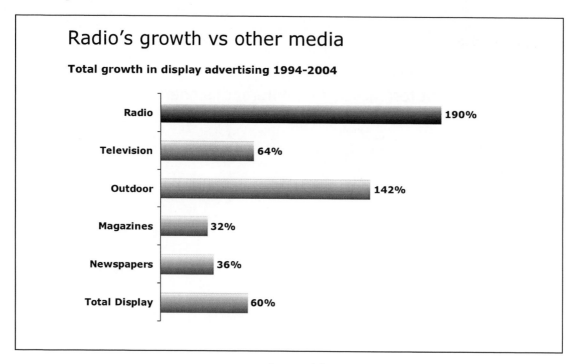

*Source: Advertising Association Quarterly Survey*

Table 5.6.1 **Radio's top twenty advertisers**

| Rank | Advertiser | Total radio spend (year ending October 2005) | Radioshare % |
|---|---|---|---|
| 1 | COI Communications | 33,729,713 | 19.4% |
| 2 | Unilever | 8,418,218 | 4.1% |
| 3 | Vodafone | 6,734,216 | 13.5% |
| 4 | Abbey | 6,373,397 | 24.4% |
| 5 | BT | 5,770,159 | 9.1% |
| 6 | 3 | 5,754,329 | 16.1% |
| 7 | Renault | 5,604,359 | 10.4% |
| 8 | Sky | 5,409,640 | 6.9% |
| 9 | Vauxhall | 5,290,815 | 8.2% |
| 10 | Ford | 5,234,829 | 8.7% |
| 11 | Sainsbury | 5,092,611 | 10.0% |
| 12 | Procter & Gamble | 5,026,103 | 2.7% |
| 13 | Camelot | 4,883,232 | 19.1% |
| 14 | Telewest | 4,402,393 | 46.2% |
| 15 | DFS | 4,120,401 | 5.0% |
| 16 | Specsavers | 3,679,658 | 13.9% |
| 17 | Toyota | 3,656,208 | 9.3% |
| 18 | Entertainment Films | 3,551,088 | 9.3% |
| 19 | T-Mobile | 3,418,393 | 8.3% |
| 20 | Nestlé | 3,416,845 | 5.0% |

Two observations on the nature of radio's top twenty spenders:

- They are mainly organisations with something to tell people – trying to get information across rather than just image advertising

- Most of them are 'response' advertisers – very few of their commercials fail to carry a clear call to action

## What will digital mean for commercial radio?

The digital era is upon us and radio is affected as much as other media. But it seems that radio is set to benefit from the change rather than suffer (as, for example, newspapers have done, with the role of classified advertising being usurped by the web).

Analysis suggests that there are three main factors that will drive further audience growth (number of listeners and time spent listening) for radio in the future:

- How radio is consumed

- Increased choice

- Increased accessibility

## How radio is consumed

More than any other, radio is an auxiliary medium. It is ideally suited to being listened to by people who are engaged in another activity at the same time (e.g. driving, cleaning, DIY, gardening and working – increasingly, using a computer) – 9 out of 10 people listen while doing something else.

So, while internet usage might mean downward pressure on the other primary media (it's difficult to watch TV at the same time as using the net), radio is set to gain. Indeed, latest research shows that one in five internet users is listening to the radio at the same time.

*Buena Vista used branded content to launch 'The Osbournes' DVD. When the first series of The Osbournes was launched on DVD the challenge was to find a way to make this more visible in a highly competitive market. The launch was publicised on Virgin Radio and extended into using live presenters playing a game with the listeners about the amount of swearing in the series! Results are confidential, but this is a good example of taking the essence of a product campaign and adapting it to suit the way radio editorial works well on-air.*

## Increased choice

We have already touched on the way increased choice of station formats has driven audience growth across the last 15 years. This choice is further augmented by the 130-plus commercial DAB services that currently exist. These roughly fall into four categories:

- Local digital simulcasts of existing analogue services

- Non-local digital simulcasts of local analogue services from other parts of the UK

- Digital-only brands developed by existing radio players (e.g. Capital Disney, Virgin's The Groove)

- Digital-only brands developed by industry newcomers (e.g. Abracadabra, Gaydar Radio)

## Increased accessibility

One of the most significant changes in radio over the past couple of years has been the growth in availability of radio through new platforms. Beyond DAB, the internet and digital television (Sky, cable and Freeview) offer significant choice to listeners. Another recent trend has seen radio receivers increasingly incorporated into other devices, such as mobile phones.

These shifts have led to a greater accessibility of the medium, creating new listening situations and occasions that in turn are contributing to greater listening – for example, listening at bus stops on mobiles.

The internet is a popular way to listen to radio, and has tended to be biased towards listening while at work, although this is likely to change as broadband households become more numerous. Internet radio users are more likely to be younger – reflecting the usage profile of computers in general.

Over half of households in the UK now have a digital television service, allowing access to radio stations as well as TV channels. The free-to-view service Freeview has been an important driver in digital television penetration over the last few years.

**Figure 5.6.5**

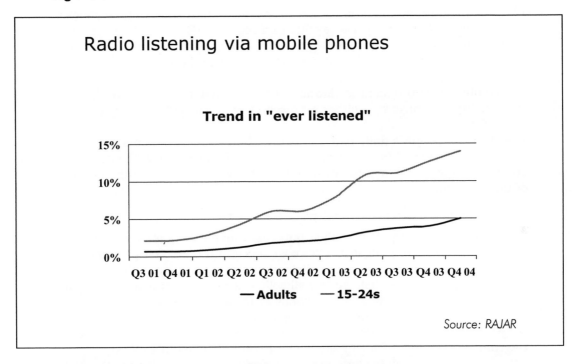

Mobile phones with radio receivers are becoming a part of everyday life, increasing opportunities to listen to the radio while on the move – again, this habit is more prevalent among younger listeners.

All these new technologies will have an impact on advertising response, so it will be vital to stay abreast of the changes as they develop. But it's important to point out that this is deliberately broad-brush advice here – these technologies and platforms are changing constantly (who would have predicted ten years ago that so many people would be listening to radio through their television set?). If you want more detail on aspects of digital listening, take a look at the websites recommended at the end of this chapter on radio.

# Radio as a communication medium

Radio has some unusual characteristics relative to other media – not least the fact that it is aurally rather than visually driven – and if you are going to use radio effectively you need to ensure you have a good grip on the way it works.

This chapter looks at the way people use the medium as listeners, and also the way media planners tend to use it in the media mix – including a look at a new study into the effects of ad avoidance, and the implications this has for using radio as an outreach medium.

## Functional and emotional needs from radio

There are two key facets to listeners' requirements from radio – the first is a functional requirement, while the second is an emotional one.

The functional requirement is the need for information – news, time checks, traffic news, weather or sports results. In a recent RAB research study, one respondent described how listening to the radio could make the difference between her journey to work taking 30 minutes or an hour and a half.

The emotional requirement is characterised by listeners in terms of the relationship they have with either a presenter or a particular show.

The reality of people's daily patterns is that the two requirements are not mutually exclusive – the balance between them changes across the course of a day according to listeners' moods, with stations being chosen according to the mood of the moment.

| | |
|---|---|
| **Breakfast** | At breakfast time, the functional element is at its highest. The most successful breakfast presenters are seen by listeners as those who are able to fulfil their functional role as a provider of news, travel and weather etc, while at the same time providing an emotional feel-good factor. |
| **Daytime** | During the daytime, radio is used in a classic background mode and listeners see this as a positive attribute. The relationship is uncritical and undemanding, with the result that the medium is used to create the right atmosphere to accompany daytime tasks. |
| **Evening/weekends** | Listening in the evening and at the weekends requires greater commitment on the part of the listener. Given the alternatives, principally television, the decision to turn the radio on is much more conscious and as such the attention and involvement levels during this period can often be higher. |

## How and why people listen

Most radio listening tends to take place when people are on their own, and doing something else as a primary activity.

It is common for radio listening to take place in a personal space such as the bedroom, bathroom, kitchen or car. Because of the solitary/personal nature of listening, they tend to personally choose the station themselves, rather than defaulting to a group decision.

The vast majority of radio listening is habitual, and occurs at the same time every day, particularly during the working week. People use radio to help them wake up, get ready and get out of the house – and then often on their journey.

This habitual listening behaviour also extends to station selection. Despite the huge proliferation in station choice, people stick to their favourites (the average listener chooses from a repertoire of 2.5 stations).

It is important to note that radio accounts for a surprisingly high share of the media day – about a third – and this is increasing as new listening opportunities arise.

**Figure 5.6.6**

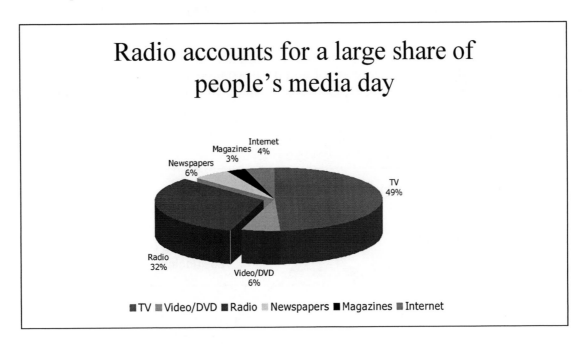

### The emotional role of radio

It should be clear by now that the emotional role played by radio in people's lives is huge. It keeps them going, lifts their spirits and alleviates feelings of loneliness or boredom during daily tasks.

This is one of the reasons why advertising on radio can make such a big impression: the advertiser is alone with the listener right inside their personal space (their kitchen or car), and at a time when the radio is being used to affect their mood.

The section on creativity offers advice on how to get the best out of this unique opportunity.

# Media planners' views of radio

The structure of the medium and the way it communicates have a direct effect on the way media planners use it in advertising campaigns: the main implications can be summarised in terms of targeting, presence and outreach.

## Targeting (audiences, modes and moods)

There are many stations which bring together listeners **who share a common interest**, be it a particular music genre such as classical or rock, jazz or dance music, sports, arts or books. Examples would include well-established stations such as Classic FM or Kiss FM, plus newer stations such as Planet Rock and Oneword.

With these stations there is a clear sense of who the listener is, both in terms of demographics and lifestyle. These stations play a valuable role in the lives of their listeners, helping them feel connected to their area of interest and defining who they are.

In terms of media effect, these stations are valuable for advertisers wanting a certain kind of positioning or set of brand associations (so, for example, a brand can begin to say something sophisticated about itself simply by appearing on a classical music station).

Figure 5.6.7

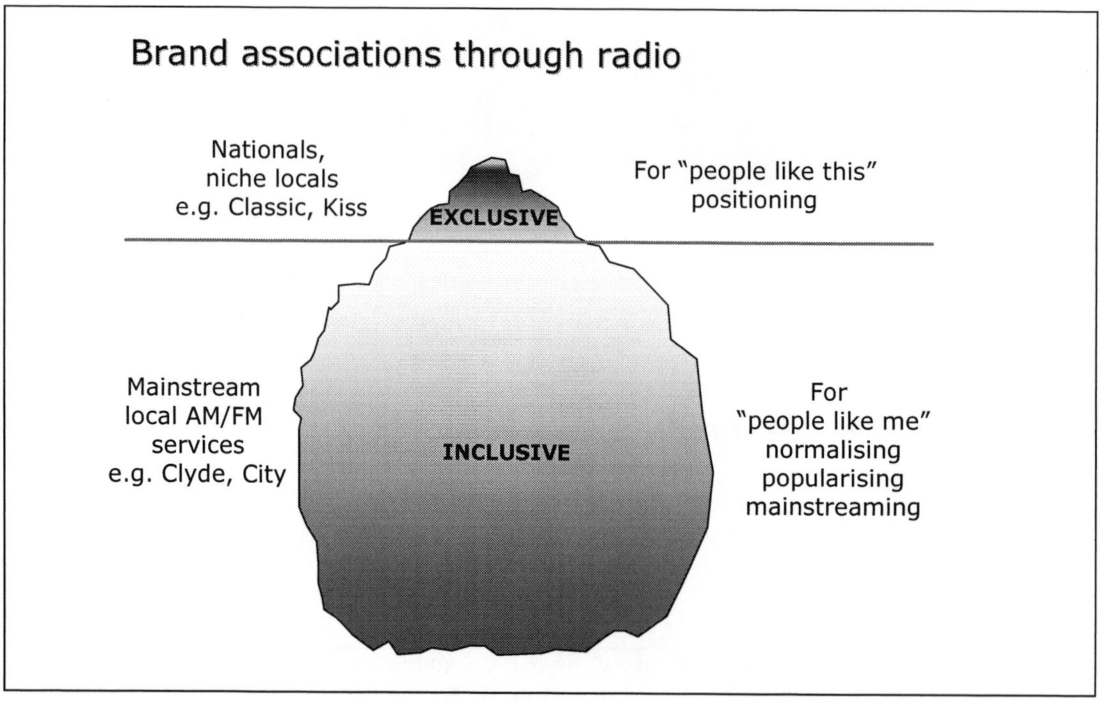

Brand associations through radio

Nationals, niche locals e.g. Classic, Kiss — EXCLUSIVE — For "people like this" positioning

Mainstream local AM/FM services e.g. Clyde, City — INCLUSIVE — For "people like me" normalising popularising mainstreaming

By contrast some stations are defined mainly by the fact that they reach people living within a certain area – typically the larger, established local stations.

Listeners to these types of stations tend to represent a broad mix of demographics, so listener image is less clearly defined. However, listeners tend to assume that the rest of the audience are 'people like me' (be that old, young, rich or poor).

The media effect of stations like these is to suggest that brands are popular, accepted and mainstream within the local culture. This acceptance is particularly valuable for newer brands and products.

Finally, because radio listening is used to accompany other tasks taking place across the day it is an effective means of targeting consumers when they are operating in a particular *mode*, or are looking to enhance a particular *mood*.

The benefit of this for advertisers is that advertising recall is higher when the listener is engaged in an activity that relates to an advertised brand – a test by Newslink showed that ad recall was 60 per cent higher among people who were doing something relevant to the subject of the advertising. (For more details see 'effectiveness research' at rab.co.uk.)

This is a particular strength of radio, where nine out of ten of those listening are doing something else at the same time.

**Nesquik making the most of school-run time:**

*Nesquik's marketing ambition is to be 'first drink home from school' and a radio campaign aimed at mothers of school-age children was devised in 2004. The campaign won awards for creativity, but one of the most important aspects was the scheduling – airtime was focused on school-run time, to catch mothers in their cars while they were contemplating what to do with their kids after school. Ad recognition scores were 50 per cent higher than those set in advance by researchers TNS as action standards for the campaign.*

## Presence

There are several factors that contribute to radio's ability to increase a brand's sense of presence or ubiquity.

Radio is often referred to as the *frequency* medium because it naturally builds higher levels of frequency than other mainstream media (e.g. TV and press). This happens even at relatively low rating levels as a result of habitual listening patterns.

Radio ads are 'on more often'

Average weekly frequency for different media
| | |
|---|---|
| TV | 1-2 OTS (opportunities to see) |
| Newspapers | 1-2 OTS (opportunities to see) |
| Radio | 3-4 OTH (opportunities to hear) |

Source: RAB/industry estimates

So radio allows brands to speak to consumers more regularly than other media. Because radio advertisers are 'on a lot' in a medium that accounts for a high share (a third) of the media day, planners often refer to radio as being good at enhancing a brand's *share of mind*.

This ability to create presence across the different dayparts is valuable for response advertisers, either because they can time their messages to be relevant for certain activities or because they can speak to people at critical moments in the day – such as the classic Monday morning moment, when matters like insurance phone calls tend to be sorted out.

For response-defined brands this can be hugely important, as the key issue is to be salient and available at the time when the consumer is in the right frame of mind...

... or approaching it; which is where we come to outreach.

### Using radio as an outreach medium

Advertising avoidance is very much a hot topic at the moment, and this has been stoked up most recently by personal video recorders like Sky+ which allow people to skim through the ads at high speed.

Some industry voices are suggesting that all this needs by way of a remedy is creativity – we need to make ads that consumers will want to watch. Many other voices think this is just too ambitious, and see the impending changes as 'apocalyptic'.

Where does advertising avoidance leave radio though? A study in the nineties by Initiative Media suggested that radio and cinema were the two media with the lowest levels of ad avoidance, but they are clearly not the same in terms of consumption – cinema is much more 'sit forward' while radio is an auxiliary activity.

So the RAB commissioned a new research project by Clark Chapman Research in 2005 to take a closer look at the way people treat the ads in different media. The study was done online, and the questionnaire asked respondents for each medium how much of the time they avoided the ads, engaged with the ads, or something in between (full details are available at rab.co.uk).

The results showed that, as in the Initiative study, radio and cinema are the two lowest avoidance media for advertising, and that ads in the static media (newspapers and magazines) are more avoided than ads in real-time media (cinema, radio and TV – although TV is far higher).

Figure 5.6.8

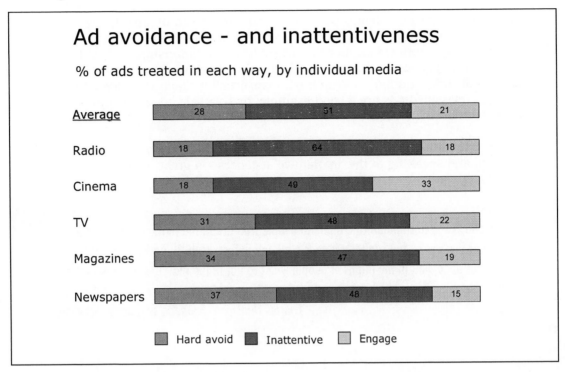

The results also showed that avoidance levels for direct mail were very high, and even higher for banners and pop-ups on the internet. For direct mail, anecdotal evidence suggests this is a function of 'junk mail' attitudes – many consumers have low expectations of the relevance or importance of direct mail. But with the internet they basically resent being interrupted in the old-fashioned way while they are trying to get something from a website.

Further analysis of the figures revealed that if avoidance levels are factored into estimates of audience reach – so in other words, the 16 to 44 TV audience would be factored down by 31 per cent, and radio's by 18 per cent – then commercial radio actually has a higher 'net outreach' than commercial TV.

Figure 5.6.9

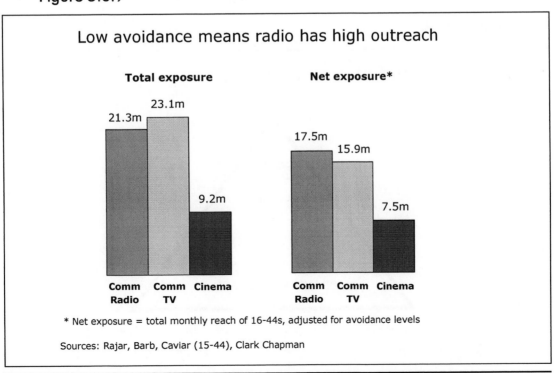

This is why radio is so valuable for reaching out to audiences.

In a world where advertising avoidance is rife, the breed of advertising which is most at risk is 'outreach advertising' – where companies are trying to reach out to new customers with whom they do not yet have a relationship. This is because people avoid the advertising which they think is irrelevant to them: they will still happily absorb- and indeed search out – advertising which they deem to be relevant (classified ads are a good example, or sofa sale ads for people in the process of buying a sofa).

Meanwhile radio's low avoidance levels mean that ads have a chance of cutting through and speaking to the 'inattentive' listeners – a great opportunity for advertisers seeking response.

"Radio allows you to communicate offers to people who are in the market to buy a phone in the next few weeks, but similarly it does a big job in just establishing your brand and some ideas about you in the minds of people who are not in the market right now, but are likely to be sometime in the future"

*Charles Dunstone, Founder, Carphone Warehouse*

# Effectiveness of radio

This section reviews what is known about the effectiveness of radio, and looks at the different forms that effectiveness measurement can take – particularly driving awareness, changing brand perceptions, driving sales and generating response.

We also include tips and hints on how to structure a test on radio to ensure the contribution of the medium is clearly identified.

For integrated advertisers, there are various levels at which advertising effectiveness can be interpreted – as depicted in the 'pyramid of effectiveness' chart, based on a project by Ocean Consulting for the RAB.

**Figure 5.6.10**

Over recent years, the radio industry has invested significant resource into demonstrating the effectiveness of radio in delivering against these different measures of success. In this section we take a brief look at the most significant effectiveness evidence.

## Driving awareness

The Awareness Multiplier, conducted by Millward Brown and published in 2000, focused on radio's ability to generate advertising **awareness**. This showed that radio was three-fifths as effective as TV on average, but at one-seventh of the price – making radio therefore potentially four times as cost-effective.

It's vital to note that these findings are based on 'the average ad' for both TV and radio – many ads will have a much weaker or stronger effect according to their content and creative approach (see the section on creativity).

The Millward Brown study also demonstrated the 'multiplier effect' – that the effectiveness of a TV budget could be improved by as much as 15 per cent, simply by redeploying 10 per cent onto radio.

Radio's 'multiplier effect'

There are many examples of campaigns where adding radio to a schedule has a multiplicative rather than additive effect – in other words, when the same advertising budget is redeployed away from TV or print and into radio, the overall total effect of the advertising is greater than in the original schedule.

The best known published examples are the Millward Brown Awareness Multiplier Study for the RAB (TV and radio), and the RAEL study in the USA where a similar finding was delivered for combining radio with print.

But why should this be?

One theory put forward is that, in a world where most marketing communications are visual, and most media are visual, radio advertising allows brands to access a different part of the consumer's mind – the non-visual, aurally-driven bit. No one has ever proved this to be true, but it does seem to make intuitive sense – sound and vision are processed in different parts of the brain.

## Shifting brand attitudes

Few norms or averages are available when it comes to assessing radio's ability to change brand attitudes (this is true of other media too). It's just not possible to average out the different effects that advertising has on different brands with different needs at different times in their cycles.

The best way to understand how radio affects brand attitudes is to look at case studies. A short list of recommended case studies is below:

**How radio affects attitudes to brands**

| | |
|---|---|
| Carphone Warehouse | Using radio as a brand-building medium |
| Make Autism Count | A bold strategy to change perceptions of autism |
| Confetti.co.uk | Using radio to create brand personality |
| Virgin Mobile | Creating brand excitement and participation |
| Freeloader.com | Creating an 'attitude' brand on-air |
| National Trust | Reinforce brand values and drive response |

All case studies at RAB online: rab.co.uk

## Creating sales effects

In terms of **sales, the most authoritative and helpful study is Dunnhumby's** *The Sales Multiplier* study. This used information from the Tesco Clubcard database to analyse correlations between sales in stores and advertising activity. It demonstrated that across a range of 17 grocery brands the average sales uplift attributable to radio was nine per cent.

**Figure 5.6.11**

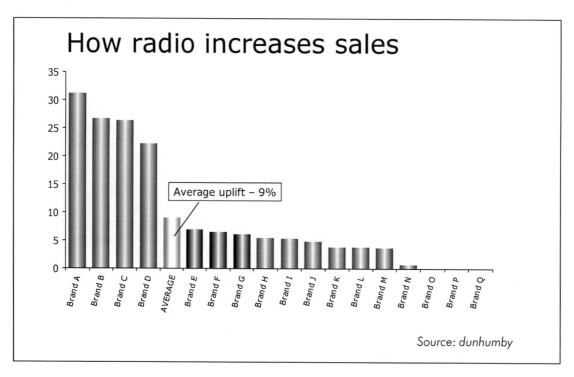

Importantly, the range of these sales effects is huge, reinforcing yet again that with radio creative approach is extremely important.

There was a further finding in the Dunnhumby study which is of special interest to people working in a response-driven or integrated advertising environment. It demonstrated that radio advertising augmented the positive effects of a brand's price promotion (it also affects competitor promotions – see 'effectiveness research' at rab.co.uk).

Figure 5.6.12

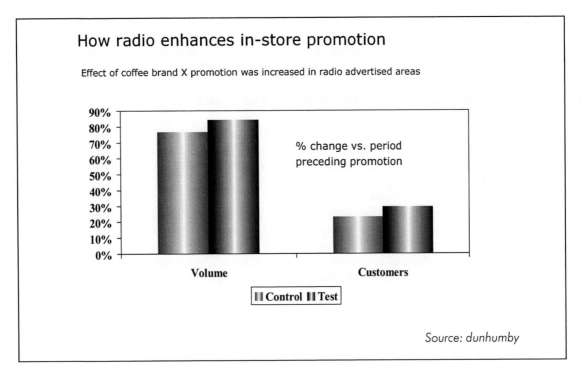

How radio enhances in-store promotion

Effect of coffee brand X promotion was increased in radio advertised areas

% change vs. period preceding promotion

Volume    Customers

Control  Test

Source: dunhumby

## *Generating response*

Before considering the rate at which consumers respond to offers on radio, it is always worth taking a step backwards.

As a listener, what would make *you* take the trouble to phone a number promoted on radio? How easy would it be to do so, especially if you were driving? How many times would you need to be reminded about the offer? Would it be easier to remember a website name than a phone number?

Remember – one in five people on the internet is listening to radio

This was revealed in a recent survey of 500 people who use the internet. Not only are 20 per cent of them listening to radio, but 57 per cent of them claim to have checked out something online after just hearing about it on the radio.

This is a very significant media conjunction, and suggests that integrated advertisers seeking response can advertise their website in the knowledge that many listeners are only a click away.

Source: Other Lines Of Enquiry, 2005

These are real-world questions which must colour any planning thought when creating response campaigns.

The key issue, as ever, is – how motivated do we expect the listeners to be when we tell them about the offer? In other words – how good is the offer? If the answer is 'not very', it's worth looking more closely at the business strategy – should the product be differentiated from rivals?

In reality, radio has been successfully used as a direct response medium from its very earliest days, when small local businesses would take money out of the till for radio ads only if there was a measurable effect. These days the principle is the same for many brands, even though the thinking has to be more sophisticated – e.g. for every £10 spent on advertising, how much is an investment in the brand values and how much is driving short-term response?

## The BT/GWR/DMA study on response radio

Case studies for direct response are very thin on the ground for radio (as they are for all media) because companies are reluctant to release commercially sensitive information which could be used in future negotiations. This study was designed to fill that gap.

It was conducted to discover what levels of response radio would elicit on average across a very broad range of campaigns. BT monitored telephone response in the minutes following the broadcast of radio advertising for dozens of campaigns (more details of the study are available at rab.co.uk) – the gross level of calls received was then compared to the number of people who were likely to be listening when the campaign was aired.

So for example, if there were 3,000 telephone responses within a quarter of an hour and the total size of the listening audience was 500,000 people, then the response rate was calculated by dividing one by the other – 0.006 per cent. This is a rather crude measure as it doesn't take account of targeting – some of the products advertised will have been irrelevant to many of the listeners – but it does offer a starting point.

Figure 5.6.13

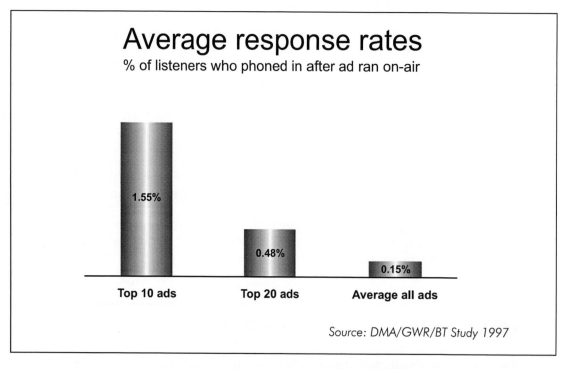

**Average response rates**

% of listeners who phoned in after ad ran on-air

1.55% — Top 10 ads

0.48% — Top 20 ads

0.15% — Average all ads

Source: DMA/GWR/BT Study 1997

As the chart shows, the variation in results was absolutely huge, with the top ten ads attracting a response of over 1 per cent (despite the irrelevance factor above) while the average for all ads was around 0.15 per cent. As this is ten times smaller, it is easy to see that some ads in the lower performing end must have been attracting very low responses indeed. This confirms yet again that, while there may theoretically be something called an average response rate, in the end it depends what the offer is, and how the offer is made.

## *Using radio for 'indirect response' (uplift medium)*

Because of the way people listen to radio – most of them are doing something else – and because radio advertising leaves no physical record behind, response ads on radio don't work in the same way as other media. People cannot select the ads as they do in the press, according to whether they decide they are relevant; they can't 'leaf through' a selection of commercials. The radio is just on, and people find themselves listening unexpectedly to those bits of the output which seem interesting.

In these conditions, what kind of role is radio likely to be most powerful at playing in driving response?

The answer seems to be an outreach role – bringing new products or ideas to the attention of people who might not otherwise be interested. Some will be interested enough to stop what they are doing and make a note of a web address or phone number, but for most who are listening, the main achievement of the advertising will be to leave them with some communication – persuaded, interested or stimulated etc.

**Case study for 'indirect response': Career Development Loans**

In the campaign for Career Development Loans (developed by COI Communications on behalf of the Department for Employment) radio was added on a regional basis to a national schedule of press inserts.

Career Development Loans constantly have to reach out to more and more new users, because they offer a one-off opportunity for people to make a career change by borrowing money at a very low rate of interest.

In the regions where radio was used, response to radio itself was not very encouraging – however, awareness of the loans doubled and response to the press inserts was 60 per cent higher than in the non-radio regions. It was concluded that radio advertising *created a climate* of awareness and interest in the offer within which response to the press inserts was accelerated.

This is an important finding, and makes intuitive sense: while the inserts were the point of contact for response mechanism, the role for radio was to spread awareness of the scheme and get people thinking about the benefits of it.

| | |
|---|---|
| Role for radio? | Is it to drive response directly, or indirectly via other media? Should the radio be literally directing them somewhere (website)? |
| Which stations to use? | Choose the stations which are best at reaching the kind of people you are targeting – radio groups can provide detailed listener data for each station, or a broader summary is available from the audience measurement website (rajar.co.uk). |
| Contact details? | People have trouble remembering numbers they are told, so it's worth considering whether people will be able to find your phone number or website themselves. Do you really need to devote airtime to spelling out contact details? |

| | |
|---|---|
| Texting, texting | Radio reaches people when they are out and about, and listeners are keen texters (most radio competitions are now dominated by text response). Can your advertising exploit the power of texting? |
| Testing, testing | In response advertising everything is a test: make sure you have structured your campaign to allow you to see what radio has contributed (see 'structuring a test'). |
| Station websites | Stations constantly direct their listeners towards the station websites: does it make sense for your response capture to focus there? |
| Terms and conditions | Remember radio has no 'small print'. If your offer requires terms and conditions to be spelt out, this will take up time in radio ads. This means that you will either have to buy extra airtime, or change the offer to avoid the need for terms and conditions – more advice is available from the RACC (see 'useful places'). |

## Structuring a test with radio

There is detailed advice elsewhere in this Guide about setting up tests for response advertising (see chapter 8.2), and radio is basically the same as any other medium – but there is one extra issue to consider. When people are asked about where they saw or heard advertising, they often hugely understate radio.

Major advertisers commonly find that people attribute advertising memories to TV *even when there was no TV activity and radio was the only medium used.*

Why is this? There is no definite answer but it seems to come down to two main reasons:

- Radio has a kind of informality about it, and there is nothing tangible left after an advertising message – if you heard about something on the radio, you may find yourself wondering whether in fact you had been told it by someone you know

- When people think of 'advertising', and particularly when they are asked about it, they tend to search visually, rather than thinking about things they might have heard

So if people can't remember that they heard about things via the radio, what can you do about it in terms of measuring effectiveness?

The simple answer is – structure the test to take account of this. For example, use radio regionally and compare the response from people in one region versus the other: then, regardless of where they think they saw or heard your message, you will be able to see the difference in response between the two regions.

**Case study**

*Broadcaster (name withheld) seeking new subscribers:*

| **REGION A** | **REGION B** |
|---|---|
| *TV campaign* | *TV campaign* |
| *Leaflets* | *Leaflets* |
| *Radio* | *No radio* |
| *Total response: 55,000 new subscribers* | *Total response: 47,000 new subscribers* |

*Radio clearly appears to have contributed an extra 8,000 subscribers when used in area A, even though many of those new subscribers did not cite radio when asked how they had heard about the offer.*

It's important, if you do this, to make sure that radio is the only variable tested – tests with several variables usually end up being impossible to read.

For more information on testing radio and advice on splitting samples go to RAB online – rab.co.uk.

# Get creative with radio!

In this chapter we review the key dos and don'ts for creativity that will really engage on radio, and look at the main points which advertisers need to bear in mind when looking at creative proposals.

## A clear role for radio

This may seem obvious but you'd be amazed how often radio advertising is used with rather vague intentions (this isn't unique to radio but because radio is seen as pretty simple, less thinking goes into strategic aspects like this).

The premise is very commonsensical – if you know clearly what radio is tasked with achieving, you will be able to tell whether it's worked or not.

Here are four different roles for radio in integrated advertising – there are more, but these will give you a starting point for clarifying your own objectives:

**Table 5.6.2**

| Role | Implication | Creative focus on |
|---|---|---|
| Change views of the brand | Make people feel differently about the brand – this is a longer term strategy unless you have some really opinion-changing news | Tone – how the brand is speaking to people |
| Familiarity/ ubiquity | Radio can create an extraordinary sense of ubiquity for a brand (because the ads are on often): this can create strong feelings of familiarity | Focus on brand identity - 'you recognise us' |
| Uplift response in other media | Radio can play a very strong role in creating awareness and interest in an offer, while actual response will come through another channel – maybe press or the web | Accessing the offer through other media – e.g. 'See today's Evening Standard' |
| Explain/flesh out an offer seen elsewhere | Radio is typically used with outdoor or TV in this respect – where a broad, eye-catching offer is made (say half-price tickets) and radio is used to explain a bit more about what kind of offer this is (e.g. how long the offer lasts, or for new customers, or for certain products) | Clarity and engagement – helping people to understand |
| Direct response only | This is where the listeners are given a very clear offer and asked to respond directly, e.g. by phone, text or web visit | Clear offer, clear response mechanism, very strong call to action (NB: Beware too much urgency on radio, which can begin to sound desperate) |

The roles are not mutually exclusive, and in fact you will see that it is quite difficult to focus on one without invoking any of the others. For example, if you focus very clearly on direct response, what might be the longer term effect on the advertiser brand? A series of short-term offers create a long-term impression.

## *Keep the brief simple*

It's a well-known motto in communications that the brief has to be simple – but radio has to be even simpler than that!

This is because of the way radio works.

Firstly you have to remember that everyone listening to the radio is doing something else, so you need to be clear and simple to make sure their attention doesn't wander back to whatever they are doing.

But the other reason is that radio is a sound-only medium, so everything has to be spelled out sequentially. This means that large amounts of detail aren't likely to get across on radio.

If you do have more complex things to say – maybe a series of different products with different benefits in the same range – make a series of ads. This allows each one of them to focus on a clear and simple thought.

> "If it's too complicated to explain easily on the phone, it's definitely too complicated for radio."
>
> *Anon*

## Ask for the team with radio skills

Radio is a challenging medium – no pictures, powerful tonal values, a writer's medium, and strongly dependent on production.

Under these conditions, it's worth making sure that your radio advertising is created and executed by people who are familiar with the medium and good at exploiting it.

## If you're not sure – ask to hear their reel

It's funny really, because radio looks easy. After all – a studio, a voiceover, a few sound effects, a bit of music … what's so complicated about that? But it's only when you have a go that you realise that *good* radio (engaging, effective radio) is quite tricky.

## Take care over tone

Radio makes a strong tonal impression, in the sense that the listener gets a feeling about the way that an advertiser is addressing them – sure-footed, professional, desperate or trying-too-hard-to-be-funny etc.

The spoken word is a very tonal medium – full of undertones and overtones. For example, think of the way people come across on the phone you get a strong sense of the kind of people they are even if you have never met them. This is less clear from, say, reading something they have written.

## Use the right judging criteria

Judging is a challenging stage of the process for advertising in any medium, but perhaps even more so with radio because it is the only medium where there are no visuals to help.

This leads to a terrible temptation to focus on the words, whereas in fact the impact or 'engagingness' of a commercial often depends on the way the words are said – which includes the pauses, and you can't see the pauses on the script.

So, how can you judge what is *not* written?

Ask for the script to be brought to life by being read out or even recorded (but note – demo versions aren't always helpful if you are trying to judge tone or feel). Storyboards can also be helpful, as can the use of audio material from elsewhere to explain the intended tone of the ads.

Having done this, you may feel confident that the commercial will engage the listener emotionally but will your brand benefit from this in the intended way? The three key questions that we recommend for judging radio ideas are:

Key questions to ask when judging creative work:

- What will make the listener zone in?

- How is this linked to the brand and its message?

- What tonal impression of the brand will the advertising leave with the listener?

Consider using these techniques when selling radio work within your own company – they are valuable for protecting the good ideas.

## Use pre-production

Pre-production is a standard practice in TV mainly because, given the amount of money that TV production requires, it is important to ensure the finished product comes out right. It's important in radio on the same basis.

Pre-production can answer really important questions before the ad gets to the studio:

- Is the script really 30"?

- How much legal copy is required, if any? What effect will this have on the overall time-length?

- What music is going to be used and are there usage issues?

- Are sound effects required? Does the studio have these and will they do the job required of them?

- Who are we casting? Why are they the most suitable person for this role?

If these questions are unanswered when everyone gets to the studio, it will cost money to answer them!

## Consider using a director

Radio directors are a relatively new and rare breed, but increasingly agencies are beginning to use them. This is primarily because of the way they lead sessions in the studio – getting the best performance out of actors, and also pulling together the input of client and agency during the session.

But directors can also be helpful further back in the process. Rather like TV directors, they can advise informally on scripts as they are developing.

Table 5.6 3    **Creative issues – FAQs**

| How many different ads do I need? | The answer is probably 'more'. The thing which most irritates listeners is repetition. Remember, the average listener hears the average commercial four times in the average week. Over a month that's sixteen times. |
|---|---|
| How many times does the website need to be repeated in the ad? | It may not need spelling out at all. If you have a website which is tricky to find, or your brand name is hard to spell, it might be worth devoting time to this – otherwise, rely on the fact that if people want what you have, they will find your website! |
| Is it possible to have direct-response commercials which also positively build the brand? | Definitely. It just means running ads which, even for the people who are not yet in the market, leave a positive general impression about the brand. |

For this creativity section we acknowledge the help of *How to be a good radio client*, presented by Adrian Reith of Radioville and Ralph van Dijk of Eardrum at the October 2004 conference *Getting serious with radio creativity*.

# Useful places to go for more information

Table 5.6.4

| Radio Advertising Bureau | Exists to guide advertisers and agencies towards the effective use of radio | Rab.co.uk(see especially sections on 'effectiveness', and 'guide to using radio for direct response') |
|---|---|---|
| Radio Advertising Clearance Centre | Exists to ensure that ad copy meets regulations | Racc.co.uk |
| Digital Radio Development Board | Promotes take up of DAB digital radio | Drdb.co.uk |
| Ofcom | Sets the regulations for commercial radio broadcasting | Ofcom.org.uk |
| Rajar | Radio audience listening figures | Rajar.co.uk |

# Getting started in online advertising

## This chapter includes:

----------------------------------------

- ❏ **An introduction to online advertising**
- ❏ **The digital networked society**
- ❏ **The online ad market**

 **The broadband revolution**

- ❏ **Setting marketing objectives**
- ❏ **Creating your campaign**

 **Setting objectives**

 **The right formats**

 **The right sites**

 **Trading models**

 **Harnessing targeting power**

 **Reach and frequency**

 **Campaign integration**

 **Measuring success**

----------------------------------------

## About this chapter

**O**nline advertising presents a richer choice of tools, targeting, messaging and engagement than any other media channel. During the first digital decade the toolkits broadened rapidly to match the benefits of all previous forms of marketing: whatever tool or objective you have in classic media, you'll now find a mirror in digital advertising.

Yet that diversity can be one of the core challenges in effectively engaging with online. Follow the classic principles of setting your objectives, building out the campaign idea and then getting creative and media teams to work together on format selection and the media plan. These same processes will stand you in good stead for online marketing, but remember to integrate the digital elements of your campaign from the start and get all stakeholders – internal and external – talking together. The good news is that harnessing this potential involves building on the traditional principles of advertising, marketing and media planning. The tools and technologies are no substitute for great marketing ideas, but when harnessed well they can accelerate the potential of what's possible.

The pace of development in online advertising has been breathtaking, outstripping the product innovation in all other media at such a vast scale that no guide will be able to give you a comprehensive picture of what is available. With that in mind I've focused on some core principles and in this chapter introduce the formats and map out the scope of what's common in online advertising. There are hints and tips for best practice and a flavour of where the industry is going as well as where it's come from. A course like this can only scratch the surface of what's possible in such an expanding and exciting market. If anything is unclear then drop me an email, mentioning the IDM Guide so I know where you found my details.

## Danny Meadows-Klue

Danny Meadows-Klue co-founded the Internet Advertising Bureau in the UK and was its first chief executive and both UK and European chairman for more than four years. He set up Digital Strategy Consulting in 2000 to help firms make sense of the rapid changes brought about by the digital world, and show them how to harness the potential of the digital networked economy. He has been an international commentator on the digital networked industries since the mid nineties and is recognised as a leading worldwide authority on digital marketing. Back in 1995 he crossed from print publishing to manage the UK's first online newspaper (telegraph.co.uk) where he stewarded it to win Newspaper of the Year repeatedly. He has helped run web businesses ranging from mass market portals and consumer magazines, to online stores and search and email services.

Alongside the UK and European IABs, he has helped launch twenty digital trade associations and initiatives around the world. He has acted as an advisor in the DTI and Home Office, and retains roles on advisory boards for digital investment funds and digital firms. He has been lecturing on digital marketing and publishing for more than a decade and has been awarded fellowships of the Institute of Direct Marketing, and the Royal Society of Arts. He is an enthusiastic educationalist and continues to teach university Masters courses and management courses. He is the inaugural chair of the examination board for the first Diploma in digital marketing, and a longstanding board member of the Journal of Digital Marketing.

Chief Executive
Digital Strategy Consulting
Danny@DigitalStrategyConsulting.com
The Digital Hub, 34 Kenway Road
Kensington, London SW5 0RR

# Chapter 5.7

# *Getting started in online advertising*

> "The changes that happen in the next five years will dwarf what we saw in the first digital decade
>
> *D. Meadows-Klue*

## Introduction

To understand the role and power of online advertising, it's best to combine the theory of marketing with hands-on experience of the models, the creative and the marketing activity that's out there. In this chapter I've outlined some of the key concepts that drive the online advertising industry, but as you read through, open up a browser, go online and look for examples of these ideas in use. Let's start right away ...

---

**A simple exercise to get us started**

To get yourself in thinking mode about online advertising, spend half an hour visiting the leisure sites you enjoy. Look at the advertising and save a copy of the banners, buttons and search messages that you find most interesting. Click through to the landing page and consider the marketing models the advertiser is using. Is this about brand building or driving response?

Think about the role of the ad, the landing page, and the next step in the journey.

Is this activity online happening in isolation, or is it integrated with other media?

---

What strikes you straightaway about online is its diversity. There's a vast array of formats and tools out there. In fact you'll find an online mirror for just about any form of marketing communications activity you could conduct offline.

Why does online prove to be so compelling?

1.  Precision in the audience you reach

2.  Certainty to reach your audience, however niche or mass market

3.  Accountability in the deliverability of the message

4.  Rapid standardisation of formats that have crossed hurdles to let your campaign run across thousands of sites unchanged

5.  Immediacy in the response, and transparency in the effectiveness

6.  Optimisation of the creative to boost returns while the campaign runs

7.  Activation in the response because you can link deeply into your own site

8.  Incredible diversity of formats and choices to match every need  a marketer has

9.  Low cost of entry through search engine advertising

10. All of which contrasts to the gradual weakening of the cost-effectiveness of traditional channels as the media landscape is transformed

### Figure 5.7.1  The online advertising mix

*Source: DigitalStrategyConsulting.com, getting to grips with online media sales,*
*November 2006*

**Some simple facts about online advertising**

If you're in any doubt about the scale of the online industry and its impact on consumers, then here are a few facts written in the autumn of 2006 to help give you some context:

•   The online ad market will be larger than national newspapers at the end of 2006

•   The online ad market is close to half the size of the TV market in the UK

•   The search engine advertising sector is larger than the consumer magazine sector

- People in the UK spend 40 to 50 days a year online

- There are more than 50,000 new installations of broadband every week in the UK

- Microsoft believes that the online ad market will be worth $51 billion by 2009, that's 9 per cent of the total US admarket for 2009

- The shapes and sizes for online ads in the IAB's Universal Advertising Package are running across more than 100,000 European websites

## *Welcome to the digital networked society*

"The explosive growth of internet advertising is about the sudden arrival of what I call the digital networked society. This step-change in the techno-media landscape has created a seismic shift in consumer behaviour. As audience attention switches into digital networked media, consumers unlock the power of near-perfect knowledge that the web delivers. They also take control of their media and ownership of their attention in a way never before seen. Let's be clear: the rules of marketing engagement have changed forever."

*D. Meadows-Klue*

### 1. Rapid growth in the number of people connected

More than 30 million people in the UK have used the internet and more than 23 million are described as being 'active', logging on at least once a month. Active users represent the addressable market because they have regular, rather than occasional, usage behaviour. The size of this group has trebled since the spring of 2000, and according to Ofcom figures published in the summer of 2005, the vast majority of these people log on several times per week. Although the total number of people who had used the internet was above 15 million at the start of 2000, for most, that use was so infrequent and light that its effects were negligible.

It is only more recently that using websites has become a routine behaviour in the mass market. This shift has taken place extremely fast. Firms operating in markets affected by internet services will only have started to feel its effects relatively recently. Growth in the number of active users continues to be strong. The behaviour of active users continues to intensify, further enhancing the effects of this migration of people's focus towards the web.

### 2. High intensity of use

Within this active group of people there has been a dramatic shift in the frequency with which each person accesses. Frequency is a good indicator of the importance people place on the media channel, because it helps reveal where their focus is. The majority of people who have access to the internet use it daily, and among those with broadband more than two-thirds are online every day. Using the web or email has become a routine experience for 23 million people and the pattern of use among individuals grows over time as they access more often and spend longer online.

**People using the web spend an average of 23 hours a week online**

# British internet users spend 50 days a year surfing web

**Bobbie Johnson**
Technology correspondent

The average British internet user spends the equivalent of more than 50 days a year online, according to a new survey that backs up claims the net is replacing television as the public's medium of choice.

The study shows net usage has risen dramatically over the past few years, with surfers now spending an average of 23 hours a week online. Web surfing is the main activity, taking up eight hours. Responses from more than 15,000 people to internet polling company YouGov found online games account for almost five hours, and users spend an average of three hours and 26 minutes on email.

Shopping and online banking register less than two hours a week but the survey found almost two and a half hours a week are spent watching online TV or video. One hour and 52 minutes go on telephone calls over the net.

"Games, TV and telephone are all driving broadband – people are seeing it as more of an access to other media, rather than just for sending email and looking at pictures of the kids," said Andrew Ferguson of broadband consumer website ADSLguide.org.uk. "Listening to the radio online is normal now, and watching television is getting more like that."

The news will concern broadcasters and telecoms companies struggling to cope with the rapid shift away from traditional delivery. The media regulator, Ofcom, has found that British people spend on average 19 hours a week watching television, but figures released this year by web portal Google suggested internet use was outstripping TV viewing.

YouGov's figures confirm that trend, a shift accelerated by recent developments in the speed of connections. Broadband has sped up rapidly over the past year as the market for internet providers becomes more competitive and BT is forced to give access to telephone exchanges. Some companies are able to deliver internet connections almost 500 times faster than traditional dial-up internet, and Britain has almost 12 million broadband users.

"It's very exciting to see Britain taking broadband by the scruff of the neck and making full use of the online world," said Chris Williams of uSwitch, which commissioned the YouGov survey.

New broadband lines are being installed at the rate of 50,000 a week but there are signs the market is slowing. Three-quarters of a million people signed up for high-speed internet in the last quarter, the lowest growth for two years.

Some analysts have blamed the slowdown on a backlog caused by products such as Carphone Warehouse's TalkTalk service, which offers free broadband if customers subscribe to one of its telephone offers. TalkTalk has activated accounts for up to 250,000 users since launching in April but it is believed up to 400,000 customers are still waiting to be connected.

**Television is giving way to the internet**

guardian.co.uk/technology »

*Source: guardian.co.uk*

## 3. Time spent with the internet continues to rise

Time spent online is another good indicator, and again research from many sources reveals a radical shift in the role of the internet. By examining the amount of time spent with each media channel, the scale of this migration can be better appreciated. The dynamics of media substitution are complicated, but the scale of the change is clear and unprecedented.

Ten years ago internet use was confined to a small academic and technical elite. By the autumn of 2004 UK internet users were clocking up 11.3 hours online each week and by January 2006, the BMRB Internet Monitor tracking study was reporting that internet users spent one-quarter of all their weekly time with a media channel, with the internet. This places the internet as the second most commonly used media channel after television, up massively since BMRB's 2004 tracker which recorded internet in third place, behind radio as well as television – though still accounting for one-quarter of all media time.

"There's an essential role for advertisers and advertising. At Microsoft we already sell over $2 billion of online advertising a year. I expect advertising to be the single fastest growing part of the revenue mix of Microsoft over the next few years; it's the priority one issue and opportunity. The online area is primarily funded through advertising. It's exploded but I see it as continuing to accelerate. During the next ten years all forms of consumer media will go digital."

*Steve Ballmer, CEO, Microsoft, October 2006*

## The broadband revolution

### 1.  Broadband: explosive growth of high-speed access

The rise in the use of broadband access is recent and its implications significant. Since June 2005, the majority of British homes connected to the internet have connected with the faster broadband connections. More than eight million homes and businesses use broadband, and according to the Office of National Statistics the UK broadband market rose by 70 per cent from July 2004 to July 2005, by which time 54 per cent of all UK internet connections were through broadband. By January 2006, BMRB were reporting this number had grown to around three-quarters of all home internet users in the UK (eighteen million people). They also noted that four million people had used a wireless connection at home. By the end of 2005 99.6 per cent of UK homes were connected to a broadband-enabled exchange (reported Ofcom), which means there is no longer a structural restriction on the potential supply of broadband.

### 2.  Why is broadband so important?

Broadband access removes previous constraints on internet use. The faster speeds let material download immediately and provide for a seamless user experience, while the 'always on' connections encourage more frequent use. Broadband accelerates online advertising.

### 3.  Are there any demographic patterns?

Broadband users tend to be higher in socio-economic status. The majority of the AB demographic group have home access, and there is a strong correlation between broadband use and high disposable income.

Figure 5.7.2 **A step-change in the frequency of internet use**

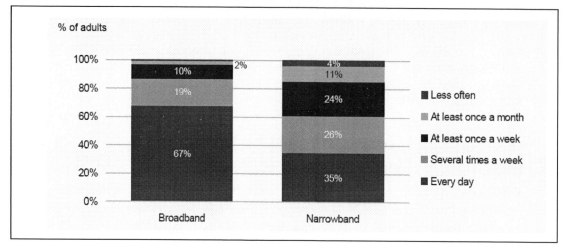

Source: Ofcom, July 2005

# Sizing up the online advertising market

## Understanding the nature of the growth

The European online media markets restructured quickly after the dotcom collapse of 2001. The resurgence that followed has been fast and steep, and has touched every country. Ten years of gradual increase in the role the web plays in people's lives has now started to be quantified. The radical change in the daily media consumption of people across the continent has seen online account for a quarter of the time most people spend with media. Among some younger demographics online has even overtaken television to become the lead media channel they choose, and the advertising markets are now responding, moving at a quicker pace than ever before to catch up with where their audiences have shifted to. The scale of this restructuring in media presents structural barriers for many firms to harness, but the trajectory of change is clear.

## €4.6 billion: the minimum total market size

European online advertising spend comfortably broke €4.5 billion in 2005 for the first time, yielding a total of €4,572 million for the markets surveyed. Data was collated from the 14 national IAB trade associations and their partner research houses, and although the methodologies and data sets vary significantly, consistent patterns still emerge. Because data sets were not available in several countries – including Sweden, Norway, most of the Balkans and the Baltic States – this represents a minimum market size.

The in-depth interviews that accompanied our Digital Europe research (DigitalStrategyConsulting.com, July 2006) revealed that a cascade effect is clearly underway as key opinion formers in each country's marketing community discover the potential of these new tools and deeply embrace online. As an innovation online marketing is poorly distributed, and it is not unusual to see two firms within the same sector behave radically differently. One may be putting more than 25 per cent of its advertising budgets into online, while another may be yet to move beyond tokenism. When the change in behaviour comes, initially it is concentrated within just a few firms. Its spread to the entire market leads to significant disparities along the way between the use of online in different marketing sectors as well as different firms.

## Why market share is the key metric

Examining the market share online enjoys of the total media spend in each country is one of the most effective ways of gauging how digitally sophisticated an advertising economy is. In 2005 online advertising took more than five per cent of all advertising spend in three European markets and more than eight per cent in one. Many more countries are closing on the five per cent threshold this year and that equates to online media spend moving ahead of other channels such as radio. We consider the two per cent threshold to be a convenient delineator for when online is considered a 'mainstream' media channel, and eight European markets have already passed this tipping point: Belgium, Denmark, Finland, France, Germany, the Netherlands, Poland and the UK.

This research only presents officially recognised data from each market, and with search engine advertising proving difficult to track in most countries, these figures probably understate the real market size. Only in the UK has an official declaration of revenues by leading search engines removed any ambiguity in the data, and this probably contributes a little to the disproportionately large share of online adspend that the UK accounts for (42 per cent of all European spend). Were search to be fully factored in, then Italy too would be reaching the two per cent threshold.

Figure 5.7.3   **The UK market – more than 40 per cent up year-on-year and half the size of TV**

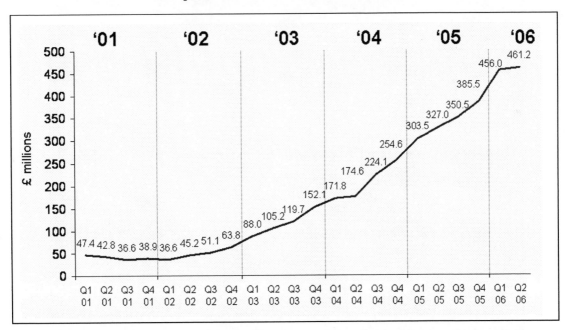

*Source: IAB UK / PricewaterhouseCoopers, September 2006*

With online advertising figures among the most accurate data sets in the digital networked economy, these figures can be used to understand much wider trends in the digital marketing industry. It may appear to be a crude technique, but the well- documented growth of online advertising acts as an excellent barometer for the wider digital marketing industry, from the switch to customer acquisition through search engine optimisation through to the migration of retention marketing into email. Back in 1997 I helped create the methodology and structure for the UK's official figures, an audit of online adspend by PricewaterhouseCoopers that has been copied around the world. This historic data set unveils rich insights that can be applied to other markets' developments. It also reveals complex patterns of seasonality and adoption by different advertiser categories. However, for a marketing channel that prides itself on accountability, there is an irony that structural weaknesses remain in most other data sets, so the figures for online advertising spend hold implications way beyond the search keywords, banners, rich media, classifieds and tenancies that they set out to count.

## Table 5.7.1

| Country | Total online adspend 2005 (€ million) | Market share (%) | Increase 2005 on 2004 |
|---|---|---|---|
| Austria• | €35m | — | 20% |
| Belgium* | €41m | 2.1% | 38% |
| Denmark | €81m | 6.0% | — |
| France | €1,100m | 5.5% | 74% |
| Finland | €36m | 3.0% | — |
| Germany | €885m | 4.4% | 60% |
| Greece | €15 | 0.8% | 25% |
| Italy | €138m | 1.5% | 16% |
| Netherlands• | €90m | 3.0% | 49% |
| Poland• | €26m | 2.0% | 60% |
| Romania* | €2m | 1.5% | — |
| Slovenia | €4m | 1.4% | 40% |
| Spain* | €150m | 1.5% | 50% |
| UK | €1940m | 7.8% | 63% |

• Annual market value based on actual figures for part of the year

\* Market value based on estimates from industry body

Please note:

- The estimate of the Austrian market is based on actual figures for H1 2005

- The value of the Finnish market does not include spend on search or directories

- The value of the French market is based on ratecard value

- The value of the German market does not include spend on classified advertising

- The value of the Italian market does not include spend on search

- The estimate of the market in the Netherlands is based on actual figures for Q1, 2 and 3 2005

- The estimate of the Polish market is based on actual figures for H1 2005

- The estimate of the Romanian market is based on actual figures for 2004

- The exchange rate used to calculate the value of the UK market in Euros was £1: €1.42

*Source: Digital Europe, DigitalStrategyConsulting.com July 2006*

## Market share reveals the Digital Giants and the Digital Sophisticats

Europe's 'digital giants' – UK, France and Germany – continue to account for more than 85 per cent of all online adspend in Europe, but the share of spend online takes within Scandinavia reflects that countries such as Denmark are also among the leaders in terms of how digitally sophisticated their marketing industry is. The UK is uniquely a Digital Sophisticat *and* a Digital Giant, and that's why the market proves such an exciting laboratory for other countries to learn from. When data for the rest of Scandinavia is available more Digital Sophisticats will be discovered.

The UK continues to lead the pack, both in terms of total online spend as well as market share which crossed eight per cent in the summer to yield an average of 8.4 per cent of all media spend across the second half of 2005. All this follows from twelve consecutive record-setting quarters.

However, the latest figures we've collated also reveal the stark contrasts between the more advanced networked economies of North West Europe and those of the Mediterranean, or the emerging faster growth markets of Central and Eastern Europe (CEE). The CEE markets are growing at relatively fast rates, and among the former Soviet Bloc countries the legacy of fewer traditional media channels, combined with an advertising industry that is both young in age and in tenure, is providing the conditions for a leapfrog effect in the use of marketing channels. With a less entrenched traditional media legacy the conversion to online will be faster.

### Figure 5.7.4    Digital Giants: the UK, France and Germany

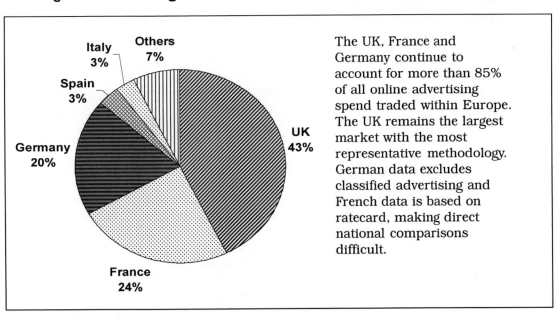

The UK, France and Germany continue to account for more than 85% of all online advertising spend traded within Europe. The UK remains the largest market with the most representative methodology. German data excludes classified advertising and French data is based on ratecard, making direct national comparisons difficult.

*Source: Digital Europe, DigitalStrategyConsulting.com August 2006*

### Search engines change customer acquisition marketing for good

Search has fundamentally changed direct marketing. Not all brands have realised this yet, and even among those who have, relatively few have gone on to unlock its full potential. What the founders of Google, Overture and Espotting stumbled upon at the very moment of the dotcom crash was the golden formula for customer acquisition. In the UK last year the search engine market was worth more than the whole radio advertising sector, and this year it should top consumer magazines. All this just six years after Google hired its first international employee in London. It's still staggering when you reflect on the pace of that growth.

The switch to search engine keywords is not just a switch to an entirely new advertising format; it's the switch to a model native to the medium. Since 2000 at Digital Strategy, we've been talking about the Digital Networked Economy, and the unique aspects of how it behaves. Search exemplifies this, harnessing social networking with customer empowerment and transparent pricing. Frictions in the supply of advertising are removed, and through dynamic bidding the price paid equates to the customer's value.

But it's also the switch back to an old direct marketing model, but one enriched by new efficiencies. Paying a fixed price to acquire a customer, and then bringing them straight into the sales pipeline of the business is a powerful offer. Harnessed with a web analytics engine and under the control of smart marketers, what you have is no longer 'advertising' spend, but a new factor in the cost of sales. Press your foot down to acquire more customers, and take your foot off the gas when your firm reaches capacity constraints; marketers are truly driving the business.

The explosive growth of search engine listings is strongest in the UK, but a common theme across Western Europe and Scandinavia. As Google and Yahoo build out their offerings in Central and Eastern Europe, a combination of increased supply and ramped- up marketing, will see direct marketing in those countries flip even faster than it has in France and Germany.

(For a thorough explanation of Search Engine Marketing, see chapter 5.8.)

"We can develop ways to target consumers by their preferences. The consumer and the advertiser have exactly the same intent in this space. The advertising isn't interruptive, it's part of the consumer experience."

*Steve Berkowitz, Senior Vice President, Microsoft Digital Advertising Solutions, October 2006*

## Building stronger brands

Ironically, one key challenge that held the industry back was its diversity. Because online can support any aspect of the marketing mix, the breadth of choice can be daunting. Smart online marketers realise it's about more than having a successful website. They've discovered how online marketing can support every step in the customer's journey – from the early stages of raising awareness of a brand, through the sale itself, and into the after sales service. That's why the proportion of investment into online continues to grow as more and more firms discover the power of web advertising as both a branding and direct marketing medium. This explains why not only is the growth unstoppable during the next five years, but the way agencies work needs to change.

"The world of media is changing and agencies across Europe need to be braver in crafting a new mix of media that really explores the rich variety of digital tools available and the vast European audiences you can reach with them."

*Nigel Morris, President Worldwide of the communications agency Isobar*

## Advertisers: take a second look

All this has profound implications for client-side marketers. If the last time you thought about online was six months ago, then whichever country you are in, it's time to take a fresh look. This is a medium that does anything but stand still, and the reason it remains the fastest growing marketing channel in history is the power of its results. Whether for brand building or direct response, firms are turning to online, upweighting its role and using the expanding range of tools to create the right digital media mix for them.

## Media substitution clearly underway

The migration of advertisers from one channel to another is now clear. Much of online's growth has been at the expense of other channels; with spend migrating from the printed newspapers, magazines and directories into online properties. Some new spend has come from sales promotion and PR budgets, and search is benefiting from a reappraisal of direct mail. New models of integrated media are emerging, but as yet, while they remain intuitively smart, they usually lack the analytics to quantify the optimisation of each media channel. Gradually this will change, and as it does, those who need the structure of currencies and ratings to support their media planning decisions will have the confidence to fully embrace online. The new formats will enable the transition of television campaigns to the web, initially building frequency and extending the reach of existing TV campaigns, but later routinely creating new television style assets as a core element in all TV campaigns.

"It's no longer a question of whether to invest; it's now a matter of how much. Marketers have realised there is no escaping the enormous impact that digital is having. The key now is to work out how to fit this new opportunity into the rest of the marketing mix."

*Michael de Kare-Silver, Managing Director of the AKQA*

The role of direct mail continues to suffer as acquisition budgets are redirected into search, and retention budgets into email (the spend which is not currently quantified). Meanwhile classified advertising in newspapers and magazines is finally migrating to the web and although recruitment is the largest single advertising sector online in several markets, much of the ad spend simply evaporates as the customer communication takes place either through the client's own website or through the vast range of free-to-place services like CraigsList.org and GoogleBase. While there are good examples of traditional media firms that are mounting good responses to this 'disintermediation' – the Guardian, Business Week, the International Herald Tribune, Haymarket Consumer Publishing, for example – the actions of most media groups remain either inherently weak, or reflect pragmatism over strategy.

Figure 5.7.5    **Restructuring the media industry: tracking year-on-year growth for the first half 2006**

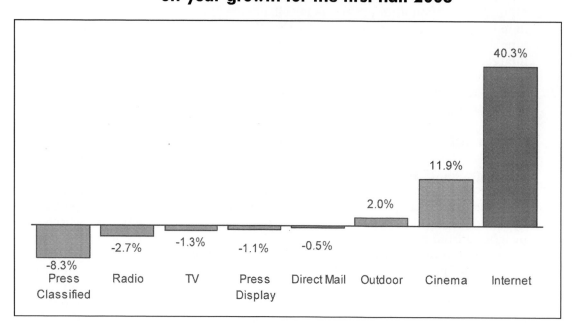

*The change in advertising spend year-on-year for comparable half years January to June 2006 versus January to June 2005:*

Source: PricewaterhouseCoopers / Internet Advertising Bureau UK, The Advertising Association / WARC

## Client sectors: who tops the charts?

Financial services and recruitment are the largest two client categories in many countries. Their products are a natural fit with the early web environments and as the firms refocused their marketing to include the web, audiences found the services useful and a virtuous circle developed. This has changed a great deal from the early days when IT and telecoms dominated the market. In the mid-nineties their products were a perfect fit for the first wave of web users whose interests and employment were heavily skewed in favour of the same sectors. Then came the sectors whose products could be reviewed, inspected, compared and even sold, without the need to touch them: books, CDs and travel among the higher profile movers. Although every sector has its own early adopters, the migration in the marketing industry's focus only happens when enough firms realise the potential of the new marketing channel.

Structural barriers held back many sectors, and this remains the case in the less digitally sophisticated markets. For example, the lavish advertising creative of the motoring industry rendered poorly in the early online advertising formats, but the rapid take-up of video and 'rich media' since 2002 has tackled this. Fast moving consumer goods (FMCG) were unconvinced initially because of concerns over the audience reach of online, and because the model of how it drove offline sales was unclear.

Before search keywords arrived small and local firms found the internet particularly difficult to engage with and most held back for a long time. Even for the first few years after the dotcom crash they were telling us how they found it difficult to get started because there was no roadmap. Many of the routes they tried proved to be time consuming, expensive, slow to deliver results, or even devoid of benefit. However now that any firm can enjoy a basic site for almost nothing and pay for customers with keywords bought on their credit card, the barriers have been overcome. Add to that the efficiency with which Yellow Pages firms like Yell.com in the UK have bolted the web into their sales process, and the structural barriers have been conquered.

# Creating your campaign

## Setting your campaign objectives: branding, response or both?

When setting your marketing objectives there are a few things to look out for: be clear about your branding objectives and your direct response objectives. What are the messages you want to get across? Examine what you want to achieve with your customer acquisition and retention objectives. Remember to make them SMART objectives: specific, measurable, achievable, relevant, and time-bound. Here are some simple examples:

Figure 5.7.6    **Setting clear campaign objectives**

*Example 1*
Raise awareness of our product: We aim to reach 100,000 of our target audience with a message introducing our new product in the first two weeks after its launch.

*Example 2*
Get 5,000 sign-ups to our credit card over the next six weeks at an average cost of £25. Achieve this by getting 250,000 clicks on our landing page at a conversion ratio of 50:1.

To set yourself a smart direct response marketing objective try using this simple formula:
Getting X thousand sales, from Y leads, from Z clicks, at an average price of A, over a time period of B.

*Source: Getting to grips with online media planning, DigitalStrategyConsulting.com, October 2006*

## The right formats for the right job

There is a bewildering mix of formats that make up the new digital media mix – from skyscrapers and roadblocks, pop-ups and pop-unders, to direct feeds and surround sessions. The key ones to know are the search tools, the graphical formats (embedded or interruptive) sponsorships, microsites, emails and virals, affiliates and syndication, e-commerce and tenancies. Don't forget that PR, events and the whole media mix offline will have a role to play online too.

Each format has its own strengths and weaknesses. Before making your selection you should be aware of what these are. You'll also want to understand the role each element plays in the journey towards a sale, so examine the media owner's website, the client's site, email and other channels, looking for how they work together.

The relationship between the media team and creative team is key, and should be taken into account as well.

In 2002 a group of us were concerned that the diversity of online's formats meant it had become hard to plan and buy. We began working on a universal package of simple graphics shapes that could be adopted by millions of websites. The aim was to give advertisers a bigger space that would give a higher impact for their image and a greater canvass for the creative teams to work on. In testing, these larger formats were proven to give stronger results than the traditional banner which had been unchanged in size since the IAB made it the industry's universal currency in 1996.

We were also keen to reduce the number of formats on a page, cutting the clutter from many sites to give advertisers an even better advertising environment. But there was also a conscious drive to make this a global currency for a global medium. It was the first time that as a group we'd consciously developed standards and guidelines at global level and it marked a watershed for online marketers.

**Figure 5.7.7**  **The IAB's Universal Advertising Package: four key graphical formats that work across tens of thousands of sites**

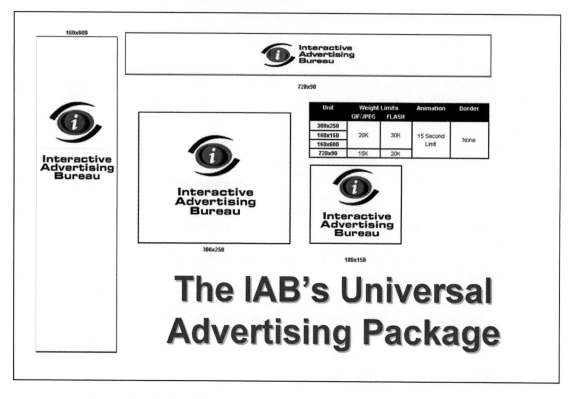

Source: Standards and best practice for online trading, IABeurope.ws, October 2006

Table 5.7.2     **Online advertsing formats**

The ten groups of online advertising formats:

1.  Text links

2.  Search listings

3.  Graphical – embedded within the page

4.  Graphical – interruptive formats that move beyond the fixed spaces

5.  Sponsorships

6.  Sites  and microsites

7.  Emails and virals

8.  Affiliates and syndication

9.  E-commerce and tenancies

10. PR, events, and the whole marketing mix

*Source: Getting to grips with online media planning, DigitalStrategyConsulting.com,*
*October 2006*

IAB Europe develops the standards and best practice for advertising formats, ad operations and online trading across the continent. 20 national trade associations have pledged to support these, so use the agreed standards to make your campaigns faster to produce and easier to transfer across markets. They have standards for video, audio, interruptive exposures, fileweights, behavioural targeting and at the time of writing are working on RSS adverts and mobile and interactive television formats.

## Selecting the right sites to advertise on

Start with a long list and include all the sites you think might work for your chosen product and audience. Be cautious about the data that you see and look for third-party verification that the numbers are accurate. This might be through official traffic audits that follow principles supported by the IAB in your country, or it could be through less rigorous third-party data reports from reputable counting providers.

Table 5.7.3 **Comparing online media**

In online, anything can be counted, but not everything that can be counted, counts.

We developed Digital's Five Ps of online audiences to help you compare websites effectively:

- People (unique users – think about the profiles and behaviour of the group)

- Pages (impressions or downloaded files and streams)

- Persistence (stickiness/duration of visit)

- Pulling power (repeat visits)

- Passion (intensity of their activity)

*Source: Getting to grips with key performance indicators (KPIs),*
*DigitalStrategyConsulting.com, November 2006*

Whittle these down to a shortlist, looking at how each site's strengths match up with your own objectives. Look out for the factors that would immediately knock a site off your list – low audience numbers, poor history of deliverability and restrictions on the creative formats. Consider the role of the editorial environment in terms of how it adds greater weight to your messaging as well as guaranteeing that the right audience is looking at it. Think about the quality, volume and reach a site can command. Because some of the more sophisticated ad formats might not be available – richmedia, microsites or sponsorships can be limited – the media team needs to be working with the creative team from the start of the campaign.

## *Trading models*

Online advertising can be bought and sold using a vast range of different trading models. Cost-per-thousand (CPM) remains one of the most popular, but a common range of options you'll encounter includes: CPM, CPD, CPC, CPA, uniques, time, sponsorship, search, email, viral, microsites and many more.

At one end of the spectrum there are trading models that revolve around the space media owners can provide (the number of impressions, views or days that a campaign is live), while at the other there are models which are drawn from sharing the revenues that come from a successful campaign. The various models like cost-per-action (CPA) or cost-per-click (CPC) that sit between these represent a balance that shares the commercial risk of a campaign between the website and the client (or its agency). The trading model you use should really depend on what your marketing objectives are. If the objective is to boost branding metrics then the sponsorship or impression models are generally most appropriate. If on the other hand the objectives are all about generating immediate leads, then models that pay on a 'per action' basis are probably more appropriate. Complex campaigns may involve several different mechanics all working at the same time and these generate a hybrid model that draws on strands from across the continuum.

## *Harnessing the targeting power of online media*

### Introducing the ten steps in the journey of targeting

To give you some context about what is possible today, I developed this ten-step history in the scope of media planning. What you see today is a fusion of these steps, with some media properties offering almost all of them combined and others just a few. The pace of development in targeting has been rapid and today's fusion with IPTV starts to deliver the long-awaited promise of convergence; that unity of media delivery that comes from the crashing together of the worlds of IT, media and telecommunications.

By giving you the history of targeting, I hope you'll be able to contextualise the tools I was familiar with when writing this and those new tools that you'll be discovering. The evolution of online targeting has been rapid, making giant strides every year with new additions to the toolkit and new processes to reach ever more specific audiences; all this while the targeting power of traditional media has barely shifted. In fact, one of the greatest challenges for experienced digital marketers can be to relate all of this back to classic media, where reach and frequency are typically guessed, where response is rarely tracked and often not even trackable, and where the level of accountability and precision is so poor that it would leave a digital planner embarrassed to recommend it.

"Digital advertising has triggered a transformation of the marketing industry into an era of precision and accuracy never before possible. Digital marketing can be challenging because the toolkits, processes and ideas we use are at the forefront of marketing, and with most of the industry still catching up, digital marketers must work hard to explain their processes and toolkits."

*D. Meadows-Klue*

**1.    Cottage industry beginnings**
When the first online media launched in the early nineties, targeting options – along with the audiences – were very limited. Initially advertisers had little choice other than being on the home page, or sprinkling the campaign throughout the site. The techniques fixed the ad to the page, rather like a magazine advert. There were no ad delivery software systems and the chances are that the editorial team would also be coding the advertisers' graphics straight onto the page themselves. Those were the days of cottage-industry web production.

**2.    Editorial environment**
From this evolved the targeting by editorial environment; matching finance brands to finance pages and travel brands to travel pages. The technology was still basic, but inventory was structured and managed with the same professionalism and process of a newspaper or magazine. Within eighteen months online targeting had covered the ground it had taken broadcast media about fifty years to reach.

**3.    Technology shifts with the arrival of ad servers**
The era of automated advertising placement began around 1996 and created a step-
change in the way web publishing worked. Although audience numbers had been large enough for some time (remember that the introduction of targeting reduces the available inventory on a publisher's site), targeting had been held back by a lack of technology to power it. The cottage industry workflow processes of the first generation of online advertising management had become increasingly

chaotic and were failing to scale. With dozens of advertisers strewn across dozens of page templates, leaving the technical tags and code that triggered the ads strewn all over the site, the arrival of the heavyweight technical solutions was warmly welcomed and filled a clear market need. With the ad serving industry up and running, advertising placements became divorced from the page content creating much greater flexibility and the potential to invent new types of schedules.

### Figure 5.7.8    **Media planners target the long tail**

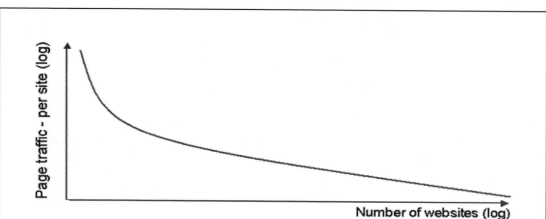

With much of the web's page inventory outside the mainstream online media, many media planners look to place their campaigns in the long tail of small websites rather than the big traffic portals and national media. The evolution of social media networks like MySpace has started to change the ownership structures of 'the tail'. Advertising partnerships through ISPs could open these sites up more effectively.

*Source: Getting to grips with media planning: Digital Strategy Consulting 2006*

### 4.    Targeting the site's granular editorial zones

The demand for targeting the diverse content environments online catapulted media planning forward as planners began harnessing the most granular of editorial environments. The ad server technology vendors helped publishers open up their inventory in a way that was cheap to maintain and highly flexible. This in turn made media planning much easier and enabled more agencies to experiment. If clients wanted just 'business people who were interested in shares' at the moment they were thinking about investments, then media planners would be able to find the editorial pages that matched up to the profile, buying, for example, the 'stocks and shares' pages of an online newspaper. If they wanted just the tourists interested in 'car hire in the south of France' then they'd just buy the travel magazine's South of France holiday pages. Print media's accurate targeting had been overtaken. The practices took several years to become widely adopted in the online ad industry, but the potential of ad servers was starting to be unlocked.

**Rethink the life of your campaign:**

When you find the perfect editorial match for your proposition look for ways of making your campaign a permanent feature of those pages. Challenge the thinking that campaigns have to be for days, weeks or months, and look for ways you can retain a relationship with this target audience for the long term. This precision targeting will reduce your inventory, freeing up budgets and media space to extend the life of your message.

## 5.    Cookies: the leap to user-centric targeting

Unlocked from about 1997 (though only implemented much later by most), came the capping of the number of exposures per viewer. This type of targeting relied upon the individual's previous exposure history to be remembered by the ad server, and the number of views (frequency) of a given ad to be restricted.

This was a leap into the new. Previously the whole history of media planning's approach to frequency (in all media) was based on modelling what a typical consumer would do, rather than making any direct link between their actual individual behaviour and how the advertising was delivered. Online planners would look at how many views of an ad the average viewer was likely to have seen, and then use those rough guides to plan the media schedule. This glossed over the paradox that a television campaign with a target frequency of say three views per person may have only been seen once by a third of the viewers and way more than three times by a small number of high-volume television viewers.

While on the one hand, the psychology of how brand impact metrics build with frequency is clear, on the other; all those good intentions were evaporating in the practicalities of how print, broadcast and outdoor media were consumed. Only direct mail – held in high esteem for its accuracy in spite of the low open rates – could be accurate with the frequency of sending, although with the majority of mailings unopened it ultimately failed to deliver on the frequency promise.

Enter the cookie. By sending one of these tiny text files to the viewer's computer, ad servers could gain a sense of memory, recognising the viewer, and the next time they served an ad, it could behave differently. If the target frequency for the campaign was three exposures then that could be set as the maximum. After the third exposure the system would tell itself to serve a different ad instead. From the media planners' perspective this freed up all those advertising impressions that would have been burned in the 'worn-out' fifth, sixth or seventh exposure to the same person, allowing them to find new sites not previously on the schedule and reach new audiences. For the advertisers it created a shift in advertising effectiveness, and for the media owner it was easy to implement. Even for the consumer it meant more effective use of the screen inventory, so it's not hard to see why capping proves popular: win, win, win and win.

But capping is just one way of using previous advertising exposures in media targeting. Storytelling through the sequencing of different creative messages had now become possible. Advertising has told stories for as long as there has been advertising, but only the brave clients – or those with heavyweight budgets – could afford wave after wave of campaign with different messages that built on what had (probably) been seen before. Yet the same tools that managed frequency could be used to deliver sequential elements in a web advertising campaign, letting the medium work harder. With ad servers and their cookies using exactly the same process to sequence the creative in a campaign, it was clear that the cookie was destined to have a major effect on ad serving.

With changes in data protection law, European websites need to have clear cookie policies in place. Ask your media owner partners to show you theirs and check that your site also has a compliant policy.

Rather than the same ad being seen three times, three different ads could be served in a managed sequence, letting the story unfold with the viewer. Although this was an easy step, it took advertisers and many media owners a long time to exploit the benefits. The model is not entirely perfect because there will always be some people who delete their cookies or even opt out of them altogether, but the tools work well for most people most of the time – especially in shorter time periods where the susceptibility to deletion is much lower.

### 6. Day parting: drawing strength from broadcast media

What might be just the right marketing message for just the right person may fall completely flat if it hits at the wrong moment. Newspapers fill up with ads for high street retails just before the weekend because that's when shoppers are receptive. Run that same campaign on a Monday morning and the message will probably be lost by the next weekend. This type of daily targeting became popular first in the US among clients whose products have natural cycles of interest. Day-based targeting continues to be a core technique for deciding the scheduling of a campaign in digitally less sophisticated markets such as New Zealand and China.

Targeting by time of day works in the same way. Get the ads for chocolate snacks before the coffee break, or fast food stores just before lunchtime, and the media planning is working hard to minimise wastage. From the late nineties it had been clear the internet was a mass reach tool throughout the working day and by 2002 in the UK it had become the lead daytime media channel.

Dividing a day into parts and then scheduling the right messages into the right time slot has been a pillar of broadcast media for decades. The same techniques have been readily available in online for years and after 2002 clients started taking advantage of them.

The smartness of the advertising systems means the time slots themselves can be set with incredible precision and manipulated with ease. That's why day parting has become standard for many online media and why we believe it will soon become ubiquitous – it's an important part of the toolkit.

> Look for ways you can target by time of day and reduce the amount of media you need to buy. Run different creative that suits these different times and consider different calls to action and different landing pages.

### 7. Geography: fusing the virtual and physical worlds together

The internet has a blatant disregard for geography. The viewers of a web page could be on the other side of the street or the other side of the world, and generally the webmaster is none the wiser. None the wiser unless they 'ask' that is.

By asking the user's browser for its internet protocol (IP) address, a unique identity can be ascribed to the user's machine. Just like telephone lines, internet connections have a unique number that identifies them. These IP addresses have been mapped, and by looking up the phone book of IP addresses it's possible to pinpoint where the customer is with reasonable geographic accuracy. Harness that to the advertising server and you can tailor marketing messages accordingly. Not only does this put global portals in competition with the local newspaper but it can expose consumer groups with unique needs.

### 8. Next stop: modelling demographics and profiling

Advertising thrives off demographics and profiling as the way of predicting customer behaviour. This fuelled the advertising industries worldwide from the 1970s onwards and while there remains a major debate about which profiling techniques will succeed in future, the reality is that the vast majority of advertising campaigns are planned based on approaches that share much in common.

The rationale is simple: in spite of everyone's individuality and diversity, people move in herds. If you spot one person heading in a certain direction then chances are you'll find the others heading there share a few things in common. When you apply this to marketing then it will reveal that people who buy similar products often share many other attributes. They might be similar in age, location, income group, aspirations or education. They might share similar interests or beliefs, and they may also share the purchasing of other brands together. Crunch the numbers and you'll have a predictive model. For example, if you find a thirty-something urban male checking their text messages on a multi-media phone over a cappuccino at Starbucks, you can safely predict they will have the internet at home. If you know their job title or income, you can probably predict the sort of car they'd be in the market for. If you looked in their grocery bag, you can probably figure out the sort of holiday they'd like to take. These are all based on correlations between individuals, their attributes and the rest of the group.

So the world of profiling – from the ABCs of simple social grade to the richness of data unlocked by supermarket loyalty cards – forms a major slice of the thinking the media planner will be doing. All that's needed is to feed in some insights about the existing customers, and out of the other end should come the principles that will drive the media plan, principles that can form a common set of descriptions all media can share. And it's relatively easy to find out about the current customers because those are the ones the brand has closest access to.

### 9.    User-centric demographics and profiling

For traditional media, that's where the story ends, but for online media there are several more steps. All this customer data sloshes around in databases, that, like the data-based phone book of a computer's IP addresses, can be hooked up to a website, and an advertising server. Whether the data has been gathered by observation or the likelihood that a person fits a certain group has been predicted by looking at other variables, the reality is that it can all link together seamlessly. That means advertising can be targeted at known individuals based on their claims or actions. Bolt on to this the ease with which websites can smartly ask their viewers questions and then store that information in a profile, and you have some phenomenal targeting potential.

Unlocking it in practice may take significant integration between the systems that store all that data and those that deliver the content to the browser, but those barriers to technical development and integration are typically the sort that quickly melt away. The real challenge is getting the accurate data in the first place, and then managing and maintaining it – a skill set the direct marketers who have raced into the industry are acquiring fast.

### 10.   Profiling through behaviour

Around 2003 the behavioural targeting engines began creeping into the European market. By harnessing cookies and noting the pages each viewer requested, they were able to build a profile of the content a viewer was interested in without having to ask explicit questions. This provides a rich insight into an individual's interests, and it does it without having to directly ask the question. Observing behaviour can be a better way to understand the viewers' interests. What's more, websites could do this without having to know anything about the identity of the individual. As long as there is a single anonymous cookie attached to the same person, that profile could continue being built.

## Trend spotting

The targeting of online advertising has stepped through these ten phases and by 2006 all of them are running in parallel inside many media. Through 2007 and 2008, contextual and behavioural targeting will be the battleground for advances in online media planning and the owners of customer data will be looking for ways to fuse that knowledge with media properties to deliver more relevant communication. The dynamics of media buying will shift as many of the tasks become automated and the knowledge of space and price undergo a transformation.

"I expect advertising to be the single fastest growing part of the revenue mix of Microsoft over the next few years. It's the priority number one issue and opportunity. The online area is primarily funded through advertising. It's exploded but I see it as continuing to accelerate. During the next ten years all forms of consumer media will go digital. There will be nothing that we will not do to understand what you [as a marketer] need and to target the audiences in the way you need, [including] software and device support for this ecosystem [that means] we need to work with non-Microsoft platforms."

*Steve Ballmer, CEO, Microsoft, October 2006*

## Conclusions on targeting

The evolution of targeting is being driven by the simultaneous need to reduce media wastage and increase campaign responsiveness. Because everything can be tracked there is much greater transparency and accountability. As more marketing spend moves into digital channels, inventory will become more valuable and targeting will become more of a necessity.

## *Appreciating reach and frequency*

Modelling reach and frequency online is challenging because there's a potential to go that much deeper in terms of accuracy. In most countries there is still no single planning tool that all parties agree to use, and although this is changing, there are still different approaches to how reach is counted.

Like all media, the first online ad a customer sees always has the biggest impact. After that the returns taper off. There are no absolutes in process, but the optimal frequency of exposures will vary due to the creative, the media plan, the reading environment, the offer and a host more factors. On the web a consensus is emerging that around three to five views works best for graphical formats. This is in contrast with cinema where the frequency only needs to be low to produce a response, and radio, where it needs to be higher. Clearly the optimal frequency will vary massively between campaigns and online marketers should experiment, test and learn what works for their own campaigns and brands.

Figure 5.7.9 **Frequency: research the optimal frequency for your campaign**

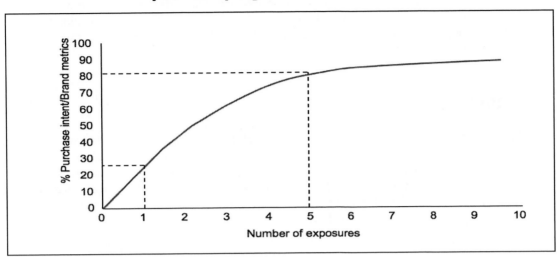

Source: *Getting to grips with online media planning, DigitalStrategyConsulting.com,*
*October 2006*

## Campaign integration: key to getting the most from your media

Integration means much more than just getting the web ads to look like the press, TV or outdoor work. That's the starting point though, and your campaign will be more effective if you integrate your marketing messages and design so the communication endorses the key points across each channel. This builds impact among viewers and gets your creative working harder for you.

*"Integration shouldn't be about the 'matching luggage' approach to media – getting the web work to share the same look and feel as the TV and outdoor material; that's only the starting point. Smart marketers know that because online has so much more potential, true integration will harness its competencies of accountability, connectivity, information capture and immediate action."*

*D. Meadows-Klue*

Let online go further in delivering greater interaction with audiences and greater impact through the extra scope all this technology brings you. Harness the advantages of online to let your campaign do more than simply replicate the design of another channel. Look for ways to go deeper, further and more interactive in the messages. Harness the return path to capture customer data and look for ways customers can interact with your messages.

As online fuses with direct marketing you're able to talk cost-effectively to ever-smaller market segments. Find ways of increasing 'dwell time' and customer engagement in your campaign. Here interaction, novelty, and community could provide some of the answers. The good news is that these are things the web can do very well. Auctioning and electronic trading are further ways to take advantage of online. And when you've run out of ideas, go back and integrate your existing strategies even more deeply.

Integration also applies to your team. Bring your creative and media teams together from day one. If you don't do this you will waste time cobbling together the different ideas later on and miss out on harnessing all their combined talents.

Remember that because online media offer so many more choices than traditional channels and media properties, there's huge scope to go beyond the simple advertising campaign models you may be used to. Consider your online and offline strategies as a coherent whole rather than as separate projects. Play up the unique strengths of each channel while making sure all elements are focused on the big idea.

## *Measuring your success*

How do you know when you've succeeded? Here's where online excels even further, and it all begins before the campaign even gets off the ground. If you start with clear, measurable objectives, and put in place a good tracking system, you'll know the exact moment when the campaign succeeds. You may be tracking leads and sales, or media metrics such as impressions, reach, plays and minutes, but by setting clear objectives, you'll know exactly when you reach them.

1. Pay attention to conversion metrics, and follow through what happens to those leads once they enter your business

2. Be careful not to attribute response to the wrong channel – if you're running a TV campaign and have a surge of activity through search engines, is that response just because of your paid-for listings?

3. Invest in web analytics well before the start of the campaign

The internet has a greater ability to measure return than any other medium. Get all your stakeholders to consider what's meaningful to track right from the start. Whether you are testing the brand effect or the direct response there are simple metrics that can be put in place.

Align your measurement to match what the campaign is doing across all media so the results can be channelled into a single dashboard. Be clear about what to count, how to count it and who should count it. Also think about your scope – do you want to measure the whole campaign, just the web channels or just one of the sites? By tracking a series of campaigns you'll be able to benchmark your performance. Direct marketers will seize the opportunity of split-run tests to quantify the way small changes to the schedule or the creative impact on the overall campaign success.

### Measuring brand and direct response

When measuring brand metrics you can either survey a group of customers before and after exposure to an ad, or test against an exposed and control group. This second approach is more popular online and without the control group you've got no starting point. The brand effect can also be tracked via purchase intent for offline decisions – someone may make the decision to buy on the strength of your web ad, but do the actual buying at the brick and mortar store instead. Alternatively they may buy online, but at a later point. And this is where post-impression tracking techniques can prove the value of the indirect leads generated.

The direct effect is more of a numbers game. The first and simplest thing to do is count up all the direct responses and their conversions. Then use total expenditure to calculate the value of every lead. From here you can model the lifetime value of the customer and get the bigger picture of what your campaign has achieved.

# Best Practice Search Engine Marketing

## This chapter includes:

------------------------------------------------

- ❏ **What is Search Engine Marketing?**
    - ❏ **Search engine optimisation**
    - ❏ **How to optimise your web site for search engines**
    - ❏ **Factors that determine search engine rankings**
    - ❏ **Content**
    - ❏ **Design & technology**
    - ❏ **The importance of links**
    - ❏ **SEO techniques to avoid!**
    - ❏ **Conclusion & SEO considerations for the future**
- ❏ **Pay per Click (PPC)**
    - ❏ **What are Pay per Click ads?**
    - ❏ **Who provide PPC services in the UK?**
    - ❏ **Where do PPC ads appear?**
    - ❏ **Why PPC can deliver exceptional ROI**
    - ❏ **The pros and cons of PPC**
    - ❏ **What PPC services exist in the UK?**
    - ❏ **How to decide What PPC networks to target**
    - ❏ **How do PPC services rank ads?**
    - ❏ **Getting started – how to build an effective PPC campaign**
    - ❏ **Successful campaign management**
    - ❏ **Web analytics**

## What this chapter is about

**P**ossession of a website is to-day a must for most companies. But if the website is to be more than just an expensive me-too accessory – if it is to add to the company's revenue – visitors must be attracted to it. Most website visitors arrive there via a search engine, which has provided them with multiple answers to their search queries. In this chapter we look at the best ways of ensuring that your website secures a prominent place among search engine listings, bringing you therefore a large share of relevant visitors.

### Mike Rogers

Mike Rogers M IDM is Managing Director of Optimize, a specialist Search Engine Marketing (SEM) agency that provides independent SEM services, consultancy and training to clients in the UK and overseas. Services include Search Engine Optimisation (SEO), Pay per Click (PPC) search advertising and other SEM related services such as Paid Inclusion and Trusted Feeds. Clients include AIRMILES, the BBC, Dyson, Kodak, Monster.co.uk, Nationwide, Parcelforce, the Royal Mail, Toshiba, Yell.com and many other small and medium sized businesses. Mike delivers all SEO and PPC training courses for the IDM and is a member of the IAB's Search Council.

# Chapter 5.8

# Best practice search engine marketing

## Introduction

**E**ight out of ten users now rely on search engines to find the information they need, according to research carried out by Yahoo! Search Marketing, Isobar and UDA in 2005. And, with up to 85% of search engine visitors coming through natural listings, today the most successful businesses realise that to maximise their Return on Investment they need to harness the benefits that integrating natural and Paid Search can deliver.

Search Engine Marketing (SEM) is big business. Paid Search now constitutes the greatest proportion of online marketing spend in the UK. According to the Internet Advertising Bureau's 'Digital Insight Report' of February 2006, the UK had an online audience of 62% of the population of 29.3 million users of which 18 million shop online. The UK now boasts 71% of home users have broadband connections. As a consequence online ad spend has soared in recent years – and spend on Paid Search is the biggest winner by far. According to the IAB Search Engine Advertising spend in the UK increased by 79% between 2004 and 2005 far exceeding all other forms of online marketing spend.

But the rise in popularity of Search Marketing hasn't been solely as a consequence of Paid Search. More and more businesses are realising that in order to be able to grow targeted traffic to their web sites in a sustainable way for the long-term, a strategic approach that incorporates Search Engine Optimisation (SEO) is also required.

Today, the greatest Search Engine Marketing success is achieved by focusing on quality and relevancy – rather than simply increasing Paid Search budgets. More time and effort is required, that's true, but gone are the days when adding a few meta tags to your home page was all that was needed to achieve top rankings. A holistic SEM approach delivers ROI exceeding any other form of marketing – either online or offline. What other marketing discipline provides an opportunity to promote your products at the precise moment somebody **actively** searches for something you sell? It's a marketer's dream.

## *What is Search Engine Marketing (SEM)?*

Search Engine Marketing (or Search Marketing as it is sometimes called) is a specialist discipline within Internet Marketing.

In essence, the objective of SEM is to achieve high visibility in search engines such as Google, Yahoo! or MSN for search queries that are relevant to your business. If your web site can be listed frequently enough and high enough in the rankings for search queries that are most relevant to your business, visitor traffic will increase.

First it is worth explaining how a search engine divides its results pages and distinguishes between listings that are paid for and those that are not. Here is a screenshot showing a search results page for a typical search carried out in Google.

# Natural/Organic SEO & PPC

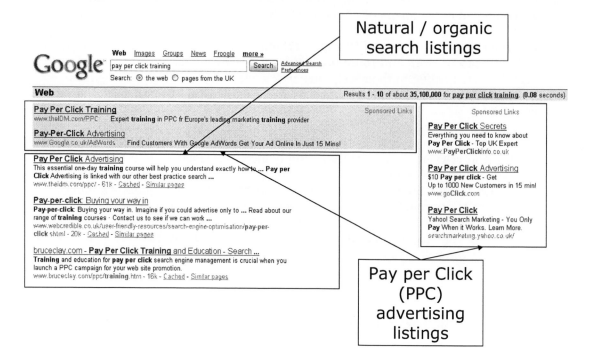

Natural / organic search listings

Pay per Click (PPC) advertising listings

Nowadays Google, MSN, Yahoo! and other search engines lay out their search results pages in a similar way. Typically, the search results shown on the left of a page are natural (sometimes called organic) listings. In most cases these are free listings. Paid for listings are, in effect, advertisements and usually appear down the right hand side of a results page. Ads are usually displayed alongside the words 'Sponsored Links' to distinguish them from natural listings. Very often you will also see a few ads appear above the natural listings as well, usually shaded in blue or another colour. These are premium paid listings and often indicate that the ads have exceeded some quality threshold.

Search Engine Marketing (SEM) covers two distinct disciplines Search Engine Optimisation (SEO) and what is often called Pay per Click (PPC) search engine advertising. Each requires a totally different approach in order to gain visibility in the search engines. These days, businesses that are achieving greatest success online are taking a strategic approach to SEM and, more importantly, they understand the importance of integrating the two disciplines.

**Search Engine Optimisation (SEO)**

Search Engine Optimisation (or SEO) is aimed towards increasing visibility in the search engines' natural search listings. Creating a 'search engine friendly' web site is the goal. In a nutshell it is a process that involves:

- Ensuring that content within your web pages is found by the search engines

- Improving the quality and relevancy of your web site in a way that will result in search engines ranking your web pages higher in their natural search listings

Each search engine uses a different algorithm – a set of rules that is used to rank listings contained within its index in response to a particular search query. Search engines frequently change their ranking algorithms, partly to improve the quality of listings they deliver but also in an effort to stop businesses from raising their rankings artificially. That said, if you are using best practice SEO principles for your web site, when search engines update their algorithms your **overall** rankings are much less likely to be adversely affected.

The higher your web page ranks in a search engine's natural listings, the greater the chance that a user will click on your listing and visit your web site. Numerous surveys show that the vast majority of Internet users prefer to submit an alternative search query rather than wade through page after page of search listings to find what they are looking for. In fact, many searchers don't even bother to scroll down a page. Therefore, ideally, you should aim to obtain high rankings on the first page of search engine results wherever possible.

"More than 60% of searchers in Google will click on one of the top three listings."

*[Source: B2B Survey]*

As more and more businesses appreciate the long-term benefits that SEO can bring, the competition to obtain high rankings for keyword phrases that convert continues to increase. Competition is already very fierce in many markets such as travel and financial services. That said, even today, many web sites are poorly optimised for search engines and so opportunities still exist to achieve a competitive advantage through SEO. This paper highlights the most important factors you need to consider to succeed in Search Engine Optimisation.

However, raising your natural search rankings may take several months – even if you do follow best practice! All search engines are in constant battle with webmasters who attempt to raise their rankings artificially.

In part, search engines respond to these attempts by not raising the rankings of web pages within a site until the site can be seen to be making progress (as far as SEO is concerned) over a period of several months. For example, search engines know that very often, as soon as a new web site has been launched, a flurry of activity follows – mass submissions here, a multitude of reciprocal link requests there. Google, for one, tries to ignore (or at least downgrade the importance of) this post-launch, frenetic activity and only reward a site with higher rankings over time. Therefore, if Google sees that a site is **steadily** adding relevant content or receiving quality links over time it will steadily raise the site's natural rankings.

## How to optimise your website for search engines

Optimising a site for search engines requires considering a range of factors. Google, for one, publicly state that they consider **at least 100 factors** when determining how to rank a page. Clearly, some are considered more important than others.

Although Google never says definitively what these factors are (or how each of these factors are weighted), it is possible that these days Google considers many more than 100 factors in their ranking algorithm. Although many of these factors may not seem important when each is considered in isolation, their combined effect can often result in a dramatic improvement in rankings. As a consequence, not only will the number of visitors to your site increase, if visitors arrive through much tighter targeting of keyword phrases they are much more likely to convert too. Overall, obtaining higher natural rankings for your most important target keywords will result in an increase to your bottom line.

## Factors that determine search engine rankings

Factors that search engines consider can be grouped into three main areas:

- Content

- Design & Technology

- Links

## Content

It's not surprising to learn that content is very important to search engines. If you have a web site that is light on content, particularly in comparison to your competitors, then you are already at a disadvantage. But taking your corporate brochures and putting the content online usually won't muster much advantage as far as SEO is concerned these days.

Not only do all search engines want content – **search engines need content** in order to ascertain what your web site is about. As Google says on its web site:

"Create a useful, information-rich site, and write pages that clearly and accurately describe your content."

In other words, the more your site contains rich and **relevant** content, the greater the likelihood that your pages will rank higher. In almost all circumstances, the more **quality** content you can provide the better it will be for your search engine rankings. If your web site has a high proportion of graphics, or it has been designed to appeal to minimalists with large areas of white space, it is very likely you will not be giving the search engines what they need. But it's not solely about the number of words you have on a page – search engines also want **quality** content!

That said, there are many other factors you must consider when designing and building your web site – look and feel, usability and accessibility issues are a few. But requirements for Search Marketing should be considered at every stage.

All search engines are obsessed with delivering pages that are **most relevant** to a search query. It makes sense for their long-term prosperity. Frequent delivery of poor quality listings will result in a poor user experience and users will swap allegiance to another search engine.

Of course, writing good prose on your web site is important for SEO. But the online world is very different to its offline equivalent when it comes to writing content.

### How to write content for search engines

First, you need to step back from your day-to-day marketing messages and the words you use to promote your business. You must try and understand how your prospective customers are likely to search for your products or services whenever they use a search engine. What keywords (more precisely, what keyword **phrases**) are they most likely to use when they enter a search query? Knowing that the number of people searching for a 'laptop' outnumbers those searching for a 'notebook' by more than 10-fold is important if you sell laptop computers.

Identifying target keyword phrases will require some research but knowing which are the best keyword phrases to include in the pages of your web site will pay dividends in the long run.

"Think about the words users would type to find your pages, and make sure that your site actually includes those words within it." (Google)

If Google tells you what it wants, then give Google what it wants! According to Hitwise, in the UK **Google accounts for more than 70% of all searches.** You can't ignore Google when it comes to Search Engine Optimisation.

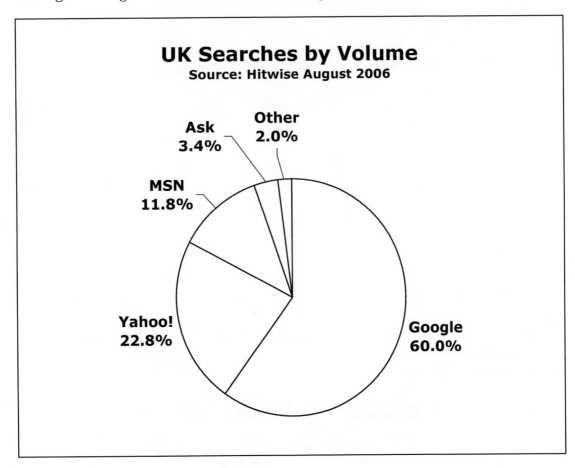

In the same way, Yahoo!, MSN and all other major search engines want and need you to focus on keyword phrases contained in your web content too. Although each search engine uses a different algorithm to determine its rankings, if you follow good practice SEO principles your overall rankings will increase on all search engines – given time!

## Keyword research

Numerous tools can help with your keyword research and many of these tools are free. Google, Yahoo!, MSN and other search engines provide keyword suggestion tools. Other keyword research tools are available commercially. One of the most popular is Wordtracker.

Although the primary objective of all these tools is to help you build a rich list of relevant keywords to target, some have unique features that can be highly beneficial. Therefore, don't restrict yourself to using one tool. Taking advantage of the features of each tool can provide assistance in improving the quality of your keyword list enormously.

For example, some tools like Google, MSN and Wordtracker use a Thesaurus to highlight synonyms or words that have a similar meaning. Wordtracker and Yahoo!'s tools show the popularity of keyword phrases so you can prioritise your keyword list.

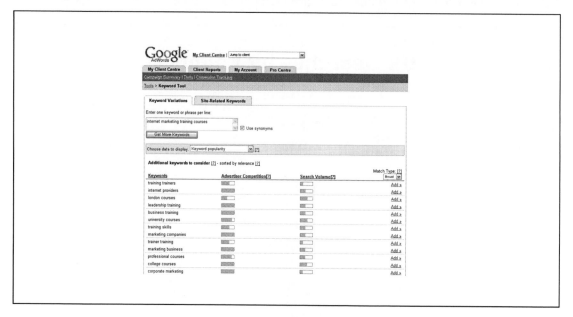

Wordtracker and Yahoo!'s tools show the popularity of keyword phrases so you can prioritise your keyword list.

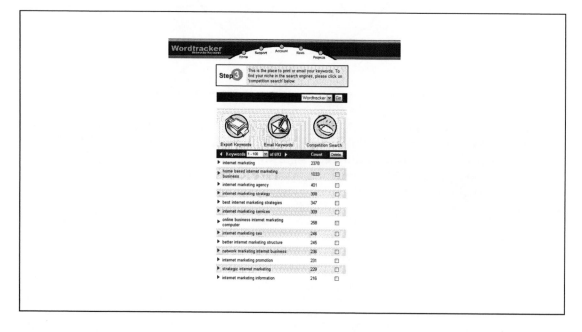

Also, both Google and MSN let you specify a page on any web site and they will identify keywords that are most relevant to that page. Why not check out your competitors' pages while you're at it. Wordtracker does something similar. It will look at a group of pages that are relevant to a keyword phrase and extract additional keyword suggestions from those pages.

All in all, these research tools are invaluable for building a list of relevant keyword phrases that you should target. With a prioritised list of keywords you can begin the process of writing content.

## The importance of understanding search behaviour

As you know, the use of search engines continues to grow in popularity. In addition, users are becoming more sophisticated in the way they search for information online. For example, now more than 50% of search queries contain three or more words in a keyword phrase.

Also, searchers also have much higher expectations regarding the results that are delivered from the searches they carry out. If they are looking for reviews and articles on a particular product they don't necessarily want to be bombarded with listings promoting your latest money-saving offers.

Consequently, it is becoming ever more important to search engines that they deliver results that have most relevance to a search query. Search engines are unable to do achieve this without you helping them on their way, and writing content that is search engine friendly.

Search queries used when researching the features and benefits of a product differ dramatically to queries used to find the cheapest price for a particular product or service. Therefore the words you use when writing a product feature page should make more references to phrases such as 'recommended by...' and 'comparison'. Whereas pages designed to encourage visitors to convert may use different language like 'best price' and 'special offer'.

So, where possible, you need to identify keyword phrases that your prospective customers are most likely to use at each stage of the buying cycle and use those phrases within the content pages of your web site, In doing so this will help you in building a clear competitive advantage.

## Where to place target keyword phrases

Search engines look at many elements of a web page to determine its context. As Google says:

"Google [uses] sophisticated text-matching techniques to find pages that are both important and relevant to your search. Google goes far beyond the number of times a term appears on a page and examines all aspects of the page's content (and the content of the pages linking to it) to determine if it's a good match for your query."

Whether it's Google or another search engine the main body copy of a page will be viewed in detail – which shouldn't come as any real surprise. Therefore, always make sure your page-specific, target keyword phrases are spread throughout the page. Ideally, target keywords should appear somewhere in the opening paragraph or, even better, in the opening sentence. References towards the end of each content page also helps, as do a few inclusions that are spread throughout the length of your page.

> However, whatever you do, **don't go overboard**! If you repeat a phrase too often, it is possible that your pages will be lowered in the rankings – or worse, banned altogether for what is called **keyword stuffing**.

Stuffing keywords into a page of content used to help inflate natural search engine rankings in the past – but generally this has little effect nowadays. Search engines discourage content that is poorly written as it does little to add value to a user's experience. In short, no search engine likes keyword stuffing. Their focus is in rewarding quality content with higher rankings.

So, how many times should you use your keywords on a page and ideally how long should your content be?

Well, the search engines don't want to tell you that – although there are commonly accepted guidelines. Pages containing 250-500 words often rank well in search engines and many of those pages that rank higher will not contain more than 5 or 6 references to a target keyword phrase. A few years ago tools that calculated the keyword density of a page were all the rage. In effect, they represented each page as a series of numbers that search engines used to calculate rankings.

Today, search engines have moved on from a relatively straightforward approach to calculating rankings and they now use much more sophisticated methods when analysing the words on your web pages. In 2003 Google acquired a company called Applied Semantics that "understands, organizes, and extracts knowledge from websites and information repositories in a way that mimics human thought and enables more effective information retrieval." Even Google would prefer you to write for humans – not for search engines! However, nowadays it is unwise to treat these two requirements in isolation – hence the growth in specialist SEO copywriters.

So, where appropriate, do include exact matches of your target keyword phrases in your pages, but don't forget to include plurals, synonyms and different word forms as well.

Search engines don't like spamming or the use of trickery or skulduggery. Those who are bent on raising their rankings artificially are viewed by all search engines with suspicion. As a consequence, search engines don't want to be too prescriptive about what works and what doesn't when it comes to rankings.

Besides, the search engines deliberately change their ranking algorithms on a regular basis. Overall, many algorithm updates result in little significant change for most web sites that follow best practice SEO. However, from time to time updates make a big impact on a large number of web sites. When that happens discussion forums start to buzz with webmasters aggrieved because they swear they have not broken the rules. In almost every situation where that happens, those who are worst affected are either relying on one or two factors to obtain high rankings or they are targeting very few keyword phrases. They don't take a holistic approach to search engine optimisation.

In the end it's all about quality and relevancy – and that's what you need to consider at all times. It is important that you 'spread your risk' so that whenever a search engine updates its algorithm you gain some higher rankings even if others fall.

## Titles & headings

Search engines view titles, headings and other key components of a page when considering how to rank a page. As you might expect, search engines treat words and phrases that appear in these areas as being important when determining the context of a page. Therefore, you must always make sure that your target keyword phrases are used in titles and headings wherever possible. Doing so will give such pages a boost in the search engines' rankings – even if only a small rise.

However, search engines also look at many other key areas within a page that include, but are not necessarily limited to:

- Headings & Subheadings

- Link Text (the actual words contained in a link to another page)

- Bullet Points

- Text in bold

Ideally each page should target one, or no more than a few, keyword phrases. If you try to include too many target phrases on a single page then you may well end up diluting any potential benefit that you could bring.

Importance of writing using the 'reverse pyramid'

When writing content on the web you only have a few seconds to grab a visitor's attention. So, you need to create an impact very quickly if you want to encourage a visitor to stay and read what you have to say.

Doing so requires following a few simple rules that become clear once you understand that most people do not read content when they first arrive at a web page – **they scan!**

According to Jakob Nielsen, the renowned authority on web usability issues, 79 percent of Web users scan rather than read a web page, picking out individual words and sentences. As the web is a user-driven medium, many users are busy and don't want to stay on a page any longer than they have to. Besides, reading from a computer screen is tiring. 25 percent read slower online than reading from paper according to Nielsen.

How Users Read on the Web
http://www.useit.com/alertbox/9710a.html

So, creating scanable text will encourage more visitors to stay and read what you have to say. If those scanable features also contain target keyword phrases then you are helping the search engines too.

Getting your web site right for usability is important – but these days it is important to make sure your site has 'sticky content' as well! Search engines have the ability to measure how long a user visits a web page. If you have installed a search engine's toolbar onto your PC you may well be providing that information on your own movements around Internet space. And, if search engines don't currently use this information as some measure of quality of a page, it may only be a matter of time before they do. In time, search engines will deliver much more personalised listings targeted to online behaviour they have identified.

So, a good usable site will support your SEO efforts. If your web site is designed with usability in mind, pages within it will stand a far greater chance of being optimised for search engines. Remember, your competitor's web site is only a click away!

## Design & technology

One commonly overlooked factor that plays a **critical** role in the success of SEO is the design and the implementation of technology within a web site. Your web site will be decidedly 'search engine **unfriendly**' if it impedes the search engines from finding, and subsequently indexing, content contained on your site.

But producing a 'search engine friendly' web site isn't always a straightforward process – particularly since developments in web site design and the use of database technology and content management systems (CMS) often hinder progress. That said, these days all providers of web technology solutions (CMS systems, databases etc...) understand the importance of SEO. Consequently, most have incorporated features that allow for the creation of search engine friendly web sites. Even so, some businesses fail to take advantage of these developments and many don't configure these systems in a way that assists the search engines.

## How do search engines find your content?

With the billions of pages that exist on the web today, the only way search engines can find and index your pages is through technology. They do so using software robots – also called spiders or crawlers. A robot is a program that 'crawls' web pages, following links to find information to index in a search engine's database. Each search engine has its own robot that will visit your site from time to time. Google's spider is called Googlebot, for example. And remember; web pages that are not indexed by a search engine will **never** be displayed in its search results.

Moreover, your aim must be to index **every** page within your web site in all the major search engines. This will greatly increase the likelihood that one of your pages will be listed as a result of a search query. To allow this to happen it is vital that you remove all barriers to search engine spiders.

## Barriers for search engine spiders

Most barriers to spiders exist because web technology has not been implemented most appropriately. But the design of a web site may also cause problems for the spiders.

Some of the biggest problems are often caused by the use of a database or Content Management System (CMS) to power a web site. Problems don't necessarily have to exist – but it is important to ensure that tools such as these are configured and implemented in a way that is search engine friendly.

In short, most search engines have problems with complex URLs (Uniform Resource Locators) – the addresses of web pages. Many CMS systems and database-driven web sites create horrendous URLs as far as search engines are concerned.

URLs containing multiple parameters with question marks and ampersands can often confuse spiders. If a spider even thinks there may be a chance of becoming confused by a complex URL it will disappear – **without** finding and following other links on your site. It is true that some search engines are more sophisticated these days, and many can handle relatively complex URLs. However, it is usually a good idea to ensure that all of your web site URLs are as search engine friendly as possible. Because each database and CMS system produces its own form of URL, it is likely you will need to talk with your supplier to find out what needs to be done for your web site. These days, all major suppliers have a response to creating search engine friendly URLs – hopefully it's a favourable one! Very often, fixing this one problem can increase the volume of traffic to your web site – often dramatically!

But your web site may be impeding the spiders in other ways too.

In order to find your web pages spiders need to be able to follow links within your site. But links on a web site can be created in a multitude of ways. A preferred link for a search engine is a text link but if your web site uses JavaScript (code that often is used to drive pop-ups or drop-down menus on a site) spiders can't always follow those links. The same applies if you use Flash technology on your site. Flash is often used to create animated web sites. They may look pretty but they will do nothing to boost your rankings.

> So, working with your web designers and technology providers is critical if you are to succeed with SEO. How they set about designing and building your site could have serious consequences for your search marketing efforts. If you are responsible for the marketing of your web site you need to make sure you are in control.

## *The importance of links*

One final piece in the 'SEO jigsaw' involves the development of third-party links to your web site. For your SEO efforts to be successful, building **link equity** is an important component.

In effect, search engines consider a link from another web site to yours as a 'vote of confidence'. But it's not simply a case of obtaining as many links to your site as possible. It is also important to ensure that each site that links to your web site has relevance to the content of your site. **Quality** links from other web sites are what search engines seek. Where they uncover quality links they will usually give a boost to your rankings.

The Google search engine was founded on technology they call PageRank – a system for ranking web pages developed by its founders Larry Page and Sergey Brin at Stanford University. To explain how PageRank works it is worth quoting from the Google web site.

### Google PageRank explained

"PageRank relies on the uniquely democratic nature of the web by using its vast link structure as an indicator of an individual page's value. In essence, Google interprets a link from page A to page B as a vote, by page A, for page B. But, Google looks at more than the sheer volume of votes, or links a page receives; it also analyses the page that casts the vote. Votes cast by pages that are themselves 'important' weigh more heavily and help to make other pages 'important.' […] Important, high-quality sites receive a higher PageRank, which Google remembers each time it conducts a search."

Google claims that PageRank is still one of the most important factors it considers when determining how to rank pages. However, Google acknowledges that 'important' pages (as determined by PageRank) have little value if they don't match a search query. Consequently (again), this is why you must take a holistic approach to SEO and treat all factors outlined in this paper with serious consideration.

## SEO techniques to avoid!

Over the years many ways have been found to boost rankings in search engines – only to find that search engines eventually respond by changing their algorithms and penalising what they consider to be dubious practices. As Google says:

> "Google's complex, automated methods make human tampering with our results extremely difficult."

But tampering is not impossible. Hence it is a continuous struggle for Google and other search engines to update their algorithms so as to ensure that 'human tampering' isn't rewarded with higher rankings. This to'ing and fro'ing between those bent on artificially inflating their rankings and the search engines continues to this day.

It is not uncommon to find references to many of these outdated methods on the web – even in recent articles! Therefore, you need to be aware which practices cause problems for search engines – and most importantly which may result in your web site being penalised, or worse banned altogether.

Some understanding of web technology will help, but you don't need to be an expert. That said, you do need to make sure you ask the right questions of your web designers, IT experts and other mission critical partners. Although no search engine reveals exactly how they determine their rankings, most do provide good advice and guidance on their web sites. Also, more importantly, they also list disapproved practices. If you have some understanding as to which practices can harm your SEO efforts you will make sure they never get implemented on your web site.

## SEO considerations & planning for future growth through SEO

Search engines will never stand still. The factors they use to boost rankings today may result in lower rankings tomorrow. Consequently it is always important to ensure you follow best practice Search Engine Optimisation at all times.

In brief, the golden rule is to create high-quality and relevant content in all areas of your web site. Search engines also want content that is fresh and up-to-date if your rankings are not to suffer. Along with a well-designed web site that does not impede search engine spiders from finding and indexing your pages, growth in the volume and quality of visitors to your web site should be sustainable – and sustainable for the long-term.

But it is very unlikely you will achieve overnight success with SEO. And that's the main challenge to Search Engine Optimisers today. All too often it can take many months to raise your natural rankings in any significant way. Therefore, you may also need to consider how you can achieve much quicker results. Pay per Click (PPC) advertising on search engines may be the answer. Not only does PPC have the potential to drive high quality visitors to your site but it can also be used as a research tool to determine what works and what doesn't in the land of search. Gaining insight from a well-structured and effective PPC campaign can pay dividends when optimising your site for natural search.

# Pay per click (PPC) advertising

Nowadays most adverts that appear on search results pages are driven through what is commonly called Pay per Click (PPC) advertising. PPC is also referred to as Paid Search, Search Advertising or Paid Listings.

The first major Pay per Click service in the Search Marketing sector was called GoTo and appeared in the US back in 1997. Google AdWords was launched in 2000. In the following year GoTo changed its name to Overture and, after being acquired by Yahoo! in 2003, is now called Yahoo! Search Marketing. Microsoft adCenter was launched in 2006. However, major PPC players didn't just follow in each other's footsteps – they innovated.

A new era in PPC advertising was heralded with a launch of Google AdWords. Google changed the PPC advertising landscape by introducing a service in which quality was deemed to be king. Although Microsoft adCenter entered the market a few years later it too was a service based around the concept of quality but it went further than Google AdWords and introduced demographic targeting of ads.

Through the introduction of services such as Google AdWords and Microsoft adCenter, advertisers with deep pockets were no longer guaranteed automatic success through Pay per Click advertising. And often those who relied primarily on automated bid management tools to help manage their campaigns found themselves at a disadvantage.

Today, the most successful PPC advertisers focus on quality at every stage of the process – something that requires human input and cannot be automated. Maximising Return on Investment should be the main driver for all advertisers to ensure they meet their PPC goals and objectives.

But before we start to look at how PPC advertising works we need to step back for a moment and cover some of the basics.

## Where do pay per click ads appear?

PPC ads usually appear down the right hand side of a search engine's results page but some search engines also show ads in other locations. Most ads are highlighted as 'Sponsored Links' or 'Sponsored Listings' to distinguish them from natural listings.

These days, on most search engines, ads also appear above natural search listings (often shaded in a colour). These are premium paid listings that usually experience higher clickthrough rates – although some search engines, such as Google and MSN, will only show premium positioned ads when they satisfy stringent quality criteria.

## Why pay per click can deliver exceptional ROI

"You only pay when your advertising works"

*Yahoo! Search Marketing Web Site*

One major benefit of PPC advertising is that you **only pay when someone clicks** on your ad and goes through to your web site. Measuring success, however, is much more than simply measuring your click costs. Maximising your Return on Investment (ROI) should be your measure of success. Consequently, you need to be able to measure how visitors interact with your web site as they progress right through the complete 'buying' process step-by-step – from when somebody clicks on your ad to the moment they place an order on your web site, for example. A web analytics solution for your web site is vital to ensure you are able to measure campaign performance. This will be discussed in more detail later.

**In addition, those who click on PPC ads are active searchers! They are actively searching for your product or service. Consequently when they arrive at your site there is a much greater likelihood that they will convert.**

## The pros & cons of PPC

### High ROI

Independent research frequently confirms that advertisers receive the highest return on investment from Paid Search when compared to email, banners and other forms of online advertising. However, that said, many, **many** businesses find that Search Engine Optimisation delivers the highest ROI overall – particularly when measured over the long term. And that includes offline marketing too!

### Quick setup

Setting up a simple campaign in services such as Google AdWords is very easy can literally mean your ads are up-and-running within minutes. Admittedly sometimes, full delivery of your ads will need to wait until your campaign has been reviewed but you can literally be receiving visitors to your web site very quickly. Setup in MSN and Yahoo! is also easy but neither will let your ads appear before they have been reviewed. It can take anything from a few hours to a few days before your ads go live.

### Disadvantages

### Expensive

Some advertisers consider PPC advertising to be expensive, but this view is often misplaced. However, it is true that average cost per click (CPC) in some competitive markets (such as in financial services) can be £10 – or even higher. But, when all is said and done, if a client win is worth many thousands of pounds to your business, even with high CPCs you can still make a healthy return. Even today in very competitive markets, many businesses are reaping huge rewards from PPC. Many more have yet to discover the full benefits they could be experiencing.

Many businesses **perceive** that their campaigns are expensive because they are running very inefficient, or very poorly managed campaigns. This is often due to lack of understanding of the complexities of the workings of PPC services. But in most cases it is because they rely on bidding higher and higher to attain (and maintain) high ad positions rather than focusing on quality – as required by both Google AdWords and Microsoft adCenter.

### Time-Consuming

Managing bids can sometimes be very time-consuming – particularly with poorly structured and inefficiently managed campaigns. As a consequence, many businesses running in-house campaigns (and also many agencies) have resorted to managing campaigns day-by-day using Bid Management software that (to a limited extent) automates the process of raising and lowering bids. A more detailed discussion on problems associated with using automated Bid Management follows but if you or your PPC agency is relying on such tools at the expense of human involvement you may have a **significant competitive disadvantage**.

## *What PPC services exist in the UK?*

The major UK Pay per Click services include Google AdWords, Yahoo! Search Marketing and Microsoft adCenter. Miva (formerly called Espotting in the UK), Mirago and a few other second tier players also exist. However, our focus in this chapter will be on the three major UK players that, together, account for more than 95% of all UK Paid Search traffic.

All three major PPC services have partner networks where their PPC ads can appear. Some also have search partners (other search engines or web sites with search features) that deliver their own PPC ads whenever a search query is entered. Other PPC services also have content partner networks where ads are displayed on web pages that are considered to be contextually relevant to keywords on which advertisers are bidding.

However, content partner ads are **not** delivered through search queries and so technically do not constitute what many regard as 'pure' Search Marketing. Suffice to say you may want to consider the additional benefits of contextual advertising. In many cases it can extend your market reach substantially.

Contextual advertising provides search engines with a very healthy proportion of their total revenues so, needless to say, they are all very keen to promote the benefits of this form of advertising. However, many advertisers find the quality of visitors that result is much poorer. Although this is not the case for all advertisers, you do need to ensure you can effectively measure the relative ROI through all your marketing channels.

Some search engines include their content partner network when quoting figures on market reach – and this isn't necessarily a true picture of their market share that is driven wholly through search advertising.

### Yahoo! Search Marketing

The PPC service that we know today as Yahoo! Search Marketing began life in 1997 as GoTo. The name was changed to Overture in 2002 and in October 2003 the company was acquired by Yahoo!. The service was rebranded in the UK as Yahoo! Search Marketing in February 2006.

If you sign up to Yahoo! Search Marketing it is possible that your ads could appear in the search results of many of the UK web sites. Unsurprisingly, this includes the Yahoo! search engine itself, but also includes AltaVista (as it happens, another acquisition of Yahoo! back in April 2003), Lycos and other, less obvious partners that offer a search engine on their site such as Orange.

Yahoo! PPC ads also **used to** be shown on MSN UK – the Microsoft search engine. However, in mid-2006 MSN launched its own PPC service – a service that had promise to change the balance of power in the PPC industry.

A few years back MSN began showing Overture ads – long before Yahoo!'s acquisition of Overture. MSN and Yahoo! secured a long-term agreement in the process. At the time Yahoo! claimed to have 80% market reach in the UK (although a significant proportion of that was through its content network).

Although Overture revolutionised online advertising when it was the first major player to launch a PPC advertising format, competitors responded by introducing their own Pay per Click services – but with much more sophisticated features.

PPC services of today fall into one of two camps. Those where ad position is determined **solely** on your keyword bid price (such as on Yahoo! Search Marketing) and those that use ad and campaign quality factors alongside keyword bids to determine ad rank – like Google AdWords and MSN. However, Yahoo! is already fighting back and its next generation PPC solution is likely to overtake both Google AdWords and Microsoft adCenter by introducing new features that neither of these provide.

Yahoo! have made public that towards the end of 2006 (or the beginning of 2007) they will be launching their new Pay per Click service. Codenamed 'Panama' it will also consider quality in the determination of ad rank position.

## Microsoft adCenter

Microsoft adCenter is the advertising platform through which you can run PPC ads on MSN Search. In time, Microsoft intends to make the adCenter the sole platform through which all forms of advertising (banner ads, video ads etc...) will be managed across all Microsoft, MSN and partner web sites.

When Microsoft adCenter launched in the UK in August 2006 a new independent PPC player entered the market. Microsoft's agreement to show Yahoo! PPC ads on the MSN search engine ended at the same time with Microsoft's own Pay per Click ads appearing in their place.

When Microsoft adCenter launched, Microsoft claimed that many Yahoo! advertisers could "lose as much as 38% of their traffic". Consequently, Microsoft was strengthening its position to battle it out in the PPC wars. Besides competing with Yahoo! head on, it also had Google in its sights.

And in many ways Microsoft adCenter is more similar to Google AdWords than Yahoo! Search Marketing ads.

Firstly Microsoft ads contain the same number of characters as Google ads. Also Microsoft adCenter considers ad quality along with maximum bids when determining how to rank ads. But the service differs in one very distinct way from Google AdWords – by providing **demographic targeting**. You have the ability to present ads to a specific customer or user segment based on day of week, time of day, gender, location, age, online behaviours, and other factors.

## Google AdWords

Google AdWords launched in October 2000 and is the most popular PPC service by far – both in the UK and globally. Google AdWords was the first Pay per Click service that introduced the concept of quality into its system.

Google also offers extensive reach. According to Nielsen/Netratings, in January 2006 nearly 19 million unique UK users used the Google search engine. And ads can appear to an even larger audience through the Google content network.

Google's search network consists of AOL, T-Online, Ask and DealTime where Google ads appear on their search results pages.

Google's emphasis with AdWords (as with Google the search engine) has always had quality as a central component. Because of this, Google AdWords introduced the concept of **quality-based bidding** – a process whereby keywords and ads that are deemed to be poor quality are disabled until ad quality is improved. Bids can also be raised to re-activate ads but doing so often requires bids to be raised to such a high level that obtaining a positive ROI becomes much more difficult. This is intentional. It's Google's way of encouraging all advertisers to focus on improving quality rather than throw money at a campaign (surprising as that might seem).

Google manages the whole process by assigning what it calls a Quality Score to all keywords and ads in a campaign. The Quality Score is determined, in part, on the performance of your keywords, ad creatives as well as the quality of your landing pages. More details on Google's Quality Score follow – suffice to say, a quality-based approach to PPC advertising is something in which all major PPC services want to succeed.

## How to decide what PPC networks to target

### Reach

According to Nielsen/Netratings, in January 2006 Google continued to dominate the search market with almost two-thirds (64%) of all search engine clickthroughs occurring on Google.

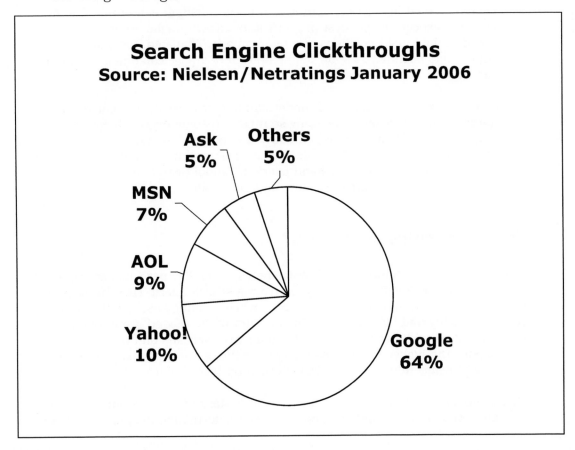

**Search Engine Clickthroughs**
**Source: Nielsen/Netratings January 2006**

Almost 19 million UK unique visitors use Google – three times as many as nearest rivals Yahoo! and MSN Search. The top search engines by Unique Audience were:

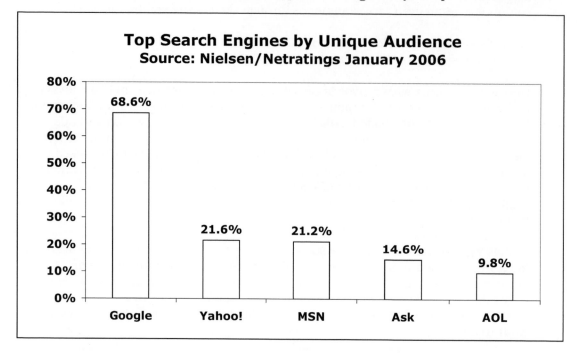

**Top Search Engines by Unique Audience**
**Source: Nielsen/Netratings January 2006**

Although these figures show the **relative volume** of searches carried out on each search engine, definitive figures that provide a breakdown of visitors coming through natural versus paid search listings are not readily available. Suffice to say, Google AdWords has the greatest market share by far – and must be considered the most important weapon in any marketer's online advertising arsenal.

Anecdotal evidence suggests that overall the proportion of search engine users who click on a paid listing (as opposed to a natural listing) is around 15%. And, as you would expect, the greatest proportion of clickthroughs are for those positioned in the top ad positions of a results page. That said, for many advertisers, ads positioned as low as the bottom of a page can still generate traffic that can be very worthwhile and profitable.

However, it is important to gain an understanding of those search engines that your target audience favours. By doing so it can, to some degree, help you to decide how to apportion your Search Marketing budget. For example, several surveys show that the 'typical' Google user is more highly educated with a higher household income. On the other hand users of Yahoo! Search are most likely to spend more time on shopping directory and guide sites.

## How do PPC services rank your ads?

One major and very important difference between the Pay per Click services is the way they rank the ads that are triggered from a search query. They fall into two camps – those that only consider your bids when ranking ads, and those that consider quality and bids together. The key aim of the second group of services is to encourage advertisers to improve the quality of their ads and overall campaigns. The higher the quality, the greater the opportunity exists to lower your costs – and hence maximise your PPC Return on Investment.

Of the three major PPC services, Yahoo! Search Marketing is the only one that considers your keyword bids in isolation when determining the position of your ads. Ad rankings in both Google AdWords and Microsoft adCenter, however, are not only determined by how high you bid but also by the quality that is associated with your keywords, ad creatives and overall campaign. Google claims to place greater emphasis on ad quality than bid price when determining ad rank. But how do Google and Microsoft determine quality?

Well, some factors that both Google and Microsoft use to determine quality are the same. However, that said, both are deliberately vague as to **all** the factors they use in their determination of quality, as well as any weighting they might give to each of these factors.

That said, both Google and Microsoft agree on one thing. One of the most important measures of quality is Clickthrough Rate (CTR). CTR is measured as a percentage and defined as:

CTR = (Number of Clicks / Number of Impressions) x 100

Their assumption is that if your ad is more appealing for a searcher to click on it, it is more likely to be relevant to their query. As a consequence the search engines consider higher CTRs to be one of the most important indicators of higher quality ads.

However, CTR needs to be measured over time – and usually search engines measure historic click activity over the most recent 1,000 impressions. Consequently, CTR will change over time – which provides an opportunity for advertisers to look at ways in which their campaigns can be improved. For very popular search queries (where ad impressions are high) CTR will change more quickly. Your objective, therefore, has to be to improve CTR in whatever way and as quickly as you can. One way to achieve this is to test different ad creatives against each other and use the ad that performs best. Google AdWords is well suited for such tests as it will let you run two (or more) ad creatives concurrently, showing each ad in equal proportions.

The most successful PPC advertisers are creating and testing new ad creatives all the time – in effect, running A/B split testing. The search engines encourage all advertisers to do the same. But this isn't pure altruism – quality PPC listings reflect well on the search engines themselves. By showing quality ads, users will return to search another day. One relatively easy way to achieve a higher CTR is to use a more relevant or highly targeted ad. Sometimes even a very small change to the wording of an ad can have a substantial uplift in CTR. Not only will higher CTRs help lower your click costs, if an ad is more relevant, those who click on it are much more likely to convert as well. A double benefit for you as an advertiser.

Now, let us look at the benefits of each PPC service, in brief to show how they work and the differences between one another.

## Google AdWords

Google AdWords was developed around the concept of quality – the same concept that was the foundation of the Google search engine. Google recognised that searchers would only remain loyal Google searchers if the quality of its advertising was as high as the natural listings it produced. As Google says:

*"...we'd rather show one less ad than to show an ad which leads to a poor user experience – since long-term user trust in AdWords is of overarching importance."*

So, when Google AdWords was introduced it provided a mechanism by which quality advertising could be rewarded from day one. This was achieved through lower costs and higher conversion rates.

Implementing this concept was brilliant in its simplicity.

First, Google wanted to ensure that advertisers are only encouraged to bid on keywords that are relevant to their campaign. Not doing so results in poor-quality ads being displayed which adds very little value to the user experience. To discourage advertisers from building untargeted keyword lists Google introduced what it calls quality-based bidding.

In quality-based bidding, if one of your keyword's CTR does not meet Google's minimum quality threshold, that keyword will become inactive and will no longer trigger the ad to which it is associated. An inactive keyword can only be re-activated if a) its quality is improved or b) its bid is raised to its 'minimum bid', or higher. Raising bids in this way can re-activate ads – but smart advertisers very rarely do so. Google knows that some minimum bids may be too high to be cost-effective. High minimum bids are Google's way of motivating advertisers to improve the quality of their target keywords.

Moreover, Google encourages advertisers to improve the quality of every component of a campaign – and to measure this it uses what it calls the **Quality Score**. The Quality Score is directly used to determine the ranking of all ads for a given search query.

Ad Rank Index = Maximum CPC (Bid) x Quality Score

The higher your Ad Rank Index, the higher your ad will be positioned in the rankings.

Once positions are determined, Google only charges for clicks on ads at a level that is required to maintain the same ad rank index. Consequently your **actual** Cost per Click can be, and very often is, lower than your Maximum bid price. Google markets this feature as a key benefit of advertising with Google AdWords.

Most importantly you will see that it is possible to increase the rank of your ad by either raising bids or improving ad quality. The most successful advertisers know the focusing on quality delivers the greatest benefit.

Each keyword, each ad creative and each overall campaign is assigned its own Quality Score. According to Google:

"Quality Score is based on clickthrough rate (CTR), relevance of ad text, historical keyword performance and other relevancy factors".

Google is deliberately vague about what constitutes those "other factors". They prefer to encourage advertisers to test, test some more and then test again and discover what advertising works best for them. If Google is too prescriptive about how advertisers can improve ad quality it knows it would encourage ads to be written that had no distinctive or individual merit. More importantly, it would restrict Google from introducing other factors into its Quality Score. They prefer to retain that flexibility – particularly since Google acknowledge that high Quality Scores have a greater influence on ad position than higher bids.

One such new introduction to the Quality Score occurred in December 2005 when Google began incorporating advertiser landing page quality into the Quality Score. Advertisers who were not providing useful and relevant landing pages saw many of their campaign keywords being made inactive by Google. A landing page is the first page a visitor sees after clicking your ad. In turn this resulted in higher minimum bid requirements for their keywords. This change created a furore amongst many advertisers who, in Google's eyes were running poor campaigns. It particularly upset the affiliate community – many of whom relied on arbitrage to generate their income. Arbitrage affiliates bought cheap ads on Google AdWords and then sent users to landing pages containing little more than dozens of ads, ads for which they received a cut of advertising revenue whenever anybody clicked through. Google made no secret that this fundamental change to AdWords was targeted at affiliates.

## MSN advertising on Microsoft adCenter

The three factors that Microsoft adCenter uses to determine ad rank are your maximum bid, Clickthrough Rate and relevance – in much the same as Google AdWords functions. And, like Google, Microsoft is vague as to how relevance is defined:

> "The relationship between an ad and its keywords, the landing page, the searcher's demographic, and the advertiser's web site."

Although Microsoft is not explicit as to the algorithm it uses to derive ad rank, it works in a similar way to Google where your maximum bid price is multiplied by an equivalent Quality Score (Google terminology) to determine ad rank.

## Yahoo! Search Marketing

Ad rank on Yahoo! Search Marketing is determined **solely** by your maximum bid – the minimum of which is £0.10. The higher you bid the higher your ad will be positioned when compared to your competitors. It's as simple as that.

Yahoo! only charges you 1 penny more than the maximum bid of the ad positioned below yours. So, for example, if you bid £2.00 and the bid of the advertiser whose ad appears below yours is £1.50 – you will only pay £1.51. Yahoo! never charges more than necessary for your ad to retain the same ad position.

Differences between the bids of advertisers appearing next to each other in the ad listings are called **bid gaps**. Yahoo! automatically removes bid gaps where it can although, in many competitive markets, large bid gaps occur infrequently.

## *Getting started – How to build a successful PPC campaign*

Now you understand how each service differs, you need to know what to consider from the moment you start thinking about running a Pay per Click campaign.

Building a PPC campaign involves a similar process for all major services. Usually the process begins by identifying keyword phrases that are relevant to your business – phrases that are most likely to be typed as search queries by those seeking your products or services.

Your target keywords should then be grouped into sets of keywords with a common theme or subject. You group according to theme because for each keyword set you need to write ad copy that is most appropriate to those keywords – something services like Google AdWords and Microsoft adCenter view as important components of quality.

The next stage involves bidding on each keyword. Each bid is the maximum price you are prepared to pay whenever one of your ads is clicked upon. Very often the price you actually pay is less than your bid, that is, in effect a **Maximum Cost per Click (CPC).** How actual prices are calculated will be explained shortly – but suffice to say, each system works differently.

> Once a campaign is underway, you will need to manage your bids. Raising and lowering bids is an important part of successful campaign management. The pros and cons of managing bids manually against using automated bid management tools will be discussed in detail later in this chapter.

Finally, you specify an ad budget and your ads should be ready to go live – subject to editorial review where appropriate.

Well, that's the abridged version. The process is much the same for any size of campaign. However, for very large campaigns consisting of many thousands of keywords (yes, you often do have to build lists of that size) taking time to define a clear structure from the outset will pay dividends in the long run. Even Google has limits on the number of keywords and ads you can place in a single account!

That said, you should never define your account structure before you have a clear idea of the objectives and goals of your campaign. To a large extent your objectives should influence how your account is structured. For example, if you are a travel agency do you categorise your keyword sets by destination or by type of holiday on offer? There is no correct answer, but your business objectives should guide you. Are you likely to raise your market budget to promote your 'Winter Sun' holiday destinations in the lead up to Christmas? If so, you need to understand how you will be able to change your budget allocations for relevant destinations in each of  the PPC services you are using. Reorganising a live and active account can take a lot of time and effort if you don't have a well-structured campaign. For many advertisers the job is too big or too complex and they need to obtain help from a SEM agency partner to manage their campaigns.

You must always be aware of limits within accounts. Running an effective PPC campaign is **never** solely about managing bids on the exact same list of keywords you used on day one of your campaign. All campaigns need active management to achieve, and ultimately sustain, a competitive advantage. As your campaign matures you will gain deeper insight into its performance. You will start to discover that certain ad creatives encourage higher clickthroughs and so you may decide to test different wording in other ads to see if they will also provide an uplift in clickthroughs. Or you might uncover that fact that some searchers who click on ads triggered by certain product-related keywords spend more when they buy on your web site. As a result you may choose to add thousands more keywords to test other product keywords. Simply put, you must actively manage a PPC campaign and so you must create a **scalable account structure** if you are to succeed with Pay per Click advertising in the long term.

### Successful campaign management

Although the most sophisticated advertisers focus primarily on improving the quality of their keywords, ads and campaigns, bids still need to be managed pro-actively.

Let's assume that you and one of your competitors are bidding on the same keyword. You both bid exactly the same amount. For the sake of argument, apart from the ad creative itself everything else is exactly the same. Over a period of time both ads will be triggered whenever somebody types in a search query that matches this keyword. If your ad is clicked on more frequently than your competitor's ad, then your keyword's CTR will rise higher than theirs. And, for a given keyword, obtaining a higher a CTR means you can lower your bid to retain the same ad position.

Of course a newly launched campaign will have no historic performance data and so will often need to bid high in the initial stages of a campaign in order to build some performance history. That said, as an advertiser you should always be looking at ways to improve the quality of your campaign. It's the smart thing to do since many of your competitors will respond to you entering the market by raising their own bids rather than focus on improving the quality of their own ads. Raising bids is a far easier thing to do – but it's not the smartest way to succeed in Pay per Click advertising.

It is not uncommon to find that some advertisers lose nerve soon after launching a campaign and terminate it soon after it started – particularly with Google AdWords and Microsoft adCenter. Starting without campaign performance history means the only way you can raise the position of your ads initially is to bid higher. In addition, new advertisers often have to bid even higher still as their competitors respond to them entering the PPC market. And, with no campaign strategy or little experience of PPC tactics, bids can very easily spiral out of control. This is the most common reason why advertisers end a campaign. They believe (often mistakenly) that the campaign is unsustainable if they carry on.

## How 'Lack of Transparency' helps improve ad quality

Google AdWords doesn't provide any indication as to how your competitors are bidding. This was a deliberate act on Google's part because they would rather advertisers focus on their own ROI rather than their competitors' Costs per Click. But many advertisers view this as a weakness. By not giving this information Google has created an issue for many advertisers – and particularly agencies that manage PPC campaigns on behalf of their clients.

Many advertisers feel they are at a disadvantage when managing Google AdWords campaigns when they do not know how their competitors are bidding. They believe they should have access to this information because Yahoo! Search Marketing provides them with some indication of competitors' bids. However, the more sophisticated advertiser who fully understands how quality-based PPC services work can deliver exceptional ROI without needing to know what an equivalent campaign is costing their competitors.

Not making bids visible to all is Google's way of encouraging advertisers to produce quality campaigns. Doing so requires testing alternatives for ad creatives, landing pages etc... at every opportunity. The last thing Google wants to do is to be prescriptive about how advertisers can improve their AdWords campaigns. Doing so would simply create a landscape where all adverts appeared the same – not something that helps to improve the user experience.

Microsoft also chose not to reveal competitors' bids when it launched Microsoft adCenter.

## Pay per click advertising is not a traditional media buy

Because of this 'lack of transparency' many advertisers and agencies realise that pay per click advertising is not the same as a traditional online media buy – such as buying space for banner ads. PPC advertising is closer to an auction where bids on keywords are dynamic during the life of a campaign. However, factors of quality that now exist in Google AdWords and Microsoft adCenter muddy the waters even more for many advertisers.

## Reliance on bid management tools

Because PPC advertising is more complicated than many advertisers imagined, some have come to rely on technology such as bid management tools as the primary means to manage their campaigns. It is true that keyword bids need to be managed throughout a campaign but managing bids to the exclusion of improving quality (through which a **real** competitive advantage can be achieved) is very short-sighted.

For one, bid management tools take away the need to change bids manually and many find their use is a great time saver. A range of different bid rules can be defined within these systems. All bid management systems should let you change bids according to ROI as a minimum. However, many also let you change bids according to where your competitors' ads are positioned. Making use of such rules can result in **bid wars** in which you and your competitors can end up paying very high CPCs unnecessarily.

Before explaining how bid wars arise and result in poorer performing campaigns for all advertisers caught up in them, we need to go back to how PPC services charge **actual** CPCs.

Yahoo! Search Marketing first calculates your ad position based on how your bid compares to your competitors' bids. Once positions are determined, the CPC you actually incur for clickthroughs on your ad will only be £0.01 more than the ad positioned below yours. Some advertisers try to take advantage of this and use an automated rule to bid £0.01 less than an ad ranked in a given position – resulting in the advertiser above having to pay their full bid price for every click. Most bid management tools let you set up rules in this way and is a technique often called **bid jamming**.

Some advertisers believe that they can force a competitor to spend its full ad budget sooner by jamming their bids. However, one key feature that providers of bid management tools promote is the facility to change bids several times per day. The problem arises when several advertisers use bid management tools (and very often the **same** bid management tools – there aren't that many of them on the market!) in an effort to compete. Bids on both sides are changed so frequently that all bids end up rising much higher than they need to. Usually, everyone caught up in a bid war ends up losing. The smart advertisers focus primarily on building quality campaigns and invariably are advertisers who manage campaign bids without complete reliance on bid management tools.

When automated bid management tools first appeared on the market, they proved very successful in removing unnecessary bid gaps for many advertisers. Saving 20% or more on CPCs made a strong case to invest in such tools. However, nowadays, where gaps between competitors' bids are much smaller (particularly in highly competitive markets) the potential gains are much lower and so the cost of investing in a bid management tool is harder to justify. Moreover, use of bid management tools are coming under increasing pressure from the PPC services themselves – in effect, they are becoming victims of their own success.

Because many bid management tools let you change bids several times a day, this uses bandwidth and Google and other PPC services don't like anything that might (cumulatively at least) have an adverse impact on performance of their servers. So, in October 2006 Google will introduce a system whereby advertisers will pay every time they use their bid management tool to make a change in their campaign. The more changes the higher the charge. Google's clear intention here is to discourage advertisers from changing bids too frequently – something that they feel it totally unnecessary. Many industry observers believe other PPC service providers will follow suit.

So for many advertisers the benefits of using automated bid management tools need to be considered against the costs incurred. Some bid management services charge a fee based on the size of an account to be managed – the more keywords the higher the cost. Because the more sophisticated advertisers build campaigns with a large number of keywords, this can often work against them when considering whether or not to use bid management tools.

## Good analytics for successful integrated SEO & PPC

However you choose to manage your SEO or PPC campaigns you will need to be sure that you have a good web analytics solution in place. And, whatever analytics solution you choose, you need to ensure that it is configured and implemented correctly. Metrics against which you measure success need to be defined from the outset but they also need to be defined in such a way that you can take actions based on their outcome. Metrics that are not actionable are of little use.

You also need an effective analytics solution if there is to be cross-pollination of insight between your SEO and PPC campaigns. For example, PPC campaigns can identify which keywords are yielding the greatest ROI quickly and easily. By acting on this intelligence, content based around those keywords can be developed for your web site that, in time, will deliver free visitors through Search Engine Optimisation. Equally, keywords that are driving natural traffic may provide an untapped opportunity for testing an extended list of related keywords in your PPC campaign.

So, knowing how many visitors arrive at your web site is only one, albeit important, metric you need to measure. Many other metrics can, and should be used to measure the effectiveness of your campaigns. And, most importantly, some of your metrics must, in some way, measure quality factors that play a part in both your SEO and PPC campaigns. For example, the number of pages viewed or the amount of time visitors spend on your web site provides some measure of the quality of content within your site. Since 'quality' is the mantra of all major search engines, particularly Google, identifying ways to improve quality at every opportunity is a never-ending process. By not doing so you will never be able to achieve a long-term sustainable competitive advantage through Search Engine Marketing.

# Email: marketing's most abused communications tool

## This chapter includes:

---

- ❑ **The tools available to an email marketer**

- ❑ **How to acquire names from a website, from customers, and from external list brokers**

- ❑ **Legal requirements when conducting an email campaign**

- ❑ **The correct components of a marketing email**

- ❑ **Testing for continuous improvement**

- ❑ **Eight steps to creating a successful viral campaign**

- ❑ **E-newsletters**

---

## About this chapter

**T**his chapter develops an understanding of the relevant technologies, marketing applications and regulatory controls needed to deliver results from email marketing, as well as techniques for the running of viral campaigns, and guidance on the design and use of e-newsletters.

All of which combine to allow you to plan, execute, measure and budget for effective email marketing campaigns.

## Will Rowan, F IDM

consultant, author, speaker and practitioner in digital marketing
email: ask@thecustomer.co.uk
tel: 020 7078 7680

When the web arrived Will worked out which direct marketing principles apply online. And which don't.

– Consultancy firm TheCustomer builds web-savvy, marketing-led business strategies that work, with clients' activities including local e-government, ethical remedies & fantasy football.

– In 2002 Will co-founded MorningPapers – an easy, clever & quick virtual typing service that delivers overnight typing for a blue-chip client list.

– TheCustomer's partner organistions deliver rapid & effective business decisions, Virtual Team Insights workshops, and a full-service marketing communications agency – through a virtual company, of course!

Will is the author of *Digital Marketing* (Kogan Page, 2002) and *The eCommerce Pocketbook*, which is available in 6 languages, with two editions in Chinese.

# Chapter 5.9

# Email: marketing's most abused communications tool

## Introducing email as a marketing tool

**I**f online marketing's rise to prominence in recent years has been remarkable, email marketing has been the most visible driving force behind the growth of digital marketing.

Online marketers have a varied toolkit at their disposal – from straightforward information emails to prospects, to service emails for customers, surveys, e-newsletters and viral mails. Whether email is used business-to-business, for PR, to customers, prospects or staff, it can be a powerful marketing tool.

Email is used so universally that first timers often assume that marketing by email is no more complex than sending a single message, many times over. Not only could nothing be further from the reality of email marketing, that single misconception is at the root of the difficulties in planning and executing a campaign with success.

The power and problems of using email as a channel to market are in the ease with which huge volumes can be assembled and despatched. Take care to minimise spam risk at every stage of executing a campaign.

Email can rapidly damage a company's reputation. The risk of spam is considerable – even if it is unintentional. Not only do the systems which individuals and companies put in place to protect themselves from unsolicited email make it increasingly difficult for the legitimate marketer to reach their marketplace,but a company which spams its marketplace will find that its everyday business emails don't get delivered.

This chapter examines how successful email marketing campaigns are put together, from the success factors of planning, timing, targeting and offer, to tracking and measurement, to working through all the stages of a comprehensively developed email marketing programme.

Successful email, viral and newsletter campaigns create new and nurture existing customers at low cost. Exceptionally strong programmes can change how customers react to marketing communications, from seeing them as promotions, to welcoming each email as relevant information and privileged treatment.

## Plan campaigns around permission and request marketing

Permission marketing is about much more than an opt-in box: it is a different approach to marketing that relies on gaining and keeping your customers' trust. The continuing popularity of Seth Godin's book Permission Marketing (Godin, 1999) is well deserved. However, remarkably few marketers who claim to practice permission marketing have actually read and understood the book. In the last five years, adoption of web and email by marketers has increased so dramatically that there is a danger that, if email marketing is not practised sensitively, it will become interruption marketing – exactly the problem that Godin suggests should be avoided.

The permission in permission marketing is granted through an individual opting in to communications by proactively agreeing to receive communications.

### Reduce interruption marketing.

Seth Godin says: "Permission marketers spend as little time and money talking to strangers as they can. Instead, they move as quickly as they can to turn strangers into prospects who choose to opt in to a series of communications."

All marketing channels can interrupt when they are used – interruption marketing (see http://www.marketingterms.com/dictionary/permission_marketing/ for useful definitions) is the traditional communications process of interrupting what a recipient was doing at the point of viewing your communication. The interruption goes a step deeper than mere intrusion: it fails to take account of what the recipient was recently doing or thinking, or any preferences and interests that have been expressed.

Godin describes four tests of permission marketing:

1.  Does every single marketing effort you create encourage a learning relationship with your customers? Does it invite customers to 'raise their hands' and start communicating?

2.  Do you have a permission database? Do you track the number of people who have given you permission to communicate with them?

3.  If consumers gave you permission to talk to them, would you have anything to say? Have you developed a marketing curriculum to teach people about your products?

4.  Once people become customers, do you work to deepen your permission to communicate with those people?

The permission marketing concept suggests that communications requested by customers have a greater impact and higher response rates than the many unsolicited communications which bombard us each day through print, mail and TV. Seth Godin says that permission-based communications are anticipated, personal and relevant.

As many have pointed out, and as Godin recognises, interruption will always be needed for customer acquisition and when starting a dialogue with potential customers. The initial interruption should seek to reduce the need to interrupt again in the future. To that end, registration forms exist for a purpose – to engage customers with your marketing process. If a customer has not opted in, do not send them email. Do not ignore the information gathered in databases – it can make every email more relevant to the recipient.

How does your last email campaign fare on Godin's four tests?

1.a   Does it create a learning relationship?

1.b   Does it invite customers to 'raise their hands' and start communicating?

2.   Is there a permission database?

3.a   Does your marketing system listen, hear and react to the information provided by respondents?

3.b   How does that change future marketing communications to those respondents?

4.   How does the marketing relationship change over time?

## Think 'request marketing'

Email campaigns should be planned to encourage customers to ask for more emails in the future. That's likely to mean offering them a choice of which emails they are sent.

The internet changes the central power source in marketing, from the seller to the customer – the web is far more customer-centred than the high street.

Web usability expert Jakob Nielsen argues that online marketing should not be about the company gaining permission, but the customer requesting information; a subtle, but important distinction.

"The web must reverse the traditional direction of marketing. Instead of a company generating messages when it wants to reach its customers, with request marketing the company sends only messages that users ask for. Request marketing is especially suited to the mobile internet, where intrusive messages are ultra aggravating."

*Full column at: http://www.useit.com/alertbox/20001015.html*

Nielsen gives the example of the facility on Amazon where a site visitor can request email notification about future books from an author.
Notifications requested by the user can also be shown on the website on future visits in what Nielsen refers to as 'an information control panel'.

Notifications and alerts could include a wide range of information that's useful to a customer:

a) New products

b) Product updates

c) Service updates

d) Contract renewal approaching

e) New local shops

f) Public advertising and promotions

g) Customer-only advertising and promotions

## Illustration

Email is more effective when users are able to choose their own interests.
If the aim of permission, and request, marketing is to make marketing more useful, it makes sense to let recipients request which emails they want to receive.

Four of the main options for communications preferences are offering selections by:

1. Format – text versus HTML

2. Frequency – individual emails, daily, weekly, monthly, quarterly or alerts

3. Content – news, products, offers and events

4. Channel – email or direct mail

Of course, there are resource implications for tailoring communications, so you will need to consider which give the best benefit. Frequency and format are probably the options that will give the best response for the least resource cost.

Customers are far less likely to treat email as unwelcome spam if it is useful – and they are likely to request information that's useful to them.

## Example

Wippit offers a choice of HTML and text email delivery. The same email is shown below, in two versions: HTML graphics and plain text. Visitors to Wippit can choose their preferred email format before they take out a paid subscription:

### Figure 5.9.1

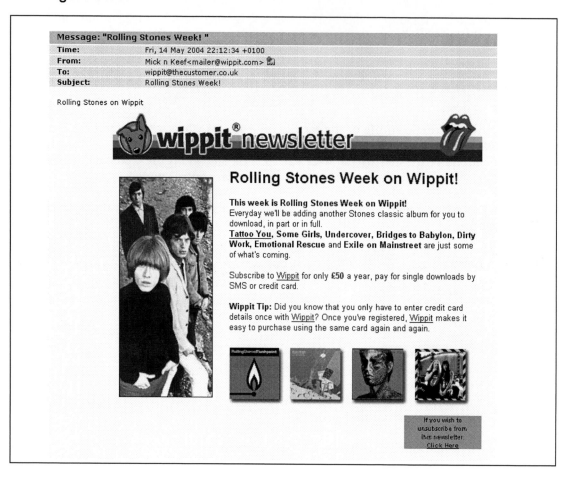

### Figure 5.9.2

| Message: "Rolling Stones Week! " | |
|---|---|
| Time: | Fri, 14 May 2004 22:12:34 +0100 |
| From: | Mick n Keef<mailer@wippit.com> |
| To: | wippit@thecustomer.co.uk |
| Subject: | Rolling Stones Week! |
| Format: | Show HTML-version |

Rolling Stones on Wippit

Rolling Stones Week on Wippit!

This week is Rolling Stones Week on Wippit!
Everyday we'll be adding another Stones classic album for you to
download, in part or in full.
Tattoo You, Some Girls, Undercover, Bridges to Babylon, Dirty Work,
Emotional Rescue and Exile on Mainstreet are just some of what's coming.

Subscribe to [1]Wippit for only £50 a year, pay for single downloads by
SMS or credit card.

Wippit Tip: Did you know that you only have to enter credit card details
once with Wippit? Once you've registered, Wippit makes it easy to
purchase using the same card again and again.

If you wish to
unsubscribe from
this newsletter:
Click Here

1. http://wippit.com/

Though the two emails are largely the same, the text version is a summary of the HTML version text – it hasn't been edited to be as clear as possible. The HTML version is therefore easier to understand.

Some customers may not want a weekly email; they may only want to hear about new product releases. Their choice will be personal and the sending company cannot really make a judgement on the recipient's behalf.

## Checklist

Which of these alert activities does your organisation collect and tell customers about? When could your company offer customers requested email?

### Table 5.9.1

| | | By email | By another channel (which one/s) |
|---|---|---|---|
| a) | New products | | |
| b) | Product updates | | |
| c) | Service updates | | |
| d) | Contract renewal approaching | | |
| e) | New local shops | | |
| f) | Public advertising and promotions | | |
| g) | Customer-only advertising and promotions | | |

On what other occasions could your company gather and use alert information that would be useful to customers?

# *The marketers' email toolkit*

By the end of this section you will have seen all the components that can be included in a successful email marketing campaign, and examined the contribution that each part of the toolkit makes to the overall success of a campaign. You will be able to plan an effective email marketing campaign, and understand the importance of planning a campaign from end to end before it begins.

You will discover:

- Assessing the most appropriate targeting for a campaign

- Identifying an offer

- Understanding how to develop a measurable campaign

- The value of testing

## Components of a campaign

Email marketing is a primary digital communication channel for marketers. To be effective, marketers must get and keep their recipients' trust. They must also balance the ability to deliver rapid and inexpensive marketing emails against the respect for recipients and the marketers' own need to test effectively, and learn to develop their communications programmes.

The cornerstone of any successful email campaign lies in its planning – which should begin with permission-based principles and detail every step of the campaign before the first email is despatched. (http://www.permission.com)

The core elements of an email marketing campaign:

acquiring and storing email lists.

## Build permission email lists through a mix of communications channels

There are many ways to add email addresses to your database – with permission to use them – and buying external lists is not the only route to building your in house email database. Email can act as a powerful channel in the communications mix – and customers will often prefer to respond online, which builds the email database for future activities.

Emails cannot be sent without a contact email address. It is absolutely practical to use an email address list without knowing the names or any further information about the recipient.

The email address may well have been provided by a customer:

- Directly at a physical point of purchase

- By telephone

- Through an online channel – website, email or SMS

Alternatively, the recipients' names may be bought through a broker. Where traditional direct mail lists are often segmented by interests and geography (proximity to the business), it is most likely that an email list will be sourced by interests and recent behaviour.

Email lists decay much faster than analogue marketing data: buy and use email addresses that are as new as possible.

Table 5.9.2     **Sourcing customer data, channel by channel**

Recipients of emails do engage with communications that they have proactively agreed to receive. Responsiveness to permission email campaigns is supported by these trend reports:

- Doubleclick (EMEA) http://emea.ie.doubleclick.net/uk/research.asp. Average open rate across Europe is 40 per cent with an average clickthrough rate of emails opened around 10 per cent.

- Doubleclick (US) www.doubleclick.com/us/knowledge_central shows that clickthrough rates are not declining despite SPAM.

- Clickthrough

In spite of 70 per cent plus of all email sent being spam, email response rates have not experienced the dramatic decline in response seen with banner advertising over its first five years.

There are other alternatives to using email marketing to gain permission online apart from renting email lists:

- Advertise in a third-party e-newsletter. This can help you learn about targeting and the types of offers that will work.

- Co-branded emails, such as one sent out by a mobile phone company to its subscribers but featuring a credit card company, are another alternative.

- Online advertising through traditional graphical online advertisements.

- Pay per performance or pay per click advertising on Google AdWords Overture or Espotting.

- Microsites on third-party or advertiser sites will get better opt-in response rates than a clickthrough to an opt-in on your own site.

Any method, such as reciprocal linking or natural search engine listings, which gains visitors to your site is an opportunity to gain permission. Smart companies which practice e-permission marketing design their websites to showcase offers which encourage permission to be gained from all digital footfall on the site.

Of course, it is not only online tools that help gain permission online. Many campaigns have shown that email marketing produces the best response when offline media are used first to build campaign awareness.

Email used to support a product launch:

> When JD Edwards launched a new CRM product they started offline,
> promoting the event in print, and offering a choice of response channels:
>
> a)   Direct mail and print ads were used to build awareness about the
>      event
>
> b)   Emails were then sent to house and external lists
>
> c)   Email generated the most acceptances for attendance at a launch
>      event
>
> d)   The web form for booking referred to in print communications was
>      the most popular response mechanism from print
>
> Future campaigns will benefit from an enlarged inhouse email database

## Acquiring names and email lists

### The difference between inhouse and third-party lists

House lists should always outperform an external bought-in list: recipients on an inhouse list should have some affinity with the company, and will have signed up and given specific consent for the company to write to them. They are more likely to open and respond to an email. Having given personal information and the consent to use it in the past, they are more likely to keep that information up to date – which means that the list will continue to be a likely better performer than an external list.

Proper uses of an inhouse mailing list:

When prospective recipients consent to receiving your company's emails they should understand what it is they are signing up for. Normal purposes would include:

• Service updates

• Product updates

• Product and service offers from your company

It would be an abuse of the recipient's consent if your company sent email every time there's a change in the product range or price list. Customers are rarely as interested in company products as you are!

Send email about products and services that customers say they are interested in.

When recipients are adding themselves to your mailing list, ask them for some information that helps filter in product and service mailings. Please note, that's filter in: assume that customers have no interest in the company's products, and that it is the company's duty to find out what they're interested in, rather than assuming that customers will be interested in receiving information on everything you sell – they won't and the company's emails will soon be treated as spam.

When opt-in is not required:

If the recipient has purchased a product or service from your company, strictly there is no need for opt-in consent to mail them with information relating to the delivery of that contracted product or service, or to similar products and services. However, we have all become so accustomed to seeing privacy statements and opt-in boxes at the point of purchase, that it would seem odd if these questions were not asked. Anything that reduces a customer's trust of the company is best avoided, so best practice suggests asking for consent even when it is not required.

The Information Commissioner describes this in relation to the Privacy and Electronic Communications (EC Directive) Regulations 2003:

"This strict opt-in rule is relaxed if three exemption criteria are satisfied.
These three exemption criteria are as follows:
1. The recipient's email address was collected 'in the course of a sale or negotiations for a sale'.
2. The sender only sends promotional messages relating to their 'similar products and services'.
3. When the address was collected, the recipient was given the opportunity to opt out (free of charge except for the cost of transmission) which they didn't take. The opportunity to opt out must be given with every subsequent message."

*From the Information Commissioner's website at*
*http://tinyurl.com/342h6*
*www.informationcommissioner.gov.uk*

(For fuller guidance on this subject, see chapter 12.2.)

Tesco shows how to make opt-in easy for their prospects:

Tesco have created a very simple registration process – the first page asks for just three facts:

- Email address

- Postcode

- Loyalty card number

Customers without a Clubcard account are offered a pop-up box, confirming that by registering online they will create a virtual Clubcard.

## Figure 5.9.3

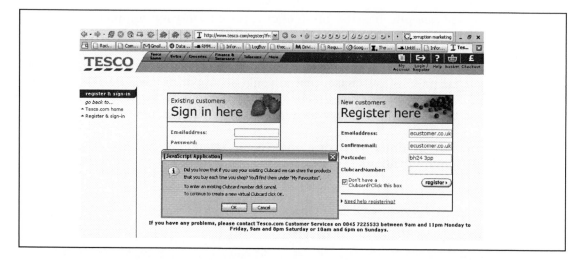

The second screen asks only four more questions, three of which are necessary to fulfil the service that's being signed up for. Customers are also asked where they heard about the service – the only question which is not strictly needed to deliver an online shopping order, but quite a reasonable request.

## Figure 5.9.4

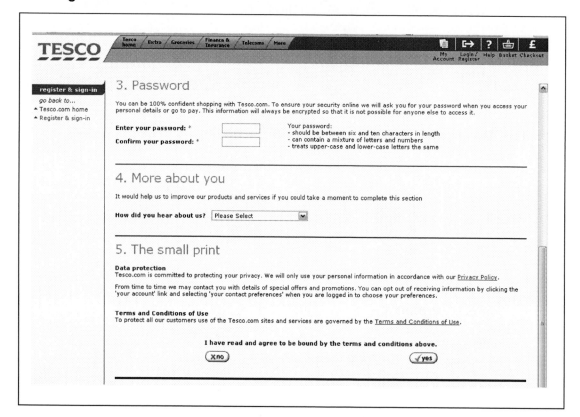

Tesco have done away with a tick box, replacing it with a colourful green 'Yes' checkmark – it performs the same task as an opt-in box, without the same privacy connotations. Even the smallest design detail matters when a company is asking for permission from their customers.

### How to maintain and grow an inhouse list

Respecting customers' privacy is the strongest way to maintain a list's integrity: do not send mail when it's convenient for the company – send it when it's likely to be useful to the recipient.

Make sure that your emails help recipients keep their information up to date. Add footers that allow recipients to:

- Unsubscribe, in one click

- Update their details

- Forward to a friend or colleague

If your company respects recipients' privacy, and makes proper use of their data, recipients will keep their details up to date, and are much more likely to forward email to their network. Recipients who have these options are also less likely to unsubscribe. The proportion of bounce backs will also reduce.

A consumer company added 'update your details' and 'forward to a friend' links to their emails. Over a three-month period, unsubscribers dropped from some five per cent to under two per cent, every mailing produced information updates from three to four per cent of recipients, and new 'forward to a friend' subscribers replaced the numbers lost to unsubscribers.

### Abuse of an inhouse list

Because house lists tend to perform well, it is tempting to abuse them. Abuse might take the form of:

- Over-frequent use

- Sending emails 'for the sake of it', with no content of value to the recipient

- Offering unrelated products or services from the company

- Offering unrelated products or services from a third party

An abused house list will not only deliver progressively lower opening and clickthrough rates, it will also lose the recipient's trust.

### Pros and cons of external lists

A third-party list cannot offer the same level of commitment or brand engagement as a house list. Recipients will have signed up for 'accepting offers from trusted third parties'. They may have been busy trying to win a competition, or have attended a trade exhibition. However, a third-party list can quickly boost the size of an email campaign. That may be invaluable if your company is launching a major initiative or a product into a new market area.

There are three types of external list:

- A 'shared interests' affiliate list, provided by a related business with customers who share interests or needs

- A 'profession' list, which may be built from exhibition or subscription lists

- A compiled list, built by reviewing directories or telephone canvassing

Some consumer lists resold by brokers are compiled from competition entrants. The best of these will share interests – the least committed will perform at the level of compiled lists. DMA member brokers offer assured standards of service, should clean all data against suppression lists before supply, and can participate in practice audits of business lists.

See http://www.dmabusinesslistaudit.org.uk/Content/BLA_Intro.asp

External lists can add:

More names to a house list, more quickly than other routes, as recipients respond and add themselves to the house list
Numbers, to create a bigger campaign

They will also add:

Spam risk, as recipients have mail that they didn't ask for
Wastage, as targeting will be notably poorer

External lists – affiliate arrangements

Sharing lists with relevant companies may offer a compromise route to expanding a house list, without the same levels of creating spam for their customers. Affiliate lists work well where there are clear associations between two companies' brands and customer interests.

## Legal issues – lists, transparency and notification

(NB: For a fuller discussion of the legal issues surrounding direct marketing, see Section 12 of this Guide.)

Some email address lists for sale have been compiled by spidering company websites. It would be in breach of the Data Protection Act and the Electronic Communications Directive to send email to these addresses. Always purchase lists from warranted brokers who are members of the Direct Marketing Association (DMA).

Though we often refer to the European data protection regulations – and take that to mean the European Union – your data's boundary includes not only the 25 EU member countries, but also Norway, Iceland and Liechtenstein – the totality being the European Economic Area (EEA). The EEA was maintained because of the wish of these three countries to participate in the Internal Market, while not assuming the full responsibilities of EU membership.
See http://europa.eu.int/comm/external_relations/eea/

Lists acquired within the EEA may be moved among member states without restriction, within the terms of the EU's Data Protection Directive. Moving data outside the EU may require specific consent from the list owner or the individual subjects.

In practice many companies handling data outside the EEA are willing to commit contractually to the same data protection standards as any company within the EU, which usually addresses privacy concerns for non-sensitive data.

Data moved to the US should be covered under a Safe Harbor agreement. For Safe Harbor information, visit: http://www.the-dma.org/safeharbor/ (See also chapter 12.1 on the need for legal advice.)

## Registering with the Information Commissioner

If you're storing any email addresses for commercial purposes, your company should check its data protection registration status: exemptions from registration are possible for small and not-for-profit businesses. An assessment process is available at http://www.ico.gov.uk/eventual.aspx?id=2662.

Without proper data storage routines a marketer can quickly breach the Data Protection Act. Store addresses carefully, so that their origin can always be traced, to minimise the chances of sending inappropriate messages to:

- An address which has requested that they be unsubscribed

- Duplications of the same addressee

- An address which has repeatedly been undelivered

If your business holds personal or company data – even if it is simply a business card – the company may need to notify the Information Commissioner. The Bar Council has a good summary of the legislation here: http://tinyurl.com/6jm5j It notes that direct marketing by email is regulated by Regulations 22 and 23 of the DPA.

Regulation 2 defines electronic mail as:

> "Any text, voice, sound or image message sent over a public electronic communications network which can be stored in the network or in the recipient's terminal equipment until it is collected by the recipient, and includes messages sent using a short message service".

Regulation 22 describes the requirement for prior opt-in as:

> "A person shall neither transmit, nor instigate the transmission of unsolicited communications for the purposes of direct marketing by means of electronic mail unless the recipient of the electronic mail has previously notified the sender that he consents for the time being to such communications being sent by,or at the instigation of, the sender."

However, there is an allowable 'soft opt-in', where email can be sent if:

1. Contact details were gathered during a sale or negotiations

2. The email is only for similar products and services

3. The recipient had a simple means of refusing when the details were first collected, and with every subsequent communication

New rules on email marketing;
What do they mean for individuals?

Since December 2003, two new rules have applied to email marketing when the Privacy and Electronic Communications (EC Directive) Regulations 2003 came into force:

First new rule
This rule applies to all marketing messages sent by electronic mail, regardless of who the recipient is:
- The sender must not conceal their identity
- The sender must provide a valid address for opt-out requests

Second new rule
This rule only applies to unsolicited marketing messages sent by electronic mail to individual subscribers:
- Senders cannot send such messages unless they have the recipient'sprior consent to do so

*From the Information Commissioner's website at*
*http://tinyurl.com/342h6*
*www.informationcommissioner.gov.uk*
*(http://www.itspublicknowledge.info/ for the Scottish Information Commissioner)*

Visit the Business Link website and complete their notification tool, using your company's use of data to complete the questions.
http://tinyurl.com/55hpf
http://www.businesslink.gov.uk

## Opting out of email marketing

Consumers may opt out of receiving email by registering with the email preference scheme, run jointly by the UK and US Direct Marketing Associations.
http://www.dmaconsumers.org/emps.html
Businesses using consumer lists should clean their lists against this register:
http://preference.the-dma.org/products/

## *The email*

Emails always comprise a number of elements:

- The sender's name

- The subject line

- The return address

- The body of the email

- And, normally hidden from the recipient's eyes, routing information

The email may also optionally contain:

- Images, delivered with the email

- Images, drawn into the email from an external source when it is opened

- Attachments, normally delivering supporting information

- Sound and video, delivered with or streamed to the email

- A signature file

- Account administration information, describing how to unsubscribe and update the user's details, or to subscribe

## Sending out an email

The simple process of sending an email becomes complex when many messages are sent together.

Sending a single email is quite straightforward. You will need:

### Table 5.9.3

a) An account to send your email from

b) An email address for the recipient

c) An address to which they can reply

d) A subject line that gets their attention and tells the recipient what's in the email

e) Some content

Sending multiple emails adds several complexities.

If the emails are to be sent from your own company's email system, then:

f) Check that sending large volumes of email does not breach your contract with the company ISP

g) Be sure that the number of email you're sending, and replies you receive, will not interfere with colleagues' normal work routines

h) Decide if it is possible to personalise the emails you're sending

i) Decide if you're going to send a text or HTML version, or both

j) Be prepared to send your emails in small batches of less than 20, to reduce the likelihood of being caught in spam filters before the email reaches your recipient's email inbox

k) Make sure the links in your email work, and that the landing pages are online

l) Plan how to manage responses:

  – The response that you intended

  – Unintended responses – recipients will ask 1001 questions by email, phone, post and in- store

  – Unsubscribe requests

m) Set down how you're going to measure how effective the email campaign has been, remembering that some of the impact will be by post, phone and in-store, as well as on your website and by email

If your emails are being sent out by a third party, then:

n) Ensure that they manage your inhouse lists and any external lists responsibly, cleaning them against relevant databases – http://www.dma.org.uk/content/Prf-Introduction.asp

o) Make sure you have a way of properly reimporting the lists, with their correct permissions and history, after the campaign

p) Brief the mailing house on how to handle:

   – Hard bounces, that don't leave their server; usually an improperly formed email address, which can be fixed by software or manual checking

   – Soft bounces, where the receiving mailbox is found, but cannot be delivered to right now. How often should the email be resent?

q) What charges will you pay for:

   – Set up costs to import data to the mailing house's systems, any cleaning and personalisation charges

   – Setting up creative versions – text, HTML and test versions

   – Any charges for establishing or hosting landing pages

   – Testing of as many or few parts of the campaign as you request

   – Sending out the emails

   – Returning cleaned lists (or lists and cleaning activity) for reloading to your inhouse database

## The landing page

Landing pages (or splash pages) should be purpose-built for each email marketing campaign.

Visitors to the landing page will normally be asked to:

- Register for more information

- Provide for sales follow-up

- Make a purchase

The intention is that the recipient will complete any personal information or purchase details, and submit these to the company. Best practice is to acknowledge that recipients will feel most comfortable if they have the option to explore further information about the product, the company and its support services, before completing their registration or purchase.

If the email is sent to existing customers as a service announcement, then the landing page may contain full details of the new information, links to downloadable documents, or links to a software update, where these would be too large to include in the original email.

Once visitors have completed their task and submitted their information, they would expect to be shown a confirmation page, which conventionally thanks them for what they have just done, and offers a comprehensive set of links to other relevant parts of the company's website.

Most visitors would expect, if they have given any form of information or made any payment, that they will receive a confirmation email, almost instantly.

The same email filters that folk and their ISPs use to block spam can block information and marketing email that they've signed up to receive.

Many of your subscribers will not be familiar with how their ISPs' email filters and mail programmes' white lists work. Here's a clear explanation:

Filters are looking for a number of key criteria, against which they scour every email which passes across their servers. These criteria are likely to include –

- The number of emails despatched from a server at any one time

- The 'to', 'from', and 'reply to' fields of the email

- The header information in the email

- Whether the email draws images or similar content from another internet server

- The presence of attachments, which are likely to be virus checked

- The obvious filter points of subject, and body copy of the email

Useit.com's registration process explains filters and white lists, to make sure that customers receive future emails:

## Figure 5.9.5

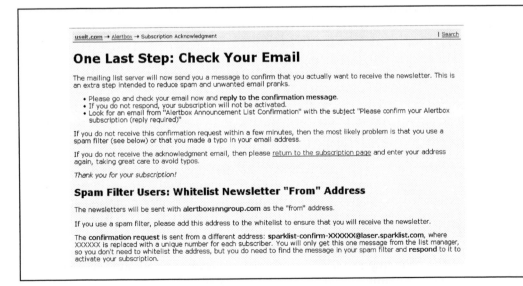

Without straightforward advice like this every subscription list is at greater risk of having subscriber email go undelivered.

## *Response objectives and mechanisms*

The most conventional response route is an HTML link to a landing page on the company's website. Some emails will contain a response device – a phone number, form to complete, a clickthrough to an external web page, or simply inviting a reply to the email. More sophisticated marketers are likely to create a microsite, which might be specific to the campaign or to a product or brand.

Your recipients could be asked to do a number of things once they have opened your email.

They could be asked to update their personal information, register for future product or service news, for promotions, or to participate in a website promotion; or even to place an order for your product.

Online, their response mechanism might be to:

- Complete a form in your email, and return it

- clickthrough to a landing page on your website, using a text or image hyperlink in your email

- Send an SMS

Offline, they might respond by:

- Phoning your company

- Printing off and posting an application form

- Printing a voucher you've emailed to them, and using it in-store

- Being more likely to notice and use an on-pack promotion in-store

- Visiting a shop to make a purchase

While email marketing campaigns should be planned around a direct response and purchase, the internet is not simply used to make purchases. At different times customers may prefer to use the web for research (which might be triggered by receiving an email) and to make their purchase in some other way – by phone or visiting a shop.

Landing pages should be built to a template, so that they are quick and inexpensive to change. A landing page should be changed so that it reflects the email which directed the visitor to the landing page. If the offer changes, so should the landing page.

An ad campaign's landing page should never be the corporate home page of a company website. The internet is a user-driven medium, and making life more difficult for users will simply result in a reduced response.

Each way of sending out the email campaign will have costs and benefits. These should be considered very early in the planning process, alongside the promotion's objectives and the response mechanism you've selected.

## *Response management*

The system to track the response to an email campaign needs to be set up well in advance of the first email being dispatched. Most email response is delivered within the first two hours, and there is simply no time to correct any errors once a campaign has been despatched. The measurement system should show:
Bounce rates – the number of emails sent that were not delivered
Opening rates, for HTML emails
Clickthrough rates, where the recipient has clicked on a link in an email and conversion rates, where the recipient has followed the hoped-for activity from the email
Website tracking, to see which routes recipients took after they had landed on the company's website at the landing page

As well as measuring the activity that the email campaign has generated, the measurement process should be able to track the value of that activity. Notional values may be attached to email addresses which were delivered, opened and responded to, generating traffic on the website. A new visitor, or retained customer may be assigned a value: a new purchase clearly has a value that can be attributed to the email campaign. If printable vouchers or promotion codes are used, the email campaign's sales impact can be measured in the store, and by telephone sales as well as through the website.

## Table 5.9.4

| Planning checklist | Yes or no | Issues and improvements |
|---|---|---|
| For campaigns sent out internally: | | |
| a) Check ISP contract | | |
| b) Bandwidth check: Can colleagues continue working? | | |
| c) Will emails be personalised? | | |
| d) Create text version | | |
| e) Create HTML version | | |
| f) Despatch batch size | | |
| g) Test links | | |
| h) Test landing pages | | |
| i) Managing responses: | | |
|   – Intended | | |
|   – Unintended | | |
|   – Unsubscribers | | |
| j) Measurement process: | | |
|   – Email | | |
|   – Other channels: | | |
|     a. Post | | |
|     b. Phone | | |
|     c. Store | | |
|     d. Website | | |
|     e. Email received outside the campaign's channels | | |
| If your emails are being sent out by a third party, then: | | |
| k) Responsible list management contracts | | |
| l) Post-campaign list handling | | |
| m) Brief the mailing house on: | | |
|   a) Hard bounces | | |
|   b) Soft bounces | | |

# Testing email for continuous improvement

Regular testing delivers incremental, progressive improvement. It is rare – but welcome – to uncover a single element that multiplies the response to an email. More often, improvements come from careful, systematic evolution through testing.

Every email programme should consider:

- Which components of an email are worth testing?

- A logical sequence to test for improvement

- How to measure and evaluate responses

- How testing changes other parts of your business

Testing lies at the heart of any direct marketing activity. Email is inherently measurable, and so is a natural communications tool to be tested and measured for improvement. Yet its flexibility and implementation speed make it all too easy to develop too many tests, too quickly to be able to properly understand either what is being tested or the results that they indicate. A structured testing programme can deliver regular incremental improvements to the overall impact and profitability of any new marketing campaign.

## What to test?

### Testing technology

The first staging post on testing technology in email is to consider whether HTML or text is the right route to go – for most people. However, it is far from the most significant technical challenge for an email marketer. It is far more important to construct emails which are likely to be delivered and viewed by the recipient as your team intended. This is a considerable technical challenge.

Before an email lands in the intended recipient's mailbox it must first successfully leave the sending server, pass across the internet, arrive at the recipient's mailbox host – usually their ISP (but not always) – and be opened by the individual. Along the way it must avoid being detected as a piece of UCEM (unsolicited commercial email):

- Any server on the internet might have detection software on it to identify mass mailings; and ISPs' servers are extremely likely to have filters in place over which the sender or end-user have no control

- Any corporate or personal firewall

- The recipients may well have their own spam filtering software

If the programming used to create and the technology used to send the email at any stage makes it appear as either unsolicited or mass marketing, it will not be delivered.

In practice, it is far easier to have a simple text email with a hyperlink direct to a website landing page than it is to achieve delivery of creatively designed graphic HTML emails. The added technical complexity of the HTML email means that, without care and experience, it is more likely to be treated as UCEM than a simple text email.

## Creative testing, creative content

Unlike technology, testing creative is the art of testing all the components that a recipient does see. The likely principal creative elements to test are:

- Sender's name

- Subject line

- Reply to

- First two lines of copy

- First screen of copy

- Final screen of copy

- Administration elements

Creative content has a role to play in making sure that emails are delivered, as well as encouraging recipients to act on what they see.

### Sender

The sender's name is a consistent and visible anchor to your email marketing programme. It is best to treat it as the only element which will never change. So, as early as possible in developing a programme, make sure that the sender's name is something which is useful and recognisable to the recipient.

It is important to make a conscious choice whether the sender should be a department or a person. If it is a person, is it a real person, who actually works at your organisation, or a fictitious one who will never leave or be on holiday – whose email box will always be answered.

- Recipients are quite likely to set up filters based on your chosen sender's name

- Change your sender's name and in future emails are more likely to be treated as UCEM.

It may be useful to establish naming conventions – that sales and marketing emails always come from a named individual; while service, support and contract renewal messages are from a named company department.

### Subject line

Testing the subject line can yield significant increases in opening and clickthrough rates – 50 per cent leaps have been reported as part of structured testing programmes, simply by changing the order of the words as they appear in a subject line.

Many subject lines are written as if they were headlines in press advertising – one or two lines of copy. The default width of an email subject line is likely to be between 30 and 35 characters. Though your subject line may be longer than 30 to 35 characters, it is important to make sure that the message is communicated in the likely visible space.

For some years the DMA members' Code of Practice has recommended that commercial emails start with ADV – as do some state laws in the US. This practice does not appear to have become conventional. It may, however, often be a useful test to run, particularly on a cold list, to establish whether being transparent in the subject line, and indicating that it is a commercial advertising email improves opening and clickthrough or not.

For more, see http://www.emaillabs.com/articles/email_articles/ writing_email_subject_lines.html

## The email's body copy

The first two lines of an email are extremely important. Many computer users set up their inbox to display the first two lines of an email in a 'preview' mode.

Using the first two lines of an email:

## Figure 5.9.6

HWC has sensibly put their offer into the first two lines of this email – it's the same in the text version.

Any recipient using the preview setting in their email client will be able to see the offer straightaway.
Since these lines are a hyperlink, recipients can click straight through to the website without actually opening the email.

If your proposal is visible in those first two lines, before a recipient has even opened an email, and includes a hyperlink, you will increase the response to the email. The first two lines are likely to be a straightforward statement of the campaign offer, and a clickable link.

## Lead/opening/first paragraph

The first paragraph must:

- Engage – when reading this, perhaps in the auto-preview window, recipients are deciding whether to delete or read further. So, as for any creative, the opening needs to be powerful.

- Add detail to the subject line or the headline – repetition is less important in email than in direct mail since it is processed so quickly – the recipient will remember the gist of the subject line, and it is always there at the head of the email, so reinforcement is the main objective of the message here.

- Summarise the whole – the opening of an email is often compared to the opening of a press release which typically uses an 'inverse pyramid' structure to summarise the main points of the message, in decreasing order of importance, as briefly as possible.

- Include a call-to-action – if the reader likes the offer or wants to know more, we shouldn't make them scroll down to find an elusive link – it should be there in the first paragraph. This is a mistake often made by email 'newbies' – leaving the best until last.

### Figure 5.9.7 Short, effective copy from Boden

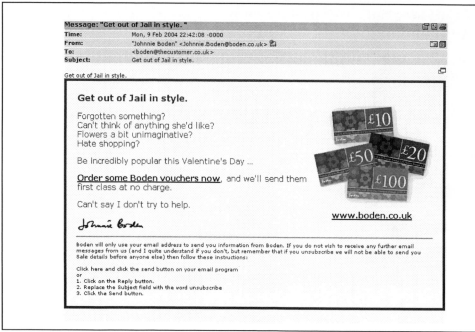

Boden has a chummy relationship with its customers, which sets the tone for their emails.

The whole of this message is visible in a single screen – this format is often known as a postcard. The copy is short and simple to understand at a glance. And hyperlinks are clearly formatted.

## Body copy

As for a direct mail piece, the main body of the email typically details the features and benefits of the offer in order to encourage a response.

With email, we shouldn't describe the offer in too much detail – the best place for detail is arguably the website – we can encourage clickthrough to find out more.

A common approach is to use a bulleted list in the main body to describe features and benefits. Some emails seem to take this too far though, with the email becoming little more than a series of bulleted lists.

Although most would agree that 'brief is best' when it comes to email, we do need to make the body copy long enough to create engagement, set the tone and explain the offer – bullets alone are often not the best way to do this.

Northern Light explains a complex message. It can't be easy to relaunch a service that's been dormant for several years. Yet that's the challenge facing Northern Light.

Their email:

- Reminds past subscribers that they were a subscriber

- Explains the new service

- Goes on to instruct recipients in how to use the new service

- Sets out an incentive for reactivating their account

## Figure 5.9.8

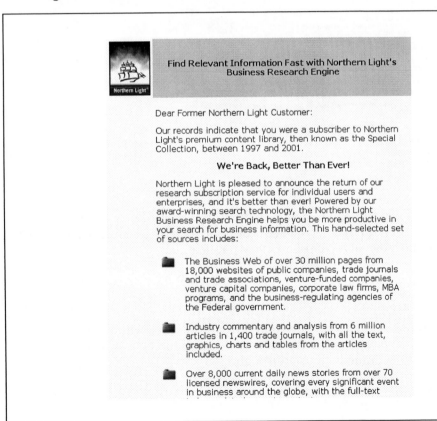

The body should also 'explain' and 'instruct':

- Explain – you may have developed a great offer and method of redemption, but it may be too complex for the embattled recipient wading through hundreds of emails. You need to clearly explain how the offer works.

- Instruct is related to explain – most of us seem conditioned to follow instructions – they make our lives easier. So the main body copy can instruct the recipient what to do next to receive the offer.

## The close

Again, as for direct mail, the 'close' should encourage 'action', so the call-to-action should be repeated here.

The Economist's clear call-to-action:

### Figure 5.9.9

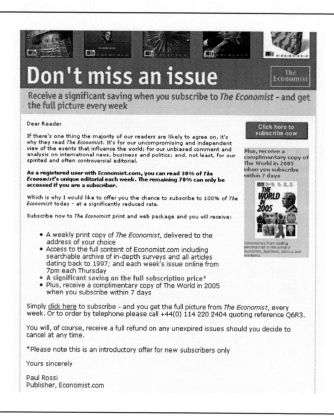

The Economist's offer and call-to-action is there in the headline and twice in the body copy. It's backed up by a telephone order line as well as online clickthrough, and there's the incentive of a complimentary publication.

The close – 'Simply -click here to subscribe' is succinct and clear. Just like the publication.

The call-to-action should encourage action now so the close will often include a secondary offer to encourage clickthrough, or perhaps the offer will be time-limited, to encourage immediate clickthrough.

## Sign-off

Sign-off can be personal or impersonal. It is best to be personal – from a named person – especially if the recipient knows an individual in your organisation such as an account manager or a customer service representative.

Alternatively, if the company has a well-known figurehead – the email could be from them, but many would think this was false familiarity unless the copy is written to avoid this. An impersonal sign-off is often more appropriate for rented lists.

Figure 5.9.10  **The right sign-off to a subscribers' list:**

| Message: "Ensuring our subscribers are satisfied " | |
| --- | --- |
| Time: | Wed, 6 Oct 2004 06:24:05 +0100 |
| From: | evo.subscriptions@dennisnet.co.uk (evo subscriptions) |
| To: | evo@thecustomer.co.uk ( ) |
| Subject: | Ensuring our subscribers are satisfied |

Dear Mr Will Rowan

Tell us about our subscription service and give yourself the chance
to win GBP25,000.

I want you to be 100% happy with your subscription. That's why we
regularly monitor every aspect of our service to you, from the
packing and despatch of your magazine, to how effectively we deal
with your enquiries.

As one of our most valued readers, your views on the service are
extremely important. So this month I'd like to ask for your help.
Please complete our brief online survey and give us your feedback on
how we can provide you with a better subscription service.

To thank you for your time, as soon as you submit your completed
questionnaire, we will automatically enter your name into a FREE
prize draw to win GBP25,000.

Click through to the following web address now to give us your
feedback and for your chance to win.

<http://www.demographix.com/surveys/TWHI-SQ67/HZY5929A>;

Thank you in advance for your help.

Julian Thorne
Customer Services Director

\*\*\*\*\*\*\*\*\*\*\*\*\*\*\*\*\*\*\*\*\*\*\*\*\*\*\*\*\*\*\*\*\*\*\*\*\*\*\*\*\*\*\*\*\*\*\*\*\*\*\*\*\*\*\*\*\*\*\*\*\*\*\*\*\*\*

Evo magazine's marketing team make a nice job of incentivising their subscriber
research:

- The campaign is reaching out to print subscribers by email

- Their request is clearly put

- The incentive – with its time close – is placed at the head and foot of the
  email, making sure it will be visible on screen at any point of the text

- The sign-off is from a named individual – a real person – with his job title.
  And the tone of the email is in keeping with his position

## Creating and measuring successful tests

The marketing in email marketing

While it is important to get the technology copy landing pages, and all the other
paraphernalia of an email marketing campaign correct, and to test them regularly,
campaign planners should never forget the marketing in email marketing. Having
the right sending, the right timing, to the right list, with the right offer, and the
correct creative will always have a significant impact on results. Without making a
product attractive to a potential audience, no amount of detailed testing of text
versus HTML, subject lines or landing pages will make a campaign profitable.
Testing body copy is far more a creative process than a technical one. The
approach to testing body copy must be right otherwise confusion will reign.

Whatever tests are planned they should be set out in a matrix showing all the tests, technical and creative, the target audiences, and timing. In a perfect world the full results of any single test will always be known before the next is deployed. Although most response to email campaigns are received within 48 hours of despatch, and the results are measured in real time, it is not always possible to carry out analysis that quickly nor is it necessarily wise to do so. However, many tests run at any one time; it is critical that the results should be able to distinguish the source of any impact – test one significant element at any one time. If an email campaign is likely to consist of several different tests, it is worth trying to assess how many can be run simultaneously without conflict, and evaluate groups of single issue tests together.

The email's body copy should be viewed as a series of screens – the size of the screen is determined by the campaign's audience – probably the most common screen resolution size that the companies' websites are viewed in. (This information is available from the company's web statistics package.)

Every screen in the email should have a hyperlink to a landing page: ideally, each link should be coded differently, so that it is possible to tell whether respondents are clicking through from the first, second, middle or last hyperlink of the email. Conventionally 50 per cent of the response is likely to come from the first screen of the email, and only 15 per cent of recipients are likely to reach the foot of the email.

## Measuring test campaigns

The spreadsheet extract below shows how these metrics relate to each other for two different campaigns where 10,000 emails were sent.

Campaign one is much more successful than campaign two. This is because email marketing involves multi-step conversion magnifying the effect of poor response at each stage of campaign two. More and detailed evaluation of the different performance ratios is needed to improve the performance of the campaign.

### Figure 5.9.11

| | Campaign 1 | Campaign 2 |
|---|---|---|
| Number of e-mails SENT from list | 10,000 | 10,000 |
| Receipt rate | 98% | 90% |
| Number of e-mails RECEIVED from list | 9,800 | 9,000 |
| Reader rate (open rate) | 60% | 40% |
| Number of e-mails READ or opened | 5880 | 3600 |
| Response rate 1 (CTR of readers) | 30% | 10% |
| Response rate 2 (CTR of recipients) | 18.0% | 4.0% |
| Response rate 3 (CTR of number sent) | 17.6% | 3.6% |
| Number of CLICKTHROUGHS to landing page | 1,764 | 360 |
| Completion rate | 80% | 60% |
| Response rate 4 (Responses of number sent) | 14.1% | 2.2% |
| Number of FORMS COMPLETED (RESPONSES) | 1,411 | 216 |
| Referral rate | 10% | 2% |
| Number of REFERRALS | 141 | 4 |

represents rates that will vary according to the success of the campaign.

This spreadsheet is available from www.marketing-insights.co.uk.

# Eight steps to creating a successful viral campaign

## 1 Designing the campaign process

Although it is clearly important to write and design the viral email carefully, careful planning of parallel activities, before and after the first viral email is sent, would add to the overall impact of the campaign.

Although a viral campaign usually exists online, the recipient of viral email lives in the real world! The viral campaign should be consistent with current brand positioning, and marketing goals. In developing a campaign, it is important to ask whether the brand positioning is new, distinct, a reinforcement of an existing position, or part of a repositioning exercise. The answers to these questions will determine the visual and copy style of the campaign.

Careful planning will avoid unintentional brand conflict. For example, it is possible to plan a viral campaign relatively quickly, certainly more quickly than the design of a corporate website can be changed. For a viral campaign – carrying new brand logos or icons – hyperlinking a recipient to a corporate website with the prior branding, will confuse a respondent. When confused, people are less likely to respond.

Any email campaign should be planned around the profile of its likely recipient: a viral campaign should in particular consider recipient's usage and attitude. Do they have broadband? Are they likely to provide three names, or ten? How much product and service information might they be comfortable to provide as part of a viral campaign?

It is worth considering which other media channels can be used to support the viral campaign. In particular, online and offline public relations are likely to accelerate the take-up of the viral activity. A well-managed online PR campaign would involve relevant communities as well as post news articles.

Finally, in designing the online campaign, are there opportunities to allow participants to take a voucher of reward to a retail shop? If a viral campaign is successful, there is no doubt that it will have a positive influence on sales activity through offline channels: if possible, design the campaign to include the mechanics which will recognise online participants when they give information on a purchase offline.

## 2 Resources used

If a viral campaign's activities are carefully planned, it will grow successfully with little or no impact on other areas of an organisation. When insufficient, scaleable resource is not in place, a viral campaign can cause significant problems for other parts of the organisation. By planning additional resources – bandwidth, server capacity and customer support – in advance, the opportunity for a viral campaign's success to disrupt other activity is reduced.

By monitoring activity of the campaign in real time, and website statistics (and perhaps even call centre calls) it will be possible to plot activity trends and anticipate and prevent problems. These bottlenecks can only be avoided if the extra capacity is planned in advance. The impact of a successful viral campaign can be felt in many different parts of an organisation – even postal activity to a customer service address can increase.

The first time any campaign is run, it can raise an internal resource question, which should be decided in advance. For example: if there are additional data management costs, how will be these be allocated? Can the existing systems allocate them to every involved department's satisfaction? If a campaign is successful, what is the impact on other channels, what are their costs, and who is responsible for them? If there is an associated increase in fulfilment costs, how are those allocated?

## 3 Legal implications

The Data Protection Act applies to online communications, as it does to offline.

Data protection is covered in detail in chapter 12.1.

There are a small number of specific privacy issues which relate to viral activity.

- Remember that an email address is personal data, even when it cannot clearly be associated with an individual person.

- The campaign's privacy statement must be clearly worded and visible, ideally at points where participants add personal data and submit it to the campaign.

- Verify that the privacy statement is carried out in practice. It particularly applies to making the source of any viral invitation clear: did it come from a company or their friend/colleague?

- When the campaign forwards an email on somebody's behalf, and the new recipient is not on the company's database, is that new recipient data held in such a way that it is clearly marked as not being available to the company for any purpose?

## 4 Managing the digital environment

A viral campaign is not just an email! Before sending the first mail, check that the viral campaign's content is truly promoted in the brand, product and privacy statement on branded websites, micro sites, any e-newsletters, and personal email if they are being despatched.

Similarly, is every part of your customer's network being used to promote the campaign? Are there banners, buttons and branded signatures available for supporters to put in to their personal email, their blocks and the communities they participate in.

Is it possible to make the campaign more visible on search engines, by:

- Separate search engines, by creating a campaign microsite communities basis, by feeding posts, perhaps in advance of the formal campaign start date?

- On news pages, by submitting press releases?

Any of these customers and independent online sites which 'hyperlink' to a dedicated viral campaign site will quickly and rapidly increase the visibility of the campaign beyond the initial mailing database.

## 5 Nurturing a campaign to success

Very few viral campaigns are instant overnight successes – they are carefully nurtured to success. The process of good campaign management is akin to that of good public relations and website management. Monitor the activities that were generating traffic, and seek to do more of the same.

Where individual recipients are particularly helpful, either by forwarding a campaign to many contacts, or promoting it through their own websites, recognise, thank and support those people.

If an element of the campaign appears to be underperforming, analyse it to try and understand why; if it is possible, improve it!

## 6 Campaign measurement

The most successful viral campaign is likely to ask just for an email address at the initial point of forwarding. In many cases, that may allow newly acquired information to be matched to existing customers or prospects, and those databases updated accordingly. However, customers, existing prospects and new prospects will also appear on the data.

The campaign should be designed to encourage them to notify the company of their more complete identity. That might be done through a voucher. A voucher reward for participating in the viral campaign may be an effective way of encouraging users, known only by email addresses, to voluntarily add further information. They might use this incentive voucher online or offline.

A campaign's success in generating activity would normally be measured through website statistics: the number of visitors to campaign pages, the number of times the viral activity is used, the number of unique users and the number of names it is forwarded to.

Ratios to monitor include:

- Infection rate – the ratio of email received to the number of email sent. An infection rate of one would mean that for every email received another one is sent.

- Commitment rate – the measure of the number of recipients who achieved the marketing goals of the campaign – to register, apply for further product information or request a sales visit.

- Conversion rate – the proportion who achieve the commercial goal of the campaign – usually the purchase.

To establish the commercial viability of the campaign, measure the cost to acquire prospect and customer data, comparing this cost to other online and offline channels. In particular, compare the cost of acquiring a valid email address and a paying customer. Where possible, identify the cost of reactivating a previously lost contact through viral activity.

If an organisation runs brand tracking studies for awareness and attitude to the company and its products, it may be possible to track changes in those attitudes among campaign participants.

### 7 Testing viral campaigns

A successful campaign is likely to be repeatable. The 'big idea' may need to be renewed. The structure and approach of a campaign can be tested and measured, with best practice captured for future use.

### 8 Ending a viral campaign

Successful viral campaigns can roll on, and on, and on. Almost unwelcome, this may not be the best use of your audience's attention. Before complete fatigue sets in, give participants something else (new and exciting) to look at. Thank participants and direct them towards this new activity. In doing so, do not take down the old campaign's web pages – redirect them to point visitors towards a new campaign.

# Ten planning decisions that include e-newsletters in your email activity

Many thanks to www.davechaffey.com for the original 10 point list and additional materials for this section.

## Introduction

E-newsletters provide simple, regular mechanisms for marketers to update their registered prospects and customers on their marketing programmes.

### First decision – planning an e-newsletter

The starting point for planning an e-newsletter has to be to examine, or re-examine, why you are publishing it. You will probably have a primary objective such as boosting sales on a site through clickthrough, or building a brand by providing value to customers, but what about other objectives?

The 5Ss of Smith and Chaffey (2001) originally applied to a corporate website, provide a good way to think about e-newsletter objectives:

a)   Sell – grow sales (the e-newsletter often acts as both a customer acquisition tool and a retention tool)

b)   Serve – add value (give customers extra benefits online, such as online exclusive offers or more in-depth information about your products or industry sector)

c)   Speak – get closer to customers by creating a dialogue, asking questions through online research surveys, and learning about customers' preferences through tracking (that is, what type of content are people most interested in?)

d)   Save – save costs (of print and post). If you have a traditional offline e-newsletter, can you reduce print runs or extend its reach by using email?)

e)     Sizzle – extend the brand online. An e-newsletter keeps the brand at 'front-of-mind' and helps reinforce brand values. Added value can also be delivered by the e-newsletter in informing and entertaining customers.

All the e-newsletter design decisions discussed below should, of course, be controlled by the main objectives of the e-newsletter.

Five contributions your e-newsletter can make to your company's marketing:

- Use the e-newsletter to preview future offers and product developments before other media. Highlight unique web offers – this will be an incentive for audiences to open the e-newsletter.

- Use the e-newsletter to reinvigorate recent or current campaigns or promotions that were first highlighted in other media.

- Use the e-newsletter to give more detail than the offline e-newsletter or house magazine – refer visitors to the online version and reduce the size and cost of the offline communication. Alternatively, put the whole magazine online as with http://www.easyjetinflight.com.

- Rather than referring the media or other audiences to press releases or a media centre, refer them first to an e-newsletter item. This will give them a more complete picture of what the company stands for, and your current news.

- Adding a theme to each edition of your e-newsletter will increase readership. The subject line can stress the theme and this will give a higher open rate for hot topics or great offers. Choose themed content that delivers a greater response, and then give it precedence.

## Decision two - measuring success

When thinking about the objectives, think about how you will judge the success of your e-newsletter.

The following metrics are commonly used to assess the effectiveness of e-newsletters through time:

- Open rates (for HTML e-newsletters)

- Clickthroughs to more detailed content or promotions

- List churn – the numbers of new subscribers and unsubscribers

- Number of updates to profiles

- Numbers forwarded to friends

- Website traffic generated

While it is easy to automate collection of these metrics, think about whether these really relate to the goals from decision one.

Automated measures do not give the full story – they cannot measure the value that recipients place on the e-newsletter. Consider conducting surveys to determine softer measures related to how the customer perceives the e-newsletter and how it impacts on the brand. Of course, the survey can be a part of the newsletter's content.

What do you measure?

Find out which of these measures your company tracks:

## Table 5.9.5

| | measured | not measured |
|---|---|---|
| 1. Open rates (for HTML e-newsletters) | | |
| 2. Clickthroughs to more detailed content or promotions | | |
| 3. List churn – the numbers of new subscribers and unsubscribers | | |
| 4. Number of updates to profiles | | |
| 5. Numbers forwarded to friends | | |
| 6. Website traffic generated | | |

Now check what's done with the measurements? Are they put to good use?

## Decision three – proposition

The proposition defines how value will be delivered to the main audiences. It should relate to your offline proposition – and may even be the same. The proposition could include showing how your e-newsletter will deliver value to subscribers through:

1.  Saving time by providing a single, up-to-date source

2.  Learning – increasing knowledge and solving day-to-day problems

3.  Saving money – for instance through exclusive offers or offering new ways of working through a company's products

4.  Entertaining – all e-newsletters can and should be fun for their audiences – this is not only the preserve of consumer e-newsletters

5.  Trust – you will also need to demonstrate that you are a reliable, knowledgeable source and that the customers' data is safe

For business-to-business e-newsletters, think about how you can add value by acting as a filter for information about your market sectors. Your e-newsletters can potentially:

•   Alert

•   Aggregate

- Inform

They do this through market alerts, industry trends and in-depth best practice case studies.
Delivering this information-based value will not be cheap as the content will have to be:

- Up to date

- Relevant

- Accurate

- Concise

- Clearly presented

Your e-newsletter's name should reflect its proposition. There are many e-newsletters called E-newsletter, eNews or eAlerts, so think about using a name that stands out. The name should summarise the proposition and be a clear differentiator.

It may be sufficient to use your company's brand name. E-newsletters traditionally mirror all aspects of an organisation's branding in terms of brand name and brand image. The tone of voice and style should also be consistent.

In some cases, brand variants can be used to appeal to the reader, and may be more in keeping with the informal nature of internet email.

Using well-defined audiences and products, what three e-newsletters would be useful (and profitable) to distribute?

Identify the audiences and the e-newsletter propositions that would interest them; name specific products or product groups if appropriate.

|   | Audience | Proposition | Product group (optional) |
|---|----------|-------------|---------------------------|
| 1 |          |             |                           |
| 2 |          |             |                           |
| 3 |          |             |                           |

## Decision four – audience

Before deciding on the proposition, content and structure of the e-newsletter, think about your readership. Who are you writing for?

Most e-newsletters must try to accommodate two audiences – existing and potential customers. It's unlikely you'll perfect your view of the e-newsletter audience in a single analysis: spend some time examining these four factors, and expect to revisit them regularly:

- Assess the proportion of subscribers who are existing customers or potential customers. If the majority of subscribers are not customers one of the main measures of e-newsletter success is the conversion rate achieved from e-newsletter subscribers to customers.

- Analyse the subscriber base to assess whether they fit into existing customer segments. For example, by interest, geographic, life stage or product ownership.

- Build up subscriber profiles in order to benefit from segmentation by asking simple questions, such as their postcode.

- Analyse readers' preferences by seeing how they use your e-newsletter – customers and prospects may click through to different sections.

## Decision five – content

As for any printed publication, the e-newsletter will live or die according to its content.

Think carefully about the type of content which will get and keep regular readers, and will stop them unsubscribing. What special offers or nuggets of information can be provided by your company, and are indispensable?

If you already have an e-newsletter, you can assess which types of content receive the greatest number of clickthroughs. What's New in Marketing (www.wnim.com) conducted a survey six months after launch to ask readers' views of the content – what was good, bad or missing, and found that content should be included for specific reasons:

- The balance of content provided should be driven by the objectives, audiences and proposition

- Often it won't be possible to accommodate all factors in a single e-newsletter

- The most enticing content needs to be 'above the fold' when the email is opened

- Start with what you feel are the strongest articles for your audience

- Have regular features plus new, topical articles in each issue

- Unlike a print e-newsletter though, your pages are not of a fixed length: the e-newsletter can be as long or short as each issue's content merits.

## Decision six – resourcing

A worthwhile e-newsletter will not write itself.

It will usually take at least a day of one person's time just to compile the e-newsletter. This will involve going out to the people in the company and asking them to contribute copy or develop offers.

The e-newsletter may not be perceived as a priority by these content providers, but a way has to be found to communicate the importance of the e-newsletter to the brand to ensure that good quality content is contributed.

Costs of broadcasting must also be considered. If an external provider is used there is wide variation in cost and capabilities for targeting and tracking, so it is worth making sure you get the best balance of cost/performance.

### *Decision seven – format, layout and structure*

The vast majority of e-newsletters are sent out in HTML format.

- HTML e-newsletters should be used if resources allow. Not only do HTML emails tend to get the highest response rates, they also provide options for a multi-column layout which is a much better way of delivering the 'sell versus inform' balance.

- Text-only may be the best option for a technical audience, particularly if the email is brief and limited to alerts. Often limited resources will be the only reason for a text-only e-newsletter option.

- The usual solution is to send out a multi-part MIME email which will be displayed according to the recipient's preferences. That gives your readers a choice.

A strong layout that helps deliver the right content to the right audience to meet the right objectives is important. If you look at a range of e-newsletters, they have common features:

#### 1. Header block

This graphical area at the top brands the email and can be used as a navigation element. It often includes a different headline for each issue to help gain engagement – rather than having the same header each month.

#### 2. Table of contents

A compact TOC is a must, but this is often missing.
The TOC should include links to the content in the email.

**Iconocast uses a contents listing to navigate a long e-newsletter:**

Figure 5.9.12

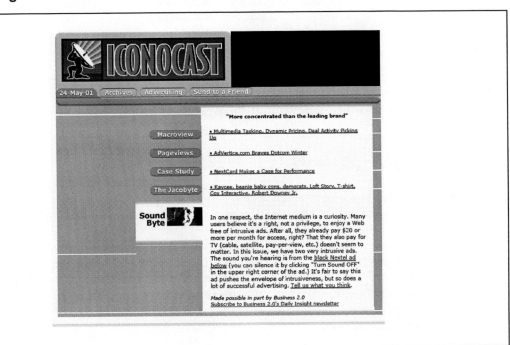

The Iconocast e-newsletter runs to many screens. By creating just four contents sections – Macroview, Pageviews, Case Study and The Jacobyte – it becomes easy for regular readers to find their way around the e-newsletter.

**3. Website features.**

Using part of your web pages' layout in an e-newsletter can help readers feel comfortable when they click through to the full site.

For instance, Amazon uses the familiar search box from the website on their e-newsletter to prompt an action. Menu options from the website can be included, although this can confuse if they are not directly related to the e-newsletter content.

**L.L. Bean picks up on website layout to make its e-newsletters familiar:**

Figure 5.9.13

L.L. Bean's seasonal e-newsletter echoes its website's layout – which makes the presentation instantly familiar to customers, and reduces the time it takes newcomers to find their way around the website when they click through.

## *Decision eight – personalisation and tailoring*

If you only offer one e-newsletter, ask whether a 'one size fits all' e-newsletter is really delivering what the organisation and its subscribers are looking for.

One way to assess the need for different e-newsletters is to analyse clickthroughs to different types of content according to different types of subscribers. Alternatively, you can use the profiling information to assess the balance between different audiences; for example, customers who have adopted different products or services, prospects, media and employees. A simple opt-in form can be used to acquire this information.

## *Decision nine – frequency and timing*

Think of the frequency of most e-newsletters you receive. They tend to be daily, weekly or monthly. Why is this? Perhaps we are we still in the print mentality of dailies, weeklies and monthlies?

We don't have to limit ourselves to fixed frequencies. Where different email e-newsletter options are offered for different audiences or different needs then the frequencies can of course vary. You also won't have to search so hard for 'newsworthy' topics each week or month; instead, major announcements and news can form the basis of the e-newsletter.

### PalmSource delivers offer-timed e-newsletters

PalmSource delivers regular e-newsletters, with product updates – and since the precise delivery day is less important their timing is more often based by weekends or holidays, or by a specific product offer.

**Figure 5.9.14**

Closely related to frequency is timing – time of the day, week or month.
In many cases, a regular consistent timing for e-newsletters is something to strive for, so our brand can become part of the recipient's routine. How many organisations actually achieve this regularity? More often it is Tuesday one month and Thursday the next.

Deliver your e-newsletters when the audience is most likely to be using their PC or PDA. This tends to increase response rates. For businesses, this means during office hours and for consumers, during the evening or weekends.

## Decision ten – listening

While we can use the clickthrough and website outcome data to second-guess how well our e-newsletter is working and what our customers think of us, there is no substitute for asking the question: "what do you think?" face-to-face or through a structured survey within your e-newsletter or in a separate email.

Since e-newsletters can become a large element of how your brand is perceived, it is important to know what people really think. Online brands such as Tesco.com and lastminute.com poll their audiences regularly to find this out.

Find out the health of an e-newsletter by using a mixture of 'watching and asking'. Listen to your readers to make sure the e-newsletter is valued.

The Tesco.com e-newsletter seems to be in good shape judging by these 'watching and asking' metrics (Parekh 2003):

80 per cent of customers rate as excellent
65 per cent open rate (individual average of <20 per cent)
50 per cent read the entire email
20 per cent purchase due to email
Additional 37 per cent considering purchase
13 per cent forward to friends/family
5 to 10 per cent average clickthrough rates
<1 per cent unsubscribe

## Summary – top ten e-newsletter dos and don'ts

**Dos:**

1.   Start with the business objectives

2.   Remember the diverse audiences, e.g. customers and non-customers

3.   Get the sell/inform balance right

4.   Work hard to research powerful customer-centric content

5.   Send out multi-part MIME formats, or give a choice at opt-in

6.   Use template layout to distinguish content for different audiences and different marketing offers

7.   Give your e-newsletter a distinctive brand related to the core brand

8.   Offer choice of opt-in to different content and frequencies if your resources and technology permit it

9.   Use a regular time for delivery – same time of day and same time of week or month

10.   Clearly define the proposition to encourage opt-in and clarify offer

**Don'ts:**

1. Underestimate the resource implications of creating email e-newsletters

2. Personalise for the sake of it – different content areas can appeal to different audiences at a lower cost

3. Use a frequency that is too high to justify the returns – quarterly may make more sense than monthly

4. Underestimate the effect of timing – don't broadcast the email at midnight on Sunday

5. Forget to clearly theme individual e-newsletters to showcase the offer

6. Forget to prepare a long-term programme of themes or incentives through time

7. Forget to plan integration between other online and offline media

8. Forget to measure success using qualitative data such as views, clickthroughs and unsubscribers

9. Forget to research qualitative feedback on e-newsletter

10. Forget to use a closed-loop approach to continuously improve email marketing

## *Bibliography*

Permission-based Email Marketing That Works, Kim MacPherson, Dearborn Trade 2001

Email Marketing, Jim Sterne and Anthony Priore, Wiley 2000

Ideavirus, Seth Godin, available at http://www.ideavirus.com

Designing Web Usability, Nielsen, 2002

Digital Marketing, Will Rowan, Kogan Page 2002

http://www.cluetrain.com

# Mobile marketing: A mainstream medium for every brand

## This chapter includes:

- - - - - - - - - - - - - - - - - - - - - - - - - - - - - - - - - - - -

☐   **What mobile marketing covers**

☐   **Mobile marketing is mainstream**

☐   **Examples of brands using mobile marketing**

☐   **What mobile marketing can achieve**

☐   **Mobile data technologies demystified**

☐   **Developing your mobile marketing campaign**

☐   **Golden rules of mobile marketing**

☐   **Mobile marketing legislation**

☐   **Closing thoughts about mobile marketing**

- - - - - - - - - - - - - - - - - - - - - - - - - - - - - - - - - - - -

## About this chapter

The phenomenal spread of mobile phones, to almost everyone, almost everywhere, has opened up a whole new world of marketing opportunities. Mobile marketing is still maturing, but it is certainly already extensively used by many brand categories and the others are catching up. This development is being driven by the ubiquity of this interactive medium as well as above average response rates and low implementation costs.

Initially this medium was perceived as a youth-orientated, entertainment-focused technology but the last few years have proven otherwise. A myriad of applications have sprung up and are touching people of all ages in their everyday lives. As of June 2006, at least ten car manufacturers in the UK have run direct response TV or print campaigns using a mobile response mechanism; the National Health Service is installing text message (SMS) appointment reminder software in GPs' surgeries; energy companies have launched services to allow customers to submit gas and electricity meter readings by text message; Google, the world's largest internet search engine, has launched a search tool accessible through the mobile internet and charities raised millions of pounds in a matter of days, by text donation, following 2005's tsunami in Asia.

In this chapter we will show how to develop successful mobile marketing communications across a wide spectrum of possible interaction between organisations and their customers; not just initial acquisition and brand building, but also ongoing relationship management for retention purposes and even transaction handling. We will not cover the altogether different subject of mobile entertainment; the selling of 'wallpapers', 'ringtones' and games by publishers (as opposed to their inclusion in marketing campaigns) nor mobile betting or mobile TV.

## Jonathan Bass M IDM

Jonathan founded mobile marketing agency Incentivated Limited, with James Hubbard, to bring a traditional marketing approach and rigorous commercial analysis to this new medium. Clients include British Airways, The Carphone Warehouse, Hilton Group, The Mayor of London, Transport for London and Samsung as well as many of the UK's direct marketing, media and interactive agencies.

Jonathan Bass
Managing Director, Incentivated
e: jbass@incentivated.com
w: www.incentivated.com
t: 0845 130 3985

# Chapter 5.10

# *Mobile marketing: A mainstream medium for every brand*

## *What mobile marketing covers*

**T**he use of mobile phone data services by organisations to interact with their customers, efficiently and regardless of place or time, is what we broadly define as mobile marketing. The enabling technologies will help you achieve your campaign objectives but in themselves should not be intimidating. After we discuss how and where mobile marketing works, we will demystify the technology.

Mobile marketing has the potential to influence all aspects of the organisation's relationship with the customer, be that acquisition, transaction or retention. Since all customer-facing departments can use the mobile channel, including before, during and after the point of sale, the subject matter of this chapter is wider than the reader might first think. Some more precise definitions will be helpful and those we will use in this chapter are: the narrower definition of 'mobile marketing', which is distinct from but complementary to 'mobile commerce' and 'mobile customer service'. For convenience we refer to these three under the 'mobile interactivity' or 'mobile channel' umbrellas.

The graphic below shows how these can be interrelated when the entire customer journey is considered. Since a number of banks are working on just such an example, I predict that at least one will have implemented the mobile channel in all three areas, for a single product, before the year is out. (Note, where content is distributed as part of a campaign we include it within 'mobile marketing'; however, when it is distributed directly from the publisher to the consumer for a fee, we include it within 'mobile commerce'.)

Figure 5.10.1

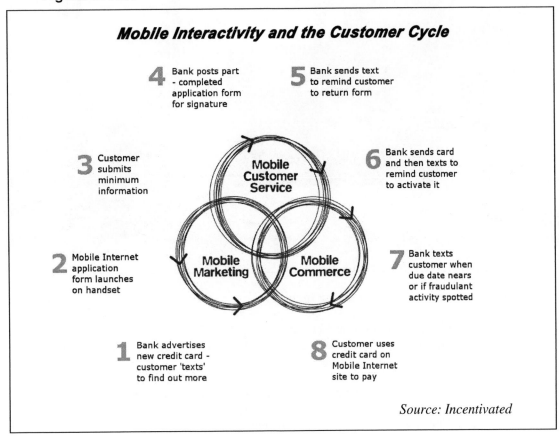

Now let's look at these three component parts of the mobile channel in greater detail:

## (i)   *Mobile marketing*

Mobile marketing is the use of text and picture messaging, location-based services and the mobile internet, for advertising, direct marketing, direct response and sales promotion purposes. Mobile marketing can originate from either the organisation ('push') or the customer ('pull') and will often include both the sending and receiving of messages.

The graphic below shows two examples of customer-initiated mobile marketing: a direct response mechanism (advertising a voter registration form on a credit-card sized handout distributed on London's Oxford Street) and the Google mobile internet search portal.

Figure 5.10.2

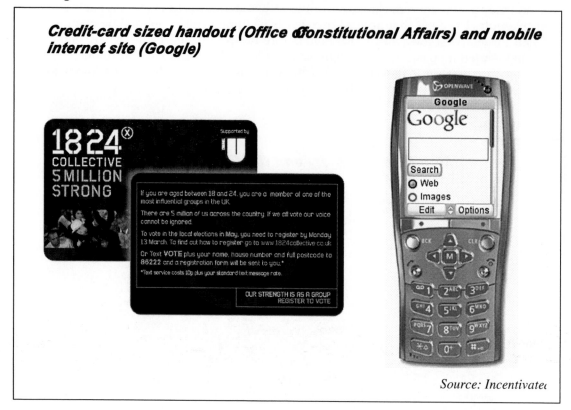

**Credit-card sized handout (Office Constitutional Affairs) and mobile internet site (Google)**

*Source: Incentivated*

Other forms of mobile marketing include:

- Targeted promotional and cross-selling offers sent in a text message by the organisation to existing customers or those whose opted-in details have been obtained from a bona fide third party

- Customer ordering of printed materials or electronic brochures

- On-packet prize draws and instant win sales promotions

- Multi-media content delivery as part of a campaign

- Interactive 'brochureware' mobile internet sites

More information on mobile marketing, including case studies, can be found in the section 'What mobile marketing can achieve'.

## (ii) Mobile commerce

Mobile commerce or 'm-commerce' is important because advertising budgets are moving out of home and closer to the point of sale and the mobile acts as both a marketing communications channel and a device for facilitating a transaction, i.e. at the point of sale.

The graphic below shows how 'barcodes' can be shown on a mobile phone screen for use in a sales promotion campaign (redemption) or as an entry ticket (proof of purchase). One-dimensional barcodes, which can be delivered in multiple text messages, are the traditional codes you see on packaging and work with most existing scanners; however they are limited in terms of uniqueness. This can cause a problem when trying to run a promotion across multiple retailers, especially for FMCG products. Two-dimensional barcodes are actually not bars but more like small chess or draughtboards, giving far more number combinations. Although they offer more flexibility, few retailers support 2D barcodes at the time of writing and they are most often used at live events.

**Figure 5.10.3**

*Mobile phone 'barcodes'*

One dimensional 'barcode'     Two dimensional 'barcode'

*Source: Incentivated*

At the time of writing, mobile network operator O2 was using mobile phone barcodes to issue tickets for the 'O2 Wireless Music Festival 2006' in London and Leeds and a number of airlines are considering issuing mobile barcode boarding passes.

Mobile commerce also includes the secure processing of transactions made by mobile phone for goods and services consumed both on and off the phone, the collection of payments by premium rate text message (PSMS) and content delivery to the handset, e.g:

- Fraud alerts and new product registrations

- Account or credit top-ups

- Credit card authorisation

- Donations to charity

- Auction bidding

Possibly the most well-known example is that of London's Congestion Charge, payment for which can be triggered by text message.

### (iii)  Mobile customer service

The addition of the mobile channel can enhance existing customer service processes and reduce costs in call centre operations, by using text messaging where simplicity is required or a mobile internet site for more complex situations. Examples include:

- Receiving pictures and videos sent in by the general public, as used by television broadcasters and local councils

- 'Find my nearest' services, such as dealer or retailer location

- Appointment reminders or delay and cancellation notifications

- Submission of meter readings or other data entry

- Booking and voting

Figure 5.10.4

**Flight cancellation text message (British Airways)**

*Source: Incentivated*

At the time of writing, the Conservative Party had just announced that they would allow London's registered voters to select a candidate for the 2008 London mayoral vote by text message. While some will worry about the trivialisation of politics, others will see this as a natural extension of the explosion in reality TV voting which has led to figures such as one in four people having voted for something, often a TV show, by text message.

# Mobile marketing is mainstream

Mobile marketing is still maturing, but it is certainly already used regularly by many leading brands and the others are catching up. We estimate that one in three larger organisations have run at least one mobile marketing campaign and the proportion is even higher for small and medium-sized consumer-facing enterprises. It has gone beyond the phase of early adoption, which, like the internet, was characterised by 'girls, games and gambling', and has recently become mainstream.

It is in use across the corporate, not-for-profit and public sectors and for interactions with all age groups. The breadth of applications, like the ones above, that touch ordinary people every day as well as the wide range of sectors in which it has been employed suggest mobile marketing has arrived. By the end of 2008, a majority of European businesses are expected to have adopted mobile marketing as part of their ongoing marketing activity. Despite this and partly due to the size of the screen, mobile marketing is unlikely ever to eclipse online advertising by value spent on it.

## Current situation and recent history

Estimates for current European expenditure by businesses, on the wider definition of mobile marketing (i.e. all mobile interactivity including mobile marketing, customer service and m-commerce, but not entertainment or the value of goods and services themselves sold via mobile) range from 110 million euros to 500 million euros in 2005 (sources: Jupiter Research, Vision Gain Intelligence and Yankee Group).

Incentivated estimates that the UK's share for 2005 represented approximately £35 million or about £0.50 per head per annum. This is equivalent to between one and two marketing, customer service or transactional messages per person per month, for every adult in the UK. The above figures, just as this chapter, do not include peer-to-peer messaging or paid-for-mobile content.

Of the total population of Western Europe, 76 per cent were mobile phone subscribers in 2005. In the UK this figure was 79 per cent, or 47 million people. Excluding the very young and very old the percentage penetration is nearer 90 per cent and in urban areas as many as 97 per cent of the population are said to have a mobile phone, according to Metro newspaper, while some people have two or more handsets. (This is why you will sometimes see a figure of more than 100 per cent penetration, i.e. there are more handsets in use than people in the UK and most Western European economies). The mobile phone therefore compares very favourably with other interactive choices such as internet access (55 per cent) and interactive TV (31 per cent).

The total number of text messages sent for all reasons, a figure that has astounded most people, continues to grow. In the month of December 2005, 3.1 billion text messages were sent in the UK, which was a 10 per cent increase on the previous month and 25 per cent up on the previous year. In the same month over 1 billion mobile internet (WAP) page impressions were served. (Both sources: the Mobile Data Association.) In 2005 the mobile network operators had as many customers accessing mobile internet content as most of the large internet service providers had online, although frequency is lower.

There is a perception that mobile marketing is a youth medium, but this is incorrect. Just as there is little difference in mobile phone ownership by age bracket, there is also only a small difference in monthly spend on mobile data services and awareness of sophisticated mobile services, across age groups under 65.

### Table 5.10.1 Mobile marketing is relevant to all ages

| Age bracket | Mobile ownership | Average monthly spend on mobile data services | Awareness of mobile news services |
|---|---|---|---|
| 15-24* | 88% | £3.61 | 82% |
| 25-34 | 88% | £2.70 | 82% |
| 35-44 | 85% | £2.46 | 79% |
| 45-54 | 76% | £2.42 | 79% |
| 55-64 | 70% | £2.06 | 62% |
| 65-74 | 53% | | 44% |

*For average monthly spend, this age group is 18-24

Source (in order): Oftel (2003), Yankee Group (2005), NOP for O2 (2004)

Although ownership is broad across all age groups, just as with other media, openness to usage does show higher levels among the under 40s. According to a recent survey by Ireland's Mobile Marketing Forum 55 per cent of 25 to 35 year olds would consider purchasing goods and services by mobile phone. Another recent survey, this time by Enpocket/Harris Interactive, showed 57 per cent of 18 to 34 year olds have interacted with a company via a 'short code' and 60 per cent have used the mobile internet in the first quarter of 2006. Still, a wider survey of all age groups concluded 84 per cent of all mobile subscribers are open to the prospect of mobile marketing when the message is targeted and the campaign conducted on a voluntary opt-in basis (source: Empower Interactive 2004).

However, of all the media that an organisation can use to communicate with customers, the mobile channel is the most personal, and therefore badly targeted or unwanted messages can have a strongly negative effect on a brand. Specifically, subscribers are interested in local promotions, information about products from national brands and updates of a customer relationship management nature, according to the same Empower survey.

In another survey of 50 leading European brands, 40 per cent had already used SMS for marketing purposes. Another 24 per cent were regular users and 18 per cent had already used some form of multi-media messaging (MMS). (Source: Airwide Solutions, Jan 2006.)

However, just 18 per cent of advertising agencies offered mobile marketing as part of their standard media offering in 2004 (Empower Interactive, 2004) and according to the Airwide survey, 70 per cent of agencies have never proposed mobile marketing campaigns to their clients because they know so little about it. A lot more work needs to be done by the 'creative' suppliers to educate advertising agencies and clients.

"At the moment I don't think the brands or their agencies have been introduced to the opportunities that are available."

*Julie Jeancolas, Account Director (Digital Media), Carat, 1st September 2005*

Interestingly, small and medium-sized enterprises (SMEs) have shown a greater propensity to adopt mobile marketing, compared with larger brands. Of the SMEs surveyed by the Mobile Data Association (MDA) in 2005, 91 per cent regularly used SMS for business purposes and 9 per cent used MMS. Of the messages sent, 26 per cent were to customers and of the messages received 16 per cent were from customers (the rest were between the organisation and employees or between members of staff). Of the total messaging, 23 per cent was for marketing or customer service reasons. The benefits mentioned by those interviewed included: time saving (convenient for group messaging), cost effectiveness, and non-intrusiveness and discretion.

## Medium-term outlook

Forecasts for European expenditure by businesses on the wider definition of mobile marketing (again, all mobile interactivity including mobile marketing, customer service and m-commerce, but not entertainment or the value of goods and services themselves sold via mobile) range from 700 million euros to one billion euros by 2010 (source: Jupiter Research  and Yankee Group). Incentivated estimates that the UK would represent at least £150 million by then. In comparison, Juniper Research estimates that 87 million consumers will spend $63 billion between them on mobile commerce in 2010, driven by mobile ticketing and retail mobile internet sites.

Most forecasters believe that mobile phone ownership is close to peaking in Western Europe; however, usage of mobile data services will continue to grow strongly. Forrester expects the number of text messages sent nearly to double (growth of 92 per cent) over the next five years, i.e. almost 15 per cent per annum. This is consistent with the networks' forecasting of a more than doubling of revenues from mobile data services over the next five years (source: Yankee Group).

The age profile of mobile phone owners is expected to change only marginally, despite an aging population, since penetration among the 55 to 64 age group is already 70 per cent.

Adoption of mobile marketing by organisations is expected to change the most over the next few years as the mobile interactivity revolution takes hold in all sectors of consumer society. Of the 50 leading European brands surveyed, 89 per cent said they intended to use mobile marketing by 2008 (source: Airwide Solutions, Jan 2006). Nearly a third planned to spend over 10 per cent of their communications budget on mobile marketing. This coincides with Incentivated's recent experience at a new media supplier forum, where 58 per cent of senior level attendees, with budgets to spend, asked to meet a mobile marketing supplier.

"Mobile phones will replace TV as the most important medium for advertisers. We are rapidly getting to the point where the single most important medium that people have is the wireless device."

*Andrew Robertson, CEO BBDO, Financial Times, 7th April 2005*

The 50 leading European brands surveyed also said they expected that seven per cent of their total sales would result from mobile marketing expenditure in five years, compared with 38 per cent from internet advertising and seven per cent from interactive TV and the rest from traditional channels (source: Airwide Solutions, Jan 2006). While the quote below was never intended to be a serious commitment, it does highlight one of the arguments for mobile taking a larger part of the media-cake over the next few years.

"As a way of connection, it ought to be phenomenally powerful and more important than TV. So we should be spending 50 per cent of our marketing budget within decades."

*James Eadie, Marketing Manager Coca Cola UK, Mobile Marketing Conference, 2005*

## Examples of brands using mobile marketing

As with any new marketing solution, some sectors adopt it more quickly than others. What is surprising is the fact that more than half of the volume car manufacturers selling in the UK are already regular users of mobile marketing, even for luxury models. Other sectors showing strong recent growth include the charity sector, the public sector, entertainment, travel and FMCG. Sectors that are expected to catch up in 2006 and 2007 (based on discussions and trials taking place now) include financial services, utilities and pharmaceuticals. Sectors like beauty products (as opposed to beauty services) and fashion have shown relatively little interest to date; however, someone will come up with an innovative and creative use of mobile marketing in these sectors, of that we are sure.

The following table lists some of the major users of mobile marketing, but is far from exhaustive. Not included are the obvious users such as the broadcasters and producers (e.g. BBC, Big Brother, Pop Idol and X Factor), record labels (who make their content available as ringtones, e.g. EMI) or the mobile phone companies (both networks and handset manufacturers).

### Table 5.10.2 Major users of mobile marketing

| Sector | Organisation or brand and product |
|---|---|
| Automotive | Audi, Fiat, Ford, Jaguar, Mercedes-Benz, Peugeot, Shell, Smart, Suzuki, Toyota and Vauxhall. |
| Charity and not-for-profit | Cancer Research, Comic Relief, Disaster Emergencies Committee (Asian tsunami appeal), Live8, Macmillan Cancer Support, NSPCC, Oxfam, RSPCA and SSPCA. |
| Financial services | Barclaycard, Barclays, First Direct, Insure and Go, Lloyds TSB, Nationwide Building Society and Mastercard. |
| FMCG and retail | Adidas, Bacardi, Budweiser, Cadburys, Coca-Cola, Smirnoff, Demon Tweaks, Horlicks, JJB Sports, MFI, Muller, KitKat, Tampax, Red Bull, Reebok, Selfridges, Tango, Tesco, Walkers and Woolworths. |
| Healthcare, pharmaceuticals and public sector | Army and TA, NiQuitin (GSK), Greater London Authority and Mayor of London, Hammersmith and Fulham Council, NHS*, Transport for London and Westminster Council. |
| Media, publishing and entertainment | Electronic Arts, FHM, Luminar Leisure, Smash Hits, Ubisoft, and Xscape. |
| Property | Countryside Properties, Galliard Homes and Savills. |
| Sports, fitness and beauty | Cannons, Esporta, LivingWell and Holmes Place. |

| Travel and holiday | AA, BAA, British Airways, National Rail Enquiries, Qantas, Virgin Trains and Zingo. |
|---|---|
| Telecoms and utilities | 118 118, Dial-a-Phone, IDT, Onetel, Primus, Scottish Power and The Carphone Warehouse. |

*Source: Incentivated*

*A recent study, funded by Vodafone and carried out by Imperial College London, found 150 examples of the use of text messaging in the delivery of healthcare around the world. It is claimed that text message reminders reduced the number of missed appointments with GPs by 26 to 39 per cent and with hospitals by 33 to 50 per cent. Text messages were also being used to remind patients about blood tests, dental appointments and frequency of prescription in the case of diabetes. In Iraq mobile marketing was being used to support a polio vaccination campaign and in Kenya to control tuberculosis (source: The Economist, 25th March 2006).

Case studies of some of these uses appear in the next section.

## What mobile marketing can achieve

We have seen that major brands are already demonstrating that mobile marketing's capabilities are wide and deep enough to support their interactions with customers throughout the cycle of acquisition, transaction and retention. For them, mobile marketing might well form part of a fully integrated communications campaign, or be entirely standalone.

The same processes can equally be applied to bring 'real world' benefits and efficiencies to smaller organisations. Indeed, it can be argued that mobile marketing has proportionally greater leverage potential in smaller scale organisations with tighter budgets where it can be employed as a standalone campaign to greater effect. The following table demonstrates the advantages of mobile marketing for both customers and organisations, large and small, throughout the customer life cycle:

## Table 5.10.3 Advantages of mobile marketing

| | Additional functionality or convenience (for customer) | Enhanced response rates (for organisation) | Reduced operating costs (for organisation) |
|---|---|---|---|
| Acquisition | • Offers interactive response mechanic in support of out-of-home advertising such as posters.<br><br>• Greater reach than interactive TV for in-home direct response.<br><br>• Simpler and more accessible interaction compared with online, when PC not booted up.<br><br>• Low environmental impact (no paper waste) compared with printed matter. | • The customer can respond immediately on sight of the advertising and is less likely to forget the contact details.<br><br>• Generates immediate traffic to call centres if human interaction is required (call backs).<br><br>• At present the vast majority of text messages are opened, unlike email where only 25 per cent are opened.<br><br>• Digital opt-in rules encourage willing participation through clear protection. | • Messaging costs measured in pennies — lower than telemarketing and direct mail.<br><br>• Unlike manual data entry, mobile marketing enables automatic insertion of information into a database and so reduces labour costs and rekeying errors.<br><br>• Measurement is accurate and detailed, at no additional cost. |
| Transaction | • Premium rate SMS or WAP billing are inbuilt micro-payment mechanisms.<br><br>• Mobile can be used to trigger credit card payments or set up direct debits.<br><br>• Once-off charity donations can be topped up by Gift Aid declaration. | • Services run on credit, e.g. long distance calling cards, see more top-ups when this can be done by text message rather than returning to the shop to buy more credit.<br><br>• 'Always on' medium creates purchasing opportunities. | • Compared with handling a simple purchase through a call centre, e.g. paying the Congestion Charge, the mobile channel can be quicker and cheaper.<br><br>• Confirmations sent by text message following a voice call remove the need for a callback. |
| Retention | • Customer given additional response choices in order to generate accurate bills, e.g. utility meter readings.<br><br>• Relying on organisations to remind you of appointments or prescription frequency. | • Automated follow-up reminders which are targeted generate incremental sales from cool or supposedly dead leads.<br><br>• Mobiles are rarely shared and therefore the organisation knows who they are reaching. | • Appointment reminders result in fewer missed appointments.<br><br>• Checking whether a mobile is turned on before calling reduces call centre costs.<br><br>• Shorter lead time reduces campaign costs. |

*Source: Incentivated*

The adoption of mobile marketing by large and small businesses has led to two different business models for delivery; 'off the shelf' (or DIY) mobile marketing applications and managed campaign solutions offered by agencies, be they specialists or other media, direct and interactive agencies. The managed campaign tends to appeal to major brands, while for a few hundred pounds an SME client can start sending text messages for promotional or informational reasons or for a couple of thousand pounds include a call to action in the local newspaper. Even for larger businesses the cost of a simple, robust and compliant direct response mechanism should not exceed a few tens of thousands of pounds. More sophisticated campaigns will cost a couple of hundred thousand pounds and the largest to date, the Walkers Text 'n' Win campaign, probably cost £1 million.

Mobile marketing can be used in conjunction with other media or on a standalone basis. This explains why there is debate over whether mobile is a medium in its own right. In fact it is both a medium in its own right and a communication channel for making traditional media interactive – for turbocharging other media. Direct marketing through text messaging and mobile internet advertising sites are examples of mobile marketing operating on a standalone basis. Adding interactivity to TV advertising in order to enable a customer to order a brochure is an example of where mobile marketing can act as the glue between the elements of a multi-media campaign. It also plays this role in conjunction with the other traditional advertising media: radio, outdoor, cinema and print.

## Mobile marketing in support of other media

What mobile marketing can achieve is in part defined by how it has been integrated with other media and the role it has been given. A mobile call-to-action buried in the small print at the bottom of a poster, or requiring complicated instructions but appearing for just a moment on TV, will not generate responses, for obvious reasons. Common sense applies to mobile marketing just as it does to other forms of direct marketing and when mobile is given a supporting role the same tried and tested rules that apply to creative production apply.

Some of the uses where mobile marketing can reinforce other media include:

- Direct response mechanism for ordering printed material (brochures and tickets) or electronic material (e-brochures)

- Sales promotion mechanism such as instant wins, prize draws and coupon-redemption schemes

- Callback request

- Vote handling

- Donations

- 'Find my nearest' and 'find out more' services

## Mobile in support of outdoor advertising

The same rules apply to mobile marketing as apply to any other calls-to-action included on a poster. Leading outdoor advertising media owner Clear Channel recommends that the call-to-action should be in 120-point text at the very least, since "you have five to ten seconds to get your idea and message across – copy should be short and sharp." So concerned are they about bad creative execution impacting response rates they have developed a tool for potential outdoor advertisers to use to test creative propositions. ([http://www.clearchannel.co.uk/creativity/creativesimulator/.](http://www.clearchannel.co.uk/creativity/creativesimulator/.))

Figure 5.10.5

### Quick case study – Recycle for London

*For a couple of years, Recycle for London had been running an outdoor advertising campaign, advising Londoners that their local council offered kerbside collection services. The problem was that every borough collected different materials from different roads at different times. This information could not be displayed on a single poster. A text call to action was added, asking Londoners to text their postcode to find out what could be collected. The campaign saw:*

- *More text requests than calls to the 0845 hotline (though the website generated the highest number of requests);*
- *Substantial cost reduction of request handling compared with hotline and postal methods;*
- *Clear pattern of requests near poster sites, revealing which outdoor advertising sites were working and which were not.*

*Source: Incentivated, Recycle for London*

## Mobile in support of broadcast advertising

Direct response TV (DRTV) now has a new acronym: MDRTV or 'mobile direct response TV'. As interactive TV has yet to become ubiquitous and few internet-enabled PCs are in the same room as the average family's main TV, mobile marketing offers a simple and effective way to respond to advertising on TV and indeed radio.

For mobile marketing to work with TV advertising, the call-to-action, which typically appears for only a second or two, should be quick and simple and the contact number as memorable as possible. This precludes the use of full-length mobile numbers and means a short code (four or five digit number) must be used.

## Figure 5.10.6

### *Quick case study - Peugeot 1007*

*When car manufacturer Peugeot launched the innovative 1007 (with ingenious sliding doors) they choose an innovative medium to complement the car. The objectives of the campaign were to raise awareness and generate brochure requests and test-drives. The TV advertisement ran for 6 weeks, with a 1.5 second mobile marketing call-to-action at the end using the branded shortcode text number 81007. The results of the mobile direct response TV campaign were:*

- *30,000 requests for information were made by mobile, resulting in some 24,000 visits to the campaign mobile internet site;*
- *from the mobile microsite 1,400 brochures were ordered and 300 test drives were booked, which "exceeded expectations" (typically 1 in 10 test drives results in a purchase);*
- *brand recall was 10x higher for people who participated via mobile compared with the other response options;*
- *the campaign went on to win Campaign magazine's 2005 Digital Awards.*

*Source: Vodafone, Marvellous*

Response volumes in the tens of thousands are not unusual:

- Ford Motor Company received 40,000 responses from six 30-second spots highlighting a wider campaign to give away a car (source: ITV)

- The mobile marketing campaign in support of the Oliver Twist drama series received 3,000 responses in two and a half weeks and saw the video clip downloaded 1,800 times (source: Channel 4)

- Transport for London received 30,000 requests for local licensed minicabs following two four-week radio and poster campaigns with a mobile marketing call-to-action (source: Incentivated).

## Mobile in support of print advertising and PR

The message in magazine and newspaper advertising can be more detailed than poster or television advertising and the call-to-action more sophisticated, if required. For example the organisation might offer customers information in three different formats (physical, online and via mobile internet) and offer three different calls-to-action. In addition, terms and conditions can be explained on the page rather than taking up valuable space in a text message reply. Using mobile marketing in support of print advertising is commonly used by small and medium-sized enterprises as the budgets required are small. Together mobile and print offer a low risk entry into interactive marketing.

### Figure 5.10.7

### Quick case study – Live8

When Live8 and Comic Relief, Bob Geldof's follow-up concert to Live Aid 20 years earlier, wanted to give away tickets but also raise money for the campaign in a very short time period, they ran a text and win promotion. The mobile channel was probably the only way of achieving their goal of charging everyone a very low price for the chance to win tickets and yet generating a large figure overall.

- More than 2 million people entered the draw at a cost of £1.50 each.
- £2.6m was raised in a week.
- The campaign cost just £35,000 to run, due to in-kind donations from O2 amongst others.
- The campaign went on to win NMA's Grand Prix in the 2006 Effectiveness Awards.

Source: O2, Evening Standard 6the June 2005

## Mobile as sales promotion mechanic

On-pack promotions using mobile marketing, typically 'text and win' campaigns, generate the highest volume of responses. This is due to the number of packs in circulation for FMCG products, point of sale advertising on supermarket shelves and distinct packaging which often mentions the prize. To replicate such response rates on television would be prohibitively expensive.

In percentage terms, response rates are typically higher than through other mechanisms due to the swiftness of entry (a few seconds) and the instant gratification possible using an interactive medium. (In the case below there was no charge for entry beyond the cost of a standard text message, therefore the mobile channel compared favourably with the usual stamped, self-addressed envelope entry mechanism. Had the promoter wished, they could have made a small charge for entry using Premium SMS – premium rate text messaging – although this would have complicated matters since a 'no purchase necessary' entry mechanism would have been required as well for legal reasons. The response rate would have been reduced correspondingly.)

**Figure 5.10.8**

### Quick case study – Walkers Crisps (Frito Lay)

*When Walkers wanted to break the record for an on-pack promotion they chose a combination of mobile (text) and web entry mechanisms during Autumn 2005. The result was the largest mobile marketing sales promotion campaign to date, anywhere in the world.*

*The campaign was elegant in its simplicity – every five minutes a prize draw took place and one person from those who had sent their unique code (one of 900m codes) by text message or entered it online would win an Apple 'iPod mini'. Since the chances of success were affected by the number of entries in each five minute interval and the text message reply would mention the quietest and busiest times of the previous day, repeat purchases were encouraged. The results of the on-pack mobile sales promotion were:*

- *17m responses, making the mobile marketing campaign the world's largest;*
- *over 7% of the UK population entered, which is double the response of the most successful TV promotion;*
- *the campaign has since been extended to The Netherlands and Belgium.*

*Source: Sponge*

## Mobile in support of email

Mobile marketing has also been used to harvest other contact details. For example, organisations have sent text messages to their entire database of mobile numbers asking individual customers to reply with their email address so they can be sent an electronic newsletter. This is an example of a multi-media approach. Response rates to this kind of campaign are often of the order of 10 per cent.

## Standalone mobile direct (push) marketing

So far mobile marketing has been discussed as a support mechanism for campaigns using other media. Of course, the organisation can also send text and picture messages to their or a third- party's opted-in database of mobile numbers without a request from the customer immediately preceding it. Called mobile direct marketing, or mobile push marketing, this use is what people often first think of when mobile marketing is mentioned. It is also a usage that is heavily regulated and subject to negative feedback if abused.

However, direct marketing by text message to your own or a third-party's opted-in database can be highly cost effective. Typically the text message asks the recipient to call a telephone number in the message, visit a website or reply with another text message.

In the case of mobile direct marketing the same rules about accurate targeting and clear message that apply to direct mail also apply here, even if the message is limited to 160 characters.

Response rates vary from a few per cent to one in four, though they typically fall within the range of one to three per cent. When the cost of sending the message is taken into account, cost per response figures can vary from less than £1 when using your own data, to between £1 and £10 for third-party data. (Third-party data sources vary greatly, from the lists owned by the mobile phone ringtone companies – which are often just mobile numbers – to those owned by the lifestyle survey companies who sell high-quality postal and email lists.)

Figure 5.10.9

### Quick case study – Cannons Health Clubs

*In the fiercely competitive health & fitness sector, finding the 25% of people who have an interest in keeping fit requires ingenuity. Cannons, like many other membership products, send text messages to carefully selected partner databases. In the same way that they buy direct mail lists, they profile their good customers and buy data from partner*

*companies who are able to conduct the necessary socio-demographic profiling to identify more of these people. One recent campaign generated the following results:*

- *1.7% response rate*
- *£12 cost per response*
- *ROI of 44%*

*Source: Incentivated*

## Mobile marketing as advertising medium in own right

With the arrival of the third-generation mobile phone networks (3G) the mobile internet is far richer than it used to be. The eight per cent of the UK's population with a broadband mobile phone access a rich and colourful 'home page' each time they turn on their phones and on this page the networks now sell advertising space. Banner advertisements similar to what are seen on internet websites are displayed in order to encourage people to 'click through' to a campaign microsite on which more information can be found about the product. One of the first advertisers to pay for a banner on the 'Today' page of the '3' portal was Apple when they launched the 'iPod' portable digital music player.

### Figure 5.10.10

**3G mobile network '3' charges advertisers to appear on their home-page**

*So successful is 3's mobile internet portal that it is now Europe's second largest retailer of music downloads after Apple's iTunes. The traffic that this and other content generates has enabled 3 to sell banner and microsite advertising on its portal in the same way that websites sell electronic display advertising.*

*In April 2006, one million tracks were downloaded from the 3 portal, or 76% of all mobile music downloads in the UK and 17% of the entire digital music download market. Including music sales on all formats 3 is now a formidable channel for the music publishers with a 4% market share of total singles sales, including on CD.*

Source: 3, The Official Chart Show Company

## Standalone mobile customer service

As a customer service medium the mobile channel is suited to time-sensitive and short updates, such as flight disruption notifications or warning such as credit card fraud alerts. As a global standard (GSM, or the Global Standard for Mobiles) delivery to the four corners of the world is entirely possible. There are even websites that allow you to schedule text messages to remind yourself of your appointment, if the doctor or dentist is not going to do it for you. Healthcare and drug brands, which are restricted in how they can advertise, are looking at mobile customer service messages as a subtle – and legal – way of getting their marketing message across.

### Figure 5.10.11

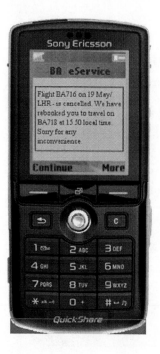

### *Quick case study - British Airways passenger disruption notification service*

*Following significant investment in email marketing, the airline discovered that 48 hours before takeoff, email was not a good enough communication method for urgent disruption notifications. The airline established the need to develop an instantaneous communication channel for disseminating updates to the flying public, logistics firms and staff. After extensive trials, text messaging proved to be the best solution, for the period less than 48 hours before scheduled departure time.*

*The project's main objectives were twofold:*

- *contact more people in the time required than is feasible to contact by calling them;*
- *increase customer satisfaction by letting people know about cancelled or delayed flights while they are still at home, rather than have them find out at the airport.*

*The solution had to be:*

- *instantaneous medium;*
- *global reach;*
- *cost effective;*

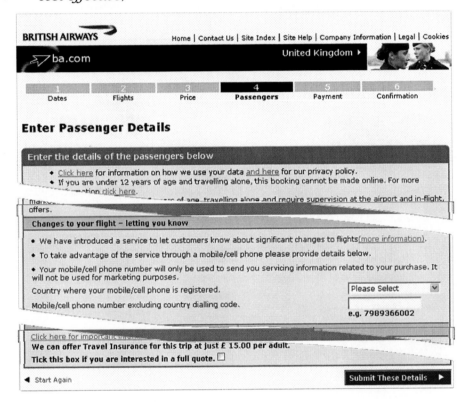

*Results from the first three months of operation have exceeded initial expectations and usage continues to grow. The passenger disruption notification service was launched just in time; as a result of an oil depot fire nearby and a combination of fog and ice, many planes were affected over the weekend of 10th & 11th December 2005 and text message alerts sent to 3,288 people in 59 different countries/languages. Consequently many passengers were able to wait at home instead of in the airport lounge.*

*Since the launch, a further 8,953 passengers in 81 countries have benefited from the service. The number of people being advised of flight delays or cancellations has reached, in some cases, 30% of those on a flight (typically flights with large numbers of business travellers or long haul flights). For example flight BA9043 (Düsseldorf to Heathrow) was cancelled on 11th Dec 2005 and 46 people (or 29.8% of the typical loading of 155 people on a Airbus A310) were sent a text message telling them not to go to the airport but to call BA instead.*

*Source: Incentivated*

## Standalone mobile commerce

Mobile commerce typically takes one of two forms:

- Paying for something by directly charging the customer's account with the mobile phone network (both prepay and monthly contract).

- Authorising a transaction whereby payment is collected through another system (e.g. triggering a credit card charge or initiating a direct debit payment).

Examples of the first include charitable donations, purchases of mobile content and topping-up of calling card accounts.

### Figure 5.10.12

**Quick case study – Macmillan Cancer Support**

*As well as on-going direct-debit donations from individuals, charities rely on ad hoc donations. This works when the fund-raiser is face-to-face with the donor, but is more difficult using traditional advertising, especially if the charity wants to benefit from spontaneous expressions of generosity. A simple micro-payment mechanism is required and Macmillan Cancer Support chose Premium SMS (premium rate text messaging).*

*Although it is too soon to assess the overall results of this mobile commerce fund-raising drive, early results are very promising: of the total responses to a trial newspaper campaign, Macmillan received 43% of the donations by text message, 40% by post and 17% by credit card through the call centre. Not only did the mobile channel generate more donations, but the administrative cost for the charity was lower on a unit basis. At present, it is unfortunate that the mobile phone networks take a revenue share from theses donations, (which almost consumes the Gift Aid/ tax reclaim!) , though several parties are putting pressure on the networks to reduce their charges.*

*Source: Incentivated*

Examples of the second include payment of the central London Congestion Charge, bidding on auction websites or taking out a magazine subscription by filling in a mobile internet direct debit form.

**Figure 5.10.13**

### Quick case study – Central London Congestion Charge

*The aim of the scheme, which went live in February 2003, was to reduce traffic in Central London by 15 per cent and speed up journey times by 25 per cent by getting people to shift to public transport. Prior registration by residents of their credit card details, number plate and mobile phone number allows them to pay by text message. By sending a text message from the same handset, containing the last four digits of the credit card number, the resident is authorising Transport for London to take the daily charge of £8 off their credit card.*

- *170,000 drivers are registered to pay by SMS and in 2005 3.5m text payments were made.*
- *23% of the 300,000 drivers who enter the zone each day pay by text message, compared with 28% through the website, 28% via Paypoint shop-fronts and 14% through the call centre. The rest forget and get fined!*
- *You are more likely to remember to pay if you can do so from your mobile phone shortly after entering the zone, than waiting till you are next online.*

*Source: Transport for London*

# Mobile data technology demystified

There is a compelling case for adopting mobile marketing across the marketing spectrum, but as with any new medium, there is also the inevitable concern that technology will prove a barrier to rapid take-up. A recent survey confirmed that there is a significant gap between the expectations of brands interested in adopting mobile marketing and their capability to do so. Of these brands 60 per cent were unsure how to implement or measure mobile marketing and, significantly, 70 per cent of their advertising agencies were in the same boat (source: Airwide Solutions, Jan 2006).

We should not be surprised that with mobile marketing we are seeing a repeat of the 'technophobia' that first greeted the widespread arrival of personal computers and, later, the internet. Of course, virtually everyone now simply sees PCs and the internet as enabling tools that they use naturally, without having to understand the detailed technology behind them. With that hindsight, it is only a matter of time and familiarity before mobile marketing is just as easily accepted.

The role of the mobile marketing agency, or specialist function within a full service agency, is to instil confidence in the client that the technology is being handled correctly, leaving the client to concentrate on business objectives. The bottom line on mobile technology is to leave this to the specialists: the mobile interactivity expert companies who can recommend the appropriate tools to support the development of your mobile campaign.

In essence, these specialist agencies can, as a minimum, enable their clients to exploit the standard offerings of both the network service providers and the handset manufacturers to achieve usefully interactive mobile marketing. Beyond this, some specialists offer enhanced applications that leverage these 'as standard' network and handset offerings to create flexible, fully interactive and robust web-based campaigns.

The table below provides a 'layman's overview' of the key technologies behind mobile data services and networks, but has been intentionally left at a high level to avoid confusion.

## Mobile data services

The communications mechanisms that are built into handsets by their manufacturers and which are already recognised by the layman are as follows:

## Table 5.10.4

| Mobile data service | Description |
| --- | --- |
| SMS (Short Message Service) | Free, standard rate or premium rate text messaging familiar to most people. Suitable for receiving messages from consumers or sending messages to consumers, in many languages and using different character sets. These messages are sent from or sent to short codes, usually of five digits, or long codes, i.e. normal 11-digit mobile numbers, which would start 07 in the UK. A text message can also be sent from an originator that is not a number but a word, e.g. a brand. One text message is limited to 160 characters but most modern handsets will allow you to exceed this limit and the two or more text messages are joined together upon receipt. Joining two or three text messages together allows enough information to be included to transmit a mobile phone barcode. While SMS texting has a universal appeal, much as emailing does, it clearly has limitations which in the marketing context provide only the most basic experience for the customer. For simple direct response or sales promotion campaigns this is all that is needed and some of the biggest mobile marketing campaigns have relied on SMS only. |
| MMS (Multi-media Message Service) | Sometimes simply called 'picture messaging', MMS delivers a range of content from sounds to slide shows of still images and video. MMS messages can be sent to or received from the consumer. Picture messages and video clips sent to the brand by consumers are fuelling a wave of user-generated content campaigns at the time of writing, including one linked to the football World Cup. (Note, sending multi-media content to consumers can also be done in other ways, such as WAP Push – see below.) Superior to SMS in terms of the amount of data that can be transmitted, but due to those data limitations, MMS is still reasonably expensive. |
| WAP (Wireless Application Protocol) | Hailed as the 'mobile internet', WAP is a protocol that enables applications on the handset, e.g. an internet browser, to access information from online servers connected to the wider internet. WAP is used for mobile websites, portals for content or gateways to private information, such as online billing records. WAP and the mobile internet is clearly the future of mobile marketing wherever a superior customer experience or brand building is the objective. It makes sense for any organisation to ensure that their website is mobile-enabled and in fact many will be able to achieve this without significant investment in rebuilding. |
| WAP Push | A WAP Push is a link to a mobile internet site or a file such as a piece of multi-media content, sent in a form of text message. This link makes it easier for the consumer to access the site rather than typing the address directly into the handset's browser. In fact a WAP Push is a specially encoded text message that tells the handset which WAP site page to open, rather like a hypertext link you might find in an email. A limited amount of space is left over, after inclusion of the link, for a brief explanation of where the link goes. Typically WAP Push messages are sent to the consumer in response to a text message request from the consumer. |
| LBS (Location Based Service) | To work a mobile phone has to remain in contact with an aerial belonging to your mobile network operator. This aerial might be a few hundred metres away or even a kilometre or two, but rarely further. The area of coverage of one of these aerials is called a cell, hence another name for mobile phone technology which is cellular telecoms. Since the aerial does not move around the location of the handset can be pinpointed approximately. As you are passed from one cell to another, it is possible to track your whereabouts. This ability to determine from where a text message was sent allows companies to run location-based services, such as 'find my nearest dealer' or 'child tracker' for parents. |

Figure 5.10.14

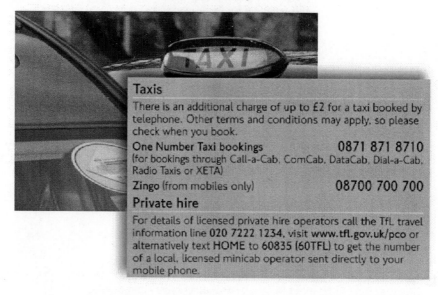

> **Quick case study – Location Based Services (find my nearest licensed minicab, TfL)**

Taxis

There is an additional charge of up to £2 for a taxi booked by telephone. Other terms and conditions may apply, so please check when you book.

One Number Taxi bookings          0871 871 8710
(for bookings through Call-a-Cab, ComCab, DataCab, Dial-a-Cab, Radio Taxis or XETA)

Zingo (from mobiles only)          08700 700 700

**Private hire**

For details of licensed private hire operators call the TfL travel information line 020 7222 1234, visit www.tfl.gov.uk/pco or alternatively text HOME to 60835 (60TFL) to get the number of a local, licensed minicab operator sent directly to your mobile phone.

*This is the world's first text message service to promote safer use of minicabs; providing telephone numbers of licensed London minicabs based on the location of the sender of the text message. This is an example of the mobile data technology known as 'Location Based Services' being used to turn a non-interactive campaign into an interactive one in a way only the Mobile Channel could facilitate.*

- *"I am committed to improving the quality of peoples' lives in London and to enabling a 24-hour society with people able to get home safely after a night out in Central London. Adding the HOME mobile phone service to our Safer Travel at Night campaign has helped reduce the number of assaults and rapes by illegal minicab operators and has delivered, for the first time, a simple solution for people to access legal and licensed minicab firms across the Capital." Ken Livingstone, The Mayor of London*

*Source: Greater London Authority, Incentivated*

## Developing your mobile campaign

As you begin to think through the specific details of your own mobile marketing campaign, it will be no surprise to realise that a 'one-size-fits-all' approach to mobile interactivity does not work. No two advertising agencies want to run the same campaign and no two organisations' CRM databases are the same when they need to be integrated. As a result, a number of different techniques and commercial products are available to the mobile marketing practitioner. These include off-the-shelf, gateway and tailored solutions alongside 'full-service' managed campaigns and consultancy from specialist agencies. Whatever approach you take, you do not need to start with a database of mobile numbers.

## Online applications

Also known as ASPs, these are a range of off-the-shelf products, hosted on a supplier's server and accessible online from any PC. Normally these products must be used on a standalone basis, however sometimes they can be integrated with the client's systems. The client's data usually resides in a ring-fenced database on the supplier's server. Costs vary from nothing (often overseas suppliers offering little support and with no regard to the legislation) to a few thousand pounds per month for a 24/7 service level agreement with many additional features.

## Gateway access

Clients can use a supplier, often called a cross network aggregator, to access a wide variety of mobile data services via a 'gateway'. Gateways are designed for use by the client's own developers and require the client to build an application to manage the campaign.

## Tailored or sector-specific solutions

Bespoke solutions are often required when a campaign is intended to break the mould or the client does not build their own service. Typically built upon the supplier's modular infrastructure and either hosted on the supplier's or the client's servers, these solutions use the supplier's existing network connectivity.

## Managed services

Clients will often choose this option for a short-term campaign or where they do not like the do-it-yourself approach. An account manager at the mobile marketing agency will run the campaign, on the client's behalf, using the supplier's own platform. The client will probably be heavily involved in the campaign design as well as testing and will be able to access results in real time through an online console. Post-campaign analysis is often included in the brief.

## Consulting

Most suppliers are happy to provide consulting services to clients wishing to build and maintain a system inhouse. The supplier can recommend an appropriate architecture and even design a solution taking into account the client's existing set-up and the project's objectives.

There are therefore multiple options, but the essential choice is between what you might call the DIY approach using proprietary software where there is the time, inclination and lower budgets, versus the bespoke or managed campaign outsourced to a mobile interactivity agency. The latter will be appropriate where complexity, quality and budgets dictate.

## *Some golden rules*

Planning:

- Plan your mobile marketing as a total campaign; avoid piecemeal implementation and keep a record of what you have offered or sent to whom.

- Ensure your basic customer data is accurate, relevant for the campaign and cleaned in advance (using a network lookup product if available).

- If you want the best response rates from cold lists, buy opt-in lists of mobile numbers from the professional data companies, not ringtone vendors.

- Mine your data to ensure messages will be relevant and thereby avoid excessive messaging queries. The best results come from databases built by the brands themselves.

The message:

- Keep your mobile messages simple and use plain English.

- Avoid over zealous use of exclamation marks and capitalisation.

- Do not put spaces in telephones numbers but include them as a single number so they can be dialled easily from within the message.

- Include a call-to-action in the message by way of a telephone number, website or WAP site link.

Maximising campaign effectiveness:

- Offer a mobile option alongside other response methods advertised in traditional media – let the consumer choose the medium through which they wish to communicate with you.

- Promote the mobile option on all marketing communications to reinforce the option.

- Consider an incentive for choosing the mobile channel, especially if your operational (acquisition and service) costs are reduced through this medium.

- Always reply instantaneously when someone sends your organisation a text.

- Being completely transparent with your message recipients is by far the most effective way to turn them into customers. Let them know what they are letting themselves into.

Keeping it legal:

- All messages to be pre-authorised and easily cancellable by the recipient.

- Allow opt-outs via text, web and through your 'front desk' and highlight these clearly.

- Train all customer-facing staff in your permission and privacy policy including how to manually record opt-outs.

Housekeeping:

- Clean your database after three broadcasts (using delivery receipts).

Get help:

- If you have questions about the technology, the legislation or likely consumer acceptance, then call an expert mobile marketing supplier who offers account management.

## *Legislation*

(NB: For a fuller discussion of this area, see chapter 12.1 below.)

There are several pieces of legislation and various industry 'best practices' that are relevant to communicating with customers by mobile marketing. What applies to email marketing also applies to mobile. Existing clear guidelines mean that customers are well protected and this should give marketers comfort. The good news is that the law is fully supportive of legitimate organisations running bona fide, mobile marketing campaigns and is only designed to stop unwanted 'spamming' by unscrupulous operators.

Broadly speaking, one commonsense principle can be applied to ensure both legality and good practice and it is that 'all mobile communications should be pre-authorised and easily cancellable by recipients'. The key to achieving pre-authorisation by the recipient, is to be certain whether or not they are considered to be an 'existing customer' and then applying the appropriate means for them to opt in and opt out of your communications.

### Opting in

By giving you their mobile number by whatever method, your existing customer, or someone you are already discussing a sale with, is consenting to be recontacted by you at a later date (Clause 22 of the Privacy and Electronic Communications Regulations). This is sometimes known as the 'soft opt-in' because the consumer has not physically ticked a box, rather some other action on their part is deemed an opt-in. They might have given you their mobile number verbally, sent you a text message, or filled out a contact form. Subject to always allowing them to opt out and with a restriction that you cannot sell these numbers, you can market your goods and services to these people following a soft opt-in. Customer data captured via the soft opt-in process cannot be sold on to third parties, unless those customers are specifically asked to consent in a second text message.

In all cases where people have not had previous dealings with the organisation or are not engaging in discussions regarding a sale or participating in a sales promotion for example, the recipient must give explicit, prior consent to mobile marketing contact by that organisation or third parties; this is known as the 'hard opt-in' process.
This consent should be achieved transparently and simply, for example by ticking a box either to give or to deny permission and plain English always used, rather than formal legalese, to explain your intention.

### Opting out

Whichever way your message recipients have opted in ('hard' or 'soft'), you must enable them to opt out easily from any further communications, if they so require, in order to comply with the law. Providing you handle the opt-in correctly, and keep your messages well targeted, you will not have large numbers opting out. For whatever reason opt-out rates are presently running at about 10 per cent per annum. Obviously this does not include numbers that have ceased to work and these numbers should be suppressed within six months, before the mobile network operators recycle the numbers. (Note, be wary of old data as it is possible that someone opted in to your service, then gave up their mobile number and it was later recycled. In this case, as long as you have evidence of the opt-in and allow the new owner of the number to opt out you will be fine.

The actual opt-out methods are not defined in the legislation. We therefore suggest you offer one or more of the following:

- Contacting your organisation and asking to be removed or 'blacklisted', which requires manual updating of your database

- Entering their mobile number into your website, for auto removal

- Sending a 'STOP' request from their mobile phone to a long or short code, for auto removal

## Mobile customer service

As the customer usually initiates this type of communication and pre-authorisation is only needed for 'marketing messages', the organisation is left to decide the frequency and nature of customer service messages. None of the above legislation deals with non-marketing, service messages. Although these are not subject to the same opt-in, opt-out legislation, you might want to treat them in the same way. The exception might be a bank who does not want to be prevented from chasing a bad debt by someone opting out!  Providing any follow-up communications are restricted to customer service (e.g. a text message appointment reminder), there is no need to offer an opt-out, although the organisation might choose to do so, as good practice. Whenever an organisation combines customer service with advertising its own products and services in the same message, it is subject to the opt-in, opt-out rules for mobile marketing above.

## Mobile commerce

Mobile commerce is subject to much the same legislation as transactions made over the internet and distance selling legislation applies. In addition, ICSTIS has a set of rules governing premium rate SMS services, including subscription services, while the recent e-money legislation covers the use of prepaid mobile phone credit for the purchase
of goods and services not consumed on the mobile phone. This warrants a chapter in its own right and will not be covered in detail here.

## Data Protection Acts

Transmission of any data you hold on individuals outside the European Union is a particular concern. One of the key principles established by the DPA Information Commissioner is often overlooked but is highly significant for mobile marketing sourced from overseas. It requires that data about UK individuals are:

- 'Not transferred to countries outside the EU area unless the country has adequate protection for the individual'.

This is an area of considerable complexity: if you are in any way involved in exporting personal data from the UK to any other country, you will almost certainly require legal advice. In any event, you should read chapter 12.1 below, with reference to the section on 'exporting personal data'.

## Closing thoughts

- Mobile marketing has come of age: initially perceived as youth and entertainment- focused, it is now mainstream with countless applications capable of touching all age groups in their everyday lives

- There are high profile success stories across the private, not-for-profit and public sectors

- Despite proven success across all sectors and huge potential growth projections, traditional creative agencies can be slow to propose mobile marketing to their clients

- In its first five years, mobile marketing has been a powerful, direct response tool, driven by the familiar technology of text messaging and this will continue for a long, long time

- Going forward, the next 'big thing' is clearly the mobile internet

  - More than 75 per cent of UK mobile subscribers can now access the mobile internet

  - Many things online that previously required a PC for access, can now be replicated on a mobile

  - High resolution screens and browsers designed to mimic the online world, have created branding opportunities in the palms of consumers' hands

  - Interactive advertising can be taken 'out-of-home' and closer to the point of sale

  - The mobile internet has the potential to be a mainstream advertising medium

  - Cross linking your traditional media and mobile internet site will maximise their combined effectiveness

  - The good news is that that it should be possible to drive your online and mobile internet presence from one combined web and WAP site content database.

We'll leave you with two final quotes:

"Only 13 per cent of all written communication is now using pen and paper; 48 per cent is via email, 29 per cent via SMS text and 10 per cent via internet instant messaging."

*Institute of Practitioners in Advertising's TouchPoints survey, late 2005*

"The advertising industry is failing to understand the scope and scale of change that is going on in the digital age. It is a cop out to talk about children and grandchildren having different media habits – it's happening now. The failure to react is because people who run the major media and ad groups, who are mainly in their 50s and 60s, are reluctant to change. Take note: in the Chinese version of 'Pop Idol', 800 million votes were cast by mobile phone during the final episode, even though China has only 400 million mobile phone handsets."

*Sir Martin Sorrell, CEO WPP Group, at the IAB Engage Conference 27th October 2005*

# Integration – bringing the media plan together – or making it all work – really well!

## This chapter includes:

--------------------------------------------

- ❏ **Introduction**

- ❏ **What is integrated marketing communications?**

- ❏ **Media neutral planning**

- ❏ **Defining the advertising objectives**

- ❏ **Defining the communication objectives**

- ❏ **Defining the target audience**

- ❏ **The media selection process**

- ❏ **Campaign timing**

- ❏ **Final selection criteria**

--------------------------------------------

## About this chapter

**H**ere we try to bring together the threads of the previous chapters in this Section, which have dealt with how to communicate through direct mail, the press, door-to-door, telemarketing – and so on for each direct marketing medium. The aim of this final chapter in this Section is to indicate the importance of not just optimising one's use of a single medium, but of optimising the media mix, such that all the company's communications are singing from the same hymn-sheet.

### Beverly Barker

Beverly is an entirely over qualified communications planner having started in the business as a broadcast buyer with Ogilvy & Mather in 1984 and, after moving through a succession of agencies that were assortedly acquired and merged to make the large conglomerates of today, spent from 1992-2002 as Head of Direct and Interactive at Carat Direct.

Beverly now combines academia with practical commercial operations, working as a senior lecturer in Marketing at London Southbank University and a regular tutor for the IDM, alongside being a Managing Partner in Everythingville, where she provides a strategic customer insight consultancy to both UK and International clients in customer management, customer insight, proposition development and integrated communications planning.

## Chapter 5.11

# Integration – bringing the media plan together – or making it all work – really well!

## Introduction

Now you have read about all the different media disciplines in great detail. Section 5 has brought you a wealth of information about the strengths and weaknesses of direct mail, how to target door-to-door deliveries, how to prevent attrition in your press campaigns, who to call, and different ways to use TV and radio, along with all the many possibilities of the internet. On top of all that, we have made you think about the benefits of floor panels and washroom ads and getting closer to different types of consumers.

But how do you decide which of these media vehicles to use to achieve your objectives? This final chapter is designed to give you the principles of media planning at the inter-media level – that is, at the point when you are looking to see what is the most impactful way in which to engage with a certain segment of your audience.

Two phrases will be central to this: integrated marketing communications (IMC) which reminds us that all communications activities, whether direct marketing, sponsorship or sales promotions, should be planned to work together and enhance the overall effectiveness, and media neutral planning, a framework that dictates that we do not choose the media vehicles that we like, but the ones that the target audience engage with and pay attention to.

# What is integrated marketing communications?

There are numerous definitions of IMC bandied around and I have listed a few of them below:

## Definitions

- IMC is the co-ordinated planning of communication for each customer, community or public to achieve creative harmony of messages, customer interest and marketing objectives across media, at each 'touchpoint' and over time. *Jenkinson, 2004*

- IMC is a strategic business process used to plan, develop, execute and evaluate co-ordinated measurable, persuasive brand communication programmes over time with consumers, customers, prospects, and other targeted, relevant external and internal audiences. *Schultz and Kitchen 2000[1]*

- IMC is the integrated management of all communications to build positive and lasting relationships with customers and other stakeholders. It is a customer-centric approach to marketing and branding that stresses the use of multiple, intersecting forms of media and technology.

## The common themes are ...

- Management – co-ordination – planned – strategic business process

- All customers and stakeholders – publics – each customer – prospects

- Customer-centric – customer touchpoint – intersecting forms of media

- Lasting relationships – over time

The aim is to build a strong brand identity/sales message through tying together and reinforcing all the company's messages, positioning, images and identity, ensuring these are co-ordinated across all marketing communications, media and channels, so the consumer receives a consistent positioning and message and the marketer an improved ROI.

This means that IMC is an active role that links all of the communications activity of the company or brand, and the adoption of this best-practice approach for all of your 'internal' and 'external' communications seeks to gain positive advantage from synergy and make 1+1+1=5.

IMC incorporates all of the best elements of media planning, whether it be for direct mail, TV or press, i.e. the need to get the advertisement in front of the right person at the right time, but also the co-ordination of all communication activity, across all disciplines and all customer contact points from call centre and point of sale through to customer services or call out engineers. This ensures that there is a harmony that makes every contact with your customers and prospects a profitable one.

[1]Schultz, D.E. and Kitchen, P.J. (2000a), *Communicating Globally: An Integrated Marketing Approach*, Macmillan, Basingstoke, pages 3, 32, 62 and 188.

Figure 5.11.1 **The wide range of promotional disciplines available**

## *Media neutral planning*

So integrated marketing communications requires that all communications (PR, awareness, or lead generating) should integrate with the main business positioning: therefore the tone, imagery, quality and appearance should reflect the main corporate theme and prevent fragmentation of messages.

Media neutral planning requires integrated and unbiased planning that reflects how different media and disciplines work, the preferences of customer segments at different touchpoints isolating the optimal media combination, time sequence and contact strategy for each segment, enhancing cost-efficiency and avoiding confusion, with clear evaluation criteria defined for each element.

However, planners work in a constantly changing marketplace.

In the mainstream the number of TV and radio stations keeps growing, digital broadcasting is creating new interactive possibilities, magazines come and go, and the internet continues to introduce us to new ways to reach our customers and prospects. On the periphery, petrol forecourts now have TV screens and ads on the pumps and our corner shops take advertising on their carrier bags and egg boxes.

Within each medium, there are lots of options too: there are over 400 TV channels, more than 300 radio stations, around 11,000 magazines and papers and about 180,000 poster sites; on top of which there are ambient opportunities everywhere and endless potential internet sites and a multitude of digital innovations

All of the options will deliver audience impacts (opportunities to see) and the vast majority will have carried a direct marketing advertisement at some time or another.

Figure 5.11.2 **Numerous different media vehicles**

TV, Video
Cinema
Team Shirts
Outdoor
Transport Road-side
Web
Email
Mobile
SMS MMS
WOM
Friends
Celebrities
Showroom, Kiosk
Point of Sale
Newspapers
Magazines
Ambient
Beer Mats
Wash Rms
Direct
Mail
Leaflets
Books
Brochures
Personal Selling
Sales Reps
Radio - On-line, In-car,
store, home or mobile


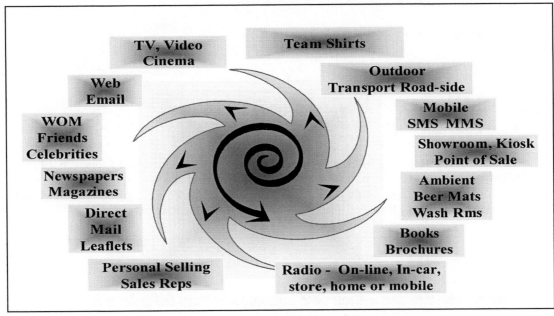

People are exposed to an extraordinary amount of advertising every day and an individual's 'media consumption' does not remain the same for long, as people move through different life stages and develop new interests.

- Planners have to understand who sees what and when, learning from the past to try and predict the future and interpreting how a medium might work in the context of a specific campaign.

Figure 5.11.3 **The media planning process**

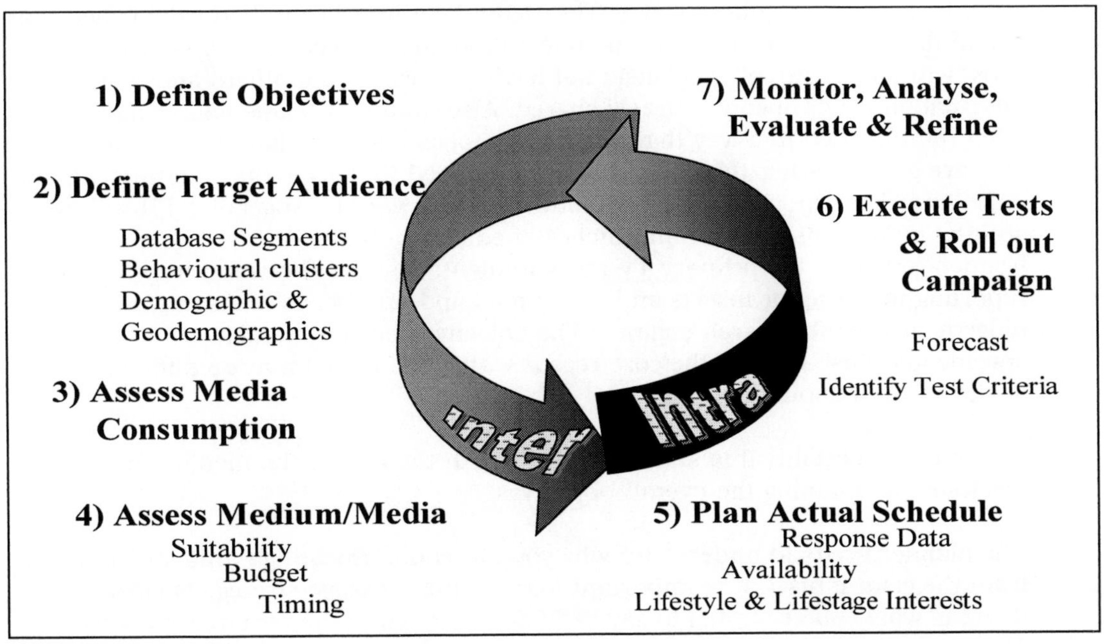

1) Define Objectives
7) Monitor, Analyse, Evaluate & Refine
2) Define Target Audience
Database Segments
Behavioural clusters
Demographic &
Geodemographics
6) Execute Tests & Roll out Campaign
Forecast
Identify Test Criteria
3) Assess Media Consumption
Inter
Intra
4) Assess Medium/Media
Suitability
Budget
Timing
5) Plan Actual Schedule
Response Data
Availability
Lifestyle & Lifestage Interests


There are a number of key features that the planner looks at as they have the greatest impact on overall effectiveness of response volumes and cost of response:

- Communication objectives

- Campaign objectives and strategy – including offer, incentives, endorsements and creative

- Target market

- Budget

- Timing

- Past results

By following a rigorous but straightforward process, as detailed in figure 5.11.3, planners ensure that they have researched and armed themselves with as many relevant facts and figures as possible, at the end of which certain conclusions and directions become clear.

> The media neutral bit ...
>
> Identifying what consumers, customers and prospects see and hear and prefer to do.
>
> Maximising individual media and building media synergy to maximise the effectiveness of each segment of a campaign.

## Defining the advertising objectives

Work by Professor Jenkinson and The Media Planning Group had established that one of the biggest reasons why true integration fails is because people work in silos, with one group of specialists not having access to the others and therefore information is not openly or freely shared. Also, different teams and agencies are often remunerated in a way that make them focus on what share of the budget they are getting rather than what budget they need to deliver the communications objectives. The reporting accountabilities will also vary by speciality. PR will be seeking to maximise the column inches of editorial obtained; coverage and frequency may be the primary TV measurement, cost per thousand may be a key reporting measure for inserts and direct mail and number of leads may be the judgement used for search engines. The objectives become vehicle- and discipline-specific and this is one of the core reasons why IMC is much more difficult to achieve than it should be.

Within each speciality it is still vital to establish the role of the medium or discipline in attaining the overall objectives.

The planner needs to understand why you are communicating – this should come from the central brief. It is important that the full message strategy is clear, defining what you are trying to say or to do and what is the required response. The element of response is important because prospects and customers may well be at different stages in their relationship with the organisation and where they are in the communication cycle.

As detailed in figure 5.11.4 an organisation will need to communicate with suspects who may not be aware of their offer as yet, as well as move other individuals along from consideration to purchase or repurchase. This element will reoccur in the discussion of target audience identification, but it is vital to start thinking of this issue at the very beginning as it will start to shape the overall communications mix.

Figure 5.11.4 **Defining the communication objectives**

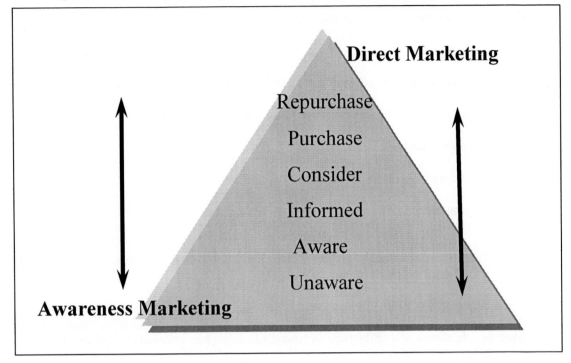

Individual targets and evaluation criteria can be detailed for each target segment and objective as outlined below:

## Brand awareness objectives for launch of new product

To Inform/persuade audience

Brand advertising using strategic, paid-for programme, designed to inform, influence and sell

### Awareness targets

- Meet coverage and frequency targets of X

- Heighten awareness by Y%

- Deliver spontaneous recall of Z%

- Reach prompted recall level of Z+20%

- % change in attitude

- % sales uplift

## Direct response objectives

Targeted, quantifiable, sales-orientated, informative and actionable

## Response targets should be SMART

Specific, Measurable, Achievable, Agreed, Realistic and Time-framed ...

By understanding the overall objectives, the response-orientated media objectives can be established. Within direct marketing the objectives are predominantly orientated around the amount of business that is needed and the need to refine that which has gone before.

Therefore specific media objectives may include phrases like:

- Generate X number of leads at £Y CPL

- Increase quality of conversion by X% via targeting and segmentation

- Increase value of sales/donations, by Y%, etc

- Construct test matrix to identify…

Plus identifiable objectives for acquisition and retention

- Acquisition objectives: generate X new calls/leads, convert to direct sales of £Y value

- Retention objective: to reduce churn by X%, to earn Y% more, to re-enrol Z% of existing customers

These objectives can also be combined, e.g. to make direct sales and build awareness; or to produce volume enquiries and support other media. However, there is a fundamental difference between planning for awareness and driving pure direct response.

## 1)   Generating awareness

If the key objective is to heighten awareness, the media will be planned to optimise the 'coverage' (the number of people within the target group who see the advertising) and 'frequency' levels (the number of times that those individuals see the advertising) within the budget.

With successive insertions or spots, a campaign delivers a mixture of repeat exposures to some people while reaching other new people for the first time. In this way coverage and frequency levels will grow during the campaign.

**Figure 5.11.5   Awareness grows steadily with incremental exposure**

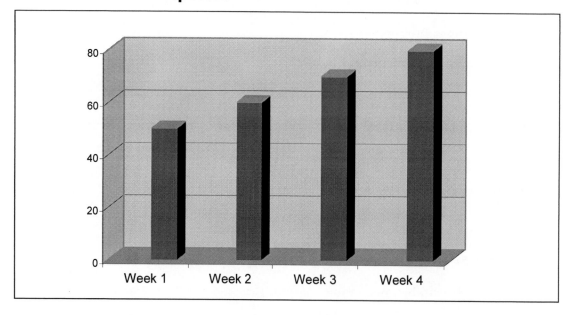

Logically the more diverse the audience reached with each advertisement, the faster the coverage will build as new people are reached. Conversely, the greater the level of audience duplication between two successive ads (for example – by using the *Daily Mail* two days running) the higher the frequency level achieved.

The target frequency level will be dependent upon such issues as:

- Creative impact and cut through of a particular creative execution and message within its product category

- Level of competitive activity

- Product purchasing cycle

Obviously in today's market the boundaries between pure brand and pure direct response have blurred. Many planners have to balance the need to drive brand recognition with generating cost- efficient leads.

One way to do this is to undertake regular awareness studies (both promoted and spontaneous) to quantify the effect that reported increases or decreases have on response generation.

Brands such as Direct Line work at a very high level of awareness and proposition understanding, which inevitably increases the rate at which people respond to their advertising.

Figure 5.11.6 **Varied degree of response versus brand requirements**

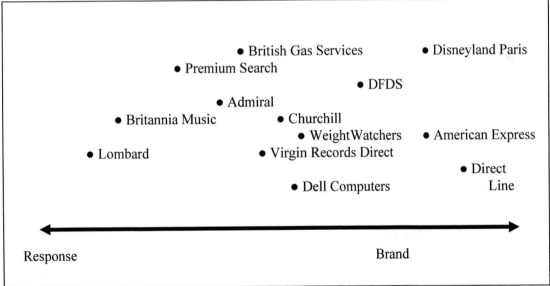

### 2) Driving response

Years of tracking have demonstrated repeatedly that the maximum response from any vehicle will often come from the first or earliest insertions. Successive insertions, mailings or broadcast 'spots' increase the frequency, which is synonymous with 'attrition' – the reduction in response from one insertion to the next. The key to successful direct response planning therefore is to understand how to keep the response at the same level as that of the initial or best responding insertions.

Figure 5.11.7  **Decreasing response with repeated activity**

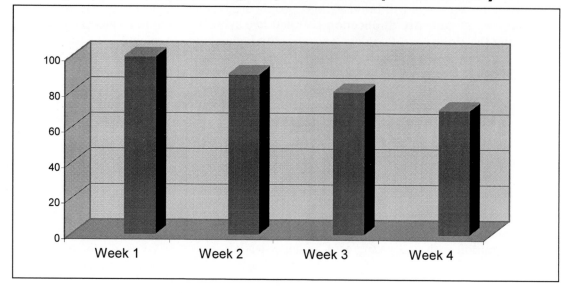

Techniques for maintaining high response levels include:

- Avoiding overuse of one vehicle

- Minimising duplication between media options

- Working with a variety of creative executions

- Varying the positions, day of week and time of day used within a single publication or television channel

However, the easiest way of understanding how attrition is affecting a campaign is to construct a carefully phased test. Cells can be established to track the response decay over successive insertions or spots. In this way it is possible to identifying the optimum time allowable between exposures. The results will vary from one medium to another and from one product or service to another. Mail order jewellery or collectibles may find that anything between 9 to 12 months should elapse before the same product is promoted to the same audience.

By contrast someone operating in the insurance field may well be able to advertise every week because new prospects enter the market each month by virtue of their need to renew their policy.

## Constructing a test matrix

Including a campaign test matrix into any campaign is the primary starting point for all DM planners.

New product campaigns may commence with an inter-media test that will help refine the apportionment of budget for rollout.

An ongoing campaign may include tests to refine the media schedule and targeting (such as publication selection, position, or day of week) or creative elements (such as headline, proposition, size and colour versus mono). In this way the planner will work through a process of testing, measurement and replanning. This process should be adopted regardless of the size of the organisation or of the budget.

Figure 5.11.8  **Simplistic comparison between awareness and direct response**

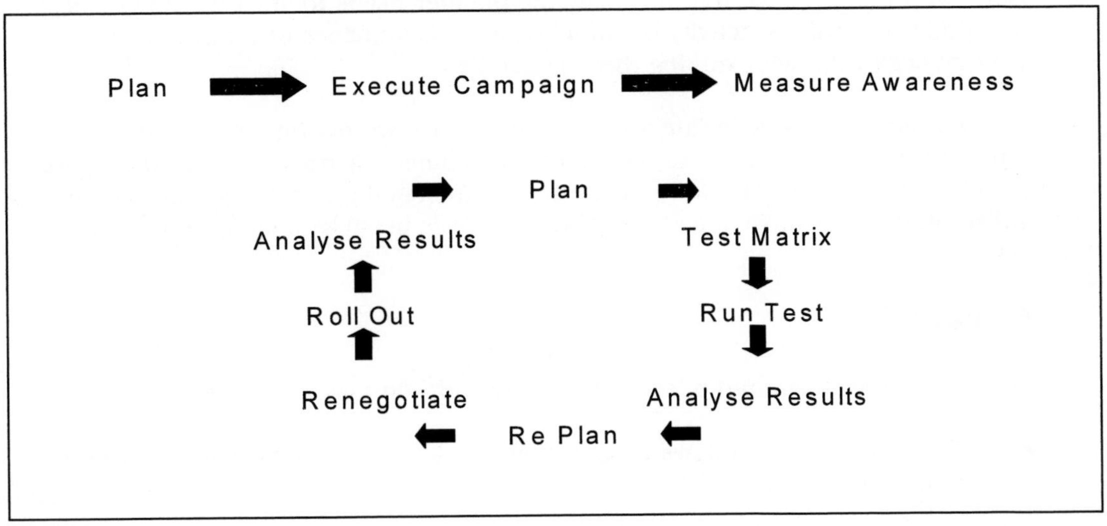

Plan  ➡  Execute Campaign  ➡  Measure Awareness

➡ Plan ➡

Analyse Results          Test Matrix

⬆                ⬇

Roll Out               Run Test

⬆                ⬇

Renegotiate          Analyse Results

⬅  Re Plan  ⬅

This topic will be reviewed in more depth later in this and the individual media chapters.

## *Defining the target audience*

In any form of advertising the most important factor is that of targeting. No matter how good the headline, illustration, offer or incentive, it will not work if the right person does not see it.

The results below are taken from a very large consumer direct mail campaign, where over 1,000 test calls were created to identify the relative value of various factors.

Table 5.11.1  **Targetting: the most important element**

| List targeting | x 6 |
|---|---|
| Offer | x 3 |
| Timing | x 2 |
| Creative | x 1.35 |
| Response mechanic | x 1.2 |

As demonstrated in table 5.11.1, and elsewhere in this Guide, the most successfully targeted list was six times more responsive than the least. Elements such as the 'offer' and 'timing' generated variations in response by factors of two or three, and only minimal impact was seen from changes in the response mechanic. Theoretically, getting everything right would be over 58 times better than getting it all wrong!

Such evaluation has been carried out numerous times and while the precise numbers may vary from test to test, the sequence does not. List targeting or media selection always comes out on top.

In identifying the target audience the media planner must try to define the key prospects as tightly as possible and there are many sources that can be used to assist with this process, but primarily the planner needs to start making choices straightaway – will the activity be targeting a mass audience or a number of discrete segments, with varying lifestyle profiles?

To help define the appropriate audience, there are two options; firstly to access primary data relating to the organisation's customers or donors, and interrogate on relevant selection criteria to derive profile information. It is also possible to utilise industry data, such as that collected by the lifestyle database companies or TGI.

## Primary data

- Profile/segmentation of customers/enquirers on own database

- Focus groups, interviews or questionnaires to understand triggers, interests and motivations

## Secondary

- Profile from lifestyle database sources (e.g. Acxiom and Experian) detailing product usage, propensity to buy and geodemographics

- Profile industry research including customer/prospect profiles and media consumption habits via TGI

- Media specific research such as NRS, BARB, POSTAR, etc

## *Profiling existing customers*

Section 2, chapters 2.3 to 2.6, explain in great detail the benefits of, and techniques for, profiling and segmenting customer data. Once the nature of different segments is fully understood, decisions can be taken as to which ones are to become the target audience for the campaign under discussion.

Files will identify the characteristics of:

- The average customer

- Prospects likely to be best, high-value customers

- Individuals likely to be low value/bad risk customers

If the profiles of the two latter groups are different then it is possible to bias activity away from the bad risk individuals and target the better quality prospects. Similarly, customer segmentation might show that purchasers of different products have different profiles and therefore these can be used to refine future activity. It is even possible to see which customers have responded to different stimuli/advertising vehicles in the past if the data has been collected.

All of this enables you to target the right people for a particular message or offer; construct different offers for different clusters of customers and target copy more accurately, e.g. by gender and life stage.

External data sources can be purchased to overlay and enhance a customer base. These can be very useful; to build more detailed clusters and to refine profiling with geodemographic or lifestyle indicators. Lifestyle data can be a good indicator to an individual's channel preferences, helping the planner to decide between using the internet or direct mail for a certain cluster. In addition, details relating to hobbies, age of children and type of car can be pointers to the preferred magazine environments, programme genre or list selections that should be used, all of which could improve the targeting and, with it, the response.

Analysing the database may also provide information on:

– Customer geography and postcode clusters – by ITV, ISBA regions, towns and vicinity to stores

– Basic demographic – by age, class, sex, marital status, household income and household and family composition

– Behavioural patterns – by purchasing activity such as recency, frequency, types of products, payment methods, credit history and response history

– For business-to-business – SIC code, client company turnover, payment history, order cycles, repairs, upgrades and complaints

– Geodemographic patterns – neighbourhood types via ACORN and MOSAIC etc. (See chapter 2.5.)

However, many advertisers do not have an existing customer database or may be looking to take old products to new markets or launch new products. For whatever reason, there are many occasions where advertisers will refer to the available industry research for the profile and media usage information.

## Industry research

There are a number of pieces of research that can help the media planner to identify and cluster individuals. However, the Target Group Index (TGI) studies are the most popular for defining an initial marketing audience. The studies aim to combine demographic data, media consumption and product usage, together with a large number of lifestyle statements and are described in greater detail below and also in chapter 5.2 in relation to selecting press titles for campaigns.

Planners can also use data from the various media-specific research studies, all of which are described in greater detail in the respective media chapters in this section and include:

– NRS (National Readership Survey) and BBS (British Business Survey) for press

– BARB (Broadcaster Audience Research Board) for TV

– RAJAR for radio

– POSTAR for posters

– CAIVAR for cinema

Alternatively it is possible to undertake bespoke research such as:

–       Individual customer and prospect focus groups

–       Omnibus surveys and tracking studies

## BMRB's Target Group Index series of research surveys

The TGI research is a very good starting point for defining an initial marketing audience. The research is collected through self-completion questionnaires and provides a single source measurement of consumer product/brand usage and media exposure together with respondent attitudes and motivations. It allows us to construct a multitude of target audience descriptors, from the simple to the complex, for example:

Definitions may be broad social demographic descriptions:

–       ABC1 adults aged 35-plus

They may be more specific, with lifestyle or attitudinal overlays:

–       ABC1 adults aged 35 plus who have children and agree with the following lifestyle statement: 'I think it is important to be well insured'

The audience may be segmented to define regions, age ranges or product variations:

–       ABC1 adults aged 35 to 44 in the Granada TV region

–       ABC1 women, retired, aged 60-plus, who are motor insurance decision makers

–       ABC1 men retired, aged 65-plus, who have higher than average savings

Or they may be solely product related:

–       Customer of 'Brand X'

To gain the required detail, there are four major segments to the TGI research:

1)      The Target Group Index (TGI): (sub-divided into three studies – Great Britain (GB), Republic of Ireland (ROI) and Northern Ireland (NI))

2)      Premier TGI (AB adults aged 20-plus)

3)      Youth TGI (7 to 19 year olds in three age bands)

4)      TGI Gold (50-plus year olds)

There are a number of media-specific studies such as TGI Wavelength and more information on TGI can be obtained by contacting BMRB, Saunders House, 53 The Mall, Ealing, London W5 3T3 (Tel: 020 8576 3060) http://www.bmrb.co.uk/

## The Target Group Index (TGI) UK

With a sample size of circa 25,000 interviewees, aged 15-plus, TGI provides information on the use of over 4,000 brands in 500 product areas. TGI data is collected on a rolling quarterly basis.

Table 5.11.2 below outlines a short excerpt from a cross tabulation of lager drinkers by broad demographics. It shows us a number of things about the populations and lager drinkers:

Table 5.11.2 **TGI extract – which is your 'preferred canned lager'?**

| A | B | C | D | E | F | G |
|---|---|---|---|---|---|---|
| | | Total | Budweiser Most often canned lager | Grolsch Most often canned lager | Heineken Most often canned lager | Heineken Export Most often canned lager |
| Adults | 000's | 45350 | 1326 | 396 | 3263 | 328 |
| | Sample | 25296 | 649 | 203 | 1724 | 157 |
| | % Profile | 100.0 | 100.0 | 100.0 | 100.0 | 100.0 |
| | %Penetration | 100.0 | 2.9 | 0.9 | 7.2 | 0.7 |
| | Index | 100 | 100 | 100 | 100 | 100 |
| Men | 000's | 21899 | 847 | 294 | 1815 | 210 |
| | Sample | 11687 | 395 | 144 | 936 | 104 |
| | Profile | 48.3 | 63.9 | 74.2 | 55.6 | 64.0 |
| | Penetration | 100.0 | 3.9 | 1.3 | 8.3 | 1.0 |
| | Index | 100 | 132 | 154 | 115 | 132 |
| Women | 000's | 23451 | 479 | 102 | 1448 | 118 |
| | Sample | 13623 | 254 | 59 | 788 | 53 |
| | % Profile | 51.7 | 36.1 | 25.8 | 44.4 | 36.0 |
| | % Penetration | 100.0 | 2.0 | 0.4 | 6.2 | 0.5 |
| | Index | 100 | 70 | 49 | 86 | 7.0 |

Column C details the population base against which the specific product data is compared. In this case all adults are aged 15-plus, totalling 45,350,000 individuals across the research period, with a sample size of 25,296. Men represent 48.3 per cent of this, at 21,899,000 (based upon a sample of 11,678), and women 23,451,000, at 51.7 per cent.

Columns D, E, F and G detail the product data. Heineken, column F, has the highest number of regular drinkers at 3,263,000 and Heineken Export, column G, the fewest, at 328,000. As a percentage of the population these represent 7.2 per cent and 0.7 per cent respectively (% penetration)

1,815,000 Heineken drinkers are men, and 1,448,000 are women, demonstrating a 55.6:44.4 male/female spilt (% profile). Compared to the population (48.3:51.7) this indicates a male- biased profile, and can be expressed simply as an index, in this case 115.

---

**55.6% ⌄ 48.3% = 1.15 x 100 = index of 115**

---

By contrast, Grolsch is only drunk regularly by 0.9 per cent of adults (396,000 individuals). It demonstrates a more male-orientated profile with a male index of 153 derived from its 74:36 male/female split. But in looking at high indices it is important to remember that this still only represents 1.3 per cent of all men and

0.4 per cent of all women - numbers which detail the respective 'penetration' of this product. Equally, when the sample size becomes less than 30 or 40, sampling error should be accommodated.

We could extend this example to detail age, class, household income, regionality, readership and viewing patterns, internet usage, geodemographic through MOSAIC and ACORN, and much more.

Therefore TGI can be used to build up a picture of the buyers and consumers of different brands and products and is valuable for both the creative and media strategy.

A second example demonstrates the use of the index to read profile bias at a glance. Table 5.11.3 details two different groups, firstly 'individuals making pensions contributions AVC' and secondly 'people who have shopped at a household furnishing chain in the last 12 months'

**Table 5.11.3   Comparison of targeting information compiled via TGI**

|   | Rank Order I Individuals making Pensions contributions AVC | | Rank Order II Shoppers at a household furnishing store in the last 12 months | |
|---|---|---|---|---|
| 1 | AB | 154 | AB | 133 |
| 2 | C1 | 113 | C1 | 115 |
| 3 | C2 | 100 | C2 | 106 |
| 4 | DE | 47 | DE | 70 |
| 1 | 45-54 | 157 | 25-34 | 177 |
| 2 | 35-44 | 153 | 35-44 | 143 |
| 3 | 55-64 | 124 | 20-24 | 134 |
| 4 | 25-34 | 103 | 45-54 | 92 |
| 5 | 20-24 | 51 | 15-19 | 80 |
| 6 | 65-99 | 39 | 55-64 | 49 |
| 7 | 15-19 | 20 | 65-99 | 19 |
| 1 | h/i 40-49999 | 279 | h/i 50-99999 | 292 |
| 2 | h/i 50-99999 | 224 | h/i 40-49999 | 247 |
| 3 | h/i 35-39999 | 214 | h/i 25-34999 | 181 |
| 4 | h/i 25-34999 | 195 | h/i 35-39999 | 175 |
| 5 | h/i 15-24999 | 124 | h/i 15-24999 | 115 |
| 6 | h/i 10-14999 | 76 | h/i 10-14999 | 74 |
| 7 | h/i 1-9999 | 36 | h/i 1-9999 | 45 |

At a glance assessment tells us:

- Pension contributors are generally 45-plus, with a household income in excess of £15,000, but more significantly from £25,000-plus, and tend to be ABC1s

- Shopping for household furniture is broader; ABC1C2 being significantly younger and primarily 20 to 44 years.

Further data in table 5.11.4 goes on to show us that:

- Nearly 70 per cent are married and two per cent are engaged - which represents nearly 10 per cent of all engaged couples, demonstrating a strong bias to this relatively small group of people. There is a slight female bias.

- The group goes to work - whether full- or part-time, with only five per cent of non-working individuals visiting this store, although they make up 31 per cent of all the stores' shoppers.

- There is a bias to London and the South, which reflects the chain store locations.

Using this data it is possible to describe the profile of the current customers of the retail chain.

If a planner were given the following brief and the accompanying TGI data there are a number of initial insights and targeting statements that can be made.

**Table 5.11.4  Extended TGI analysis of household furnishing shoppers**

| TGI Shoppers at a household furnishing store in the last 12 months | | | |
|---|---|---|---|
| Demographic | Profile % | Penetration | Index |
| Engaged | 1.6 | 9.6 | 125 |
| Married | 68.1 | 8.3 | 109 |
| Men | 47 | 7.4 | 97 |
| Women | 53 | 7.8 | 103 |
| Work - not | 31.8 | 5 | 66 |
| Work1-29part-tm | 12.8 | 9.2 | 121 |
| Work 1-8 part-tm | 1.9 | 10.2 | 134 |
| Work 30+full-tm | 53.5 | 10.3 | 136 |
| Central Scotland | 6.28 | 5 | 101 |
| East of England | 7.33 | 5.06 | 102 |
| London | 26.53 | 6.69 | 135 |
| Midlands | 15.1 | 4.64 | 94 |
| NE Scotland | 1.83 | 4 | 81 |
| North East | 4.62 | 4.5 | 91 |
| North West | 11.82 | 4.77 | 96 |
| South | 9.6 | 5.17 | 104 |
| South West | 2.49 | 4.01 | 81 |
| Wales/West | 5.54 | 3.48 | 70 |
| Yorkshire | 8.12 | 4.05 | 82 |
| Border | 0.74 | 3.44 | 69 |

Assume that the campaign objective is to take the core retail proposition and launch the direct sales operation - with products being available via a 375-page catalogue and the internet; TGI data can be used to define the current customer profile. This can become the base target audience of those who are most likely to be interested in buying the same products, but directly...

*'ABC1 working women aged 20 to 40, with a household income in excess of £15,000'*

A bias to London and the South can be seen in the TGI data, but this is known to be due to store location. Therefore, the campaign could take on a national platform. However, the campaign might seek to identify whether the response from the London and South areas is affected, either positively because of greater familiarity with the chain or negatively because they have the retail option.

## Formalising segments to meet business objectives

By understanding the broad audience and potential sub-audience segments, the planner will be able to start to shape some of the initial selection criteria. Some segments will be more desirable to reach, others may like to receive regular contact and some may prefer to be in control of their own actions. This will determine the degree of proactivity or reactivity that the message and media strategy needs to accommodate. Figure 5.11.9 outlines an example of a segmented strategy that starts to identify the audiences based upon the type of media that they may respond to, but is filtered by the preferred contact style.

### Figure 5.11.9  **A new focus for segmentation**

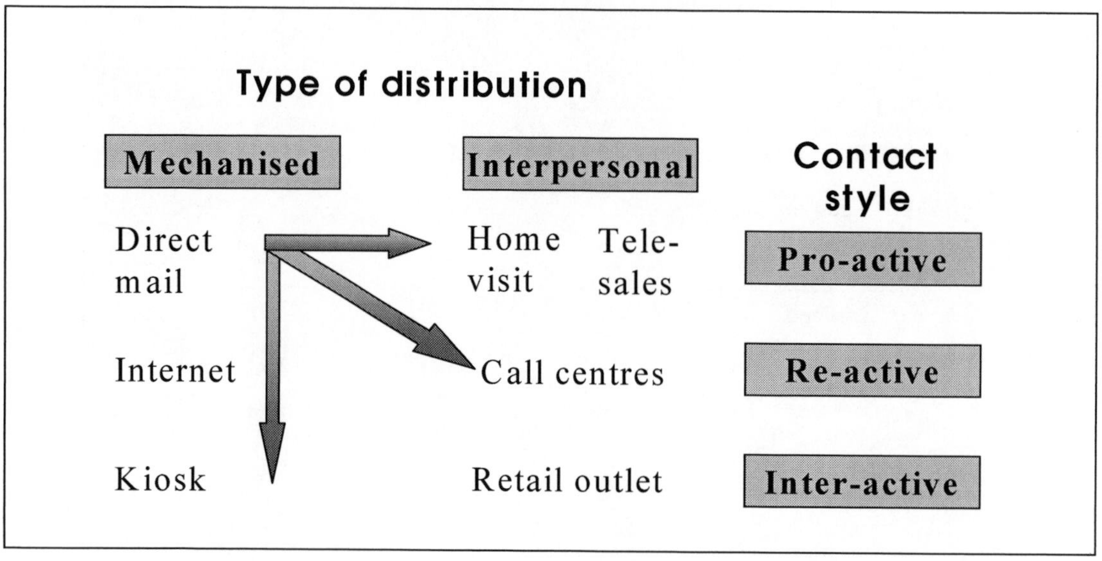

### Business audiences

Business audiences also require a further dimension, to ensure that all of the individuals involved in the decision making are provided with the right information. Business targets segments are therefore more complex decision making groups as detailed in figure 5.11.10 and require a broad range of research to understand them fully, including customer data, industry data and personal contact information.

Figure 5.11.10 **Example of key audiences for business campaigns**

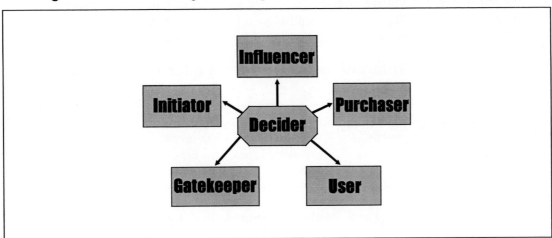

Most importantly each will require a different proposition to ensure that the right benefits are explained in each case. Table 5.11.5 outlines an example of how the audience and proposition development might look.

Table 5.11.5    **Business audience/proposition matrix**

| Title | Role | Interest | Proposition |
|---|---|---|---|
| CEO/President | Overall company performance | + productivity<br>- costs | Company Focus<br>(Credibility/brand) |
| Financial Director | Management of company finances | Income, expenditure, cash flow, risk | Company Focus<br>(Competitive, stability) |
| IT Director | Management Information Systems | Integrity of systems<br>Needs of users | Product Focus<br>(Performance, compatibility) |
| Line Manager | Achievement of personal targets | Productivity, morale, best tools for job | Product Focus<br>(Performance, support, running costs) |
| Office Manager | Management of office support functions | Availability of equipment and supplies | Product Focus<br>(Reliability, supplies deliveries) |
| Users (secretaries) | Producing reports and letters | Speed, quality, reliability | Product Focus<br>(Speed, quality, reliability) |

# The media selection process

There is an enormous number of media vehicles available to advertisers, all of which have the ability to drive a response if required to. However, the response volume and cost of response will vary dramatically depending upon the suitability and closeness of match between the role required and the target audiences' level of involvement with that medium.

Therefore, understanding which are likely to be the most effective is vital to the success of a campaign.

The planner's first step therefore is to identify which media vehicles are most suited to a specific target audience and message - known as the inter-media decision process. Figure 5.11.11 outlines an example of how this may shape up, remembering of course that targeting in all instances is key.

Figure 5.11.11 **Different tactics perform better for different objectives**

| Acquisition | Retention | Branding |
|---|---|---|
| Search engine | email | banners |
| Press space | website | PR |
| DRTV | mobile | Cinema |

This is done by looking at a number of elements that, together, help identify the best solutions:

- Media consumption/targeting

- Media/audience research - research data (NRS, TGI, BBS)

- Intrinsic qualities of the medium

- Results analysis

- Competitor analysis, MMS/AC Nielsen and other observation

- Production/creative

- Budget

- Media, production, follow-up materials and fees

The final schedule construction will rely on a further level of refinement, the intra-media decisions, which will be based around elements such as:

- Cost-effective coverage of the target audience

- Known responsiveness of a specific vehicle

- Environmental endorsement and tone

- Tactical use of editorial and environmental opportunities

A planner might use a table such as that outlined below to accumulate the answers to the various questions, scoring elements with fours and eights, or ranking elements from one to ten. Whichever method is used, tables such as these make it very easy to see at a glance which media options are better suited to a campaign, as outlined in table 5.11.6. This type of analysis is frequently done via a computer program that builds a campaign delivery model based upon all of the inputs. However, although planning is based upon a great deal of research, it is still probably more of an art than a science. The intrinsic qualities to be gained from one environment over another while understanding the overarching message strategy will be more beneficial to a campaign than an extra theoretical coverage point.

Table 5.11.6 **Spreadsheet example of planning criteria**

| | Media Consumption | Environment | Involvement | Response History | Competition | Creative Available | Lead Times | Budget/Cost | Timing | Response Times | Accountability | TOTAL |
|---|---|---|---|---|---|---|---|---|---|---|---|---|
| Direct Mail | | | | | | | | | | | | |
| Press | | | | | | | | | | | | |
| 3rd Party | | | | | | | | | | | | |
| Take Ones | | | | | | | | | | | | |
| Door-to-door | | | | | | | | | | | | |
| TV | | | | | | | | | | | | |
| Radio | | | | | | | | | | | | |
| Internet | | | | | | | | | | | | |

## *Media consumption/targeting*

Media consumption essentially means understanding which media are 'consumed' by your target audience - i.e. what they choose to view, read and interact with.

TGI and the other related media-specific research such as BARB or the NRS can provide a great deal of data relating to the media that the target audience interacts with. TGI is, however, the only single source data that can give cross-media comparisons. Generic measures such as whether the group are high, medium or low consumers of TV or the national press, and what their opinion is of a medium can help steer the direction of the media selection - the inter-media decisions.

TGI media quintiles are particularly useful for this, as demonstrated in figure 5.11.12 which provides comparable and easy-to-use media measurements from a single data source that splits consumers of each medium into five equal-sized groups, based on their level of consumption of that medium.

Figure 5.11.12 **Example of TGI media quintile data**

## Quintile 1 (Highest)
## Own an MP3 Player

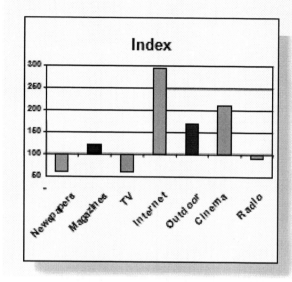

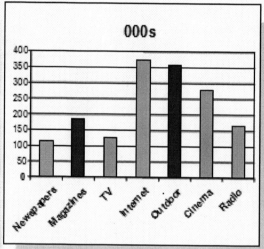

It can be seen that when targeting individuals who own an MP3 player the internet would be a good choice, supported by outdoor and cinema, all of which show high indices and volume reach. Where a medium does not look as strong, such as magazines or radio, it would be important to review the detail of specific niche stations and publications which may on their own be very popular among the target if the vehicle were believed to have some inherent qualities that would enhance the campaign.

Table 5.11.7 details the top-line media consumption information for the target group 'ABC1 working women aged 20 to 40, with a household income in excess of £15,000', i.e. shoppers at a household furnishing store in the last 12 months, discussed previously.

Table 5.11.7    **Media consumption information compiled via TGI**

| II Shoppers at a household furnishing store in the last 12 months | | | | |
|---|---|---|---|---|
| Demographic | Individuals in 000s | Profile % | Penetration % | Index |
| Totals | 2292 | 100 | 4.96 | 100 |
| Ch4 none | 197 | 8.6 | 5.34 | 108 |
| Ch4 light | 1325 | 57.81 | 6.02 | 121 |
| Ch4 medium | 549 | 23.95 | 4.16 | 84 |
| Ch4 heavy | 221 | 9.64 | 3.01 | 61 |
| Ch4 all | 2095 | 91.4 | 4.92 | 99 |
| | | | | |
| itv1 none | 48 | 2.09 | 5.83 | 118 |
| itv1 light | 1249 | 54.49 | 6.21 | 125 |
| itv1 medium | 637 | 27.79 | 4.95 | 100 |
| itv1 medium/heavy | 225 | 9.82 | 3.43 | 69 |
| itv1 heavy | 133 | 5.8 | 2.26 | 46 |
| itv1 all | 2244 | 97.91 | 4.94 | 100 |
| | | | | |
| Poster Heavy>9 H/wk | 727 | 31.72 | 4.4 | 89 |
| Poster Med 4-8.5H/w | 992 | 43.28 | 6.46 | 130 |
| Poster Light<=3.5H/w | 561 | 24.48 | 4.2 | 85 |
| | | | | |
| London Underground: Ever All | 1121 | 48.91 | 8 | 162 |
| LU Heavy >=1 P/Mth | 240 | 10.47 | 7.89 | 159 |
| LU Med >=1/6 Mths | 222 | 9.69 | 7.31 | 148 |
| LU Light < 1/6 Mths | 659 | 28.75 | 8.31 | 168 |
| LU Non | 1171 | 51.09 | 3.63 | 73 |
| | | | | |
| Rarely notice poster Ads | 730 | 31.85 | 4.55 | 92 |
| Expect Ads to be entertaining | 1013 | 44.2 | 4.83 | 97 |
| I fast forward through Ads when watching video | 1842 | 80.37 | 5.77 | 116 |
| Enjoy TV Ads as much as programmes | 515 | 22.47 | 4.86 | 98 |
| Rely on papers to keep me informed | 721 | 31.46 | 4.37 | 88 |
| Read financial pages of my paper | 427 | 18.63 | 4.68 | 94 |
| Extra sections make papers interesting | 725 | 31.63 | 6 | 121 |
| Cannot resist buying magazines | 362 | 15.79 | 7.22 | 146 |
| Usually look at free papers | 1405 | 61.3 | 5.19 | 105 |
| Always listen to radio in car | 1470 | 64.14 | 6.95 | 140 |
| Enjoy listening to commercials on radio | 951 | 41.49 | 4.84 | 98 |

Based upon the target audience of 'ABC1 working women aged 20 to 40, with a household income in excess of £15,000'

We can summarise the following from this information:

They are light viewers of the television, who are out and about and travelling around gaining good exposure to posters. The London and South bias is also producing good results for London Underground.

Attitudinally:

- They believe themselves to be advertising aware.

- They know that they notice the posters they are exposed to. This is demonstrated through the lower than average index to a question that is asked in a negative fashion.

- They don't expect too much from ads on TV or radio.

- They love buying magazines and reading supplements and are not too opposed to local newspapers/free sheets which might bode well for a door-to-door test.

TGI details individual publication and programme data that can then assist with the schedule refinement – the intra-media process. However, it is at this point that many planners incorporate the media-specific research, such as NRS, BARB and RAJAR, as they provide a great deal more detail than the TGI. Use of each of these studies is detailed in the individual media planning chapters (see 5.2 to 5.6).

Table 5.11.8 demonstrates a more detailed look at a single medium, listing national newspapers and household magazines, out of which some strong patterns emerge.

Home-orientated, parenting and wedding magazines show some very high indices, reflecting the young engaged/married status that was incorporated into the target audience. This information is not only useful for the selection of magazines but also for informing the selection criteria for other media such as direct mail.

Younger quality/mid-market newspapers are popular. The previously seen interest in the 'extra section' combines to indicate that supplements in these titles might be a good option.

You will note that the column previously headed profile is now termed coverage. This is because profile indicators have to be mutually exclusive, i.e. if a person is a 'C2' they cannot be anything else. If they are aged 30, again, that is what they are. However, if someone is a reader of The Independent, they can also read ten other titles. So it is now described that: four per cent of the audience read The Independent, i.e. The Independent delivers four per cent coverage of our target group. Our target group shows a bias towards the younger, quality newspapers, particularly The Independent.

Table 5.11.8    **Publication consumption information compiled via TGI**

| II Shoppers at a household furnishing store in the last 12 months | | | | |
| --- | --- | --- | --- | --- |
| Demographic | Individuals in 000s | Coverage % | Penetration % | Index |
| Independent on Sunday | 101 | 4.41 | 11.23 | 227 |
| Sunday Times | 294 | 12.83 | 8 | 161 |
| Mail on Sunday | 339 | 14.79 | 5.54 | 112 |
| Sunday Telegraph | 105 | 4.58 | 4.54 | 92 |
| Sunday Express | 115 | 5.02 | 4.05 | 82 |
| News of the World | 406 | 17.71 | 3.54 | 71 |
| Sunday Mirror | 210 | 9.16 | 3.21 | 65 |
| People | 114 | 4.97 | 2.36 | 48 |
| Homes & Ideas | 252 | 10.99 | 17.99 | 363 |
| House Beautiful | 189 | 8.25 | 17.42 | 352 |
| Brides/Setting Up Home | 40 | 1.75 | 15.38 | 310 |
| Inspirations | 50 | 2.18 | 13.77 | 278 |
| Wedding & Home | 32 | 1.4 | 13.06 | 264 |
| Mother & Baby | 107 | 4.67 | 12.62 | 255 |
| Ideal Home | 215 | 9.38 | 12.24 | 247 |
| Good Housekeeping | 271 | 11.82 | 11.82 | 238 |
| Homes & Gardens | 162 | 7.07 | 9.93 | 200 |
| House & Garden | 123 | 5.37 | 9.53 | 192 |
| BBC Homes & Antiques | 56 | 2.44 | 9.21 | 186 |
| Woman & Home | 103 | 4.49 | 7.5 | 151 |
| Country Life | 17 | 0.74 | 4.83 | 97 |

## Intrinsic qualities of the medium

The planner must understand the principal strengths and weaknesses of each media route; the intrinsic qualities that a medium will bring to a schedule and whether the tone and environment will enhance or detract from your communication. Also whether it is good for long, detailed copy and explanation or better suited to demonstration, and how complex the message is.

## Complexity of message

There are many situations where a medium will look very strong when reviewing TGI data, but in reality it would not be right for the creative interpretation of the message.

A poster site alongside a major road could carry a very short, simple message with a highly memorable phone number, e.g: 'Want cheaper car insurance? Phone 0800 080 080'. But a longer, more complex message would be more difficult to get across, due to the way in which the medium is consumed.

Alternatively, an underground poster could carry much more in-depth information very effectively due to the increased reading time allowable and the higher frequency with which posters in a similar position may be seen. It is still necessary to consider the audience and their capability to absorb and remember the message.

Financial service advertising is a good example of how individual products drive media selections. A simple motor insurance message can be seen on TV and in small press ads. However, more complicated investment packages may be better communicated via inserts and direct mail where there is the scope to outline all of the required detail, draw competitive comparisons and include application forms and all the required legalese.

## Environment

Statistics show that more ABC1 men read the News of the World than The Times. However, an investment advertisement may carry more weight in The Times than the News of the World, gaining additional credibility from its environment. Chapters 5.2 to 5.10 outline the strengths and weaknesses of each medium and review intra-media planning issues in detail.

## Results analysis

Media research is an excellent starting point for planning a campaign, but results will become one of the most important ongoing currencies for refinement and negotiations. Thorough analysis will quantify the actual response rates, conversion levels and respective costs attributed to each medium. Actual results can completely alter the perception of how much it costs to reach the target audience. Table 5.11.9 demonstrates that the buying cost-per-thousand bears little relation to the final cost-per-lead.

Table 5.11.9  **Comparison of possible response and resulting costs**

| Media type | Circ' volume 000s | CPT £s | Cost £s 000s | Response rate % | No. of responses | Cost-per-lead | Rank |
|---|---|---|---|---|---|---|---|
| National | 300 | £50 | £15,000 | 0.02% | 75 | £200 | 5 |
| Press inserts | 25 | £160 | £40,000 | 0.2% | 50 | £80 | 3 |
| Telephone | 5 | £5,000 | £25,000 | 5% | 250 | £100 | 4 |
| Direct mail | 15 | £500 | £7,000 | 1% | 150 | £50 | 2 |
| Mail and phone follow-up | 5 | £5,500 | £27,500 | 15% | 750 | £36.5 | 1 |

## Competitor analysis, MMS/ACNielsen and other observation

The monitoring of competitive activity can give a clear insight into a market and its use of the media.

Monitoring competitive activity is about seeing where they are advertising, what sort of messages and offers they are communicating, and trying to understand their strategy and tactics. The simplest monitoring is to track category trends and individual product activity; assessing whether things occur regularly or as 'one-offs' can be useful.

If an entire category of advertisers is using the same media vehicles it could be safe to assume that they work quite well; for example, many motor insurance advertisers use DRTV, directories and direct mail. It would be safe therefore for a new advertiser in this category to assume that this media mix would make a good launch platform for them too.

If a competitor is seen to try something new but does not repeat it, it might be because the results were poor.

There are a number of ways to assess competitive activity:

– Collect all or the main publications on a regular basis and review the advertising seen therein.

– Buy industry reporting research such as BARB for television, or a competitive analysis report from a specialist supplier such as Nielsen Media Research. These will report all advertising appearing in the consumer press, on TV, cinema, radio and outdoor and report monthly on the majority of business-to-business sectors including medical and agricultural publications. They also have a substantial UK-wide panel that provides information on addressed and unaddressed direct mail and third-party mailings that they receive, and PDF copies of all creative executions can be obtained.

– It is also possible to subscribe to cutting and show reels services that can compile reports of actual ads.

## Production/creative

A planner must always keep in mind what creative executions exist for a campaign and what creative routes are planned. This may have a major impact on what can and cannot be included in the selection, and also is directly linked to the budget and timing requirements. Television production is a lengthy, and in the main, expensive process in comparison to the development of a press execution.

## Budget

The budget can be a major determinant in the shape of a final schedule. The budget may be fixed, with the task to deliver the maximum number of leads. Conversely there may be a target number of sales to be made and the budget could be said to be 'task-related'; that is, whatever it takes to achieve the sales target. The latter usually comes with the caveat of 'while minimising the cost-per-sale', etc.

Financially the planner must know what the budget is based upon. If you have been given a budget, you need to know whether it is gross or net. Most media owners offer 10 to15 per cent commission to recognised agents/brokers. A net budget would be the amount before commission and the gross amount the total sum including commission.

## Media and production variables

For this it is important to know which media have fixed production costs and which are variable. If the television commercial is budgeted at £40,000 it will cost that irrespective of whether the television schedule costs £2,000 or £20,000. However, if a direct mail pack costs 50 pence then the final production cost will be a direct multiple of the number of names used.

There are also a number of distant but related costs that some clients like to include, such as television repeat fees for the artists or music used, postage and leaflet transportation to distribution depots. Therefore, where required, a provision should be made for these.

## Media, production and fees

Some fees are fixed monthly amounts; others are based upon hours worked, and some based upon a percentage of money spent. The latter is obviously the easiest to calculate at the planning stage, being a multiple of the schedule expenditure. The others, however, may require setting aside an allocation that is incorporated back into the final total costs and amortised across all the activity.

## Including or excluding VAT

VAT is added to the majority of invoices that relate to advertising campaigns. Currently the Royal Mail is a zero-rated supplier for household distribution, but there are very few other exceptions. To many companies the inclusion of VAT into a budget is an accounting requirement to ensure that purchase order amounts match to the penny, and the finance department has allocated the total sum required for payment. However, it is not a 'cost' because the same company will make a VAT return at the end of each quarter and offset the VAT paid out to the suppliers against VAT it has been paid by its customers. However, to the financial services business, and a number of other sectors, it is a real cost. Their customers do not pay VAT on the products or services; therefore there is no VAT collection against which to offset the payments.

# Campaign timing

Constraints may relate to the timing over which the budget should be spent, such as the campaign period, or the financial year. There may be a requirement to launch a new product and therefore the need to construct an initial test and learn quickly which media to rollout into.

## Annual and seasonal planning

In general most marketers work to annual objectives. Results are reviewed quarterly and incorporated into schedules going forward.

Many annual plans demand a continuous and steady stream of leads to be generated to ensure that the considerations of the call handling and sales staff are met at the same time as delivering the annual business targets. Others may have significant peaks and troughs as they take advantage of seasonal fluctuations in either consumer behaviour or the media marketplace.

Annual planning means that there is the opportunity to use all of the appropriate media options, including those with long lead times or limited availability. In addition, fluctuations in the cost of media can be amortised over the course of the year to deliver a target annual cost-per- lead/sale etc. This is particularly beneficial where television advertising is concerned, as the price variation between months means that November airtime can cost nearly twice as much as January airtime. Annual plans can also benefit from annual volume price negotiations with contractors and publishers.

Some products and services have a distinct seasonality to their purchasing cycle – motor cars, holidays, ISAs and woolly jumpers, for example. Planning well ahead ensures that you can secure exactly what you want to stand ahead of your competitors.

## Tactical requirements

Tactical, short-term requirements often need to be addressed. However, to advertise a special offer next week TV may not be a practical solution, unless you already have the creative ready and are prepared to pay a heavy cost premium for booking at short notice. The newspaper business may take this option to exploit a particularly good story through TV but a direct marketer may find it a prohibitively expensive way to run a campaign. Press, on the other hand, could meet the short-term demands, combining fast production of new copy with short booking and copy deadlines. For these reason it is one of the first choices for tactical solutions.

Many advertisers will, in fact, leave a proportion of their annual budget in a tactical 'pot' to enable them to take advantage of opportunities that may arise in the press. This includes firstly, reduced price 'short-term' offers for advertising space and secondly, taking advantage of relevant stories and surveys that may be published that provide an especially suitable environment for the copy.

## Production lead times

The issue of copy deadlines and lead times is examined in detail in the individual media chapters, but as a guide the media planner must watch out for:

- TV advanced booking deadlines – usually requiring eight weeks prior to the month of transmission to ensure the desired airtime selection at the best price – see chapter 5.5 for more details on TV-specific issues.

- Direct mail production, including the time required for merging individual lists, deduping and adding personalisation to the mailing piece.

- Magazine deadlines, particularly for heavily demanded editions such as in the spring and autumn. Planners must also be wise to the fact that the date patterns for monthly magazines can be somewhat confusing. For example, the December edition of Cosmopolitan is on the street on the first Tuesday of November; the Christmas edition is therefore also the January cover-dated publication. Schedules must therefore reflect cover dates, on-street dates and copy deadlines if mistakes are to be avoided.

- Tube cards are booked notoriously far in advance, often six to nine months, and therefore cannot be 'popped' onto a schedule without checking long-term availability.

The simple issue of timing can therefore end up being one of the key determinants in the media selection, particularly where there are short-term tactical requirements.

Compiling a table of the key deadlines in relation to a specific campaign, such as that demonstrated in table 5.11.10 below, is often a worthwhile exercise. Such data can be sourced from BRAD, either from its published volumes or the web, but published guides must always be overlaid with notes relating to the specific campaign objectives and the reality of media availability.

### Table 5.11.10  Outline example of key dates table for you to complete

| Medium | Booking deadline | Copy deadline | Production time |
|---|---|---|---|
| Television | 6 to 8 weeks prior to month of transmission | 1 week prior to transmission | Min. 4 to 5 weeks |
| National daily newspapers | | | |
| National Sunday newspapers | | | |
| Monthly magazines | | | |
| Women's weeklies | | | |
| Local radio | | | |
| Cinema | | | |
| Inserts | | | |
| Door-to-door | | | |
| Tube cards | | | |
| Bus sides | | | |
| Direct mail | | | |
| Email | | | |

It can prove a good reference point when tactical solutions are needed, but can also highlight media that are being missed due to lack of forward planning. Systems can therefore be changed to ensure that this does not continue to happen.

# Final selection criteria

## Buying and negotiation

Negotiating the best prices for all media is obviously a primary requirement to maximising the success of a campaign.

However, best price must never be confused with biggest discounts or cheapest space. There are many reasons why a media owner will give you the biggest discount but it is usually achieved because the rate card is overpriced, the audience is declining or demand has fallen away. None of these are guarantees for success. The same is true for short-term offers. They only represent good value if it is a short-term offer for something that you had planned to put on your schedule. With the press short-term may represent an additional insertion in something that you use regularly, or may be an incentive price to allow you to try something that you have previously thought to be overpriced.

Essentially there are only a handful of things that affect the cost of media:

- Date

- Position

- Size

- Colour

- Market demand

- General media inflation

- Volume

Advertisers can generally achieve a lower price if they are offering:

- A reasonable volume

- Booking flexibility, be it by date, position or day part

- Equal or greater share versus a competitive media owner

- Booking in advance

In addition, with advance booking it is also possible to secure the best positions, get the right phasing and co-ordinate copy rotation properly. Advance booking is popular with media owners because it makes it easier for them to manage their 'inventory'.

A premium is generally charged for:

- Low volume

- Lack of flexibility – fixed day or fixed position

- Short notice

- Unusual sizes

- High-demand placements

- Prime television programmes such as *ER* or *Coronation Street*

- High traffic press positions – outside back cover (OBC), inside front cover (IFC), TV page, early right-hand pages, solus or semi-solus on a page or spread, facing matter, within features or front of section.

It is also important not to allow the simple pricing commodity of cost-per-thousand to be the driver to shaping the inter-media decisions. CPTs between media are not always comparable currencies, as they do not take into account the targeting and responsiveness. As detailed in figure 5.11.13 the lowest CPT media often deliver the lowest response rates as they are the least targeted, and conversely the targeting of a medium such as direct mail is accompanied by high perceived CPTs, but also complemented with high response rates.

### Figure 5.11.13 **Common relationship between targeting, cost and response**

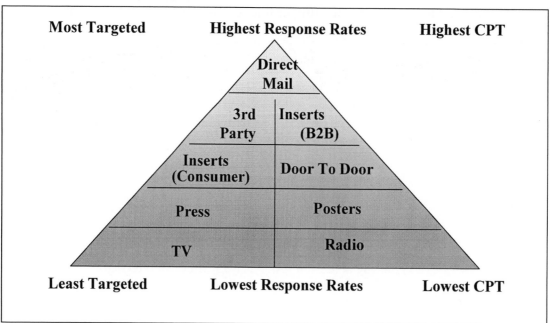

However, this type of model will vary for different audiences. If text messaging were included with the direct mail options, it is easy to conceive that the results could vary dramatically.

In addition, there will sometimes be compromises to be made. The highest response rate and lowest cost-per-customer may come from a specific mailing list or from personal contact through your salesforce; however, it may not be appropriate to tackle the entire market in this way. This is why segmentation is so important, as it enables decisions to be made between those prospects and customers that require proactive push activity and those that will be reactive to pull media such as the internet.

Figure 5.11.14 **Trade-off between cost-per-contact and conversion potential**

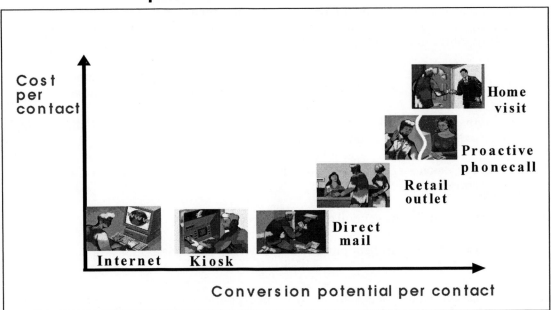

## Per response (PI) deals

PI deals are available for a number of media. These deals are based on the advertiser paying the media owner a fixed rate for each enquiry ('inquiry' in the US, hence PI), lead or sale generated.

So, for example, if a week's activity generates 2,000 leads at an agreed price of £10-per-lead, then the advertiser will pay the TV contractor £20,000. However, many contractors are unwilling to trade in this way; firstly, because they become dependent upon the lead information supplied by the client. To overcome this the advertisers should allocate a dedicated telephone number to every medium that they wish to agree a PI deal with, to ensure that responses and sales can be accurately reported. Secondly, because no one has the means of judging how well a product will perform: too few responses and the advertiser will have had a cost-efficient test but the contractor will not have met their revenue targets. Some advertisers call this 'sharing the risk', but the majority of media owners do not need to share the advertiser's risk – they have a very solid trading platform and can afford to maintain it.

Most importantly, when laying down a test matrix it is worth paying to ensure that insertions and spots appear when you planned them to. If the test was worth constructing it is worth running. For example, if 'day of week' is thought to be an influencing factor then it is important to run and track a number of insertions on the different days of the week. If there is no discernible difference then it is possible to negotiate a 'run of week' package and make future savings that way; in addition, short-term offers could be accepted for any day. However, if Thursday and Friday are significantly better performers, then it may be better to negotiate a rate for those days or a discount for the weaker days.

Test cells and negotiations should work to inform future negotiations and ensure improvements in the cost of the business going forward.

Individual media negotiation issues are reviewed in detail in the respective media chapters.

## Monitoring performance

It is important to monitor the performance of a schedule to ensure that it is running smoothly. Seeing the advertising in situ is essential. Although rare the sort of things to look out for are:

- Press space – wrong position, not appearing at all, negative editorial, competitive clash or clutter, poor reproduction and A/B copy mixed up

- Inserts and leaflets – not distributed or inserted properly or at all, leaflets delivered to the wrong clusters or delivery delayed

- Television – spots moved outside of call handling times and wrong copy running

- Outdoor – sites vandalised or obscured

- Door-to-door leaflets put out in the wrong postcode sectors, or not put out at all

- Direct mail leaflets sent out with the same telephone number as was being used for the radio campaign

The physical environment will have a bearing on the results. If there is a popular film cover-mounted on the outside of a national Sunday newspaper, the sales could be increased by up to 25 per cent. When the results are analysed an Excel spreadsheet or computer will merely divide the results into the circulation. The circulation figure will be derived from the monthly average and not reflect the uplift of the CD. The response rate will look high, but will not be a sound basis for forecasting unless it is recorded that the CD boosted the circulation and that tactically future editions with a promotional CD would be worth seeking out. Equally, taking a TV example, if the results seem to show an ongoing reduction in response rate as impact levels increase, there are two scenarios – 1) that higher rating spots don't work as well, or 2) that you are losing calls at the exchange when they go over a certain level. By monitoring the call data regularly for lost calls, queuing time and average call length, as described in chapter 5.5, a better interpretation can be put on the data for evaluation. Monitoring is likely to show that you are having increased call loss as the spot impacts increase.

## Evaluation

The most important thing to remember with media evaluation is to make it meaningful. There are lots of mnemonics that can be used but they work best if they describe the relationship with the service or product being advertised. Therefore, if you are driving policies for an insurance company or donations for a charity, the key criteria may be CPP (cost-per-policy) or CPD (cost-per-donor) rather than the cost-per-response (CPR). Evaluation is described in detail in each media chapter, but it is important to bring all the information back together for comparison and also to identify over time where one medium is affecting another. Table 5.11.11 outlines a very simple evaluation chart, but it is meaningless unless it is time-bound and trends are identified as well as snapshots.

**Table 5.11.11  A cross-tabulation that provides all of the relevant information**

|  | No. of leads | Response rate % | Cost-per-response | Conversion % | Sales | Cost-per-sale | Average value |
|---|---|---|---|---|---|---|---|
| Overall |  |  |  |  |  |  |  |
| By medium<br>DRTV<br>Press<br>Direct mail<br>Door-to-door<br>Directories |  |  |  |  |  |  |  |
| Press genre<br>Newspapers<br>Monthly magazines<br>Local newspapers |  |  |  |  |  |  |  |
| Press space size<br>Full page<br>25 x 4cm<br>Inserts |  |  |  |  |  |  |  |
| Creative by genre<br>Copy A<br>Copy B<br>Copy C |  |  |  |  |  |  |  |
| Average order value |  |  |  |  |  |  |  |
| Value by product<br>Value by section<br>Value by medium<br>Value by publication |  |  |  |  |  |  |  |
| Avg. no./value |  |  |  |  |  |  |  |

When evaluating, don't use the data to put all of your activity into the lowest cost-per-sale medium unless you are 100 per cent sure that it has done all the work itself, which is entirely unlikely.

Directories are notoriously good for large motor insurance companies. However, out of the 15-plus pages of motor insurance advertisements in the average copy of *Yellow Pages* why do certain companies get selected? Brand reputation, credibility and familiarity all play a very large part. A company like Direct Line is well known and people use the directory to find the number; it is not the directory that sells the proposition but the directory will deliver a very low cost-per-lead when evaluated. So, if all the other advertising for Direct Line were taken away would the directories remain as successful in generating leads in the long term as the awareness and reputation of the company fades?  This is unlikely.

Use tests to try and understand the relationship between the media vehicles to ensure that your evaluations are accurate and not misleading.

Even the biggest brands can identify how changing the media mix improves sales over time, as demonstrated by the final example for this chapter:

Figure 5.11.15 **IMC working for KitKat**

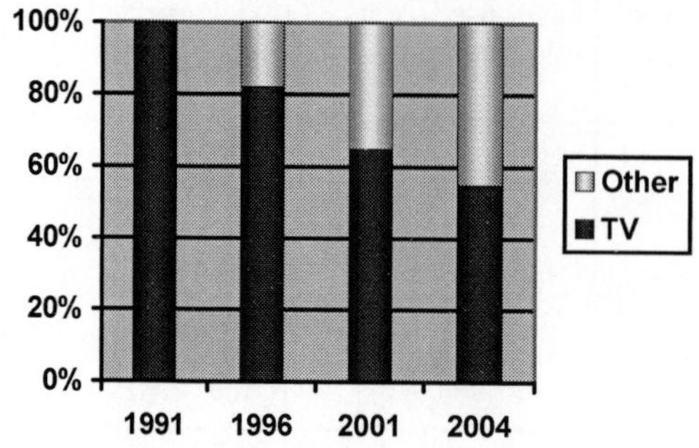

As a traditionally heavy user of TV, Nestle started to incorporate other media executions within the media mix as outlined in figure 5.11.15, culminating with a fully integrated mix as detailed below:

| | |
|---|---|
| TV | 22 weeks of advertising, 8 executions |
| Posters | 6 months of advertising |
| Press | 12 weeks of advertising, 6 executions |
| Radio | 16 weeks of advertising, 8 executions |
| Internet | 6 months of advertising and sponsorship |

The results speak for themselves. Using a mixed media schedule the coverage was increased; an acknowledgement that we don't all sit in front of the TV any more, and this generated a higher level of awareness of the products which in turn increased sales (source IDM 2005):

• Coverage up 92 per cent in any given month across all media

• Awareness up 12 points since 1999

• Sales volume up 25 per cent between 1998 and 2000

There is no evidence that increased awareness drives sales, but for a popular product, being reminded that it is around can prove successful.

# Section 6: Customer acquisition

**■ ■ ■ ■ ■ ■ ■ ■ ■ ■ ■ ■ ■ ■ ■ ■ ■ ■ ■ ■ ■ ■ ■ ■ ■ ■ ■ ■ ■**

**S**ince the 1990s there has been a constantly repeated mantra in the industry that money spent on customer retention earns a higher ROI than the same sum of money spent on customer acquisition. This is a half-truth: spending on customer retention is inevitably subject to a law of diminishing returns; the more one spends on it, the less the ROI. To state the obvious, one cannot retain customers who die. Every business that wants to maintain a stable market share must acquire new customers - at the very least in sufficient numbers to offset deaths. And every new business, or business that wants to expand its customer base, must also acquire new customers.

So the first chapter in this Section deals with the fundamentals of customer acquisition: how to plan for it, how to calculate allowable marketing costs (AMC) and then ROI, and how to project future costs and returns over a period of years. All of these principles are illustrated by the use of two case studies.

Chapter 2 deals with the factors that make for success in acquiring customers - the drivers of response to marketing blandishments. These drivers are analysed, regardless of individual medium, through the classic 4Ps – product, price/offer, place (e.g. channel) and promotion.

Chapter 3 is concerned with recording and analysing results – an activity that could be said to define direct marketing. Once again, the same principles are applied – albeit with minor differences – to both offline and online media.

# ROI-driven customer acquisition

## This chapter includes:

---

- ❏ Acquisition and retention

- ❏ The direct marketing acquisition plan

- ❏ Allowable costs and return on investment

- ❏ Setting targeting priorities by expected return

- ❏ Case one: an established home shopping business

- ❏ Projecting payback on customer acquisition

- ❏ Case two: projecting the ongoing value of new customers

---

## About this chapter

**T**his chapter gets to the heart of direct marketing – whatever medium is used - because all direct marketing is measurable so the marketer can measure their return on investment – or ROI. To be able to understand direct marketing it is important to grasp the mathematical concepts of allowable costs, yield and return on investment.

We begin this chapter with a reminder of why and how direct marketing focuses on the acquisition/retention cycle. We then look at the measurements that are commonly used in direct marketing acquisition forecasts and results analysis.

In this chapter we see that it is not necessarily a good idea to place acquisition and retention in separate compartments or departments. Traditionally this has happened because it appears to be a sensible 'split' for the companies doing the business of direct marketing. But this approach fails to appreciate that the customer should be pre-eminent in any relationship and so the company should look at the whole of a customer's life from beginning to end. If this approach is taken – more of a CRM approach – then to split acquisition and retention makes little sense. And of course, as we all know, it is cheaper to retain a customer than recruit a new one.

The chapter concludes with two case studies. The first shows how priorities are decided. The second, which includes all the detail required to make a business case, shows how future customer values are projected in direct marketing.

---

### Joanna Reynolds

Joanna has over 25 years' experience in direct marketing and publishing.

In September 2005, she set up consultancy ReynoldsBusbyLee with two colleagues. RBL specialises in direct marketing and publishing – from high-level strategic reviews to hands-on doing – in the UK and abroad.

Joanna has worked across the whole range of direct response channels and has in-depth knowledge of direct mail, DRTV, telemarketing and online. Most recently, she has been CEO of three European businesses – IMP, Time Life and

HCI – all of which specialise in continuity direct marketing. Each posed different challenges, but in all three both the core business, and the staff structure, required review and change.

Previously Joanna worked for Reader's Digest and Which?. At Reader's Digest, where she was Director, Magazines, Joanna was responsible for all aspects of the magazine portfolio as well as financial services and online. Her Which? career spanned 10 years, the last four as marketing director.

Joanna sits on the board of the Direct Marketing Association (DMA), which she chaired for 3 years. RBL are patrons of the IDM.

# Chapter 6.1

# ROI-driven customer acquisition

## Acquisition and retention

**T**he question is, how easy is it to identify when a customer is acquired? Although in some markets this can be difficult – where there is frequent brand switching as in FMCG – for many of us it is relatively easy to identify the moment of acquisition and thereafter to record customers' activity while their business is retained.

Of course, to record the moment of acquisition and the period of retention, we need a customer marketing database that incorporates transactional history as well as other customer behaviours.

---

**Customer's transactional record**

- Date acquired

- Source – e.g. direct mail, DRTV, telemarketing, online, fax or SMS

- First transaction value

- Number of transactions

- Average transaction value

- Cumulative transaction value

- Date of last transaction

- Payment method preference

- Anything else?

---

If we know the cost of acquisition, we can measure how long it takes for the new customer's business to repay that cost. To do this we will also need to know our profit margin on the transactions and the cost of further marketing to retain the customer's business.

Knowing these facts and figures enables us to bring scientific method to customer acquisition. As we said at the beginning of the chapter, this is at the heart of direct marketing.

## Acquisition media

Due to the changes in database building, management and data sharing etc, we need to define what we mean in this chapter by your 'own' customer database. Within your database you will have existing customers, lapsed customers, prospects (i.e. people who have communicated with you but not bought) and also data gained via third-party data sharing agreements.

With four exceptions, acquisition involves trawling for customers outside of your own customer database. The four exceptions are:

1. Conversion of previously unconverted prospects

2. Recovery of lapsed customers – customers who no longer do business with you

3. Referrals of new customers from existing customers

4. Conversion of prospects from shared data

All other sources of new business lie outside of your database. So what are they?

Direct marketing uses all media – including direct mail, inserts, DRTV, telemarketing, online, fax and SMS. New ways to market constantly evolve, so in the time it took this Guide to come to press, another medium could have appeared. All media that can be used cost-effectively to generate response are sources of new business.

All marketing communications need to either acquire (or help to acquire) new business or to maximise (or help to maximise) net earnings from existing business.

The direct marketer's dividing line

Many direct marketers draw a line in their marketing communications between acquisition and retention. But even this line can be crossed. For example, established customers may respond to a direct response advertisement designed to acquire new customers or visit your website, and click on an acquisition site.

## Corporate image building

Many marketing communications tasks appear to have little connection with acquisition or retention. For example British Airways spent a reported £60 million on an attempted repositioning as a 'world' airline. BP has since undertaken a similar exercise. Arthur Andersen rebranded its consultancy empire as Accenture. The business case for such initiatives may include consideration of the short-term effects on staff morale, distribution channels or the City, but unless they can also be justified as paving the way for more effective *customer acquisition or retention*, they are a waste of management time and shareholders' money. BA later decided to reverse its decision when the 'world' positioning failed to win or keep business.

### Direct marketing may operate anywhere in the buying process

Direct marketing can be applied successfully at all stages of the customer's buying cycle, from generating awareness to clinching the sale.

Direct marketing often undertakes the whole of the acquisition activity. For example, in the case of Amazon, there is no pure awareness or image building. Amazon's advertising and website establishes awareness at the same time as it makes the direct offers to sell books, CDs, DVDs and a range of other related products.

Increasingly, advertising carries a direct response mechanism even where direct response is not seen as the primary task of the advertising. With the increasing presence of web marketing, response is becoming more key.

Direct marketing needs to dovetail with advertising to help ensure the prospect receives the information needed to make a purchase. An example is a car advertisement bearing an 0800 phone number. Responders receive a brochure and an invitation to take a test-drive with a named dealer. The prospects' names may also be passed on to the dealer to fix a convenient time.

# The direct marketing acquisition plan

## Why it's interesting

Because direct marketing communications produce responses, the direct marketing executive has a continuous stream of performance data to inform planning.

By its very nature, this data is back data. It provides a record of what has already happened. Although the data may be refined in analysis, it is broadly true that the direct marketer assumes that what has happened will be repeated in the future unless some change is made. Alternatively, the direct marketer assumes that the current trend will continue. Except when the marketing environment changes suddenly, or unexpected competitive action causes discontinuity, these assumptions are usually correct, plus or minus a few percentage points.

The reason for such accuracy is that the supply of performance data is immediate and continuous so that changes are spotted very quickly. To enable changes to be acted upon immediately, the planner tries to avoid committing all available funds too far in advance.

Table 6.1.1 points up the basic difference between general and direct marketing campaign analysis. Each individual campaign is important – and will still need to be tracked – however, it must be noted that increasingly marketers are interested in the lifetime value of the individual customer and therefore look beyond the results of an individual campaign. Results of a campaign or event taken in isolation could be unprofitable, while the lifetime value of the customers acquired more than repays the initial investment.

**Table 6.1.1**     **Marketing analysis: how two disciplines compare**

| General marketing | Direct marketing |
|---|---|
| Whole campaign | Each event |
| Whole effect | Contribution per event |
| Tracking studies | Response analysis |
| Qualitative research | Testing |
| Market behaviour | Individual behaviour |

## General marketing

General marketers tend to measure the results of whole campaigns and look at the overall effect.

Tracking studies are used to reveal the awareness of advertising among the target audience as well as changes in perception caused by the advertising.

Qualitative research is used to check out the content and presentation of the advertising.

Market behaviour, i.e. sales and brand shares, will generally be the measure of success or otherwise – after attempting to isolate the variables within and without the marketing mix (e.g. changes in distribution levels).

## Direct marketing

**By event** – the direct marketer (who may also use the above methods) generally prefers to 'take a campaign apart' event by event.

**Contribution per event** – the contribution of each component is then looked at. This will usually be the response or revenue stream created by an individual advertisement or mailshot to a specific list.

(Individual events are not viewed as contributors to a campaign; individual events can only be justified by their own return on investment.)

**Response analysis** – direct marketing is concerned with measuring *response*. However, the analysis will not end with immediate response.

**Testing** is used to compare the response effectiveness of various communications (although these may also be subjected to qualitative research before testing).

**Individual behaviour** – the behaviour of each customer is tracked.
Analysis at the direct marketing level depends utterly on computer power: the
analysis of one large direct marketing campaign can involve sifting through
literally millions of data items. The point of going to all this trouble is, of course,
to optimise the return on future marketing expenditure.

Figure 6.1.1 shows the loop that is followed for planning both acquisition and
retention activity. (Analyse-plan-implement-control-analyse-plan etc.)

Although direct marketers often refer to 'campaigns,' the business of
acquiring and trying to avoid losing individual customers is most often
continuous. Even when it is not (as in a Christmas campaign), the planning
loop is a continuum.

Figure 6.1.1    **The direct marketer's planning loop**

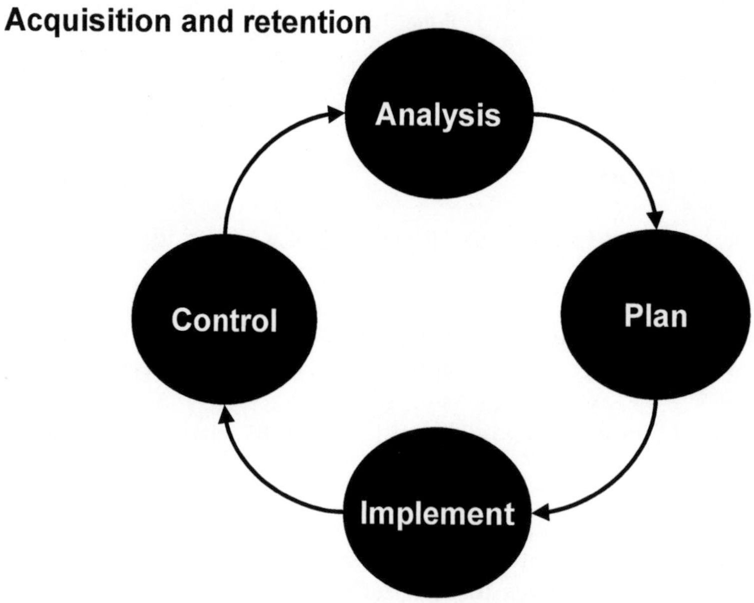

**Acquisition and retention**

Analysis

Plan

Implement

Control

Using this loop enables the direct marketer to exercise the direct marketing
principle of control. This is one of the four principles on which direct marketing
depends. Control depends utterly on recording interactions.

It follows that the close examination of each result is an essential part of
planning the next advertisement, mailing or campaign etc.

While it may appear simplistic, and is indeed simple in concept, the idea of a
continuous loop is fundamental to the direct marketing method.
In practice the analysis of simultaneous events does not necessarily take place at
the same time. There are three situations:

1. **Results of events that could have a bearing on immediate plans. Daily reviews.** For example, the first of a planned series of advertisements in a daily newspaper produces an unexpectedly low or high response. We might want to cancel our plans, renegotiate the space cost, increase the size or frequency of our spaces or order more fulfilment material etc.

2. **Results that are immediate but not immediately actionable. Regular review.** For example, a seasonal emailed invitation to prospects produced more or less response than expected.

3. **Results that will take time to mature. Repeated reviews.** For example, when 'pay up' needs to be determined – response is clear but the net number of customers will take time to mature due to a delayed offer – e.g. a three-month free trial offer.

# Allowable costs and return on investment

## Measurement

Measurement of direct response effectiveness depends on attaching a unique source code to each advertisement. For direct mail the source code will either identify the list or the creative/offer. In DRTV, allocating a separate telephone number to each channel or offer will enable you to record response accurately. If response is received online from an offline offer you can either use a unique URL for every individual offer or ask where the advertisement was seen. The former is more accurate.

## One-step and two-step response

When the advertisement makes a direct offer for sale, measurement is simplified. When it merely invites an enquiry (e.g. a request for a catalogue), it is more complex. It is now necessary not just to measure the response but the conversion rate as well. Conversion rate measures the number of people who actually order rather than simply respond.

## Results recording and analysis

All direct marketing activity, via whatever medium, will generate a stream of data capable of analysis:

- Clickthrough and clickstream data

- Responses/enquiries/leads

- Further information requests

- Orders and order value

- Order to enquiry ratios

- Sales and sales values

- Sale to order ratio

- Returns and bad debts

This stream of information is monitored, allowing immediate comparisons to be made between one medium and another, one offer and another and so on. Adjustments to planned expenditure are likely to be made as a result.

A major benefit is that controlled testing of new media and offers (and even countries) can take place before too much money is put at risk.

However, none of this information takes us to the bottom line, to answer the question, "was it profitable?" or the equally important question, "will it be profitable?" To answer these questions, we need to track newly acquired customers' transactional behaviour.

There are two useful measures of the efficiency of marketing investments. They are:

1. Allowable marketing cost (AMC)

2. Return on investment (ROI)


In many ways these measurements overlap and both can be used in your business.

What is the 'marketing allowable'?

The concept of the marketing allowable or **AMC** (allowable marketing cost) is familiar to nearly every direct marketer. It is usually expressed as a formula, as show in table 6.1.2 below:

### Table 6.1.2    The AMC formula

| | | | | | |
|---|---|---|---|---|---|
| £ | Sales value_____ | e.g. | £ | 50 | (100%) |
| less £ cost of goods | | | – | 30 | (60%) |
| less £ cost of distribution | | | – | 5 | (10%) |
| less £ required profit margin | | | – | 5 | (10%) |
| = £ AMC | | | £ | 10 | (20%) |

This simplified formula works well when we expect to make a profit on each transaction. But what if the first sale to a new customer is made at a loss? This can and often does, happen. For example:

- When you are running a continuity programme – the price for the first product can be reduced to entice the buyer to purchase. Examples would be book clubs, coin collection or magazine subscriptions. The profit is made on subsequent purchases from the same series.

- When you are running a programme where the first product is a way in for cross-selling your other products; for instance, office supply companies..

- In the automotive market, it has often been quoted that it costs five times as much to make a 'conquest' sale (a sale to a new customer) as it does to make a repeat sale.

In such cases what is the marketing allowable to capture a new customer?

If your offer has a continuity or cross-sell element, you need to calculate the lifetime value (LTV) of your new customers – how much will they be worth over their lifetime with you? You can then calculate how much you can afford to spend to bring them in, taking into account the costs of recruitment and renewal efforts.

The lifetime value calculation will be based on the buying and retention history of previous customers recruited in the same way. Lifetime value therefore needs to be recalculated on an ongoing basis. (For a fuller discussion of lifetime value, see chapter 3.5.)

## Customer acquisition and 'cash burn'

The reason dotcoms were once so overvalued is because the investors did not understand how to estimate future customer values. A high marketing spend was thought to guarantee success. For example, at one point Freeserve was valued at £700 per 'customer' even though the customers had paid nothing to join. No direct marketer would have believed that the average lifetime value of Freeserve's customers, in direct and indirect revenues, could reach even one-tenth of this figure, yet customers were Freeserve's main asset.

## Return on investment (ROI)

Return on investment (ROI) is one of the most commonly used performance measures in business. Therefore it provides a useful yardstick, not only enabling marketing investments to be compared with each other but also with any other investment the business might make.

ROI answers the question: *"How well did we use this money?"*

The way ROI answers the question is by showing *the eventual return* on the money that has been spent. Unfortunately, business moves too fast to allow the whole return to be achieved before making a judgement on the investment.

Therefore, the *rate of return* is plotted at different intervals from the investment and the trend is used to forecast the eventual ROI:

$$ROI = \frac{\text{£ future contribution}}{\text{£ expenditure}}$$

The *contribution* figure in future contribution is the net margin on sales (or profit before operating costs). The net margin on sales will take account of the costs involved in making the sales and providing customer service.

### Table 6.1.3    Measuring rate of payback – ROI

$$\frac{\text{£ contribution over 12 months}}{\text{£ acquisition cost}} = \text{ROI} \qquad \text{e.g.} \qquad \frac{\text{£45}}{\text{£60}} = 75\%$$

So how do we calculate contribution? Let's assume sales are £300 and the gross margin is £120 (having deducted the cost of acquisition). This is how we calculate contribution or net margin.

| | | |
|---|---|---|
| Sales (£) | 300 | |
| Gross margin | 120 | (Having deducted the cost of acquisition) |
| Less distribution | 30 | |
| Less returns | 30 | |
| Less handling | 15 | |
| Net margin | 45 | |

## Profit and loss statements

Where do P&L statements fit in? In many business situations, it is more appropriate to use P&L *forecasts* when planning campaigns and P&L *statements* when all the results are in. That is because the object of the campaign may be to sell a specific quantity of a product at the lowest possible cost. Customer acquisition will then be seen as a by-product.

Examples might include:

✔    The event organiser staging a business conference

✔    The collectibles producer marketing a commemorative plate

✔    The specialist tour operator marketing a new holiday

In all of these cases, the marketer will want to measure the success of the venture by its overall contribution. Many of the sales may be made to established customers (because that will help to reduce marketing expense). The ongoing value of new customers who book conference places, buy plates or take holidays is excluded from the P&L calculation.

In general, the aim in these situations is to avoid making a loss on any of the sources of business that are tapped. However, the marketer may be prepared to take a small loss on sources that add new customers to the database. To justify this, a calculation of the likely future value of new customers *must be made*, although it will not appear in the P&L statement. (However, where a business counts the calculated lifetime value of its customers as a physical asset, the acquisition of new customers will have a positive effect on the balance sheet.)

## The value of reactivation

Sales made to established customers are said to *reactivate* them. They may prevent defections and may be almost as valuable in maintaining customer strength as sales made to new customers.

Note that the P&L forecast sets the AMC for the product. The AMC may be exceeded in the case of new business sources, but sales made to established customers will be (or are expected to be) made at less than the AMC.

The P&L statement will show the *product* ROI. It will not usually show the *customer* or lifetime ROI, as it only looks at current year revenue.

## *Setting targeting priorities by expected return*

Whether the object is to meet a product sales target or a customer acquisition target, best direct marketing practice involves prioritising target groups by potential responsiveness (or potential ROI if we can project this).

If the object is to meet a sales target, the aim will be to maximise those sales that can be made at little or no cost (inevitably sales to established customers) before giving consideration to other target groups.

If the object is to meet a customer acquisition target, the aim will be to maximise intake from the most responsive target groups before focusing on the less responsive.

In either case, the most responsive target groups of all will be those with whom some sort of business relationship exists or has existed. Earlier in this section we noted that, with four exceptions, acquisition involves trawling for customers outside the database. The four exceptions were:

1.   Conversion of previously unconverted prospects

2.   Recovery of lapsed customers

3.   Referrals (of new customers) from established customers, e.g. viral marketing

4. Conversion of prospects from shared data

99 times out of 100 these four sources of new customers will be cheaper than all others. It therefore makes sense to do what we can to maximise return from these sources and reduce our dependence on more expensive external media.

### *Targeting by value, not responsiveness*

Sometimes the targeting priority is determined by *potential value* as opposed to responsiveness. For example, FMCG marketers may prioritise those who use competitive brands *only*. Although members of this target group will be expensive to convert, return on investment can be improved by selecting only those who are *heavy users*. Data from lifestyle surveys or field marketing exercises will be used to select target group members.

Once priorities among broad target groups have been established, selection continues at a micro level *within* target groups, e.g. *The Sun* versus *The Daily Mirror* or even taking a fourth ad in *The Sun* versus a third ad in *The Daily Mirror.*

## Case one: an established home shopping business

*For this example, we take a fairly small home shopping company trading from seasonal catalogues and a website. About 80 per cent of the business is offline.*

*In the home shopping business, marketing costs depend on the required rate of growth. That is because it is much cheaper to market to identified and established customers than to secure the initial order from new customers. When the enterprise starts trading, all the customers are new and so marketing costs are very high. As the enterprise matures, more and more business comes from established customers and marketing costs reduce. Eventually, however, the business may reach saturation level and it will again become expensive to acquire new customers at a greater rate than old customers are being lost.*

Table 6.1.4    **Case one: established home shopping company**

### Target groups in order of responsiveness/profitability

| | |
|---|---|
| **1. Active customers** | purchased in one of last two seasons |
| **2. Lapsed customers** | not purchased in either of last two seasons |
| **3. Unconverted prospects** | requested last catalogue but made no purchase |
| **4. External media** | |

The definitions of active and lapsed customers used in table 6.1.4 are fairly typical. Target groups are prioritised in order of potential profitability (in making the next sale) and this will equate to responsiveness adjusted by sales value.

*The more recently a customer has ordered, the more responsive the customer is likely to be.* Therefore, lapsed customers will be mailed or emailed for as long as it is profitable to do so. Eventually, they will be removed from the mailing file.

Unconverted prospects are likely to remain on file for a much shorter period because they are, in general, less profitable as a target group. They will include people who requested a catalogue but did not order, people who abandoned an online order and others who ordered but then returned the goods. (The behaviour of these subgroups
will be analysed separately in case they are very different – for the sake of simplicity we are assuming they will behave similarly.)

Table 6.1.5 **Case one: home shopping company – full year (two seasons) sales forecast**

| Target group | Sales forecast | Marketing cost | Cost to sale (%) | Gross profit | Net contribution |
|---|---|---|---|---|---|
| Active customers | £5,000K | £400K | 8.0 | £1,500K | + £1,100K |
| Lapsed customers | £750K | £150K | 20.0 | £225K | + £75K |
| Unconverted prospects | £350K | £105K | 30.0 | £105K | Nil |
| New business | £1,000K | £400K | 40.0 | £300K | - £100K |
| TOTAL | £7.1m | £1.055m | 14.9 | £2.13m | £1.075m |

In this example in table 6.1.5, the gross profit is profit *before* marketing and is taken as being 30 per cent of sales value. In order to grow the business (or stop it shrinking), we are prepared to make a loss on new business and break even on converting previously unconverted prospects. We do this in the expectation of making a profit once these new customers join our profitable 'active customer' target group. In effect, all the profit comes from active customers. However, we are bound to lose some of these active customers.

In the next table, 6.1.6, we see the population within each target group. This shows how the less profitable target groups are used to repopulate the most profitable target group. The anticipated loss of 30,000 active customers is replaced by 37,000 new or reactivated customers, producing an overall projected gain of 7,000 active customers; this amounts to a seven per cent increase.

Table 6.1.6 **Case one: home shopping company – customer strength forecast**

| Target group | Total population | Number of enquiries | Number of buyers | Gain/loss |
|---|---|---|---|---|
| Active customers | 100,000 | - | 70,000 | (-30,000) |
| Lapsed customers | 90,000 | 36,000 | 12,000 | +12,000 |
| Unconverted prospects | 60,000 | 24,000 | 5,000 | +5,000 |
| New business | 7,000,000 | 80,000 | 20,000 | +20,000 |
| TOTAL CUSTOMERS | | | 107,000 | +7,000 |

The active customers are not shown as enquirers because they all receive catalogues without requesting them.

Who are the seven million people who are in the new business target group? They are the potential customers who receive cold mailings, see off-the-page ads or inserts, receive a cold telephone call or email campaign or who visit the website.

These population statistics say more about the dynamics of the business than the cash contribution figures. Now we can see that our active customer loss rate is 30 per cent (let's say over a year). Assuming the enterprise is fairly stable in size, we can see that we are targeting about three years' worth of lost customers in our lapsed customer mailings. (90,000 = 30,000 losses x 3.)

But we are only targeting about a year's worth of unconverted enquiries (table 6.1.6 shows that it takes 80,000 new business enquiries to create 20,000 customers – therefore there must be 60,000 unconverted enquiries). Looking at the conversion rate, we see that this group is just as responsive as the lapsed customer group, but that they are less likely to buy. This is what one would expect – our unconverted prospects failed to buy before.

If you had just bought the home shopping company in this example and wanted to accelerate its expansion rate, what would you do?

Judging by the forecast, the least productive action to consider is spending more on external media, because this is the most expensive source. So what are the alternatives?

**Table 6.1.7    Case one: home shopping company – alternative marketing tactics**

| Target group | Objective | Proposed action |
|---|---|---|
| Active customers | Reduce loss rate | Identify non-buyers and incentivise |
| Lapsed customers | Increase orders | Send catalogue unrequested |
| Unconverted prospects | Increase conversion | Offer incentive for first order |

Before proceeding you would set objectives for each action and cost it out. You might then test in one season before rolling the action out against the whole target group in the next season. For example, you might send unrequested catalogues to all of the most recent lapsed offline customers but not to the older-lapsed customers. Then you might *test* sending unrequested catalogues to a *sample* of the older-lapsed customers and ask the remaining offline lapsed customers (*the control group*) to request a catalogue. Finally, you might email all lapsed online customers with a personalised offer available only on the website.

## Lessons from this case

✔    The case illustrates that *customer acquisition* is not easily separable from *customer retention.* We need to do both, but saving old customers reduces the need for new customers. However, we must take care to avoid giving away too many incentives to customers who would order anyway at full price.

✔    Simple P&L projections are an excellent way of illustrating the effects of alternative tactics. However, they do not show the ongoing value of increased customer strength. We need to bear in mind that adding to customer strength is likely to reduce short-term profit but increase longer term profit.

✔    It is crucial to project differences in *customer strength* arising from alternative tactics. It is an important refinement to project the different potential values of customers derived from different sources, e.g. lapsed customers who are recovered may be worth less or more than new customers.

## Projecting payback on customer acquisition

### The launch situation

In case one we reiterated the need to project the potential value of newly acquired customers. Doing so is crucial for a new business – and much more difficult.

Also in case one (table 6.1.5), we see that it costs five times as much to sell to unidentified prospects as to established customers. This is fairly typical of a mature operation and poses a problem to anyone starting a new business.

A degree of compensation exists in two respects:

1.  Every market includes early adopters who are more responsive to whatever is new.

2.  The fact is that some new business sources prove to be very much more productive than others. A new business can begin by tapping the best media sources.

By following the *test philosophy* described in chapter 8.2 it should be possible to contain customer acquisition costs. However, the established business with a portfolio of satisfied customers will always enjoy an advantage.

## Case two: projecting the ongoing value of new customers

In case two, using real-life projected sales and costs we shall track the forecast achievement of another home shopping catalogue business over 18 catalogue issues (say three years) from its inception. The forecast is from the original business plan and has not been modified in the light of trading experience. The business plan proposes that the company acquires customers through one-stage activity, using ads and preview catalogues, and sends more substantial catalogues to the customers.

In this projection, no online trading is included, the presumption being that a website will be built once offline trading justifies the additional investment.

Table 6.1.8 shows the projection for the first year:

Table 6.1.8 **Case two: three-year projection of customer values (using one-stage customer acquisition) – year one**

| Year 1 | Issue 1 | Issue 2 | Issue 3 | Issue 4 | Issue 5 | Issue 6 | Total |
|---|---|---|---|---|---|---|---|
| **Active customers** (000s) At start of period | - | 78 | 146 | 190 | 199 | 233 | - |
| New customers | 78 | 68 | 44 | 51 | 71 | 58 | 370 |
| Customers lost | - | - | - | 42 | 37 | 24 | 103 |
| At end of period | 78 | 146 | 190 | 199 | 123 | 233 | 267 = catalogues |
| **Acquisition costs** | | | | | | | |
| Per customer | £13.24 | £11.72 | £15.48 | £12.63 | £10.80 | £12.98 | £12.64 |
| Total (000s) | £1,033 | £797 | £681 | £644 | £767 | £753 | £4,675 = £1.09 each |
| **Retention costs** (000s) | | | | | | | |
| Catalogue production and postage | £84 | £159 | £207 | £217 | £254 | £290 | £1,211 |
| Origination, incentives, other print | £97 | £85 | £55 | £64 | £88 | £72 | £461 |
| **Total marketing costs** (000s) | £1,215 | £1,040 | £943 | £924 | £1,109 | £1,116 | £6,347 |
| **Sales** (Number 000s) | | | | | | | |
| New customers | 78 | 68 | 44 | 51 | 71 | 58 | 370 |
| Repeat sales | 24 | 46 | 56 | 63 | 75 | 82 | 345 |
| Total | 102 | 114 | 100 | 114 | 146 | 140 | 715 |
| **Sales** (Value 000s) New customers | £1,950 | £1,700 | £1,100 | £1,275 | £1,775 | £1,450 | £9,250 = £25 av value |
| Repeat sales (catalogue) | £607 | £958 | £1,172 | £1,317 | £1,571 | £1,714 | £7,339 = £25 av value |
| Add-on sales (from other stationery) | - | £146 | £190 | £199 | £233 | £267 | £1,035 = £20 av x 5% response |
| Postage and packing | £72 | £135 | £166 | £185 | £220 | £242 | £1,020 = £2.95 per order |
| **Total sales** | £2,629 | £2,939 | £2,628 | £2,976 | £3,799 | £3,673 | £18,644 |
| Marketing cost: sales | 46.2% | 35.4% | 35.9% | 31.0% | 29.2% | 30.4% | 34.0% |

## Table 6.1.8 The first year

In this model, active customers are defined as (a) new customers who have bought from a one-stage ad or preview leaflet, or (b) repeat buyers who have bought from the catalogue mailings not more than six months ago. If you look at the *customers lost* line (line 3) you will see that no customers have been lost during the currency of the first three catalogues. That is because customers are defined as active if they have ordered within the last six months. Since the business is less than six months old, no customers can have been lost.

The customers who will be defined as lost at Issue 4 will never have ordered from the catalogue – they will only have ordered from an ad or a preview leaflet. Once lost, they will go back into the customer acquisition pond and some will be enticed back by lapsed customer mailings.

By the end of year one, there are 267,000 customers defined as 'active'. This is the number to whom Issue 7 of the catalogue will be mailed.

Looking down to *acquisition costs*, we can see these are expressed as *cost-per-customer* as well as being shown as totals. Alternatively, it would have been possible to show the costs as a marketing ratio. Expressing the cost as 'per customer' is very typical of direct marketing. The fact of winning a new customer is seen as being more important than the value of the first sale.

Note, too, that in the next section of table 6.1.8 ongoing customer communications costs are captioned *retention costs*. Here we see that retention costs start very low compared with acquisition costs, but gradually increase in line with the growth in the number of active customers.

Along lines 9 and 10 we see the *number of sales*. Number of sales appears in the table because each one represents an active customer. The more customers who remain active, the healthier future prospects will be. Repeat sales overtake new business sales with the third catalogue issue. The exact balance of acquisition to repeat activity is affected by seasonal factors and so the growth of the repeat business share of sales is not on a straight-line basis.

In the *sales value* section of the table we can see that more than half the total sales value arises from new business. This causes the marketing cost ratio to remain quite high throughout the first year. For the sake of simplicity, the sales shown are net sales, not orders. The difference between value of orders and value of sales can be considerable.

### More demand than sales

Orders are always higher than sales for three reasons:

1.    Some credit orders may be refused

2.    Some orders cannot be met because goods are out of stock

3.    Some goods are returned unwanted within a free approval period or for a refund

Table 6.1.9   **Case two: three year projection of customer values (customer acquisition stripped out) – year two**

| Year 2 | Issue 7 | Issue 8 | Issue 9 | Issue 10 | Issue 11 | Issue 12 | Total |
|---|---|---|---|---|---|---|---|
| **Active customers** (000s) At start of period | 267 | 221 | 167 | 125 | 105 | 82 | - |
| New customers | - | - | - | - | - | - | - |
| Customers lost | 46 | 54 | 42 | 20 | 23 | 18 | 203 |
| At end of period | 221 | 167 | 125 | 105 | 82 | 64 | 64 = catalogues |
| **Acquisition costs** Total (000s) | - | - | - | - | - | - | - |
| **Retention costs** (000s) | | | | | | | |
| Catalogue production and postage | £241 | £182 | £136 | £115 | £89 | £70 | £832 = £1.09 each |
| Origination, incentives, other print | £91 | £68 | £51 | £43 | £34 | £26 | £313 |
| **Total marketing costs** (000s) | £331 | £250 | £188 | £158 | £123 | £96 | £1,1,45 |
| **Sales** (Number 000s) | | | | | | | |
| New customers | - | - | - | - | - | - | - |
| Repeat sales | 67 | 54 | 42 | 36 | 28 | 23 | 251 |
| **Sales** (Value 000s) Repeat sales (catalogue) | £1,395 | £1,1,35 | £898 | £776 | £609 | £499 | £5,3`` = £25 av value |
| Add-on sales (from other stationery) | £221 | £167 | £125 | £105 | £82 | £64 | £764 = £20 av x 5% response |
| Postage and packing | £197 | £158 | £124 | £107 | £84 | £68 | £739 = £2.95 per order |
| **Total sales** | £1,813 | £1,460 | £1,1,47 | £988 | £775 | £631 | £6,814 |
| Marketing cost: sales | 18.3% | 17.1% | 16.4% | 16.0% | 15.9% | 15.2% | 16.8% |

## *Table 6.1.9 The second year*

Looking now at the second year in table 6.1.9 you will notice that *customer acquisition* appears to have been cancelled. It seems the business is being bled for profit and is being allowed to go into rapid decline.

This is not the case at all. The reason for stripping out customer acquisition is to show the *ongoing value* of the customers who were recruited in the first year. By showing only the costs and value associated with their repeat purchases, the company can see the rate at which it is paying back the customer acquisition cost.

To determine the effect of continuing customer acquisition at the same rate as in the first year, it is simply necessary to add the two years together. This produces sales of £25.458 million with marketing costs of £7.492 million, a ratio of 29.4 per cent. In practice a slightly better position could be expected because the pool of lapsed customers could be fished to produce cheaper new business than would be available from outside media and lists.

Without any new business, the second year would begin with 267,000 customers and end with just 64,000. Meanwhile, the marketing cost ratio falls to about 15 per cent by the end of the year.

Table 6.1.10  **Three-year projection of customer values (customer acquisition stripped out) – year three**

| Year 2 | Issue 13 | Issue 14 | Issue 15 | Issue 16 | Issue 17 | Issue 18 | Total |
|---|---|---|---|---|---|---|---|
| **Active customers** (000s) At start of period | 64 | 54 | 44 | 35 | 32 | 29 | - |
| New customers | - | - | - | - | - | - | - |
| Customers lost | 10 | 10 | 9 | 3 | 4 | 3 | 39 |
| At end of period | 54 | 44 | 35 | 32 | 29 | 25 | 25 = catalogues |
| **Acquisition costs** Total (000s) | - | - | - | - | - | - | - |
| **Retention costs** (000s) | | | | | | | |
| Catalogue production and postage | £59 | £47 | £38 | £35 | £31 | £28 | £239 |
| Origination, incentives, other print | £22 | £18 | £14 | £13 | £12 | £10 | £90 = £1.09 each |
| **Total marketing costs** (000s) | £82 | £65 | £53 | £48 | £43 | £38 | £329 |
| **Sales** (Number 000s) | | | | | | | |
| New customers | - | - | - | - | - | - | - |
| Repeat sales | 22 | 18 | 15 | 16 | 15 | 15 | 101 |
| **Sales** (Value 000s) Repeat sales (catalogue) | £565 | £485 | £407 | £433 | £417 | £402 | £2,710 = £30 av value |
| Add-on sales (from other stationery) | £68 | £54 | £44 | £41 | £36 | £32 | £274 = £25 av x 5% response |
| Postage and packing | £64 | £54 | £45 | £47 | £45 | £43 | £299 = £2.95 per order |
| **Total sales** | £697 | £593 | £496 | £521 | £498 | £477 | £3,238 |
| Marketing cost: sales | 11.8% | 11.0% | 10.7% | 9.2% | 8.6% | 8.0% | 10.0% |

## Table 6.1.10 The third year

In table 6.1.10 we see the third year position, still showing only the business that arises from the year one recruits. The decline now starts to taper off as the most active customers tend to remain on board. The projection allows for this by increasing the number of sales-per-customer by about a third and the value of sales by about 20 per cent. To arrive at a view of year three with customer acquisition, it is just a matter of adding the three tables together. Sales are now £28.741 million with marketing costs of £7.821 million, a ratio of 27.2 per cent.

## Points to note

The marketing costs look very high early on because the required growth rate is very rapid, forcing the level of new business activity up.

The plan shows a consistently high response rate to catalogue mailings and the company may be planning to withhold distribution from non-buyers prematurely. At a cost of £1.09 per catalogue, mailing any database segment that responds at a rate of 10 per cent or more will be cheaper than replacing lost customers with new ones. That is because the cost-per-sale will be £10.90 compared with an average of £12.64 from new business.

Thus, the company might do well to consider ways of keeping customers on board for somewhat longer. This would not make a large difference to the marketing ratio, but it could have a significant impact on the bottom line.

Clearly, there would be benefit in adding online trading, because this would enable some customers to be reactivated without incurring the expense of additional catalogue distribution.

## Applying the case two model

Case two shows all except one of the figures needed to show the ROI on new customer acquisition over a three-year period. The missing figure is contribution. By making an assumption on gross profit (say it is 40 per cent), it is simple to add a bottom line to the tables showing contribution. This will be 40% of sales, less the percentage on marketing.

The value of this model is that it illustrates how ongoing customer values are projected. The model can be applied to most situations but the marketing cost ratios are peculiar to the case and not realistic for other types of business. To discover the true cost ratios, industry research is needed to set a benchmark, and this needs to be followed by live testing.

# Success factors for customer acquisition on and offline

## This chapter includes:

--------------------------------------------------

- [ ] **What is a direct response?**
- [ ] **Why do people respond?**
- [ ] **The elements of success**

   **Product - the whole package**

   **Price/offer**

   **Place – targeting and channel**

   **Promotion – creative and format**

- [ ] **Summary - the elements of success**

--------------------------------------------------

## About this chapter

**T**his chapter is focused on response. Response, and the measuring of response, is the unique aspect of direct marketing. Other marketing and advertising does not have to stand up and be counted.

So what makes people respond? This chapter looks at the important drivers for response and makes an assessment of which is the most important. The major drivers are the classic *4Ps*: product, price/offer, place (targeting and channel), and promotion (creative and format).

## Joanna Reynolds

**Joanna's biography appears at the start of the previous chapter.**

### Chapter 6.2

# Success factors for customer acquisition on and offline

## What is a response?

**When** planning a campaign it is important to be clear what you mean by a response. It can be anything from a hit on your website to a phone call with credit card details for immediate payment. If you do not know what response you need to make your campaign cost-effective, your efforts will be wasted.

Most of us would prefer to plan campaigns with one-step response – i.e. the order happens immediately in response to the offer. However, sometimes direct marketers are forced into two-step campaigns; for instance, currently in France you cannot sell directly off the TV screen. So the initial advertisement has to ask the viewer to call in for further information. Clearly, this makes it much harder to run cost-effective DRTV campaigns in France!

Response which does not result in an immediate purchase is usually called two-step response; in practice, it may be multi-stage. There may be a number of communications between buyer and seller before the transaction is completed.

### One-step responses

These are not always purchases. The four main types of one-step transactions are:

---

✔   **Purchases:** usually accompanied by immediate payment unless B2B

✔   **Trial orders:** invoice or direct debit payable after expiry of free approval period

✔   **Enrolments/subscriptions:** responder takes out renewable membership or subscription, e.g. magazine subscription

✔   **Applications:** responder applies for product, e.g. a credit card, usually without guarantee of acceptance

---

### Two-step responses

Many responses are two-step but they are not all the same:

---

✔ **Information requests:** usually requests for brochures or catalogues

✔ **Volunteered information:** responder provides personal information in exchange for a benefit, e.g. website registrations and lifestyle survey responses

✔ **Enquiries:** responder requires specific details prior to purchase, e.g. insurance quotes

✔ **Sales leads:** responder requests information to be supplied by salesperson, often fixing appointment

---

In two-step response, the second stage is as important as the first. The sale will depend on the effectiveness of the catalogue, the website, the call centre, the store, the dealer or the sales team. This in turn will depend very largely on the information technology and logistical support underpinning the sales process.

# Why do people respond?

Despite the hurdles that direct marketers face, there are distinct advantages for direct sellers.

Prospects may choose to deal direct in order to:

✔ Acquire a unique product or a personally specified version of a product.

✔ Acquire an everyday product in a unique configuration, e.g. with different accessories or, perhaps, personalised with their initials.

✔ Acquire a product at a lower price or with better payment terms or incentives.

✔ Save on procurement through online exchanges, reduced transaction costs and superior supply chain management (B2B only).

✔ Enjoy bargain hunting and comparison shopping on the internet.

✔ Enjoy better guarantees, e.g. pay nothing if not satisfied.

✔ Enjoy a wider product selection, e.g. from a catalogue or website.

✔ Shop without consuming valued leisure time, without car parking hassle and with an option to try out goods at home etc.

✔ Preserve privacy; avoid embarrassment.

✔ Be better informed: direct marketing offers can be accompanied by more expansive information than is available from other channels.

✔ Enjoy an ongoing dialogue: many prospects enjoy 'belonging', whether to a club or a less clearly defined community; they enjoy receiving correspondence and engaging in feedback. This is a special advantage of interactive marketing.

## The barriers to buying direct

In the past, consumers had serious and deep-rooted concerns about buying direct. This was especially true if the purchase was over the web and needed credit card details. However, many of these doubts have lessened as we have all become used to distance buying and online purchasing.

But it can depend on the purchase – people may still want to see, touch and try on merchandise – if it is clothes or shoes etc. When buying white goods, frequently a retail outlet will be visited and then the purchase made online. But few of us are concerned about buying books, CDs or DVDs, or booking holidays, flights and hotels online.

But there are still hurdles when we sell direct and these need to be overcome. And the perceived 'risk' is most pronounced at the time of the first purchase. This is an important difference between direct marketing and other sales methods.

Reasons for non-response include those causing a 'no sale' in any other situation, i.e. wrong product, wrong price or wrong audience. But with direct marketing there are additional obstacles resulting entirely from the remoteness between seller and buyer, for example:

✗ Prospects may not be able to see or handle the product, or sample the service, until after it has been ordered.

✗ Prospects cannot easily assess the integrity of the seller or the seller's organisation. Bricks seem safer than clicks.

✗ Prospects may not be able to interpret the literature. Questions thus remain unanswered, which is highly destructive.

✗ There may be fears in relation to payment: is it safe to order online by credit card? Will I be able to secure a refund if the goods are returned?

✗ There may be worries about delivery. When will the goods arrive? Will I be at home to receive them?

✗ There may be concerns about data protection and privacy.

✗ There may be specific fears about becoming more involved. Will I be expected to buy more books or CDs than I can afford? Will I be pursued for further orders or donations?

All of the above negative perceptions must be overcome before a prospect becomes a first-time buyer. A large part of customer acquisition communication is directed towards overcoming objections.

## *How people react to advertising*

Having suggested why prospects respond, now let's consider their attitudes and responsiveness to different direct marketing channels.

The following research was carried out by the Future Foundation in 2004. It looks at positive and negative attitudes as well as responsiveness by channel.

Figure 6.2.1   **Positive/negative reactions**

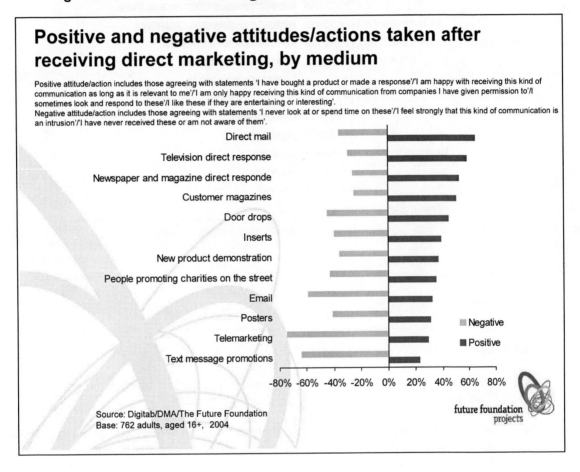

Figure 6.2.2    **Proportion that claim they have bought**

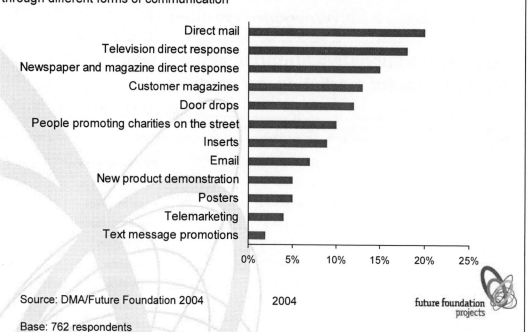

## Proportion that claim they have bought a product or made a response in the past year as a result of different communications

The proportion of respondents who "have bought a product or made a response in the past" through different forms of communication

Source: DMA/Future Foundation 2004          2004          future foundation
projects

Base: 762 respondents

What do these graphs tell us?

- Many direct response channels are positively regarded by the consumer. The more established channels are most 'acceptable'.

- Marketers need to make sure that their message is well communicated and not intrusive. And they need to ask themselves how acceptable their message is to the recipient.

- If the direct marketing industry ignores consumers' concerns, legislation could follow.

- The second graph shows that there is significant response to direct marketing offers. Around a fifth of the population has bought via direct mail or DRTV.

- New channels are emerging all the time – SMS (text) already shows a response of around 2.5 per cent of the population.

The primary aim of direct advertising is to generate a response. However, many direct marketing-only brands are well known – e.g. Amazon, First Direct, Egg, Direct Line and easyJet. So although the object is to generate response, direct advertising can also build brand awareness.

"A conventional advertisement, designed to influence the greatest number of people, has to be aimed at as many people as possible. A direct marketing advertisement, designed to achieve sales as cost-efficiently as possible, has to appeal more strongly to only those people most likely to purchase."

*John Watson, Successful Creativity in Direct Marketing*

# The elements of success

To begin a relationship with a customer, the direct marketer must make a sale. So what are the elements of a successful customer acquisition programme? Like all marketing strategies, we come back to a version of the classic *4Ps*: product, price, place and promotion.

1. **Product** (the brand, positioning and packaging etc.)

2. **Price/offer** (general pricing policy, discounts, terms of offer and incentives)

3. **Place: targeting and channel** (direct mail, DRTV etc. and timing or seasonality)

4. **Promotion:** creative and format

All of these elements are closely linked and work together. Most direct marketers would agree that product and price/offer are the most important elements with place/targeting a very close second. Promotion/creative, which can be the area which has most focus and attention, is the least important.

We will now take a look at these success factors one by one:

## 1. Product – the whole package

The product defined

Product means:

- Branding

- Packaging

- Positioning

Product can mean a physical product or a service – for example, a music CD or insurance.

### Successful products

In the pioneering days of mail order, the definition of the ideal product was quite prescriptive. For example, it was expected to be either unique, difficult to find in shops or embarrassing to buy face-to-face. Furthermore, it needed to be light in relation to its value, not fragile, and be perceived as a bargain even though the mark-up needed to be at least 200 per cent. Incontinence pads, left-handed scissors and courses in English grammar met the criteria and helped fill the bargain pages in the weekend newspapers.

Today, a wide variety of products and services are sold via direct marketing and the explosion of the web – and latterly SMS – will only increase the range. Everything from wine to holidays and flowers to clothes is sold direct. Nonetheless, there are still attributes that a product or service can have which increases the chances of success:

**?** Is it unique or does it feature an added unique benefit?

**?** Can it be personalised or configured to meet the buyer's specification?

**?** Is it a niche product that is difficult to find or embarrassing to buy in shops?

**?** Can it be successfully described in marketing communications?

**?** Can it be satisfactorily delivered?

**?** Does it carry sufficient margins to support direct promotion/distribution?

When deciding whether to test a product via direct marketing, it is worth answering the questions asked above.

## 2. Price/offer

The price and offer is a vital part of the marketing mix. The way you price your product or service will position it in the consumer's mind – are you a premium brand or a competitive/cheap alternative? Do you offer a cut price as an incentive to 'join' or hold the pricing even at the initial stage. These are questions you need to ask before you start to direct market.

### Offers

Below is a selection of different offers that can be used:

✔ **Sample** product – 'send for a sample of the product before committing to a purchase'. Examples: demonstration cassette for language course, free first issue of magazine and sample size consumable product.

✔ **Free trial** – 'try the product at home for 10 to 30 days; return undamaged if not satisfied'. Often expressed as 'send no money'. Another form of free trial is the *deferred direct debit.* For example, the subscriber receives a monthly magazine free for three months before the direct debit mandate takes effect. The subscriber can cancel during the free trial, paying nothing. To cancel, the subscriber must contact the bank.

✔ **Money-back** guarantee – 'if at any time you are not satisfied, return the product for a full refund'.Usually an enhanced version of statutory rights, featuring elements such as 'no questions asked' or with no time limit on returns.

✔ **Invoice** – 'send no money now; we will invoice you with delivery'. Example: magazine subscription (often allied to 'cancel at any time' option, offering refund of unexpired portion of subscription payment).

All these offers can help to lift orders substantially but will not necessarily lift net sales *proportionately*. Asking for payment upfront will bring in fewer orders than sending an invoice with the goods, but will offer some compensation by eliminating bad debt, speeding cash flow and reducing administration expense.

## Promotional offers

However good the product, an added incentive to purchase will usually prove effective. It will help to overcome the inertia which otherwise characterises the direct response process.

Incentives include:

✔   Premia (gifts)

✔   Prize draw or competition entry

✔   Promotional discounts

The extra costs of premia and gifts should be offset by an increased response. The cost of the premium that can be afforded will depend on the price of the product and the level of risk. If goods are offered on approval or free trial, make the premium available only on payment.

**Two-step premia**

A small gift may be offered just for responding to an ad or mailing, for example to request a catalogue. This will increase response at the expense of increasing catalogue wastage. Such a gift is often teamed with another, larger gift that is conditional on purchase. In combination, the two offers can increase both response and conversion rate. The first gift is often time-restricted and is then called a 'speed premium' or 'early-bird offer'.

Generally speaking, more generous offers produce better returns, even after the cost of the premium has been taken into account. Table 6.2.1 demonstrates the effect of a low-cost premium. It is also an example of an 'everybody wins' situation. The direct marketer sells more and makes more profit; the purchaser receives an extra item free.

## Table 6.2.1

| (Direct mail or email) | Without incentive | | With incentive | |
|---|---|---|---|---|
| Mailing quantity | 400,000 | | 400,000 | |
| Net sales | 24,000 | (6%) | 28,000 | (7%) |
| Selling price | £12.95 | | £12.95 | |
| Total revenue | £310,800 | | £362,600 | |
| Extra revenue | | | + £51,800 | |
| Less premium | | | - £14,000 | @ 50p each |
| Net extra revenue | | | + £37,800 | |

Successful marketers offer premia tactically to achieve specific objectives, e.g. for higher order values or for orders from specific ranges of goods. 'Early bird' or 'speed' premia are offered for response within a reasonable but short period of time.

## More on offers – what makes a good premium?

The ideal premium has a *high perceived value* and *low actual cost*. Information is often a very effective premium, e.g. booklets and videos. 'Hard' premia (jewellery and watches) will give higher response but at a higher cost; it is best to avoid mechanical items.

Choosing the right premium is important. A premium linked to the product (e.g. a tape measure with a DIY product) will often work well but, as long as the premium has a perceived value much greater than its cost, the 'fit' between it and the product does not have to be precise. If the product and the marketing have wide appeal, the premium must also have wide appeal.

> Beware of 'freeloaders' – not all response is good. Conversion rates need to be measured carefully when rewarding people to respond.

## Discount offers – powerful but dangerous

The most powerful incentive of all is often a lower price, or, more precisely, a reduced price. However, discounts are also the most expensive incentive: a discount of £5 means £5 less profit unless the discount is linked to an increased order, in which case it may pay for itself in the same way as a premium.

Many catalogue marketers successfully use volume discounts to increase profitability per sale, for instance:

✔ Buy two, get one free

✔ Postage and packing free on orders over £20

✔ 5 per cent discount on orders over £10, 10 per cent discount on orders over £20

However, discounts can be counterproductive, especially when used with quality products. A unique product should sell on its excellence or rarity value. A discount may signal that we are having difficulty in disposing of the stock, unless a logical explanation is offered. The most convincing and enticing explanations add exclusivity to the offer, e.g. 'we pass on the savings of selling direct/on the internet to you'.

Special deals for members of affinity groups or customers of affiliates are among the most convincing and effective, e.g. 'offer exclusive to Members of the Institute of Direct Marketing'. Needless to say, exclusive offers must be genuinely exclusive, although they need not always be discounts. Such offers are invariably close-dated, allowing them to be made to another affinity group at another time.

## The lowest cost offers: prize draws – or sweepstakes – and competitions

For the larger scale marketer, prize draws can prove to be highly cost-effective as response boosters. A £50,000 prize fund spread over 500,000 entries costs only

10 pence an entry. If it has boosted the response from 250,000 to 500,000 the cost per incremental response is still only 20 pence. The downside is that prize draws can be used to attract response only, not paid orders. Entry cannot be conditional on purchase.

Briefly, the crucial distinction between prize draws and competitions is:

### A prize draw:

✔ Calls for no skill on the part of participants and must not be conditional on the purchase of a product or ticket

✔ The cost of a phone call or stamp to enter the draw does not count as a purchase

✔ Lucky numbers may be pre-drawn or post-drawn, i.e. before or after entry

✔ The lucky numbers will normally be drawn by computer

### Competitions:

✔ Competitions (contests) are games of skill where there must be a significant application of skill and judgement

✔ Competitions can be linked to purchase; entries may be charged forü   They are often less effective compared with prize draws

Users of prize draws or competitions/contests are advised to take legal advice and ensure they are set up correctly. (See also chapter 12.3)

Prize draws are best used in direct mail and inserts, where pre-drawn numbers can be printed on documents. Although prize draws normally involve pre-issued numbers, this is not a requirement, and it is possible to offer prize draw entry through other media.

## Table 6.2.2

| Model based on 25% increase in order rate | | |
|---|---|---|
| | Non-prize draw | Prize draw |
| Mailing quantity | 400,000 | 400,000 |
| Order rate | 5.00% | 6.25% |
| Mailing cost per '000 | £750 | £750 |
| Total mailing cost | £300,000 | £300,000 |
| Prize fund | | £ 40,000 |
| Total promotional cost | £300,000 | £340,000 |
| Orders | 20,000 | 25,000 |
| Cost per order | £15.00 | £13.60 |

Prize draws have lost much of their former popularity due to the impact of the National Lottery and, more significantly, to the replacement of the post as the chief response medium. Nevertheless, they can sometimes lift initial response by 100 per cent or more. A draw can run for many months, so amortising its costs over a number of promotions. The terms of entry must be made clear to entrants.

The most popular prizes are cash. But a prize draw can be run with a relatively small prize, or by offering products as prizes.

Prize draws boost initial response at the expense of poorer conversion to sales. Therefore their use demands a strong conditional-on-purchase offer. For example, major home shopping companies may ally a prize draw to a choice of free gifts that can be claimed against the new customer's first purchase.

### Charities

Charities are effective users of direct marketing and are publicly held to account over their marketing expenditure, so their donor and member acquisition must be efficient.

Below, there are examples of two very different approaches to the challenge of generating donor revenue cost-effectively.

The first, for Action Aid, is a deceptively simple, unfussy, straightforward request for money. There is a long letter outlining the need for the money, a gift aid response and a reply envelope. Nothing apparently fancy, few bells and whistles; but highly effective nonetheless.

### Figure 6.2.3

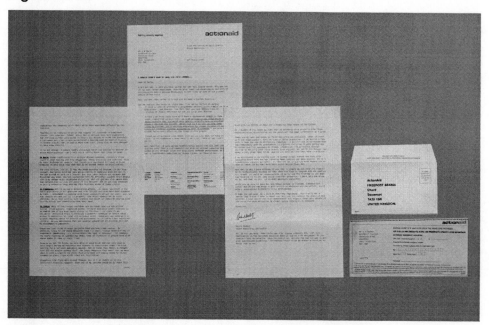

The second is for RNID. This offers a free gift – a calendar – but attached to each month is a gift aid form reminding the recipient to donate. As well as the calendar, there is a long letter with an attached response form and a reply envelope.

Figure 6.2.4

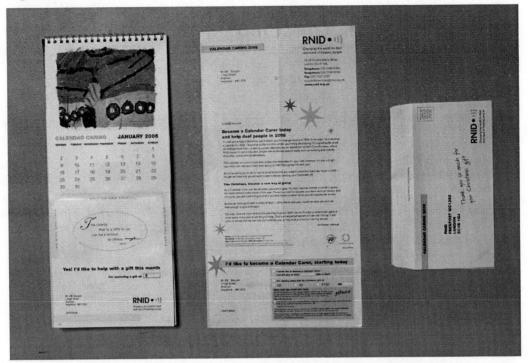

In both mailings the reply envelope is prepaid but the copy states that if you use a stamp it reduces the costs to the charity.

These two mailings are interesting for many reasons.

- Very different creative approaches can be successful

- Long letters work

- Gift aid is important – it can significantly increase the revenue to the charity

- A simple response device which is clear and easy to fill in

- Enclose a reply envelope – offer Freepost but ask for a stamp!

- The free gift can provide a longer term branding opportunity – for example, the RNID information on the calendar

## 3. Place: targeting and channel

### Targeting – effectiveness and efficiency

Almost every medium can be used for new customer acquisition – with varying levels of response and effectiveness. When deciding what channel to market to use, reach, response, payment method, and creative approach all have to be taken into account. And the most important consideration will be the cost of the media.

Targeting is very important. In any campaign, using any medium, direct marketers should use all their knowledge of the product and previous response to target as best they can. Clearly, targeting is easier in, for instance, direct mail or telemarketing, than a DRTV or insert campaign. So cost can make the difference. The cost of newspaper space and TV airtime is cheaper per thousand people reached (cost-per-thousand) than direct mail and so the marketer can afford a lower response.

Just a word on online marketing. The most effective online marketing is constantly changing. Initially, banner advertisements had widespread use. Deals were also made with affiliate companies and payment was made (where possible) based on a cost–per– sale. Recently, banners have become less effective and online marketing has moved towards charging on a cost-per-click basis. The 'click' can be driven via 'keywords' sponsored on a search engine or via deals with sister companies. Clicks do not necessarily become customers – in fact, conversion can be very low – so it is important to negotiate a deal which limits the cost paid per click and agrees the total number of clicks driven to the site.

Unless the quality of customers proves to be very different when we compare one source with another, what matters most is the *cost per customer*.

The best media bargains are often found in unfashionable media: the media that non- direct response advertisers ignore. It is harder to sell space in unfashionable media, so it represents a buyer's market. Similarly, it is easier to make DRTV work on satellite channels (which are cheaper and more targeted), than terrestrial. On terrestrial channels, it is easier to make DRTV work in unfashionable daytime (or night-time) slots.

## Selecting the right audience

Experienced direct marketers use what is known about their existing customers to attract new customers. One of the benefits of a customer database which tracks individuals by their personal details, transactions and promotional history, is its value in forming acquisition strategies, especially in respect of targeting.

Knowledge of current customers improves media decisions. While many media can be made to work at the right price, they may not all be available at a price that is affordable. Some media, such as door-to-door distribution and direct mail, are largely non-negotiable. Distribution and postage costs are constants. Thus, targeting decisions become critically important.

The technique used for identifying the characteristics that differentiate all customers (or best customers) from the population at large is known as profiling. Existing customer knowledge is the must crucial bit of data, but other profiling tools include:

- ✔ Socio-economics

- ✔ Geodemographics

- ✔ Lifestyle and psychographics

- ✔ Source analysis (acquisition media usage)

- ✔ Offer analysis (acquisition offer usage)

The 'identikit' profiles of known customers, built up from the above, are compared with the profiles of media readerships, lists and geographic areas (postcodes) etc. in search of a close match. The closer the match the more likely it is that the people targeted will behave like our established customers. In this way, the target audience can be defined with some precision.

The last two items shown in the profiling tool kit above (source analysis and offer analysis) are used when attempting to match suspects with the *best* customers. A disproportionate number of the best customers may have been acquired through particular media or particular offers.

A risk involved in profiling is that the profile of current customers may have been distorted by biases in the targeting of previous acquisition activity. In direct mail acquisition, responders are often profiled against the entire mailing base (which naturally is composed mostly of non-responders) and this gives a very precise picture of which characteristics are associated with response.

## Targeting by customers – member-get-member

Customer referrals are an interesting extension of the profiling principle. Suspects identified and recommended by customers (e.g. friends, neighbours, relatives and colleagues) by means of a 'member-get-member' (MGM) scheme usually share many similarities with the people who put forward their names. Referral marketing should be considered within the overall marketing mix.

A more informal (and potentially effective) version of the MGM is *viral marketing.* This is any marketing technique that gets websites or users to pass on a marketing message to other sites or users, creating a potentially exponential growth in the message's visibility and effect.

But beware: bad news travels even faster than good news. Viral marketing can be a two-edged sword.

One of the most important pieces of advice that can be given to new direct marketers is to remember the principle of profiling: normally what you are looking for is not new and different types of customer – but more of the same.

However, the pool of matching suspects can dry up – or become tired with overuse. There is then no choice but to widen the target market. Now it may be necessary to identify and target secondary characteristics that could discriminate between good customers and others. This may even involve modifying the product and changing the offer. When more than one change is proposed, each variation must be tested separately.

## Targeting for start-ups

What if there are no customers to profile? And no existing customer characteristics?

Even when the company is new, the techniques of profiling can be used to match the anticipated profile of our likely customers (drawn up from research, observation and focus groups etc.) with the known profiles of media readerships, geographic areas and so on.

## Targeting – let's be realistic

Targeting is vital to direct marketing and so much a factor in its success that the term is often overused. In practice, targeting can range from the very specific (e.g. direct mail to known individuals), to the very loose (e.g. newspaper advertising directed at a broad readership which shows only a slight bias towards the customer profile), to the almost non-existent (e.g. terrestrial TV airtime bought very cheaply to reach as wide an audience as possible).

It is a common error to assume that all targeting is precise – direct marketing has not yet reached that utopian goal. In fact, it pays not to assume too much personal knowledge of a prospect or even a customer, because getting it wrong can cause offence.

**Don't assume too much**

A supplier was forced to sue its client for non-payment, covering the costs of a direct mail campaign. The client counterclaimed on the grounds that the list it had been supplied was not wholly made up of retired people as it had hoped, being based solely on geodemographic codes. The court, having read submissions by advertising experts, decreed that it was unreasonable to expect any form of targeting to be 100 per cent accurate.

Never assume, therefore, that because a list comprises a higher than average percentage of people of one or other characteristic, that all its members will fit that description. Don't make the mistake, as another marketer did, of opening your letter 'Dear Retired Person' simply because it was being targeted to a geodemographic area with a high retired population. Around 60 percent of recipients were not retired.

Nonetheless, the 'loose' targeting of newspapers, television, radio and the internet can serve acquisition programmes very well It might not always be clear who will be attracted to a product or service, especially if it is new or has been relaunched. Therefore, reaching as many people as possible (within a controlled marketing spend) allows the market to define itself. These responders can then be used as a base for developing the future direct marketing strategy.

## 4. Promotion: creative and format

### Formats – sizes, colours, shapes, animation and lengths

Should the banner ad be animated? Should the DRTV commercial be 60 or 120 seconds? Should the page ad be full colour or black and white?

The word 'format' is used to cover everything from the size or length of an advertisement to the number of pieces in a mailing pack. It includes the use of *involvement devices* such as stamps, peel-off stickers and scratch cards. Often, the format of an ad or mailing will outweigh the copy and surface design in its importance. Naturally, however, the format and creative treatment are linked. In both cases the winning formula will have to be discovered through experimentation.

Fairly short and simple messages work to generate two-step enquiries. Longer, more detailed messages are required to complete a one-step sale. Since direct response advertising does not thrive on overindulgent space sizes and use of colour etc. for impact, *two-step formats are usually small*, short or simple and *one-step formats tend to be larger*, longer or more complex.

## Why are smaller ads more efficient?

People filter out what doesn't interest them more or less unconsciously. Ads that are relevant to an immediate interest or need will probably be noticed, however small they may be. Ads that are not relevant will probably not be noticed or recalled, however large they may be.

Unless a big (or long) ad is bought for much less per column centimetre or per second, it is not usually going to be as efficient as a smaller ad, unless the extra size or length is needed to tell the story. A longer size or length is likely to be needed when a lot of convincing needs to be done – that is, when selling one-step.

## Creative – copy and design

The final element in the success of customer acquisition is the creative treatment given to the ads, mailings and so on, used to attract and convert suspects into customers. While this element is widely regarded by experts as less important than the targeting or even the promotional offer, it still plays a crucial role. It is the creative execution that will attract the suspect's attention and communicate the benefits of the product and the excitement of the incentives and offers.

To become a customer, the prospect must buy the product. The product might not just be a physical thing; it will also have features that add value. The creative proposition turns the features into benefits – and benefits turn prospects into customers.

"The secret of persuading readers to buy can be summed up in one simple equation:

$$\frac{Benefits}{Price} = Value$$

What readers unconsciously do is divide benefits by price. The result is the value they place on the product you are selling ... If ... the benefits outweigh the price you have probably made a sale. It's as simple as that."

*Stuart McKibbin*, The Business of Persuasion

The creative treatment should identify the key benefits of the product and the offer and express them in a way that will attract, excite and convince the suspect. In a one-stage advertisement, copy will usually be long. The ad has to take the customer from knowing little and being wary about the product, through the benefits, overcoming objections, all the way to phoning, posting, faxing or emailing the order.

The creative process is highly disciplined and starts from a clearly defined proposition. The most important single benefit will be included in the proposition.

"A proposition is a short statement that gives a clear reason, backed up by some brief arguments why the target audience will respond.

It is therefore a 'why' statement. 'Why' should someone respond?"

John Watson, Successful Creativity in Direct Marketing

John Watson, a founding partner of WWAV Rapp Collins and latterly of Watson, Phillips and Norman, says there are three types of information required before writing the proposition:

1. **Past response data** – what has worked before and what has not

2. **Competitive ads** – what appears to be working for them

3. **What the marketing requirements demand**

The most important of these three is the first one. Nothing teaches like results.

The proposition is *not* copy. But it may well be adapted to make a headline and provide the bedrock for the selling argument.

*One-step* ads and mailings are usually structured to the well-tried AIDCA formula. AIDCA stands for Attention, Interest, Desire, **C**onviction and Action. *Two-stage* ads need to devote less effort to supplying conviction and that is why they can often work with short copy. Detailed description and evidence are highly reassuring and are, therefore, critical components of one-stage creative work. In two-stage response, the burden of supplying conviction may be left until the second stage.

One simple but vital thing to remember: it must be easy for a prospect to respond.

Although the majority of *print media* response may come in by *phone*, including a well-designed *coupon* with lots of room for information will usually boost response. It emphasises that the advertisement is soliciting response (an attraction to readers) and allows those readers who prefer not to telephone to respond. Furthermore, the information requested from the responder in the coupon alerts the phone responder to the questions he or she will be asked.

The postal coupon may also double up as a fax-back form. A web address is powerful especially when used in combination with DRTV – as much as 30 per cent of the response can come via the web and it is cost-effective as it saves the cost of the telephone call. So make sure all coupons request email addresses where possible.

What is true, is that the most effective response mechanism – effective must take both response and performance into account – should be given the most prominence in the advertisement.

## Summary – the elements of success

1.  **Product** – the whole thing, whether it's a physical product or a service. Branding, positioning, packaging and configuration.

2.  **Price/offer** – cost, any discounting, term of subscription and payment methods.

3.  **Place: targeting/channel** – determining the most cost-effective way to reach potential customers.

4.  **Promotion: creative/format** – turning product features into benefits, making it easy to respond.

# Recording and analysing the results

## This chapter includes:

------------------------------------------------

- ❏ **Monitoring**
- ❏ **Media results reporting for offline campaigns**
- ❏ **Website data collection and application**
- ❏ **Typical offline home shopping conversion procedures**
- ❏ **Data analysis: using back data for forecasting**
- ❏ **Using data results in negotiation**
- ❏ **Summing up**

------------------------------------------------

## About this chapter

**R**esults are, of course, what direct marketing is about – results that are predictable (within limits), quantifiable, and measurable. But results are important not just for themselves, but for how they can help us to improve the performance of future campaigns.

In order to achieve this, it is essential to record the results of each direct marketing activity in considerable detail, and to analyse this data so as to obtain insights into what worked, what didn't, and why. In this chapter we look at some of the requirements inherent in monitoring, recording, and analysing results.

**Joanna Reynolds.**

Joanna's biography appears at the start of chapter 6.1

# Chapter 6.3

# *Recording and analysing the results*

## *Monitoring*

Results are the key to successful direct marketing campaigns, whether they are online-based, telephone, television, off the page, inserts, direct mail or SMS. Their performance must be monitored continually – at the very least, on a daily basis.

The first figure to establish is the initial response, sometimes called the gross response. Once this is in, monitoring can be extended to include net response (also known as conversion or 'pay up'), representing the number of people who actually buy the product. Some campaigns, especially those with a continuity element, can be effectively measured only at this stage, as the direct marketer needs to know how many customers are recruited, not how many leads are generated.

Planning and media buying can be carried out in many ways: inhouse, or via a direct marketing agency, media agency, media independent or list/email broker. However it is done, it must be agreed in advance how response will be captured and fed back by individual media or source code. It must also be clear who is responsible for analysing the response.

Although all media expenditures will (or should) have a forecast result, the actual result will rarely match this. Nothing goes completely to plan. The forecast will be based on previous results, if any, and history never repeats itself precisely. From test to rollout, response levels almost always fall, yet it can be difficult to predict this fall accurately. Unanticipated external factors, such as a flood, terrorist attack, postal strike, competitive launch or royal wedding, can impact the response.

As a result, adjustments must continually be made to a current programme. As far as possible, the planner will book media at the last possible moment (some media are more flexible than others) to take account of events in the outside world. The best planners will never put all spend on one media type – or one list/channel etc. within a type; and they will leave some money, around 10 to 20 per cent of the total media budget, to test new media.

## Continuous monitoring is critical

Monitoring is a key part of successful planning and buying. Results from one campaign will shape future activity. The planner/buyer needs to know:

- Which media worked best – by individual list/channel etc.

- Which creative was the most successful – including tests that beat the control

- Whether a certain position or day part works best – for example, how does the outside back cover (OBC) compare with a right-hand page (RH); or early morning airtime with late night

- Which was the most efficient newspaper space size or TV spot length

- What response mechanisms were most effective – post, phone or web etc.

Because each single advertisement is an event in its own right, many pieces of information need to be collected to evaluate each part of the campaign.

# Media results reporting for offline campaigns

Although, for ease of understanding, this section is split into offline and online campaigns, in the real world many campaigns are multi-media. It is not intended to suggest that a campaign should not be monitored as a whole across all the media used. Good practice used in traditional offline media applies equally to online campaigns.

Meticulous data collection is the key to effective campaign analysis. Direct marketers should keep an accurate record of everything from the product promoted to the creative execution, media use and costs, and response. A lengthy, but not necessarily exhaustive, list of variables to record includes:

## Product/offer

| | |
|---|---|
| Product | What you are selling. |
| Offer | The promotional offer. |
| Copy/creative | The control copy and creative. All tests must also be recorded. |

## Media

| | |
|---|---|
| Medium | The medium used and the individual title/channel etc. within it. For example, not just 'press' but the title of the newspaper or magazine used. |
| Date | When the advertisement appeared. |
| Circulation/audience | For press, the current six-month average. For broadcast, the number of impacts (viewers reached), although accurate TV broadcast data is not currently available for 10 days. |
| Size/length | How big the press advertisement or insert was, how long the TV commercial lasted etc. |
| Position/time | Exactly where the advertisement was placed. For TV this must include date of transmission, not just day part. |

## Costs

| | |
|---|---|
| Design copywriting cost | For the control, the costs will be for updating. For a test, a rollout cost should be used and the costs for creating the new approach recorded elsewhere – maybe under test costs. |
| Media cost | The actual cost paid for the media. This will usually be lower than the rate card cost. |
| Production cost | This can vary considerably by medium. For example, the production cost of a loose insert could represent as much as 50 per cent of the total cost, whereas for a space advertisement it can be as little as five per cent. |
| Total cost | This brings together all expenditure. It is needed to calculate the cost-effectiveness of the campaign. |

## Response

| | |
|---|---|
| Identifying code | The numeric or alphanumeric code given to the individual advertisement, such as 'DT3'. The code will be printed on coupons, reply cards and response devices. Most response will quote this code – especially if it is paper- or online-driven. In some media, such as DRTV and telephone, it is unusual to code the individual commercial. Instead each commercial can feature a different phone number, indicating to the inbound agency or company monitoring website response where the commercial was seen or heard. |
| Gross response | Gross (or total) response is the most useful measure of success or failure for day-to-day monitoring. Response isn't just orders; it is important to record all contacts/calls/clicks. Before a campaign starts, some advertisers will estimate likely response, helping them to determine at an early stage whether or not the response will reach the |

expected level. Of course, not all responders will go on and buy something, which is why conversion or net response (see below) must also be calculated.

**Response by type**  Break down response by channel. Phone, mail and internet etc. should be monitored separately.

**Net response**  Net response, also called conversion or pay up, is the number of people who actually buy the product. It can take some time for conversion percentage to be calculated but it is a key measure for calculating the profitability of the campaign. When calculating the profitability, it is important to include all costs for the conversion. These can be high if, for instance, a sales person has made a follow-up call.

**Sales value**  A sale can be a one-off purchase, a purchase that starts a series or subscription (so continuity) or a number of sales made at the same time, for example from a catalogue. Its value will vary accordingly.

## Other events

**Competitive activity**  It is important to monitor any marketing by rivals.

**Other**  Record any unforeseen events – acts of God, royal births/ deaths/weddings or winning the World Cup!

## Displaying results for analysis

Results should be assembled in user-friendly formats, allowing marketers to see which activity has been most effective. This could be listing advertising cost: sales ratios, as in table 6.3.1. If we were more interested in the cost-per-customer acquired, we would use a ranking headed by the ads that recruited customers at the lowest cost.

### Table 6.3.1  **Displaying results**

| Publication | Size | Date | Total cost (£) | Sales (£) | Advertising : Sales ratio (%) |
|---|---|---|---|---|---|
| 1 Daily Mirror | 25x4 | 30.04.01 | 10,600 | 28,980 | 36.6 |
| 2 The Sun | 25x4 | 01.05.01 | 14,600 | 32,860 | 44.4 |
| 3 Daily Mirror | 25x4 | 15.05.01 | 10,600 | 23,670 | 44.8 |
| 4 The Sun | 20x2 | 14.05.01 | 6,000 | 12,960 | 46.3 |
| 5 The Sun | 20x2 | 08.05.01 | 6,000 | 12,120 | 49.5 |

At the end of a campaign or specific time period, results may be tabulated to show such rankings, but grouped by media, space size or length or offer etc.

## *Response to catalogues*

Catalogues are complex and expensive direct response advertisements. Analysing their effectiveness is complicated.

The performance of each item in a catalogue is assessed through its sales: space ratio. If an item occupies two per cent of the space allocated to products, yet pulls four per cent of the business (by pound sterling value), then its sales: space ratio is two (dividing the first figure by the second figure). This good result may be explained by the pulling power of the product or by a favourable position within the catalogue.

The performance of each page and double-page spread is also recorded. Over a series of issues it becomes clear how valuable each position is, because items are rotated and changed between issues, ensuring that the same item does not stay in the same place. This review of page and position is called pagination analysis.

Commonly, the performance is analysed by sales value, margin and number of sales, broken down in the following ways:

- Individual items

- Product category (e.g. horror book or Greek holidays)

- Price band

- Page and position

- Size of space

Over a number of issues, this analysis helps determine the optimum size and design of the catalogue, as well as assisting judgements about which types of product to feature in 'hot spots' (the best positions).

## *Special opportunities of addressable media*

A direct mail campaign most commonly uses all names available from previously tested lists (rollouts), as well as sample test names from a few new lists (tests). An example appears in table 6.3.2. For the sake of simplicity, this shows only a couple of rollouts and three tests, although there would usually be more. There is no significance in the list sizes; they might be 10 times larger or smaller. The mailing cost: order value ratio in the right-hand column allows mailing performance for different lists to be compared in financial terms. It also allows overall mailing performance to be compared with the cost: order value ratio of other media.

Table 6.3.2 **List results format**

| List | Quantity | Response (number) | Response (%) | Orders (£) | Mailing cost:order value (%) |
|------|----------|-------------------|--------------|------------|------------------------------|
| Rollout 1 | 43,500 | 896 | 2.1 | 43,904 | 59.4 |
| Rollout 2 | 26,850 | 594 | 2.2 | 33,858 | 47.6 |
| Test 1 | 5,000 | 94 | 1.9 | 4,418 | 67.9 |
| Test 2 | 5,000 | 145 | 2.9 | 7,250 | 41.4 |
| Test 3 | 5,000 | 71 | 1.4 | 3,564 | 84.2 |

Other columns could be added to show, for example, cost-per-customer acquired or the cost of mailing to each list.

The results in table 6.3.2 suggest that tests one and three have failed. However, profiling against the whole mailing file (which includes the non-responders) could improve all the results. The explanation of how the results could be improved is outlined below.

## List deduplication and profiling

To assemble the mailing file for the mailing in table 6.3.2, the names on each list would have been deduplicated against:

- The database of existing customers, lapsed customers and prospects

- The other rollouts and test lists

Deduplication ensures current customers are not mailed with an acquisition offer and ensures that a person is not mailed more than once. This saves them the irritation of duplicate mailings, and the advertisers the extra cost.

During the deduplication process, significant features of the names and addresses are compared by the 'intelligent' software to detect duplicates. This is necessary because names and addresses are not always written in exactly the same way. This processing leads to the creation of a mailing file which is an edited version of all the lists used.

The deduplication report will show the profile of the mailing file in terms of:

- Title (Mr, Mrs, Ms, Miss, Dr or Rev etc.)

- Gender

- Address type (street number, house name or farm etc.)

- Postal area

- Area demographic or lifestyle type

In B2B mailing files, the profile may include:

- Job title

- Company/organisation suffix (Ltd., plc or LLB etc.)

- SIC (Standard Industrial Classification) or type of business

When results of the mailing are in, the profile of respondents can be compared with the profile of the entire mailing base. For this reason, a record of the files used for direct mail, email and telemarketing should be retained until after the results are in, although this must be agreed with the list providers. Responders can then be profiled against the whole file to see how they differ.

These profiles can vary significantly as the following true examples, taken from Direct and Database Marketing, show. The product was computer software with academic and commercial users:

### Table 6.3.3

**Best company type was four times as good as worst:**

| Group | Response index |
|---|---|
| School | 163 |
| Engineering company | 154 |
| University | 134 |
| Bank | 30 |

**Best job title was 15 times as good as worst!**

| Job title | Response index |
|---|---|
| Professor | 300 |
| Manager | 39 |
| Computer job title | 20 |

By comparing the profile of responders with the profile of the mailing base, we can see how to edit all of the lists during future deduplication runs to improve their performance.

**Net name deals**

Because of the likelihood of duplication, direct mail users negotiate 'net' name deals with list owners or via list brokers. These ensure that the user does not pay for all the duplicate names. Usually, a minimum price is agreed, which can be as high as 85 per cent of the price for all the names.

The list user can also specify desirable characteristics at the time of rental – recency, frequency and monetary value being the most common (so getting names at their most responsive). Other specifications include gender, geographic location and car owner etc.

# Website data collection and application

Websites suck in data like industrial-strength vacuum cleaners. Not all of the data is worth keeping but nearly all of it is useful for diagnostic purposes. For example, if there are 200 unique visits for every order, it is not worth using each visitor's clickthrough data to personalise the site for a possible return visit. Instead, marketers analyse the clickthrough data for a sample of visitors periodically and use the results to guide redesigns of the site.

## Server log file data

> Lines in the server file log record 'hits'. Each represents a piece of information downloaded from a web page. It is possible to track the progress of a visitor within pages as well as between pages. The data identifies:
> - The visiting computer
> - The date and time of the visit
> - The visitor URL

In addition, a good deal of technical information is included.

Analytical software is needed to make sense of the mass of data recorded in the log file. This software enables analyses such as:

| | |
|---|---|
| **Total unique visitors** | How many people visited the page/site |
| **Total page impressions** | The total number of pages they viewed |
| **Page impressions by day and time** | The most popular days/day parts |
| **Length of visits** | The average time spent on the site |
| **Most popular pages** | The most visited parts of the site |
| **Exit pages** | The pages viewed immediately before visitors left the site |
| **Document trails** | How visitors progressed through the site |
| **Referring site details** | The visiting URL and, where relevant, the search word used to find the site |

The exit pages and document trails are particularly useful pieces of information in guiding site design. The information can be used on an aggregate basis or, where the visitors are identified customers, used to personalise the site.

## Identifying prospects

To the direct marketer, a visitor to a website is only a computer until that visitor has logged in by taking part in an online game, or ordering something. There is no certainty that a repeat visitor in the log file is the same person, or two people sharing a PC. Conversely, a single person with a PC and a laptop may count as two different people – although they should be matched via their email address.

You turn visitors into prospects by persuading them to log in – to receive a newsletter, a special offer, a competition entry, a free sample or some other benefit. Now you have a record on them as an individual.

## Tracking and converting prospects

Once a website visitor has logged in to a website, that person is a bona fide prospect in the same way as a press or direct mail responder. Prospects must give their permission for you to contact them with offers etc. This is the beginning of the conversion process.

The conversion process may involve:

- One or more sales calls (usually in a B2B scenario but not always)

- Introduction to a dealer or retailer

- Outbound telemarketing

- Emailed, or possibly mailed, information

- A combination of media and channels

The conversion effort expended will depend on two primary considerations:

- How quickly the prospect converts

- How valuable the prospect's business is likely to prove

## Tracking prospects in real time

Interactive marketing has brought a new dimension to tracking prospect status. The simplest kind of two-step transaction occurs when a prospect visits a website with a view to making a purchase or requests a catalogue. When a prospect requests a paper- based catalogue there is no way of knowing how long they will spend looking at it, or which pages will interest them and which they will skip. They may not even bother to look at the catalogue at all. All we know is that some people ordered and some did not. But when prospects log on to the online version of our catalogue, we can trace their progress from home page to checkout, so adding to our buying information enormously.

The majority of would-be buyers abandon their shopping carts before reaching checkout. Tracing their progress, and identifying the most common exit pages, may supply clues as to why they failed to shop and suggest changes to website design and navigation, guarantee wording and security reassurances. However, striking a balance between simplicity and reassurance is not easy.

## One-click shopping

For marketers, one-click shopping with all the buying information available to the seller, is the ideal scenario. Amazon, and others, allows customers to repeat-buy online without having to key in their credit card and delivery details each time they shop. Interestingly, when Amazon introduced their '1-click' button many customers saw it as too good to be true, emailing to query the automation. The answer: a simple 'thank you' screen, confirming that the transaction has indeed been processed. Of course, one-click shopping can only take place once customer payment and delivery details have been captured.

# Typical offline home shopping conversion procedures

Smaller home shopping catalogues and holiday brochures etc. are not usually followed by a conversion programme. If the initial sale is offline, and no email address has been collected, the cost could not be justified. Instead, the next issue will usually be sent to unconverted prospects and further issues may also be sent, depending on the economic viability of doing so

Major catalogues or fulfilment packages for major purchases (e.g. language courses) can be followed by a conversion series. This is often a combination of mailings, telephone calls and, if email addresses are captured, emails. First follow-up activity should occur within three weeks of the original despatch date of the first catalogue.

A variety of offers can be made during the conversion series. The offers, timing and content of the follow-ups will be tested, making accurate reporting of prospect behaviour crucial.

If all conversion attempts fail during the conversion series, unconverted prospects will remain on a prospect file and seasonal attempts will be made to reactivate them as long as it remains cost-effective.

## Typical sales lead follow-up procedures

Most sales lead follow-up situations occur in B2B marketing. Typically, leads will be qualified before deciding how to continue the follow-up. Leads may leave sufficient qualifying information on the website or at the call centre. Usually they will then be contacted by phone to establish their potential value and willingness to receive a sales visit. Appointments will be made with relevant prospects. Other prospects could be invited to do business through the call centre or website. They will then receive a telephone call and possibly supporting emails.

The meticulous recording of prospects' product interests, channel preferences, profiles and status is essential. This information will be made available to all marketing and sales staff who need it, via the web.

## Follow-up and fulfilment

In all continuity marketing – whether catalogue, book, DVD or collectibles for example – the quality of the follow-up programme is critical. It can add on 20 per cent or more to the conversion rates, often at very little additional cost, as the cost of acquisition has already been paid.

Yet all but the most experienced direct marketers usually fail to test alternative follow-up methods, offers and timings. Many even fail to monitor their follow-up to ensure that timings or content are not being allowed to slip. Monitoring involves planting 'seed' names in the prospect file (whether the campaign is offline or online). A seed name is a name and address belonging to the campaign team so that they can monitor when the marketing message arrives and what then happens in the fulfilment process. It is also important to listen in to call centre and customer service calls. Without continuous monitoring and management, any conversion programme will deteriorate over time.

Some prospects may phone or email queries prior to making a purchase. Monitoring involves checking that these queries are handled in a helpful and timely fashion.

Best direct marketing practice involves regular 'road testing' of competitive fulfilment and follow-up with a view to importing or bettering any good ideas.

# Data analysis: using back data for forecasting

Direct response planning differs from conventional advertising media planning:

- It includes results forecasts based on extrapolations from past results

- It prioritises actions by projected return on investment

- It treats each advertisement in each medium as a separate event that must be justified by its individual contribution

It is time to return to the topic of forecasting. Wherever possible, forecasts are based on extrapolations from past results. However, if a new medium is being tested, a new space size, a new spot length or a new offer, there is no back data. And sometimes past results look strange and incorrect to experienced planners. Therefore, forecasting is not simply extrapolation from past results; it also involves judgement calls.

## Analysing the data: unscrambling the variables

The first step towards forecasting future results by looking at previous performance is to make sure there is reliable data on campaigns – both rollout and test. All the information must be recorded in detail.

The second step is to check the detail to avoid misinterpreting the results. This means analysing the data and extracting variables that may have distorted the results. Here is an example:

| Media | Size | Day | Position | Copy | Response |
|-------|------|-----|----------|------|----------|
| Daily Mail | 25x4 | Monday | Early LHP | A | 464 |
| Daily Express | 25x4 | Wednesday | Late RHP | B | 321 |

The off-the-page advertisement in the Daily Mail pulled 143 more enquiries than the advertisement in the Daily Express. Can future response be forecast from these results? The space taken in each newspaper is the same but there are three variables recorded which pose three questions:

- Is Monday a better response day than Wednesday?

- Are early left-hand pages (LHP) better than late right-hand pages (RHP)?

- Does copy A outperform copy B?

Because there are three variables in the above example it cannot be a true test. When testing, only one variable at a time should be adjusted otherwise the results cannot be read with any certainty.

## How should the test have been set up?

1.  Different advertisement sizes should have been tested in the same newspaper, at the same time with the same copy

2.  Wednesday versus Monday should be tested in the same newspaper, with the same size advertisement with the same copy

3.  Left-hand page versus right-hand page should be tested in the same newspaper, on the same day with the same copy.

4.  Copy A versus copy B should be tested in the same newspaper, on the same day with the same size advertisement.

Only when disciplined testing has been conducted can results be read with confidence.

But direct marketers do not always operate in an ideal world. Often there is not enough data in any one campaign to provide for reliable analysis. This makes it even more important to keep back data from previous campaigns. Some variables, for instance page and position, are unlikely to change from one campaign to another.

Press advertising is used in the above example but the principles apply to all direct response media. Only test one thing at a time. For the very first campaign for any product or service, keep it simple. Then take the best responding offer, creative and list and test out from there. Again, keep it simple. Too often, too much is tested and therefore the results cannot be read accurately.

## Rollout campaigns

The most effective offer, creative and media have been identified. Testing will be carried out against this 'control'. But how certain can the planner be about predicting the control results? For a period of time, results can be predicted with some accuracy. However, over time, all creative approaches tire. The experienced direct marketing planner knows that it is imperative to find a new creative approach that beats the existing control before the marketplace becomes too used to the existing control. In other words, change is essential – the same offer and creative will not work for ever.

One other important point on rollout and testing: generally the uplift seen at the test phase is not repeated in its entirety when the creative or offer is rolled out. So if the test indexes at 130 versus control, assume only an uplift of 115 when forecasting the rollout results. This is important, especially if the test is more expensive than the control and an index of 130 is needed to pay for the increased cost.

## Insurance against the uncertain future

Nobody can ensure that forecasting and planning will be totally accurate – these disciplines are by nature somewhat uncertain – but there are ways that we can protect our forecasting against an uncertain future:

- Only test one thing at a time, either creative, offer or media.

- Test small. If it's creative or offer, take a small, random sample of media to test. If it's a new medium, take a small sample of names or data.

- When forecasting the result of a test to rollout, take only half of the uplift observed. So if the test indexed at 130, take an uplift of 115.

- 'Controls' tire over time, so test to find the new creative or offer to take over from the current control.

### Forecasting conversion and yield

For some organisations, it is important to forecast upfront response as well as back-end conversion. For any company with a continuity offer – and that could include insurance companies as well as collectibles – the marketer needs to know what the initial response is and then how many people go on to make subsequent purchases. Clearly in this situation it is important to track activity for a longer period of time and apply the results to the upfront offer, creative or media.

# Using data results in negotiation

Media owners usually publish advertising rates for their space, time, list, channel or data. These rates may not coincide with what the direct marketer can afford to pay. Unlike non-direct response advertisers, direct marketers know what they can afford to pay for their advertising media. Or at least they know what they could afford to pay last time and have forecast what they can afford to pay in the future. This knowledge guides the media buyer in negotiations with the media owners, allowing them to turn down media that would not be cost-effective.

Unless it is a sellers' market for the required media – i.e. TV time in the lead up to Christmas – there is scope for negotiation. Two types of deal may be agreed:

- A straight reduction in price

- Payment by results

It is far more common to negotiate a reduction in price. Media owners are usually unwilling to take a risk on the advertisers' business as well as their own. However there are exceptions, especially when negotiating online deals:

- Cost-per-click (CPC)

- Cost-per-inquiry or per lead (CPI/CPL)

- Cost-per-sale (CPS)

Although all these models are used when negotiating online deals, CPI and CPS deals predate digital media.

## *Summing up*

Planning and buying are pragmatic disciplines. Value for money and cost-effectiveness is what counts for direct marketers. And only through the meticulous recording and analysing of results can future acquisition advertising be planned and bought successfully.

Most customer acquisition campaigns have an optimum level. This is set by the optimum format, the optimum frequency and the number of media that can be relied upon to produce cost-effective results. Beyond this optimum level results begin to decline. Ideas for new offers, media, formats and creative treatments have to be tested in an effort to counteract diminishing returns.

The wheeling and dealing is usually left to specialist groups but the process of direct response planning is inextricably linked to marketing. It is about acquiring and keeping customers and selling products and services.

There are three ways in which planning for direct response differs from conventional advertising media planning:

- It includes results forecasts that are based on extrapolations from past results

- It prioritises actions by projected return on investment

- It treats each advertisement in each medium as a separate event that must be justified by its individual contribution

In multi-media campaigns, it is important to make sure that overall the campaign is cost-effective and that each channel used is tracked separately.

And finally, to repeat once again, testing should be kept as simple as possible. Only test one thing at once. Be sure that the results can be accurately read by coding each test. But remember, control offers, creative and formats will tire, so testing is not a luxury, something to be done when there is enough money. It must be done continually to ensure the continued success of the direct marketing activity.

Recording and analysing results accurately and in detail are central to successful direct marketing. Using the information to forecast future results is key to fighting for marketing budgets. It may not be the sexy end of the business, but get it wrong, and little else will matter.

# Section 7: Customer retention

------------------------------------------------

**A**s Joanna Reynolds has already commented in the previous Section, it makes little sense to regard customer acquisition and customer retention as wholly separate subjects – leave alone as separate responsibilities within a marketing department. These are truly two sides of the same coin, whose value lies in its ability to optimise the long-term return on investment in the maintenance and growth of a customer database. But if the principles and objectives of these two activities are the same, the techniques involved are somewhat different – which is why we have devoted a separate Section to each.

In chapter 1 we examine the concept of loyalty. The assumption here is that a high level of customer loyalty – that is a substantial and continuing predisposition to a brand – is the best guarantee of a high level of customer retention. We look at the importance of emotional loyalty, and at the very mixed record of today's businesses in fostering customer retention. In particular we look at the need for commitment of employees at all levels within the organisation itself, and – as always in direct marketing – at the importance of measurement.

Chapter 2 is about the customer experience – first understanding how customers actually view organisations with which they do business, and then considering what can be done to enhance that experience *for the customer*. Once again, the importance of the right attitudes in the company's staff is stressed.

Chapter 3 returns to the question of loyalty, and recognises five different 'types' of loyalty (of which only the last is labelled 'true' loyalty), discussing each. It castigates the common business practice of treating all customers identically, insisting on the importance of discrimination, and the concentration of effort on those customers who are actually or potentially the most profitable. And we insist, yet again, on the importance of measurement.

# Customer loyalty – more a philosophy than a technique

## This chapter includes:

---

- ❏ **What are retention and loyalty?**
- ❏ **Managing loyalty**
- ❏ **Aligning the organisation to generate real loyalty**
- ❏ **Customer behaviour**
- ❏ **Customer commitment**
- ❏ **Managing the customer experience**
- ❏ **Employee commitment, engagement and behaviour**
- ❏ **Corporate context for customer management**
- ❏ **A systemic approach to business organisation and measurement**
- ❏ **Measurement tips**

---

## About this chapter

### Customer retention is a business philosophy, not a programme

This chapter provides an overview to what retention and loyalty are, looks at the philosophy of developing loyalty and establishes the concept of enterprise-wide alignment to achieve better customer retention and loyalty.

Customers are knowledgeable and savvy. They talk to other customers, and customers of your competitors about their experiences. They have a healthy scepticism of 'advertising promises', they generally understand when they are being misled or 'ripped off' and worst of all they hate being let down. They have *feelings* about the experiences they have, and although they may not express them to your company through formal channels, strong feelings will make a big impression on them. A 'wow' feeling will get noticed, as will a 'miserable' feeling. Those feelings will have an impact on whether they buy from you again and whether they talk to others about you, positively or negatively. Loyalty cannot just be about a short-term sales promotion, or sending a 'valued customer' communication out, nor is it about low price. It is about developing an appropriate experience through all transactions with a customer, particularly the transactions that are most important to *high spending* customers. Let us talk here about how leading organisations are beginning to align themselves to do this.

### Neil Woodcock F IDM

+44 7785 2205004
neil.woodcock@w-c-l.com

Neil Woodcock is a director of change management consultancy WCL (www.w-c-l.com). He has co-authored several research reports and five books on Customer Management, the latest of which, The Customer Management Scorecard, describes CMAT™ and its findings in some detail.

He is involved at an advisory level in several strategic projects. He was the inspiration behind QCi's CMAT™ and has had a lead role in its evolution to improve its ability to deliver real business benefit for clients.

Neil is on the editorial boards of the International Journal of Customer Relationship Management and the Journal of Database Marketing. In 2000, he was elected as an Honorary Life Fellow of the Institute of Direct Marketing and is on the Institute's Council of Management.

## Chapter 7.1

# Customer loyalty – more a philosophy than a technique

## A definition of loyalty

References to 'loyalty' can be found in the early years of marketing[1]. 'Brand loyalty' was a term commonly used in marketing before the wide adoption of the principle of relationship marketing. 'Loyalty' as used by marketers does not have the full significance of loyalty in interpersonal relationships. It is better interpreted as:

'A positive disposition or commitment to a brand that transcends transactions, making repurchase likely (but not certain) even in the face of adversity'.

"Adversity' might be competitive offers, convenience, or immediacy, and it may prove too much for the consumer to resist, with so called 'disloyal' behaviour

[1] Styan G P H and Smith H (1964), Markov chains applied to marketing *Journal of Marketing Research* February 1964 pp 50-54

resulting. In some markets, such as power supply, telephony or motor insurance, switching benefits vary from year to year and the barriers to switching are low. Only in certain categories (e.g. some utilities) is a consumer likely to spend 100 per cent with one particular brand, so loyalty is perhaps best described as a *share of mind*, and measured by *share of category spend*.

In almost all categories today, there are so many providers of products and services that it is hard for the consumer to investigate and compare them all. Consumers who are ready to carry out comparisons themselves, rather than choosing the most recent offer, will typically only review offerings from a shortlist of two to four brands that they feel most comfortable with in the category. Getting customers on that 'most comfortable' list, especially if they are high spenders in your category, can make or break your brand, as we shall see below.

## The concept of emotional loyalty

There are a number of studies which show the importance of emotional loyalty (where the customer *feels* good dealing with a brand and sees it as 'my brand'). Perhaps this is best represented by research from Ogilvy's Loyalty Index (OLI)[2] programme, including its BRANDZ brand equity consumer research study. This shows that there is a very strong link between emotional loyalty, financial value and market share. The word *emotional* is important here. It refers not to price discounts, sales promotions or other temporary loyalty techniques, but to a belief by the customer in the brand and its products, value and service.

The OLI shows that customers who are most strongly bonded to a brand (whether that brand is a retail store, consumer product or service), can be worth up to twenty times more than other customers. Brand leaders have more customers who are bonded to them – the correlation is strong. In the UK in 2005, two out of the top 10 bonding brands were retailers (Boots and Tesco). The relationship between bonding and market share in retailing is given in figure 7.1.1.

Figure 7.1.1

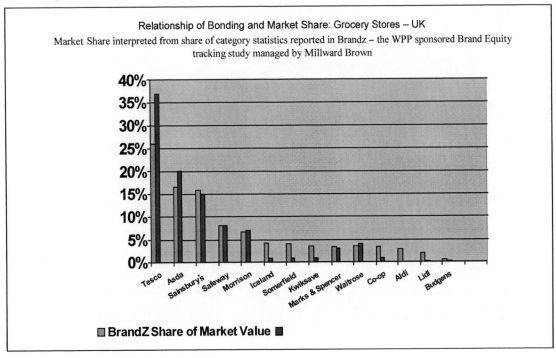

Source OgilvyOne and Millward Brown 2005

[2] www.ogilvy.com

The extensive global OLI research database shows that the correlation between emotional loyalty and market share is apparent across most categories and across most geographies. So, if emotional loyalty is so important, it needs to be designed into the 'system and processes' of customer management and managed carefully. The question then becomes what drives loyalty and how can it be managed cost-effectively?

# Managing loyalty

## How well do companies manage customer retention

Facts and figures used in this chapter show that despite studies like the one above, the ones discussed in chapter 7.2, and the enormous attention that has been paid to customer retention in the academic and management press and elsewhere, much is lacking in practice. Many companies that claim to consider customer retention as an important business objective do not define it well or measure it.

### Table 7.1.1

- Only 16% of senior management have regular contact with customers

- 63% of companies do not know how many high-value customers they lose

- 75% do not know the reason why key customers are lost

- In most markets, just 1% of customers are worth about 30% of total margin, but 58% of companies do not have any special development plans for these key customers

- 85% of companies do not measure the big changes in individual customer spend

- In more than 90% of companies, staff who are responsible for talking to customers could not articulate why customers should buy from them

- 43% do not measure service levels against key elements of the proposition. They can have no idea whether they are delivering their proposition consistently

- 41% of companies do not record customer contact channel preferences, let alone contact customers through their preferred medium

- Only 35% bother to thank new customers

- Only 10% of companies can measure cost to serve at a customer level

- Although 52% look at the quantity of customers acquired, only 8% look at the quality of customers acquired

- Only 4% have regular winback programmes, despite the fact that the majority of our research sample found these campaigns to have a high profitability — because customers often receive worse service from the competitor. Are companies embarrassed to go back to previous customers?

- 47% do not have any sales lead distribution agreements, implying that enquirers are liable to get lost and not followed up, particularly by third parties. In fact only 14% of companies are able to close the loop of campaign feedback/results

- 29% have a robust business case for their $mm IT programmes

- Only 4% of companies have an enterprise-wide customer information plan

- 67% of senior managers do not give clear, visible leadership in achieving excellence in customer management

*Source: CMAT™ statistics in QCi's State of the Nation II[3]*

[3] Woodcock, N., Starkey, M. Stone, M., Weston, P., and . Ozimek J. *The Customer Management Scorecard - State of the Nation II*: 2002: How companies are creating and destroying economic value through customer management

These statistics are averages from around 800 large company assessments carried out across the world, using the CMAT™ methodology. If you are surprised by these facts, or are sceptical about them, remember that CMAT™ assessments are evidence-based, so these statistics are the nearest you will get to the reality of customer management today[4]. We have fed these results back to the Boards of large organisations, and they justify what we have said, so they do represent the true picture of business today. They indicate that basic business practices are not as robust as they should be – from understanding which customers are being lost and why, to following up on potentially high-value enquiries. Profit is haemorrhaging from most companies that we assess. Each failure to observe good practice contributes to this.

Most companies claim a stronger focus on retention than acquisition, yet only around 25 per cent have a clear definition of retention (e.g. many banks measure the number of accounts, rather than the number of customers with accounts that have been used in the last three months). This may explain why only half of those rating retention as more important than acquisition go on to measure it; also why retention measures are often basic, behavioural and short-term focused. Database analyses are limited, with profitability and lifetime value rarely calculated and behavioural warnings and signs of disaffection unnoticed. Fewer than half had activities to understand what drives loyalty or loss, or examined the impact of retention on profit. Chapter 7.2 in this section discusses this in more detail.

## Aligning the organisation to generate real loyalty

### Overly focusing on profit and growth may actually destroy customer loyalty

Let's start at the top. Organisations should align their capabilities around their driving goal, which for most companies is delivery of 'profit growth'. The driving goal of the enterprise might be to make a profit, but the problem comes when companies have an overriding focus on it! This is because:

The need to focus on short-term profit can be overwhelming. There is often an uncomfortable relationship between the need for short-term returns, to appease the demands of shareholders, and the requirement for long-term investment and sustainability. We know from the Enron, Worldcom and Equitable Life scandals that the balance sheet can be misleading. P&Ls can give a false picture of 'business performance'. A company can make excellent profits this year and look good on the balance sheet if it cuts customer service standards to increase productivity, fires 30 per cent of its staff, cuts its marketing budget by half, fails to invest in product development and cuts all of its IT development budgets. The focus on short-term profitability will compromise the company's long-term sustainability to say the least!

A focus on profit naturally encourages a focus on the most obvious *components* of profit, rather than the underlying causes of it. Thus the focus is on:

- Cost reduction, rather than longer-term investment in customers, channels, products and people, and productivity – often at the expense of customer service and employee motivation

- Short-term sales revenue, squeezing another sale out of customers now that isn't balanced by nurturing customer commitment and longer-term value

[4] Please refer to www.qci.co.uk

Through focusing on profit in these ways, current measurement approaches (even so-called 'balanced scorecards') inadvertently destroy sustainable profit! Companies worry about profit too much, and spend too little time worrying about the systemic drivers of profit such as customer behaviour, loyalty and commitment and employee capability and engagement. Customers are normally the largest single source of profit (alongside the sales of assets, capital efficiency and investment performance), and for smaller companies, the only source. Our premise is that, by focusing on a system of measures of which a key output is profit, rather than on profit alone, managers will achieve a balance of short- and long-term performance. 'Customers' must be central to this measurement system. To align themselves effectively and efficiently, organisations must develop a 'Line of Sight' of measures to their ultimate profit objectives. 'Line of Sight' is a term we use in WCL to describe a systemic approach to business and business measurement that is underpinned by a fundamental belief that:

---

**Sustainable business performance** is achieved through gaining **commitment** and **sales** from **customers** who are, or can become, **heavy spenders in a category**

Commitment is gained through **delivering a distinct and appropriate customer experience (the right blend of functional, rational, sensory and emotional elements)** to these customers

This is done **most effectively through engaged and motivated employees or partners**

Employees and partners work **within the context that the company sets** which encourages the appropriate customer management approach (e.g. budgets, policies, products, pricing, clear proposition, environment, processes, IT infrastructure and measures)

This **'system' must work in harmony** so that the organisation is aligned to deliver sustainable business performance

---

Figure 7.1.2 **'Line of Sight'**

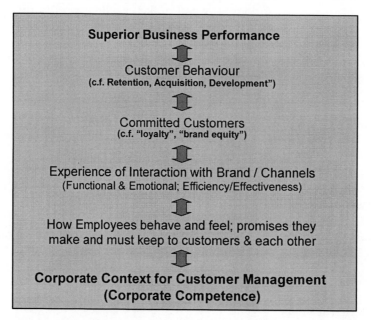

In our experience, although most companies would agree at least in principle to this, few see all the components as part of a 'system' that needs to be actively managed. We describe these areas in more detail below and we believe that the concepts will be useful to senior managers serious about transforming their businesses.

## Customer behaviour

*(more on this in chapter 7.2)*

Figure 7.1.3

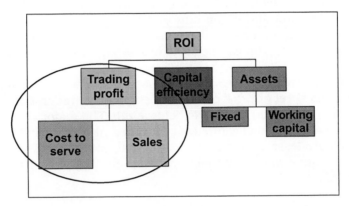

Trading profit is for most companies the major source of profit, along with profit from capital efficiency (e.g. investment and assets) and comes from sales to customers. As far as profitability from customers is concerned, the Pareto rule (80/20) holds true for almost all categories of product and service. 12 per cent of a bank's customers are responsible for 119 per cent of the bank's profit. 18 per cent of supermarket shoppers are responsible for 65 per cent of margin and so on. The only exceptions include pure subscription-based services, although cross-sales and upsales to the basic subscription service can skew the relative value of customers towards Pareto levels. Five per cent of customers in your company will make or break your profitability and 50 per cent will have minimal impact on profitability.

Figure 7.1.4    **Decile analysis: manufacturer**

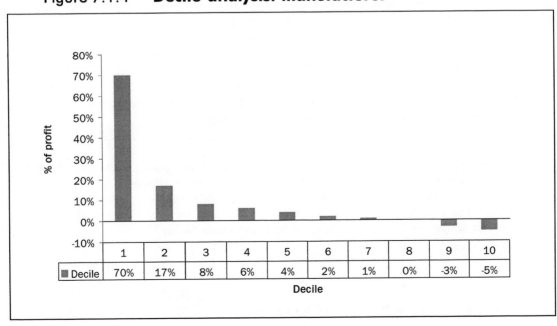

| Decile | 1 | 2 | 3 | 4 | 5 | 6 | 7 | 8 | 9 | 10 |
|---|---|---|---|---|---|---|---|---|---|---|
| Decile | 70% | 17% | 8% | 6% | 4% | 2% | 1% | 0% | -3% | -5% |

Figure 7.1.4 shows that losing just five per cent of the most valuable customers may account for up to half of overall profitability, whereas losing 50 per cent of the least valuable may have an insignificant effect or, in this case, may even increase overall profitability! If 10 per cent of the best customers shift half of their spend somewhere else, then this is likely to result in a 35 per cent fall in profit. It therefore makes sense for a company to focus on:

- Holding on to their most valuable customers: the heavy spenders, and developing their value where possible

- Attracting prospects with most potential value, rather than attracting everyone

A company can do this by understanding who their most valuable customers and prospects are (both now and in the future), how they behave, their attitude to the category and their commitment to the brand. If you can then determine what drives this commitment, you can begin to design an effective, focused proposition.

If this is done well, studies show[5] that it is possible for a large company to double profit in three years! Yet only 21 per cent of companies understand customer management well enough to be able to achieve this. The majority of companies may have different marketing campaigns for different customer groups (the activities which are least important to customers), yet they will treat them all pretty much the same when it matters, i.e. when the customer has an issue or requires service.

---

### Essential senior management insight required to understand: customer behaviour

Senior management needs to know:

- Their own Pareto in terms of volume and profit

- Who their heavy spending customers are

- The share of spend of this group, versus competitors

- How the company manages this heavy spending group, tracks their spend levels and takes remedial action if necessary

- When and why the heavy spenders reduce their spend with you, or leave you altogether

- The relationship of the dynamics between retention, penetration, acquisition and cost to serve, by value group

---

A company needs to understand why its best customers and prospects behave in the way they do. For instance, in retail markets, a senior manager may ask: "which of my best customers stopped buying, or reduced their buying, from my store?" The next logical question to ask is: "why did they stop buying; was it the product range, service, store location or some other factor?"

[5] Woodcock et al; *State of the Nation IV* 2005; Chapter 1

A review of behavioural metrics will enable senior managers to ask the questions that will explain behaviour. If they can do this, they will be getting to the heart of increasing business performance. This is where the overlap with the next element in 'Line of Sight' – customer commitment – begins. Why do customers behave the way they do? How can we influence this? And then the killer question: how can we increase the commitment of high spending customers to our brand, rather than someone else's? Emotional loyalty is not necessarily the be-all and end-all. For instance, in retailing, store location is a strong component that can skew behavioural loyalty strongly. So even if a customer has developed a strong loyalty to a particular retail brand (particularly for convenience shopping goods such as grocery foods), shopping patterns will still be dominated by ease of access.

# Customer commitment

Customer satisfaction is a commonly used and important measure. Applied correctly, customer satisfaction measures tell how satisfied customers are with a particular interaction (i.e. touchpoint). However, they are misleading in that the overall 'satisfaction score' rarely predicts, or even correlates with, repeat purchase behaviour and therefore business performance. Customer commitment is different. Customer commitment, measured in a variety of different ways, does have a clear link with business performance and is a first-class barometer of the overall impact of organisational activities. A number of 'commitment' studies[6] (e.g. Ogilvy Loyalty Index™, ACSI™, Net Promoter™ and Conversion Model™ ) show conclusively the worth of developing customers who are committed to the brand. Not all customers will become committed, but the aim of the organisation must be to get a large percentage of heavy spenders, and potential heavy spenders, committed to the brand.

As discussed briefly above commitment is likely to be based on a set of:

- Functional and rational elements (e.g. price, product features and process-type success of the transaction, i.e. interaction delivered on time, in full, on specification)

- Emotional and sensory elements (e.g. how do I feel about what happened?; do I like the look and feel of the product/package/advertisement?)

In increasingly global and commoditised markets, the balance of power is shifting towards the emotional and sensory side of the equation[7].

## Need to measure both customer commitment and satisfaction

Is it possible to measure how a customer feels about a brand (product or service) so that their future purchase behaviour can be predicted? In the course of our CMAT™ assessments and work in customer management, we have come across a few measurement mechanisms that provide a much closer understanding of these relationships. Our CMAT™ work shows that 21 per cent of companies have some sensible measure of customer commitment (even though some may call it customer satisfaction measurement).

[6] Woodcock et al; *State of the Nation IV*; Chapter 2 - Customer satisfaction, commitment, brands and profit
[7] Woodcock et al; *State of the Nation IV*; Chapter 6 – Line of sight; key messages for implementers, section 6.4.3

Leading companies appear to measure commitment by looking at one or more of the following questions (with a range of answer options):

- Have you recommended us recently and how many times?

- Will you continue buying from us?

- Might you buy other things from us, if we recommend them?

- If we increased the price by 20%, would you still be interested in buying?

- How much more would you be willing to pay for the brand than for a private label?

- If you needed the product and alternative brands were available but ours was not, how likely would you be to purchase an alternative?

- Does our product/service do everything you want it to?

- Do you enjoy the experience of interacting with us?

- If you have had a complaint recently, was it handled really well?

- Do you really care about the product you bought from us?

- Do you believe other companies can provide you with the same or better product and service?

Measuring customer commitment will rarely provide explicit evidence about a service pressure point, or broken process, although this may be implicit in how the customer answers some of the questions above. Commitment measurement does not replace customer satisfaction or event-driven measures, but it is an essential addition. WCL believes that customer commitment measurement is so powerful that it should be used by all companies, so as to have a better understanding of whether their customer management is effective.

While 84 per cent of companies measure satisfaction, only 21 per cent measure commitment, despite its importance. Of these 21 per cent, less than half measure the commitment of their best customers as a disparate group.

---

**Essential senior management insight required to understand: customer commitment**

Senior management need to know:

- What percentage of your heavy spending customers are committed to your brand (not just 'very satisfied'?)

- How many, and which, of your heavy spending customers are vulnerable (weakly bonded with you) or very likely to shift some or all of their spend elsewhere?

- What makes heavy spenders in your category committed to a brand in your category?

- How well does the brand advertising deliver on commitment (e.g. differentiation, relevance, esteem and involvement) and how important is this for heavy spending customers and prospects?

---

# Managing the customer experience
*(more on this in chapter 7.2)*

Customers interact with an organisation at many different levels, both passively and actively. They will see advertising and communications in all their shapes and forms. They may 'interact' when they enquire, purchase or complain about the product. They will experience the product or service. They may see, from PR or directly, the impact a company is having on their community, country and the world. Many of these interactions will wash over most of the market. But for some customers a more lasting impression will be made. The brand and direct personal experience they receive shapes their commitment to the brand. A great customer experience is not necessarily an intimate one. It must support the top customers' values and belief systems and deliver against their functional and emotional needs.

Effectively, the link between the customer experience and business performance will be measured through customer commitment and sales behaviour. The challenge facing senior managers is to design both:

> Brand approaches to bring valuable prospects into the brand 'franchise' *and* customer management interactions to keep them there

Figure 7.1.5    **Impact of brand approach versus customer management interactions, by customer lifestage**

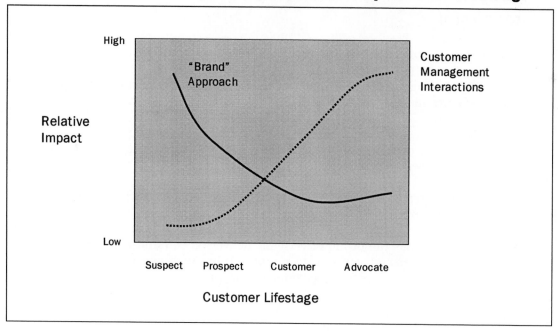

© QCi Assessment Ltd 2004

In most markets, brand awareness ('early' commitment) is developed initially through advertising and word of mouth, but then commitment is developed through the experience the customer has when they interact with the brand (this is a little different in fast moving consumer goods markets, where brand advertising has a higher impact on commitment). New media can help to build the 'good brand feelings' that lead to brand preference by involving the consumer in ways that mass media never could. They make it easier to create meaningful 'engaging' brand experiences to different audiences.

Any interaction or communication may have an impact on the customer experience, and therefore customer commitment and therefore business performance. Some interactions are more important, in the customers' minds, than others. The interactions need to be designed to develop commitment and sales, rather than just sales. Without a systemic approach, the *short-term profit* focus discussed earlier may provide an overwhelming challenge to the cost of ptoviding good service. It may also encourage the achievement of short-term revenue at the expense of a nurtured longer-term customer relationship, which will in turn lead to a poor customer experience, lower commitment and lower sales.

"We must adopt the mentality of permission marketing and creative advertising that is so appealing that consumers welcome it into their lives"

*Jim Stengel, CMO P&G 2004*

An understanding of what drives commitment and behaviour is the starting point for the development of the appropriate customer experience. Companies can then manage their channels against the desired customer experience. To deliver the appropriate experience, brand, reseller, customer management, direct marketing and other communities your company needs to:

- Share data and insights on customers and the market

- Work together to understand the implications of their actions and impact, not just on sales and behaviour, but on commitment

- Work with other functions such as HR, finance, planning, manufacturing and IT to understand each others' roles in delivering business performance, using the 'Line of Sight' framework as the backbone

This should be orchestrated by a core team, but implemented company-wide, across functions. Few companies work this way, and instead, provide dysfunctional delivery of the desired customer experience. Often departmental measures will clash with the overall goals of the organisation (e.g. measuring call centre people on call time may degrade the customer experience of best customers and undermine the initiative of employees.

Attempting to control the experience provided through indirect, or third-party channels is much harder and success is dependent upon the level of influence you have over the channel, the investment you make in the channel or the level of additional business you can provide it.

Developing a distinctive customer experience, either directly or through channels, is discussed in chapter 7.2.

---

### *Essential senior management insight required to understand: customer experience*

Senior management need to know:

- Which events, journeys or touchpoints your top customers perceive as critical or important

- How well you deliver the functional and emotional experience at each touchpoint

- What organisational barriers exist to delivering the desired experience?

- How aligned are the measurement goals of individual functions to ensure that they are all pulling towards your overall business objectives?

- The efficiency and effectiveness of your communications from both the short- and long-term sales perspective, and from the customer experience perspective[8]

---

[8] Woodcock et al, *State of the Nation IV*; Chapter 6 - Line of sight: key messages for implementers, section 6.5.2.1

# Employee commitment, engagement and behaviour

The customer experience is delivered through a variety of interactions as described above. The majority of employees will impact on the brand experience in some way because they will be involved in a customer interaction 'process' in some shape or form - either impacting on the content of the interaction (e.g. pricing and proposition), the speed of it (e.g. back office and IT), the delivery of it (e.g. marketing and sales, operations) or the cause of it (e.g. manufacturing and logistics).

Customer-facing employees, and their immediate back office support functions, will impact on both the functional/rational side of the commitment equation ("they did the job for me", "they were knowledgeable", "they processed my application quickly") and on the sensory/ emotional side ("the design looks great", "they made me feel really good", "I enjoyed that").

Other staff, or suppliers, will be involved in designing or delivering processes or systems which need to deliver the ingredients of commitment.

For example:

- Designing the advertising and communications that shape customers' and prospects' perceptions

- Designing websites used by customers and staff

- Providing systems which will be used by customers and staff to provide them with the necessary information, on time and in full

- Providing decisions or documentation in the full understanding of what drives customer commitment

- Presenting information (e.g. financial) to the market in a way that engenders trust and esteem

They too need to understand what drives customer commitment and what they need to do to achieve it. But are they capable of doing it, and do they care?

An increasing body of research shows that the attitude, engagement and commitment of staff towards the brand and, ultimately, to the customer has a large impact on business performance:

- Companies with highly engaged employees generated 200 per cent higher three-year total returns to shareholders than low-commitment companies between 1999 and 2002[9]

- Over the past five years, companies which employees rate as great places to work have shown 25 per cent growth in share and dividend returns, compared to 6.3 per cent for the rest of the All-Share index[10]

- 70 per cent of customer brand perception is determined by experiences with people[11]

[9] Watson Wyatt Work USA 2002 Survey
[10] *The Sunday Times* Great Place to Work Survey, March 24 2005
[11] Ken Irons, Market Leader, Winter 1998

- 41 per cent of customers are loyal because of good employee attitude[12]

- UK retailer: 1 per cent increase in employee commitment = 9 per cent increase in monthly sales[13]

"I worry about employees first, customers second and shareholders third"

*Richard Branson, in his autobiography*

As basic as it may sound, a warm, helpful, caring and knowledgeable person on the phone, or in the retail outlet, makes a big impression. Somebody designing the website who really understands what customers need, what makes them committed, what other choices they have, how they are likely to use the site - someone who is engaged in the brand - will do a much better job than someone who doesn't really care or understand.

The Vivaldi Brand Leadership study[14] shows that if customers rate your brand highly you will outperform the market by a factor of 1.6, but if customers *and employees* both value your brand highly, you will outperform the market by a factor of 3.2 times! Proof indeed of the value of engaged employees!

All this provides overwhelming evidence of the power of employees in delivering the brand.

---

### *Essential senior management insight required to understand: employee engagement*

In terms of the employee commitment, engagement and behaviour, senior management need to know:

- Which employees you want to keep, at all levels, in the company

- How many of these are committed to the company?

- How many of these are engaged with the proposition?

- What positive and negative impact employees can have on the brand experience

- Have employees been instrumental in defining what good customer experience looks like?

- Do HR, coaches and the training department know what the right customer experience looks like?

---

[12] MCA The Brand Ambassador Benchmark Survey, MORI 1999
[13] Enterprise IG presentation to Loyalty Futures 2003
[14] Woodcock et al *State of the Nation IV* 2005; Chapter 4 (Section 4.2.1)

## Corporate context for customer management

Employees can only work within the 'context' set by the company. If the strategy, policies and processes are incorrect or undefined; if they do not have the appropriate support tools; if they are working in a scruffy, poorly managed, demotivating environment, then they will not be able to manage customers well.

Setting up the appropriate customer management infrastructure is the foundation (but not necessarily the starting point) for 'Line of Sight'.

Customer management impacts significantly on business performance and profit. Research[15] has shown that between 29 to 61 per cent of any common profit indicators (e.g. ROA, ROCE, OM, NM) may be described by the way a company is set up to manage customers! It is therefore critical to get this right. It sets the context for the whole of customer management.

Table 7.1.2 illustrates the areas which need to be considered to set the right context for customer management. These areas form the basis of the CMAT™ assessment, and doing them well has a clear link with business performance.

**Table 7.1.2    Setting the right context for customer management**

| | | | |
|---|---|---|---|
| **Analysis and planning** | • Customer management strategy and business case development<br>• Customer value analysis<br>• Customer and prospect segmentation<br>• REAP analysis planning activity | **Customer management activity** | Retention<br>• Welcoming and getting to know<br>• Identification of a new customer<br>• Customer welcoming process<br>• Information capture and sharing |
| **Proposition** | • Customer needs research/ analysis<br>• Moment-of-truth identification<br>• Proposition development<br>• Emotional commitment<br>• Brand stretch<br>• Proposition communication | | Retention activity<br>• Building customer understanding<br>• Customer ownership<br>• Customer involvement<br>• Rewarding of loyalty<br>• Risk of loss monitoring |
| **Infrastructure** | Customer information<br>• Data feed management<br>• List management<br>• Information planning<br>• Data quality standards<br>• Privacy regulation compliance<br>• Data security<br>• Tacit knowledge management<br><br>Technology support<br>• Access to the customer database<br>• Exploitation of new technology<br>• Integration of new technology<br>• Technical architecture<br>• New technology planning<br><br>Process management<br>• Process documentation<br>• Process checking<br>• Continuous improvement<br>• Radical change | | Managing Problems<br>• Problem definition<br>• Culture of complaint management<br>• Complaints process<br>• Root cause analysis<br><br>Efficiency<br>• Control of proposition creep (e.g. giving high value/high cost propositions to low-value customers)<br>• Customer activity-based costing<br>• Cost to serve targets<br>• Cost of poor quality |

[15] Woodcock et al., *State of the Nation IV* 2005; Chapter 1 - What impact does customer management really have on business performance?

| | | | Acquisition<br>Targeting<br>● Influencer and prospect targeting<br>● Integration of sales targeting and campaign targeting<br>● Over-targeting policies<br>● Targeting agreements with channels |
|---|---|---|---|
| **People and organisation** | ● Leadership and culture<br>● Organisational structure for customer management<br>● Competency frameworks<br>● Training plans and activity<br>● Measures frameworks<br>● Staff recognition and reward<br>● Outsourcing strategy<br>● Supplier management | | Conversion<br>● Enquiry capture and qualification<br>● Sales lead distribution and reporting<br><br>Sales conversion winback<br>● Last minute loss prevention activity<br>● Customer exit management<br>● Winback timing and programmes |
| **Measurement** | ● Customer management KPIs<br>● Measures cascade<br>● Campaign effectiveness<br>● Channel effectiveness | | Penetration<br>● Use of lead products<br>● Customer development strategies<br>● Cross-selling to inbound contacts<br>● Key account management |
| **Customer experience** | ● Customer experience blueprints<br>● Channel consistency<br>● Measuring customer satisfaction and commitment<br>● Event-driven customer research<br>● Mystery shopping<br>● Experiencing the organisation | **External environment** | ● Competitor information collection<br>● Competitor analysis<br>● Customer management benchmarks |

---

### *Essential senior management insight required to understand: corporate context for customer management*

Senior management need to know:

- Whether their company is a top-quartile performer in their sector, in terms of how they manage customers against the criteria in table 7.1.2

- Do all functions work together as a cohesive unit and are they aligned behind sustainable business performance, not just profit?

- Are all business units sharing best practices?

- What is the 'Line of Sight' for your organisation?

# A systemic approach to business organisation and measurement

'Line of Sight' is a very different business philosophy and measurement approach in which everyone can understand and align with the overall purpose and aspirations.

Although each element of 'Line of Sight' correlates with business performance independently, the overall effect is to focus on optimising the system as a whole - aligning the organisation behind business performance optimisation and changing 'the way we do things around here'. It reduces or even removes the conflict and confrontation common between pseudo-independent organisational functions.

The measurement approach has an emphasis on forward-looking prediction and insight to help people understand and improve performance (e.g. to improve customer commitment) and their role in delivering it. It is not designed to provide a rear-view mirror to what happened in the past - although it must not ignore the lessons from the past.

'Line of Sight' links in the critical 'people' angle, omitted from most measurement systems. It applies the same principles to employee measurement as it does customer measurement; measuring commitment and behaviour (as well as satisfaction), and trying to keep those that are most valuable now and in the future.

The process of developing 'Line of Sight' builds engagement and encourages self-motivation, again contrary to the top-down management 'command and control philosophy' of "tell them what to do and make sure they do it". Do it with them, not to them! It provides the opportunity to continuously improve, based on customer and employee feedback, and creates improved business performance, rather than simply reacting to circumstances. Those who have to deliver the changes become directly involved in shaping them.

'Line of Sight', like any measurement system, needs to be used carefully and it will only work if the measures are used intelligently by managers. As an example, a call centre manager will need to look at average call time to answer questions such as: "how many people are required to manage the call centre?" An agent will also need to be measured on this but in the context of other measures, such as revenue generated and customer satisfaction. A good supervisor or coach will recognise the balance of measures and coach people to improve appropriately. A focus on any one of these measures to the exclusion of others will break the system.

'Line of Sight' positions profit as an output of the system; not the sole focus of it. This will be a leap of faith for many. The preferred approach of WCL is to encourage Board level and general management interest not just in profitability, but in all of the elements of 'Line of Sight'. It is only in this way that a sustained 'business change' can occur.

# Measurement tips

Analysis and measurement in retention is discussed in more detail in chapter 7.3

## *Align functional measures to overall business goal*

The nature of control in large organisations is to manage the organisation by departments or functions; and measures throughout the organisation rarely align to the overall business goal, but to functional goals. A focus on sales in some departments, service in others and cost and productivity in yet others invariably causes dysfunctional behaviour in the organisation, with functions and departments often working to conflicting objectives. This is illustrated in table 7.1.3. In each of those areas the functional goal may be eroding customer commitment to the brand.

We have probably all seen several of these in our organisations, and undoubtedly we have been on the receiving end of many of them as customers!

### Table 7.1.3    **Misdirected measures**

| Measure | Behaviour | Likely customer reaction | Outcome |
|---|---|---|---|
| Call centre agent targeted on 2 minutes average per inbound telephone call | Agent tries to end call, sometimes (often?) before the customer is ready. May not capture key information required | Customer feels rushed, processed, cheap and unwanted | Unfulfilled, frustrating experience which ends up with the customer calling back[16] an additional time or not bothering to and going somewhere else |
| Branch 'teller' being measured on the system prompts, which provide 'offers' to the customer in front of them | Attempts to sell the product even though there is a queue in the bank | Frustration for people in the queue because each transaction appears to take a long time. When they get to the front of the line, they want the transaction to be as quick as possible and are in no mindset to buy any more | Frustrated customers and lower sales results than could have been expected |
| Claims department in an insurance company targeted on reducing original claim value | Adjuster 'questions' the claim in detail, arguing with many small points | Customer feels distrusted, annoyed and frustrated at a sensitive time | Customer has such a poor experience at such a critical time, that they vow never to renew their policy |
| Mortgage processing measured on number of cases processed per day (or any service function) | Staff will process applications on a first come first served basis. Urgent, larger applications or more complex applications, even from valuable customers, cannot be prioritised | Valuable customers, or ones with a particular time pressure, likely to be frustrated | Customer assuming she has the choice, likely to go to a mortgage company who can process her application more quickly |
| Collections department focused on reducing days outstanding, without consideration of circumstance | All customers with outstanding debt contacted in similar ways depending on level and age of debt | Customers with previous exemplary payment history, who have missed a payment through forgetfulness will be upset | Customer feels distrusted and slightly annoyed. Certainly doesn't feel 'valued' as the communications keep telling him he is! |
| Sales people targeted on sales revenue generated[17] | Sell a product to a customer every time they can. May not be the right long-term product for the customer. Customer also might not want to be sold to | Increasingly annoyed with company for keeping trying to sell to him. Encourages him to believe that there is no relationship, it is simply based on sales | Will have less loyalty to the company |

## *Worry about high level customer metrics at Board level*

From our CMAT™ assessments we know that only 26 per cent of companies regularly view customer measures at Board level, alongside profit, sales and cost figures. The following customer behaviour measures should be the concern of senior management across the business, but are rarely considered:

- Retention of high-value customers

- How many valuable customers stop or reduce buying and what are their reasons for leaving?

- What is the acquisition volume of the right (high-value) customers?

- How successful are we at cross-selling rates?

- What is the overall cost to serve (sales + operational costs)

- What is the commitment of my most valuable customers - as opposed to the satisfaction metrics that senior managers increasingly review?[18]

- How engaged are my employees?

- How capable are my employees?

- What is my employee product holding?

- How well am I set up to manage customers?

## *Suggested operational 'Line of Sight' metrics*

We have explained how senior managers at leading companies are beginning to think about 'Line of Sight' as a way of aligning their organisations. Some of the metrics they should be considering are included in the tables below:

[16]  John Seddon of Vanguard Consulting coined the term 'failure demand'. He cites a financial services firm that discovered an astonishing 46% of calls were caused by their own failure. Seddon states "The distinction between 'failure demand' - demand caused by a failure to do something or do something right for the customer, and 'value demand' - what the call centre exists to provide, is a distinction that few call centre managers make". www.lean-service.com/6-12.asp

[17] Commission-based selling was the root cause of the 'Pensions Mis-selling Scandal'.""The debacle has arisen because a commission-hungry salesman persuaded thousands of people to leave generous occupational schemes for personal pensions in the late 1980s and early 1990s. By December 1996 just 1% of 558,000 victims identified had received compensation". This quote from the *Financial Times*, 20 March 1997 was used in a presentation by M.W. Starkey *"Moving away from commission-based remuneration for sales people"*, at the Institute of Directors conference, "Successful strategies for your sales team" 19th June 1997. One co-presenter felt this was putting forward communist thinking!

[18] Woodcock et al; *State of the Nation IV*; Chapter 2 - Customer satisfaction, commitment, brands and profit

**Table 7.1.4    'Line of Sight' metrics for customer behaviour**

**Retention performance ( R )**

- Customer retention rates by decile value group

- Changed sales (>50%) up or down by customer (as they give you a smaller or larger share of their spend in your category)

- Reasons for loss (or reduced sales) for top 10% of customers

- Customer commitment levels of key customers (see below)

**Efficiency performance ( E )**

- The cost of customer management for all customers (cost of acquisition and management)

- Marketing effectiveness measures

**Acquisition performance ( A )**

- The number of customers acquired

- The quality/likely value of customers being acquired (i.e. how many are being attracted to the top deciles?)

- Availability of key prospects

**Penetration performance ( P )**

- The amount of category of product that is being sold to customers as a % of their available spend ('share of wallet')

- The number of products sold to each customer versus market norms

- All these can be analysed by segment, customer value group and/or decile

## Suggested 'Line of Sight' commitment metrics

Table 7.1.5 outlines some possible 'Line of Sight' commitment metrics for overall commitment of customer and prospects, the perception of brand and the perception of direct personal experience.

### Table 7.1.5    Suggested 'Line of Sight' commitment metrics

**Overall commitment of customer and prospects**

- Overall % customer commitment levels to the brand and identification of vulnerable customers (or customer types) - for best customers and others (e.g. 55% of your largest 20% of customers are committed to your brand and unlikely to defect. However 45% of the largest customers vulnerable, of which 20% very vulnerable)

- Overall commitment levels of prospects to competitive brands and identification of available customer types and vulnerable competitors - for best customers and others (e.g. 40% of target marketing committed to competitor brands, but 60% available, of which 25% are readily available. Competitor A's customers look most available to you

**Perception of brand**

- Customer and prospect perception of critical brand components of commitment - for best customers and others (e.g. low differentiation, high relevance, high esteem, high trust - need to be clearer about delivering our unique customer experience)

- Internal compliance against critical brand experience components of commitment (e.g. we have met all of our social and corporate responsibility goals)

**Perception of direct personal experience**

- Customer perception/satisfaction of critical direct experience components of commitment - for best customers and others (e.g. we hit perception targets for order management, invoicing, handling technical requests, but failed in logistics)

- Internal compliance against critical direct experience components of commitment (e.g. target performance for order management and invoicing, below targets for invoicing and technical requests, poor performance for logistics)

## Suggested brand experience metrics

### Table 7.1.6    Suggested brand experience metrics

- Functional and emotional compliance versus key clusters of touchpoints (e.g. events) - internal and external (e.g. emergency boiler repair; top scores for functional performance; below average on emotional rating)

- Functional and emotional compliance of key touchpoints - internal and external (e.g. handing of customer 'help me' calls exceeds performance for functional and emotional targets)

- Achievement of customer 'think, feel and say' goals for key events (e.g. all goals met for complaints handling event)

- Effectiveness and efficiency of activities - absolute and relative

## *Suggested employee engagement metrics*

Table 7.1.7    **Suggested employee engagement metrics**

- Retention by employee value group

- Engagement to the proposition - by value group, and team (e.g. most valuable employees highly engaged across the organisation, except in some call centre teams

- Commitment to the company - by value group, and team (e.g. most valuable employees have medium commitment to company on average - needs action)

- Product purchase advocacy - by value group (e.g. all employees score 9/10 on 'would you recommend a good friend to buy our products?')

- Percentage compliance against key behaviours

- Recruitment percentage versus 'talent' targets

- Pay index versus key competitor(s)

## *Suggested corporate infrastructure metrics*

We recommend that companies carry out a fundamental review of their capability against 'best practice'. Use of an assessment model such as CMAT™ may fast-track this process. CMAT™ assessments have been carried out on over 800 companies. The methodology has a proven link to business performance and covers all of the areas above. It provides organisations with an integrated view of how to align business units and functions: a 'Line of Sight'.

# *Conclusion*

This chapter begins to define loyalty and describes how companies can obtain more success through a systemic approach to customer retention and loyalty - focusing on the enablers of business performance rather than on the profit objective in itself. Of course, organisations should still measure and worry about profit but as an *output* of the work of the organisation (the system). They should not focus solely on its achievement or even maximisation, as bizarrely this may destroy the process of achieving it! WCL does not propose that companies blindly adopt a systemic approach, but develop the measurement systems and management co-operation that this approach implies.

Some companies like HSBC, Tesco, Royal Bank of Canada and Richer Sounds are applying system thinking in their approach to customer (and business) management. Their success is clear to see. Others will struggle to persuade sceptical managers that a systemic approach is appropriate. Perhaps in these companies it will be worth an evangelist, or a team of customer management professionals, developing the linkages discussed in this chapter and slowly convincing their Board. Normally, when this is done, the story for systemic management becomes pervasive. Key messages from this chapter are:

- Loyalty is a state of mind, built over several interactions

- Emotional loyalty of customers can make or break a brand

- Board members should *worry* about profit and growth, but *focus* on the system of measures that lead to profit and growth

- Managing the dynamics of customer behaviour (REAP) will lead to improved business performance (see chapter 7.3)

- Customer satisfaction does not predict business performance, but customer commitment does - both need to be measured

- Design the customer experience to do the job, functionally, but try and incorporate some emotion in the design as well (See chapter 7.2)

- Leading brands have higher level of emotional bonding from their customers

- Employee commitment and engagement need to be measured - employee satisfaction surveys rarely lead to increased commitment

- Employee behaviours need to be designed with employees, so that they know what it looks and feels like to 'live the brand' - coaching,, managing and measuring against a clear set of behaviours is more straightforward

- Map a 'Line of Sight' to business performance that crosses functional boundaries - this will help create inter-functional co-operation

# Customer experience: getting under the skin

## This chapter includes:

- - - - - - - - - - - - - - - - - - - - - - - - - - - - - - - - - - - -

❑ **Defining the experience from the customer's perspective**

❑ **Understanding what customers value**

❑ **How to influence customers**

❑ **Creating an experience blueprint – who, what, why, how and where?**

❑ **Improving the experience through customer journeys**

❑ **Engaging staff to improve and deliver the experience**

❑ **Five 'must dos'**

❑ **Ten principles to deploy in your programme**

- - - - - - - - - - - - - - - - - - - - - - - - - - - - - - - - - - - -

## About this chapter

**T**his chapter is all about how to get under the skin of customer experience; what it means to customers, how organisations need to approach designing it and how to influence colleagues and front-line staff to deliver it.

In a world where product quality and price differences have narrowed in virtually all categories, delivering a distinctive and relevant customer experience is the factor that can win the hearts and minds of customers and create competitive advantage for brands.

This chapter describes what a good experience is from a customer's perspective, exploring what customers truly value and how they can be influenced. It then looks from an organisational perspective at how to gain alignment to a new experience design by establishing an experience blueprint. We focus on how to get started and then how to improve customer experiences through customer journey mapping and management. Employee engagement is key to delivering great experiences and we set out five principles to ensure this is achieved. Finally, we conclude with a checklist of the five 'must do' things to get your customer experience improvement programme up and running.

## David Williams

+44 7968 854764
davidw@h2x.biz

David Williams is CEO of H2X – How to Experience, an experience-consulting company that specialises in coaching organisations how to practically design and deploy compelling customer and employee experiences. David actively leads customer-focused transformational change programmes for clients across many sectors. His experience includes working with clients such as British Gas, Royal Mail, American Express, and Royal Bank of Canada. He has contributed significantly to the State of the Nation series and written many articles on customer experience and marketing effectiveness. He draws on 10 years' experience at BP, where he led and delivered international business transformations. A co-founder and ex-Vice Chairman of QCi, he still remains an associate, having successfully taken the company into the WPP group in 2001.

## Chapter 7.2

# Customer experience: getting under the skin

## Defining the experience from a customer's perspective

### Good and bad customer experiences

> Start by thinking about when, as a consumer, you last had a great experience. What was it about the way that this company managed you that really pleased you? Was it the product/price performance? How easy it was to use? The way in which they treated you? The consistency over time? The physical environment/ambience?
>
> Next, make a list of those brands where you have had a bad experience – and why.

Firstly, I bet the second list is longer than the first! We are far more likely to remember and tell others about a bad experience than a good one. There's a minimum level of functional performance and service that we expect and many brands in many categories do not deliver it.

A recent consumer council survey of 2000 consumers which took place over an 18-month period, defined five attributes of both the 'smart' company and the 'stupid' company. They may resonate with your lists:

## Figure 7.2.1    **Smart and stupid companies**

| Stupid | Smart |
|---|---|
| Inflated expectations and broken promises | Provide continuity and ownership |
| Sell, sell, sell | Show respect and honesty |
| Sneaky and dishonest | Give the personal touch |
| Impersonal and robotic | Reward existing customers |
| Incompetent and ineffectual | Provide aftercare |

This survey is actually great news for you, the reader, and your brand. It reinforces the fact that if you do get the experience right, you really can differentiate yourselves from the majority and that applies to whichever category your brand is in.

Expectations are key and are shaped, not just by what we promise, nor by what others in the category are delivering, but by the best companies in other categories. First Direct sets the standard in telephone dialogue, Tesco in face-to-face care, Amazon in personalisation online.

So consumers use three comparison points:

- Against what we expect from the brand based on the specific promise that was made (and our past experience of delivery)

- Against what we expect from the category

- Against what we expect from leaders

Think about where your expectation and delivery gaps are against these three, and do not set your sights on being 'best in category'.

Let's revisit your bad experience list. The words 'careless neglect' may well summarise how you felt on many of these occasions. And that language is interesting in itself. Consumers describe good and bad experiences in the way that they feel (their emotional out-take). So to design good or even great experiences we have to not only deliver good functional products and services, but also think about how we want the customer to feel.

"If you are in the service business you are there to serve the customer. If all your competitors have all the functional things sorted out, then the only thing you can focus on to win is the customer experience, the emotional piece."

*David Mead, ex-Chief Operating Officer, First Direct*

If you don't believe this, sit in on a focus group or simply listen to some calls from disappointed customers and listen to the language customers use.

## A customer experience model

"A brand is what a brand does."

*Arun Sarin, Chief Executive, Vodafone Group PLC*

How a customer feels about a brand is affected by what they perceive the brand to be, what they hear about the brand, and the many and various interactions they may have with it. Their experience is made up of a blend of the company's physical performance and the emotions evoked and measured against customers' expectations across all brand interactions.

Figure 7.2.2 **Customer experience model**

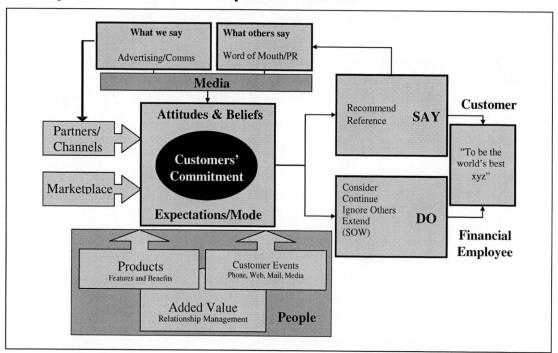

Interactions can be delivered at a hygiene level (getting the basics right) or with a 'wow' factor (either delight at something better than obtained elsewhere, e.g. premium or value-added, or surprise – unexpected service beyond the call of duty). Some interactions are more important than others in the customer's mind, either because they are generally more important (resolving an error is always more important than making one) or because they are more important to the customer at that point in time (a lost credit card on a business trip, for example).

How customers feel emotionally and rationally has a direct impact on how committed they are to a brand and in turn, what they say and do. That is, their level of recommendation and future purchase behaviour, which will be the manifest proof to all stakeholders whether the brand has met its corporate objectives.

Figure 7.2.3 **Leading brands differentiate themselves through experience in both practical and emotional ways**

1. Delivering the basics consistently across all touchpoints in line with customer expectations (accurate statementsand meeting promises etc.) e.g. Fedex

2. Resolving problems/queries positively on first contact, e.g. Rolls-Royce and Bentley

3. Recognising the customer appropriately – understanding and dealing with emotional motivations, e.g. First Direct

4. Making a personal connection at the point of contact, e.g. Gap and Richer Sounds

5. Formally delighting on low-cost factors that can differentiate with high impact, e.g. removing shoes when entering a home (British Gas) or staff who smile (Disney)

6. Delivering a distinct experience that is unmistakably from that brand, e.g. South West Airlines and HBOS

7. Delighting through 'random acts of kindness or fun', e.g. El Al and Ritz Carlton

8. Involving customers in the category and making them care, e.g. Saturn, Coke and Intel

9. Leading the industry and reinventing the service delivery model, e.g. Tesco, Virgin Atlantic, Amazon and Dell

10. Having committed staff who care and are aligned to the organisation's objectives, purpose and brand values, e.g. Richer Sounds, Prêt a Manger and REI

Oscar Wilde defined a cynic as "a man who knows the price of everything and the value of nothing."

Under this definition there are a lot of cynical companies out there! Almost all companies have a clear understanding of their costs, yet 75 per cent of companies have significant gaps in their understanding of what their customers truly value.

## Universal service needs

Although we always advocate organisations to design experience based on research and insight, our work across countless brands and categories always leads to a set of universal service needs, regardless of category. Time and time again customers say:

> "Give me products and services that are value for money, reliable and easy to use."

> "Do what you say you will do."

> "Show me that you care. Appreciate and value my business."

> "Treat me as an individual, not a number."

> "Demonstrate that you know me."

> "Anticipate my needs, regardless of where and when I interact with you."

> "Be there when I need you."

Or put another way customers want value for money and to feel respected, valued and if appropriate, recognised.

How does your experience live up to these universal service needs?

## Getting under the skin

Understanding what consumers value is fundamental to developing a distinct experience. Traditional qualitative and quantitative research techniques are key to eliciting the important, ranked needs between segments. The best organisations conduct trade-off (conjoint) analysis to understand the interplay of these factors and then construct the proposition accordingly. But this is only part of the story.

To really understand needs we need to get deeper into the customer's psyche. Fast moving consumer goods (FMCG) companies know this well and regularly spend time in their customers' homes. There they understand customers' everyday attitudes to the problems their products solve (or create!) and how they are actually using them.

HBOS, the successful financial services provider, is another company that understands this. It uses a range of 'consumer closeness' techniques to bring the voice of the customer into the organisation.

### Figure 7.2.4 **HBOS customer closeness techniques**

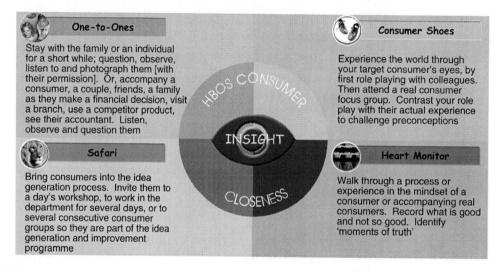

How close are you to your customers? Which of these techniques could you use?

## Value gaps

"Reaching the parts of value that 'customer focus' can't reach" – that's what Alan Mitchell and his co-authors say their book[1] is partly about. They say there is a widening gap between the individual's demand for 'value-in-my-life' and traditional businesses' ability to supply that value. Mitchell identifies seven forms of these 'value gaps'.

[1] *The New Bottom Line; 2005;* Mitchell A et al

In the past we have used the term 'customer sacrifice' to describe what customers have to do to buy or use products and services. What is clear is that if you think about sacrifice from a customer's perspective (hassle, wasted time, worry, cost and uncertainty about value) the types of solutions you consider do change from those derived from more traditional techniques.

## Figure 7.2.5 **Value gaps**

| Value gaps | Description | Costs | Benefits – examples |
|---|---|---|---|
| Transaction | The activities involved in acquiring a good service | The costs incurred in transacting | Delight in a smooth and friendly process |
| Integration | Integrating various ingredients together to achieve an overall solution | The costs incurred in integrating; pleasure in exercise of ingenuity. | Reassurance that a scenario will unfold smoothly and seamlessly comfort of a close fit; pride in being recognised as an individual |
| Customisation | Achieving the best fit to what is needed, rather than just the least worst 'off the shelf' fit | the costs incurred in customising what has been acquired; pleasure in creation and use of craft skills | |
| Buyer-centric information | Information needed to understand a given situation and make choices for the best outcome | The costs incurred in finding and assessing the information; delight in exploration and discovery; pleasure in problem solving and pattern recognition | Reassurance that a situation has been properly understood and informed choices have been made; confidence that the wool has not been pulled over one's eyes |
| Authentic emotions | Responding to emotional needs | Artificially stimulated emotions; negative emotions (e.g. irritation, boredom and jealousy) | Positive emotions, eg delight, reassurance, pride and belonging |
| Economies of scale and automation | Tasks still done manually (such as washing and ironing), where economies of scale or automation have not yet been brought to bear | Costs incurred in performing them; the time taken, their tedium; pride in homemaking, neatness and know-how | Saving of time, tedium; removal of the guilt of chores not done; reduction of physical effort |
| Personal assets | Assets such as 'my time', 'my money' or 'my personal information' | Costs of assembling, understanding and managing these assets | Optimal use of personal assets to get the most from life |

When British Airways and other airlines recently introduced online check-in from home they were addressing a transaction value gap. There was no value to the customer in standing in a line to check in and actually not that much to the company either. Traditional research would have told them to open more check-in desks and improve check-in processing time, thereby reducing queuing times. The real solution takes away the inconvenience and time associated with a transaction and also for the brand, the cost of dealing with it.

What customer value gaps exist in your marketplace? How could you or others fill them?

## Some interactions are more important than others

Some experiences have more impact than others in customers' minds. These were coined 'Moments of Truth' by Jan Carlzon[2] at Scandinavian Airlines. Figure 7.2.6 shows how the feelings provoked at various key stages (MOTs) of the airline journey can be mapped. Getting these interactions right allows companies to reap the benefits; getting them wrong results in erosion of the quality of relationship with the customer. Identifying these and their relative importance is key to focusing on the right interactions. These MOTs are the points where brands are made or broken.

### Figure 7.2. 6    Assessing moments of truth – an airline example

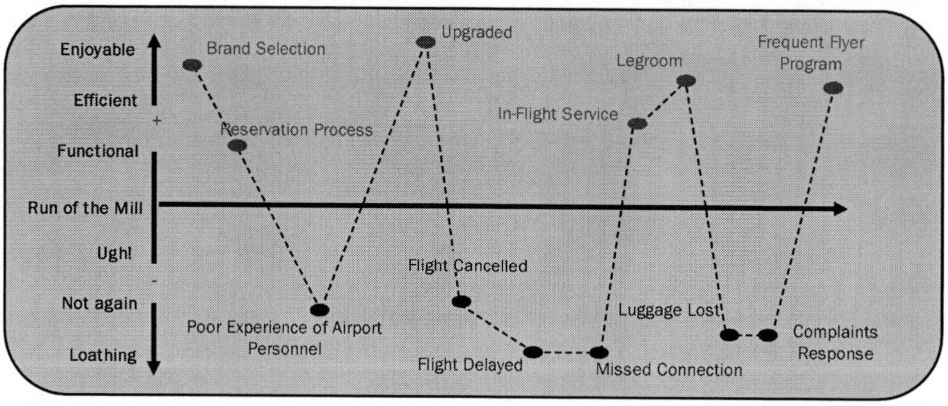

Enjoyable

Efficient

Functional

Run of the Mill

Ugh!

Not again

Loathing

Brand Selection

Upgraded

Legroom

Frequent Flyer Program

Reservation Process

In-Flight Service

Flight Cancelled

Poor Experience of Airport Personnel

Flight Delayed

Luggage Lost

Missed Connection

Complaints Response

Source: OgilvyOne

At moments of truth, consistency of brand promise and brand behaviour is absolutely essential. In the example above, a brand cannot promise a better airline experience if the staff are poorly trained, ill-tempered and rude.

## *How to influence customers*

### Sensory  and emotional

To know how to influence customers you first need to consider how customers think.

"The tangible attributes of a product or service have far less influence on consumer preference than the subconscious sensory and emotional elements derived from the total experience."

Dr. Gerald Zaltman, Harvard Business School, Laboratory of the Consumer Mind

[2] The phrase 'moments of truth' was coined by Jan Carlzon, the former president of Scandinavian Airlines. His book 'Moments of Truth' first published in 1987 by HarperCollins. Reprint Edition published by Perennial Currents (February 15, 1989) ISBN: 0060915803

According to Zaltman, customers 'sense' first then 'rationalise'. In his book, 'How Customers Think!', Dr Zaltman asserts that 95 per cent of our processing takes place at a subconscious level. Essentially, we've thought about it before we know we've thought about it!

This means that we have to examine the subconscious messages we send and what customers feel through all their senses (see, hear, smell, touch and taste). Lewis P Carbone in his book Clued In:How to Keep Customers Coming Back Again and Again, writes extensively about embedding 'clues' into the experience to deliberately elicit the right sensory and emotional responses.

Airlines have long understood that the cleanliness of the cabin and the tray table is important. Not just because it's nice for customers, but the message it would send if it wasn't clean might be: "if they can't even take care of the inside of the cabin, how well are they looking after the engine?"

Some banks who redesigned their branches to be more like retail outlets pump the smell of money into them to make them feel like branches to customers.

---

What clues are you sending your customers through your various touchpoints? Think about product design, appearance, environment, IVR, contracts, language, behaviour and paperwork.

---

Often the most frequent communication channel an organisation has with its customers is its operational communications. Generally, this is the least 'sexy' part of marketing and is consequently neglected. One company carried out analysis to understand the various levels of dialogue that it had with customers. It chose four representative customers and then laid out the correspondence (operational and promotional marketing) exactly as it had been sent on a timeline. It then tried to determine the message the customer had received. If you haven't done this recently, I suggest you do. You might find it rather revealing!

## How do customers buy?

Next you need to know how customers approach a category. You need to build this mental model into:

- How you lay out your goods and services in all channels

- How you navigate customers through the category and into the various detailed choices

The best brands use this to understand the various stages of the buying process and how customers use various channels to finally make their decisions.

If there is one place where all organisations can make money quickest, it is improving the enquiry management process. Think about how you can capture and follow up customers who have expressed an interested but not yet bought. We've never seen a company that couldn't improve it!

One of the best examples of this understanding being brought to bear is the Dell website ( www.dell.co.uk ). An enquirer enters by choosing a category: 'home', 'small user' or 'enterprise'. You can then navigate further by type of product (notebook, desktop or printer etc) or via a promotional offer. Ultimately as you navigate you end up with three choices that you can then add further options to. The choice is made manageable through the understanding of needs and the buying process. This is built into the architecture of the site. Throughout, they entice you to continue to the next level with messages around great value. Customers customise their own solution and generally end up paying a higher price than they would have otherwise paid, but for something that they genuinely want. Well-designed experiences generate additional revenue and save costs.

> "Help customers to find the principal item they want to buy. Once they find it, they'll relax into the shopping experience and that's the point where retailers have the chance to build basket size."
>
> *Craig Phillipson, CEO Shopworks.*

---

Does your enquiry management process help your customers buy easily?

---

## Experience stages: perception, interaction and recollection

Finally you need to manage all stages of the experience.

There are three stages to any experience:

- The **perception**: what the customer expects to happen when they interact with the brand

- The **interaction**: what actually happens

- The **recollection**: what the customer remembers after the interaction

Research shows that although companies spend 80 per cent of their resources on influencing perception, it is recollection that creates the highest customer loyalty.

Indeed, most experience-projects focus on fixing specific interactions. Few actually focus on designing the experience in such a way that it is truly memorable.

Small touches can make the difference. Recently, the service engineer who set my wireless network up for me, left me with a branded one-page diagram of my network with useful settings should I need them in the future. A good example of something that is practical, cheap and easy to deliver that was unexpected but reinforces that the company cares. It probably also has a by-product, that it reduces irritating (for the company and me) future calls if there is a problem.

---

How could you make your experience truly memorable?

---

## *The experience perception cycle*

The experiences we have form our attitudes and these change our very perceptions, thus tending to reinforce attitudes. This is why first impressions and first real experiences are so very important in any relationship, personal or otherwise. It is also why many companies find it so difficult to change the behaviour of existing customers; because they have started off on the wrong foot.

For example, in a test of beer drinkers, it made a huge difference to the evaluation of the beer whether the drinker thought that he was drinking his favourite brand or whether it was a blind taste test. Consumers consistently rated their favourite brand above the same drink unlabelled. It is this principle that is behind the famous Pepsi challenge, in which consumers try unlabelled Pepsi and Coke drinks. The majority choose Pepsi even though Coke enjoys brand leadership.

ServiceMaster, a leading home cleaning firm, identifies customer hot spots; the key things that they want cleaned and how, and prioritise these parts of the job. Then when the owner returns to review the work, they are more likely to be impressed and more quickly learn to trust the work of the cleaners.

**American Express –**
**An intentional experience leads to intentional consequences**

*American Express is a company with a history of delivering premium value to its customers and its business partners. It realised that customer experience was one of the key differentiators and so set about transforming its entire end-user customer experience. But where should they start, and with which customers? After much discussion, it realised that it had to focus on the first 100 days of the relationship – to start right, right from the start. The theory being: if you set the customer relationship right upfront, the behaviours and attitudes would flow through in business results immediately and then over time. American Express is famous for differential service to its highest value customers and it goes out of its way to recruit disproportionately more high-income, high-value card members. So it focused on high-potential customers first and looked at the various servicing and marketing treatments it could influence in the first 100 days. After detailed analysis, it piloted various approaches across seven major markets.*

"The result was impressed customers, who consequently uplifted spend significantly. An intentional experience led to intentional consequences."

*Simon Chrisp, Vice-President, Customer Experience, American Express International*

The implications for marketers are simple. Get the purchase, on-boarding and first product experiences designed to deliver as well as they possibly can.

# Creating an experience blueprint for your organisation

"If you think you can give experience management to a project team in some far-flung corner of your organisation, think again. To reap the benefits of embedding experience into your value proposition, you'll need to make it a corporate priority and get buy-in from every nook and corner of the organisation. It takes continuous cross-functional collaboration to deliver a great customer experience. Otherwise, you can expect your experience management programme to pass like a ship in the night."

*Stephen Blanchette, Director Brand Experience, Vodafone*

Defining a blueprint for success requires a business to be clear about the following elements:

Figure 7.2.7  **Customer experience blueprint framework**

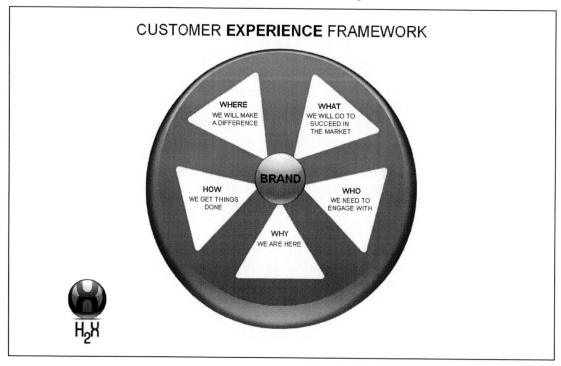

If we define all of these, then everyone in the organisation will be clear what the desired customer experience will and will not be. Working this through with the senior management team can be tough, but is vital if you are to gain true alignment. It will also determine where you are going to start. This model also acts as a great framework for communicating simply to staff what you have decided. This section will examine the components of these elements further:

Figure 7.2.8    **Customer experience blueprint framework detail**

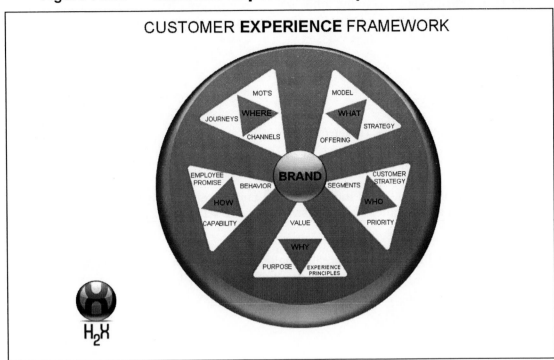

## Who?

Defining *who* the brand's target customers are and *what* they truly value is a vital first step.

How an organisation decides to segment its market and the degree of differentiation in the way it goes to market (propositions, marketing and servicing) is one of the most important decisions a business will make.

> Almost all business can be optimised if they address a differential approach based on value and potential.

> "In almost every category a small number of high-spending bonded customers make or break a brand."
>
> *Ogilvy Loyalty Index[3] and BrandZ, Millward Brown*

CMAT™[4] studies show that in most companies 1 per cent of customers are responsible for 30 to 50 per cent of the profit margin of a company. The next chapter in this section shows this in more detail.

The implications are stark – companies must focus on capturing the hearts and minds of high-category users. Hence, the starting point must be to look at the experience of high-value or high-potential customers. Their needs and transaction patterns are often very different to the 'average' customer.

[1] www.ogilvy.com
[2] www.qci.co.uk

Having a clear customer strategy to drive clear objectives is the next step. The best organisations overlay the following factors (normally categorising each high, medium and low) to build specific segments from which they can build a customer strategy:

- Current value

- Potential value

- Vulnerability (risk of defection)

- Credit risk (if appropriate)

You would probably spend more time and energy retaining a high-value customer at risk than a low-value one and less time cross-selling to a low-potential customer.

Think about which customers really make a difference or where there is most potential for value improvement – focus on these first.

## What?

All businesses need to be clear about their strategy, offering and business model.

We cannot go into depth about corporate and market strategy as this is not the purpose of this chapter. Brands must understand the core category benefits that are required to be delivered. The point we need to make here is that the customer experience needs to be designed to deliver this strategy and these benefits. It needs to be designed within the real *competitive* context.

As an example, in an intermediated insurance business, price and performance are fundamental factors that have far more influence on overall performance than experience. So, the service strategy needs to enhance these factors, not work against them by adding in unnecessary complexity.

In their book *Simply Better*, Paddy Barwise and Sean Meehan set out a compelling argument for simply focusing on delivering the core category benefits better than other companies.

Brands meet these category benefits through a range of products and services and a clearly articulated customer value proposition. It is vital that the brand understands what drives attraction and loyalty as well as dissatisfaction and defection and addresses the root causes. It's also important that the brand understands the drivers of both customer and product profitability so that the experience enhances the business performance. The business model needs to be crystal clear as does the service model and standards that will fit behind it.

HBOS has an internal 'communication card' that lets all staff know:

- Who its customers are

- What promises it needs to make to customers so they choose HBOS

- How they will deliver the brand promise 'EXTRA'

## Why?

The purpose of a brand must be clearly defined for a customer. This must be predicated on customers'attitudes to the category and their use of the products.

All brands should have a set of values that sum up the brand's essence and what it stands for to its stakeholders. These values should direct and pervade the promise that the brand creates through its advertising and promotion, and be delivered through various interactions. These are the building blocks the experience must deliver on if the promise is to have any meaning.

When Royal & SunAlliance launched its new and invigorated retail insurance business in the UK under the 'more than' brand it followed this approach. In developing its propositions it asked groups of employees how it could be 'more than' a normal insurance company, across the key moments of truth.

Experience principles are derived from both brand values and the emotional out-take that the brand wants customers to feel. The best companies deploy them in a checklist format for staff to judge whether or not the experiences being provided and those being considered are 'brand true'.

Orange ([www.orange.co.uk](www.orange.co.uk) ) sets out its experience principles to be *'easy to use'*, underpinned by *simple, intuitive and personal* products and services. You see this in their communications and products (e.g. the efforts they put into the usability of the product).

Royal Bank of Canada sums up its purpose as 'always earning the right to be the customers' first choice'. Similar to the Oskar case study it also defined three words that described how it wanted its customers to feel after every experience and used these to guide the design.

---

What three words should define your experience?

---

### Oskar – a brand experience designed to fulfil customers' emotional requirements

*Oskar, was the Czech Republic's third mobile provider, bought by Vodafone in 2005, now being renamed and rebranded Vodafone. Its strategy was and is based on delivering a distinct branded experience and its approach is one the most impressive and comprehensive we've seen.*

*To start with, Oskar elicited from customer emotional reflection interviews a 'motif' – an emotional end-frame of how Oskar wanted its customers to feel. This, along with the company's brand essence and business model, served as the basis for its experience design.*

*The Oskar management team established a cross-functional team to drive the programme. It then set about auditing its various touchpoints to understand the current experience and look at how well it amplified these principles. Throughout all of this it balanced the customer and employee dimensions. The techniques used included:*

- ***Experience scanning** – identified the sensory clues they were giving their customers through observation and listening*

- **Video observation** – *reviewed how the customers and employees interact with each other*
- **Employee focus groups** – *explored how employees were trained, managed and compensated and how this impacted their ability to deliver the experience*
- **Preference model** – *categorized all of the touchpoints in terms of their negative, positive or neutral impact on customers*
- **Customer research** – *drew heavily on existing customer commitment research, complaint analysis and mystery shopping*

*As a result Oskar redesigned its interactions (touchpoints) with the objective to:*
- *Create positive memorable brand experiences aligned to the 'motif'*
- *Enhance business effectiveness*

*The experience design focused on environmental design, process and employee enablement as well as delight tactics. Standardised 'sales maps' simplified the sales process and made the experience easier to navigate for staff and customers through all channels. The roles, attitudes and competencies of all staff were clarified and these were embedded in new hiring and training programmes. To sustain this, they have integrated other good practices from Prêt a Manger and Ritz Carlton such as 'daily line-ups and ongoing refresher training for front-line staff.*

*Incorporated into a new retail design are:*
- *Queuing systems that allow customers the freedom to browse while they wait.*
- *Innovative seating areas with live handsets which enable customers to interact with merchandise.*
- *Improved signage and category display.*
- *Barriers were removed. The traditional counter was replaced with interactive stations designed with the customer and staff collaborating together side by side.*
- *Online self-care was integrated across all channels.*

*The commercial results were and still are impressive:*
- *57 per cent of visits are now spontaneous (unplanned)*
- *98 per cent of customers leave the store with positive or very positive feelings*
- *90 per cent of customers found what they were looking for*

*Oskar won the 2005 DBA design effectiveness award:*

*"Wonderfully fresh design and engaging approach that obviously made an impact."*

*Christian Cull, Marketing Director, Waitrose*

## Where?

It's really important to understand which channels, touchpoints or journeys have most impact so that we can determine where to start.

A customer journey traces the diverse experiences of a customer with a company over a period of time and records everything from the customer's point of view. It normally is made up of a series of events that involve a number of individual touchpoint experiences.

To do this it is necessary to understand the importance of the various touchpoints by looking at volume/frequency, the impact of failure and the degree to which the touchpoint can drive satisfaction or remove dissatisfaction. Once the current performance from a customer's perspective is overlaid decisions can be made.

The size of the bubbles in figure **7.2.9** represent the frequency of transactions and the shading represents the priority areas (light to dark representing low to high priority).

In this business-to-business example this company sends invoices for what is despatched rather than what is received by the customer. These very rarely reconcile because of distribution process issues. Their clients often complain about the administration issues involved in reconciling invoices with their accounts systems and constantly dispute invoices. It is a major *dissatisfier*. The complaints department's policy is that 'we are right' unless the customer can prove us wrong. There is a major opportunity to delight in the first instance by providing an excellent service recovery.

Figure 7.2.9    **Impact of touchpoints**

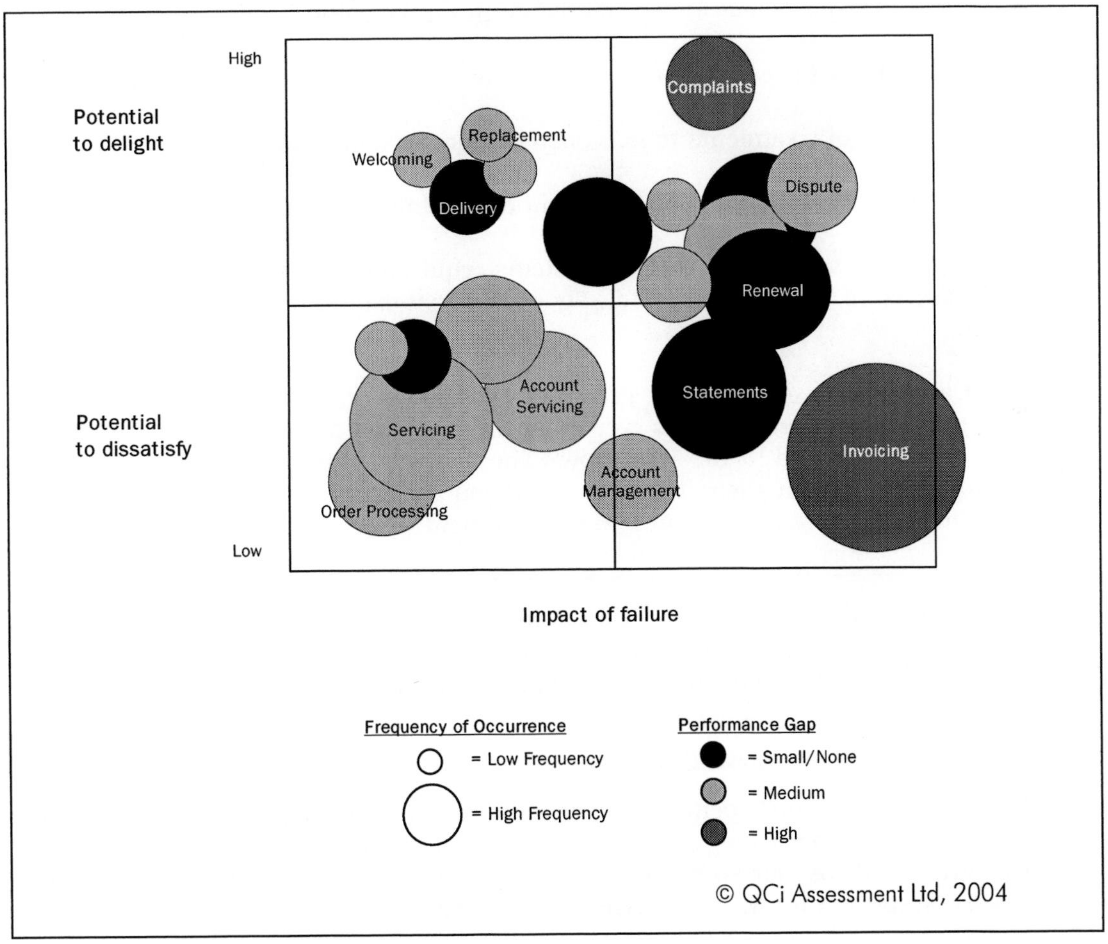

In prioritising where to start, we always recommend getting the basics right first, then working on issues that have a high potential to dissatisfy, before moving onto those that might delight. If areas cannot be fixed quickly then mitigate them as best you can and put in a good service recovery process. Further priority should be placed on those actions that will have high impact from a business and customer perspective and that can be implemented quickly.

## *How?*

When you've worked out what it is that you want to do you have to determine *how* you are going to do it. This requires motivated staff enabled with capabilities, skills and behaviours to deliver the required experience.

To do this effectively you really need to work out your vision in a reasonable level of practical detail. What are you actually going to do differently to customers? Then you can work backwards to what you need your people to be able to do and the capabilities required to support them. In practice, these discussions are iterative as you work out what you want and what is feasible.

For example, we decide we want to give more *relevant* experiences to our customers. Specifically, we want to use service events to trigger marketing communications (through mail, web, SMS and other media), specific web messages and conversations in the contact centre.

We have already determined:

- A data requirement to identify the event on the same day

- The ability to recognise the customer and flag at the point of contact

- A series of treatments to demonstrate the personalisation

- The ability of the operator to act upon the information appropriately

But before you scream out that the systems requirements are far too complex to get delivered in your lifetime, think about how you can do it quickly without these.

Ritz Carlton manages to deliver great personalised service without complex systems. A new guest is always greeted at the reception desk by their name before they have introduced themselves. How? The doorman checks the tags on the luggage and radios it ahead to reception. If you are creative you can often deliver close to what you want without major investment.

Make your mistakes before you commit lots of money. The most successful system developments always go through a prototyping stage where users can trial the concept and functionality. It helps users clarify and tighten requirements.

Many companies don't spend nearly enough time on working out what they really want their customer-facing staff to do and how practical it is to do it real time. If it's simple and easy for staff to do it, so long as you've engaged them and lined up reward systems, they will do it. Are your staff enabled to offer great service?

However, customer-facing systems and processes are often hugely complex. It is often the softer customer service functions and features that get de-scoped and staff end up unable to provide the service required. This has a knock-on effect on the customer's experience.

Audit the employee experience just as you did the customer experience and deal with the hygiene issues first.

# Improving the experience through customer journeys

Journeys have to start from the customer's perspective. In defining a customer journey it is first necessary to understand the customer context. Therefore, understanding the buying cycle and the customer needs during it, is crucial. These, of course, are category- and product-specific but can be generically summarised in table 7.2.1:

Table 7.2.1    **Customer buying cycle**

| Searching | Buying | Using | Disposing |
|---|---|---|---|
| Becoming aware of a need | Negotiating | Learning | Reorder |
| Searching for solutions | Transacting/paying | Consuming | Selling/waste |
| Making portfolio choice | Configuring/ preparing receiving/delivering | Servicing,renewing | Switching |

© QCi Assessment Ltd, 2004

Looking at this from the customer's perspective leads us to think about the experience in very different ways. It is necessary to consider the overall use customers are putting the product to and the overall outcome they are trying to achieve.

This is never more apparent than when thinking about the consumption of goods, as customers go through different life stages, which include all of the major life events which result in brand and service re-evaluation:

- Consumers:    job start/change, house move, birth of children, retirement

- Businesses:    business formation, office relocation, business sale/ merger, international expansion

An example of this for consumer goods brands would be to track the changing motivations and needs of both baby and mother as the baby progresses through various food and activity stages and the mother moves from full-time childcare back to work.

In financial services, many companies understand how the needs and motivations (and therefore the products they buy) are very different for people getting married and buying their first home (not necessarily in that order!) than for someone accumulating wealth and preparing for retirement or preserving wealth afterwards.

## Mapping and evaluating customer journeys

These six tests of each key touchpoint can help uncover whether or not the desired and distinct experience is being delivered:

- Do we deliver on our brand promises by achieving most or all of our chosen customer experience principles?

- Is the level of proposition delivery differentiated from our main competition for our (highest spending) customers?

- Is it relevant to our (highest spending) customers?

- Is the desired experience being consistently delivered?

- Can we measure internal compliance and external perception for major components?

    - Functionally

    - Emotionally

- Do we deliver or exceed performance?

### Telco Case Study

*A telecommunication company dramatically improved its SME customer experience and the process they went through was typical of leading companies. Firstly, they looked at customer profitability and determined that 5% of companies were responsible for 55% of their profit and the top 15% for 95%. They were undecided as to whether to differentiate service, recognising that it is not easy to offer a differentiated service proposition in a large Telco, but they decided to carry out a customer journey mapping exercise with the top 15% of customers in mind. Their thinking was that if they got the customer management process right for these companies, they could go on to determine the cost of service provision for different touchpoints and decide if and where they should develop a differentiated customer management/service strategy.*

*They pulled together and sifted through recent research documentation, looking for customer satisfaction, customer moments of truth and so on. This provided some factual content for the work to come, such as current pressure points and long term 'hygiene' issues. They also pulled together the customer management KPIs they had to identify any obvious opportunities/issues.*

*The next step was to hold a senior management workshop to understand the scope and context of all customer touchpoints, and the possible business impact of an incoherent customer approach. This resulted in a high level Customer Journey map across the whole organisation, and the identification of a large number of touchpoints across all functions and major partners, and some recognition of the possible business benefit of improving the experience. The output of this workshop was a clear framework for what touchpoints, functions and partners should be included in the more detailed journey mapping exercise to come. The reality of this type of work is that the high level journey map should be carried out looking at all touchpoints, but that the scope of the detailed work should focus on key touchpoint areas.*

*Key touchpoints were identified through the use of a scoring matrix (see table 7.2.2), which was designed to identify a rating of the 'likely impact on the business'. Intuitive scoring rules and weighting are used.*

**Table 7.2.2    Key touchpoint scoring matrix**

| Criteria | Score 5 if...Score 5 if | 4 | 3 | 2 | Score 1 if...Score 1 if |
|---|---|---|---|---|---|
| Customer perception | This is a vital customer step. Failure here will upset the customer. We are much better than competitors | | | | This is not particularly important to customers |
| Value to us | Score 5 if revenue value of getting this right is >£x | | | | Score 1 if revenue value of getting this right is <£x |
| Cost to us (should include working capital) | The cost of this step is >£x. | | | | Minimal cost incurred |
| Error rate (% of times the process fails to deliver the desired outcome) | The error rate is >x | | | | Insignificant number of errors |
| Cost of re-work (cost in fixing what went wrong to deliver desired outcome) | The cost of rework is more than £x | | | | Minimal cost of re-work |
| Therefore: likely impact on the business | High impact on the business | | | | Low impact on business |

Most companies notice that key touchpoints (ones with high customer impact, high value, high cost, high error rate and high rework cost) generally involve multiple functions and partners. In the 'telco', work groups were set up to examine each of the key touchpoints (KTs) in detail. Table 7.2.3 shows the type of information that was examined for one of the 50-plus KTs.

**Table 7.2.3**    **Engineer maintenance site visit: customer requested**

| High level process description | Relative cost customer perception ranking & vital MOTs | Relative re-work | Cost of re-work. Success/ error rate | Reason for suggestions/ targets | Improvement |
|---|---|---|---|---|---|
| Customer calls service centre for unplanned (not in contract) engineer visit.<br><br>Engineer (or contractor under certain circumstances) visit scheduled using schedule+ and date time (half day window) confirmed with customer<br><br>Engineer submits visit report<br><br>Visit report logged<br><br>Explanatory letter and invoice sent to customer (if applicable)<br><br>Log summaries sent to contractor/product provider/ service review team | High<br><br>Engineer visit cost £170<br><br>Contractor visit cost £220<br><br>Product renewal cost £50<br><br>Customer complaint if invoice received and customer feels wronged £75 | High<br><br>Engineer to turn up on time<br><br>Engineer visit to be free of charge<br><br>Time window should be reduced (perhaps to 2 hours)<br><br>Problem should be fixed first time<br><br>No unsightly damage to premises | High<br><br>Engineer revisits, product replacement<br><br>Explanations of invoice | 42% successful, completed visit<br><br>34% engineer could not gain access<br><br>9% catastrophic product failure. Revisit<br><br>5% need to return with missing part<br><br>3% engineer do not arrive on time<br><br>35% of invoiced customers complain | 15% (mail/tel confirmation of appt)<br><br>7% (product review with supplier)<br><br>3% (review contractors' support kit)<br><br>1.5% (improve contractor 'sickness' process)<br><br>18% (clearer contract; engineer explains on site; clearer letter; no invoices to group 1 customers) |

KPIs (e.g. error rates, costs and customer perception ratings) were available from current work/analysis in less than 50 per cent of the KTs areas (which is indicative in itself!). For the >50 per cent of KTs where this information was not available, the KPIs had to be determined. This is a major area of project benefit and risk. Facts and figures are vital for this exercise. Some organisations use tools to structure and hold all this data in an easily accessible manner. Samplings and old-fashioned work studies are normally set up to provide approximate figures. Absolute accuracy in the figures is not required. This is where the project manager's previous experience is very beneficial in customer journey mapping.

A review of the 50-plus KT tables identified which were the priority actions, and these were built into project plans in the normal way. The journey maps and KT work have become a fundamental part of training in this 'telco'. It is a requirement that any new system/process project identifies where the new process fits within the customer journey.

## *Designing the future journey experience*

Leading companies often apply a five-step process to do this. The example shown in figure 7.2.10 (on page 23) is from a consumer home appliance 'warranty' event. The company carried out a workshop with a cross-functional group of people who are involved in the delivery of the event. The process used with front-line employees was to ask the following questions:

- If we wanted someone to say we were 'experts' in this event what would we want them to think, feel and say?

- To get them to say this, what do we have to do?

- To do this, what promises would we need to make to the customer and each other?

- What capabilities would we need to do this?

- What's getting in the way, or stopping us from doing this?

Figure 7.2.10 **Mapping brand values to individual touchpoints**

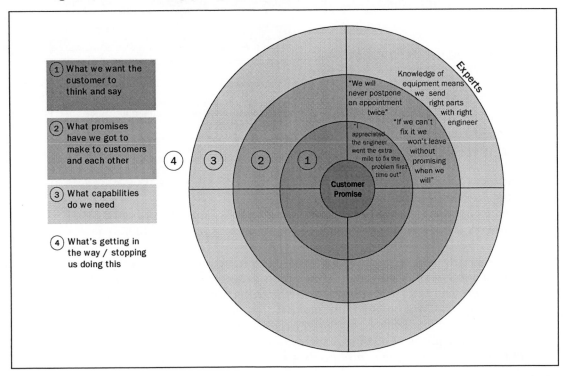

QCi Assessment Ltd, 2004

The result was not just a well-designed experience, but a set of engaged people who truly bought into, and helped design, the outcome.

**British Gas – 'Doing the Right Thing'**

*Several years ago, British Gas embarked on a major mission to transform its customer experience, taking its people on this journey under the 'Doing the Right Thing' banner.*

*The starting point was to understand the current customer journeys. It identified around 25 journeys (e.g. getting through to the right customer service adviser, interim boiler breakdown, home move and the debt process). It then carried out high-level analysis on what was broken in these journeys and approximately how much it was costing the business. The first view showed that there was £100 million of 'value at stake' in its various customer journeys. This focused management attention on the issues and helped prioritise which journeys to focus on first. It was helped in this process by the fact that its research data is tagged (anonymously) to behavioural data so that it could model which factors made the most impact on customers. It could also model its service profit chain so it knew how an improvement in satisfaction and its various components would flow through to the bottom line.*

Figure 7.2.11 **Journey improvement process**

*It started fixing the basics first, removing areas of dissatisfaction before focusing on the drivers of satisfaction. It had a specific and very pragmatic sequential approach to the redesign of the touchpoints:*

*Understand it – Mend it – Brand it – Protect it – Differentiate it – Re-engineer it*

*A cross-functional team went through a systematic journey improvement agenda for all the journeys. This established the key metrics (external perception and internal compliance) and British*

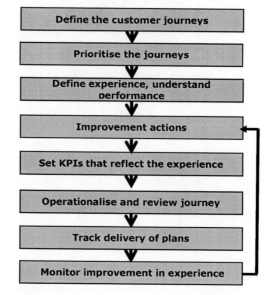

*Gas brought these onto the management agenda via a dash board that made all these metrics and journey improvement plans visible.*

*However, there is no point transforming a journey without a set of guiding design principles. These were built around the brand values and set into a set of service principles, which were not only communicated but also embedded into the business change process, as an additional sign-off criterion. Employees were engaged around the 'Doing the Right Thing' agenda in a series of events. A series of hero stories brought this to life in various offices and the content was embedded in training.*

"British Gas has made major improvements in its customer experience. It continues to encourage its staff to 'Do the Right Thing' for its customers and through its customer experience improvement agenda, its shareholders too."

*Andrew Reaney, Head of Customer Experience, British Gas*

# Engaging staff to improve and deliver the experience

"In a service business like ours you can only look after the customer by looking after your staff. So the route to creating value from customers is through the management of your people. Good retailers always understand this instinctively and we, at Tesco, regard it as a major priority."

*Terry Leahy, CEO Tesco 2002[5]*

Figure 7.2.12   **Great service brands know that people are key to delivering the customer experience**

| |
| --- |
| How staff represent their company/brand directly affects consumer loyalty |
| How customers are treated by staff is the number-one reason why people are put off from purchasing |
| Yet only one in 10 consumers say staff show pride in their products and services |
| Moreover, staff is one of the top three reasons why customers repeat purchase |

Source: Brand Ambassador Study: MCA, 1999 (now part of Enterprise IG)

There are five key principles that the best brands use to engage staff:

1.   **Bring customers alive**
2.   **Make it real for me**
3.   **Align, lead and direct**
4.   **Attack beliefs**
5.   **Maintain momentum**

## Bring customers alive

We discussed earlier the series of techniques that HBOS uses to get closer to customers. The output of these types of initiatives needs to be brought alive to staff in accessible and innovative ways. The more these are dramatised in stories, the more impact they generally have.

A telling question to ask is: when did your senior team sit in and observe a focus group. Videoing and showing edited highlights to management can be another way to make this information more accessible.

If management need convincing that there is a problem the best way is to bring alive customers' real experiences. This is best done in multi-media formats: transcripts of conversations, photos of locations/packaging, hidden cameras (the shakier the better!), or voice recordings of complaints.

Tesco sends its management 'back to the floor' for at least one week a year to ensure managers stay in touch with the real world. They are expected to make suggestions for improvements on their return.

[1] Milligan, A. and Smith, S., *Uncommon Practice: People Who Deliver a Great Brand Experience*, Prentice Hall 2002, p64

Another organisation gave all senior head office staff the ability to dial in and silently monitor contact centre calls.

> You need to bring the pain alive enough to get people to want to act, but actually a customer experience programme should be a positive programme. Ensure you keep the balance in your communication and celebrate success when you have it.

## Make it real for me

Once underway, engaging people behind the defined customer experience is critical to the success. There are a number of robust frameworks for building employee engagement that mirror the approach marketing organisations take consumers through when winning their advocacy to their brands.

### Figure 7.2.13  Major insurer engagement framework

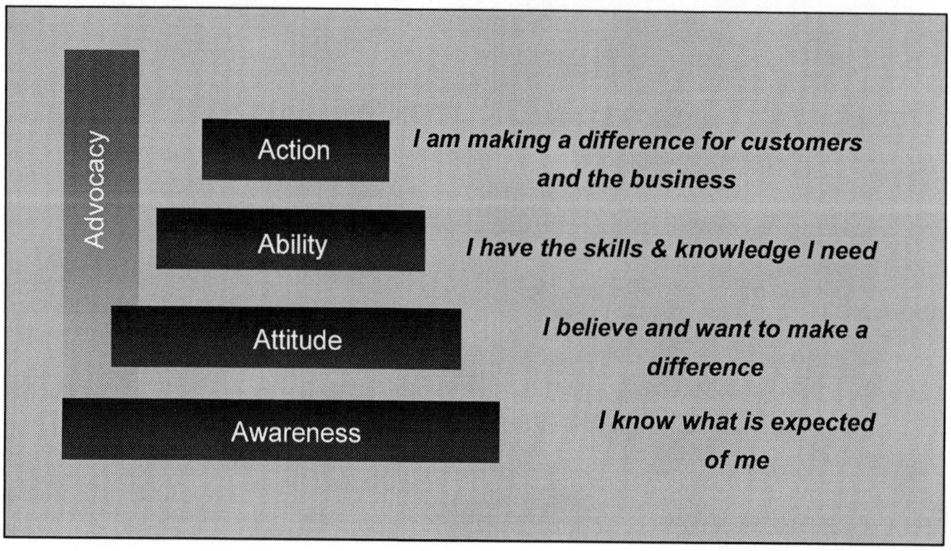

Advocacy

Action — *I am making a difference for customers and the business*

Ability — *I have the skills & knowledge I need*

Attitude — *I believe and want to make a difference*

Awareness — *I know what is expected of me*

Source: Enterprise IG, 2004

The framework in figure 7.2.13 is established on a number of building blocks:

- **Awareness** Everybody should have a clear rational understanding of the case for change, the magnitude of the journey and what it means for teams and individuals.

- **Attitude** We have started positively to shape people's beliefs and feelings around the change. We are starting to engage their emotions around the customer experience and brand promise.

- **Ability** People feel confident that they have the personal competences and skills to put the new behaviours in place and start to 'live' the experience.

- **Action** There is actual behaviour change as people start to make the brand promise and customer service experience a reality, internally and externally.

- **Advocacy** People 'own' and champion the behaviour changes, spreading enthusiasm for them and the business.

'Make it real for me' is all about showing people what this wonderful customer experience vision means to them today, in the near future and next year.

The mistake many organisations make is to simply communicate the vision and assume that everyone will work out for themselves that this is a wonderful thing. You must answer the WIFM question for all stakeholder groups (what's in it for me!).

One of the most effective ways to engage people is to actually bring to life the future experience. Storyboards or video role plays that help people see, rather than just imagine, what the future looks like can be very effective. This is especially true if you involve staff in its creation. The British Gas 'Doing the Right Thing' video makes such an emotional impact that it actually brings a tear to most viewers' eyes.

## Align, lead and direct

Great leaders lead from the front and back their words up with actions. They 'walk the talk'. When I work with organisations the first place I look is the senior management team. Are they serious about delivering a great experience and does that manifest itself in what they talk about and what they actually do? What's on their weekly and monthly management agendas? I also ask them what their most important business issue is. If customer experience isn't integrally connected to that issue then there is a problem.

Linking customer experience to the key corporate objectives is critical. If you can't do this then you simply won't get the support. And if by chance you do, and the business climate changes, you can be pretty sure that it'll be the non-core programmes that get de-prioritised or cut.

If you follow the guidelines around developing an experience blueprint you should achieve alignment. Sometimes though, you need some success to be able to get into a position where you can have the conversation about creating a blueprint. If you're in this place then you need to find some quick wins within your sphere of influence that show the benefits of a focus in this area. You will also want to start building a business case to help do some persuading (see the 'value at stake' point in the British Gas case study). Using best practice organisations to informally benchmark and show the art of the possible can also be a powerful motivator.

Once you've got them on board you need to provide them with the means to manage and direct the experience. Often this means different metrics and management reporting mechanisms.

"People don't do what you expect; they do what you inspect."

*Lou Gerstner*

While at BP many years ago, we had many sub-process metrics in our manufacturing and distribution chain. Each one of them was more than 95 per cent against the established standard, which every department deemed to be acceptable, and yet our customers were continually telling us we were not delivering. We established a new end-to-end metric – ISOTIF – In Spec On Time in Full. It was only when we established this end-to-end measure that it became clear that we were systematically failing more times than we were delivering. It helped convince everyone all was not well and created a real focus. The overall metric that matched the way the customers judged us climbed steadily and quickly as we understood the many interdepartmental issues.

The second place to look is front-line supervisory management. If these people are well trained, competent, enabled to do their jobs and have the appropriate spans of control to manage their people, then whether the service is good now or not, it will be in the future. A key objective of any programme is to help these supervisors to coach their people and demonstrate to them what the experience should be. If you can motivate these people to deliver your message to the front line on a daily basis you will succeed.

Invest in tools that will help supervisors direct their people to deliver the right experience.

## Attack beliefs

Organisations that take the customer experience truly to heart are able to make changes that positively affect the very DNA of that company. However, to achieve this you almost always need to attack and shift one or two of the core beliefs of the organisation. People take their cues about what is important from a wide range of formal and informal sources (just like customers!).The following model shows how many different factors shape these beliefs. You really need to address all of them.

In thinking about each of these, think about how these get the organisation to behave. It will give you a clue as to which ones are causing the most problems. What gaps do you have? What do we need to do personally?

### Figure 7.2.14  **Cultural model**

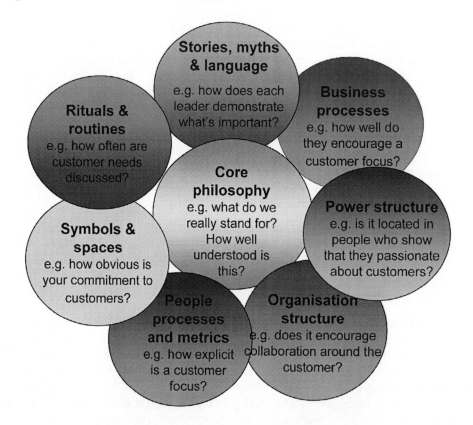

Adapted From: Johnson G, and Scholes K, Exploring Corporate Strategy, Prentice Hall, 1999

You've thought now about the beliefs that are driving the wrong behaviours in the organisation. One of the most effective ways to build momentum in an organisation is, early on, to find what we like to call a 'dramatic symbol of change'.

Figure 7.2.15 **Dramatic symbols of change**

| Makes a difference for customers | Attacks staff belief system |
|---|---|
| Manifestly supports distinct experience | Puts money on bottom line |

In response to declining customer satisfaction scores, a large home shopping company established a cross-functional customer experience team. Early meetings were interesting but you could tell that the body of senior managers assembled didn't really believe the organisation was serious. The belief, built from management decisions over the last few years, was that commercial considerations always overrode customer considerations. They made a list of the key things driving complaints and dissatisfaction. This included the perennial issue of the opaque wording on invoices that didn't label credit charges as clearly as they should. When this was raised, the director in charge 'couldn't understand the hesitation' and simply instructed the change. This small and seemingly irrelevant change was a clear symbol of change. The news 'leaked' out of the group and went a long way to attacking the belief.

What's your dramatic symbol of change that will convince your sceptics that your change programme is serious?

### *Maintain momentum*

Too many customer focus programmes are one-hit wonders that are great when they get kicked off but quickly dissipate once real business issues start to apply pressure. The key is to sustain the activities we discussed earlier in this section and embed the programme into key organisational processes. This always requires an ongoing internal engagement programme that is tailored to the various audiences.

When the author led the drive to 'world-class customer service' for Mobil across Europe, we developed a very simple mantra. Start right, right from the start. You'll remember American Express used this to describe the customer experience and it's no surprise that the employee experience is built on similar principles. You might not have responsibility for HR policies and processes but influencing them is really important if you are going to positively change over the long term.

**HR checklist: have you changed or influenced the following?**

✔  **Recruitment profiles**

✔  **Competencies and behaviours**

✔  **Job descriptions**

✔  **Training and induction programmes**
    **(for front-line staff and team managers)**

✔  **Task and role design**

✔  **The employee joining experience**

✔  **The reward and recognition systems**

✔  **Coaching and appraisal processes**


A brave way, to ensure that there can be no retreat, is to make your commitment visible to customers.

AAMI, an Australian insurer, has a great approach to sustaining its commitment to continuous improvement of the customer experience. It publishes a customer charter that sets out what customers can expect from AAMI. If AAMI breaches any of its commitments it compensates its customers with a $30 payment. The majority of these payments are actually initiated by staff rather than customers. Now in its tenth year, the charter sends a clear message to customers and staff that the brand is committed to doing what it says it will.

**Have you embedded the five principles in your programme?**

✔  **Bring customers alive**

✔  **Make it real for me**

✔  **Align, lead and direct**

✔  **Attack beliefs**

✔  **Maintain momentum**

# Conclusions

There are five 'must do's'

1. **Bring the current experience alive**
   Find creative and financial ways to bring home both the pain of the current experience and the opportunity if it is improved.

2. **Ground the vision**
   Establish a blueprint. Be clear about what the organisation is trying to achieve, what role the experience plays in these goals and what the barriers are to its achievement. Paint a picture of what the future might look like and get the senior team to sign up to the direction.

3. **Mobilise the organisation around priority customers and journeys**
   Carefully determine where maximum impact can be attained for customers, employees and the business and set up a cross-functional team to map these touchpoints and journeys and determine detailed solutions.

4. **Fix the basics and deliver quick wins**
   Remove the 'dissatisfiers' first and get the basics right. Ensure that you find some dramatic symbols of change that make a difference to customers and really attack existing beliefs.

5. **Enable your staff to deliver**
   Focus on the elements that prevent staff delivering the experience you want and remove them. Review and change metrics to align with what you want. Involve and engage staff in designing solutions.

Figure 7.2.16 should help as a good aide-memoire for you in designing and delivering your new customer experience.

### Figure 7.2.16  **Top 10 principles to guide your customer experience design**

1. Customers - be clear what you want customers to think, feel and say as a result.

2. Focus and differentiate - focus on highest value/potential customers first.

3. Moments of truth - all interactions are not created equal: some are more important in driving commitment than others - focus on these.

4. Events - think about clusters of touchpoints.

5. Hygiene before delight - fix the rotten things first. If you can't, be brilliant at service recovery.

6. Brand - amplify your unique brand through embedding brand values and customer experience principles into touchpoints.

7. The experience does not have to be expensive to be good.

8. Think big, start small - you might want to re-engineer your experience in its entirety but you can improve it immediately tomorrow.

9. Outcome-focused - make sure it changes how you manage your customers. The project must be customer outcome-focused with agreed milestones.

10. Address beliefs - to change both consumer and employee behaviours we must address beliefs.

Further reading:

1.    National Consumer Council Survey. The stupid company. How British businesses throw away money by alienating consumers, Philip Cullum, 2006. www.ncc.org.uk

2.    *State of the nation IV*: QCi www.qci.co.uk

3.    *The New Bottom Line*, Alan Mitchell et al.

4.    *How Customers Think, Essential Insights into the mind of the market*, Gerald Zaltman, Harvard Business School Press, 2003

5.    *Clued In: how to keep customers coming back again and again*, Lewis P. Carbone, FT Prentice Hall, 2004

6.    *Simply Better, Winning and keeping customers by delivering what matters most*, Patrick Barwise and Sean Meehan, Harvard Business School Press, 2004

7.    Milligan, A. and Smith, S., *Uncommon Practice: People Who Deliver a Great Brand Experience*, Prentice Hall 2002

8.    Johnson G, and Scholes K, *Exploring Corporate Strategy*, Prentice Hall, 1999

# Retention and loyalty: how do your customers measure up?

## This chapter includes:

- ❏ **What is loyalty?**

- ❏ **Why is measuring retention and loyalty important?**

- ❏ **What are you trying to retain?**

- ❏ **Who are you trying to retain?**

- ❏ **The importance of potential value**

- ❏ **The impact of digital marketing and the internet**

## About this chapter

**I**n this chapter we look at retention and loyalty – in the first instance at five different types of loyalty, only the last of which is truly significant. We consider why it is important to measure loyalty; how to distinguish those customers we should be trying to retain, and the importance of potential (or lifetime) value. We look at the concept of REAP planning (Retention, Efficiency, Acquisition, Penetration). We consider the concept (introduced by Peppers and Rogers) of Return on Customer (ROC as distinct from ROI), and finally we examine the impact of the internet on the practicalities of measuring and enhancing customer loyalty in order to provide for the retention of our most valuable customers.

## Mark Say M IDM

Tel: 07799 065762
E-mail: mark.say@qci.co.uk

Mark is a senior consultant within the QCi network and is a CMAT™ instructor and assessor. Prior to his consulting work, Mark had a broad range of experience gathered primarily in blue-chip sales and marketing departments, including Hyundai, American Express, Yellow Pages and Freemans mail order. He has worked in both B2B and B2C and has over 17 years of direct marketing experience.

Over the last five years, Mark has worked primarily for business-to-business clients, especially in commercial insurance and support services, where he has led projects involved with customer analytics and insight generation, defining customer strategy, segmentation, developing propositions, creating innovative contact strategies and helping clients launch and implement tactics designed to drive and retain customer value and advocacy. He has led consultancy engagements all over the world including the United States, Scandinavia, the Far East and Latin America.

# Chapter 7.3

# Retention and loyalty: How do your customers measure up?

## Introduction

"A fuzzy sense of what matters is far more important than a precise calculation of the irrelevant."

Tim Ambler (Senior Fellow, London Business School)

Historically, marketers have frustrated managing directors and finance directors by being unable to prove which half of their marketing budget actually works! Apart from causing frustration and minimising accountability, it has been one of the main reasons why marketing's credibility around the Boardroom table has been low and why so few marketing-orientated individuals have gone onto the most senior positions in the world's biggest companies – only 11 of the FTSE 100 companies have marketing representation on their Board (Marketing; December 2005).

In direct marketing, quantification has been part of the discipline's stock in trade. The very real danger for direct marketers is the other side of the coin – too often 'analysis paralysis' sets in as testing and control groups seem to be more important than the real reason why the campaign is being put together. The balance between the commercial objectives of the campaign and worthwhile, meaningful testing and measurement is too often lost.

The great news is that technological advances now allow all organisations to manage their most important source of profit – their customers – much more efficiently and effectively (and in most cases for the very first time). Unfortunately, as QCi's CMAT™ benchmarking assessments continue to show, 'knowledge of good customer management techniques and practices is not widespread'[1].

# What is loyalty?

A newly appointed customer retention manager in an automotive company in the UK was just starting to brief the director of a marketing research agency on some work, so that a retention programme could start to be constructed. The rather prickly researcher shot back a question that left the poor retention manager scrabbling for an answer, as he realised with a rising sense of panic that he had not really thought it through enough. The question she asked was:

"What does 'loyalty' mean...to you?"

Was a little old lady who had owned and driven her car for 15 years more or less loyal than the family man that religiously changed his car every three years and bought the same brand every time?

Certainly, both the little old lady and the family man would both perceive themselves as extremely loyal customers, but what was the car company's point of view? Let's see what you think by the end of this chapter.

Before attempting to measure the loyalty and retention of customers, you must be able to have a 'single view of the customer' – in other words, you must know how much each customer spends with your company across all its products and services. If you only have transactional information on one product or service then you are effectively measuring product retention and not customer retention.

This does not mean that you have to spend £millions on a CRM system, as it is feasible (in the short term) to take an analytical single view by gathering the relevant data together offline, and if you work for a company that only has one product or service then your product retention measure will be your customer retention figure (and cross-sell may be a bit difficult).

## The five types of loyalty

As we can see in the simplistic example of the little old lady and the family man above, loyalty means different things to different people. Likewise different organisations mean different things when they refer to loyalty.

Consider your own organisation – which of the following five different types of loyalty is relevant to your organisation?

- Fake/artificial loyalty

- Inertia/lazy loyalty

- Price-/incentive-based loyalty

- Fashion-led loyalty

- True loyalty

Let's consider some of the differences between these types.

### Fake/artificial loyalty

Angus Jenkinson puts forward the case of the East German carmaker Brabant. In mid-1989, Brabant had a 19-year waiting list. However, within three months of the fall of the Berlin Wall, Brabant was bankrupt. East German necessity might look like loyalty, but it certainly doesn't feel like it and when finally customers did get the opportunity to benefit from genuine choice, they displayed their true sense of loyalty by cancelling their orders.

Included in this type of loyalty is what others have called 'monopoly loyalty'. Certain airline and train operators may feel that they have wonderfully loyal customers due to the fact that the 'planes and trains are so full and evidently in demand. However, certain routes (especially local commuter routes around London in the train company scenario) are operating as a monopoly and in these instances customers have no choice but to be 'loyal' to the supplier. Perhaps, as Chris Daffy suggests, these customers should be called more accurately 'hostages'!

Other organisations, such as the Royal Mail, are such a part of our lives that even though their market has opened up to much greater competition this year, it is not possible that either consumers or businesses will stop using all the Royal Mail's products and services totally. So what would loyalty mean to the Royal Mail? Perhaps loyalty must be centred around customers continuing to use certain key product lines and services.

### Inertia/lazy loyalty

This type of loyalty takes place when obstacles exist (or are created) that make switching suppliers difficult or inconvenient. One of those obstacles may even be because customers can't be bothered to try and find an alternative. Customers will stay 'loyal' until they are either so dissatisfied that they are willing to overcome the 'pain' of changing supplier or until a new entrant comes into the marketplace and takes some or all of that 'pain' away.

New online banking entrants have taken most of the pain out of switching bank accounts by offering to handle the changeover of all direct debits and standing orders from the customer's existing provider into their new current account. Companies, such as Intelligent Finance, have made this a key part of their customer proposition.

### Price-/incentive-based loyalty

Not all customers are the same. In any market, there will be those customers who buy purely on price (but it is not as big a proportion as some people might have you believe). As long as your price is the lowest, then this type of customer will be 'loyal', but as soon as somebody undercuts your price, these customers will start to switch.

Chris Daffy cites Kwik Save as a good example. As soon as the likes of Aldi, Costco and Lidl appeared in the UK in the late 1980s, he maintains that price-loyal customers then switched their allegiance.

Loyalty cards do offer an incentive for a customer's loyalty and as some commentators have suggested a few customers will become 'loyal' to the loyalty scheme rather than the company running it. However, in the longer term, it must be remembered that loyalty schemes are only a mechanic and must be viewed as part of an overall package of initiatives and focus on the customer. In the 1990s, the UK press produced comparison tables and articles comparing the different rewards of different schemes – this does not happen any more. As the creators of the rightly much-vaunted Tesco Clubcard point out:

"No one would contend that a card-based loyalty scheme is a credible alternative to being the right price, offering excellent service, innovative products and customer care — because any business that neglects factors like these is extremely unlikely to have long-term success in achieving customer loyalty. Innovative customer care programmes offering services that customers want will develop loyalty. The important point is that these initiatives and a card-based loyalty scheme are not mutually exclusive."

*Humby, Clive, Terry Hunt and Tim Phillips; 2003; Scoring Points; London: Kogan Page; p17*

## Fashion-led loyalty

The latest trends and fashions create a loyalty of their own; the trouble is that it tends to be ephemeral. The amazing rise of the Burberry label in the last five years is a case in point and it will be interesting to see how the management of the brand contend with its downmarket associations that have rapidly built up.

In the early 1990s, Sol lager was all the rage (drunk from the bottle with a wedge of lemon pushed down its neck), but the brand has now lost favour and custom.

The owners of Tie Rack must be praying that the current male business trend for not wearing ties will disappear soon!

## True loyalty

True loyalty is when, even in the face of many competitors (some of whom may be offering advantageous incentives and may be making it very easy to switch), the customer is willing to continue buying and buy more from the company that they are loyal to over a long period of time. They are 'bonded' and are advocates of the brand.

It is this type of loyalty that this chapter focuses on, because if a company manages to achieve this type of loyalty with its customers, then it replaces and supersedes all the other four types of loyalty.

## *The two axes of loyalty*

As you have already seen, loyalty is a complex beast and it is not always synonymous with satisfaction levels. There are two further factors that you need to take into account:

- Behavioural loyalty

- Attitudinal loyalty

**Behavioural loyalty** is the name given to the actions and behaviours that a customer can exhibit that demonstrates loyalty. It means that the customer behaves in the way that the brand wants, e.g. spending money; we will consider the many and various measures of behavioural loyalty later on in this chapter.

**Attitudinal loyalty** is the term given to the attitude, feelings and emotions felt by the customer towards the brand, be it satisfaction, delight, hate, apathy or advocacy. This is covered a little in chapter 7.1 and a lot more in chapter 7.2 on 'Customer Experience'.

## Figure 7.3.1 **The two axes of loyalty**

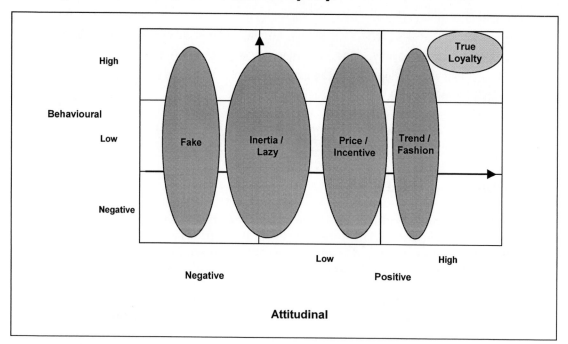

Angus Jenkinson captured the dynamic between these two aspects of loyalty very neatly when he wrote:

"Perceptions and emotions drive behaviour. Loyalty involves customer behaviour and depends on customer attitudes: what they think and feel and do in relation to your brand or service."

## Customer loyalty's 'golden nuggets'

There are certain 'truisms' that have been proven time and again across all types of industry. Don't try to re-prove them; accept them, build them into your business cases and allow them to steer and guide your thinking. They are:

- **Loyal customers are assets** – Doyle reports that a customer who generates a cash flow of £1,000 in its first year is likely to have a net present value of approximately £50,000 if retained over 10 years.

- **Loyal customers are more profitable** – they buy more of the company's products, are less costly to serve, are less sensitive to price and bring in new customers.

- **Winning new customers is expensive** – it can cost up to six times as much to acquire a new customer as to retain an existing customer.

- **Increasing retention has a dramatic effect** – increasing customer retention by as little as five per cent can double the lifetime value of customers.

- **'Delighted' customers repurchase; merely satisfied customers do not** – delighted customers are six times more likely to remain loyal than those who merely rate themselves as satisfied. The advocates tell others.

- **Dissatisfied customers tell other people** – and unfortunately, they tend to tell two to three times as many people as those who are delighted!

- **Most dissatisfied customers do not complain** – for every complaint received another 26 customers will have had a problem and about six will have had a serious problem.

- **Handling and resolving complaints well increases loyalty** – those who have a complaint handled well and resolved to a customer's satisfaction tend to be more loyal than those who never had a problem.

- **Few customers defect due to poor product performance** – two-thirds of customers leave due to indifferent or inaccessible service people.

Source: Peter Doyle; (2000) Value-Based Marketing; Chichester: John Wiley

# Why is measuring retention and loyalty important?

If the 'golden nuggets' of customer loyalty above weren't enough reason for measuring loyalty and retention, then let us consider the following aspects that reinforce why measuring retention and loyalty is critical.

> "Profit does not come from products or service. They are the vehicles through which it is created, but the profit comes from whoever is found to pay more for them than the cost. That obviously is the customer."
>
> *Chris Daffy, Consultant and Author*

## Driving customer value through REAP

There are only four levers that you can pull in order to drive customer value or profit – they are:

- **R**etention

- **E**fficiency around costs

- **A**cquisition

- **P**enetration

Try this exercise in setting REAP objectives and targets:

---

**Let us say that your company has the following characteristics:**

**This year:**

- Turnover: £10 million
- Fixed and variable costs: £2 million
- Number of customers: 10,000
- Retention rate: 65 per cent

**In your plan for next year:**

**Show how you would get *higher* turnover and *profit* from fewer customers using all elements of a REAP framework:**

- Costs don't change.
- Retention can only improve to 70 per cent

**See a worked-through example at the end of this chapter.**

---

REAP is an extremely powerful concept and one that most organisations still do not grasp fully. Your ability to measure retention is at the core of your organisation's ability to drive its business performance. Here is a thought that people should realise but don't:

If your retention rate is lower than 50 per cent, your company is, at best, treading water or, at worst, about to drown!

That's a bit alarmist, isn't it? Well, no. If you are losing more customers than you are retaining, then the third 'truism' in the 'golden nuggets' of loyalty should be borne in mind, as you are likely to be disproportionately dependent on acquisition – acquisition is painfully expensive.

A mail order company in the UK had a retention rate below 50 per cent and had just managed to achieve revenue growth over a five-year period (which kept the city happy), but was looking at making a loss for the first time in living memory. The marketing budget had risen from £28 million per annum to nearly £80 million in that period and was totally focused on acquiring new customers or reacquiring its old customers who had lapsed. A real case of throwing mud at the wall and hoping that some of it sticks!

The only time that a retention rate of less than 50 per cent is acceptable is when you are actively trying to manage specific customers out of low-value segments – and the main learning point should be is that you are managing this and not reacting to it.

"Shareholder value is determined by the company's growth rate and its ability to achieve an operating margin above its threshold level. For most companies, customer loyalty is the single most important determinant of long-term growth and profit margins."

*Peter Doyle, Professor of Marketing and Strategic Management,*
*University of Warwick Business School*

OK – hopefully none of that will have come as too much of a surprise to you. However, this may well do so:

**63 per cent of companies still do not measure retention rates and ...**

**Only 19 per cent of companies understand and apply lifetime value measurement**

Woodcock, Neil, Merlin Stone and Bryan Foss (2003) The Customer Management Scorecard: Managing CRM for Profit; London: Kogan Page; page 50

These facts are shocking in their own right, but when you consider this next section, you will start to see why not measuring these metrics could be considered negligent – if shareholders knew how much profit is being lost because companies are mismanaging their customers, the AGM would become quite interesting! Perhaps it is as well that the majority of Board directors are unable to quantify this lost opportunity, because if they were able to, they would have some very serious questions to answer

## The growth/margin multiplier effect or 'The Loyalty Effect'

If the effect of customer loyalty on growth is high, the effect on operating profits is extraordinary. Frederick Reichheld in The Loyalty Effect identifies six reasons why loyal customers are more profitable:

1. **Acquisition cost** – obtaining new customers is more expensive as we have already seen and Reichheld has estimated that it is typically a ratio of 6:1.

2. **Base profit** – base profit is the earning on purchases before allowing for loyalty effects – therefore the longer the customer is retained, the greater the total sum of annual base profits.

3. **Revenue growth** – loyal customers will increase their spending over time. As trust increases and they get to learn more about the company they are then more inclined to spend with it.

4. **Operating costs** – as customers become more loyal the cost to serve them decreases.

5. **Referrals** – customers who become advocates become a very important source of new business.

6. **Price premium** – loyal customers are normally less price conscious than new customers. The new customers may have had to be attracted by discounted offers/prices.

If we call increasing retention rate the growth effect and the impact of loyal customers' spending over a longer period of time the margin effect, when you combine the two together – in other words, holding onto more of your most profitable customers for longer – magic starts to happen!

As you hold onto more of your customers each year (the growth effect), their 'customer lifetime value' or CLV (how much profit you make from them over time – covered later on in this chapter) is almost certain to increase as well (the margin effect). As you multiply the two together the results can be startling. For example:

- Increasing the retention rate from 90 to 95 per cent in a moderate growth market would increase the number of customers by 55 per cent over a ten-year period. This is the growth effect.

- In addition, the average duration that a customer stays with the business would double and their average lifetime value would grow by 84 per cent. This is the margin effect.

- The net result is to almost treble the value of the business.

| Value with 90 per cent retention | | Value with 95 per cent retention | |
|---|---|---|---|
| Customers | 100,000 | Customers | 155,000 |
| Average CLV | £280 | Average CLV | £515 |
| Business value | £28 million | Business value | £80 million |

Peter Doyle, Professor of Marketing and Strategic Management,
University of Warwick Business School

If further evidence were required as to why measuring retention and loyalty is so critical, please refer to QCi's State of the Nation IV report, chapters 1 and 2 (www.qci.co.uk).

So, why is measuring retention and customer loyalty important? Because if you are not measuring and in control of these metrics, your business is more likely to be seriously underperforming.

## *What are you trying to retain?*

"Where there is less emphasis on quantification, there is more wastage.
In marketing, the unwatched kettle never boils."

*Graeme McCorkell, Author, Consultant and ex-Chairman of the IDM*

At first sight, the title of this section might appear a bit strange. However, it is critical to appreciate and understand what the facets of customer behaviour/ attitude are that we are trying to get more of, repeat, hold onto for longer and maximise (or minimise).

Certain measures will have greater resonance in particular industries and some sectors will have their own particular 'quirks'. You need to think through what your measures will be and how you will measure them. Some may be difficult to measure, but you have to know the impact that your sales, marketing and service activity is having.

Let's work through the possibilities (see figure 7.2.2). But before we do, it is worth restating that:

You must measure *customers* and not products or services.

On numerous occasions, during feedback sessions at the end of a CMAT™ assessment, the directors of XYZ company have asserted that they do measure customer retention. They are then somewhat shocked when it is pointed out to them that they are actually measuring policy retention, account retention, service retention or some such product-siloed measure.

## Behavioural measures of loyalty

Figure 7.3.2    **Behavioural measures of loyalty**

| Measure | Notes | Remarks |
|---------|-------|---------|
| **FRAC measures** | Frequency of purchases<br><br>Recency of last purchase<br><br>Amount of purchase (both as volume and margin)<br><br>Category of product | These are the very basic foundation stones of any retentative measurement. They are used to monitor any significant volume changes both in the short term (such as order frequency) and the longer term (such as year-on-year changes).<br><br>Frequency and recency measures are key in industries such as retail and mail order. |
| **Repurchase rate** (often most associated with what is termed retention rate) | This often needs thinking through in more detail – how does this measure apply to your industry?<br><br>Does it? | E.g. in the automotive industry, the repurchase cycle may be a number of years – so although this is a key measure, you would still need to measure what is going on in the interim. How much are they continuing to spend with you on servicing/ parts/accessories/repairs/ insurance/finance?<br><br>Another issue in the automotive industry is being able to measure repurchase rate. You know when a customer sells their car and buys again from you, but you will struggle to know how many customers have sold their car and then bought another marque. |
| **Number of customers** | This may appear too basic, but some companies do struggle to be able to define what a customer actually is! Too often the automotive Industry confuses cars for customers. The driver may not be the person who actually paid for the car.<br><br>A 'customer' could be a named policyholder, a user of the product, an intermediary, a broker, a partner or a corporate organisation. | NB: You may have a 100 per cent customer retention rate but your business will still be in terminal decline if:<br><br>They are not increasing their spend with you<br><br>You are not managing the cost to serve your customers<br><br>You are not acquiring new customers<br><br>Therefore 'number of customers' is a basic but essential measure.<br><br>Do you know how many your business has?  Has the number increased or decreased over the last 12 months?  Was the increase/decrease planned or did it just happen?  Did you acquire the right type? |

| Measure | Notes | Remarks |
|---|---|---|
| **Average value of each customer** | This measure is too often overlooked. When analysts and CEOs focus on customer metrics they usually quote satisfaction, churn and numbers of customers, but rarely average value.<br><br>At worst this could be average revenue per customer, but ideally this should be profit per customer. | NB: Number of customers x average value/customer = operating profit.<br><br>Therefore, a fundamental metric has to be how much you have managed to increase the average value of your existing customer base.<br><br>E.g. as a basic first step in the insurance industry, value must be gross written premium (across all policies) less claims (across all policies) – in this industry, it is critical to be looking at a basic profit measure such as the impact of claims on customer profitability. |
| **Average number of products per customer** | This is sometimes a proxy measure for average value/customer.<br><br>Simplistically, it may be a useful measure of cross-selling success or failure.<br><br>Make sure however that your products are relevant to the customer (see remarks column)<br><br>In companies with a lot of products, increasing higher margin product uptake could be a worthwhile measure. | A direct personal insurance company in the UK set its people the goal of increasing cross-sales and plans on measuring success by the average number of products held by each customer. Primarily, they had a motor insurance product and a home insurance product.<br><br>The problem was that the motor product was for safer, older drivers and the home product was designed for first-time buyers.<br><br>Unsurprisingly, the underwriters refused almost all the first-time buyer customers' motor insurance and customers were left wondering whether the left hand knew what the right was up to! |
| **Stamina or tenure** | Either the number of purchases a customer would make before dropping out…<br><br>Or, the length of time that a customer has been a customer. | Stamina – book clubs and continuity series marketers (such as collectibles) tend to use this measure.<br><br>Think of the little old lady driver at the beginning of this chapter. |
| **Cost to serve/cost to retain** | This is often put in the 'too difficult to do' box by marketers.<br><br>Without appropriate systems or any activity-based costing this will be difficult, but rough estimates are better than nothing at all. | There are three points to note here:<br><br>Don't aim to attribute cost to each customer down to the nearest penny; to the nearest £50 or £100 will do in the short to medium term.<br><br>Remember that you can refine and improve your precision over time.<br><br>Don't just do nothing. |

| Measure | Notes | Remarks |
|---|---|---|
| **Share of business/ wallet** | This is a good measure of the potential or the headroom of a customer.<br><br>Again it is perceived by some as difficult to find the information, but although various clever proxies may exist, it is often wisest just to ask the customer – you would be amazed at what they are prepared to tell you! | In the automotive industry, this is referred to as 'share of garage'. This is an attempt to think at a household level in order to identify where the potential exists.<br><br>With B2B customers, an annual account review is an excellent place to gather this information, but too often the information remains in sales and does not permeate through to marketing.<br><br>In intermediated industries, this is a critical measure – there is no point pouring investment into an intermediary in order to maximise your share of their business if you already have close to 100 per cent of it. Instead you would want to help them grow their business, in order to expand yours, which is a very different business strategy. |
| **Current value** | Some 'experts' call this 'net present value'. However, what we mean here is the sum of all the profits and any losses that the customer has made for your company since they first started trading with you to the present day. | This measure takes into account the profit/losses generated and the tenure of the customer.<br><br>Therefore it takes into account historical value plus profits generated and expected in the current year. |
| **Potential value:(net present value and lifetime value)** | Different academic experts and authors seem to contradict and confuse these metrics.<br><br>Some suggest an overly simplistic extrapolation of current value over a reasonable period of time…to vastly complex equations that use discounted cash flow, fully allocated cash flow or marginal cash flows etc.<br><br>Whatever method you choose to employ, remember three principles:<br><br>You are attempting to predict which customers hold the most potential value to you…<br><br>So that you can prioritise which customers to target and…<br><br>Understand how much to invest in retaining them or acquiring customers like them. | The other factor to remember is that, as this is a prediction of the future and of potential, the only certainty is that you will be wrong…or at least not 100 per cent correct!<br><br>Therefore, exercise good commercial judgement as to how much effort and resource you are willing to put into determining this metric. Do not try to be too precise but at the same time, too simplistic an approach will only wash for so long.<br><br>The only other definite is: you must work your way towards this measure. You must be able to understand where to invest, which customers to prioritise and how much to invest – otherwise it is like driving a car while looking in the rear-view mirror all the time – you must be able to see where you are going or you will crash sooner rather than later! |

| Measure | Notes | Remarks |
|---------|-------|---------|
| | | For a full discussion of CLV, see chapter 3.5. For an excellent (and detailed) discussion see the Peter Doyle and Don Peppers' books in 'further reading/references'.<br><br>The only other factor to remember is that you should take into account the time value of money – in other words a pound now is worth more than a pound in the future. Again an excellent interpretation of discounting and the value of future cash flows can be found in Appendix 1 of Don Peppers and Martha Rogers' *Return on Customer*.<br><br>Some people get wary of the term 'lifetime' – if you prefer, call it 'long-term value' and perhaps the metric might appear less daunting. The main factor is that you are looking forward over a commercially reasonable period of time. |

## Attitudinal measures of loyalty

- 95 per cent of companies collect customer feedback

- 30 per cent make decisions using this insight

- 10 per cent deploy those decisions and improve

These findings are taken from research carried out by ResponseTek, who produce software that captures customer experience feedback. So most companies do measure customer satisfaction, few learn from it and even fewer then do anything about it. Again, this is probably not any great surprise to you.

Until recently, the main customer attitudinal measures have been limited to customer satisfaction measurement, and the word 'limited' is probably very appropriate.

As we have seen in other chapters, customer satisfaction is often misused and does not predict repeat purchase, retention or loyalty.

### When should customer satisfaction be used?

Every interaction between a customer and your company is a touchpoint. Some touchpoints are more important to the customer than others and can be determined as critical points in the relationship when the customer will really judge your performance.

These are called 'Moments of Truth'.

In defining your proposed customer experience (chapter 7.2) one aspect you will focus on is how you will handle these moments of truth.

Ongoing customer satisfaction research is a good method of measuring how well your specified customer experience is being delivered at these critical customer touchpoints and other key events.

For example, in most industries, handling customer complaints and dissatisfaction is almost certainly a moment of truth. Measuring customer satisfaction upon resolution of the complaint would be a good use of this type of attitudinal measure.

## Customer commitment and advocacy

It is worth bringing out a number of recent findings by Marsden, Samson and Upton:

- Customers enjoying higher levels of word-of-mouth advocacy (higher net promoter scores), such as HSBC, Asda, Honda and O2, grew faster than their competitors in the period 2003/2004

- Every one-point increase in net promoter score correlated with an £8.8 million increase in sales for the average business in their analysis

- A one per cent reduction in negative word of mouth would lead to £24.8 million additional revenue

- Companies with high advocacy rates grew four times as fast in 2004 as companies with low advocacy rates

Marsden, Dr. Paul; Alain Samson & Neville Upton, (2005) *Advocacy Drives Growth: Customer Advocacy Drives UK Business Growth*; Accepted for publication in Brand Strategy: Nov/Dec 2005; distributed on www.insightexec.com March 2006

Customer commitment does seem to have a clear link to business performance and both satisfaction and commitment will drive some of the behavioural metrics outlined above.

Commitment derives from a combination of functional and emotional experiences at the customer touchpoints and it is harder to achieve if the customer is not satisfied, not involved with the product or service and perceives the competition to be the same or better than your organisation.

Best practice companies measure both customer satisfaction and customer commitment.

# Who are you trying to retain?

Not all customers are the same.

However, most organisations that do not practice customer management seem to assume that they are. They tend to manage to the lowest common denominator.

Most organisations invest roughly the same amount of money on each customer. They may be aware of their biggest few customers and invest a little more there (see figure 7.2.3.), but that is only because they feel they have to (or the customer has demanded it!).

## Good customer management 'tilts the line'

Figure 7.3.3    **Tilting the line**

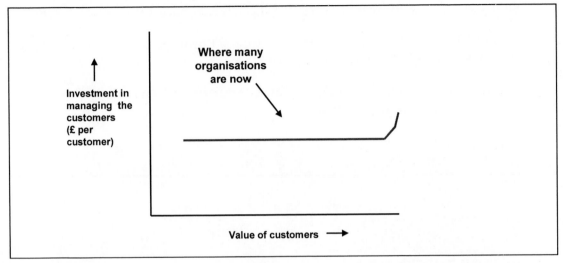

Source: QCi Assessment Ltd

In the diagram above, this is sometimes called 'hockey stick' investment for obvious reasons – what customer management tries to do is 'tilt the line': so the higher value customer may receive more investment, but most importantly, the lower value customers are managed more cost-effectively (see figure 7.2.4.). Good customer management should be as near to cost-neutral as possible.

Figure 7.3.4    **What good customer management tries to achieve**

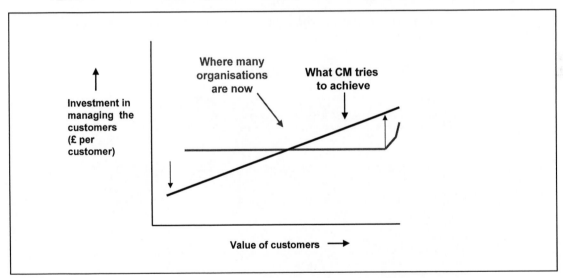

Source: QCi Assessment Ltd

So not all customers are the same. Firstly you have to understand what 'shape' your customer base is in.

## Decile analysis

Too few marketers in too few organisations use this very simple technique to analyse their customers. You could use quartiles (four) or quintiles (five), but the maths gets really easy when you use deciles!

Firstly you have to rank your customers in order – in order of spend (if determining how much profit each customer makes your company is too difficult at present) – then divide your base into ten divisions.

So if you had 10,000 customers, each division would have 1,000 customers in it.

This example of a decile analysis is taken from a European oil lubricants company – they did not know this information.

## Figure 7.3.5 Decile analysis for European lubricants organisation

Report 001 - Decile Analysis On Margin
==============================

Reporting Period : 199507 for 12 months.
Selected Customer Classification Type : Primary Classification Code

| Dec | No of Customers | Total Margin | % of Total | Cum Margin | Cum % of Total | Average Value of Customer | No of Trans- actions | Average No of Trans- actions per Cust | Average Value of Trans- actions |
|---|---|---|---|---|---|---|---|---|---|
| 1 | 229 | 72548471 | 63 | 72548471 | 63 | 316806 | 42387 | 185 | 1712 |
| 2 | 229 | 17946713 | 16 | 90495184 | 79 | 78370 | 12772 | 56 | 1405 |
| 3 | 229 | 10086663 | 9 | 100581847 | 87 | 44047 | 8989 | 39 | 1122 |
| 4 | 229 | 6454351 | 6 | 107036198 | 93 | 28185 | 6874 | 30 | 939 |
| 5 | 229 | 4159540 | 4 | 111195738 | 97 | 18164 | 4682 | 20 | 888 |
| 6 | 229 | 2508023 | 2 | 113703761 | 99 | 10952 | 2979 | 13 | 842 |
| 7 | 229 | 1324798 | 1 | 115028559 | 100 | 5785 | 1741 | 8 | 761 |
| 8 | 229 | 628358 | 1 | 115656917 | 100 | 2744 | 974 | 4 | 645 |
| 9 | 229 | 171566 | 0 | 115828483 | 101 | 749 | 520 | 2 | 330 |
| 10 | 235 | -625399 | -1 | 115203084 | 100 | -2661 | 230 | 1 | -2719 |
| | 2296 | 115203084 | | | | 82148 | 36 | | 1402 |

They were even more surprised when the customer attrition rate was plotted by each customer decile:

## Figure 7.3.6 Attrition rate by decile

**Report 005 - Decile Analysis of Attrition**
==================================

| Decile | |
|---|---|
| 1 (largest) | => 3% |
| 2 | => 5% |
| 3 | => 6% |
| 4 | => 15% |
| 5 | => 19% |
| 6 | => 22% |
| 7 | => 4% |
| 8 | => 3% |
| 9 | => 3% |
| 10 (smallest) | => 20% |

The analysis showed that the company was holding onto its most valuable customers; its least valuable customers were leaving; but customers in deciles 4, 5 and 6 were leaving disproportionately. An investigation quickly showed that a competitor was offering incentives to less bonded customers.

Decile analysis really comes into its own when it is produced graphically. The following decile graph shows a general insurer in the B2B marketplace in the UK.

Figure 7.3.7    **Graphic representation of decile analysis**

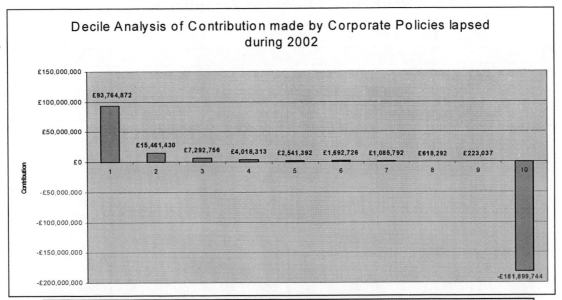

> Decile Analysis of Contribution made by Corporate Policies lapsed during 2002

**Between 1999 & 2001 the bottom 10% of customers wiped out the profit of the other 90%!**

Once you know which customers are producing your profit and which are losing you money, you can start to use REAP planning to manage customer value and drive business performance. Decile analysis is a very simple and effective tool that will start to show you who you want to retain.

## Differentiation produces yet more financial magic!

Earlier on in this chapter, we covered the extraordinary impact that the growth effect and the margin effect have on longer-term business performance in a company that manages to hold onto its most profitable customers for longer. That was at an overall business level.

The growth/margin multiplier is even more apparent, but this time in the short to medium term, when REAP strategies are applied using 'differentiation' within the customer base.

The best example of this can be seen below in figure 7.2.8. A European telecom company worked with QCi to determine the impact of REAP strategies on their customer base at a decile level. The effect was extraordinary.

By tweaking performance at a decile level, profits would double over three years!

Figure 7.3.8 **REAP target table for European telco**

| REAP Target table. Figures THEN (year 0) vs. TARGET (year 3) | | | | | | | | | | |
|---|---|---|---|---|---|---|---|---|---|---|
| | Retention | | | | Efficiency | | Acquisition | Penetration | | |
| Decile | Attrition % *₁ | | Satisfaction % *₂ | | CTS *₃ | | % of customers acquired *₄ | SOW% *₅ | | |
| | Then | Target | Then | Target | Then | Target | | | Then | Target |
| 1 | 3 | 2.5 | 85 | 98 | £300 | £400 | 20% | | 50% | 60% |
| 2 | 5 | 3.5 | 85 | 98 | £250 | £350 | 20% | | 40% | 60% |
| 3 | 5 | 3 | 85 | 97 | £250 | £350 | 20% | | 30% | 55% |
| 4 | 8 | 5.5 | 85 | 95 | £250 | £300 | 10% | | 30% | 50% |
| 5 | 10 | 8 | 85 | 90 | £250 | £300 | 10% | | 30% | 30% |
| 6 | 15 | 15 | 85 | 88 | £250 | £200 | 5% | | 30% | 25% |
| 7 | 26 | 30 | 85 | 88 | £250 | £100 | 5% | | 30% | 25% |
| 8 | 25 | 30 | 85 | 86 | £250 | £100 | 5% | | 30% | 25% |
| 9 | 28 | 35 | 85 | 85 | £250 | £50 | 3% | | 30% | 10% |
| 10 | 40 | 48 | 85 | 85 | £250 | £50 | 2% | | 30% | 10% |
| Benefits YEAR 1 | 18% increase in Revenue | | | | -9% reduction in costs | | Incremental 6% increase in revenue | Incremental 2% increase in revenue | | |
| Est. Benefits YEAR 2 | 24% increase in Revenue (vs. Year 0) | | | | -4% reduction in costs | | Incremental 6% increase in revenue | Incremental 2% increase in revenue | | |

Producing something like the above might appear daunting for your organisation, so why not aim to be in a position to be able to fill this matrix in (see figure 7.2.9). Divide your customer base into three groups – low, medium and high-value – then apply REAP planning, objective, targets and measures. You will then unlock the latent profit within your customer base, rather than wasting resource trying to hold onto those that you don't want to.

Figure 7.3.9 **REAP target matrix**

| Decile | Value Group | Retention | Efficiency | Acquisition | Penetration |
|---|---|---|---|---|---|
| 1 | | | | | |
| 2 | High | Plans, tactics and measures | Plans, tactics and measures | Plans, tactics and measures | Plans, tactics and measures |
| 3 | | | | | |
| 4 | | | | | |
| 5 | Middle | Plans, tactics and measures | Plans, tactics and measures | Plans, tactics and measures | Plans, tactics and measures |
| 6 | | | | | |
| 7 | | | | | |
| 8 | | | | | |
| 9 | Low | Plans, tactics and measures | Plans, tactics and measures | Plans, tactics and measures | Plans, tactics and measures |
| 10 | | | | | |

**Focusing at the margins of your customer base
will have a dramatic impact on your margins!**

*Hyundai Car (UK) Ltd was established in
September 1993 and used to be part of the
RAC Group plc (which in 2004 had turnover
of £1.5 billion and made profits of £71.2
million – RAC has since been sold to Aviva in 2005).*

*In 1993, around 8,000 cars were sold in the UK and this has steadily risen
until in 2004 nearly 40,000 cars were sold in the UK, gaining a market
share in the extremely competitive UK market of 1.5 per cent. These are
predominantly distributed to customers through 160 independent dealers.
Hyundai has been one of the fastest growing car brands in the UK over the
last 10 years.*

*HCUK's strategic intent was:*

***"To win and retain our chosen customers through the unbeatable
value of the products that we sell and the intimate ownership
experience that we provide."***

*Although they were selling more cars than ever before, the Board knew
that they had to deliver on the 'intimate ownership experience' and
therefore employed a customer retention manager. His brief was:*

- *To build an effective database – it was offline, full of duplication and
  not good enough to produce a mailing list from*
- *To understand why Hyundai kept and lost customers*
- *To establish what the KPIs were and how the company was
  performing*
- *To develop a clear and deliverable strategy within brand guidelines*

*The retention team were unable to do any meaningful value analysis due
to the poor data and systems in the organisation. Research and analysis
took place that allowed Hyundai to segment its customers – one segment
was called 'Free Spirits'. These customers readily admitted that they had
bought certain models such as the sports coupé for the car's looks and
they maintained that they did not want any 'relationship' with either
Hyundai or their local dealer.*

*The most obvious insight was that due to the margins on this particular
model, any customer who bought a new coupé would immediately fall into
Hyundai's top 10 per cent of customers by value and yet they were likely
to be the most disloyal customers. The retention team knew that they had
to try to build a dialogue with these customers even though they had said
they wanted no such thing.*

*The retention team put together a programme of which one element was
called 'Design Track'. It was piloted on a special edition coupé – the F2
Evolution. Design Track invited customer input and then gave details to
the dealers and allowed them to continue a dialogue that had been
started by HCUK.*

Each of the selected customers received a large A4 folder that looked like a work-
in-progress project folder. Inside there were photographs, rough illustrations of
spoilers and mudguards, colour charts and a questionnaire.

*The questionnaire proclaimed that "everyone will have an opinion about the F2 Evolution...yours will actually count".*

*On opening it up they found that they were being asked to input into the design of the car: which spoiler, which style of wheel and which exhaust?*

*The questionnaire covered such things as what sound system they wanted, which accessories might they be interested in, how much they would expect to pay for it – and the learning for Hyundai?*

*A small design change to that which was already planned and the price could go up! The product manager learned how concerned the customers were about the security of the car – so a top-of-the-range alarm was added as standard and the price went up further!*

*The campaign ran for almost seven months – during which time the team got to learn more and more about the customers. A feedback pack went out in June, and to those who requested it in the original questionnaire, a limited edition signed print of the car was sent out as well – 93 per cent of men requested a print and 87 per cent of women.*

*These customers (remember the non-responsive, disloyal ones who wanted no relationship) kept up a dialogue with the company and the dealers for over seven months – the response rate was a staggering 47 per cent (in later versions of Design Track to much more loyal and responsive groups, the response rate was over 66 per cent).*

*All this information was fed into the customer database and individual dealer lead sheets could be produced for each customer. These detailed what price they were prepared to pay, their first choice of colour, whether they liked accessories (and which ones if they did), and what additional sales might be made – such as digital rolling encryption locking! All the dealer had to do once his demonstrator arrived on the forecourt was to phone up his customer and say: "you know you took part in that exercise to design the Coupé special edition – well I have one on the forecourt; do you want to come and have a drive?"*

*The customer retention rate rose from 26 per cent in 1997 to 32 per cent in 1998...to 56 per cent in 2000.*

*Coupe Design Track had an ROI of over 14:1. Hyundai were only spending an average of £10 per customer in their total retention programme and this particular element – Design Track – cost about £5 per customer.*

Source: Hyundai Car UK Ltd

> The first customers you must start to try and retain are your high value customers – the 80/20 rule is reinforced so strongly by the distribution of customer value, that if you try to retain lesser customers (or easier customers), then commercially you would be putting the business at risk.

## The importance of potential value

Measuring what has already happened is vital, but if you don't have an appreciation of what and where the potential value is in your customer base, then you could be investing time, effort and resource in managing the wrong customers.

If you do not have an understanding of the potential value of each customer, it can be likened to driving a car while only looking in the rear-view mirror – you can see where you have been, but you cannot see where the next bend in the road is. This could make the journey quite tense and unpredictable!

Once you have an understanding of potential value, then it is relatively straightforward and simple to start to plan and implement different strategies to different sections of your customer base (see figure 7.2.10).

### Figure 7.3.10  The current/potential value matrix

|  | | |
|---|---|---|
| High<br><br>**Potential value**<br><br>Low | **Develop business through upsell and cross-sell strategies** | **Develop effectiveness strategies or exit** |
| | **Retain and develop business through upsell and cross- sell strategies** | **Retain business** |
| | Low      **Current value**      High | |

### Simple lifetime value models

Understanding potential value is not an exact science – the only certainty is that your measures of potential value will be wrong (or at best, not 100 per cent correct). Much time, effort and resource can be spent generating potential value measures using complex data and techniques. Over time you could and should look to test, evaluate and enhance your measures of potential value, but not having all the information must not prevent you from making a start.

Proxies can be used as long as they are commercially sensible. Think of the little old lady, and the family man who changed his car every three years that we mentioned at the start of this chapter. Obviously, the family man has more potential value to the car company.

Simple information such as age, the model being driven and geographical location could create a reasonably powerful measure of potential value without tying a marketing department in knots. A thirty five year old driving an executive model and living in Surrey would have a higher potential value than a pensioner driving a hatchback in the Outer Hebrides.

## Lifetime value algorithms

There is no set 'equation' for lifetime value (LTV). Every business in every industry anywhere in the world could create an LTV model peculiar to itself.

At its most basic, LTV refers to an estimate of a customer's future economic worth. There are a number of alternative definitions that abound in academic literature that can be confusing.

For example, is LTV the net present value of the future stream of fully allocated profit from a customer, or is free cash flow better, or marginal financial contribution? Each has advantages and disadvantages and the arguments as to which is better could keep the finance team busy for a long while, but as a marketer you should understand the principles that in essence are:

- This is customer-led (so all revenues from all products per customer)

- You are looking forward over a commercially sensible time period

- Don't allow defining LTV to prevent you from getting on and doing 'stuff'

- You must refine, test and evaluate your LTV model over time

(For a full discussion of lifetime value, see chapter 3.5.)

A more strategic view – Return on CustomerSM

Recently a new metric has been put forward as a key strategic customer measure. Retaining loyal customers will obviously be a key input to that measure.

The measure is called Return on Customer (ROC) and has been put forward by Don Peppers and Martha Rogers (see 'references'). Whether the financial community accept and demand the measure from corporations is not certain yet, but it does make very good sense and reaction so far has been positive:

"Finally – business metric that can drive better management and higher stock price. I predict that you'll soon be hard-pressed to find a  company that isn't tracking ROC."

*Larry Kudlow, co-host of CNBC's Kudlow & Company*

Although quite complex to calculate, the best way to understand it is to think of owning shares. Total Shareholder Return (TSR) is a precisely defined measure in current use – in essence it looks at the overall return that a shareholder earns from their shares in a company over a period of time.

TSR shows how much return an investor gets from their shares in a company – so their dividends that are paid out to them plus the underlying change in the value of the shares in a period of time (let's say a year) are expressed as a plus or minus percentage of the opening value of the shares at the start of the period of time.

ROC adopts the same principle. How much you earn from the customer (cash flow) plus the change in its lifetime value (discounted cash flow) are expressed as a plus or minus percentage of the opening LTV.

Return on CustomerSM is a registered service mark of Peppers & Rogers Group, a division of Carlson Marketing Group, Inc.

The main benefit of the measure is that it would force senior management and the city to take longer-term customer value into account and it could start to move publicly listed companies away from the 'short-term-ism' of quarterly reporting. We can all think of instances where the Boardroom has taken decisions that destroy customer value and goodwill in order to hit the short-term numbers.

## The impact of digital marketing and the internet

"Organisations that are succeeding in using the internet to create customer loyalty haven't created new techniques to do this. They are simply applying the existing, well-proven techniques to this new medium."

*Chris Daffy, Consultant and Author*

Although Chris Daffy is right that the digital age has not changed how customer loyalty is created (nothing has changed in what makes customers loyal or disloyal after all), the internet and digitisation does have an impact on how things are done.

These technological advances should allow companies to adopt customer management and customer value-based marketing more wholeheartedly.

Figure 7.3.11 **Changing technologies and the evolving marketing concept**

| | Marketing concept | | | |
|---|---|---|---|---|
| | **Distribution** | **Selling** | **Brand management** | **Individual relationships** |
| **Products** | Single product | Few | Many | Huge' customised |
| **Market size** | As big as possible | National to global | Target segments | Individual customer |
| **Competitive tools** | Price, costs | Advertising, selling | Positioning, segmentation | Dialogue, customisation |
| **Key technology** | Mass production | Television, media | Market research | Internet |
| **Key measures** | Production costs, volume | Market share, margins | Brand equity | Customer lifetime value |

Peter Doyle
Professor of Marketing and Strategic Management
University of Warwick Business School

In the above table, Peter Doyle argues that over the past century there have been three changes in the orientation of marketing: distribution, selling and then brand management. He maintains that:

"The internet is consolidating the fourth stage of marketing's evolution: marketing as managing individual relationships with customers."

Doyle produced this table over five years ago and perhaps some amendments could be made to reflect recent developments. They are that the 'key technology' should be digital/internet as the advances in digital printing and photography etc. further reinforce his assertion. Secondly, the 'key measure' could be return on customer (ROC) rather than lifetime value as discussed above.

## Some impacts on customer retention and loyalty

"Price does not rule the web; trust does."

Frederick Reichheld and Phil Schefter
Harvard Business Review
July/August 2000

### Don't forget the basics

The technology, advertising banners, a sexy home page and links to other sites are important, but nothing is as important as customer focus and delivering what your customer wants. Make sure that you know what their needs are and don't get carried away by technological possibilities.

### Customisation

Because the technology allows product and service customisation, there is no reason why you should not be able to meet your customers' needs and make the proposition personalised and relevant to them.

### Speed

It is no longer a story of the big beating the small – the digital age is about the fast beating the slow. A premium marque car distributor group in the UK, has said that 45 per cent of all their phone calls requesting a test drive now originate from the web. The company also maintains, that in customer research, if any sales lead is not responded to within the day, the lead can effectively be deemed a 'cold' lead again.

### Richness and reach

The technology allows companies to offer customers almost unlimited information at virtually zero cost.

### Managing the E of REAP

Communication strategies that aim to retain customers through an ongoing dialogue suddenly become much more cost-effective. Self-service can turn marginal customers into profitable customers.

### Greater convenience for the customer

Having an integrated contact strategy that makes use of digital technology allows you to talk to customers when it is most convenient to them (and therefore when they are most receptive) 24/7.

With all this personalisation, customisation, speed and convenience – one aspect acquires even more importance and if carried out poorly can have a massive impact on customer retention and loyalty – the importance of managing customer data and information effectively is vital.

# Conclusion

Effective measurement of customer loyalty is a business imperative.

In today's business environment, the opportunity for organisations to be customer-led (rather than product-led) has now been enabled by technology. What marketers must do is to be effective at driving customer value and be better at realising the existing profit within their customer base. At the moment too much profit is squandered through inappropriate allocation of resource.

If marketing is to deserve and get a seat on the Boards of the biggest and best companies in the world then it has to be able to demonstrate, through effective measurement, that it is capable of driving superior business performance.

Superior business performance will only take place if a company can hold onto its most profitable customers for longer and be able to increase the value of those customers cost-effectively.

Learn to Measure and Measure to Learn!

**Possible answer to REAP exercise:**

- Retention rate rises from 65 to 70 per cent = 7,000 retained customers

- Assume a penetration increase of 20 per cent; therefore the average spend of each customer was £1,000 x 1.2 = £1,200 (either cross-sell or upsell)

- Therefore 7,000 customers x £1,200 average value = £8.4 million

- Acquire 2,999 customers at an average spend of, let's say, £600 = £2.1 million

- £8.4 million plus £2.1 million = £10.5 million

- Efficiencies around cost mean your budget has stayed the same

Therefore your objectives were to get:

|  | This year | Next year | Achieved? |
|---|---|---|---|
| Higher turnover | £10 million | £10.5 million | ✔ |
| Higher profit | £8 million | £8.5 million | ✔ |
| Fewer customers | 10,000 | 9,999 | ✔ |

**References:**

Daffy, Chris (2001) *Once a Customer, Always a Customer*; Dublin: Oak Tree Press

Doyle, Peter; (2000) *Value-Based Marketing: Marketing Strategies for Corporate Growth and Shareholder Value*; Chichester: John Wiley & Sons Ltd

Gamble, Paul, Merlin Stone and Neil Woodcock (1999) *Up Close and Personal?: Customer Relationship Marketing* @ Work; London: Kogan Page

Humby, Clive and Terry Hunt with Tim Phillips (2003); *Scoring Points: How Tesco is winning customer loyalty*; London & Sterling, VA: Kogan Page

Jenkinson, Professor Angus (2002) *The Interactive and Direct Marketing Guide*: London: Institute of Direct Marketing; Chapters 6.1 and 6.2

Marsden, Dr. Paul; Alain Samson and Neville Upton, (2005) *Advocacy Drives Growth: Customer Advocacy Drives UK Business Growth*; Accepted for publication in Brand Strategy: Nov/Dec 2005; distributed on www.insightexec.com March 2006

McCorkell, Graeme; (1997) *Direct and Database Marketing*; London: Kogan Page / Institute of Direct Marketing

Murley, Peter (editor); (1997) *Gower Handbook of Customer Service*; Aldershot & Vermont: Gower

Peppers, Don and Martha Rogers (2005) *Return on Customer: creating maximum value from your scarcest resource*; London: Marshall Cavendish Business/Cyan

Reichheld, Frederick (1996) *The Loyalty Effect*; Boston MA: Harvard Business School Press

Woodcock, Neil, Merlin Stone and Bryan Foss (2003) *The Customer Management Scorecard*: Managing CRM for Profit; London: Kogan Page

Woodcock, Neil, Merlin Stone and Michael Starkey (2000) *The Customer Management Scorecard: State of The Nation – A strategic framework for benchmarking performance against best practice*; London: Business Intelligence

Woodcock, Neil, and Michael Starkey (2004) *State of The Nation IV – The five-year global study of how organisations manage their customers*; London: QCi Assessment Ltd

# Section 8: Campaign planning and management

**▄ ▄▄ ▄ ▄▄ ▄▄ ▄▄ ▄▄ ▄▄ ▄▄ ▄▄ ▄▄ ▄▄ ▄▄ ▄▄ ▄▄ ▄▄ ▄▄ ▄▄ ▄▄ ▄**

**I**n Section 3 of this Guide we dealt with strategic planning considerations. In chapter 1 of this Section we look at converting strategy into action plans. We consider how to write, manage and action the plans we devise, and how to forecast, monitor, control, measure and analyse our results.

Chapter 2 is all about testing – its uses, benefits and methodology, including the statistical principles that underpin it. While separate consideration is given to direct mail, as possibly the most advanced test bed of all, and to testing in the press, in non-print media generally and in digital media in particular, nevertheless we emphasise throughout that the principles of testing are media-independent.

Chapter 3 deals with the sources and nature of data required for the successful implementation of any campaign. Again, though the detailed needs of different media may diverge, the common principles remain constant.

Chapter 4 is about printing, print production, print buying and choosing a print supplier.

# Campaign planning and management: – converting strategy into action plans

## This chapter includes:

-------------------------------------------------

- ❏ **Introduction**
- ❏ **Communication strategy**
- ❏ **Writing the plan**
- ❏ **Managing and actioning the plan**
- ❏ **Defining the status of a campaign**
- ❏ **Measurement, analysis, forecasting and control**
- ❏ **Supplier relationships**
- ❏ **The brief**

-------------------------------------------------

## About this chapter

**T**he implementation of strategy is an integral part of the marketing management process. Customer acquisition and relationship management requires that every customer touchpoint with your organisation be effectively and efficiently managed.

As part of the strategic planning process, we have addressed and tried to answer the following questions:

– Where are we now?
– Where do we want to be?
– How can we get there?

We are ready to answer the communications tactical planning question:

– How do we ensure we arrive?

## Kate Boothby BA (Hons), MSc dip, M IDM.

E-mail: kateboothby@msn.com

As a Senior Consultant for the IDM, Kate's roles have included managing the Education Department, advising a college about their marketing database and defining structure and content for a graduate website.

Kate has written material for the IDM's certificates in e-marketing and customer relationship management and has most recently edited the IDM's digital marketing diploma and certificate for online delivery.

Kate has been a tutor for the IDM's distance learning diploma in direct marketing for many years and has delivered lectures on such subjects as leisure and tourism and database marketing.

Previous roles have included Sales and Marketing Manager for Canvas Holidays, Direct Marketing Manager for Portland Holidays and a variety of marketing roles for some leading UK charities. While at Portland, Kate managed a database replacement project that came in on time and under budget!

# Chapter 8.1

# Campaign planning and management: — converting strategy into action plans

"Planning is about making it happen."

Sir John Harvey Jones, Consultant, former Chairman, ICI

## Introduction

**The** implementation of strategy is an integral part of the marketing management process. Customer acquisition and relationship management require that the customer is effectively and efficiently managed at every touchpoint with your organisation.

As part of our strategic planning process we have answered the following questions:

✔ "Where are we now?"

✔ "Where do we want to be?"

✔ "How can we get there?"

We are now ready to answer the communication tactical planning question:

**"How do we ensure we arrive?"**

Direct marketing tactics have been defined as:

> 'The manoeuvring of the specific resources of the company within a framework defined by the overall strategy'.

This part of the planning process spells out the precise details for delivering the objectives of the plan. Responsibilities are allocated, budgets are set and timings agreed.

The process of translating strategy into action can be divided into two phases. The first is the creation of a written document, the *tactical communication plan*. This document includes sufficient detail for management approval to be gained for the proposal. The approved document is central to the subsequent communication and briefing process which begins the second phase, that of *implementation*. The implementation phase encompasses diverse management tasks. The most important task is two-way communication with all key personnel involved in the campaign.

In earlier chapters we discussed the hierarchical planning process with each stage leading back into the corporate and marketing objectives. This process repeats itself at the tactical planning level.

Tactical communication planning takes its lead from the marketing objectives. Depending on your level of responsibility within your organisation you may be involved in setting both strategy and tactics or you may be presented with the strategy and asked to action it.

## Objectives, strategies and tactics – the essential differences revisited

Let us recap and revise the stages of the strategic marketing plan, reminding ourselves of the difference between objectives, strategies and tactics.

**Objectives** describe destinations: "where are we going?" Usually they are stated in revenue and profit terms. There can be multiple objectives.

**Strategies** set out the route that has been chosen, or the means for achieving the objective: "how do we get there?" Each objective will have an identifiable strategy, although some strategies may contribute to meeting more than one objective.

Strategies are:

✔ Theoretical

✔ Descriptive

✔ General

✔ Guidelines

**Tactics, action plans or campaigns** constitute the vehicle for getting to the destination: "how do we ensure we arrive?" They form the detailed, precise plan that allows for the execution of the strategy. This stage also encompasses the management responsibilities and techniques required for the effective execution of tactical plans.

Tactics are:

✔ Operational

✔ Specific

✔ Detailed

✔ Costed

## Communication strategy

To produce a tactical communication plan you will ideally be working within the framework provided by the *communication strategy*.

The communication strategy should have considered the following factors, either separately or under a generic communication strategy heading, depending on the plan's scale and complexity.

Where possible, your tactical planning process should work in the context of the following strategies:

1. **Communication objectives and strategy** – this should define in high-level financial terms, such as return on investment (ROI) or revenue forecasts, what target your tactical communication plan must achieve. The communication strategy may incorporate guidelines regarding the division of the total communication plan budget between acquisition and retention. This fundamental question must be decided before any detailed work begins on communication tactics. The decision will be based on the results of the situation analysis and the strategic direction of the company.

2. **Segmentation strategy** – the target audience has been identified. Your tactical plan will use these broad segments as a starting point for defining precise target segments.

3.  **Positioning strategy** – this defines the parameters for the creative, offers and messages you will develop in your tactical communication and contact plans.

4.  **Database strategy** – investments and developments relating to the marketing and corporate databases, as well as other technical issues such as the digital and telemarketing capability, will have a big impact on your ability to plan and implement your communication tactics. You need to be aware of existing and planned capability that could support your plan. Your formulation of a detailed tactical plan may well lead to your making recommendations for new requirements in these areas.

## *Writing the plan*

Tactical communication planning incorporates *campaign* and *contact plans*. Various terminology is used and this can be confusing. Fundamentally, regardless of the terminology employed, *a tactical communication plan defines precisely what you will say, to whom, and when*. You are also defining resources and responsibilities – to ensure the plan is actioned effectively – and forecasting the results.

The typical components of a tactical communication plan are:

1.   Tactical communication objectives

2.   Target audience selection, profiling and segmentation

3.   Media selection

4.   Products, services and pricing

5.   Offers

6.   Media format

7.   Creative positioning and messages

8.   Fulfilment and response management

9.   Budgeting and forecasting

10.  Contact plan

11.  Communication action schedule or timing plan

12.  Testing

"It is rare for there to be an online-only digital marketing campaign. Typically, at campaign level, digital needs to be integrated into the overall campaign plan. There are many specific issues relating to the digital component of the campaign that must be referenced. In extreme cases, the digital element could be large enough to warrant its own campaign."

*Dave Chaffey, IDM Diploma in Digital Marketing, 2005*

The detailed, specialised requirements of a digital marketing plan are outside the scope of this chapter. The need for a separate digital plan will be determined by the organisation's resources and the level of digital marketing development.

Whether a combined or separate digital marketing plan is created, it is essential that digital communications are incorporated as part of a fully integrated approach to customer communications. (For more on digital communications, and on integration of communication media, see appropriate chapters within Section 5 of this Guide.)

Once approval has been gained for the plan, actioning the plan involves management skills to ensure the plan is carried out effectively:

1.  Measurement, analysis and control

2.  Resourcing, including management, supplier selection and briefing

The above list may look complicated but many of the elements can be combined in tables to summarise and present a clear contact plan:

Table 8.1.1

| Example contact plan - in table headings | | | | | |
|---|---|---|---|---|---|
| Segment | Media | Offer(s) | Message | Test | Fulfilment requirements |
| Segment 1 | | | | | |
| Segment 2 | | | | | |
| Segment | Volume contacted | Total cost | Forecast response | Cost per response | Forecast revenue | Return on investment (ROI) |
| Segment 1 | | | | | | |
| Segment 2 | | | | | | |

## *Tactical communication planning – step by step*

### 1.  Tactical communication objectives

Tactical communication objectives conform to the same SMART principles as those for strategic objectives. Ideally, these objectives should be expressed by segment and activity.

These objectives are important for two reasons:

✔  They help you to *gain approval* for your plan by showing how you intend to meet the corporate and strategic marketing objectives, i.e. they feed back into the original high-level targets set for your activities. Your plan should always link objectives with the budget by using the same financial measures. This gives your proposal credibility.

✔  They allow you to *forecast, monitor* and *evaluate* which activity will be most profitable and which segments should be pursued for future activity.

## 2. Target audience selection, profiling and segmentation

You now need to bring your audience to life by describing them in ways that will paint a clear picture of their main, differentiating characteristics. This will enable you to create a communication plan that is relevant to them. For example, the enquirer segment for a financial product may evolve into several distinct sub-segments; females aged 25 to 35, with a part-time job, a mortgage and two young children; and financial directors, aged over 35, prepared to listen to a proposition if it addresses questions which are relevant to the company.

*Digital media* can allow you to define and contact micro segments more cost-effectively than traditional direct media.

*Business-to-business* activity segmentation can be complex, involving several different people who each need to be influenced using targeted media and tailored messages.

If you have existing customers you would usually begin by evaluating them first, as they are likely to be your most profitable target group. Profiling techniques can be used to try to find prospects who share a profile with your most profitable customers. Research may be used to fill in information gaps.

## 3. Media selection

The area of media selection involves assessing how best to reach your target segments most effectively using the media available. Media planning is one of the most (potentially) complex areas within a tactical communication plan. (See also Section 5 of this Guide.)

If your target segments are already customers you are likely to use *personalised* media, such as *direct mail, phone, website interaction* or *email.*

For *acquisition* media you may not be able to target activity so precisely. Digital marketing has added a plethora of communication alternatives to consider alongside traditional direct marketing approaches. For example:

Figure 8.1.1

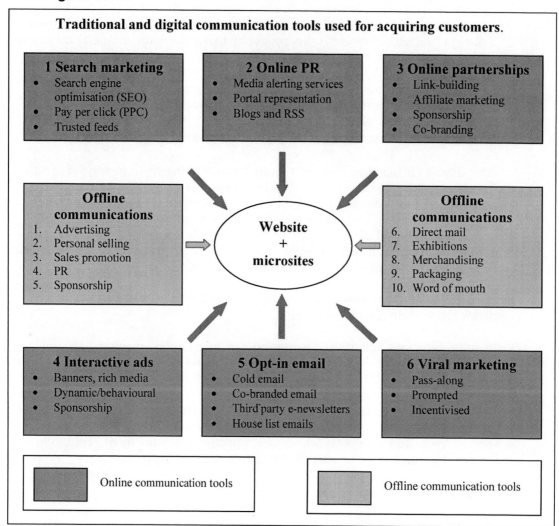

Traditional and digital communication tools used for acquiring customers.

**1 Search marketing**
- Search engine optimisation (SEO)
- Pay per click (PPC)
- Trusted feeds

**2 Online PR**
- Media alerting services
- Portal representation
- Blogs and RSS

**3 Online partnerships**
- Link-building
- Affiliate marketing
- Sponsorship
- Co-branding

**Offline communications**
1. Advertising
2. Personal selling
3. Sales promotion
4. PR
5. Sponsorship

**Website + microsites**

**Offline communications**
6. Direct mail
7. Exhibitions
8. Merchandising
9. Packaging
10. Word of mouth

**4 Interactive ads**
- Banners, rich media
- Dynamic/behavioural
- Sponsorship

**5 Opt-in email**
- Cold email
- Co-branded email
- Third party e-newsletters
- House list emails

**6 Viral marketing**
- Pass-along
- Prompted
- Incentivised

Online communication tools

Offline communication tools

*Source: Smith and Chaffey (2005)*

## 4. Products, services and pricing

It is likely that you have single or multiple products and services to offer to new and existing markets. You may have some scope to create tailored products and services for some key segments, or to channel customer feedback into the product development process. The interactive functionality of the digital channel lends itself to delivering high levels of personalisation and collecting feedback cost-effectively.

Keep in mind that digital and traditional direct marketing is customer-led. If there is no scope to tailor products and services to meet customer requirements, the success of your plan will hinge on your ability to find customers who will value your existing offering.

Products and services should be matched to customer and prospect segments and required actions incorporated into your tactical plan. Pricing and repackaging are powerful tools for marketing your products and services, but the scope to alter these elements may be circumscribed by the strategic plan.

## 5. Offers

An offer can comprise any combination of elements, e.g.

? Promise of the solution to a specific problem

? A specific (sometimes timed) promotional device, e.g. an incentive or discount

? Quality and value

? Reassurance

? Service superiority

Offers can be expressed very simply, e.g. *"The solution to your problem ... "* or in much more detail. You do not always have to think in promotional terms – simply telling the right story in the right way to the right person will often be sufficient.

It is vitally important to distinguish between a proposition and offer. Most marketers are confused and treat both as the same. The following example shows a very distinct difference between a proposition and an offer:

**The proposition:**

*'Learn French in 30 days'*

This is the basic business proposition we are making to customers.

**The offer:**

*'And receive a free cassette/CD'*

This is the offer which supports the proposition and adds the incentive to act. You can obviously combine both:

*'Learn French in 30 days and receive a free cassette/CD'*

(For more on the proposition and the offer, see chapter 3.2.)

## 6. Media format

This defines the detail of the size and appearance of your communications in the media you have selected.

For example, *direct mail packs* can vary from a simple, personalised letter to a luxurious multi-insert pack, designed to present a complex or high-value product or service. *Press advertising* can range from a full-colour double page spread to a tiny, mono-classified ad. If you have a *website*, a website redesign or update may be part of the campaign plan.

## 7. Creative positioning and message

Your overall creative positioning is usually determined by corporate level strategy. The creative you select for your tactical communication plan will reflect this but there is often considerable scope for development of creative approaches to meet the needs of different customer groups within a campaign. (Creative development is covered in detail in Section 10 of the Guide.)

## 8. Fulfilment and response management

This vital part of communication planning is often neglected. And yet there is little point in expending valuable time and money on creating enquiries and sales if no thought has been given to how customers and prospects will be treated when they contact your company.

In a survey conducted by Sistrum, 184 major companies were researched on their ability to respond to email requests for information via the internet. Only eight per cent of companies responded by email efficiently and quickly; 50 per cent took several weeks to respond, while 42 per cent did not respond at all.

Fulfilment and response handling incorporates:

✔ Order handling

✔ Payment processing

✔ Data capture (including research)

✔ Enquiry handling

✔ Sales conversions

✔ Complaint handling

## 9. Budgeting and forecasting

The budgeting process for a tactical communication plan begins in a similar way to that of a strategic plan. Budgeting is a cyclical process and you should expect to go through at least several iterations before finalising your proposal.

You begin with high level ROI (Return on Investment) targets and fundamental decisions regarding how to divide your total budget between acquisition and retention activity. This may need to be revisited once you have forecast your responses.

Beginning with customer segments you forecast likely responses to your activity, including ROI. What is the shortfall against your total target? This shortfall must be made up with acquisition activity. Acquisition activity is then planned in descending order of cost-effectiveness, usually beginning with 'recommend a friend' as a cost-effective source of new business. Once the broad acquisition media groups have been decided the budget must then show detail down to *individual media level*.

Return on investment and break-even calculations should be included to justify your proposal.

## 10. The contact plan defines in detail:

1. Customer/prospect segments

2. Medium

3. Message

4. Offer

5. Fulfilment

6.  Budget

7.  Review of objectives

You may start your contact plan with a broad statement of intent, for example:

***The campaign will use:***

> ✔ Press relations to build awareness and generate confidence among senior management people
>
> ✔ Direct response advertising to generate enquiries by telephone or email
>
> ✔ Search engine and affiliate marketing to drive enquirers to website
>
> ✔ Coupon analysis and website interaction to qualify enquirers
>
> ✔ Direct mail, email, SMS and telephone to stimulate non-converted prospects
>
> ✔ The salesforce to produce additional leads
>
> ✔ Recommendation of offers to existing customers to produce new prospects

Important issues that require consideration as part of your contact plan are:

1.  **Integration** – truly effective integration employs each marketing discipline to carry out the functions it does best, while pursuing a common communication objective

"The task set for each advertisement within an integrated campaign is different ... this imposes an additional task: to ensure that each element reinforces the others without compromising its own effectiveness."

*Graeme McCorkell*

2.  **Single- or multi-step contact** – you may be able to achieve your objective(s) using a single communication, but more often your campaign will involve several stages including follow-ups and reminders or offers.

    Note that at this level individual media (i.e. titles) are not specified – these are part of the communication action schedule.

## 11. Communication action schedule or timing plan

This is the *implementation schedule*, showing each action you and others need to take, and setting these out in an easy-to-use chart.

> NOTE – because it is an action reminder and planning tool the schedule does not carry all of the minute details.

The schedule gives broad details, e.g.

✔ Target categories – customer segments and prospects etc.

✔ Media outlines – women's magazines and national newspapers etc.

✔ Timings, e.g. week commencing 4 January

✔ Briefing dates

Because the schedule carries only action points it must be supplemented by a number of other documents such as:

✔ Individual campaign summaries – details of a precise campaign objective and the action plan, e.g. 20,000 information requests from press advertising and 25,000 requests from DRTV

✔ The media plan – giving details of channels, formats, timings, precise dates and costs etc.

✔ Details of the briefings – e.g. customer service, creative and response handling

✔ Detailed estimates – e.g. costs and expected returns, responses, conversions and average order values

✔ Production schedules and supplier details – artwork, commercials, print, mailings and website development

The table below gives an example of a Campaign Schedule:

Table 8.1.2

## Example of campaign schedule

| Action | Jan | Feb | Mar | Apr | May | Jun | Jul | Aug | Sept | Oct | Nov | Dec |
|---|---|---|---|---|---|---|---|---|---|---|---|---|
| | | 5 12 19 26 | 5 12 19 26 | 2 9 16 23 30 | | | | | | | | |
| **Press campaign - Spring 2006** | | | | | | | | | | | | |
| Creative work | Finished a/w ready 10 Dec | | | | | | | | | | | |
| Media bookings – main titles | Confirmed by 30 November | X X X | X X X | X X | | | | | | | | |
| Response handling and lead qualification | Briefing/ training January | | | | | | | | | | | |
| **DRTV campaign - Spring 2006** | | | | | | | | | | | | |
| Creative designs | Designs approved by January 7 | Production completed 15 February | On air X X X | | | | | | | | | |
| Response handling and lead qualification | | Briefing/ training February | | | | | | | | | | |

## 12. Testing

This is an important, cyclical activity that hones your marketing to achieve the most cost-effective use of your budget.

Test the most important elements first: list, media, timing, offer, format and creative execution.

Remember, tests must have clear objectives to deliver profit or develop the product. Testing represents a sizeable investment of budget and carries a risk of poor return on investment. For this reason the test budget is usually no more than 10 per cent of the total media budget.

Limit sample sizes to sufficient minimum quantities, so that the majority of the customer base can be contacted with the most proven and profitable control packages as a means of maximising revenue. (For a full consideration of testing, see chapter 8.2.)

# *Managing and actioning the plan*

## *Process management in an imperfect world – running campaigns without an overall marketing plan*

We have seen that campaign planning *should* start when marketing planning starts. In practice, many companies' marketing plans lack the basis for this approach. A plan may be too general, lacking the detailed objectives required. It may be produced too early and be irrelevant by the time it is applied. Or it may be produced too late. If we were to recommend a process which depended totally on the existence of a properly documented marketing plan, its advice would be dismissed as irrelevant by half its readers!

So, in what follows, we describe how campaigns can be handled irrespective of the state of your marketing plan. A good marketing plan will help you handle campaigns better. But you can still develop and run good campaigns without a proper marketing plan, provided you *do your bit* professionally. However, if your company doesn't give you the right support for campaign planning, you must develop an approach of your own. If you don't get clear guidance on objectives and priorities you must develop them yourself.

Campaign planning and co-ordination are not theoretically complex. It is just a question of making sure that your campaigns deliver messages, the content and timing of which are co-ordinated and which contribute to the development of your brand(s). This means co-ordinating every aspect of campaign development.

Important: Remember to co-ordinate your direct (offline and online) and non-direct marketing activities!

### Co-ordinating targeting and contact strategies

In companies whose main marketing channels are direct and which have good customer databases, co-ordinating selections is the key activity. This is so important that some companies treat access to the database(s) as the most important marketing decision. Brand managers and sales managers are required to submit their briefs to the database manager. The manager's job is then to determine the best prospects for each campaign and when they should be contacted, taking into account the targeting, timing and offers of other campaigns as well as the potential profit generation for the company.

In some companies, the database manager suggests which campaigns should be run and what contact strategies should be used. He moves from being a *gatekeeper* of the database to the *initiator* of campaign ideas. By analysing the database he can determine what campaigns are required.

### Co-ordinating and organising the team

> Co-ordinating and forewarning personnel is the most important single function of a campaign process.

Many companies organise their co-ordination by committee. Incoming briefs are collated and submitted to a campaign co-ordination committee. This meets regularly (typically monthly) to review all briefs and slot them in. In other companies a planning department receives all briefs and allocates them a budget and timing slot.

Whichever approach you use, the most important achievement is getting briefs submitted in good time and ensuring that the output of the planning process is properly communicated, so that the whole team knows what it must do and when.

As part of a truly integrated process, external agencies and suppliers should be included at the initial briefing stage, alongside internal departments.

# Defining the status of a campaign

## Where are you at today?

Because it takes time to decide whether and when a campaign should be run, a campaign can have different statuses, from being a *gleam in the eye* of a product manager to being finished. It is essential to recognise this in your process.

Below, we set out the kind of status that a process may have, which can be easily determined by anyone who needs to know. We have divided the possible statuses into *operational* and *management*. The table shows the key eight operational statuses you may find:

## Table 8.1.3

| The eight operational statuses | |
| --- | --- |
| Provisional | The campaign has been identified as needing consideration, but has not yet been submitted for formal consideration by your campaign co-ordination process. Normally, a deadline for such consideration should be set. The campaign proposal should contain an outline brief, timing and suggested budget. |
| Submitted | The campaign has been formally submitted for consideration through your campaign co-ordination process, with the brief and timing firmed up. Again, a deadline for approval or otherwise should be set. |
| Approved | The campaign has been approved by the campaign co-ordination process, with timings for development, launch and close agreed. |
| Budgeted | Although an outline budget should be considered when a campaign is at earlier stages, we believe that you should not budget until you have received quotes from suppliers. There is no point in getting detailed quotes before the campaign is approved, because this wastes suppliers' time, and may slow down other projects. The outline budget should be based on your experience with earlier campaigns. An outline budget also stops you wasting time if your suppliers think your requirement is totally unfeasible within the outline. |
| Under development | Serious work has started on the campaign, suppliers have been briefed, and money is being spent! |
| Live | The campaign has hit the market. |
| Completed | The campaign has been completed, and no further actions in the market will be undertaken. |
| Closed | The results of the campaign have been analysed and properly documented. |

The eight operational statuses describe where a project has reached in its normal process of development. However, things do not always run so smoothly. Campaigns may be cancelled, deferred or even absorbed into other campaigns. So we need four further statuses, known as management statuses, as laid out below:

## Table 8.1.4

| The four management statuses | |
| --- | --- |
| Current | The campaign is at one of the above statuses and progressing normally. |
| Cancelled | The campaign will not go ahead. This may be determined at any stage before the campaign is live. You should keep a record of work done for the campaign as it may be needed later. |
| Deferred | The campaign is deferred. No new timing has been specified and it will require resubmission through the co-ordination process. |
| Absorbed | The campaign has been absorbed into another campaign. |

### Who makes the decisions?

Who is responsible for making the decision at each stage and managing the campaign through depends on how you are organised. What we call *authorities* at each of the main campaign statuses might be allocated:

## Table 8.1.5

| Who does what in the campaign process? | |
|---|---|
| **Status** | **Person responsible and action required** |
| Provisional | The person initiating the request (the brand or product manager, sales manager, service manager, database manager etc.) is responsible for providing an outline brief, requested timing and likely budget. |
| Submitted | The person initiating the request is responsible for submitting the campaign unless you have some more formal process of allocating the progression of projects. |
| Approved | The manager of the campaign co-ordination process is responsible for making it happen. Any revisions to the brief agreed during the process – especially targeting and timing – should be circulated by him. |
| Budgeted | This depends on how you are organised. If your promotional budgets are centralised, this may be the responsibility of your financial controller. If budgets are allocated to internal customers (e.g. brand managers), they may be the appropriate authority. |
| Under development | The campaign manager is finally responsible for all work during this and the next two stages: live and completed, and for documenting the results at campaign close. |
| Cancelled, deferred and absorbed | The manager responsible for the last stage of a campaign is responsible for maintaining the data available. However, ideally the data should be centralised with the manager responsible for campaign co-ordination. |

## ... and who carries out the various tasks?

One of the most neglected aspects of direct and digital marketing management is recognition of the different functions needed to ensure that campaigns are delivered properly. We have already discussed some implicitly, e.g. the campaign manager – the person responsible for co-ordination. But there are other roles that management must fulfil. These include:

✔    Initiation/origination: coming up with the ideas for campaigns

✔    Workload/resource control: ensuring that the resources of the team – including suppliers – are adequate to meet the demands upon them, and that work is scheduled so as to optimise these resources

✔    Campaign administration: ensuring campaigns are correctly documented and communicated, and that everyone in the team meets their deadlines

✔    Delivery/production: actually bringing the campaign to market

✔    Sponsoring: providing the funds

✔    The internal customer: the person benefiting from the campaign; typically a product, service or sales manager

In some companies, all the above functions and roles are combined in the job specification of the direct or digital marketing manager. But in very big companies heavily committed to digital and direct marketing the roles are often split. The most underrated of all these functions is *campaign administration*. Although a relatively junior person often occupies this role, a good campaign administrator is worth their weight in gold.

## Table 8.1.6

| The Campaign process – key information areas and responsibilities | |
|---|---|
| 1. Campaign definition and accountabilities | Describing the requirement in brief, at a high level, and saying who is involved in delivering it: staff, suppliers and internal clients. |
| 2. Campaign coverage | Testing and market coverage issues. |
| 3. Objectives and strategy | Where the campaign fits in overall marketing and promotional strategy and what the campaign needs to achieve. |
| 4. Product or programme detail | What exactly is being promoted, and what its features and benefits are. |
| 5. Market detail | Who the campaign is targeted at, what their perceptions are, who the competition is and what they are offering. |
| 6. Campaign elements | What are the detailed requirements of the campaign? |
| 7. Initial estimates | What you think the campaign is going to cost and what revenue you expect. |
| 8. Management and media timing plans | The main management and media milestones in the campaign. |
| 9. On- and offline media, website and telemarketing timing plans | The main milestones for digital and direct marketing media implementation, including website development. |
| 10. Formal agency quote | Agency response to the brief, outlining approach and quote! |
| 11. Outbound list selection brief | Which specific customers you want to target, off- and online from your database(s). |
| 12. External list selection brief | As 11, but for list rental. |
| 13. Contact and fulfilment strategy | What you are going to do with each group of customers or prospects. |
| 14. Contact and fulfilment details | How you are going to implement 13 in detail. |
| 15. Contact strategy diagrams | A diagrammatic representation of 13 and 14. |
| 16. Data format and delivery | How you want the data to be provided by your customer database system. |
| 17. Reports | What reports you want from the database? |
| 18. Systems feedback report | How many customers have been chosen by your selection criteria? |
| 19. New data fields requirement | It is important to ensure that any newly collected data can be added to the database. |
| 20. Outbound telemarketing | Detailed brief to telemarketing agency for outbound calling. |
| 21. Enquiry and complaint management off- and online | As above, but for inbound. Are you expecting enquiries through your website? |
| 22. Questionnaire summary | To record details of questions asked in telemarketing, mailing programmes or internet surveys. |

| 23. | Media briefings; for example, broadcast media, press and search engine agency | Detailed brief to media buyers for TV, radio and press and search engine optimisation agency. |
|---|---|---|
| 24. | Fulfilment pack summary | Details of contents and suppliers. |
| 25. | Fulfilment letter summary | Details of letter/literature to accompany pack. |
| 26. | E-fulfilment | Details of e-newsletter and email content. |
| 27. | Print production and distribution | Handling of printed items. |
| 28. | Print delivery advice | To ensure print gets to the right place. |
| 29. | Campaign close report | The results! |

# Measurement, analysis, forecasting and control

## Keep a close eye on your performance

Digital and direct marketing work through measurement. Measurement during campaigns helps you to check if your strategy is working. Measurement after a campaign enables you to find out what worked and what didn't. In setting up your campaign, you need to make sure that the *right information* is reported at the *right time* to the *right people* (i.e. those who are in a position to do something about it). This means you should:

✔ Decide what key performance indicators you wish to use. They must, of course, be measurable as well as useful.

✔ Make sure that these indicators are actually measured. Ideally they should not require special measuring techniques but be picked up as a normal part of the campaign.

✔ Make sure that the results are communicated to the right people.

## What should you measure?

The information needed to monitor a campaign is fairly straightforward and derives from the logical flow of a campaign. Below are some examples. Note that many of the measurements are simple checks on the volume of flows (of communication) or stocks (of material to be communicated). The measures are as follows:

✔ The number of customers actually selected by your selection criteria (or the number of valid names on a list of customers for mailing or emailing)

✔ Availability of stock of mailing material; check that numbers match selection/list numbers

✔ Volumes actually despatched; record timings of despatches

✔ Where the first communication is – through digital, broadcast or published media; e.g. record whether the print or pop-up ad appeared according to schedule

✔ Media timings achieved

✔ Numbers responding to the first communication, by category of response

✔ Availability of response packs

✔ Website functionality; internet server performance, failed links and navigation errors etc.

✔ Response mailings – timing and volumes (applying to every subsequent action step)

✔ Results of response mailings or emailings (category and timing), e.g. sales

## Where does this essential information come from?

This information comes from many sources. Where it comes from suppliers (e.g. media buying, mailing, response handling and email bureau), the contract should include the supply of high- quality, up-to-date statistics. Potential problems concerning data collection and availability can usually be easily avoided by attention to detail at an early stage of campaign planning.

Failure to obtain these statistics from suppliers means that no one knows the exact status of the campaign at any given point. Supply of these statistics should therefore be part of the conditions of the contract, and also specifically detailed in the brief for each campaign. Most of the problems in this area are caused by campaign managers failing to specify their requirements in enough detail.

Each supplier should be told:

✔ The data required

✔ The frequency of reporting expected

✔ Procedures for signalling problems

One of the most important skills for a direct/digital marketer is knowing what to do when initial results do not meet with expectations. You should therefore consider contingencies for such a scenario. Examples include:

? Responses too high or low

? Problems with stocks of mailing or fulfilment material

? Media schedules altered for reasons beyond your control

? The internet server out of action for a significant period of time

For example, *if response is too high*, fulfilment pack stocks may run out. Can additional stocks be ordered quickly (this needs to be established during initial negotiations with suppliers), or can a later wave of outbound communication be deferred? Before taking a snap decision the *reason* for the high volume needs to be established. Was the outbound mailing larger than expected? Was there a special reason why more people than usual might have seen the press advertisement? Has there been a high volume of responses from *friends and family* as well as from the target respondents?

*If response is too low*, the achieved media and mailing schedules should be checked. So should the selection criteria or list used. Perhaps there were delays in the outbound communication. Were all the components of the pack included? Did the right response packs go to the right respondents?

*If your internet server is down* in the period during or immediately after an email communication goes out, this will affect the number of customers who click through to your website.

The problem with learning after the event is that you may already be onto the next campaign. Control statistics may be forgotten. *Therefore they should ideally be kept in a simple graphic format, as a permanent record of the campaign's progress.* This will help you to review, for example, the performance of particular agencies over several campaigns.

## Learning from your final results

During a campaign we usually evaluate *basic flows and stocks* (responses in and packs out); after a campaign we typically evaluate *rates and ratios* (e.g. profit per contact and return on investment per segment).

There are many ways to measure a campaign's effectiveness. Some are non-monetary (e.g. response rates). Some are cost ratios (e.g. cost per response and relative media cost/productivity).

Using intermediate measures, the campaign could be evaluated by:

?	The number of customers reached

?	The number of responses generated (of each type)

?	Number of bookings/orders generated

?	Incremental profit from the campaign

?	Effect on customer lifetime value etc.

Each campaign must be evaluated against, as well as in conjunction with, other campaigns. Thus, you might evaluate direct mail *against* email, or *with* email as a combined contact strategy.

The *cost/productivity* statistics we use to judge the effectiveness of different inputs into the marketing process include:

✔	Cost per 1000 mailed, called, emailed or contacted via SMS

✔	Cost per decision maker contact

✔	Cost per lead or clickthrough

✔    Cost per sale

✔    Return on investment

These should be compared for different media. The cost of different elements of the sales process (outbound contact, enquiry handling and fulfilment, and concluding sale) should also be evaluated. These should be set against revenue and margins achieved (including any selling of products which were not the subject of the promotion).

Quality statistics should also be accumulated. These include database quality statistics (e.g. gone-aways) and measures of the quality of the response handling process (e.g. average elapsed time before fulfilment pack sent out).

# Supplier relationships

(For further specifics on working with particular types of supplier, see Section 9 below.)

Relationship marketing and value chain theory, along with the interest in partnership and backward integration has led to renewed focus on the importance of supplier relationships. In direct and digital marketing, with the range and complexity of relationships involved in the implementation of campaigns, supplier relationships have become increasingly important. To achieve a truly integrated approach, suppliers should be included at the earliest briefing stage so that they can contribute to the plans before they are finalised.

Both consumer and business-to-business marketers are evolving ways of rewarding suppliers for working co-operatively with each other, as well as with the client; for example, by introducing rewards for 'co-operation' and fully integrated objectives for total campaign rather than individual performances.

The range of suppliers that direct and digital marketers deal with is vast, including some or all of the following:

✔    Database agency

✔    Advertising/interactive advertising/direct marketing agency

✔    Research agency

✔    Web/direct marketing design agency

✔    Consultancy

✔    On- and offline PR

✔    Affiliates

✔    Legal representatives

✔    Trade bodies

✔    Reprographics house

✔    List brokers, including email

✔ Off- and online media owners (e.g. search engines and portals)

✔ Media buyers

✔ Mailing houses

✔ Email marketing bureau

✔ Internet service provider (ISP)

✔ Web analytics

✔ Printers

✔ Laser bureau

✔ Royal Mail

✔ Freight forwarders

✔ Order and enquiry fulfilment

✔ Banks

✔ Credit card companies

✔ Credit reference companies

Given that it is rare that a job goes precisely to plan, a supplier who will go the extra mile for you, who will take the time to understand your and your customers' needs is invaluable.

There are several guiding principles to help ensure supplier relations are harmonious:

✔ Respect them – they will do a better job.

✔ Involve them early – they will offer ideas.

✔ Share information and news; communicate through the project.

✔ Create shared performance objectives.

✔ Share results and rewards on a 'team' basis.

✔ Try to get people you like on the business. Or at least people you can work with.

✔ Be tough on price but remember they have to make a profit too.

✔ Make an effort to understand their business; try to set realistic goals for them.

It is in everyone's interests to ensure the job goes smoothly. However, in the event of problems, a motivated, well-informed team is more likely to produce the extra effort required to solve the problem and may prioritise your work over that of your competitors.

## *How to choose suppliers*

### 1.  Draw up a list of five to ten potential suppliers

?  Previous suppliers.

?  Recommended suppliers: by colleagues or contacts.

?  Trade association members.

### 2.  Review your list

?  What has their work been like in the past?

?  What other clients do they have?

### 3.  Create shortlist

✔  Draw up a shortlist of three or four.

✔  Take up references – volunteered or not.

✔  Arrange to visit them for a chat and a look.

✔  Invite selected suppliers to pitch/quote. Issue a concise brief.

✔  Check trade association membership.

### 4.  The pitch

✔  Consider confidentiality.

✔  Agree realistic timings.

✔  Allow questions and answers.

✔  Insist you meet the individuals who will handle your business.

### 5.  Final selection

✔  Price is never a good measure of quality. Paying peanuts attracts monkeys.

✔  Price is important but reputation in the industry is at least as important.

✔  Beware of cost differences – insist on standard format where possible.

✔  Do you need the additional services they offer? – if not ask them to strip them out of their quote.

✔  Can they do the job themselves or will they outsource part of the work?

✔  Are they accessible? Will you be able to go and see them if there are difficulties? Face-to-face still works well.

✔  Are they competing against you? Are they working with competitors?

✔  Do they meet required quality standards?

✔    Do their software systems talk to yours?

## 6.    Finalising the contract

✔    Agree all costs and contractual details up front.

✔    Agree evaluation criteria too.

# The brief

## The supplier briefing process

A comprehensive brief is a vital part of the campaign management process. It is always better to provide too much information than too little. Briefing documents provide protection when problems occur and, more importantly, minimise the chances of anything going wrong. The need for a brief applies to internal departments as well as external suppliers.

Once you have defined the internal and external campaign team(s) you need to brief them properly. The checklist below outlines the key elements of a briefing document.

## Briefing checklist

1.    What is the background to the campaign? Provide as much information as possible, including customer research and defined customer benefits.

2.    State the overall objectives and a clear quantified objective for the task.

3.    Provide an outline of considered approaches to the campaign, e.g. media options.

4.    Set a budget. This may be specific or a reasonably narrow band.

5.    Fix a timetable for the presentation of response to the brief and completion of the job.

## The briefing form

The brief should be written. Using a form helps you make sure you have included all the key elements and guides your thinking through the various issues.

The best forms, like the best deals, are those that satisfy both parties:

✔    Consider a *round table* briefing for all parties.

✔    Provide all necessary information in writing.

✔    Too much information rather than too little.

✔    Encourage contribution and debate.

### *The mailing schedule*

It is never too soon to put all the key dates onto a mailing schedule, and make sure that all the relevant parties have a copy – of the most recent version! Always include draft number and date of issue

### Figure 8.1.2 **Mailing schedule example**

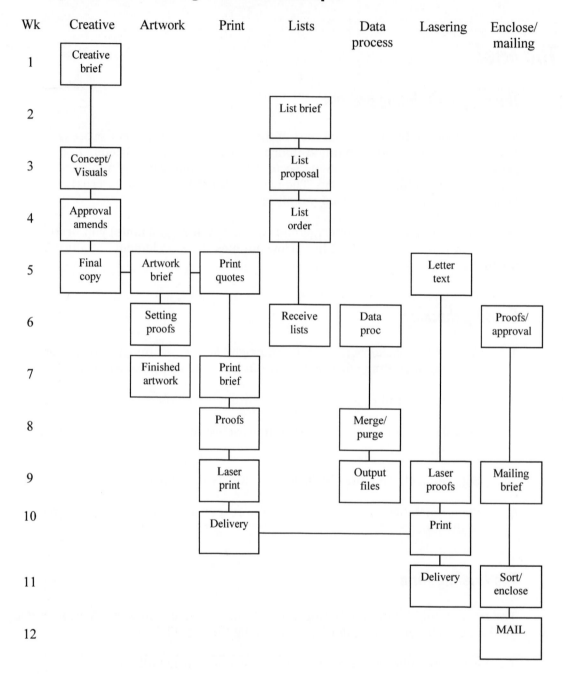

Table 8.1.7

| Direct Marketing Campaign production schedule | | |
| --- | --- | --- |
| Creative presented to client | Date XX/YY/ZZ | Responsibility or date completed |
| Visuals sign-off | | |
| Purchase order received | | |
| Final list approval presented | | |
| Lists ordered | | |
| All copy signed off | | |
| Artwork to client | | |
| Artwork comments back to agency | | |
| Artwork sign-off | | |
| Artwork to printer | | |
| Internal and external tapes to data processing bureau | | |
| Print proofs – presented            – approved | | |
| Data processing complete | | |
| Laser stationery to laser bureau | | |
| Mailing tape(s) to laser bureau | | |
| All print to mailing house | | |
| [Loose inserts to publications/leaflets to distribution company] | | |
| Laser proofs– presented            – approved | | |
| Lasering commences | | |
| Lasering complete | | |
| Enclosing commences | | |
| Mailing despatched | | |
| [First responses received] | | |

## Checklist: tasks and stages in a direct marketing campaign, including digital

Different campaign types may differ in terms of what tasks are required and in what order. Many tasks may run in parallel, so this checklist of principal tasks is arranged by topic.

If a campaign has already been tested, many stages may be omitted (e.g. creative/media development and market targeting etc.) As mentioned previously in this chapter, digital may be allocated separate treatment or be fully integrated as just another customer touchpoint.

**A test campaign should involve the same tasks as a rollout campaign.**

**Communication plan – senior management tasks**

✔  Develop marketing plan

✔  Within marketing plan, determine market focus for campaign

✔  Identify customer needs in target market

✔  Select product or service for promotion

✔  Check customer database system for previous similar campaigns: type, product, customer coverage and level of success etc.

✔  Confirm consistency with timing of other campaigns

✔  Run trial selections to confirm numbers in target market

✔  Determine budgets

✔  Set up outline campaign on database and management system(s)

✔  Prepare draft timings (main milestones, not detailed project plan)

✔  Circulate draft timings to all suppliers and internal customers

✔  Deliver 'start-up' campaign team briefing

✔  Receive supplier and internal customer comments and modify draft timings

**Communication plan – management tasks**

✔  Determine project management accountability – overall and in each supplier/department

✔  Prepare contact list and circulate to all suppliers, off- and online

✔  Confirm product and service details

✔  Agree campaign timing

✔  Prepare draft agency brief using forms

✔  Issue draft brief to agencies. The timing of briefing will vary if competitive tender and/or fully integrated approach is being used

✔  Invite agency comments on draft brief

✔  Finalise brief and confirm

✔  Agency to develop strategy, concepts, proposals and detailed timings

✔  Prepare detailed project plan in consultation with suppliers

✔  Prepare reporting forms

✔  Review forms with management

✔  Agree forms

✔    Agency to submit initial recommendation (creative and media etc.)

✔    Select agency (if competitive pitch)

✔    Evaluate costs of recommendations against expected response

✔    Comment on recommendations, using checklists provided in this section

✔    Agency to revise recommendations?

✔    Agency to present revised creative and media proposals?

✔    Agree agency creative proposals finally

✔    Agree agency media proposals

✔    Prepare campaign flowcharts

✔    Circulate campaign flowcharts to all suppliers/departments

**Mailing and fulfilment**

✔    Prepare copy and layouts (letters, brochures, envelopes and emails etc.)

✔    Prepare illustrations and photographs

✔    Review copy and layouts using checklists

✔    Revise copy and layouts if required

✔    Approve final copy (text)

✔    Prepare artwork

✔    Check artwork

✔    Revise artwork

✔    Approve artwork

✔    Prepare complete pack dummy (off- and online)

✔    Check pack dummy

✔    Approve pack dummy

✔    Print sample run for distribution to all involved in campaign

✔    Distribute samples

✔    Order all print for production runs

**Internal communication**

✔    Brief all sales and marketing staff

✔    Brief all customer-facing staff

✔    Brief all technical staff, including database and website administrators

✔ Receive confirmation from customer-facing and technical staff that briefs received, understood and agreed and that mechanism exists for handling results of campaign (lead-handling and follow-up)

✔ Schedule training and motivation meetings if required

✔ Prepare training and motivational material

✔ Hold training and motivation meetings

**General and system logistics**

✔ Make go/no-go decision

✔ Check campaign logistics with all suppliers, including mailing, telemarketing, response handling, email bureau, search engine optimisation agent and fulfilment agencies etc.

✔ Check data links between all parties

✔ Agree selections/lists

✔ Determine testing strategy (including test and control cells)

✔ Determine list size

✔ Select contact strategies

✔ Confirm selection rules and timing for initial target customer groups for each action/treatment; allocate codes and enter into system

✔ Confirm rules for allocation to follow-up groups; allocate codes and enter into system

✔ Write custom selection routines if required

✔ Run trial extract/selection on test basis

✔ Check trial extract/selection

✔ Modify extract/selection programme if required

✔ Run extract/selection on production basis

✔ Check output file

✔ Transfer to desired medium

✔ Despatch output

✔ Check with recipient(s) that output correct/readable

✔ Go live!

✔ Update promotion histories

✔ Receive updates from fulfilment/telemarketing and online agencies

✔ Update contact records

✔ Report production

✔ Report campaign closed

✔ File outstanding enquiries for future

✔ Prepare final campaign report and issue

**Print and (e)mailing logistics**

✔ Brief mailing, emailing and fulfilment houses using briefing format

✔ Develop print production and online production schedules

✔ Issue production schedules

✔ Prepare artwork/design for print and online

✔ Prepare laser letters with variations to match source and targeting and (for fulfilment letters) outcome of customer response

✔ Check sample letters

✔ Confirm outbound mailing envelope description

✔ Confirm fulfilment pack envelope description

✔ Define mailing and fulfilment packs on system

✔ Confirm media slots and timing

✔ Issue final media schedule

✔ Print outbound mailing

✔ Check samples of outbound communications using checklists

✔ Deliver outbound packs to mailing house

✔ Outbound stock arrives and correct stock level confirmed

✔ Print fulfilment packs

✔ Check samples of fulfilment packs and emails using checklists

✔ Deliver fulfilment packs to fulfilment house

✔ Check fulfilment stocks arrived and confirm correct stock levels

✔ Plan and buy media

✔ Check advertisements appeared correctly

✔ Send mailing tapes/data to mailing house

✔ Despatch outbound communications

✔ Receive response to media advertising/mailing/telemarketing/emailing/ search engine marketing etc.

✔ Process response information to determine required fulfilment

✔ Initiate fulfilment

✔ Print personalised laser letters

✔ Make up fulfilment packs to customer requirements and despatch

✔ Monitor fulfilment stocks and replenish if required

✔ Receive progress reports and monitor

✔ Dispose of unwanted print stocks after campaign close

**Telemarketing**

✔ Prepare draft telemarketing agency brief

✔ Issue draft brief to telemarketing agency (or agencies if competitive tender being used)

✔ Receive agency comments on draft brief

✔ Finalise brief and confirm

✔ Receive agency recommendation on campaign approach

✔ Select agency

✔ Evaluate costs of recommendations against expected response

✔ Comment on recommendations

✔ Agency to revise recommendations

✔ Agency to develop decision trees

✔ Circulate decision trees internally and to client for comment

✔ Agency to present revised decision trees

✔ Agree decision trees for testing

✔ Agency presents draft scripts

✔ Scripts circulated internally and to client for comment

✔ Agency to present revised scripts

✔ Agree scripts for testing

✔ Design script screen displays

✔ Check screens

✔ Brief training and phone room management, and receive comments on screens

✔ Amend screen displays and implement

✔ Determine data entry procedures, including return of questionnaire data to customer database

✔ Implement data entry procedures

✔ Select test team

✔ Train test team

✔ Make test calls

✔ Check hard copy output

✔ Revise trees and scripts after testing

✔ Revise screens and data entry procedures after testing

✔ Agree final trees and scripts

✔ Confirm target customers

✔ Set live date!

✔ Determine customers to be called and provide telephone numbers

✔ Select main calling team

✔ Train calling team (products and offer etc.)

✔ Confirm timing of calling

✔ Begin calling

✔ Despatch call results to system for processing

✔ Check tapes and follow up

✔ Receive progress reports and monitor

**Digital marketing campaign**

✔ Prepare draft briefs for online agencies and suppliers, including website designers, online PR, partners, email bureau and online advertising agency or principal digital agency; this is the point for competitive tendering process if appropriate

✔ Issue draft briefs to suppliers

✔ Receive feedback on briefs

✔ Finalise brief and confirm

✔ Receive supplier recommendations on campaign approach

✔ Select suppliers

✔ Evaluate costs of recommendations against expected response

✔ Comment on recommendations

- ✔ Suppliers to revise recommendations

- ✔ Suppliers to present draft plans

- ✔ Detailed proposals circulated internally for comment

- ✔ Suppliers present revised proposals

- ✔ Agree website design, formats and online marketing approaches for testing

- ✔ Design email or SMS messages, redesign/update website

- ✔ Check functionality and legal compliance

- ✔ Brief fulfilment, internal and external

- ✔ Determine data entry procedures, including return of e-questionnaire data to customer database

- ✔ Implement designs and online communication plans

- ✔ Implement data entry procedures

- ✔ Tests and checks

- ✔ Final revision of all campaign elements, including website design (navigation, interaction and links etc.), media plans, data entry and fulfilment.

- ✔ Confirm target segments

- ✔ Set live date!

- ✔ Confirm timing

- ✔ Issue email(s), SMS, search marketing, affiliate marketing and viral campaign, etc.

- ✔ Receive progress reports and monitor

- ✔ Monitor fulfilment data including responses, queries and orders

# Testing, testing, testing

## This chapter includes:

------------------------------------------------

------------------------------------------------

## About this chapter

**I**n this chapter we look at testing, across *all* direct marketing media; its uses, benefits and methodology – and the science which underpins it. Each medium has its own technical complexities which we explore, but the fundamental principles are the same for all – from direct mail to email and SMS, from press to radio to DRTV, to telephone.

Today the old conflict between 'pure' research and 'real life' testing has all but evaporated. Modern direct marketers appreciate that the two disciplines are both complementary and indispensable: whereas market research seeks to tell us why people behave in certain ways, testing tells us how they actually behave and, more to the point, how they are likely to behave.

## *Robin Fairlie F IDM*

This chapter has been written by Robin Fairlie and David Hughes, using also a quantity of material provided by Terry Forshaw.

Robin Fairlie graduated in history from Cambridge and joined the infant computer industry, leaving to become the first computer manager for Reader's Digest, and eventually serving on the Digest's UK Board. In 1980 he became Managing Director of the country's largest library supplier; in 1983 he was asked by the Post Office to serve as Chief Executive of the Direct Mail Services Standards Board, which aimed to improve ethical and professional standards in the direct mail industry.

In 1987 Robin became a freelance consultant. In this role he procured agreement between the Post Office and the industry on the detailed implementation of Mailsort, negotiated the formation of the DMA, and introduced the Mailing Standards Levy, which pays for the direct mail work of the ASA and for the Mailing Preference Service.

Robin helped to found the Direct Marketing Centre (predecessor of the IDM) and lectured on its diploma courses for many years. He has written two books and many articles on direct marketing, besides lecturing on MBA courses in the Far East. He is a Fellow of the IDM, the author of the Institute's Code of Conduct, and currently serves as co-editor in chief of the IDM's international Journal of Direct Data and Digital Marketing Practice.

Robin Fairlie, Tel 020-8340-2528;
e-mail: robin@idms.co.uk

## *David Hughes Dip DM, M IDM*

David Hughes runs an independent digital marketing consultancy, Non-Line Marketing, and has over 8 years experience of email and internet marketing. His areas of specialisation include on-line data gathering, developing email marketing communication programmes and integrating email marketing with traditional direct marketing channels.

For the past 5 years he has been a Strategic Consultant with Emailvision, a European email technology provider, helping client and agency partners with the strategic, technical and operational issues affecting email campaign success. He works with companies such as Telegraph, Kangol, Institute of Directors and 3M and has experience of email in both the BtoB and BtoC sectors. David is also the Director of the Tank! On-Line Marketing Action Group, delivering thought leadership programmes for the client marketing community and is author of the DMA UK Email Marketing Benchmarking Report.

David spent 7 years at Claritas (now Acxiom) as the European Data Acquisition Manager generating over 8 million survey responses per year across 7 countries, both on and offline. He gained an IDM Diploma, with Distinction, in 1992, is a regular speaker for the Direct Marketing Association on email issues and is a member of the IDM Digital Marketing Examination Board and a Course Tutor for the IDM Digital Marketing Diploma.

davidhughes@nonlinemarketing.com
01737 218171

# Chapter 8.2

# *Testing, testing, testing*

## *What is testing?*

**T**esting is the activity that sets direct marketing apart from all other forms of marketing. All marketing is about communicating with individuals; direct marketing alone make it the foremost aim to elicit a *response*, and offers the tools which enable the marketer to measure the cost-effectiveness of that response.

But we can go one stage further: using these tools, marketers can ask *questions* about product and marketplace (testing); provide *answers* to these questions (measurement) and make statistically reliable *predictions*. These three functions – testing, measuring and predicting – are the subject of this chapter, and they lie at the heart of any proper understanding of direct marketing.

Despite its unsophisticated label, testing is a sophisticated form of research. At its simplest, testing means a direct one-to-one comparison between two marketing options, e.g. between a high price and a low price.

For example, by presenting two different offers to identical samples of a target audience, an exact measure of the selling power of each offer can be obtained. Similarly, by presenting an identical offer to two different market segments, the responsiveness of each audience can be measured.

The simplest test of all would be to compare a single isolated variant with a known control. The example below in table 8.2.1 shows how a simple test programme can be developed to evaluate marketing options:

**Table 8.2.1    Simple test programme**

| Control | List A | Proven offer |
|---------|--------|--------------|
| Test 1  | List A | New offer |
| Test 2  | List B | Proven offer (as control) |

A simple set of tests such as that above, sheds light on a potential new market (list B) and a new offer (e.g. a lower price or a new incentive). So long as the samples are representative and the sample sizes are sufficient, the proper measurement of test results can predict the likely outcome of future marketing activity.

But testing is not a one-off event; it is a way of life, and should be conducted on a cyclic basis:

Figure 8.2.1 **Testing – a source of continuous improvement**

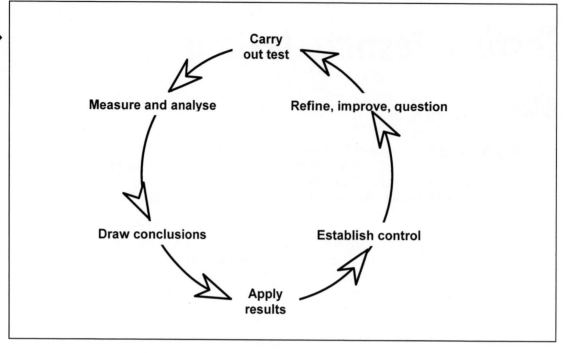

## Why test?

### If it ain't broke...

A memorable way of looking at the benefits of testing is to turn that popular adage "If it ain't broke, don't fix it" on its head. As Graeme McCorkell has pointed out, the huge advances made in Formula 1 racing car technology would never have occurred if things that hadn't broken were never replaced. Science advances precisely because innovators constantly pose the question: "How can we improve what is already working very nicely?"

So in direct marketing the rule is:

If it ain't broke yet, it will be one day. So study now how to fix it so it works better still and is even less likely to break in the future.

## The first rule of testing

Many tyro direct marketers – and non-direct marketers with a smattering of knowledge – become preoccupied with their new toy: measurable response. All too often they channel all their creative energies into formulating (and testing) relatively unimportant variables, almost always those involving creative elements, e.g. copy style, layout and design, paper folds and envelope colours. Such tinkering rarely, if ever, pays off.

The golden rule of testing is that tests must be meaningful. *Only significant marketing variables should be tested.* As one of the modern industry's founding fathers puts it:

"Test the BIG things"

*Bob Stone*, Successful Direct Marketing

Testing *marketing* variables will normally have a much more dramatic impact on response and profitability than any esoteric creative test, and your test programme should reflect this.

## *The seven key marketing variables*

The following seven factors in table 8.2.2 are the key elements responsible for the success or failure of *all* direct marketing ventures, regardless of medium. Later in this chapter we deal with specific issues relating to press advertising, to DRTV, to radio, to web advertising and to email. However, the principles on which we are now embarked (which have their broadest application in the context of direct mail and email) are applicable to all these, and to telephone testing as well (which has the added advantage over other media of person-to-person contact, allowing assessment of *reasons* for testees' behaviour.) We can rank these key elements in the following order of importance:

Table 8.2.2    **The seven key marketing variables**

| | |
|---|---|
| 1. Product/service – nature and quality of | equal 1st |
| 1. Target audience (list, media) | |
| 3. Offer (e.g. price, incentives, terms) | |
| 4. Format | |
| 5. Creative | |
| 6. Timing | |
| 7. Response mechanism | |

Fortunately, this hierarchical order of importance corresponds with the normal chronology of planning and implementation, i.e. in a normal sequence, product and audience are planned first and creative treatment later. So there is no excuse for overlooking the most important variables.

However, because these so-called 'leverage factors' describe incremental gains, over time less incremental gain will come from testing the higher-ranked variables and more incremental gain will come from testing lower-ranked variables.

**Testing is not only about maximising response**

Bear in mind, as we discuss the impact of each of the seven chief marketing variables, that their impact will vary greatly from one situation to another. Remember also that we are not simply concerned with which will deliver the highest response.

As well as response, our test plans should take into account:

✔ Potential cost savings, effect on profits

✔ Outlay costs, absolute expenditure – affordable or not

✔ Competitive pressures (change may be unavoidable)

✔ Risks incurred or avoided (not necessarily financial)

✔ Long-term implications (you cannot always go back)

✔ Overall marketing objectives (not always response and immediate profit

**Matching test objectives to marketing objectives**

Company A's marketing objective was to recruit 10,000 new clients at a cost per new client of £10 each; its list/media test programme was structured to identify new lists or media to generate new clients within this threshold using a proven offer/creative approach.

Company B's marketing objective was to reduce mailing costs by 10 per cent while maintaining volume. The variables it selected for testing included cheaper formats and fewer enclosures per mailing.

We now look at each of the seven key marketing variables in turn:

## Key variable: product/service

In many situations the product or service on offer will be predetermined. Test programmes will be built around the other six key variables.

However, the benefits of testing can be profound in the area of product design and development. If the product or service has insufficient appeal then all else will fail, and small-scale product tests will have limited the cost and risk at the launch stage. More significantly, testing can take place prior to expensive product development. This may involve *dry testing*.

Using dry testing, a number of product concepts and promotions can be tested simultaneously. Only successful products need go forward to more expensive product development stages.

What is dry testing?

Dry testing means developing a product concept and promotional package without having produced the final product. Promotions must make clear to prospects that the product will not immediately be available and should not request payment until the order has been fulfilled. To overcome negative reactions, dry-test products are often offered on special terms, e.g. a pre-launch discount. Subsequent production can be based upon responses to dry tests. Beware! Dry testing can cause serious hostility among prospects if it is not fairly and openly conducted.

## Key variable: target audience

The selection of lists and choice of media (and programme content in the case of TV and radio) are absolutely critical to the success of direct marketing. The wrong creative approach to the right audience may succeed, but the right creative approach to the wrong audience is doomed to failure.

Mailing list test options include:

✔ Customer lists

✔ Enquirers

✔ Lapsed or dormant customers

✔ Affinity groups

✔ Lifestyle databases

✔ Cold lists (i.e. bought or rented lists)

Other addressable media that can also be tested include:

✔ Phone

✔ Electronic media (e.g. email lists, visitors to websites, responders to SMS messages)

## Key variable: offer and price

The best offer you'll ever make your customers is the intrinsic promise of your brand. But few brands are so strong that an additional offer won't greatly enhance a product's appeal and increase its sales. As Jim Kobs says, *"The right offer can sell almost anything"*. The key word is 'right'. The offer needs to be relevant to the target market.

Offers may be as simple as the product at an attractive price. Or they may be multi-faceted including optional extras, special packaging, incentives, terms, payment options and guarantees etc.

Importantly, offers not only affect response, they also impact other variables, i.e. different offers produce different levels of ongoing customer performance. For this reason, sophisticated marketers track the results of offer tests for several years.

Price is often as critical as the product itself in terms of whether or not a sale is made. Its effect is something which most experienced exponents find impossible to predict without testing. For example, a high price can occasionally pull the best response, while a low price may not guarantee you a sufficient number of orders. For this reason, and because of the impact of price on profitability, price testing should be considered wherever possible. To non-marketers, the concept of price testing is often suspect, but if the exercise is carried out sensitively there should be no problem. After all, the aim of price testing is not to find the highest price at which goods can be sold; it is to find the *profit maximising* price and this may well be a lower price than customers might otherwise expect to pay.

In a direct high/low price test, it is important that customers buying the product at the higher price are refunded the difference and the reason for the lower price should be explained, e.g. lower production costs resulting from higher volume responses.

If you test only two prices against each other, and the low price proves to be more profitable, what have you learnt? Perhaps a still lower price would do even better....So, always test three prices, with the one you consider most likely in the middle.

## Key variable: format

The physical format of a mailing piece or advertisement is another important area for testing. For example, it has been known for a large C4 pack to more than double response when tested against a smaller DL pack. Conversely, small packs have triumphed over large packs in different situations, especially when their lower costs are taken into account.

Possible format tests include size, number of components, paper weights/ qualities, types of envelope (e.g. paper or polythene), and addressing method. The equivalent in email marketing might be length of message, text versus HTML, and so on.

Experience shows that the following tests are not usually significant: colour of paper, label versus direct addressing, blue versus black signature, name and style of signature, franking versus preprinted postal impression etc. – yet all of these are regularly tested by blinkered marketers at the expense of more meaningful marketing variables such as, for example, payment methods.

## Key variable: creative treatment

Although low on the hierarchy list, creative elements (copy, layout, typography and colour etc.) can significantly affect results. However, care must be taken when drawing conclusions. A well-written letter clearly stating benefits, proposition, product details and action required may increase response, but it is easier to conclude *that* it works rather than *why* it works.

### Whose garden is it anyway?

A manufacturer of garden tools decided to find out whether results were affected by the use of male or female gardeners in illustrations. To his surprise, although his garden implements were heavy and difficult to handle even for professional gardeners, both enquiries and sales were enhanced by some 20 per cent when female models were employed. This does not necessarily mean more gardeners are female, although it might mean that. It is a typical example of how testing shows what happens, while research is needed to know why it happens.

### So what to test?

The list below demonstrates only a fraction of the number and variety of tests regularly carried out by direct marketers:

✔ Product, product name, with and without accessories, deluxe or standard versions

✔ High price versus low price, payment terms, paid or free trial, size of discount

✔ Free gift versus no free gift, nature and number of gifts, reason for gift

✔ Prize draw: nature and value of prize(s)

✔ Media tests, e.g. newspapers versus magazines, positions, sizes, timing

✔ Lists

✔ Formats, e.g. envelope size, number of components, use of colour

✔ Copy, tone, positioning, length

## *Key variable: timing*

Although timing tests are often neglected in test programmes, timing can play a very significant role in direct marketing success and failure. There are obvious situations where the product has a link with seasonality, e.g. a gardening product, a Christmas hamper, a holiday or an educational product coinciding with the commencement of the academic year.

However, seasonality is often far more subtle. For example, when would you expect private motor insurance applications to peak – at the beginning of the registration year, in January, at the beginning of summer or none of these? Certainly until recently the peak was in March, one explanation being that motorists used to lay up their cars for the duration of the winter!

Clearly it is difficult to generalise about timing. Some mail order companies' tests have shown July to be a strong selling period – maybe as a result of less 'clutter' in the press and mail from competitors. Others typically favour January to February and September to November. Timing should therefore always be included in any serious test programme if results are to be maximised. Not surprisingly, media owners have become aware of these peaks and troughs and now adjust their rates accordingly, so that planning should take into account savings from using less popular, cheaper time slots.

One of the surest guides to seasonality and timing is directories such as Yellow Pages, where an advertisement may sit unchanged year in, year out. A simple tracking of enquiries/sales will accurately pinpoint peaks and troughs of interest.

**Some like it hot**

When would you expect swimming pool enquiries to peak? Remember a pool may take several months to plan and build and so, to be ready for the first hot day of summer, you might expect prospects to make their plans just after Christmas, or perhaps March at the latest. When do they peak? Many suppliers report enquiries peaking on the first hot day of summer! No doubt the same goes for other summer-related capital goods: sun awnings, conservatories and garden furniture etc.

### Key variable: response mechanism

Time was when direct mail only offered coupon response. Tests of coupon therefore focused on the size of the coupon or creative considerations, e.g. whether or not to repeat the offer or call to action in the coupon.

Nowadays, however, there are many more ways your prospect might respond, notably by phone, fax or email. So, you might wish to test Freephone versus STD or fax *plus* email against fax *or* email.

In testing any of these combinations, though, remember the general rule of response: the more response options you offer, the higher response volumes are likely to be.

One final thought: important though response volumes and rates are, it is the cost of the response and its quality that will matter most. The volume of response is quickly measured, but the quality of the response takes much longer to determine.

# How to design a test programme

Before we begin to design a test programme we need to fully understand the campaign of which it is to form a part.

In table 8.2.3 below a 12-step checklist for planning and executing a test programme has been compiled, from initial campaign objectives to final analysis and reporting on test results. We now explore the three practical steps in setting up a test programme: steps 4, 5 and 6 from that master checklist.

### First establish the control

In direct marketing generally, the control is simply your best-performing package, insert, advertisement or script. It is the base against which all test results should be measured. The control is the approach you would use if you were unable to test alternatives; what some exponents term 'the banker'. Test programmes should monitor the continued effectiveness of the control while at the same time trying to beat it – the 'beat the champ' principle.

If yours is a new venture you will have to research industry norms to establish a control; using direct mail you will probably start with a fairly standard pack (e.g. letter, brochure, order form, outer and reply envelopes). This need not inhibit you from being more adventurous – it simply means that you will have a baseline against which to judge more ambitious departures. Hopefully you will conserve your creative energies for testing the key marketing variables!

An important reason for testing – perhaps *the* most important reason – is that at some point your control will tire and cease to perform adequately. At this point you will need a replacement control, developed and honed from your test programme.

Table 8.2.3    **The 12 steps in building a test programme**

| Step 1 | Define the overall campaign objectives. | What is important to the campaign's success? What are the *real* objectives? |
|---|---|---|
| Step 2 | Understand the parameters of the campaign as a whole. | How many mailings? Available list size? Opportunities for testing? Budget? How responses to be handled? Time span? Is response device logical and clear? Data to be captured etc? |
| Step 3 | Decide list selection criteria. | Remember test lists must be representative of the market universe. See Part III of this section. |
| Step 4 | Establish the control/s. | See details in the text. |
| Step 5 | Decide the test strategy. | See details in the text. |
| Step 6 | Construct test matrix. | See details in the text. |
| Step 7 | Carry out tests. | Is any cell responding far better than others? Can this be explained? Are all cells contacted at the same time? Is bad weather affecting overall response? Note your conclusions for future reference. |
| Step 8 | Observe responses. | Was the programme executed as planned? If changed, will this affect results? |
| Step 9 | Check back. | Plot key variables and record what worked and what failed to meet objectives. |
| Step 10 | Analyse results. | Can you spot any correlations between winners and losers? Any key variables among responders to tests, e.g. age, gender? |
| Step 11 | Study analysis. | Try to gain a subjective view of who is responding to tests, and why. |
| Step 12 | If possible, undertake other forms of analysis, e.g. regression analysis. | Begin the process again. |
| Step 1 | Define overall objectives for the next campaign. | |

### Next decide the test strategy:

**Test strategy statement**

Project name: SPRING 2001 WIDGET MAILING

Issued: 11/09/2000

Control: C4 control pack with 2-page letter, control brochure and reply card

| | Test | Objectives | Method |
|---|---|---|---|
| 1. | Format test: C5 versus C4 outer | To reduce mailing pack costs while maintaining control response | All internal elements as control pack, folded to fit C5 outer envelope |
| 2. | Free gift added – lowkey presentation | To improve response and profitability by offering a free gift, without affecting the basic tone and structure of the control pack | Mention free gift in the letter copy and PS |
| 3. | Free gift added – heavy emphasis | To improve response and profitability by offering a free gift and featuring the gift heavily throughout the pack | Include separate fourcolour 'free gift' flyer. Refer to gift in the letter and copy and PS and include an order card with illustration |
| 4. | New creative | To achieve a 'breakthrough' against the existing control by using a very different approach | All new elements |

An important rule when constructing a test strategy is: *do not test more than one variable against control at a time*. If, for instance you change, say, the offer and the creative in one test and you get a significant uplift in response, to what can you attribute that uplift, the offer or the creative?

There are, however, two major exceptions to the rule of single-variable testing:

1.  In some situations it may be wise to break right away from earlier thinking and test a completely new approach, in which case the more different the new approach, the better. This should never be done in the absence of a strict control, or the effect in future years may be literally to lose one's bearings and not know which way to turn next ('wandering').

2.  Multi-variable tests can be carried out if a strictly scientific basis is used to determine sample size and test structure, as we explore below.

### Finally, construct your test matrix – direct mail and email only

At the most advanced level of direct marketing, where large amounts of money are at stake, multi-variable test matrices are constructed and monitored by statisticians. For the lay reader, some guidance is given below on compiling direct mail test matrices to compare several variables at once.

Let us suppose you want to compare three lists (A, B, C) and three offers (1, 2, 3). Strictly speaking you would need to cover all possible combinations of list and offer, each to a statistically significant sample. If your minimum sample size was 6,000, your test matrix would look like that in table 8.2.4 below. It would consume 54,000 valuable names (always assuming that you had 54,000 names available!).

### Table 8.2.4 **Test Matrix I**

|  | Offer 1 | Offer 2 | Offer 3 | Total |
|---|---|---|---|---|
| List A | 6,000 | 6,000 | 6,000 | 18,000 |
| List B | 6,000 | 6,000 | 6,000 | 18,000 |
| List C | 6,000 | 6,000 | 6,000 | 18,000 |
| Total | 18,000 | 18,000 | 18,000 | 54,000 |

Consuming too many names in a test, even if available, can be a serious error, and so an alternative matrix may be needed. It is possible to reduce the number of test names used by making some careful assumptions.

If we assume that the three lists (A, B, C) are sufficiently similar and the best offer is likely to work across all three lists (i.e. the lists and the offers are independent variables), then the test matrix can be revised as in table 8.2.5. Test Matrix II uses only five test samples and reduces the name requirement to 30,000 overall. The likely outcome of the blank cells can be extrapolated from those mailed.

### Table 8.2.5 **Test Matrix II**

|  | Offer 1 | Offer 2 | Offer 3 | Total |
|---|---|---|---|---|
| List A | 6,000 | 6,000 | 6,000 | 18,000 |
| List B | 6,000 | - | - | 6,000 |
| List C | 6,000 | - | - | 6,000 |
| Total | 18,000 | 6,000 | 6,000 | 30,000 |

However, an even more efficient method is a *block design* which can be used to combine all the test variables in one matrix and further reduce the number of test names used. In Test Matrix III in table 8.2.6 below, only 18,000 names have been consumed. The minimum mailing quantities of 6,000 per test are arrived at by adding up the columns. The required results are the totals for each column, both horizontally and vertically.

### Table 8.2.6 **Test Matrix III**

|  | Offer 1 | Offer 2 | Offer 3 | Total |
|---|---|---|---|---|
| List A | 2,000 | 2,000 | 2,000 | 6,000 |
| List B | 2,000 | 2,000 | 2,000 | 6,000 |
| List C | 2,000 | 2,000 | 2,000 | 6,000 |
| Total | 6,000 | 6,000 | 6,000 | 18,000 |

The benefits of multi-factor or block designs like the one above (Test Matrix III) are two-fold:

1.   The total sample size is kept to a minimum.

2.   Some light may be thrown on the effects of different combinations of factors. Remember, for these interactive effects to be statistically significant, each

individual cell total would need to be 6,000 names, which brings us back to Test Matrix I and a total of 54,000 names.

By keeping the numbers within each test cell to a minimum you run the risk of an occasional freak result. If, in a multi-factor test matrix comprising small volumes, the result of one of the cells is abnormally different from the other cells, it may be wise to ignore the result for that cell. The discrepancy may be caused by some operational problem and not the test variable itself – known as 'statistical error'. Alternatively you would need to investigate the 'freak' result very carefully and ascertain the likely cause.

### Table 8.2.7     **Test Matrix IV**

|         | **List 1** | **List 2** | **List 3** |
|---------|-----------|-----------|-----------|
| Offer 1 | Copy A    | Copy B    | Copy C    |
| Offer 2 | Copy B    | Copy C    | Copy A    |
| Offer 3 | Copy C    | Copy A    | Copy B    |

For Test Matrix IV – a 'Latin square' – we see that *nine* variables have been included: three lists, three offers and three copy variants. To test these nine variables in straight 'head-to-head' tests, i.e. testing one element against each other at a time, for the results to be meaningful, would involve 36 paired comparisons and 216,000 names.

But by using a Latin square, these tests can be carried out with only 45,000 names, or 5,000 per cell, saving hundreds of thousands of pounds on the programme.

Note each offer, list and copy variant appears in three cells. To design and evaluate the results of a complex matrix like this requires either a software package or a statistician.

# The statistical principles of testing

All prediction based on the outcome of tests relies on the theory of probability. The theory is used to assess the chances of a given test result being repeated.

By using statistical probability direct marketers can interpret response data and make decisions on the basis of objective criteria. Statistical principles provide a better decision-making foundation than 'gut feel' or partial experience. *By balancing statistical probability with sound judgement direct marketers can make the best possible decisions.*

## The role of statistics

Statistics are used to *generalise*, e.g. to summarise the behaviour of customers in a particular target market. In direct marketing, the aim is normally to *measure* the behaviour of past and present customers in order to *predict* the behaviour of future customers, although the direct marketer should never forget that predictions based on test results are conditional on other factors remaining equal.

The three statistical concepts discussed in this chapter are:

1.  Inference

2.  Significance

3.  Confidence

## 1. Inference: accuracy depends on sample size

Direct marketers not only generalise from past and present customers to future customers; they also use part of their target market to stand for their entire target market. This process of generalisation is called 'statistical inference'. The term 'inference' is used for good reason: it is never possible to prove that a future response rate will be X per cent. This can only be inferred. The smaller the group that is studied, the less certain one can be that the inference is a good one.

Because analysing the whole of a target market is usually expensive, time-consuming and often impractical, tests are performed on *samples*. A sample should be of sufficient quantity, and of a suitable character, to render it unbiased and wholly representative of a total 'universe'.

## 2. Significance: is that test difference meaningful?

Significance is what you are hoping for when you plan and execute a test: you want to know if one course of action is more productive than another, by how much, and – this part is often overlooked – whether the result is *statistically* significant. Not whether it is significant to you but whether it is significant scientifically, i.e. not simply the effect of chance. In other words, a statistically significant result is one that cannot be explained by sampling error.

## 3. Confidence: how reliable is the test overall?

Because all tests are probabilistic, we need one more assessment of the accuracy of a test before we can be sure of its value. This is the confidence level, which represents the degree of assurance that the test sample and its result are representative of the total market.

The probability that a test response truly lies within a given range is its *confidence level*. Most often 95 per cent confidence is the chosen level of confidence – implying that only once in 20 times will an identical campaign produce results outside the range inferred from your test. (There is of course, no such thing as a 100 per cent confidence level.)

As the marketer you must set the level of confidence required – that is, how confident you need to be of the significance of your test results.

# *Samples and sampling methods*

Ideally, the job of selecting a proper test sample should be given to a trained statistician. For small direct mail practitioners, or users of email, that may not be feasible. They then, above all others, must understand clearly the statistical methodology on which good sampling depends.

Users who can rely on good professional statistical help should also, for their own protection, know the principles that underlie the method. Since this chapter is in no sense a handbook of statistics, it is to these principles, together with some simplified rules of thumb, that we will now address ourselves.

The normal method of obtaining a random, representative sample in direct marketing – e.g. from a list of names and addresses – is to select every 'nth' name in the list. (You can safely ignore any jumped-up mathematician who tries to tell you this is not satisfactory.) Thus, if you have a list of 100,000 names, and you require a sample of 5,000, then you will take every 20th name for your sample.

How do we determine the required sample size? First, let's dispose of a common fallacy: it is sometimes alleged that sample size should be related to the size of the universe from which it is taken – 10 per cent or some such. This is nonsense. (If it were true, Gallup, in order to produce a valid sample of electors for a political opinion poll, would have to interview several million people.)

The criteria for determining minimum sample size are:

The confidence level required (usually 95 per cent)

The percentage variance above or below your observed test result which you will tolerate

The approximate expected response rate

That is, if the response rate is $c\%$ we wish to be $a\%$ certain that $c\%$ of our universe, plus or minus $b$ will respond in the same way.

There is a completely generalised formula for working out the correct sample size (S) for all possible values of $a$, $b$, and $c$ – but it is complex. So long as we are working with a 95 per cent confidence level, a simple formula will do:

$$S = \frac{3.8416 \times c\,(100 - c)}{b^2}$$

Now try an example. Imagine a list of prospects from whom we must get a response rate of 4.5% in order to break even; the best estimated response is 5% and the limit of error we can tolerate is 0.4%. Then our sample size must be:

$$S = \frac{3.8416 \times 5(100 - 5)}{0.4^2} = 11,405$$

But if we expect a better response – say 5.5% – we can afford a wider margin of error without risk of falling below break-even. Our formula might then become:

$$S = \frac{3.8416 \times 5.5(100 - 5.5)}{0.9^2} = 2,465$$

Always choose a value for $c$ which errs on the high side, and a low value for $b$. This may give you a larger sample than necessary, but this may be better than ending with a statistically invalid result.

Once the *actual* response to your test is known, the formula can be transposed in order to indicate what the real margin of error in your result is. Thus:

$$b = \sqrt{\frac{3.8416 \times c(100 - c)}{S}}$$

Then, if the actual test response were 5.2%, with a sample of 11,405:

$$b = \sqrt{\frac{3.8416 \times 5.2(100 - 5.2)}{11,405}} = 0.41$$

I.e. we can be 95% certain that a mailing to the universe of which this sample is representative will (other things being equal) produce a response of 5.2% plus or minus 0.41 – that is, between 4.79 and 5.61%.

Or, with our smaller sample

$$b = \sqrt{\frac{3.8416 \times 5.2(100 - 5.2)}{2,465}} = 0.88, - \text{ a result between 4.32 and 6.08\%}$$

It is worth noting that, for most practical purposes we are really operating at a level of 97.5 per cent confidence rather than 95 per cent. This is because our variance can be either above or below our test result. Most practitioners worry about checking the low point of their expectations, which they can be 97.5 per cent sure of exceeding, and are less worried about the 2.5 per cent chance of getting a result above the maximum variance.

The foregoing examples show how to set sample sizes and project rollout responses from test samples. In practice, rollout conditions are rarely consistent with test conditions, and many factors need to be considered when assessing the viability of rolling out a test. For example, the timing of the rollout, the level of competitive activity, and general economic circumstances, could all significantly affect response. So be careful: this is where judgement must come to the aid of statistics!

## Testing alternative approaches

So how do we determine statistically valid differences between alternative approaches, e.g. when more than one sample is being mailed?

### Is the difference significant?

A test sample of 10,000 was mailed with Pack A and a further 10,000 received a variation that we shall call Pack B. The question is: are the different results statistically significant?

The response percentages were:  Pack A  2.14%  (+/- 0.283 – i.e. 1.857 – 2.423)
Pack B  2.68%  (+/- 0.316 – i.e. 2.364 – 2.996)

Since there is potential overlap between these results (Pack A could go as high as 2.423%, while Pack B could be as low as 2.364), we cannot be 95% confident that Pack B will perform better. (We could, however, be 90% confident: rework the formula using 2.706 in place of 3.8416 for a 90% confidence level; the overlap now disappears.)

## *Using statistical tables*

We have made much of the statistical formulae in this section to demonstrate the principles involved. In day-to-day direct marketing it is far more likely that you will refer to published tables of sample size and probability.

Below in table 8.2.8 you will find a useful table of sample sizes covering responses from 0.5 per cent to 10 per cent, the range most frequently found in consumer direct marketing. The table shows the minimum sample size required for different response rates and accuracy levels.

To use the statistical table, given the most commonly used 95 per cent confidence level, you need to have a broad idea of the response rates that you anticipate. This will probably be based on previous controls. As the minimum size of sample increases with higher response rates you should slightly overestimate your anticipated response levels when deciding on sample size.

Then, you must decide on an acceptable level of accuracy. The accuracy will affect any calculations of break-even or profitability. For example, are you going to be satisfied by results which are within + 0.5 per cent of your expected response, or do you need to be sure to within 0.2 per cent? The decision often depends on the lower limit as this may represent break-even or budget cut-off points.

**Table 8.2.8**  **Table of minimum sample size for a test or control mailing 95 per cent confidence level**

| Anticipated response rate to the mailing | Acceptable plus or minus error on anticipated % response | | | | | | | | | | | |
|---|---|---|---|---|---|---|---|---|---|---|---|---|
| | 0.1 | 0.2 | 0.25 | 0.3 | 0.4 | 0.5 | 0.6 | 0.7 | 0.75 | 0.8 | 0.9 | 1.0 |
| 0.5% | 19,100 | 4,800 | 3,100 | 2,100 | : | : | : | : | : | : | : | : |
| 1.0% | 38,000 | 9,500 | 6,100 | 4,200 | 2,400 | : | : | : | : | : | : | : |
| 1.5% | 56,800 | 14,200 | 9,100 | 6,300 | 3,500 | 2,300 | : | : | : | : | : | : |
| 2.0% | 75,300 | 18,800 | 12,000 | 8,400 | 4,700 | 3,000 | 2,100 | : | : | : | : | : |
| 2.5% | 93,600 | 23,400 | 15,000 | 10,400 | 5,900 | 3,700 | 2,600 | : | : | : | : | : |
| 3.0% | 111,800 | 27,900 | 17,900 | 12,400 | 7,000 | 4,500 | 3,100 | 2,300 | 2,000 | : | : | : |
| 3.5% | 129,800 | 32,400 | 20,800 | 14,400 | 8,100 | 5,200 | 3,600 | 2,600 | 2,300 | 2,000 | : | : |
| 4.0% | 147,500 | 36,900 | 23,600 | 16,400 | 9,200 | 5,900 | 4,100 | 3,000 | 2,600 | 2,300 | : | : |
| 4.5% | 165,100 | 41,300 | 26,400 | 18,300 | 10,300 | 6,600 | 4,600 | 3,400 | 2,900 | 2,600 | 2,000 | : |
| 5.0% | 182,500 | 45,600 | 29,200 | 20,300 | 11,400 | 7,300 | 5,100 | 3,700 | 3,200 | 2,900 | 2,300 | : |
| 5.5% | 199,700 | 49,900 | 31,900 | 22,200 | 12,500 | 8,000 | 5,500 | 4,100 | 3,500 | 3,100 | 2,500 | 2,000 |
| 6.0% | 216,700 | 54,200 | 34,700 | 24,100 | 13,500 | 8,700 | 6,000 | 4,400 | 3,900 | 3,400 | 2,700 | 2,200 |
| 6.5% | 233,500 | 58,400 | 37,400 | 25,900 | 14,600 | 9,300 | 6,500 | 4,800 | 4,200 | 3,600 | 2,900 | 2,300 |
| 7.0% | 250,100 | 62,500 | 40,000 | 27,800 | 15,600 | 10,000 | 6,900 | 5,100 | 4,400 | 3,900 | 3,100 | 2,500 |
| 7.5% | 266,500 | 66,600 | 42,600 | 29,600 | 16,700 | 10,700 | 7,400 | 5,400 | 4,700 | 4,200 | 3,300 | 2,700 |
| 8.0% | 282,700 | 70,700 | 45,200 | 31,400 | 17,700 | 11,300 | 7,900 | 5,800 | 5,000 | 4,400 | 3,500 | 2,800 |
| 8.5% | 298,800 | 74,700 | 47,800 | 33,200 | 18,700 | 12,000 | 8,300 | 6,100 | 5,300 | 4,700 | 3,700 | 3,000 |
| 9.0% | 314,600 | 78,700 | 50,300 | 35,000 | 19,700 | 12,600 | 8,700 | 6,400 | 5,600 | 4,900 | 3,900 | 3,100 |
| 9.5% | 330,300 | 82,600 | 52,800 | 36,700 | 20,600 | 13,200 | 9,200 | 6,700 | 5,900 | 5,200 | 4,100 | 3,300 |
| 10.0% | 345,700 | 86,400 | 55,300 | 38,400 | 21,600 | 13,800 | 9,600 | 7,100 | 6,100 | 5,400 | 4,300 | 3,500 |

## Testing for smaller users

Many smaller users will, of course, never achieve the minimum sample sizes required, to be 90 or 95 per cent confident about their test results.

This does not mean that small operators should not test. On the contrary, testing is as important for small users of direct marketing as it is for the giants of the industry. It simply means that you should not accord too much credence to isolated tests. You should also not attempt to test minor departures from your control, but only major marketing differentials.

The golden rules for smaller operators include:

✔   Repeat important tests several times

✔   Validate test results by other research methods, e.g. follow-up interviews, customer feedback and staff reports

✔   Keep tests to absolutely significant differentials

✔   Test only one or two major departures per campaign/season

✔   Keep tests to criteria which cannot be verified by other means

## Testing when response rates are low

There are, unfortunately, circumstances in which the mathematical formulae discussed above do not hold. This is the case when response rates are very low – below 0.1 per cent. This will not often occur in direct mail or email (although it might in the case of a very high priced product) but will be the case in most space advertising. (The same is also true in radio or TV advertising when you are testing the response from one region against the response from another – i.e. the audiences being tested are not matched samples.)

In these circumstances, the procedure for comparing the results of two tests (or a test and control) is as follows:

1.   Total the responses from the two tests

2.   Determine the confidence level (90 or 95 per cent) required

3.   Then, for the difference between the two responses to be significant, the larger response rate must constitute a proportion of the total as shown in the table below:

Table 8.2.9 **Significant percentage share for confidence level of:**

| Total response | 90% | 95% |
|---|---|---|
| 100 | 60 | 61 |
| 150 | 58 | 59 |
| 200 | 57 | 58 |
| 250 | 56 | 57 |
| 400 | 55 | 55 ½ |
| 600 | 54 | 54 ½ |
| 1,000 | 53 | 53 ½ |

In other words, with a total response of 200, the difference between the two tests would be significant at 95 per cent confidence only if the larger of the two responses were 116 or more. (This method is a form of the chi-squared test, and should be used, instead of the significance-testing method described earlier, whenever you are dealing with a response rate below 0.1 per cent or are testing two unmatched audiences against each other.)

# The cost of testing

Testing has a cost – and therefore requires a budget. The cost of testing stems from such items as:

✗ Higher print and production costs. Shorter runs and more variants inevitably result in higher unit costs.

✗ Loss of discounts. Variations of materials and timing can lead to forfeiture of volume discounts on print, postage and media buying.

✗ Executive time. The cost of devising, implementing, controlling and reporting upon a complex test programme is extremely significant and should not be overlooked.

✗ Higher proportion of fixed costs. Developing a number of new test approaches can involve additional fixed costs, such as creative origination charges or agency fees.

Your test budget should be seen as an investment in the future, and the less you know about your market, the more you would invest in testing.

It should also be remembered that testing is not necessarily expenditure that cannot be recouped. As part of an ongoing programme, tests may well earn a higher return on investment than the remainder of the programme even in the short term, if the tests have been well chosen and implemented.

# *Monitoring and evaluating test results*

A carefully structured test programme will count for nothing if the results are not properly monitored, analysed and evaluated.

Monitoring and evaluating systems can be divided into five stages as follows:

>Stage 1.    Information processing
>
>Stage 2.    Response summaries
>
>Stage 3.    Results analysis and evaluation
>
>Stage 4.    Programme reviews and reports
>
>Stage 5.    Campaign library maintenance

## *Stage 1.   Information processing*

Personnel who physically handle responses must be briefed with relevant campaign details (products, timing and source codes) and should also appreciate the need for accuracy.

The response handler's brief should include:

? When response should be counted (daily or weekly).

? Exactly what should be recorded (single/multiple orders, order values and source codes).

? Checks to be made to ensure source codes are not wrongly captured. The system should recognise current promotion codes and input data should be verified.

Where the campaign is being conducted through digital media, response tracking can be handled automatically – provided that the requirements are thought through and fully specified in advance.

## *Stage 2.   Response summaries*

When the first orders or enquiries are received, systems should be in place to provide ongoing response summaries. Although it is dangerous to draw too many conclusions from early results, where response is exceptionally high or low, early warning allows immediate adjustment of fulfilment resources. The following should be considered:

? Will response actuals be shown against response projections?

? Who will perform what analyses and how often?

? Has an analysis schedule been set up?

## Stage 3.   Results analysis and evaluation

Once campaign results are final (or if final results can be accurately projected), they should be carefully analysed. Results analysis is two-stage:

1.   **Initial response analysis** establishes that results are statistically sound, i.e. the absolute number of orders received is adequate and differences statistically significant.

2.   **Back-end (subsequent customer performance) analysis**. Once all campaign costs are known and performance rates established (e.g. conversion from enquiries to sales and bad debts), the profitability of the test programme can be calculated. Depending on test objectives, it is often not until this stage that meaningful conclusions can be drawn.

For example 'two incentives' may outpull 'one incentive' at the enquiry stage, but a poor conversion rate may mean that 'one incentive' is the most profitable approach.

Remember, when test results are analysed, additional costs attributable to testing must be taken out of the calculation. Rollout cost projections should be compared with control costs to establish which is the more cost-effective, test variation or control, in the long haul. Higher origination costs, higher costs associated with smaller print runs and discounts etc. need to be deducted to reflect the rollout conditions.

## Stage 4.   Programme reviews and reports

To avoid some of the problems outlined in this section it is important to set up formal review meetings or, at the very least, structured test programme reports in order to:

✔   Confirm the validity of test results.

✔   Objectively assess results and evaluate against test objectives.

✔   Balance the results with judgement and past experience. Do any external variables or circumstances need to be considered?

✔   Agree key decisions affecting future marketing activity and adjust future programmes accordingly, i.e. should the control be changed, should you adopt the low price, do you retest or drop the new incentive?

## Stage 5.   Campaign library maintenance

A well-maintained campaign library is essential and should provide a permanent record of all key marketing information for future reference. Details of test programme results and objectives, analyses, recommendations and decisions taken should all be accessible, together with appropriate sample packs or advertisements.

All too often such an information base is not properly maintained or is made the responsibility of a junior member of staff. Having invested time and money in acquiring direct marketing knowledge, you should carefully record, maintain, and refer to it regularly.

## How to ensure the reliability of testing

At several points during this section we have stressed that test results should be valid when compared to control all else being equal or, as the scientists say, 'subject to consistent conditions'.

We have dealt with statistical error, but what about operational error and other factors outside our control? The graphic in figure 8.2.2 draws attention to some of the many factors which can lead to predictions being rendered inaccurate and thus to disappointing outcomes:

### Figure 8.2.2    How testing and forecasting can go wrong

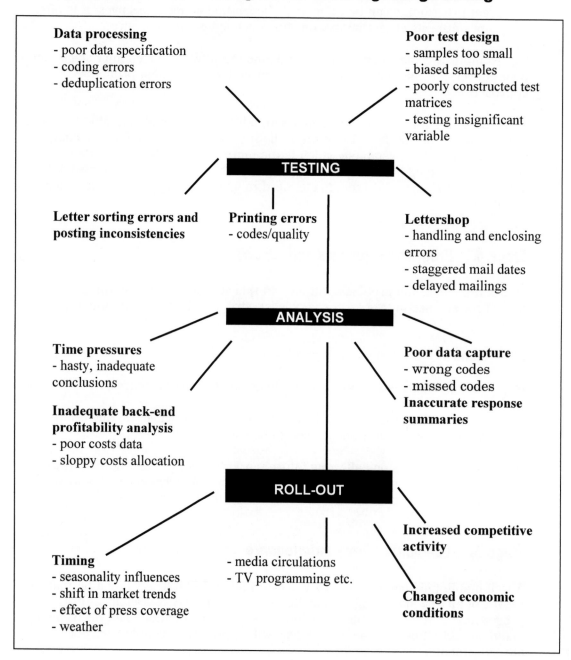

**Data processing**
- poor data specification
- coding errors
- deduplication errors

**Poor test design**
- samples too small
- biased samples
- poorly constructed test matrices
- testing insignificant variable

**TESTING**

**Letter sorting errors and posting inconsistencies**

**Printing errors**
- codes/quality

**Lettershop**
- handling and enclosing errors
- staggered mail dates
- delayed mailings

**ANALYSIS**

**Time pressures**
- hasty, inadequate conclusions

**Inadequate back-end profitability analysis**
- poor costs data
- sloppy costs allocation

**Poor data capture**
- wrong codes
- missed codes

**Inaccurate response summaries**

**ROLL-OUT**

**Timing**
- seasonality influences
- shift in market trends
- effect of press coverage
- weather

- media circulations
- TV programming etc.

**Increased competitive activity**

**Changed economic conditions**

### The role of judgement

The theory and principles behind direct response testing are sound. The statistical concepts used are reassuring. However, it must be stressed that testing is an aid to judgement and not a replacement for it. Test-based experience must be modified with judgement in order to reach decisions.

---

**TEST RESULTS + JUDGEMENT = DECISION**

---

Testing can provide invaluable guidance and can dramatically improve long-term profitability, but it is an imperfect science. Many variables outside your control can and do affect test results. It is as well to be as aware of the pitfalls of testing as of the opportunities it affords.


# Press testing

For direct marketers developing customer acquisition programmes across a range of media, testing in space advertising can be as important as direct mail testing.

But, whereas direct mail permits testing a wide range of variables very quickly, space advertising opportunities for testing are fewer. Advertising tests must accommodate the physical limitations of print media. Several techniques are used for testing advertising in space and inserts, as follows:

## Perfect splits using inserts

A number of versions of an insert can be interleaved or ganged up at the print stage before being supplied to the publication. In this way a number of options (usually not more than six) can be tested in any one issue of the host medium. This method is ideal for accurate testing of such variables as product, price, incentive, headline, copy and illustrations etc. – anything printed on the surface of the insert (figure 8.2.3):

## Figure 8.2.3    Perfect splits using inserts

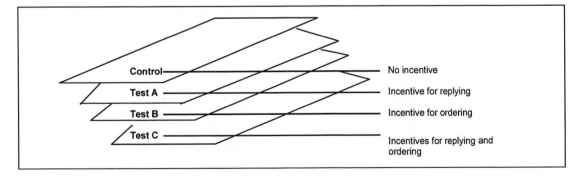

It is more difficult to test different formats of inserts (e.g. unequal sizes, shapes or thicknesses) by this method, since printers and publishers cannot easily arrange random distribution of different items. However, many publishers do offer test facilities for unlike inserts by ensuring that batches of test inserts are delivered to matching areas in equal quantities (figure 8.2.4):

Figure 8.2.4   **Testing formats of inserts**

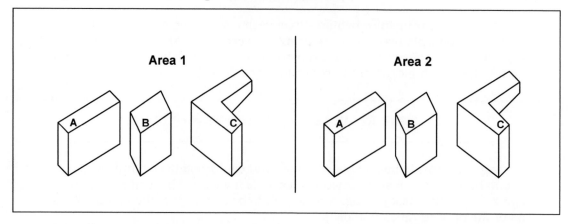

A further advantage of insert testing is that any number of media can be included on the test schedule with no increase in cost or complexity. Results can be measured not only by test, but also by medium. Interaction between medium and test can also be observed in this way.

NB:   Similar procedures can, of course, be applied to door-to-door testing.


## Space advertising: A/B splits

Many publications are printed two-up, meaning the printer produces two copies simultaneously from each machine. By changing a plate affecting half of the press sheet, a perfect 50/50 or A/B split can be achieved. In this way you can arrange for each alternate copy of a publication to contain either advertisement A or advertisement B.

Some publications offer split-run facilities using several machines printing simultaneously. You can arrange for half the machines to print your A copy and half the machine to print your B copy (figure 8.2.5).

NB:   Not all publications offer A/B splits: in fact the number that do has declined over time. For up-to-date information on this situation, you should apply to the 'newspaper publishers', or the Periodical Publishers' Association.

Figure 8.2.5   **A/B Splits**

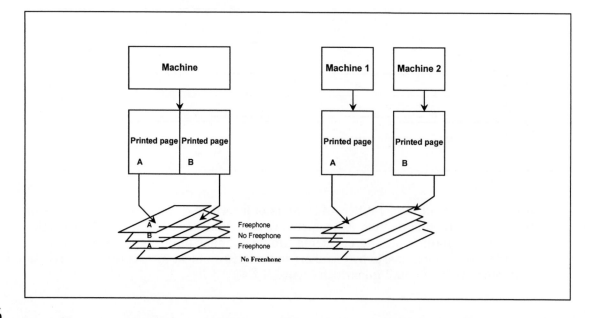

A/B splits can be used to compare a wide variety of variables but always two at a time. In theory, A/B splits are perfect samples, since each alternate copy of the publication contains copy A and copy B retrospectively. Excellent samples of several million copies can be achieved with national newspapers or combinations of magazines.

However, the results of A/B splits, while extremely useful, are not individually reliable. For example, due to breakdowns or other operational reasons, a printer may not always print equal numbers of your A and B advertisements, although this fact will be unknown to you. A/B splits are a facility offered to advertisers at a nominal cost and are generally outside the publisher's legal obligations. Therefore no redress will be available.

### A cautionary tale

Some years ago, the agency for Plumb's stretch covers booked a split run in a national newspaper for their client. By mischance, they sent the same copy for each half of the split-run test. The only difference was the key or code number in the coupon on each ad (used to identify the source of responses). One key number pulled 14 per cent more replies than the other key number.

Earlier in this chapter we devoted much space to a discussion of assessing test results. We gave particular attention to assessment of results where the response rate is very low – as is normally the case in space advertising. But whatever the response rate may be, and whatever the statistical methods employed, the golden rule of A/B splits, especially when using newspapers, is not to attach too much credence to a single result. Always repeat important tests several times before drawing far-reaching conclusions, above all if the results are counter-intuitive.

Many newspapers mark their editions with a small 'A' or 'B' at the top or bottom of pages on which split copy occurs so that you can spot A/B splits by acquiring several consecutive copies.

## Cross-over testing

Cross-over testing is a technique sometimes used where individual publications do not have A/B split capabilities but where tests are important for the product. Cross-over testing can also be used for testing pairs of advertisements which are different in size, position and use of colour etc. It is, however, less reliable than A/B split testing and far less reliable than testing with inserts.

Using two similar publications, advertisement A is first run in one magazine with advertisement B running in the other. Then, in a subsequent issue, the advertisements are switched. The results are aggregated over the two issues and comparisons drawn, as in table 6.2.10:

Table 8.2.10 **Example of a cross-over test**

| | Magazine 1 | | | | Magazine 2 | |
|---|---|---|---|---|---|---|
| | Copy | Response | | | Copy | Response |
| 1st issue | A | 240 | | | B | 120 |
| 2nd issue | B | 180 | | | A | 160 |
| Total | | 420 | | | | 280 |

Clearly, extrapolating results from this cross-over test is not an entirely satisfactory basis for an important decision. As with A/B splits, it is unwise to base decision making on isolated tests but to repeat important tests several times if possible.

## Press testing: a summary

When testing a publication, use your control advertisement where possible.

✔ If your control advertisement is particularly expensive, experiment with smaller or cheaper spaces.

✔ Different media and copy often produce widely varying ongoing customer performance (the so-called 'back end'). It is therefore wise to calculate back-end results carefully before settling on control advertisements and media.

✔ Never rely on single press test results. The more critical the decision, the more tests should be carried out (say four to six). Fewer tests than this may yield inexplicably contradictory results.

✔ Where two advertisements regularly produce similar, satisfactory results regard this as a good outcome. It could mean you have a second winner!

In summary, testing in press (inserts or space) offers less flexibility than direct mail testing. It is also less reliable in its results. But there is no other way to compare the response-inducing power of advertising in newspapers and magazines. The important point is to be aware of the deficiencies and to retest frequently.

# Testing in non-print media

The principles of testing are the same whether the medium is direct mail, press insert, DRTV, email, SDMS or whatever. The test must:

✔ Be measurable

✔ Have the minimum number of variables at play

✔ Have test criteria clearly identified for post-campaign evaluation

However, across the individual media options there are many factors that affect the type of testing and evaluation that is possible.

The internet, on the other hand, has the ability to provide an audit trail to rival all others. The downside is that in the majority of cases the profile of the audience and impacts can only be assumed by association with the site content, as there is very little site audience research, except where visitors have to carry out a detailed registration process.

## Television and DRTV

In drawing up an initial test we need to identify which are the factors that are likely to have the greatest bearing on the overall results, and which can be considered opportunities for further refinement. TV has a robust electronic audience measurement system, BARB, which gives us accurate impact data, audience demographics and programme and advertiser details against which to correlate response information. The aim must be to minimise the capital risk while maximising the response information available for robust analysis.

**Cost of entry: what airtime might we use, and what might it cost?**

?      Who are the core prospects? When do they watch?

?      Do we need to chase a specific audience or can we track down low-cost airtime?

?      When do the competitors advertise?

?      How long do we need to run the schedule to gain a robust insight?

Cost is influenced primarily by the choice of station, the time of year, the daypart and the commercial length. For example, across the ITV stations alone, the regional and monthly variations, combined with the difference in station universe, mean that the capital cost of 100 x 30-second TVRs could vary from as little as £4,000 to as much as £150,000. Cost-per- thousand (CPT) could be as little as £1.50 and as much as £20.

So, to give our test the best chance of success, we need to construct our schedule so that it delivers the required audience at the most cost-efficient price. A schedule constructed from a selection of the many satellite stations is definitely a good route when possible, and using the cheaper months, such as January and February, rather than say, September, is an easy but significant way to reduce initial costs.

Let's work through an example:

| | |
|---|---|
| Advertising category: | Mail order |
| Product category: | **Manchester United 1999 Treble Collection** |
| Price: | £295 inc. VAT, for boxed set of four coins |
| Payment; | Credit card or cheque, in full or instalments |
| Proposition: | Commemorative limited edition, 24-carat gold-plated |
| Media objective: | To test DRTV as a marketing option |
| Budget: | Not more than £70,000, including media, production and call handling, excluding costs of product |
| Target returns: | 130 per cent of spend (i.e. £100,000), sales of at least 400 boxed sets |
| Evaluation criteria: | All costs associated with creative and production to be amortised across test campaign |

**Cost of entry**

✔    Target audience research shows that the product purchasers from press and direct mail advertising are male biased.

✔    A planning consideration should be to investigate whether results are stronger from the more male-orientated stations; however, as the male bias is only marginal, it would be wrong to ignore the female audiences in the test stage. The influence of station profile should be reviewed in the response analysis.

✔    BARB audience data can be used to understand the audience profile and assist with the selection of stations for the test schedule.

Table 8.2.11 below shows a snapshot of how BARB data can help us understand the profile of stations. This is from the Sky media site and is updated monthly http://www.sky-skymedia.com/advertising/airtime.

## Table 8.2.11    **BARB data extract**

| Station | Male | Female | Rank |
|---|---|---|---|
| History Channel | 63% | 37% | 5= |
| National Geographic | 63% | 37% | 5= |
| Tara | 65% | 35% | 3= |
| Sky 1 | 53% | 47% | 7 |
| Sky News | 65% | 35% | 3= |
| Total Sky Sports | 70% | 30% | 2 |
| Total Sky Movies | 51% | 49% | 8 |
| Sky Travel | 34% | 66% | 9 |
| TV | 83% | 17% | 1 |

✔    A review of MMS data indicates that competitors advertise primarily in daytime airtime, across a broad spectrum of stations.

✔    The media recommendation is to construct the test across a broad range of stations, utilising a large percentage of daytime airtime, taking advantage of lower-cost audiences.

✔    Airtime negotiation resulted in 10+ stations being selected across six contractor groups. Some stations were agreed on the basis of 'CPT agreements' and others on 'spot costs'. The result was four weeks of 60-second airtime, with a regular spread of spots going out.

**Response predictions**

✔    Response calculations are based upon the press results. Response rate increased as TV is likely to generate more 'enquirers'. Conversion to sales decreased correspondingly. 0.01 per cent set as planning target, at 65 per cent conversion.

✔    The selected satellite channels consistently show average daily impacts of less than 200,000 or One Adult TVR, generating a maximum predicted spot response of 20 calls per spot. At the same time the stations are sufficiently large to ensure that the response analysis will be statistically reliable.

**Results**

✔ Response rate differed widely by station and ranged from 0.015 to 0.002 per cent.

✔ The response rate showed a strong uplift from sports-orientated channels, but not consistently from those with a male bias.

✔ ROI varied dramatically by station, ranging from 192 to just 30 per cent.

✔ The lowest CPR came from a male-biased station with a CPT index of +90 above the average for the campaign – by no means the cheapest.

✔ The two lowest cost stations produced opposing results. The mass entertainment channel delivered a high response rate with low conversion and the other, a more male-biased station, a lower response rate but good conversion to sales and a better CPR.

**Conclusion**

✔ The DRTV test was highly successful on 50 per cent of the selected stations and sufficient data was recorded to ensure that rollout campaigns could be refined to take advantage of the successes.

✔ Targeting, at the right price, delivered the best results.

✔ The cheapest airtime did not deliver the best results.

Once a product has been tested and it has been proved whether TV can produce viable business results, it is time to look at the evaluation data and isolate the aspects that can be refined.

In our above example, we found that sports-orientated environments produced good quality enquiries, converting to sales at a higher rate than those from more general entertainment environments. Many of the entertainment stations produced excellent response rates, but not of sufficient quality to lead to a sale – which after all is the end-game. The test also proved that the buying CPT was a factor that helped reduce the cost-per-response in some cases, but it was not the biggest determinant of success. In constructing future activity, the media planner can build on these factors, introducing additional stations that match the profile indicators. In addition, the next schedule can be constructed to enable evaluation of other influences, such as times of day, days of the week and break patterns, in order to see how future campaigns can be further improved.

Below we have summarised a checklist of a number of the criteria that can influence the success of DRTV campaigns:

✔ Channel and station: ITV regions, Ch4, Ch5 and GMTC macros

✔ Regionality: North versus South etc

✔ Programmes: genre (e.g. sport versus film), audience profile etc

✔ Day of week: weekday versus weekend

✔ Time of day

✔ Break position: end breaks versus centre breaks etc.

✔ Positions in breaks: first ad, last ad or just 'in there somewhere' ad

✔    Effects of proximity pairing: commercials close to each other, in the same programme or clock hour, versus more random spacing

✔    Short-term and long-term frequency effects over days, weeks and months

✔    Creative executions and creative testing are usually longer-term issues than media testing, but the following are common criteria to evaluate if you can: commercial time lengths, use of cut downs, call to action reminders, phone number types – i.e. Freephone versus lo-call, duration of phone number display, voiceover and copy rotation.

## Digital TV and iTV

Tests that are currently taking place all require much higher levels of investment than for traditional DRTV, principally to cover the cost of the computer software programming part of the equation.

**The scenarios that are possible include:**

Having a presence on one of the interactive areas such as Open. Clients using this Portal iTV include Domino's Pizza and Woolworths. To enable the interactivity of this area the viewer needs to plug their set-top box into the phone system, prior to which the viewer is receiving a continuously broadcast, navigable stream of text and video from the open satellite. So for Domino's you can select your pizza topping and flavour of cold drinks, but the order has to be placed 'online'. The open database reads the delivery address and identifies the nearest Domino's franchise, and sends them the order details. The 30-minute guarantee is still maintained and the system appears to work very well.

On the ITVDigital terrestrial platform (formerly OnDigital), CarltonActive clients have tested interactive commercials on Carlton Food Network and Carlton Cinema. Prompted by the on-screen strap, the feature allows viewers to get more involved with the commercial message. A number of major brands have taken part to date:

✔    **Max Factor**: make-up tips and product information, plus redeemable coupons for viewers.

✔    **Bounty**: the kitchen towel. Details on product range, with tips, celebrity endorsements and a chance to win a holiday to Florida.

✔    **M&G**: detailed information on M&G's financial products.

✔    **AA**: information and quotes on insurance policies, with special promotional offers

These tests did not take the viewer out of the programme stream but are non-transactional.

Where platforms offer a return path (phone, cable link or 'web on TV' access via ONnet) it is possible to pass captured data from the set-top box to an online server and pass data back to the set-top box from the server for presentation to the viewer. TV banking is a good example.

At the time of writing, testing interactive response is both complicated and expensive. This may change as the services become more widely available, particularly if some of the common operating software is made available to work across the various platforms.

## *Radio*

Radio planning is covered in detail in chapter 5.6; however, as previously, we have detailed below the core aspects that should be included in an initial test matrix.

Like DRTV, the basic currency for radio is audience impacts, measured against a number of different target groups, such as 'all adults', 'men', 'women', ABC1s etc. derived from the RAJAR diary research. Airtime is purchased on the basis of an agreed cost-per-thousand (CPT) for the particular audience. However, pricing is much more stable than is seen with television, with minimal monthly or regional variation.

So core test criteria to include are very similar to DRTV:

**?** Who is the target audience?

**?** Which stations deliver the audience profile we need? How much do they cost? What are the impact levels?

**?** What call handling issues are there?

In response to the above questions you need to consider the following:

✔ The commercial length should be as long as is necessary to put over the sale message and the airtime selected to give the most robust test while minimising capital outlay, about £25,000 to 30,000 should suffice.

✔ Choose two or three test areas. These need to deliver audiences that are as 'average' as possible if you are looking to roll out nationally. If you are a highly regionalised brand, then choose two or three areas that are representative of your general penetration profile. It is important to try and avoid extremes, i.e. the town where you are most successful, or least successful, because this makes predicting rollout response rates more difficult.

✔ Run your commercials in all time bands that the call handling resource permits. Often daytime (ironing and cleaning time) delivers a higher response rate, but it is often beneficial to let the post-campaign statistics tell you this, and ensure you identify the best parameters for your own brand. Other factors that help response efficiency include:

– Utilising airtime at the beginning and end of the week

– Utilising airtime from midday until early evening

– Utilising airtime in conjunction with TV to establish the brand in the listeners' minds through frequency

– Utilising Freephone numbers – although this also increases the number of miscellaneous enquiries and nuisance calls, affecting statistical conversion levels, tying up the call centre unnecessarily and adding to the telephone bill!

✔ Gauging response is not always easy with radio. Consumers find it hard to recall the invisible medium as the source of an offer, and evaluation does not always show it as being as efficient as other media. But radio is an intrusive and influential medium, which has proved itself many times over for local advertisers. Therefore it can be a great help to set up an evaluation matrix that allows you to understand the effect that radio is having upon other media if you have them running concurrently, particularly print formats such as door- to-door, direct mail and directories.

We have set out below a scenario that aims to do all that ... and for less than £40,000:

**Eight-cell radio test**

1.  Scenario:
    –   Radio test for advertiser that currently has a mixed media communications campaign including direct mail, DRTV and directories.

2.  Test objectives:
    –   To test radio as an efficient response medium.
    –   To see whether radio advertising can create a climate of awareness and interest within which response to the door-to-door leaflets, direct mail and directories can be accelerated.

3.  Campaign timing:
    –   Five-week campaign to build awareness and support the door drops.
    –   Identify two to three radio areas, the final selection of which should give consideration to the weight of other media in different areas to ensure that all influencing factors are identified.
    –   Identify which stations transmit in the areas. Evaluate profile, especially AM versus FM frequencies, and size – is the area big enough to carry out all the tests you want?

4.  Campaign weight:
    –   Medium weight to ensure individual spot contribution can be measured/monitored.

5.  Campaign day and time band considerations:
    –   Airtime to run across Monday to Thursday, and Friday morning, due to call centre restrictions.
    –   Mid-morning and afternoon time bands upweighted.
    –   Morning drive-time peak spots included driving awareness and communicating the message to a wider audience. Evaluation to determine whether there is uplift from this.
    –   Evening drive-time spots to remind those who have been exposed to the proposition during the day, but who were unable to respond at the time.

**Example solution:**

✔   Granada and Anglia selected.

✔   Broadlands and Piccadilly selected: firstly due to profile match; secondly because transmission areas large enough to track DM and directory response at a postcode level and run robust door-to-door test – 40,000 leaflets targeted to each test cell. News-share and Royal Mail to be compared. Response anticipated to be lower from News-share. Need test to validate theory.

✔   Matrix with other media...

Table 8.2.12

| Region A | | | | Region B | | | |
|---|---|---|---|---|---|---|---|
| Radio station A (Broadlands 102 FM) | | No radio | | Radio station A (Piccadilly 1152 FM) | | No radio | |
| **Area 1** | | **Area 2** | | **Area 3** | | **Area 4** | |
| Norwich | | Ipswich | | Stockport | | Preston | |
| Royal Mail | News-share | Royal Mail | News-share | Royal Mail | News-share | Royal Mail | News-share |
| 50,000 | 50,000 | 50,000 | 50,000 | 50,000 | 50,000 | 50,000 | 50,000 |

Such a test matrix will identify:

✔    The recorded responses from radio

✔    The comparative response rate between two forms of door-to-door delivery

✔    Whether the door-to-door campaign is more successful with radio support or not

✔    Direct mail delivered to postcode cells both within the radio transmission area and outside can be used to judge the same potential uplift effect

✔    Monthly trends in response from directories can be compared to see if there is any change

# Online digital media

Many digital marketers argue that their channel is the perfect direct marketing medium. The low cost of campaign set-up, personalisation and contact creates a very favourable economic environment in which the individual channels can thrive. The high level of measurability and accountability really makes digital marketing stand out. Critics would argue there are limitations to even the most fundamental tracking technologies (cookies can be disabled to prevent accurate activity reporting, as can the images that track email open rates, to name but a couple).

But to focus on these failings seems petty given the sheer scale, speed and ease of online marketing reporting...and the ability to track and measure is central to all direct marketing testing. This section seeks to demonstrate that marketers can test more things, more quickly and more easily than in any other area, and these tests can deliver significant business benefit in the short and long term.

Only a few years ago there were not that many online tools to get to grips with – website design was still an evolving science, there was scarcely a critical mass of addresses to make email marketing viable, and search marketing was restricted to tweaking a site's metadata from time to time. Most of the testing was taking place in the graphical advertising space, where banner advertising was dying a slow death trying to replicate the cost-per-thousand business model of traditional media display advertising.

Today's digital marketers have a bewildering array of tools at their disposal and each one demands a high level of understanding just to deliver an acceptable ROI. Many organisations choose to outsource specific activity to specialists, and this presents a dilemma for those with a strong direct marketing culture...how to ensure testing is central to their suppliers' strategy. A recommendation is to choose partners who understand direct marketing and have a passion for testing. There are plenty of players out there, for affiliate marketing, site design, analytics, organic and paid search or email marketing. Challenge them to incorporate testing into their overall strategy and share with them what you have learned in your offline activity. In this way you will be able to enjoy the benefits of testing without the operational (and knowledge transfer) constraints of having to manage it all internally.

---

There are a huge number of digital marketing techniques that you need to understand. Every one will require a testing strategy to optimise its performance. These are just the techniques you may consider for acquiring customers:

Organic/natural search
Paid search
Affiliate marketing
Banner/display advertising
Solus email list rental
Newsletter email list rental
Blogging
Podcasting
SMS messaging
Viral marketing
Offline URL promotion
Interactive TV
Microsites
Landing pages

---

There is insufficient space in this Guide to run through testing strategies for all the digital tools and so it is best to focus on a few principles and see how they can be applied to some of the more widely used applications. Referring back to table 8.2.3 we need to ensure that we are following a business process for each of these specific applications, remembering to link our activity back to the key business objectives.

## The world wide web

The basic principles already enunciated for testing remain consistent for the web.

### Banner ads

Advertising on the web primarily means inserting banner advertisements on other organisations' websites, inciting the viewer to click through to your site. Accordingly, the first purpose of testing is to discover which websites will give you the most cost-effective results in terms of:

**Clickthroughs** (visits to your website)
**Impressions** (number of visitors times number of pages viewed)
**Registrations** (number of visitors submitting some personal details)
**Sales**

Clearly the most effective sites are likely to be those with some affinity to your own, and those will be the first – subject to cost – that you will want to test. So, if you are selling car insurance, you might go for personal finance sites; you might look at moneyextra.com, This Is Money, Money Supermarket, or at motoring sites – car enthusiasts, or those looking to buy a car – autotrader.co.uk. You can buy a good sized, four-week test campaign with a good breadth of sites to compare and sufficient budget per site to be taken seriously when entering negotiations, for £20,000 to £40,000.

Secondly, you will want to test the effect of different creative treatments – size of banner, use of colour and animation etc. Since a given banner ad, if exposed too often to the same person, quickly becomes boring, not to say irritating, at least three or four different executions should be produced and distributed to each site selected. This will help to reduce the attrition rate as well as start the creative testing process.

## Keywords

Thirdly, you should remember that search engines are a further source of visitors to your site. These visitors arrive as a result of searching on keywords submitted by you to the search engine: you may wish to test the effect of different keywords and different search engines.

## Tracking

Just as with testing in any other medium, a full evaluation of a test should take into account not merely the immediate response, but also the subsequent behaviour of the respondents. It is precisely to facilitate this that the cookie principle was invented, which allows the website owner to place a small package of data (or cookie) on each visitor's computer which can be retrieved on the next visit, allowing the site owner to identify repeat visitors and, over time, to compile a profile on each. So consider what you can track and what is meaningful to you:

- Number of registrations

- Profile of registrations

- Site traffic and visiting patterns

- Frequency and number of repeat visits

- Time spent on site etc.

Being clear about the objectives is vital on the web, and in understanding how online activity will integrate with offline media.

## *Website design*

Marketers often see the launch of a website as the end of a process rather than the start of a more important one – once a site is live the real work begins! Your new (or your current) website will probably have been subjected to much technical testing to make sure pages load at acceptable speeds, or links work from one page to another. However, these are 'hygiene' issues compared to the huge business opportunities that optimising the site will deliver.

We do not want to concern ourselves with things that have little impact on business performance – changing background colours or altering image resolution is not the kind of testing we need to concern ourselves with. Instead, think of the big issues relating to your site:

- Why do I lose 20 per cent of my visitors on a specific page?

- What would make more people continue their visit?

- How can I get more people into the 'conversion' funnel (a registration screen, signing up for a seminar programme or adding a product to a shopping cart)?

- Why do I lose 30 per cent of my shoppers at the first stage of the four-page check-out process?

- Why do only 20 per cent of people make it through all four pages to submit an order?

- How could I increase conversion rates by 10 per cent at each stage?

With these business issues identified we must try to express them in terms of potential in order to prioritise them. For example, losing 20 per cent of your traffic at one page sounds like a bad situation, but how much more successful would you be if you could reduce this to 10 per cent? If it's significant, you should develop a few hypotheses and build a test programme to improve performance, and then ensure you have appropriate tracking techniques in place to measure the tests.

Some web marketers like to think in terms of 'funnels' – creating checkpoints at certain pages and counting the traffic passing it. If you consider the whole website one large funnel you may have 100 per cent arriving at it but only 2 per cent reaching the check-out pages and 0.25 per cent converting. Looking at the check-out pages you will have 100 per cent at page one and maybe 10 per cent getting to page four. This 'funnel' analysis is easy to set up using web analytics tools and will prove insightful for a wide range of web traffic analyses, not least in suggesting where you should be focusing most of your testing energy and resources.

For simple issues you can probably construct an A/B split test to deliver the business understanding. An example of this would be running a different page layout at a crucial point in the customer journey to see if you can move more people along to the next stage. A more advanced A/B split test would be refining a four-page check-out process into a two-page process...here you are testing one check-out journey against another check-out journey, not just one page against another.

For more complex issues you may need to consider multi-variate testing. Thankfully, we do not have the costly, lengthy and complex operational issues to consider that a direct mail multi-variate test entails (see tables 8.2.4 to 8.2.7). However, we do need to plan carefully all tests and multi-variate tests need extra attention.

Let's go back to that problem page that haemorrhages 20 per cent of your traffic every day. Consider all the factors that may be affecting people moving on to the next stage of the anticipated journey: What are the navigation options? Are they easy to see? Are they lost among other more distracting images? Does the page carry advertising or affiliate links of any kind? What is the call to action to continue? How might different segments of visitor respond to this page?

By considering some of the factors that may be affecting performance it will be possible to come up with alternative page attributes – a larger navigation button, removal of affiliate advertising, moving the navigation button to a more prominent location, different wording on the navigation button and a clearer call to action. You can then feed these independent variables into a testing module and, over time, the software will present alternative versions of each attribute to new visitors and record the impact. Once an individual attribute has been 'optimised' it will look at another one, and then look at all the attributes in combination. After an agreed volume of traffic (at agreed statistical tolerance margins), the programme will have determined the best combination of attributes – your page is optimised!  This kind of testing is becoming more common and, as more technology providers offer web-based, low-cost, easy to operate tools, many more direct marketers will be able to drive up website performance.

## Driving traffic

Website optimisation is usually concerned with maximising the numbers of people passing through specific points of a site. If you are reviewing your traffic-driving techniques you may be more concerned with delivering a lower cost-per-visit. Your thinking should still follow the same process as outlined in table 8.2.3 but now you will be applying it to the world of reducing acquisition costs.

Affiliate marketing is growing in importance for direct marketers because it offers risk-free acquisition activity – the most common pricing model is one of a cost-per-acquisition. In simple terms this involves a partner website carrying your graphical advertising in the expectation of getting people to click to your site. If they do click through, a piece of tracking technology follows what they do, and if they end up purchasing from you, the affiliate website will take some commission for his contribution ... either a flat rate per sale or an agreed percentage of the order value.

In such a risk-free environment you may consider there is little need for testing but even here you should be looking at a whole raft of possible areas for improvement. Firstly, you may consider the advertisements you are using and should test smaller or larger sizes, or different offers, of different creative elements ... these small bits of graphical advertising should be treated as off-the-page press ads and subjected to similar testing regimes. Next, you may care to take a longer-term view of customer value – are any partners or any offers delivering more repeat business, or better average order values in the short term? Some of these learnings may be based on campaign analysis but again, using the process-mapping template mentioned earlier you should be able to construct a test programme for affiliate marketing:

### Table 8.2.13

| Issues | Possible issue | Test  options |
|---|---|---|
| Low first order value | Too offer-driven creative | Get affiliate to run split test on current offer and a less price-sensitive alternative |
| Low traffic volumes | Poor affiliate traffic | Offer higher commission to wider range of affiliate partners and track best volume deliverers |
| High bad debt rate | Profile of specific affiliate traffic | Test and monitor through new affiliates, maybe at a higher commission rate |

This is a test matrix for one element of one of the 'drive to web' tools at your disposal. Considering the complexities of display advertising, natural search, paid search and email list rental you can appreciate that your online activity should be heavily dependent on testing.

## *Email marketing*

Email marketing is quite a contentious medium. The issues of 'permission' and 'opt-in' versus 'opt-out' have overshadowed many of its achievements. The original internet users coined the phrase spamming to describe distribution of unrequested 'junk' email. Here is how the 'eff' describes spamming:

'An opt-out mailing in which the perpetrator involuntarily subscribes thousands of victims, bombards them with mail, and insists that they manually opt out of the list if they don't want it. Though this mimics postal junk-mailing practice, it is entirely foreign to the internet community's standards of behaviour.'

Chapter 12.2 details the current data protection and regulatory issues in the UK and the EU.

### Planning email campaigns

The overall considerations for email marketing are essentially the same as for direct mail campaigns. The database, targeting and selection issues that have been described for mailing list work should be applied to email marketing. The biggest single difference between email marketing and direct mail is cost – but it should not be thought that because the media costs of email are so tiny that any less effort is required at the planning, testing and evaluation stages than would be the case in any other medium. Indeed, given the amount of data generated in the course of an email campaign, the reverse may be true.

There are three main sources of email addresses:

1.   **Client/company's own email list**

     As a general principle, companies should try and collect the email addresses of all new customers, while setting in motion a plan of updating historic customer records and getting their email addresses onto the database as well. This way they will build up their own email list very quickly (but make sure you follow the self-regulatory guidelines, see chapter 9.1).

2.   **Commercial lists (cold or 'opt-in')**

     In addition, many of the mailing list companies are now collecting email addresses along with their other respondent data. Therefore, while the numbers on an e-list are currently much smaller than on a similarly targeted mailing list, it is now possible to email lifestyle clusters such as motor insurance renewals by month. Testing these lists now is definitely worthwhile, because they are going to grow in number very rapidly and the companies that understand how to work them will gain an advantage.

**3. Collection of new addresses**

Via online advertising campaigns, data capture banners, questionnaires or microsites using competition or games mechanics.

Once data has been collated it needs to be formatted, cleaned and deduped just like any other list.

## Handling the response

Whether you are trying to encourage people to go and see your film or to read your newsletter, once you have set yourself up to communicate with your customers by email, you must acknowledge that they may want to reply. This sounds silly, but too many companies think one way, and enquiries coming in from customers and prospects are dealt with in tardy batches or not at all. At the most general level it must be someone's job to keep on top of acknowledging and processing incoming email. There are also sophisticated software packages known as auto responders that can be programmed to carry out certain follow-up routines with a personalised sequence. These can be downloaded and run by the individual company or subcontracted to companies specialising in auto response. (See www.marketinguk.org.)

## Tracking the response

Electronic media give you the ability to track an immense amount of information, and integrated techniques can be added to the core message to gain more detail on respondents. This might be done by inviting respondents to visit a unique entry page and calculating the response rate from that. (For instance, film viewers could be given the opportunity to enter a competition based around the film content). Alternatively you can use trackable email broadcasting systems or *ad-tracking* systems.

In the past few years email marketing has matured as a direct marketing channel. Perhaps most importantly, legislation in 2003 has shaped the context within which marketers can speak to customers and prospects. This has been mirrored by a growing receptiveness of consumers and business professionals to email messaging, and house email files continue to grow at great pace. The costs of managing email communications has dropped and sophisticated web-based technologies bring advanced email techniques within reach of all marketers. Indeed, with its relatively low costs of production and high levels of personalisation, email is recognised by many as one of the most powerful direct marketing techniques.

Traditional direct marketers find testing through email offers numerous advantages:

Testing is fast – the testing phase can be as short as a few days, with some companies compressing it down to a few hours for specific kinds of testing. Immediate response and real-time reporting tools make this pace of activity possible.

Roll-out is very fast – once a winning element has been identified this can be broadcast swiftly, (many platforms broadcasting at over one million messages per hour) with none of the production lead times associated with direct mail campaigns.

Testing is cheap – the complexities of constructing test matrices and message design may be the same as offline, but the 'make-ready' and broadcast costs run to a few pence per message.

As the table below shows, email marketers are now able to set up a range of tests to deliver greater performance at every stage of an email marketing campaign:

**Table 8.2.14**

| Issues | Possible issue | Test options |
|---|---|---|
| High 'hard bounce' rates | Broadcast platform blacklisted with ISPs | Send test campaigns to problem ISPs from other technology/service providers' platforms |
| High 'soft bounce' rates | Problem delivering HTML email formats | Test sending text only versions of messages into problem domains |
| Low open rate | Lack of engagement | Test different/personalised subject lines and new 'from' fields |
| Low clickthrough rate | No compelling offers | Test pricing, product bundling, incentives for purchase |
| High unsubscribe rate | People being over-mailed | Test less frequent contact strategy with key segments |
| Low conversion rates | Too few people seem committed prospects | Test different registration incentives and track conversion rates from each one |

Finally, the email marketers achieving the greatest ROI seem to be the ones using 'advanced' email marketing techniques. These will include as a first step segmentation of your database (at the very least into customers and prospects, but should probably involve some transactional analysis). The second technique is to use the dynamic and conditional content capabilities of email marketing to deliver relevant and engaging messages based on individual registration and purchase activity. Finally, marketers should seek to weave their email activity into the recipient's life cycle with your organisation – specific messaging based on date of purchase or likely replenishment/renewal times have proved to deliver higher ROI than 'monthly newsletter' campaigns. However, as with all generalisations, some of this may not be true for your organisation. You should seek to build testing programmes that identify the optimum ROI through segmentation and personalisation, bearing in mind that at some point the effort expended to deliver another personalised segment will not yield a corresponding return. Only by testing will you determine your email marketing ROI boundaries.

## Viral marketing

Not to be confused with a computer virus, the term apparently came from the 'hotmail', free email system, because every outgoing email was branded with a link back to 'hotmail', and an advert for their free email service. Since then, viral marketing has quickly become a hot buzzword in e-marketing circles, due to its innately efficient marketing potential. Viral marketing is the least precise of our current selection, but if the idea is good it can be very impactful and cost-efficient.

Many people use it to stimulate awareness and drive response. TV programmers use it to attract viewers, Nike used it to extend its campaign for the 10 kilometre run, and of course companies who specialist in viral marketing such as **p@nlogic** use it. It created a fun game shortly after Mr Prescott had his punch-up, called Splat the MP, and it made it relevant for the whole election period by including figureheads from all the main parties. Marketing UK has created a page where it collects good examples of viral marketing, which is worth a visit at http://www.marketinguk.org/examplesofviralmarketing.asp

So viral marketing is the creation of an impactful vehicle, usually a game or competition emailed to a small, but targeted base. The marketer then relies on that base forwarding the game etc. onto other like prospects because they think it will be of interest or, usually, amusement. In this way, the marketing message is transmitted to a wide audience at no further cost to the marketer. This is the electronic equivalent to word-of-mouth, and is very good for member-get-member schemes.

## Emerging digital techniques

We have reviewed how testing can play a part in delivering incremental gains in some of the more popular digital disciplines. However, one certainty in this space is that there will be more tools to test as time goes on. While advances in technology for traditional direct marketing don't tend to come around too often, you will need to keep abreast of each and every new digital technology, before your competitors do. So a final observation on testing in the digital landscape is this:

> Test the new techniques as they emerge. Find out how they could help your organisation. Play around with some business models and see if they can make money for you. In the past couple of years we have seen RSS feeds, blogging, podcasting and click-to-call all play a part in organisations' marketing plans – have you tested them yet? Better still, test the next new things – before your competitors get there first!

# Campaign data: maximising the return of your campaign through excellent use of data

## This chapter includes:

-------------------------------------------------

- ❏ **How to purchase campaign data effectively**

- ❏ **Collecting data for direct marketing purposes**

- ❏ **Making campaign selections**

- ❏ **Ensuring the cleanliness of campaign data**

- ❏ **Gathering campaign response data**

- ❏ **Using data to evaluate the success of a campaign**

- ❏ **Presenting campaign results**

-------------------------------------------------

## About this chapter

**O**ne of the key aspects to the success of any campaign is the use of data. From the point that a decision is made to carry out any structured customer interaction data becomes key to the outcome, favourable or otherwise, of this interaction. From the outset, data is used to research the customers or prospects of the campaign, what they are likely to be interested in and how they can be charmed.

Obviously the main use of data in any campaign is deciding who to contact, acquiring the information needed to put the contact list together and processing this list to ensure that the data held is up to date, correctly addressed and suppressed of any records which should not be contacted.

Finally, after the campaign has been sent out and the responses start to flood in, data is again used to look at what has worked, what hasn't worked (God forbid) and how this success or otherwise can inform future campaigns.

During the course of this chapter, all of the above aspects of using data in a campaign will be covered. Throughout, it will be assumed that the campaign itself

is channel-neutral, (i.e. that the method of contact could be via direct mail, email, SMS, telephone or any other medium for that matter). However, where mention is required of specifics for a channel, this shall be done.
Your head-and-shoulders photo here

### Scott Logie – Managing Director, Occam

Scott graduated with a first-class honours degree in Statistics from Glasgow University before joining British Aerospace in the Technical Sales area. Subsequently, Scott spent several years working in various data analysis roles, mainly in Direct Marketing, for CACI and Marketing Databasics both in London and Edinburgh. He then spent six years at Bank of Scotland, initially setting up the Customer Knowledge department before moving on to manage the implementation of the bank's Data Warehouse project before taking over as Head of Research, Data and Analysis. In this role, Scott was responsible for all of the data areas of the bank.

Scott joined Occam in April 2001 to set up the Strategic Analysis offering, took over as Managing Director in February 2003, and led the current management team through a successful management buy out of the company in July of 2004.

Scott is a member of the DMA Data Council and was one of the inaugural members of the Institute of Direct Marketing Board for the West.

## Chapter 8.3

# Campaign data: maximising the return of your campaign through excellent use of data

## Buying data for a campaign

**T**he first thing you need is information about past results – and lots of it. The more examples (by previous campaign, ask, pack and incentives etc) are available, the better able you will be to determine which element of the pack is creating an effect (good or bad) or if other factors are affecting results, e.g. seasonality, regularity of list updates or overuse of particular lists.

Previous results give some benchmark as to what the targets of the campaign should be (or could be). By seeing these results, a plan can be formulated as to what the focus of the next campaign should be, i.e. increase response rates – 'get bums on seats' and then upgrade/cross-sell to them once they are customers/donors. The reverse of this strategy would be to have a much more niche approach – structuring the campaign so that although response rates are likely to be lower, the average order value/gift is significantly higher. This might be used for high-ticket campaigns or high-value donor appeals. These two different approaches have implications for campaign volumes – you are unlikely to get 250,000 names of high-value, niche individuals, but you can get this volume on the lower value, upgradeable individuals.

In order to help you understand how a list has been compiled, the data owner should be able to provide you with a data card. A data card shows basic information about a list such as source, profile, recommended users and costs. (NB. The data card is a sales tool put together by the list manager and should therefore be treated with some caution.)

**Example data card for British Dressage Members**

# British Dressage Members

British Dressage formed in 1998 and run the equestrian sport of affiliated dressage in the UK. People must be members in order to ride in competitions, own a competition horse or to judge in competitions. They are in general affluent, with time and money to indulge an expensive interest – and often more than one! They take more holidays than average, many of which are overseas and long haul. They are heavy users of credit cards, they buy by mail order and they do not have children.

## LIST PROFILE

**British Dressage Members** have a clear profile:

- 93% female
- 56% income over £25k
- 60% aged 35-55
- 62% take part in active sport
- above average on ALL cultural pursuits
- 80% own pets
- 78% buy by mail order
- Donate to Animal Welfare, Wildlife, Environmental and Health Research charities

## RATES AND DATA

| | |
|---|---|
| Active Members: | 7,206 |
| | |
| Base Rental | £125/000 |
| Selections: Gender, Geography | £5/000 |
| Delivery via email | £35 |

Minimum order 5,000 names ♦ File MPS cleaned every list order ♦ List Owner Warranty 003351 ♦ 15% commission to recognised list brokers ♦ One time usage only ♦ Mailing list is seeded ♦ Nixies returned to Occam at list users cost.

Data Card copyright

### Recency, Frequency and Value

When looking at any list, one of the main areas to look at is the Receny, Frequency and Value (RFV) of the individuals on the list for the relevant product and offer. These are still the most predictive elements to future behaviour. Buying data which has strong evidence of RFV on previous campaigns is most likely to be successful in future campaigns.

So, for example, if you are looking to buy a list of females who have bought gifts in the past, the most successful lists would have:

- Recent gift buyers (last three months plus)

- Individuals who regularly buy gifts

- Individuals who buy gifts of high value

## Known elements of lists

This is data where previous/future behaviour matches your data need, e.g. an animal charity might use consumer lifestyle data where people have indicated that they would consider donating to an animal charity. Another option would be to take data from another animal charity.

## Assumed behaviour

For an animal charity this might mean taking data such as animal book readers. It is assumed that these individuals are likely to donate to an animal charity as they are likely to have empathy with the cause.

Rental or swap?

It is possible to swap data with like organisations:

- This gives access to your direct audience

- Costs are cheaper – normally £15,000 to £ 40,000 compared to £110,000plus

- Data might not be available on the rental market – access only via a swap basis

- Mutual benefits – both parties gain individuals of worth

- Risk is lessened if you wish to try non-core markets as the price is low

## Data sources

The data can further be segmented into lists which have some element of hand-raising/ responder element, that is to say that they have already done the event we would like to happen again or have expressed an interest; for example:

Mail-order buyers

Subscribers

Lifestyle survey responders

Competition entrants

This is in comparison to compiled lists:

Companies House data

Stocks and Shares register

Professional qualifications

The first category is likely to have a much higher response rate, whereas the second category is likely to have a higher affluence and therefore a potential for higher average value per response. It is important to have a balanced campaign and to balance each of these categories with the other.

Data quality is vital. In order to assess the quality of data purchased it is important to look at:

1.    How data was put together, e.g. where did the data you are buying come from?

2.    By whom it was put together:
      Who compiled the list and how much do you trust them?  What evidence or stamp of approval from trade bodies exists for this data?

3.    When the data was collected/put together:
      How new/recent is the data you are buying and how relevant is this recency with relation to the campaign that is being constructed?

When buying data, you may wish to contract a list broker to carry out the data purchase on your behalf. List brokers live and breathe for lists, keeping up to date on which lists work best and for whom. They keep track of previous results and are expert advisors on what is currently on the market and all the pitfalls, nuances and formalities of buying data.

## *Gathering your own data for use in direct marketing*

Other than the very obvious point that gathering your own data makes it cheaper to acquire and then it can be used as often as you like without incurring further cost, the main reason for gathering your own data is controlling data quality. The key point is that it is easier to get it captured correctly in the first place and not rely on any other company to do so.

In order to maintain high data quality, ensure that you specify your requirements for data capture and ideally build some validation into this process. Think ahead and don't fail to capture data fields that you may not need today but will later wish you had collected when you had the chance to do so. Basic essentials are:

- Full name:
  ideally with a prefix and a forename – consider validation, i.e. no numerics in the name data fields, nothing other than A-Z (i.e. *no* " £ $ % type characters!)

- Gender:
  a drop-down menu may seem obvious here but is useful

- Full postal address:
  ideally verified at point of capture with some sort of QAS instant lookup

- Telephone number:
  home, mobile or work

- Email address:
  home or work

- Date of birth:
  at the very least year of birth

- Opt-in/opt-out  consent to contact in future:
  *essential* as legislation gets tougher and tougher

As often as is possible, offer tick boxes or drop-down menus to make choice and selection easy and accurate. Don't work your customers too hard; they are giving you vital information so thank them for this but most importantly, make it easy for them!

The above is a bare minimum; ideally it would be useful to capture more variables that may help you with subsequent relationship and/or sales opportunities, for example:

- Marital status

- Family composition:
  i.e. presence of children, how many and dates of birth (bear in mind age data ages!)

- Preferred communication method:
  phone, email, direct mail etc.

- Profession

- Preferred payment method:
  i.e. cash, DD, CC

Don't just think what you may need now but what you may well need in the future; it is far easier to capture it today than to attempt to backfill later.

If data is being captured online by the end-user, ensure that data fields are long enough to accommodate the information you require; for example, try and avoid 'free text' as this is difficult to process (or indeed analyse) in the future.

Don't underestimate how much data you might collect (there will be lots) and make sure that if you need to expand systems you'll be able to.

*Darwin Executive Guide to CRM*

## *Campaign selection – never as easy as it seems*

(NB For further guidance in the subject matter covered in this and the following section, see also chapter 9.6.)

Campaigns for acquisition will generally use bought-in lists or data gathered for acquisition purposes. Even in these cases it will often be possible to select subsets of prospects from such lists, based upon data contained in the list. For instance, the data card example above indicates that it is possible to select on gender, or on some (unspecified) geographic criteria. However, many campaigns are addressed to existing customers. In this case, detailed selection criteria can often be used to decide who to contact for which campaign.

If you are regularly making campaign selections inhouse and passing to your printer for Mailsort, you may wish to consider buying and using Mailsort software. It isn't expensive; it's easy to use and could save quite a bit of money!

In general, these selection criteria will first come as a set of written instructions. For example, for a credit card upgrade campaign the selection request may be:

• Please select all customers who have spent £300 or less on their card in the last three months.

This then needs to be converted to instructions which can be used to make the selection from the database. This may look like:

• Start with all active credit card customers

• Find all of those who have spent less than a total of £300 over the last 90 days

• Exclude anyone who will receive a contact within the next 10 days

• Exclude anyone over the age of 65

• Exclude any 'hygiene' flags, i.e. customers who have bad credit risk, who are flagged as deceased or as 'do not contact'

This selection would then be run, potentially, as part of a larger campaign. As a result there may need to be a hierarchy to decide whether selection for this group, or cell, should have higher or lower priority than some other selection(s) in the campaign. This hierarchy of selections is generally decided on likely return, whether short term or long term depending on the current business needs.

## Campaign selection case study – door-drop campaign

### The client

*WWF fund and manage projects throughout the world to protect endangered species from poaching and other immediate threats. They work with local people, governments and partner organisations to ensure that vulnerable habitats are not lost or degraded through neglect or exploitation. Working with governments and other policy makers, they help secure new legislation to protect species and habitats, to reduce threats such as pollution and deforestation, and to promote development that is both fair and sustainable.*
*WWF also work to raise environmental awareness among the public, whose actions impact on the environment in so many ways.*

### The challenge

*WWF use door drops as a significant method of recruitment, and were keen to continue using it as a recruitment medium in a much more targeted way. The type of supporter being recruited was important, with emphasis being placed on direct debit uptake over cash response. Occam was tasked with making the targeting more effective both in the way that areas were initially chosen to receive a door drop, and also in selecting those areas where direct debit uptake could be expected to be higher than average.*

### The solution

*Occam has been performing postal sector selections for WWF door drops for a number of years. Initially the selection of sectors for each drop was done using geographical analysis based on the penetration of WWF supporters into each sector. It became apparent that the data WWF were holding about their supporters could be coupled with other external data to create a more sophisticated selection method.*

*Extensive work was carried out looking at five years of response data from WWF, combined with Census and PAF data. Extra variables were derived from this, such as a 'measure of rurality' index (which had been seen to be significant for WWF supporters) and the number of times a postal sector had been dropped previously. The more important variables were then selected via a series of CHAID analyses, with the model being refined on each iteration, and door-drop areas were ranked.*

### The benefits

*Response rates have significantly increased from the previous campaign and the ranking has been most successful. As more door drops are performed, the results of each will be continually fed back into the model building process. This feedback loop of new data every six months will allow further refinement and improvement of the modelling.*

As part of the selections, it is advisable to set up a control group. This should be a significantly sized, representative subset of that part of your list you have chosen *not* to approach. Behaviour of this control group can be compared against your campaign audience and any differences would indicate the impact of the campaign.

# Direct marketers do it to the right people at the right time

Once your data is bought, captured or selected then you may well have problems such as identifying duplicates and ensuring the mailing list is of the highest quality. Data generally decays much faster than most people realise; each month the Royal Mail supply around 150,000 to 200,000 UK address changes to the Postal Address File. These can relate to postcode changes, new buildings, buildings being split into flats, demolitions, change of business names and occasional change of *post town* – for example, Chilcompton, *Bath* changing to Chilcompton, *Radstock*.

Add to this the fact that approximately 10 per cent of adults will move address each year – that's four to five million movers every year. As far as your campaign is concerned these are known as 'gone aways' if it is not possible to track these changes or if they do not have their mail forwarded. Also, approximately 700,000 people die each year in the UK.

If your data is Business-to-Business then the rate of turnover here is even more alarming; new businesses start up, many fail quickly, some change their trading name and many relocate to newer/larger premises. There are mergers, acquisitions, demergers, new offices set up and subsidiaries etc. Staying up to date with Business-to-Business data is a real challenge.

You will need a data maintenance strategy; neglect is not an option worth considering. Databases must be periodically cleaned, deduped and suppressed; keeping your data 'fit for purpose' will ensure that you have an asset that will add value to your company.

As far as your campaign is concerned, your final list will need to be processed to ensure all of these data quality issues are taken care of. To do this, you will need to identify a competent data processing bureau that you can trust to cleanse your campaign data. Look for a well-established bureau that has DMA membership and offers you a named account manager to work with you.

The typical data processing path for a direct mail campaign would be:

Cleaning
Deduplication
Suppression
Split into mail cells
Mailsort
Output

Cleaning is the processing of name and address data. The cleaning process will identify and qualify both name data and address data. Address data will need to be matched to the Royal Mail Postal Address File ( PAF ) and updated/enhanced if required.

Each name and address will be assigned a quality score – this allows poor quality data to be removed from your intended campaign data. A good cleaning system will also look for many other data facets within both the name and the address data, some of which you really would not wish to mail. Among these would be:

Expletives
Incomplete names
Overseas addresses – if the campaign is UK-specific
Spoof data – e.g. Homer Simpson, 123 Yellow Brick Road, AnyTown
Juveniles – Master Tom Smith
Dubious – The Late Mr Green

Once the data has been cleaned the process will move on to deduplication. This is the process of identifying exact and near-exact matching of data records. Deduplication can be run at varying match levels depending upon what is most appropriate for your campaign. The most commonly used deduplication levels would consider:

Address data only – i.e. one mail pack per address regardless of name data
Address plus surname – i.e. only one mail pack per surname per address
Address plus surname plus forename and gender – i.e. one pack per individual per address

Deduplication is usually run at either an overkill or an underkill level.

Overkill stretches the matching parameters to err on the side of caution and overkill if in doubt, i.e. you are likely to lose more records as being duplicates but have more confidence in your net mail file being duplicate-free.

Underkill sets very tight match criteria and should only bring together exact and very near-exact duplicate records; those records that could loosely be considered to be duplicates will survive into the net mail file.

Ensure you get to see the duplication reports showing both counts of records processed and quantities matched, plus also examples of duplicate records.

The net file resulting from deduplication should then be passed through suppression. Over the years the direct marketing industry has compiled numerous suppression products that contain details of individuals who are unlikely to respond to your offer as they:

a)     Do not welcome unsolicited direct marketing

b)     Are deceased

c)     Have moved address

The Direct Marketing Association (DMA ) encourages the use of suppression files – perhaps the best-known file is the Mailing Preference Service ( MPS ). This is managed by the DMA itself and contains details of people who have expressed the wish not to receive unsolicited direct mail and as such are extremely unlikely to respond to your product offer. Mailings to such records will be a waste of your marketing budget and will only irritate the recipient.

> If your campaign is a telemarketing campaign, you should note that it is illegal to make cold calls to anyone who has registered with the Telephone Preference Service (TPS). For more on the TPS see chapter 12.3. For restrictions on the use of email lists, see chapter 12.2.

There are many other suppression products that can help you identify both deceased and gone away records that may be within your intended mailing file. These are commercial products and typically charge approx 20 pence per 'match and drop' – while you have to pay for this service it is a cost that is significantly below that of the typical mail pack price – it is a cost well worth paying. Suppression should be seen as an essential tool in your data processing armoury as it will:

- Identify those records known to be non-responsive and so save your mail pack processing, printing and postage costs

- Reduce your net mailing volume and so raise your ROI

- Reduce your exposure to potentially adverse publicity and complaints

Some examples of suppression products available include:

- Mailing Preference Service (DMA)

- Telephone Preference Service (DMA)

- Fax Preference Service (DMA)

- National Suppression File (DMA)

- Mortascreen (Millennium)

- The Bereavement Register (The REaD Group)

- Gone Away Suppression File (The REaD Group)

- National Change of Address (The Royal Mail)

- Disconnect ( Equifax )

- Baby Mailing Preference Service (DMA)

- The Business Suppression File (The REaD Group)

- Experian SF (Experian)

After suppression your net mailing data will be split into the mail pack cells using the criteria you will have provided to the data processing bureau. It is likely that pack codes will be applied to each record in each cell at this point – these codes will be used later on to help measure the success of your campaign.

Each mail pack cell will then pass through Mailsort – Mailsort offers postal discounts on large volume mailings (typically those with over 4,000 mailing records). The Mailsort discount offered is dependent on the timescale required for delivery plus the mail pack weight and size.

The final stage is to prepare your data for output ready for print personalisation in a format and structure to suit this process.

When getting data processed, challenge your processing house on the order in which suppression files are run.

The responsibility for each individual contact resides with you. Make sure you check what is done before contact is made.

# *Evaluate the success of your campaign*

Quite often you intuitively know how well a campaign has gone. But how well do you really understand:

1.   Whether the campaign has achieved or even exceeded its objectives?

2.   Whether it has been cost-efficient?

3.   What type of person has responded to the campaign? Have different groups of people behaved differently?

Deeper analysis can bring even greater understanding:

4.   What has been the value to my business of this campaign in the immediate term?

5.   What are the longer term opportunities?

6.   What is genuinely due to the campaign and what has been driven by other factors or circumstances?

7.   What learning can be applied to future campaigns and strategy?

The performance of campaigns should be tracked both for reporting purposes and as part of an iterative learning process. Basic campaign evaluation should cover:

1.   Whether the campaign has achieved or exceeded its objectives

2.   Whether it has been cost-efficient

3.   Who are the people who have responded to the campaign? Have different groups of people behaved differently?

There are many different ways to measure the success of a campaign. For example:

- Response rate:
  compared to the number of individuals mailed, what percentage responded?

- Cost per response:
  How much did it cost, based on the overall cost of the campaign divided by the number of responders, for each response?

- Return on Investment (ROI):
  How much money was made in this campaign (at campaign, cell and individual level) compared to the amount of money spent?
  NB. This can be expressed as a pure £ value (i.e. income – cost) or as a ratio (i.e. income:cost)

Packages can be bought and models built that help evaluate campaigns. Below is an example of how this might work in a B2B direct mail campaign; the same principles would apply in B2C, and across all media. The model reports the overall metrics: the volume of mailings, the total campaign cost and the subsequent number of responses. From this it has calculated the overall campaign response rate along with the unit cost.

## Figure 8.3.1

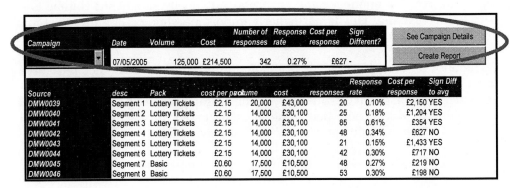

| Campaign | Date | Volume | Cost | Number of responses | Response rate | Cost per response | Sign Different? | |
|---|---|---|---|---|---|---|---|---|
| | 07/05/2005 | 125,000 | £214,500 | 342 | 0.27% | £627 | - | See Campaign Details / Create Report |

| Source | desc | Pack | cost per pack | volume | cost | responses | Response rate | Cost per response | Sign Diff to avg |
|---|---|---|---|---|---|---|---|---|---|
| DMW0039 | Segment 1 | Lottery Tickets | £2.15 | 20,000 | £43,000 | 20 | 0.10% | £2,150 | YES |
| DMW0040 | Segment 2 | Lottery Tickets | £2.15 | 14,000 | £30,100 | 25 | 0.18% | £1,204 | YES |
| DMW0041 | Segment 3 | Lottery Tickets | £2.15 | 14,000 | £30,100 | 85 | 0.61% | £354 | YES |
| DMW0042 | Segment 4 | Lottery Tickets | £2.15 | 14,000 | £30,100 | 48 | 0.34% | £627 | NO |
| DMW0043 | Segment 5 | Lottery Tickets | £2.15 | 14,000 | £30,100 | 21 | 0.15% | £1,433 | YES |
| DMW0044 | Segment 6 | Lottery Tickets | £2.15 | 14,000 | £30,100 | 42 | 0.30% | £717 | NO |
| DMW0045 | Segment 7 | Basic | £0.60 | 17,500 | £10,500 | 48 | 0.27% | £219 | NO |
| DMW0046 | Segment 8 | Basic | £0.60 | 17,500 | £10,500 | 53 | 0.30% | £198 | NO |

As shown above, the campaign has delivered 342 responses at an overall response rate of 0.27 per cent (i.e.2.7 responses per 1,000 mailed). The cost per mailing was on average between £1and £2, but the cost per response was £627.

As indicated below, eight different segments (or cells) of the population were identified in advance, and targeted in slightly different ways. Assuming the campaign has been selected as was noted above, one of these cells will be the control cell. The model also shows how these individual cells within the mailing campaign performed. These can be compared against the overall average response rate of the campaign.

## Figure 8.3.2

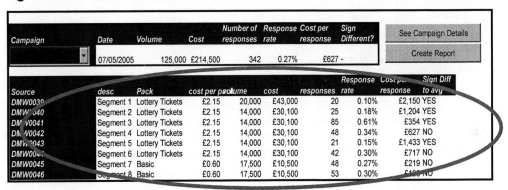

| Campaign | Date | Volume | Cost | Number of responses | Response rate | Cost per response | Sign Different? | |
|---|---|---|---|---|---|---|---|---|
| | 07/05/2005 | 125,000 | £214,500 | 342 | 0.27% | £627 | - | See Campaign Details / Create Report |

| Source | desc | Pack | cost per pack | volume | cost | responses | Response rate | Cost per response | Sign Diff to avg |
|---|---|---|---|---|---|---|---|---|---|
| DMW0039 | Segment 1 | Lottery Tickets | £2.15 | 20,000 | £43,000 | 20 | 0.10% | £2,150 | YES |
| DMW0040 | Segment 2 | Lottery Tickets | £2.15 | 14,000 | £30,100 | 25 | 0.18% | £1,204 | YES |
| DMW0041 | Segment 3 | Lottery Tickets | £2.15 | 14,000 | £30,100 | 85 | 0.61% | £354 | YES |
| DMW0042 | Segment 4 | Lottery Tickets | £2.15 | 14,000 | £30,100 | 48 | 0.34% | £627 | NO |
| DMW0043 | Segment 5 | Lottery Tickets | £2.15 | 14,000 | £30,100 | 21 | 0.15% | £1,433 | YES |
| DMW0044 | Segment 6 | Lottery Tickets | £2.15 | 14,000 | £30,100 | 42 | 0.30% | £717 | NO |
| DMW0045 | Segment 7 | Basic | £0.60 | 17,500 | £10,500 | 48 | 0.27% | £219 | NO |
| DMW0046 | Segment 8 | Basic | £0.60 | 17,500 | £10,500 | 53 | 0.30% | £198 | NO |

The different cells received different promotional packages. These had different costs attached; similar, but not identical, numbers in each cell were mailed. Each cell generated its own response rate and consequent cost per response.

Some of the cells performed significantly differently from the campaign as a whole:

- Segments 1,2 and 5 response rates were significantly lower

- Segment 3 significantly higher

Campaign analysis is already posing several questions, such as:

- Is 342 enough responses?

- Is 0.27 per cent a high enough response rate?

- Should we have mailed bigger volumes?

- Is £627 per response acceptable?

Tools can be used prior to the start of the campaign, to help the user plan with higher degrees of confidence and ensure a statistically significant volume is selected for mailing. This is particularly important when setting up a test mailing versus a control. (See chapter 8.2)

As mentioned above, ROI is one of the main preferred performance measures for most tactical marketing activity. As with any measure, it is important to be realistic in terms of what is measured. For example, include only incremental revenue/profit, not income that would have occurred anyway, and include hidden costs as well as tangible mailing costs. (Manpower etc.)

Financial services provider B2B campaign evaluation case

Following the campaign, an interactive Excel application is used to store all the direct marketing campaign results. This allows the financial services provider to split campaigns by various dimensions including the list purchased. The example below shows the list breakdown of the March 2005 campaign:

## Figure 8.3.3

| Campaign | Volume | Number of sales | Sales rate | Live | Amount | Sign Different? |
|---|---|---|---|---|---|---|
| VAN_0305 | 200,333 | 205 | 0.102% | 191 | £115,219 | - |

| List | Volume | Number of sales | Sales rate | Live | Amount | Sign Diff to avg |
|---|---|---|---|---|---|---|
| dbmp | 34,784 | 35 | 0.101% | 34 | £20,344 | NO |
| ExpBus | 131,884 | 145 | 0.110% | 134 | £68,402 | NO |
| LBM | 19,436 | 20 | 0.103% | 18 | £23,171 | NO |
| MLFS | 1,060 | 1 | 0.094% | 1 | £453 | NO |
| PFPlus | 13,169 | 4 | 0.030% | 4 | £2,850 | YES |

Through the significant tests we can conclude that the final list performed significantly worse than the average for the campaign. The financial services provider can then use this information to choose which lists to buy in the future, and also as a bargaining tool to reduce the cost of lists.

ROI should be calculated after the campaign to assess how valuable the campaign has been. This can be used both to justify the expense and help feed the thinking for future campaigns. Ideally however, it would be extremely useful to have this information in advance. In some cases, such as fixed price promotions, this is possible: "all this can be yours for £500…" However, in other cases good estimates will be possible and behaviour in previous campaigns will allow good approximations.

To understand the value to the business (ROI), and learn for future campaigns it is necessary to understand the benefit per response as well as the cost. If the average (profitable) revenue generated by each response in our example campaign were a one-off £627 then the ROI would be 1. Above this amount, ROI would be positive, below it negative. So, for example:

## Figure 8.3.4

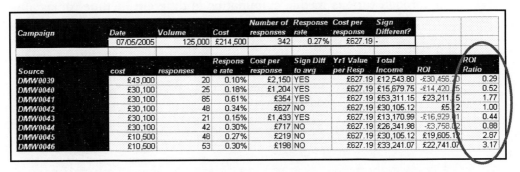

| Campaign | Date | Volume | Cost | Number of responses | Response rate | Cost per response | Sign Different? | | |
|---|---|---|---|---|---|---|---|---|---|
| | 07/05/2005 | 125,000 | £214,500 | 342 | 0.27% | £627.19 | - | | |

| Source | cost | responses | Response rate | Cost per response | Sign Diff to avg | Yr1 Value per Resp | Total Income | ROI | ROI Ratio |
|---|---|---|---|---|---|---|---|---|---|
| DMW0039 | £43,000 | 20 | 0.10% | £2,150 | YES | £627.19 | £12,543.80 | -£30,456.20 | 0.29 |
| DMW0040 | £30,100 | 25 | 0.18% | £1,204 | YES | £627.19 | £15,679.75 | -£14,420.25 | 0.52 |
| DMW0041 | £30,100 | 85 | 0.61% | £354 | YES | £627.19 | £53,311.15 | £23,211.15 | 1.77 |
| DMW0042 | £30,100 | 48 | 0.34% | £627 | NO | £627.19 | £30,105.12 | £5.12 | 1.00 |
| DMW0043 | £30,100 | 21 | 0.15% | £1,433 | YES | £627.19 | £13,170.99 | -£16,929.01 | 0.44 |
| DMW0044 | £30,100 | 42 | 0.30% | £717 | NO | £627.19 | £26,341.98 | -£3,758.02 | 0.88 |
| DMW0045 | £10,500 | 48 | 0.27% | £219 | NO | £627.19 | £30,105.12 | £19,605.12 | 2.87 |
| DMW0046 | £10,500 | 53 | 0.30% | £198 | NO | £627.19 | £33,241.07 | £22,741.07 | 3.17 |

Understanding the ROI for each segment will give insight for future focus. If the average (profitable) revenue generated by each segment in this campaign were a one-off £627 then:

- The ROI for cells 41, 45 and 46 would be positive

- For cells 19, 40, 43 and 44, the ROI would be negative

- And for segment 42 would be zero

Of course it is not necessarily the case that a response from each segment will yield the same average revenue. As revenue by segment varies so will ROI. Understanding ROI, especially in conjunction with a grasp for likely response rates, has many benefits:

- Prevent repeating unsuccessful campaigns, building on successful ones

- Future campaigns will have increasing ROI and profitability

- Can achieve same or even increased profitability with decreased mailing volumes and lower mailing costs

However, if the average (profitable) revenue generated by each segment in this campaign were not a one-off £627, but £627 a year for life, suddenly this becomes a successful campaign. Even the worst performing segment, segment 1, would have positive ROI by year four. Therefore it is important to consider the long-term effects of all campaigns and look at the likely ROI based on lifetime performance where possible. (The sum of year-by-year performance over a customer's total 'lifetime' is his lifetime value.)

Bitran and Mondschein define lifetime value as:

"The total net contribution that a customer generates during his/her lifetime on a house list."

(For a fuller discussion of lifetime value, see chapter 3.5)

When looking at customer recruitment, it's easy for marketers to measure only a year one return on investment, or a response rate, to find what recruitment method works best. A more thorough approach is to measure lifetime performance and use this as a metric on which to direct recruitment strategy.

The following graph shows cumulative average performance figures for a charity recruiting through various media, culminating in different lifetime values after an assumed lifetime of five years:

**Figure 8.3.5**

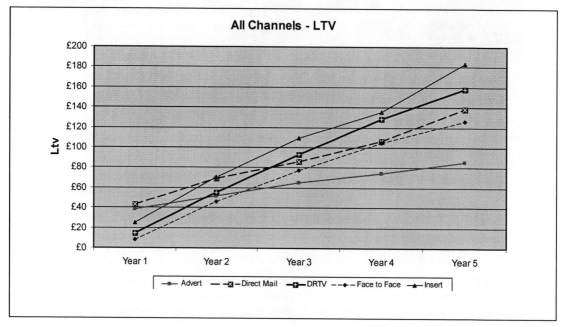

This graph shows that even though direct mail has the best, and face-to-face has the poorest, results after year one, after five years they give more or less the same results. Inserts on the other hand return only 60 per cent compared to direct mail after year one, while after five years return 138 per cent compared to direct mail.

## *Think about the future*

The results from one campaign can be used to build predictive models and segmentations for future campaigns. For example, the results can be used to build predictive models for response rates, ROI and lifetime value based on the majority of the campaign data. To do this, please remember to keep back a small but significant and representative subset of the data. Validate your modelling against this sample and further validate the model against other similar campaigns.

As a result future campaigns can be built on past learning and insight, and:

1.   Can be targeted at the right individuals

2.   Can be better planned in terms of scale and cost

3.   Can avoid non-profitable segments

4.   Can be built around long-term customer relationships as well as one-off tactical initiatives

5.   Can deliver more profit

## Brand evaluation case study

*The purpose of this analysis was to look at sales volume before and after the start of a brand advertising campaign to see what impact the campaign has had on sales. This is benchmarked against the sales development last year to account for seasonality in the data. No similar campaigns were carried out at the same time last year.*

*First graph shows sales development per day before and after campaign start, showing no sign of any impact:*

### Figure 8.3.6

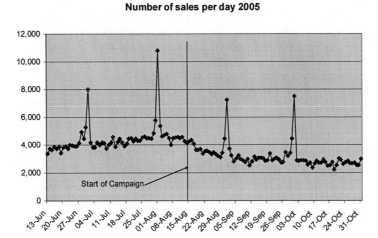

*The following graph shows the weekly sales compared to last year's sales:*

### Figure 8.3.7

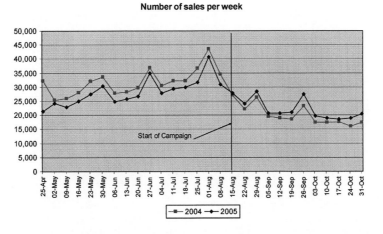

*From this we can see that there is a marked shift at the time when the brand campaign started. In fact in the 12 months before campaign start the 2005 level was about 10 per cent below 2004, while in the 12 months following campaign start the 2005 level was up by 10 per cent. There are a number of factors that are not included in this, such as competitor marketing spend, but there can be no doubting the impact of the campaign.*

# Essentials of the printing process

## This chapter includes:

------------------------------------------------

- ❑ **The eight essential steps of print production**

- ❑ **Information your printer will need**

- ❑ **Preparing the artwork correctly**

- ❑ **The six main types of paper used in direct mail**

- ❑ **Proofing: the four types of proof**

- ❑ **The six printing methods**

- ❑ **Printing technology**

- ❑ **Why use digital printing?**

- ❑ **Envelopes for direct mail**

- ❑ **Choosing your print supplier**

------------------------------------------------

## About this chapter

**A**s many authors have noted elsewhere in this Guide, there are few areas of direct marketing which do not involve direct mail. One of the chief differences between marketers in the conventional sphere and those in direct marketing is the knowledge required to implement complex print and mail campaigns. These may well involve dozens of different items of print, each produced in a different quantity, using different printing processes, different paper stocks and different finishing techniques.

In this brief but essential introduction to printing and print buying, Philip Moreland throws light on some of the terms you will encounter and the sequence of events to be followed when translating finished artwork into mailing packages ready for the mail.

Printing, like every other area of the business, is undergoing constant technological change and a knowledge of the principles will help you to keep pace with them.

## *Philip Moreland, M IDM*

Philip joined the printing industry as an apprentice in 1964 with John Waddington Ltd. He gave his first technical presentation, at PIRA, the printing industries research and development organisation, on developments in printing plate technology and has since been a regular speaker on print technology for the IDM.

In 1983 he was appointed Marketing Director of Waddington & Ledger, one of the first UK companies involved in the production of direct response products using 'in-line' finishing. In 1990 he became W&L's MD, and in 1994 he and a colleague set up Marketing Specialists to run alongside W&L. This company offers technical consultancy and print management services.

Philip has four children and six grandchildren, is a keen sailor and spends as much time as possible cruising the Mediterranean. He enjoys playing squash and in quieter moments, paints and still plays the guitar ... badly!

**Philip Moreland M IDM**
**Managing Director**
**Waddington & Ledger Ltd**
**Lowfields Business Park**
**Elland**
**West Yorkshire HX5 9DA**

This chapter, which appeared in the previous edition of the Guide, has been reviewed and amended for this edition by John Hughes

## *John Hughes F IDM*

Giving up a farm management career in Tanganyika, Africa, John returned to England in 1965 to join his mother as Managing Director for Mail Marketing, a business which she started in 1950. Over the years John has continued to work with the team to build the business into one of the UK's foremost direct marketing service companies and during the 1980s handled a large number of the government privatisation projects. John has run the business with a passion and fervour ensuring the company remained at the forefront of its industry, bringing a sense of propriety to an industry which at first struggled to become professional.

As a principal pioneer of the direct marketing industry in the UK, John was instrumental in setting up the Direct Mail Sales Bureau, was a founder member of the Institute of Direct Marketing, and one of their first Honorary Fellows; the first name on the DMA's Role of Honour, having assisted in drafting their Code of Practice, and a member of their Governance Committee. He was also a recipient of the prestigious Robert Bill Award for services to the industry. John's work continues with his passion for education within the industry and until recently he sat on the Council for Industry and Higher Education, CAM and the CBI Council for South West and was awarded an Honorary Fellow of CIM. He was presented with the first award from Royal Mail in 1998 for recognition of his contribution to the direct marketing industry.

More recently he has helped establish the Foundation and Forum for Corporate Governance and is involved with a number of charities.

# Chapter 8.4

# Essentials of the printing process

## The eight essential steps of print production

**A**ll printed work, no matter what the process or volume, should follow a set procedure if your work is to be produced exactly to your specification, on time, and to your budget.

Let us first set out the procedure, and then look at each of the stages in more detail.

The sequence you should follow is always the same. The timings, where given, are recommended minimums. Where no timing is given this is, of course, dependent on the nature of the work and will be advised at time of estimate.

1.   Estimate – two weeks prior to delivery

2.   Paper order – four weeks prior to delivery [If a making]

3.   Origination – allow two working days

4.   Plate making – allow one day

5.   Ozalid proof – allow one day

6.   Printing – will be advised

7.   Finishing – will be advised

8.   Delivery – your due date

### Factors affecting mail pack timing

The overall timings above are for a typical mailing pack comprising brochure, letter, order form and envelope etc. Special timing arrangements must be negotiated in the case of catalogues which, with perhaps 48 pages or more, are the equivalent of several regular mailings.

Factors which will affect your general timing for direct mail will include:

?   Special papers – 'makings'

?   Second and third colour proofs

?   Late specification changes

> Remember: printers' estimates assume *no further corrections* to your copy or art. Changes during production can potentially jeopardise your mailing date, although any reputable printer will lean over backwards to accommodate you. Remember to consult your mailing house regarding delivery dates needed to meet proposed mailing dates. Your start date should always be calculated backwards from the proposed mailing date.

Please note that the ever-increasing adoption of digital four-colour printing at commercially competitive quality, speed and price has had the effect of reducing lead times and proofing dramatically. PDFs (digital proofing) allow creatives to design electronic communication to printers and then press the button for instant production. Even conventional litho presses have fast 'make readies' and proofing processes that can shorten the production cycle while preserving 'fit for purpose' quality of the documents.

## Step 1: The estimate – start early

It is always advisable to contact your printer as soon as you have a rough visual, some ideas of your proposed mailing quantity, and, if possible, desired mailing date. Ideally you should ask for a printer's estimate prior to beginning artwork production. Remember an estimate is not a quote, so always get confirmation when full spec is to hand.

There are many reasons for this; for example, your printer may suggest minor changes (e.g. of fold or size) which can save significant amounts of money. These may require artwork to be prepared in a slightly different way. Sometimes your printer will be aware of new techniques which, if employed, can give your mailing a competitive edge. Just occasionally your designer may create a superlative package on paper which technically cannot be executed, or only at inordinate cost – all good reasons for calling in your printer as early as possible. Also remember if the printer is not a mailing house as well, the same applies to the collating and enclosing process. Check it can run on whatever machines are to be used.

With large-scale direct mail campaigns, or in the case of small quantity tests which may become large-scale rollouts if successful, getting an early printer's estimate is paramount, since even a small price differential multiplied by millions can amount to tens of thousands of pounds. And, of course, a large-scale plan that is held up due to an avoidable technical hitch can lead to massive shortfalls of revenue for the advertiser.

It is sensible to ask for a breakdown between set-up and run-on or reprint costs. The cost- effectiveness of a company should never be judged on a test production cost but the rollout-per- thousand to judge its viability.

Here are some of the ways in which your printer can often show you significant savings if consulted early in the process:

- Changes in format size

- Modifications to the format, e.g. inbuilt envelopes

- Alternative paper stocks

- Rationalised production methods – pre-inserted flyers and order forms

- Inkjet and laser filling or complete graphics personalisation changes including coding, offering variants and graphics etc. rather than plate changes. Sequencing can also be accomplished this way, avoiding post inserting sortation of mail to maximise postal savings

- Inbuilt involvement devices, e.g. scratch-off panels

## *Information your printer will need*

All printers and production managers require certain standard information in order to provide costings and to plan for a job. It is a good idea, since you may find yourself using several printers, to use your own standard print enquiry form.

An example of the items to be covered on a typical print enquiry/estimate form is shown on the facing page, from which you can readily create your own form. *It may be necessary to prepare a separate enquiry form for each item in your mailing or campaign* as virtually every item will be different, e.g. envelope, order form, leaflet, price list, letter and reply envelope. In some cases they will be handled by different printers.

### Cover

Remember to note whether a brochure or booklet is self-covered (i.e. same paper as text) or whether a different paper stock is required for the outside pages.

### Bleed

The amount of bleed (where ink 'runs off' the edges of the pages) can affect the cost of a print job noticeably. Your direct mail designer will be aware of the significance of bleed, but may not be aware of its true impact on costs. This also has an impact on folding and in-line cutting. Pagination is key to multi-page brochures and letters etc. Different finishing equipments use different 'mobile' attachments to achieve the result, so designer and printer must liaise if in doubt.

**Figure 8.4.1**

| Suggested print enquiry/estimate form | | |
|---|---|---|
| Job title: | | |
| ☐ Quantity | | ☐ Run on |
| ☐ Flat size | ☐ Saddle stitch | ☐ Ink-jet coding |
| ☐ Finished size | ☐ Spine glue | ☐ Scratch 'n' sniff |
| ☐ No. of pages | ☐ Remoistenable glue | ☐ Fragrance burst |
| ☐ Colours | ☐ Wet pattern glue | ☐ Silver/gold latex |
| ☐ Paper (cover) | ☐ Perforations | ☐ Silk-screen inks |
| ☐ Paper (text) | ☐ Die cutting | ☐ |
| ☐ Packaging | ☐ Coin react ink | ☐ |
| ☐ Delivery | ☐ Numbering | ☐ |
| | | |
| ☐ Artwork/film date | ☐ Delivery date | |
| | | |
| ☐ Additional information | | |
| | | |
| | | |
| | | |
| | | |
| ☐ Repro | | |
| | | |
| | | |
| | | |
| Type of proof   ☐ Machine   ☐ Cromalin   ☐ Ozalid | | |
| Diagram | | |

## Quantity

Printers will normally print a larger quantity than you request to allow for spoils, although every printer's 'overs' policy is different. It may be wise not to assume printers will deliver overs so this may need to be added to the mailing quantities. The percentage depends on the size of run and method of production. Ask your mailing house for guidance as the enclosing process may specify average requirements. Remember, a reprint is costly and causes delays in fulfilment of the order.

## Transparencies

It is often not realised how the cost of a full-colour print job increases in direct proportion to the number of transparencies used, and whether they are to be reproduced actual size ('s/s' or same size), enlarged or reduced. As digital photography has improved, more often than not images are supplied in a digital format. Designers use Apple Mac and deliver 'ready to print' (pdf) digital artwork. Changes are usually simpler, quicker and less costly to achieve. Where the printing processes are dynamic then programme data manipulation must be carefully checked or the wrong data may be married to the incorrect images.

## Paper

The weight of paper is a major factor in the weight, and therefore the postage cost, of a mailing – as well as the cost of print.
Finishing

This is a printers' term for a variety of processes that include folding, stapling, glueing and varnishing etc. Finishing can be in-line and offline. Worth checking if finishing is to be done inhouse. The amount of overs required can vary if offline complex finishing is required.

## Size

Most direct mail designers are fully *au fait* with standard paper sizes and how to get the best from them. Generally speaking the advantages of having a non-standard print size (e.g. extra impact or awareness) can be heavily outweighed by the disproportionate costs due to ordering non-standard paper and having it 'cut to waste'.

## Delivery

Coding of materials: mark the code and quantity on boxes or pallets. Never mix different print items in boxes on pallets. State all relevant details concerning delivery: quantities, destinations, method of packing (if appropriate) and so on.

## Dates

Remember to state the date at which you plan for artwork or films to be ready, if being prepared by a specialist supplier and not the printer. Invariably your printer will be able to carry out the stages known as origination on your behalf.

# *Preparing the artwork correctly*

Artwork is the image used for reproduction and is the province of the art director. However, here are a few thoughts on artwork preparation as seen from the printer's perspective:

- Always supply some form of colour proof with disc (positional guide only) – it can be low resolution.

- Make sure trim/tick marks are shown and base artwork is correct to size.

- Check against printer's laydown sheet if appropriate. (Complex finishing jobs.)

- Make sure transparencies are all together and are in focus. Check with glass.

- Check that the colour markup is complete with no areas of doubt, i.e. tint panels, headlines, key lines and whether they print or not.

- Watch out for type reversals in very small type – no less than 8pt.

- Check for 'special colours' i.e. those that cannot be achieved with the four-colour process.

- Make sure the disc provided is compatible with the repro house/printer.

- Ensure the repro house/printer carries the fonts specified on the disk.

- If any type corrections are made on or after the first proof, make sure the original disc is also corrected at some stage.

Check with your printer that he is happy with the disc and format of artwork you propose to supply.

**Digital artwork** is now the norm as most companies have desktop publishing and design systems. It is imperative that some form of colour proof is presented with the relevant artwork disk. This proof will act as the positional guide and colour markup. It is not necessary for this proof to be of high resolution for this particular purpose.

Check that the printer/repro house can handle the system disk selected.

## *Step 2: Ordering the paper*

Most printing paper is bought through specialist paper merchants and each merchant will give the paper a brand name. This brand name will be different from merchant to merchant even though the paper is the same and may have been manufactured by the same mill. Only very large printers are able to buy paper directly from the mills.

If a job requires in excess of two tonnes of paper then a 'making' is normally bought. A making is paper of a specific size, whether in reel or sheet form, and of the required weight. Such paper can take four to six weeks to manufacture and deliver. Stock paper can be bought for almost immediate delivery. However, stock paper may be the wrong size and weight for the job, possibly resulting in excessive waste. Stock papers are also more expensive per tonne to buy.

In practice, very large regular mailers (e.g. financial service organisations, publishers and mail-order catalogues) buy paper by the making, whereas most business-to-business mailers are generally forced to rely on stock papers. If you're a business mail, therefore, create your designs with stock sizes in mind. Smaller mailers should not concern themselves unnecessarily with early ordering of paper unless a very rare paper is being contemplated, e.g. antique finish or 'laid' paper (watermarked).

## The six main types of paper

There are six generic types of paper in common use for direct mail. Each has specific advantages and disadvantages of which weight and price are two – although by no means the only two.

The chart below sets out the six grades of paper together with the chief features and uses of each.

Table 8.4.1

| The 6 grades of paper | |
| --- | --- |
| **Type** | **Uses** |
| W.S.O.P. (Web-sized offset paper) | Bottom of the range<br>Low-cost, high-volume work<br>Long-run weekly magazines, eg TV Times |
| Blade coated mechanical (BCM) | Off-white, mid-range, coated<br>For run-of-the-mill colour work<br>Magazine inserts, brochures, broadsheets etc |
| Matt coated part mechanical | Off-white matt coated (cartridge)<br>Semi-high quality work<br>Letters, application forms, brochures |
| Near woodfree | Whiter than above<br>Better quality, better colour reproduction<br>Brochures, inserts |
| Woodfree | Top-of-the-range<br>matt coated   Extra white, high quality<br>Application forms, letters, brochures etc |
| Woodfree art | High gloss/high reflection<br>Prestige reproduction<br>Quality brochures, prospectuses, company reports etc |

## The effect of paper weight

Most papers used in direct mail can be bought in a wide range of weights, ranging from as low as 45 grammes per square metre (gsm) to 200gsm, or more.

Weight, generally speaking, is synonymous in the recipient's mind with quality. The heavier the weight the better it resists unwanted creasing and spoiling due to handling. But weight, of course, equals cost in postage and print terms.

The most commonly used weights of paper in direct mail are as follows:

| | |
|---|---|
| 65gsm | High-volume brochures, magazines and catalogues |
| 90gsm | Volume letters and application forms |
| 115 to 135gsm | Prestige leaflets, brochures and certificates etc. |

## International paper sizes

Everyone connected with direct mail should be familiar with the international 'A' sizes for paper and printed goods. The principle is that all stock paper sizes can be cut from a standard A1 or A0 sheet.

However, your designer will know that some paper is lost during trimming and folding and you should be certain of whether your sizes are for flat (opened-out) size or trimmed and folded size.

In the case of booklets of 8 pp (8 printed pages) and 16 pp, many print machines will print, fold and finish them in one pass – so that special sizes apply, as there may be no trimming.

On rare occasions you might be involved in printing items for use in the US, in which case be aware that international A sizes have not been universally adopted there. This can lead to mistakes and misunderstandings and is worth a special check.

Weight can affect the postage costs so it is critical, especially if one is targeting, to maximise the weight and therefore amount of material to be sent within a postal weight band.

Dependent on the printing process, paper will be ordered in sheets and reels. The allowance for set- up varies with the printing process selected.

Figure 8.4.2    **International 'A' paper sizes**

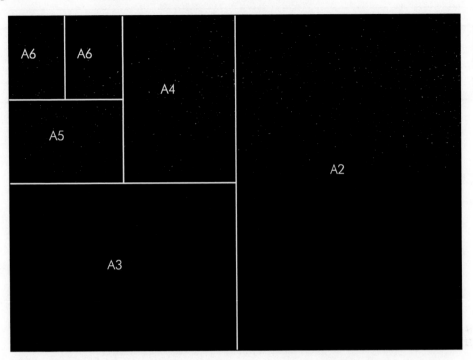

## *Step 3: Origination – colour separations and proofing*

Origination is the first stage in the print process proper, after the designer has completed his artwork and the photographer has supplied the transparencies.

Origination is the point at which artwork is separated into the four printing colours for what is called the 4-colour process or full-colour work.

The four printers' colours are:

- Black

- Yellow

- Cyan (blue)

- Magenta (red)

Figure 8.4.3

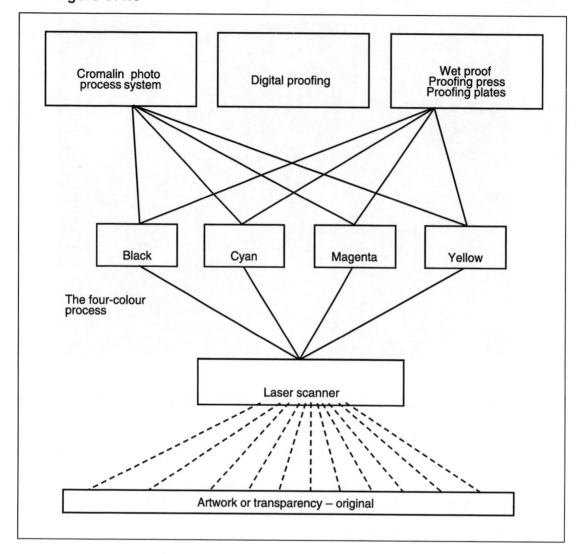

Every full-colour picture in a printed piece comprises arrangements of tiny colour dots in the four so-called process colours. To reach this stage, original artwork is usually scanned electronically by laser beam. The scanner views the originals through a series of filters which allow only one colour to register at a time. The result is four separate *positive* films; one for each of the process colours.

## Step 4 : Plate making – fixing the image in metal

In order to transfer the separated and screened images to the paper it is necessary first to produce a printing plate or cylinder.

The different types of plate are described later under 'printing methods'. Plates are generally of flexible metal and are bolted or clipped around a cylinder.

### Three types of screening

**Conventional** screening is a process in which the positive films are broken down into a series of dots. Each colour is screened at a different angle and the dots vary in size according to the depth of colour and detail present in the original.

**Geometric** screening is the same in principle, except the dots are elongated and bumped against each other to form lines, appearing as a sharp, fine-line screen.

**Full tone** is a random (stochastic) screening that excels in handling text and line work and provides outstanding rendition of fine detail.

## Step 5 : Proofing – the four types of proof

To check the quality and accuracy of the positive films, they must be 'proofed'. For most colour work there are four types of proof which you need be aware of:

- Wet proofs

- Cromalins

- Ozalids

- Digital proofs

### Proof checking

**Wet proofs** – these are produced on a small single colour printing press, specifically designed for this purpose. Each colour is printed separately and has to dry before the next one is printed down. As a general statement the wet proof is the closest we can get to the actual printing process to be used. An added advantage of the wet-proof system is the ability to proof on the actual paper stock to be used for the print run itself. Needless to say wet proofing is a costly and time-consuming process.

Wet proofing is often preferred by non-experienced print buyers, especially for quality work, because of its closer approximation to the finished job.

Please note that it is as important to proof on the paper being used as it is to check register, colour match and copy position.

Wet proofing is used when multiple proofs are required, e.g. twelve or more. In most circumstances proofs can be backed up (printed on reverse) so that dummies can be made up exactly as the finished item.

**Cromalin proofs** – the word *Cromalin* is a trade name but is now commonly used to describe methods of photomechanical proofing. In short, a light-sensitive laminate is applied to a base material. A film positive is laid on it and exposed to a bright light. The laminate is dusted with a powder dye (one for each process colour) and the excess is removed. This is repeated for each process colour. The final result is an accurate representation of the positives used.

Cromalins are quicker and cheaper than wet proofs provided that only one or two proofs are required. The nature of the proof itself, being on heavy duty paper, makes it very difficult for realistic dummies to be made up to show what the job will look like. Cromalins cannot be double-sided.

**Ozalid proofs** – in some respects ozalids are the most important proofs of all. They are taken at the plate making stage and are a black-and-white representation of the images on the printing films. If any type alterations have been made after the first proof, this is the last opportunity to examine corrections before the job goes to press. Corrections after this stage can prove very costly, particularly if a press is left to stand while the alteration is made and a new plate is made.

**Digital proofs** are now the preferred method of checking documents for positioning and content of text, images and tints throughout the creative process.

The choice of proofing technology for a particular job can be made from a list which includes laser printer (or colour laser), liquid inkjet, solid inkjet, thermal wax, dye-sublimation and hybrid electro-photographic techniques.

In the professional desktop publishing market the technologies of dye-sublimation, inkjet and thermal wax provide the basis for mid-range proofing solutions. 3M have developed the *Rainbow Proof* (brand name), a dye-sublimation process meant to simulate the offset printing process with continuous tone output.

While the traditional print buyer may consider digital proofs they still have some way to go before they become accepted as a 'proof to work to'. The process has improved to the point that most commercial colour printers can deliver a 'fit for purpose' result. Speed and cost now drive the adoption of the use of digital proofing which is why it has become acceptable.

Things to check when passing a proof include:

- Register or fit

- Colour against transparency/illustration/colour artwork

- Read the copy

- Tint panels and headings

- Spotting

- Trim lines

- Make up a dummy and trim to size

The most important point about proofing is to stipulate the type of proofing you require at the outset, as it can considerably affect the cost and time required for a job.

## Step 6 : Ready to run – the six printing methods

There are six printing processes in commercial use today, all of them employed in the direct mail business. They are:

1. Letterpress, including flexography (impact printing)

2. Photogravure

3. Silk-screen

4. Lithography: sheet-fed or web offset

5.   Laser and inkjet

6.   Digital offset colour

We now look briefly at each of the above: the differences and their chief applications:

## Letterpress – Caxton's method

Letterpress is the oldest of the printing processes and is used nowadays exclusively for very short-run work such as business cards and formal invitations. The image is in relief, the ink is applied directly onto the plate ('forme' as it is called) and the print is taken from the forme itself. This is a classic example of impact printing.

Letterpress gives printing a particularly 'crisp' look which can enhance the 'olde worlde' prestige of very short-run productions. But for all other intents and purposes you will not be concerned with it in direct mail production.

**Figure 8.4.4    Letterpress – impact printing**

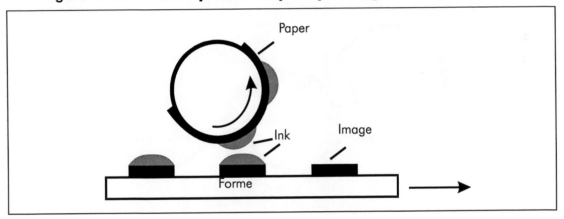

## Flexography – modern impact printing

Flexography is the modern equivalent of the Dickensian letterpress process and is used for high- volume packaging. The image is in relief on the printing forme which is inked by a roller. The paper passes between the inked forme and an impression cylinder and so picks up the image.

**Figure 8.4.5    Flexography – for volume packaging**

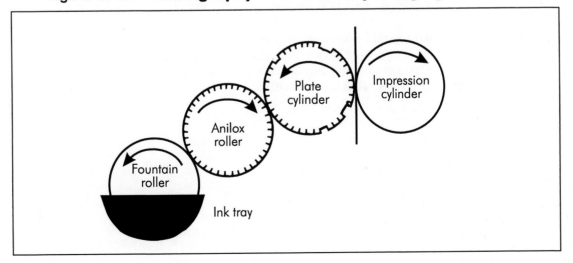

## Photogravure – the multimillion method

Like all printing processes, photogravure is very simple in principle. The image areas are engraved into the surface of huge printing cylinders. The cylinders rotate in reservoirs of ink and surplus ink from the surface (non-image) areas of the cylinders is removed with a 'doctor blade'. This leaves ink in the 'cells' of the engraved cylinders, rather like honey in a bee's honeycomb which has been rolled up with the open cells outwards.

As the paper comes into direct contact with the cylinders the ink is transferred. This takes place at extremely high speeds for each of the four colours, all colours being printed simultaneously.

Photogravure is mainly used for large volume magazine and catalogue production and can prove expensive on all but the very longest runs as the cost of cylinder preparation is high.

### Figure 8.4.6   Photogravure – like a honeycomb

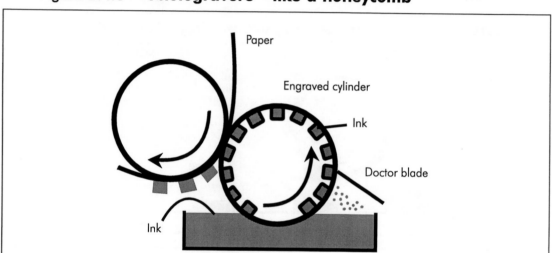

## Silk-screen – a specialist technique

Silk-screen is another simple printing process and is based on the stencil method of printing. A material with a fine open weave (screen) is stretched across a frame. On top of that frame is a stencil which blocks out areas not required to print. Ink is poured into the frame and the frame is lowered onto the material to be printed. The ink is squeezed across the screen forcing the ink through the open weave not protected by the stencil. This is repeated for each colour.

In recent years rotary silk-screen machines have been developed. Silk-screen is used for short runs on virtually any material, e.g. plastic and glass. It is commonly used for posters and any work requiring a high density of solid colour, such as portfolio covers, gifts and novelties.

Figure 8.4.7 **Silk-screen – the stencil method**

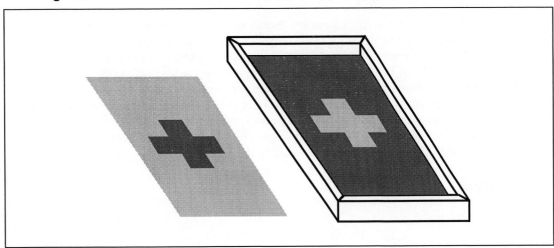

## Lithography – the direct mailers' choice

Lithography is undoubtedly the most widely used printing process and the one with which all direct marketers should be familiar. Depending on volume there is a choice of two lithographic systems: sheet-fed and web offset. How they differ can be seen in the diagram overleaf.

Both systems are based on the principle that grease and water do not mix. The image on the plate surface is grease receptive, while the non-image area (background) is water receptive. To begin with, a film of moisture is applied to the plate surface and is attracted to the non-image areas and repelled by the greasy image area. This is immediately followed by a film of ink which is greasy in nature. The ink is attracted to the image area and is repelled by the non-image area covered in moisture.

The moisture evaporates to leave the ink behind to form the image. This is then transferred onto a rubber blanket and then onto the paper. This process is repeated for each of the printing colours. The plate is totally smooth, with the image neither raised nor engraved. Because the actual printing is via an intermediary 'blanket' and not direct from the plate – it is called offset litho.

Figure 8.4.8 **Litho – the principle**

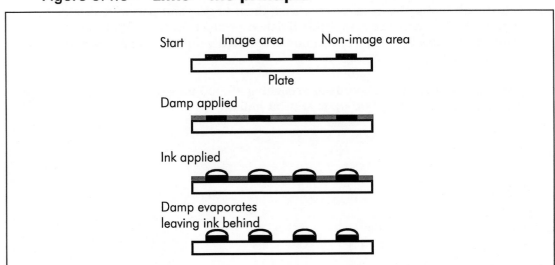

## Sheet-fed litho – one sheet at a time

Sheet-fed presses print from flat-cut sheets and deliver flat-cut sheets. Such presses are capable of printing speeds up to 18,000 sheets per hour. They are most suitable for runs of up to 50,000 impressions but this very much depends on the sheet size of the press. Presses designed for packaging applications may well produce several hundred thousand impressions. Most sheet-fed machines print from one to four colours, one side only. Specialist machines can print more colours with varnishes and some can print both sides. Sheet-fed machines can also print the board weights used in packaging, an advantage over web offset which would otherwise prove to be cheaper.

Figure 8.4.9    **Sheet-fed litho**

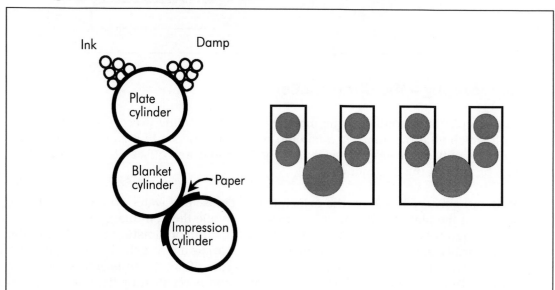

## Web offset litho – from a continuous reel

Web offset presses print from a continuous reel of paper, usually in four colours and on both sides of the paper simultaneously. The ink is dried with hot air which tends to give a high gloss finish. Quick drying enables the web to be folded on press if, for example, eight or 16 page sections are required. Some presses are fitted with in-line finishing which allows them to glue and perforate, make envelopes, and produce completely finished products at the end of the machine. Most of the novelty one-piece formats associated with direct mail are produced by this method.

Web presses can run at speeds approaching 40,000 impressions per hour and are suitable for runs of 50,000 up to several million.

Figure 8.4.10  **Web offset litho (printing on both sides)**

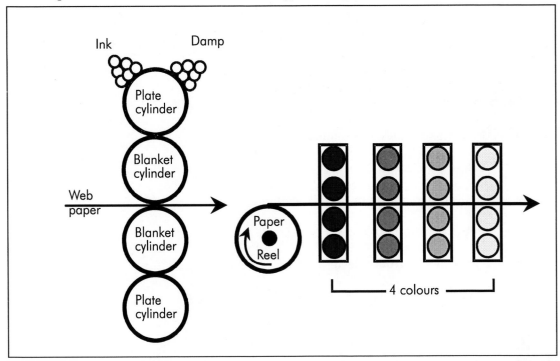

## *Sheet-fed and web – paper differences*

The table below summarises the important differences between sheet-fed and web presses. Note that each type of press calls for its own paper sizes for maximum efficiency – one clear reason for consulting your print estimator before finalising your design and artwork.

Table 8.4.3

| Litho printing presses – sizes and specifications | | |
|---|---|---|
|  | **Size** | **Specification** |
| SRA1 4-col sheet-fed | 640 x 900 <br> one side only | 4 colours |
| SRA2 4-col sheet-fed | 450 x 640 <br> one side only | 4 colours |
| 8pp mini web | Cut off web width <br> 630 x 505 | 4 colours <br> both sides |
| 16pp web | Cut off web width <br> 630 x 965 | 4 colours <br> both sides |

There are several important points of difference between sheet-fed and web, as follows:

### Sheet-fed

- Usually prints one side only

- Prints from flat-cut sheets

- Delivers flat sheets

- Ink has to dry before backing up, i.e. printing reverse unless driers used or perfector press (printed two sides in one pass)

- Paper stocks from 70gsm to 220gsm

## Web offset

- Prints both sides simultaneously

- Prints from a reel of paper

- Delivers flat sheets or folded sections

- Ink is dried by hot air, i.e. heat-set

- Paper stocks from 52gsm to 180gsm

- Some presses can produce continuous stationery

# Printing technology

## Laser printing – the 21st Century method

Laser printing is an electronic printing process, but is closer to being a high-speed computer process. Its use in direct mail is primarily to print letters by means of an online computer which 'tells' it specific information such as the recipient's name and address. This feature is used for personalising letters and order forms etc.

Laser printing (and other forms of computer-directed printing such as inkjet) is frequently employed to in-fill data on preprinted items that have been produced by one of the conventional print methods described above. The production of print for subsequent laser printing comes within the scope of any printer geared towards direct mail.

Until recently personalised printing was confined to black-and-white reproduction achieved almost always by the dry toner method, similar to that used in photocopiers.

## Inkjet printing – spray printing dots of ink

Inkjet printing is the original electronic printing process. It differs from all the others in as much as it is a non-impact printing system. Electronically charged ink particles are sprayed onto the paper.

The simplest systems apply sell-by dates on foodstuff packaging and codes on inserts, while high-end versions produce fully personalised mailings at a quality that matches many laser printers. The key strengths of inkjet in this application are speed, versatility and cost, particularly when combined with in-line finishing technology.

Over the last few years inkjet has also developed as a colour imaging system for designers, desktop publishers and repro companies. Costs for these systems vary greatly depending on the intended application. Low-end colour printers used with

Apple Mac design stations can cost a few hundred pounds. High-end printers as used by a repro house to produce colour proofs can cost several thousand pounds. Similar high-end systems are used by some companies to produce short-run posters.

## Digital offset – colour plus personalisation

Two key issues have influenced the development of printing technology over the last decade:

- The need for more targeted communications

- Shorter lead times and lower costs from design to print

## *Targeted communications*

It is well documented that personalised communications deliver higher response rates than non-personalised. Laser printers have been used to personalise mailings for many years. Laser printing technology for direct mail applications, though proven, only offers personalised text in one or two colours. The base stationery has to be preprinted by some other process before it is passed through the laser printer.

The ultimate concept is one-to-one marketing, which requires us to reach an individual customer with a personalised message. This quest is fast becoming a reality with digital printing technology – albeit at a price. However, with some users claiming response rates of between 10 and 20 per cent, it is worth a closer examination.

As far as printed communications are concerned, digital technologies were first introduced in the early 90s.

One of the first digital colour presses was the Indigo E-Print 1000 launched in 1993. There are now seven or more manufacturers of digital printing presses, some of which have up to five models in their range.

## *The digitisation of printed communications*

Over the last two decades, most organisations have invested in some form of desktop computers and or publishing equipment. These systems now allow users to send electronic files to other parts of their organisation or to printers. Today most printers receive well over 50 per cent of their jobs in electronic form.

Digital technology enables images to be stored as digital files ('dots on disc') rather than film. Photographic images can be electronically scanned or downloaded onto a computer from digital cameras or photo CDs. Other images are created on the computer using various software packages. Once the data is loaded onto a computer it can be manipulated. After correction or modification, it can than be transmitted to a printing machine in another room or even in another country if an ISDN line is used.

In experienced hands this technology has the potential to provide a much quicker and cheaper route to market than the more traditional film-based methods.

How a printer then converts the data into images on paper or other substrate depends entirely on what the communication is to be used for. Different machines have been developed for different types of printed products.

### Digital printing presses

It would be quite wrong to view digital printing as a generic process. To be specific, digital printing is any printing completed via digital files. Digital printing machines can have very different methods of applying images to paper. Manufacturers each have their own view on the technological way forward.

Some are based on a process technology called xerography. Xerographic printing uses an electrostatic image that attracts powder toner. The toner is then transferred to the paper by electrostatic or direct physical means.

Others use a development of this process and use electrostatic inks rather than toner. The imaging cylinder is exposed with a laser beam, so establishing an image that attracts the liquid ink. The image is then transferred to a printing cylinder and from there directly to the paper. The image is created from digital data that has been transferred from a computer. For each subsequent copy the imaging cylinder has to be re-exposed by the laser.

The computer can be programmed to create a different image for each copy to be printed. It could be argued that this notion is not new since laser printers have for many years offered this facility for personalised text.

The fundamental difference with this new technology is that it can also combine pictures and words. Some presses are designed to print in one colour only; others can print up to six colours.


# Why use digital printing?

### One-to-one

There are clear benefits in producing direct mail pieces with words and pictures that are relevant to the recipient only. However, while few companies are likely to have a database that is individualised to such an extent this is beginning to change and will become more common in the future. Notwithstanding this there are certain practical problems to consider:

- The creative costs for producing totally individual communications are likely to prove prohibitive, unless a very high-ticket item is being sold.

- Each mail pack would have to be checked and effectively signed off prior to printing.

- The cost and time implications of data preparation need to be considered.


### Test marketing

There could be a case for using digital printing for testing different creative ideas. Quantities of 1,000 or less could be printed and mailed in order to establish which creative to adopt for the rollout – subject to the minimum required for statistical validity. However, if it were simply a question of testing different propositions, then digital printing would not show any particular cost advantages.

## Fulfilment packs

In a two-stage campaign where fulfilment packs are mailed in response to off-the-page advertising, DRTV or inserts, digital printing may offer some advantages.

As digital printing also offers print on demand in very small quantities, it may be possible to print fulfilment packs at short notice when response levels to the advertising are known. The packs could be printed and mailed as necessary, so avoiding potential wastage.

For large-ticket items, such as cars, totally unique mailings could be beneficial. If a consumer has shown interest in a specific model and colour/trim combination, it is possible to print a single brochure for that particular customer.

On the other hand, it is most unlikely that a catalogue of hand-picked products targeted at one person would ever cover its costs, whereas to a group of 500, it may do.

As in all aspects of direct marketing, a cost/benefit analysis should be carefully undertaken to avoid using technology just because it's there!

## Figure 8.4.11  **Digital printing**

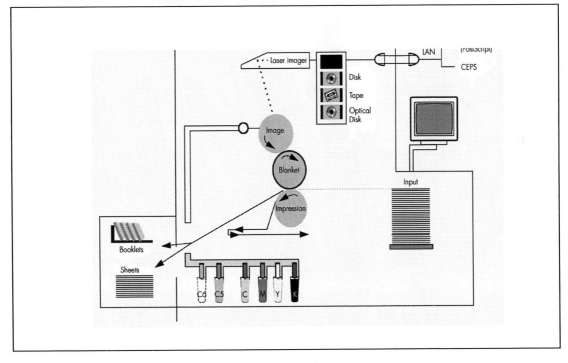

## Step 7 : Finishing

Once items have been printed they have to be cut and folded for end use. On certain products re-moist gumming and perforations may be added. In many instances this forms part of the finishing process, although these features can be incorporated while printing on specialist machines designed for volume production. Ask your printer for details of his finishing capacity when making your initial enquiry.

For small specialist finishing requirements offline is usually preferred whereas in-line is the option of choice for large volumes. It is important to ensure the printer and finishing aspects are co-ordinated, especially if done by two different suppliers.

## Table 8.4.4

| Some everyday print finishing terms | |
| --- | --- |
| Saddle stitching | Wire staples used to hold multi-page sections together |
| Spine glueing | Multiple pages glued together rather than saddle stitched |
| Re-moist glue | Applied glue for self-seal application forms or envelope flaps |
| Impact glue | Applied glue for making up envelopes or glueing two sheets together to form postcards |
| Pattern perforating | Perforating in any direction or shape |
| Trimming | Cutting leaflets or brochures to a finished size |
| Die-cutting | Cutting leaflets or pages of a brochure into an irregular shape |
| In-line finishing | Products that are folded and trimmed on press — very sophisticated formats can be produced this way (see following page for examples) |
| Off-line finishing | Similar features as above but produced from flat sheets after printing |

## *Step 8 : Delivery*

Unless specified otherwise a printer will quote ex works. It is important to be specific about your delivery address and number of 'drops' if you want an accurate costing. Note, with insert campaigns (where delivery may be direct from printer to publisher) delivery can prove to be quite an expensive item with quantities of print being despatched to various magazines around the country. It is not uncommon for such a campaign to be spread across 30 or more destinations.

## Figure 8.4.12 **Examples of finished formats**

The examples below cover almost all formats in everyday use. In the case of high-volume print runs using web offest presses, these formats can be produced on the machine, i.e. in one "pass" and can include glueing and perforation etc.

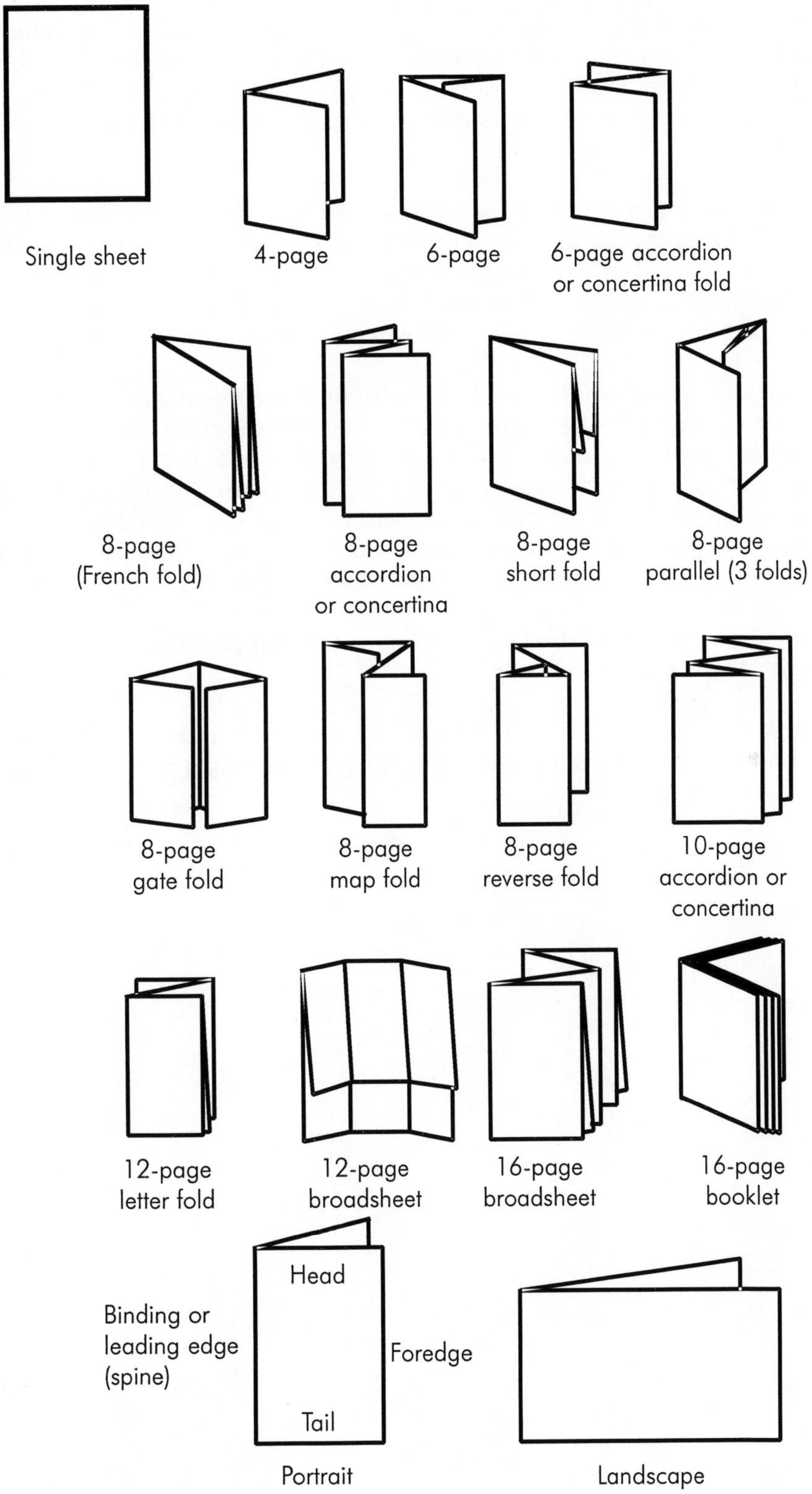

Single sheet

4-page

6-page

6-page accordion or concertina fold

8-page (French fold)

8-page accordion or concertina

8-page short fold

8-page parallel (3 folds)

8-page gate fold

8-page map fold

8-page reverse fold

10-page accordion or concertina

12-page letter fold

12-page broadsheet

16-page broadsheet

16-page booklet

Binding or leading edge (spine)

Head

Foredge

Tail

Portrait

Landscape

# Envelopes for direct mail

The most common envelopes in use in direct marketing are DL (to fit A4 folded twice) and C5 (A4 folded once). C4 (to fit A4 flat) envelopes are used on occasion. Outside of those stock sizes are bespoke envelopes, made to whatever size you require.

Envelopes can be printed in up to 4 colours. With large volume, production envelopes are printed and manufactured on a machine that accepts reels of white paper and delivers finished printed envelopes. Smaller quantities are produced by either overprinting stock envelopes or printing in flat sheets and making them up as a separate operation.

A special making of envelopes can take six to eight weeks to deliver. Overprinted stock envelopes can be produced in 10 to 14 days but are more expensive. When envelopes are filled at a mailing house they are often filled by machine. These machines require 'machine insertable' envelopes if they are to run at maximum speed. This should be borne in mind when envelopes are being ordered.

It is essential to ensure the envelope width allows enough gap on each side for the tolerance of the enclosing equipment. The thicker the pack the more room should be allowed. Most machinable envelopes are wallets, i.e. flap on long side as opposed to pockets with flap on short side. The manner in which envelopes are packed in boxes is also important to avoid damage. Good quality cartons and dividers are essential. It is worth noting that there is an increasing use of polythene for the outer wrapper. Sometimes this can have a metallic finish.

For small quantities finished 'bags' are normal with peel-off self-adhesive glue or alternatively they are heat sealed.

For large runs poly enclosing machines are used which are usually reel-fed poly and can be in multi colours. Designing for poly enclosing needs close liaison with the production house.

**Figure 8.4.13**

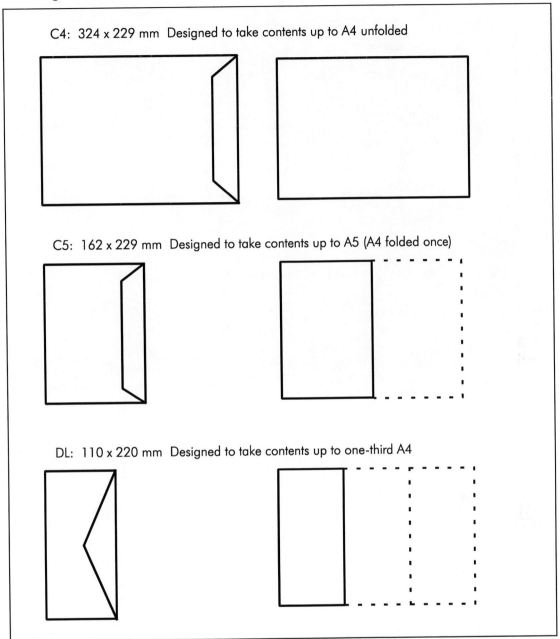

C4: 324 x 229 mm  Designed to take contents up to A4 unfolded

C5: 162 x 229 mm  Designed to take contents up to A5 (A4 folded once)

DL: 110 x 220 mm  Designed to take contents up to one-third A4

Table 8.4.5

### Leaflets – 50,000 +

**Important:** In the majority of instances, due to the size and quantity required, paper is rarely available from stock. Therefore we have to order the requirement direct from the manufacturers. Much of the UK's paper is made in Scandinavia, which requires approximately four weeks lead time.

| | | |
|---|---|---|
| Day 1 | Receipt of artwork. | Required by midday. |
| Day 2 | Proofs sent out overnight. | |
| Day 3 | Proofs to client 10am. | Approval/Amends required 4pm. |
| Day 4 | am we to amend. | Proofs sent out overnight. |
| Day 5 | Reproof to client 10am. | Approval required 4pm. |
| Day 6 | Film to printer. | Final Ozalid proof sent out overnight. |
| Day 7 | Final Ozalid proof to client 10am. | Final Ozalid proof approved. |
| Day 8 | Commence printing and folding/finishing. | On most products we would expect to complete approx. 500,000 copies per day. |
| Day 9/10 | Commence delivery. | Dependent on quantity we will notify quantity available. |

## Table 8.4.6

**Direct mailpack schedule (simple)**

Simple mail pack i.e. C5 outer, A4 or A3 stationery, t's & c's, BRE + flyer, simple laser up to four versions/letter variants per nationality.

| | | |
|---|---|---|
| Day 1 | Receipt of artwork (With sample pack mock up). | Required by midday. |
| Day 1 | Receipt of letter text. | Required by midday. |
| Day 1 | Complete DATA required. | Required by midday. |
| Day 2 | | Colour proofs sent out overnight. |
| Day 2 | | Data dumps sent out overnight. |
| Day 3 | Colour proofs to client 10am. | Approval required 4pm. |
| Day 3 | Data dumps to client 10am. | Approval required 4pm. |
| Day 4 | We to make any colour proof amends. | Proofs sent out overnight. |
| Day 5 | Reproof to client 10am. | Approval required 4pm. |
| Day 6 | Film to printer. | |
| Day 7 | Commence printing. | |
| Day 7 | Produce live lasers. | Sent out overnight. |
| Day 8 | Live lasers to client 10am. | Comments required 3pm. |
| Day 8/9 | Corrections made to laser proofs, this can take up to 24 hours. | Whenever possible we will fax the corrections but often this is not possible due to size of font i.e. caveats, in which case we will send overnight. |
| Day 10 | Revised laser proofs to client 10am. Delivery of all additional inserts and envelopes required. | Final approval required 2pm. Note; If we receive further corrections this will result in delay. |
| Day 11 | Commence lasering. | |
| Day 12 | Commence enclosing. | |
| Day 13 | Commence mailing | Commence mailing. Quantity TBA dependent on complexity of product.** |

** Mailing schedule subject to total quantity and complexity of product.

## *Print buying – the three key issues*

There are several thousand printers in the UK without looking to Europe. Apart from a few specialist printers they all do much the same thing – put ink on paper.

However, some do it on a larger scale than others; some do it cheaper and some do it faster. Your choice of printer should be based on three considerations:

1. Quality of service

2. Quality of product

3.    Price

Price should always be the last of your three considerations. The cheapest quote can easily become the most expensive job if it does not arrive on time and to the required standard.

It is important to develop a close working relationship with your suppliers. There is a trend towards 'partner' relationships between client and supplier which began in the early 1990s, with organisations working with preferred suppliers only.

Good communication is the key to a good working relationship. Poor communications between parties will lead to jobs being produced inefficiently.

> Every job should begin with a well-specified request for a quotation. If the job changes in specification or timing (as is often the case), then this should be re-evaluated by both parties, with revised costs and schedules submitted. This will ensure that the job is produced to specification, on time, and most importantly – to budget.

A good supplier should also act as an adviser and suggest alternative production approaches when appropriate.

## Choosing your print supplier

We said earlier not all jobs are suitable for the same printer. It is important to establish at the outset what each potential supplier is capable of.

Below is a checklist of questions to ask yourself and your shortlisted printer before you hand over the job:

### Table 8.6.7

| Ten questions to ask about a printer: |
|---|
| 1.  Are they recognised by the appropriate trade bodies, i.e. BPIF or DMA? |
| 2.  Do they have appropriate equipment and capacity for your work? |
| 3.  What are their materials handling and storage facilities like, and is there a general air of tidiness and efficiency about their works? |
| 4.  What experience do the sales and estimating staff have? |
| 5.  Who would be the day-to-day account handlers? |
| 6.  How do they handle production supervision and quality control? |
| 7.  Do they understand your product and its uses? |
| 8.  Are they financially stable? |
| 9.  Are there any client references and samples of previous work available to be seen? |
| 10. Are they ISO 9000 accredited? |